GUNSMITHING
TIPS &
PROJECTS

Copyright © 1989
Wolfe Publishing Company
Manufactured in the United States of America

ISBN: 0-935632-81-6

Wolfe Publishing Company

6471 Airpark Drive
Prescott, Arizona 86301

Preface

Reader demand for top quality gunsmithing articles in *Rifle* magazine over the past 20 years prompts the publishing of this book. Although covering a broad range of subjects — from metal to wood, restoration to customizing — we are aware that this volume is in no way a "complete" gunsmithing manual. And certainly it is not intended as such.

But here you will find techniques, projects and tips not found in any other reference. Hence, its purpose is to supplement the books in your gunsmithing library.

Most of the articles appear in their original form, thereby avoiding the monumental task of updating, editing and resetting each manuscript into type. Therefore, due to the two-decade time span, some products and companies may no longer exist. Addresses may have changed. We ask for your indulgence and understanding.

We have tried to include the most informative material, but in the selective process, some articles were excluded because they duplicated subject material. In a few cases the authors refer to previous articles that appeared in *Rifle*; these may or may not be reprinted in this book.

To the great variety of highly qualified authors, we offer a hearty "thank you" for making this book possible.

Dave Wolfe

Contents

Section 1

THE SHOP

STARTING YOUR

By ROY DUNLAP

I am quite sure a fair percentage of readers will be interested in my articles, for twenty years ago I wrote a thick and fairly expensive book on gunsmithing, intended solely for the American professional gunsmith. This is now in its fourth printing, which indicates one thing: that only about one of every forty purchasers could be a professional gunsmith! You "laymen" buy most of them.

Probably every gun owner at one time or another has done some work, if only rubbing oil into a stock or stoning burrs off metal parts. At least ninety-nine of every hundred professionals in the U.S. started as amateurs, working on their own firearms, calling it hobby or necessity, but *always* because we wanted something to do or to do something. In my case, I wanted guns but couldn't afford custom stocks or accessories, so I tried making them. Ten years and one war later I was in the business.

Now, after a thousand rifles and three thousand stocks, I'd much rather talk about them than work on them. What I'm getting at is that no one should be afraid to think about working on his arms, to find out how they click and, if not, why not. The man down at the gun shop started that way.

The sportsman who would work on his rifles or other equipment is limited by three factors: a place to work, the equipment he can put in it, and his own determination, meaning is he sure he will stick to a job, force himself to be slow and patient in acquiring manual dexterity, and set high standards for himself. Almost no undertaking in this work, however small, is easy to do absolutely right. I strongly doubt that the type of man who reads *The Rifle* is the type to be satisfied with crude

gun-butchery, but anyway we're going to sort of emphasize quality in work. This means primarily, *don't hurry*. Years ago when I worked in the basement of a sporting goods store and the customers were always trying to rush things, I had a standard last-resort comeback–"You can have it fast or have it right; you can have it cheap or have it good. Take your choice." This did not win me friends, but I never failed to make the point.

Unless you have room and finances to set up a few machine tools--lathe, drill press, a small milling machine perhaps--you are going to be pretty well limited to stock work and small saw-and-file jobs on metal.

The workbench is of course the first requisite, as big and as sturdy as you can get or make. If long enough, it might be combined with handloading operations, but it should mount two vises at least four feet apart, so a permanently mounted loading press may not be too convenient an addition. There are important side-effects in this arrangement, however: It will make you keep your loading equipment covered and properly stored and at the same time make you keep your bench clean.

A small bench grinder, files, chisels, gouges, etc., you buy as needed. Tool buying is dangerous--you can get hooked and sometimes you can't resist them, whether you need that particular item or not. Second-hand stores are a great place to prowl, since you can often find old tools of great value to you, of types no longer made or hard to find which are perfectly usable or easily restored. And at the right prices.

You'll need two vises, one for wood,

the other for metal. A Versa-Vise is good for stock work; the other should be as good a medium-size swivel-base machinist's vise as you can get, new or used.

Should you progress to the machine stage and aspire to lathe operations and don't know how, see if the local high school doesn't have some evening adult classes in "Machine Shop." If no instruction is available, read the book very carefully and start using the equipment. Slow and careful is the name of the game with power tools. Same with hand tools, of course, but a wood gouge doesn't have a switch you can throw the wrong way to produce instant trouble.

Two things you shouldn't go in for if you are a beginner are blueing and welding. Both are unpleasant and somewhat dangerous jobs which require working areas set aside or closed off, and are needed only very occasionally. And, unless you have professional skill and experience, unsatisfactory results are more often the rule than the exception. Find a gun shop turning out good blueing and have them do the work. You can do the preparatory work and polishing perhaps better than they can, having more time for detail, and if you do your own disassembly and assembly, the cost will be very little. For welding, look up the nearest Heliarc shop and let them do it. Welding by this system is almost foolproof in all respects--little warpage, heat discoloration, build-up to be removed, etc. It won't be cheap. Minimum charges run $7 or so, but it is worth it in the long run. A Heliarc installation costs about as much as a small sports car, so don't hint to the wife you'd like one for Christmas.

SHOP

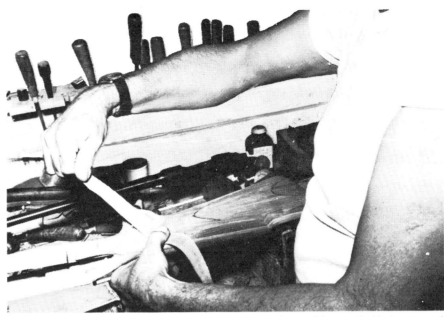

The gunsmithing shop should be stocked with a variety of screwdrivers and chisels, one to do each job right. For sanding curves in stocks, buy strip abrasive cloth. Sand by applying pressure with a finger or thumb and pull with the other hand, as shown.

Buy or borrow all the books on gunsmithing you can and read for general knowledge, mainly for directions on small tools--screwdrivers, punches, chisels, false vise-jaws, files--these are all important and vary greatly in quality. For instance, a good file will last for years--I have some I've had for thirty! A cheap one is almost worthless from the start. Files are cutting tools, not abrasives, and you move them in one direction to cut; you don't rub them back and forth over the work. Sharp files, never used on metal of any kind, are the greatest help in stock work imaginable...the vixen file, now commonly called "auto-body file," is great for working on the outside of a stock, cleaning edges, magazine openings, etc. So, if you contemplate using one of the many types of shaped and inletted unfinished stocks to complete a genuine personal rifle, get a half-dozen assorted new files.

You need screwdrivers, all the sizes you can find, and good ones. Cheap ones wreck rifles, having poorly shaped tips and often small slippery handles. A tip--most towns of any size have a MAC tool representative who calls on industrial and automotive places. They don't sell direct or retail or to stores....check with your friendly garage man (or make a friend of one!) and ask him to get you a selection of screwdrivers next time the man comes around. Prices low, quality high. Buy two each of the first four sizes, one each of the next two--don't ask for more unless you see the selection or you may end up with a three-foot job strong enough to be a crowbar!

Buy the best pin or drift punches that the best hardware store in town carries. Only the three smallest sizes will

be needed. You'll need a rawhide mallet and a small brass or lead hammer. There should be little need for a steel hammer in the home gun shop, which is good because good ones are hard to find--ball peen and claw hammers are very sad to use. The only good ones for gun work are the smaller machinist's riveting hammers, which are never carried in stock even by machinist supply houses.

Somebody has said that having the right tool is half the job. He's right.

Stock work is practically always the first step on the do-it-yourself gun road, usually refinishing or remodeling an existing stock. We'll go into just the reworking of a military stock for openers and, depending on the condition of the wood, this can be very

One of the most useful basic items in any shop is a good vise such as Will-Burt's 'Versa-Vise' shown in two positions, above and below. Leather-padded wooden false jaws protect the stock against denting.

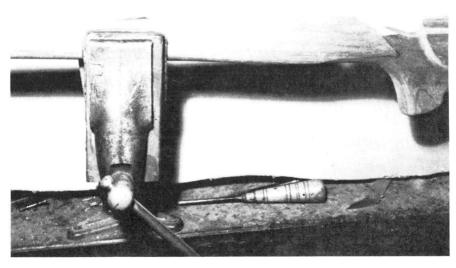

3

easy or harder'n h---, four or forty hours. Most military stocks should be given to friends having fireplaces, having been designed primarily as extension bayonet handles, however a few of the late Scandinavian types and a few of the last Mausers do have stocks that can be considered usable for a metallic-sighted sporting rifle. If the piece is to be maintained as is, for a collection or conversation item, you will want only to clean it up and as far as possible restore original appearance.

First operation of course is dismantling and stripping the rifle, removing all metal parts from the wood, excepting the metal recoil bolt usually present. These don't come out easily, and in any event you want them in place for the time being. Wash the stock with hot water and detergents to remove dirt and surface oil and grease, then use lacquer thinner, or commercial varnish removers, soaking the surface and brushing with the grain, using stiff bristle brushes of any kind handy, from old toothbrushes on up. Eventually you'll remove most of the old finish and surface stains. Finish with the water and detergent again, wipe dry, then light up the front burners on the gas stove and dry the stock over them, moving it around at about eight inches or so above flame. This will dry out most of the moisture you have put into the stock.

Now you remove the dents with steam...a hot iron and wet cloth, that is.

A large, old, long and worthless screwdriver is as good an iron as any, or you can make an iron--a short smooth bar of metal on a long metal handle. Heat red for a couple of inches, place a doubled thickness of wet cotton cloth over the dent and hold the hot iron on it just as the red color fades. The cloth will dry and char, so you must keep moving wet areas under the iron and moving the iron around slowly. Keep repeating the process until the dent is raised to the surface. The principle is that steam is forced into the wood grain and expands it to original dimensions. If the wood fibers have been broken or cut, you cannot raise the dent more than a little, and such spots must be filled in or cut down to the needed level.

This dent-raising system can apply to all stocks, requiring only that the finish be removed from the dent itself so that steam can enter the wood. A drop or two of lacquer thinner left in the dent for a couple minutes will usually cut an oil or varnish finish sufficiently. Careful use of a sharp needle, making little holes in the dent, may help. They'll close up under the steam. Of course you must refinish the spot after working on it, to match the rest of the stock. The plastic and epoxy finishes have their own solvents and touch-up systems.

And now, back to the old army stock. With the wood as clean and smooth as you can get it from cleaning and dent-removing, let it dry out for a day or two, putting it outside in warm or hot sun for a few hours if possible. Then you do any minor remodeling wanted, such as cutting the fore-end, fixing tip, filling in unwanted slots, reshaping comb, etc.

In regard to the slots and holes present in many European military stocks for sling or metal fittings, don't try to make a nice matching wood patch. You can't do it. Nobody can. It's best to reshape the opening and put in a contrasting wood plate--diamond, shield or whatever is appropriate.

Now, if possible, loosen the nut on the stock (recoil) bolt and drive back just enough to bring the head and nut flush with surface of stock, because now you start sanding and if these metal bolt-ends are flush with wood, you'll not only clean them up but they will prevent your saucering--hollowing--the surface around their inletting holes. As much as possible, use a wood block to back your sandpaper in order to keep straight lines and take off high spots.

Never buy sandpaper, only the garnet paper used for cabinet work, in 3/0, 4/0, 5/0 and 6/0. (For final finishing on hard, fancy wood, go to 7/0.) It also is now graded by numbers the same as abrasive cloths for metal---6/0 is 220, 7/0 is 240, etc.

For the little curved areas around grip and comb, invest in a roll of one inch abrasive cloth strip, 180 grit. Comes in 50-yard rolls at automotive or industrial supply stores, costs about six bucks, but a roll will last for years. If you can afford it, get a roll of 240 grit also for final finishing jobs. You tear off about a foot, hold one end to the spot you want to smooth with a thumb or fingertip, and pull with the other hand. This is the only way to sand in curved areas, around cheekpieces, in thumbholes, etc. You can do more in four minutes with strip-sanding than in an hour rubbing away with little pieces of paper. You can also get blisters on the pressure finger if you don't watch out, but adhesive tape will protect quite well. Gloves do not seem to work out, as you can't keep the "feel" of the surface under the strip.

The big thing to remember about sanding is don't overdo it--use the finest grit the surface calls for to start, and don't use the 3/0 if 5/0 will clean it up. Military stocks are always skimpy on depth so do not take much off the top or bottom of stock. If you do, metal will project above the inletting. Oh, this can be fixed up too, but it is work. You must file or grind magazine boxes and guard parts down, scrape inletting deeper, shorten guard screws and trigger tips, etc. These operations are often done purposely when slim, lightweight sporters are custom-built, but are hardly in order on our military stock refinishing program.

Anyway, after you get your ex-service stock cleaned and smoothed, it still looks kind of piebald. Stain the stupid thing. Most walnut or dark wood stains are burnt umber in solvent or raw linseed oil. Buy a tube of the color at any artist's supply, mix your own, using solvent. Or if you plan to use an oil finish, boiled or prepared stock oil such as LinSpeed, TruOil, etc., can replace the solvent. Only takes a little; wipe over the stock with cotton cloth patch. Now wipe it off with cleaning tissue or clean rags. Most of the stain will finish up to a uniform shade.

Use the stock finish of your choice, following the directions provided. If an oil finish is wanted and a really good appearance, fill the grain with oil also. Put oil on, let it gum (semi-harden) then sand wet with small pieces of 5/0 paper. Tear a sheet into six sections. Put fresh stock oil on a small area, say the size of your hand, and sand with the grain, cutting the gummed coat down to the wood, constantly changing the paper so it keeps cutting.

When you get smears of oil and wood on the stock, wipe these off cross-grain with tissue. Do this over the entire stock, two or three times, and the grain will be filled and smooth.

Finish with 6/0 paper. Put on a coat of oil all over and wipe this off with tissue. Do this a few hours or a day apart a few times and you will have a real oil finish. This sytem, with a few added refinements such as rubbing with 4/0 steel wool now and then, and the finished job with burlap, is that used by the very top custom stockmakers for the past couple of generations.

If you want an original type military finish, you just put on oil a time or two without sanding, or even use a thinned spar varnish.

This about takes care of refinishing a military stock and/or making a presentable addition for the cabinet. It will certainly be far better looking than it was to start with and you will have learned a lot about handling the abrasives and finishing. Alterations and remodeling techniques are scarcely involved, except for filling in the sling slots in butts, perhaps installing commercial swivels for a hunting sling and maybe a pad to cut down recoil effect—we'll go into fitting these at a later date.   ●

MACHINERY FOR THE HOME GUNSHOP

KEN HOWELL

Myford Super 7B toolroom lathe is smaller than lathes generally used in professional shops. Many accessories make it also a milling machine or any of several other specialty machines. Larger lathes offer greater work capacity, but the Myford is a precision tool far more capable, versatile, and precise than small lathes are generally expected to be. It is one of the best blends of compactness, capability, and fine precision as well as durability.

WHETHER YOUR gunshop is a business or a hobby, the natural hunger of the craftsman is the same — an urgent desire for good tools and equipment. Operating the shop as a business justifies equipment purchases that the hobby craftsman can only envy, as a rule, but within the usual limitations of space and cost, most serious hobby craftsmen can also afford some of the pro's basic machinery. Two warnings are in order, however: *one:* don't be fooled by the natural notion that fancier equipment will improve the work you produce; *two:* don't expect the expense to end when you install a drill press, a lathe, or a small milling machine in your shop.

Shop equipment has two basic categories: equipment that cuts in some way, to alter the shape of a piece of metal, and equipment that somehow holds the piece of metal and guides the cutting. The basic cutting tools are the file, the hacksaw, and the simple drill; the basic holding device is the vise. If you understand these and can use them well, you can also turn out good work with fancier equipment. But no matter how sophisticated a shop you may equip yourself with, you will never outgrow these simple, basic tools. You'll continue to need and use them — so frequently that you may be surprised — but your fancier equipment only facilitates certain operations, it doesn't replace skill or lessen the need for care.

I've long thought that if the manufacturers of lathes, drill presses, and milling machines could only tell who their best prospects were, they could operate nicely by *giving* away these machines and depending thereafter on the sale of tools and accessories for their profits. When you buy a lathe, for example, and get it set up in your shop, your lathe expense has only begun — from then on, for as long as you continue to operate that machine, you can expect to be buying a multitude of accessories and tooling needed for its use. Certain accessories, most of which may be included in the original purchase, equip the machine for simple turning operations. But a great many accessories also await your use — to extend the capability of your particular machine. A *complete* lathe outfit costs far more than the simple basic outfit that is most likely to be your first purchase. The same is true of the other basic machinery we'll discuss, too. Purchase of the basic machine is essentially a down payment on a *system;* some extension of the basic outfit is necessary, and there's almost no limit to how far you can extend it.

One question I'm often asked is which machine should come first: drill press or lathe? The answer is *neither,* unless you already have a very good bench grinder. Wherever cutting tools are in regular use, the means for sharpening them has to be close at hand. And the shaping of such tools is almost as important as the sharpening of them, even if the only cutting tool you have, so far, is a single chisel. As you add more cutting tools, which you are doing when you add one of these machines, you increase your need for good shaping and sharpening equipment. So the first power tool for the home gunshop has to be a good bench grinder. And just as is so with the machine tools already mentioned, this piece of equipment is only a *beginning* purchase: no grinding wheel or pair of wheels is suitable for all your needs, and no wheel holds its shape in use. You will need a selection of at least two grinding wheels and the tool for reshaping each wheel as it wears.

The Jet 1236P lathe, large enough for barrel work, is large and costly but welcome in a shop that has enough room for it. Any lathe requires a lot of space: working room around the lathe is as vital as the space occupied by the machine itself.

The six-inch Atlas is a low-cost lathe designed for small shops, small workpieces, and less than constant use. Within its capability, it turns out good results and offers good durability. Its spindle is bored to 17/32 inch, and it accepts workpieces as long as 19¼ inches — too small for some barrel work. A wide range of accessories adapt it to light milling and other work.

Also, for consistently grinding the proper angles on the tools you'll be shaping and sharpening, you will need an assortment of jigs or guides. Most of these, you'll probably prefer to make for yourself. Most are simple to make, and forms you can follow are shown in some of the guides, manuals, handbooks, and textbooks that you will also find yourself accumulating.

Start building and *using* a shop library, beginning with one of the manuals by South Bend, Atlas, or one of the textbook publishers on the subject of the machine you're considering. Check with your local schools to see what may be available in your area; schools often have some excellent shop manuals and textbooks, or at least references listing them and where you can get them. Even if you don't sign up for a local course, the books used there are likely to be good purchases for you.

First, the tool manuals and course textbooks offer a low-cost, convenient way to check out the theory and capabilities of the machines we're talking about. Beyond that, they usually cover also the basics of shaping and sharpening the particular

cutting tools you can expect to be using regularly, once you have installed that new machine, and they generally include a wealth of information that you will have to consult frequently: tables of screw threads, tap-and-drill correlations, decimal equivalents, cutting speeds for a variety of metals, and how to lay out and to hold specific kinds of work. There's no better place to learn what each machine is capable of doing, so these manuals and textbooks are the best place to begin your "shopping" for tools.

Brownell's, Incorporated, which supplies a great variety of gunsmith tools and equipment, usually carries a selection of books ranging from small specialty manuals on such subjects as small lathes or the sharpening of tools on up to a two-volume course in machine-shop techniques and some of the standard reference volumes for machinists. Atlas Press Company publishes a very nice lathe manual, which is available from Brownell's, also. The makers and suppliers of the machinery in question usually have literature that lists the specifications of each piece of machinery, so this kind of literature is a must for your

prepurchase library. Read well before you order, and you can plan your shop machinery with a maximum of wisdom now and a minimum of regret later. The more you know about what each machine can do — and can't do — the better you can decide which machines to buy, which model of each, and which to put in your shop first.

Interestingly enough, the milling machine — according to one machine-shop textbook — "was originally developed for manufacturing the small irregular-shaped parts used in the construction of firearms," but it would be the last of the three machines likely to be chosen by most of us equipping a home gunshop. The real choice of which machine to get first usually has to be between the lathe and the drill press, and the decision is as likely to favor one as the other. The space available often decides the matter; so does cost, sometimes. Fortunately, there is some overlap in the uses of these machines.

My first machine was more than a toy — but in comparison with the machines now in my shop, not much more. I had almost no space, no money to spare, and next to no

One of the first essentials for any shop that uses cutting tools is a good bench grinder with one or two grinding wheels and the dressing tool used for reshaping worn wheels. Tools must be shaped and sharpened before use, resharpened after use has dulled or chipped them. The grinder is thus one of the vital machines for the home shop. Its value grows with each machine added, since each new machine increases the number and variety of tools that need careful grinding.

Diemaker Dave Corbin also supplies a wide range of machine tools. This is one of many floor-model drill presses in the Corbin line. Choosing between floor and bench models can be tough but has nothing to do with the basic quality of the drill press itself.

Just as the Myford is a good combination of lathe and milling machine and in addition does precision drilling, a Jet drilling and milling machine from Corbin combine functions of drill press and light milling machine. Sturdier and heavier than most benchtop drill presses and much lighter than a huge milling machine, this machine provides capability and precision more than adequate for the home gunshop.

knowledge of machines for metalwork. At that time, an Austrian import called the Unimat was available. It was supposed to be about five machine tools all in one: lathe, drill press, milling machine, precision grinder, and I forget what else. Within its limits, it was a very useful tool. Most important for me, I was able to learn on it — and from it — as well as to make a great many tools and parts with it. Art Director Dave LeGate is an impresario with his Unimat: he makes things with his that I wouldn't have thought were within the capability of that tiny machine. Unfortunately, however, Dave has so little room for shop equipment that he isn't likely to move on up to larger equipment, as I have.

The Unimat model that Dave and I have is no longer imported, but several similar machines are available. Their use for work on guns is severely limited, however. The upper range of machinery suitable for gunwork extends far beyond the range of the home gunshop — to lathes, for example, capable of handling work up to a couple of feet or more in diameter and several feet long. For the home gunshop, it's probably most useful to consider those that are marginal for

work on rifle barrels — that is, those just too small and those just large enough for use in threading, shaping, and finishing rifle barrels. Drill presses likewise range from the ridiculously tiny to mighty machines large enough to require almost their own special housing. For the home gunshop, the choice is wide enough without ranging out to either of these extremes.

To supplement my Unimat, my first "drill press" was a Sears half-inch industrial electric drill, held in a benchtop stand that also came from Sears. The better of two models offered by Sears, this stand is adjustable and much sturdier than the cheaper stand. Within limits, it has served *some* of my drilling needs well. But unless you contemplate only the simplest and most limited gunwork, you probably won't be satisfied forever with so limited a piece of machinery. But let me go back now to my first warning: don't assume that better machinery makes you a better craftsman. When I had to, I've done some simple "lathe" work with a quarter-inch electric drill clamped to a steel strap by a large hose clamp, and the strap in turn C-clamped to my bench. A home-made affair held the work, and a hand-held

file was my cutting tool. This kind of rig required a lot of care and frequent checking of the work before I finally managed to finish the doodad I was making, but it did the job for me.

Makeshift and "good enough" equipment always whet a craftsman's appetite for something better. True economy lies in making your best and final choice at the beginning rather than progressing expensively upward through not-good-enough temporary outfits. Sometimes, the makeshift or the junior-grade has to come first, and it can have its value, as my Unimat certainly had for me. In an enviable position is the man who knows what will serve his needs, has the space to put it in, and can afford to put it in his shop.

In the home gunshop, the drill press seems to be the first machine usually acquired — though the lathe seems to be the machine most desired — so let's talk about the drill press first. Lower cost and smaller space are probably the factors favoring the drill press as the first choice in most home gunshops. Also, the drill press is simpler than the lathe — simpler to set up, simpler to understand, simpler to use. Therefore it doesn't awe the home

An important major accessory for expanding the role of a good lathe is the milling attachment, called a vertical slide by the English manufacturer of the Myford lathes. This senior Myford model swivels on two axes, offering more control and versatility than simpler models that swivel about only one axis. A careful craftsman can produce a variety of fine work on this kind of equipment. Size is limited, but the degree of precision and fineness of finish can be made to match the best work of professional shops.

Useful for learning basics but certain to be outgrown as your skill develops are such machines as the Unimat "universal machine tool" and the makeshift "drill press" consisting of a heavy-duty electric drill and an adjustable bench stand. Both of these are capable of good work in expert and careful hands, but they handicap anyone who is capable of using them to full advantage. At times, such temporary affairs have real value, but neither should be considered a substitute for a full-size lathe, drill press, or milling machine. They lack rigidity and power, and most such drills have only one speed.

guncraftsman quite as much, so it logically becomes a stepping stone in the development of the home gunshop.

Corbin Manufacturing & Supply offers a wide selection of drill presses, and their catalog is probably as good a place as any to continue shopping. Corbin handles the Jet line of machinery, imported from Taiwan and shipped to American buyers from about half a dozen warehouses in the continental United States. The first obvious choice is between a floor model and a bench model. Aside from cost, what's the difference? If the work you envision for your drill press doesn't require all the space that a floor model offers, between base and spindle, consider that a bench model allows room *underneath* for drawers or cupboard — in a word, *storage*. Beyond that, I'd just look over the specifications and capacities — and costs — of several models and let the choice make itself. When comparing costs, be sure to note that some drill presses come with an electric motor, and some don't. If you want to splurge where it'll count, put your money on a husky motor for your drill press, whether you pick a unit with motor included or buy one that allows

you to add the size and strength of motor you prefer.

Also, while considering cost, remember once again that the purchase of the drill press will be only the down payment on a system. The rest of the system awaits your purchase. First, even though you may have an excellent accumulation of drill bits, consider the wisdom of investing in a good set of high-speed drill bits in a case or drill index. For the best precision drilling, which after all is the reason for equipping your shop with a drill press, it's best to start with good, new drills and take good care of them. Using older drills, you're likely to thwart your own purposes and perhaps ruin parts you're making or modifying. Older drills used in less-precise equipment are subject to bending, chipping, and cracking that may not show up until after they have ruined something for you. Chancing upon an especially good deal, I outfitted my new drill press with a super set of drill bits: fractional sizes, letter sizes, and number sizes all in one big master drill index. It's a honey of a set, and it increases the usefulness of my drill press. You can be sure that I take good care of these drills, too.

They're precision tools, as precious as jewels and as carefully kept.

The next basic item for use with the drill press is a good drill-press vise. Don't try to do business on a drill press without one. With or without a positioning device, the vise provides tight and precise holding, which not only increases the life of your drills and preserves the precision of the drill press but also helps you keep all your fingers and both your eyes, with a minimum of cuts, bruises, and slivers. While I've never thought of drill-press vises as a category of collectibles, I've managed to accumulate more than a few and don't consider any of mine superfluous. Each has something in its favor not duplicated by the others, so each has its own particular usefulness. If you limit yourself to just one, it probably should be one that can be swung through ninety degrees vertically, from horizontal to vertical positioning of the work, rather than the ones that simply clamp work flat at table level.

A work-positioning table is a superb accessory for any good drill press, providing not only clamping and positioning but also some help in precision layout. Some light milling is also possible on tables that have a screw-controlled table movement. Some of these have marked index wheels calibrating the movement of work. For the stockmaker inletting a blank "from the stick," this is an invaluable accessory. It makes the basic drill press into a milling machine of sorts. Its dependability may not be as great as that of the light milling machine, but a careful worker can find it most useful. The table on my drill press is a Japanese import, available from B-Square Company. This same company, by the way, also offers another good accessory for your drill press: a tapholder for precisely guiding taps into holes already drilled on the drill press. Such a device, also available in a variety of forms from other sources, prolongs the useful life of taps, but more important is its reduction of the number of pieces spoiled and the time lost when taps break in the work. Threads so tapped are cleaner, the holes not enlarged as is often the case when taps are guided solely by hand. And B-Square is a good source for drills, taps, dies, and gun screws, too.

Choosing a lathe is seldom as easy as choosing a bench grinder or a drill press, especially when you have to fit the machine into the work plan and space of a home gunshop. The two basic foundations for choice, it seems to me, are the work you expect to do on your lathe and the space you can give it in your shop. I might add here, incidentally, that my experience has been exactly the same with all three of the major machines I've put in my shop, the drill press, the lathe, and the milling machine: each and every one requires more floor and work space than I'd thought it would. Each one is larger from front to back than I'd expected, and each requires more free space along each side than I had predicted. So my advice is either to spend a lot of time and thought on the space problem or to expect your machine to require more room than you'd first imagine.

The critical dimensions of a lathe for gunwork are the hole through the headstock spindle and the maximum length of work that can be turned between centers. Here, a caution is in order: while the ideal spindle bore is one that accepts rifle barrels through the headstock, and the ideal distance between centers is one long enough for reaming barrel chambers, much gunwork is possible with lathes that are "too small" in both these dimensions. Therefore, unless your lathe will be used quite a bit for work on rifle barrels, don't overestimate the necessity of either the spindle bore or the distance between centers.

For instance, the six-inch Atlas lathe and the seven-inch Myford lathe are "too small" in both dimensions. Yet both are excellent lathes for an astounding variety of gunwork. I used to own one of the little six-inchers from Atlas and found it to be excellent in its dependability and its precision. A gun designer whom I know uses one now for building prototypes and likes it very well. This same designer has spent some time in my shop, using the lathe that replaced my Atlas — a Myford Super 7B long-bed model, a fine English toolroom lathe. He is increasingly impressed with the Myford each time he uses it, but he is content with his Atlas and will keep it, simply because he hasn't room for a Myford in his shop. His Atlas fits, and he can move it more easily when he moves. So although he occasionally comes up against a problem his Atlas can't handle, the six-inch Atlas is a good choice for him. When he wants to thread or chamber a barrel that is too big for his little Atlas, he either has another gunsmith do it for him or temporarily borrows the use of a larger lathe in another man's shop.

Atlas makes larger lathes, big enough for any sort of work this designer would ever expect to be doing on a lathe, but he has neither the space to install one nor the *frequent* need for one so large. I wanted something a bit larger than the six-inch Atlas but hadn't the space nor the need for a twelve-inch Atlas, so the Myford Super 7B long-bed model is perfect for my shop. Another entire line of lathes that we could have considered, had we known of them at the time, is the huge line of Jet lathes handled by Corbin. These range from about the size of my Myford on up to monsters big enough to use on cannon barrels. Thus, in terms of size, the selection is large enough for the home gunsmith to find, from one of these three sources alone, a lathe to fit his shop and his budget. Myford lathes, by the way, are imported for American customers by D&M Model Engineering. I got mine directly from Myford, but importing one from England is something best handled by someone who knows more about it than I did. Direct importation cost me more than this same lathe would have cost with D&M Model Engineering handling the details. For one thing, the arrival of my lathe in Los Angeles came quite some time before I got word that it was there. In the meantime, it lay in a warehouse accumulating charges that I had to pay. Fortunately, it's a humdinger of a machine, well worth even that unnecessary extra cost. It's exceptionally well designed and beautifully made, quite versatile in the wide range of things it can do with the

accessories I got with it, and — all in all — a joy to use. I turn with it, thread with it, bore and drill with it, even mill with it sometimes, even though I also have a Jet milling machine. But all this is still possible without that needless extra storage cost that I had to pay.

Versatility is probably the most valuable characteristic of a lathe for the home gunshop, and this is one area in which my designer friend envies me my Myford. His Atlas is by no means a cheapie machine or limited only to basic turning and threading. It is available at a reasonable price — its major asset for the home shop — and can be used for a variety of machining operations with the accessories made for it by Atlas. He mills on his Atlas, for example, but his milling attachment lacks some of the adjustments and versatility of the Myford milling attachment. Mine swivels about a horizontal axis as well as around the vertical axis, for example. Also, mine has a power crossfeed for milling. More basic, however, is the difference between the ways these two lathes are converted from one threading pitch or turning speed to another: the Atlas is equipped with sets of gears that must be installed on the lathe to provide the desired setup; the Myford has all these gears installed, along with a quick-change gearbox for almost instantaneous shifting from one setup to another. Of course, there's a price to pay in either case. The low cost of the Atlas carries with it the inconvenience and grime of gear changes, as well as the necessity for storing the unused gears and the danger of losing or dropping and damaging one of the loose gears. The neatness, convenience, and protection of the Myford setup costs a few more bucks in the basic purchase.

If a good drill press *and* a good small lathe can be used to advantage for light milling, why then add a separate milling machine to the home gunshop? Having just added a Jet 15 mill to my shop, I can answer that question rather more than idly. For one thing, it's often very inconvenient to have to switch back and forth from one kind of operation to another, and back again, on the same machine. For another, the distance of travel on a milling attachment for drill press or lathe is occasionally too short for the milling to be done.

Many of the items I've made on the Myford have required both turning and milling, as well as drilling. Often, I've had to do a few minutes' worth of cutting in one setup, spend a good bit more time changing to another setup and getting everything lined-up right, then cut or drill for a few seconds, and again change the setup back to what it was. It is much nicer to have one machine set up for one operation, the other machine for the other operation, and simply move the work from one to the other and back again. To be frank, this is more a matter of luxury and pleasure than of necessity, since my shop isn't a business facility now but a hobby setup. The additional cost, if I may remind you again, is not only in the additional machine and its additional bench but also in the additional tooling required. The spindle of the Jet 15 milling machine uses arbors with a number-three Morse taper, but the Myford lathe and the Yuasa drill press use arbors with other Morse tapers. This means that even to use the same end mills in both the Myford and the Jet, I need different sets of arbors, and since these are precision-made and hardened tools, they cost a bit more, say, than a set of carpenter's chisels. Yet the new Jet milling outfit, while not exactly useless without them, is certainly handicapped by the absence of them.

It could be worse. As it is, I know a source where I can get these accessories — as well as virtually anything else I'm likely to need, from end mills and drill bits to tool steel and measuring devices — with faster delivery and better prices than I might otherwise have to suffer with: Manhattan Supply Company's catalog belongs on the bench of every gunshop where machine tools are used. Mentioning tool steel just now has reminded me also to mention another source and another caution. First, the caution: it's wise to resist the scrounger's urge and to use steels of known properties rather than salvaged pieces of unknown hardness, metallurgy, and strength. Nobody knows better than I do how satisfying it is to make something useful out of something hitherto useless. I even have my kids save any washer, bolt, nut, or the like they find on the street,

and I make things from the strangest assortment of salvaged chunks you're likely to see in any little shop. But there are times when this is simply foolish economy; sometimes, the part to be made requires that you make it from steel you know to be good for the purpose; at other times, the piece of material you've just chucked in the lathe can cost you more than the eventual part would have been worth if you'd managed to complete it. It might simply take longer than need be, simply because the steel is less machinable or tougher than you need for that particular part. In worst cases, a piece of scrap can easily ruin a valuable end mill or cutting bit worth several times as much money. And there's usually the added problem of the extra time it takes to get a new tool and the proper kind of stock delivered before you can start over again.

Sometimes, it makes good sense to make something worthwhile from pieces of scrap, and when such a project is successful, the satisfaction is enormous. But sometimes the risk simply isn't worth it, and at such times it's helpful to be able to get just the right kind of steel for the job. An excellent reference for comparing steels of various properties is the stock list and reference book available from an excellent source of good steel: Earle M. Jorgensen Company. From nineteen or more locations in the main forty-eight states and Hawaii, Jorgensen can supply any of a wide variety of steels — cold-rolled, hot-rolled, stainless, tool steel, and others — in bars, sheets, tubing — according to need. Aluminum, too.

Jorgensen's reference manual can save you a lot of grief if, for instance, you have to make some jigs, parts, or equipment for which a steel such as "Mach 5" would be suitable. The reference manual tells us that this alloy is no less than 303 percent more easily machinable than number 1212 steel, machining easily at five hundred surface feet per minute. Mach 5 isn't considered weldable, and although it can be hardened somewhat, it isn't considered a case-hardening steel. If the use you need it for doesn't require welding or hardening, you can be time and money ahead by using this easily machinable steel. Its machining requires less electricity, and its greater machinability means less wear and breakage of bits as well as less-frequent use of the grinder. Other steels are better for certain purposes; the variety offers many choices so you can select the steel that's just right for each project.

As you study gunsmith catalogs and the manuals relating to machine tools, take note of the many tools, jigs, fixtures, and accessories that you will be able to make for yourself when your shop is equipped with any of the three big machines: drill press, lathe, or small milling machine. Making these necessary extra items yourself can easily be the factor that decides which machine you can afford to put in your shop and can then use to advantage. By this means, you can cut down the total cost of your equipment, extend its useful range of operations, and increase your mastery of its capabilities. To do any less would be to miss a great deal of the value of these machines in the home gunshop.

sources:

Atlas Press Company; 2019K N Pitcher Street; Kalamazoo, Michigan 49007
Brownell's, Inc; Route 2, Box 1; Montezuma, Iowa 50171
B-Square Company; P O Box 11281; Forth Worth, Texas 76109
Corbin Mfg & Supply Company; P O Box 758; Phoenix, Oregon 97535
D&M Model Engineering; P O Box 400; Western Springs, Illinois 60558
Earle M Jorgensen Company; P O Box 6737; Phoenix, Arizona 85005
Manhattan Supply Company; 151 Sunnyside Blvd; Plainview, New York 11803

ROLLER BEARING STEADY REST

FOR INCREASED ACCURACY WITHOUT MARRING

By JOHN PARFET

GUNSMITHING JOBS such as barrel cutting and crowning, where long work cannot be supported between centers, requires the use of a steady rest which clamps onto the bed ways of the lathe. Adjustable jaws are pressed against the work at three points, holding the barrel or whatever long piece is being machined as rigidly as possible in order to eliminate chattering of the cutting tool and to make certain the piece is concentric. Most currently available steady rests have jaws that need frequent oiling and care because they rely on solid contact with the workpiece. These jaw ends tend to mar the work, for if adjusted tight enough to provide the needed support, the frictional heat generated by the turning of the workpiece causes galling and tearing, leading to rapid wear and loss of support in the steady rest itself and a rough finish on the workpiece.

While this can be tolerated in most machine shop work, it isn't acceptable for gunsmithing work, where good looks are as important as precision machining. So we made a roller bearing steady rest which has solved the problems of standard steady rests and made an efficient addition to our special purpose lathe tooling.

The roller bearing steady rest has the structure of the standard steady rest, except for the roller bearings mounted on the jaw ends, which are free to rotate at the speed of the workpiece while maintaining firm support. As the illustrations show, three sealed roller bearings, with headed pins to attach them to the jaws, support the work.

The size of the bearings depends on the smallest diameter material that is going to be machined. As an

Unlike a standard steady rest, which has a tendency to mar barrel finishes unless frequently oiled, a roller bearing steady rest will insure greater precision and damage-free rotation of the work.

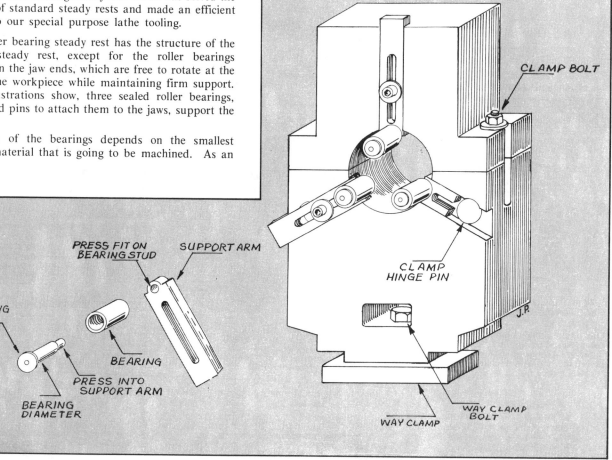

example, a bearing 5/8-inch outside diameter will support a workpiece as small as 1/8-inch outside diameter.

There are many advantages of the roller bearing steady rest over the standard steady rest. The roller bearing rest does not require frequent oiling to reduce friction for the bearings rotate at the speed of the workpiece, rolling rather than rubbing. When polishing a barrel the rest can be moved to a point along the barrel which has already been polished without marring the polish; similarly, the blue of a finished barrel which is being cut and crowned will not be damaged, as the standard steady rest normally will.

The only area of caution in using the roller bearing rest is to take care not to throw chips under the roller while machining near the support for the chips can mar the work, loosen a bearing or cause runout of the work. Otherwise the roller bearing steady rest is as simple and efficient as the standard steady rest, while it eliminates the problems encountered with the latter.

●

The
SLACK BELT SANDER

By JIM PARFET

---

a much overlooked finishing tool

BELT SANDERS are an efficient means of removing relatively large amounts of material in a short period of time, plus they can be used for holding fairly close tolerances with fine finishes, as can be seen by the work done with them in many industrial shops. But I have seen few belt sanders in home shops, and those few are used primarily for flat work, which indicates that most amateur — and perhaps professional — gunsmiths are unaware of their potential advantages, particularly of the modified "slack belt" sander.

A commercially produced belt sander using a one-inch wide belt can be modified for bench use by removing the support behind the belt, but I chose to construct my own, designed to either mount on the cross-slide of my lathe or be clamped in a vise for bench work. Construction is simple, and other than the wheels, most of the parts will be available in the shop.

Either rubber or plastic caster wheels make excellent belt sander wheels because of the radiused "crown" on their outside diameter, which tends to keep the belt centered. Three are needed, each about 2 1/2 inches in diameter by 1-inch wide; two are bored out to accept press-fit bearings and serve as idler wheels. A bushing with setscrew is pressed into the third, which is used on the motor as a drive wheel.

The basic frame can be two-inch by 1/4 angle iron about 13 inches long with a plate welded at right angles at the top to support the motor, which can be 1/8 to 1/2 horsepower, but which should turn 1,750 rpm. The stationary idler wheel is mounted near the bottom of the frame; I used a 1/4-20 x 1 1/2 hex head bolt projecting through (1) a hardened steel washer, (2) a .500 o.d. by .255 i.d. by 1.125-inch Oilite bushing pressed into the wheel, (3) a .750 o.d. by .501 i.d. by 1.062 long hardened steel bushing, against (4) a .875 o.d. by .265 i.d. x .438 thick hardened steel spacer. This assembly is held in place by a 1/4-20 hex nut and lock washer. The same bushing/spacer assembly is used to mount the second idler wheel, except the hardened steel spacer is only .188-inch thick, to offset the thickness of the support arm.

The support arm for the second idler is a 1 x 1/4 strap with a pivot point about two-thirds of its length from the idler. The strap is mounted to the frame, using a 1/4-20 x 3/4-inch bolt and Oilite bushing, at a point 3 1/2 inches from the top of the angle iron frame. Length of the support arm from the idler pulley to the pivot point is determined by the position of the drive and stationary idler wheel,

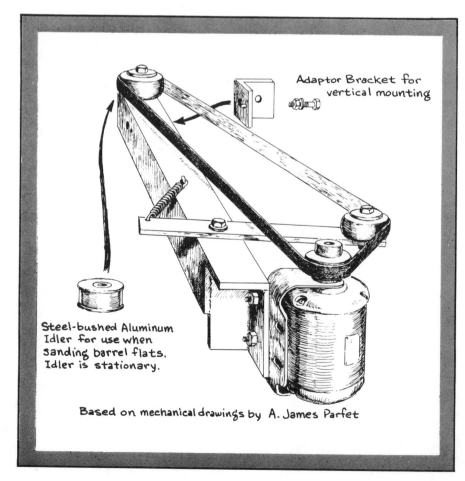

Adaptor Bracket for vertical mounting

Steel-bushed Aluminum Idler for use when sanding barrel flats. Idler is stationary.

Based on mechanical drawings by A. James Parfet

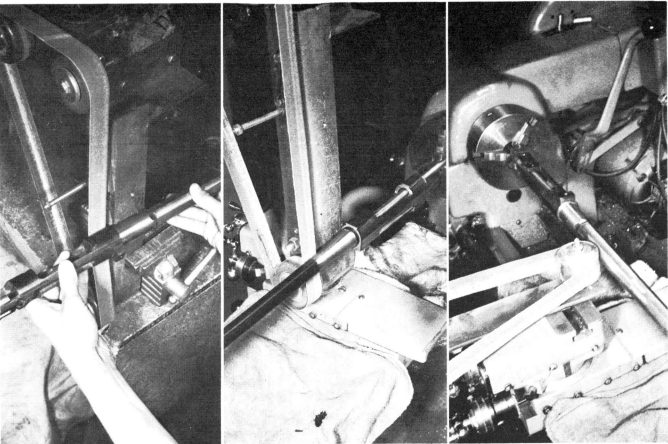

A simply made slack belt sander can be one of the most useful tools in the shop. Above left it is mounted in a vise while used for polishing the rounded top of a non-cylindrical action. At center it is mounted vertically on the lathe cross-feed for barrel polishing; due to the spring-loading of the center idler wheel, the belt will match any barrel contour. In the right photo, the sander is mounted horizontally on the cross-feed to provide ripple-free, uniform polishing of the flats on an octagon barrel.

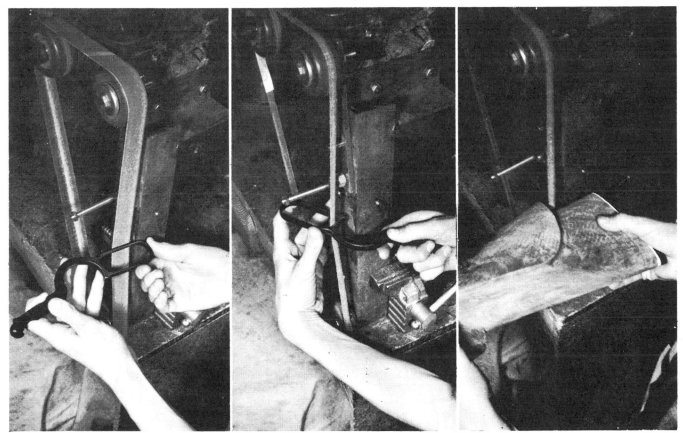

Uneven polishing of smaller-radius parts can be avoided by pressing against the spring-loaded belt to provide a radius matching that of the part, as at left. With a narrow, spliced belt, polishing of difficult-to-reach areas such as inside finger loops is easy, as in the center photo. With a paper belt designed for wood, final shaping of stocks can be done with the sander, leaving a smooth finish that requires a minimum amount of hand sanding.

since 36-inch abrasive belts will be used. An eighth-inch hole is drilled near the "tail" of the idler support arm as an eye for the tension spring. As the illustrations show, there is nothing complicated about the unit; the design can be altered as needed according to the materials that are available.

Belts are available from most industrial supply houses including Sears in the common grits of 120 to 340. Aluminum Oxide should be the only abrasive considered for metal work. The more open-grit paper belts, intended for use on wood, can be used for gunstock work.

The 120-grit belt is used for roughing work or to produce the uniform "ground" or matte type finish commonly found on medium priced arms today. This is a very serviceable finish from the standpoint of blue life. A finer "egg-shell" type finish can be produced with the 340-grit belt, while a worn out 340-grit belt will produce a soft gloss.

While a bench-mounted sander can be used to polish a barrel in much the same manner as a buffing wheel, I much prefer to mount the barrel between centers on the lathe with the belt sander mounted on the cross slide, using a 2-inch piece of angle as an adapter bracket. There is no need to draw file a barrel to remove rust pits or tool marks when done on a lathe. There is also no need to consider barrel contour or taper, on a round barrel, as the spring-mounted idler wheel will compensate for these conditions.

Stock removal is a function of the lead screw feed rate and belt grit size. A coarser grit with slow feed will remove a greater amount of stock while a faster feed, or a finer belt grit or both will remove less stock.

For finishing the action, and other non-cylindrical parts, a bench mounted sander is used. In the case of my unit I clamp it in a bench vise. On parts with a relatively large radius, like the top of the action, a small amount of pressure is used...just enough to allow the belt to match the contour of the action. On parts with a small radius, such as a trigger guard, a heavier pressure is used, again so as to match the contour.

Belts can be made narrower for those tricky inside curves by starting a cut from the underside of the belt with a knife and then tearing; belts can also be spliced with a good strong tape for use inside trigger guards, etc. Remember when splicing a belt to look for the direction of travel marked on the belt and to make a lap splice with the outside end of the belt pointing away from the direction of travel.

I find the lathe-mounted belt sander an almost indispensable tool for finishing octagon barrels. I replace the solid mounted idler wheel with a machined wheel having a straight outside diameter of a size compatable with the barrel contour to be finished. I then lay the sander on its side, and mount it on the compound slide.

The tail stock should be adjusted according to barrel taper (indicated straight with a dial indicator) so that the side of the barrel receiving the sander is parallel to the travel of the sander. The side of the barrel receiving the sander must also be parallel with the machined wheel of the sander. If your lathe has an indexing feature in the spindle, as mine does, it is relatively easy to set up the index procedure. Lock the spindle in the No. 1 index position and indicate the barrel top surface flat, then the side to be ground will be vertical.

The procedure from here on is simply a matter of index and sand, index and sand; stock removal is controlled by the cross slide feed. The cross slide hand wheel should be set to zero so all flats will be the same size. If your lathe does not have the index feature in the spindle, a four-jaw chuck can be used with a stop screw set on one of the jaws. After finish-grinding one flat, the setscrew is moved and the chuck indexed to stop with the next jaw on the setscrew. This aligns the first four alternate surfaces; to align the remaining set of surfaces they must be indicated in the same manner as the first.

The slack belt sander is good for gunstock roughing work including final contour sanding on the buttstock and forearm. In these areas a wood finishing belt is best used, producing a finish requiring only final sanding.

With proper belt selection, the slack belt sander can be used to produce any type of finish from a matte, non-reflecting surface to a highly buffed surface necessary for a glossy, highly reflective blueing job. You will also find that the slack belt sander does not "smear" lettering or holes in the surface of the metal. With a little care and practice, sharp transition lines may be maintained in areas such as on trigger guards where a radius breaks into a flat surface.

The slack belt sander does have its place in the workshop but few realize how valuable it can be.   ●

TOOLING FOR GUNSMITHING:

Jigs & Fixtures

By ROY DUNLAP

*A*NY GUNSMITH doing more than elementary hand-repair work soon finds himself in need of special tooling to make easier, or even make possible, some of the jobs that crop up — most such tooling can be made up quickly and easily by the smith himself.

Simple fixtures and jigs to hold parts for drilling, milling or fitting, made of mild steel, aluminum or even wood, are very valuable. On some jobs it takes less time to make a fixture and do the work than it would take to do the job without a fixture. The result is likely to be a better job, but it certainly will be easier — and you'll have the jig ready for next time the job comes up.

For instance, it's a lot faster to prepare a fixture for fitting parts, such as revolver or rifle triggers and hammers, than it is to repeatedly assemble and disassemble the parts in the frame until everything works properly. For milling machine use, many difficult holding problems can be solved by making such fixtures, angled or shaped false jaws for the mill vise, even shaped wooden wedges for mechanisms or magazines wells in blanks. Drill jigs aren't too easy to make, and are not needed unless you plan to go into quantity production on some small item or job.

We don't do much work with dove-tail front sights any more, but the little holder illustrated allows you to hold one in either a bench or mill vise for work without any possibility of slippage or damage to the dovetail. It takes all of five minutes to make a front-sight slot cutter from a scrap of metal.

In past years I manufactured all sorts of off-beat accessories and in self defense had to do a lot of tool-making. How do you hold a hook buttplate casting without any true flats solidly enough to permit milling a fairly precision dovetail on its base? At an angle, yet! Simple. Study your diploma from the Rube Goldberg School of Design. Sand up a batch of wooden blocks, glue together to form a pattern, have it cast in hard aluminum, mill it here and there, attach locating pins and holding arms with bolts, and you're in business. Such a fixture is really a specialized, one purpose milling vise. So you don't want to make free-rifle hooks by the hundred — how about an easy system for modernizing the ever-present Mauser action by speedlocking it? Like lightening the firing pins and shortening the fall?

The 45-degree-face angle milling fixtures shown allow milling V-grooves in the pins with any small endmill in either a vertical or horizontal milling machine, large or small. Make it of aluminum bar stock of such dimensions suited to your regular mill vise. To get the grooves all the way to the rear end you'll need carbide end mills, for the firing pins are heat-treated to real toughness on the back ends. A full set of V-slots (not sharp V—use an end mill with slight radius on corners) will take out almost 40 percent of the weight of the pin — so it'll move faster.

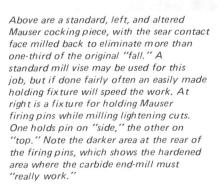

Above are a standard, left, and altered Mauser cocking piece, with the sear contact face milled back to eliminate more than one-third of the original "fall." A standard mill vise may be used for this job, but if done fairly often an easily made holding fixture will speed the work. At right is a fixture for holding Mauser firing pins while milling lightening cuts. One holds pin on "side," the other on "top." Note the darker area at the rear of the firing pins, which shows the hardened area where the carbide end-mill must "really work."

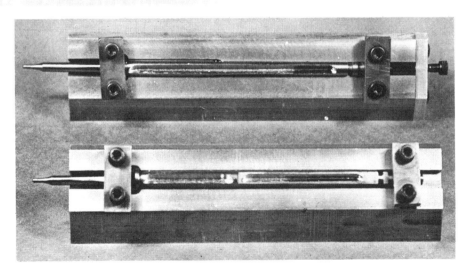

The carbide mill also will cut the faces of cocking-pieces back to shorten the fall. With military cocking pieces you may have to have the shallow cut in the bottom welded up by Heliarc, of course. On commercial straight-bottom types, just whittle them back. No, you don't have to worry about the pin warping. Yes, you may have to do some extra milling to make the safety work, depending on the type. The Mark X requires nothing at all, for instance. On wing-safety types, mill enough clearance on top of the cocking piece to allow the safety to engage properly. A one-half inch diameter carbide end-mill works nicely for this. The 3/8-inch will also do fine, with a little dial manipulation on the mill. The normal firing-pin spring, unless weakened by set-back or long use, will give perfect ignition in a fall shortened a full third.

These little home-made accessories make an easy task of producing a super-custom rifle improvement, making the Mauser comparable in lock-time to the most recently designed bolt actions. (If you're doing the job for pay, don't do it at bargain rate — those carbide and mills cost genuine money, not peanuts, but they won't spring or bend at all).

The possibilities for small shop-helpers in the form of tooling are endless, from marking templates to complicated drill-jigs. Any job you have to do fairly often may call for assistance in the shape of some gadget you can whip up in an hour or two. Even tools to help the tools. Little blocks of metal with a slot and a clamp-screw, which will slide on the toolrest of your bench-grinder, will make perfect

hollow-grinding of chisels and screwdrivers not only possible but mandatory.

A strip of metal with holes and head counterbores for scope base and sight screws, etc. allows you to grind the ends

This drilling jig is used for locating holes in line and at the correct spacing for installation of dovetail target scope bases. Note the hardened steel drill bushings.

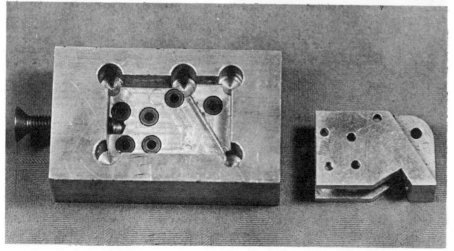

Jigs and fixtures may be as simple or complex as the job they are required to assist. The simple clamp-by-vise holding tools above are used for dovetail front sights, scope bases and guard screws. The drilling jig at left is used for precisely locating pin holes of housings (right) for the trigger mechanisms which Dunlap once made for free rifles.

of overlong hardened screws to desired length with no burnt fingertips or scarred heads from pliers — stick the screw through the proper hole in the bar and turn with screwdriver as you bring the tip against the wheel. No ruined or lost screws.

In making jigs and fixtures, any error in laying out, drilling or milling will, of course, be transmitted to all parts made in that fixture later on, so you must be pretty careful. If working with clean, bright steel or aluminum you can scribe and measure directly on the metal, otherwise you'll have to use layout dope — quick-drying red or blue liquid which has replaced, for most purposes, the 'Prussian Blue' you read about in the old gunsmithing books. "Dykem" is the best-known brand.

The most useful tool in layout is the common vernier caliper having sharp points on both the inside and outside jaws. Use the hardened points themselves for scribing center-lines, lines and cross-lines for hole-centers, etc. Use a sharpened center-punch (prick-punch) to make a light indent for centers, checking with a glass to see if you hit the center of the cross. If you didn't punch at an angle to get centered, then crater with a regular punch for the preliminary drill bit — smaller than final size.

Work up to proper hole size for the drill or drill-bushing to be used. Ordinary mild steel, unhardened, will last for hundreds of holes in a marking jig where you just want to locate and start holes. Where you must actually drill the hole all the way with the jig in place, you need the hardened steel drill-bushings sold by industrial mill and tool supply firms.

It is virtually essential, of course, that your drill and mill tables and vises are reasonably close to true — if the future fixture is not supported precisely at 90 degrees while operations are being done, you get a built-in angle that carries over into work done in the finished fixture. Use of level and indicators is required for any precision work, as always. I have a drill-press and three milling machines, with ten assorted vises which are used on one or more of each. Absolutely none combine for dead-true work without paper shims or other special setup care.

With drill-jigs it is mandatory to always use sharp bits ground correctly to center—an off-center bit, no matter how sharp, naturally wants to cut to its longest lip and the jig wants to hold it center. At best you get wobble of everything; at worst a damaged jig or even broken bit, if it is a small size.

For deep-drilling with a jig, the bit must be brought up and shavings cleared often to prevent them packing between the work and the jig, possibly forcing the jig away from the work and thus changing the hold position or angle. When using drilling fixtures, be very sparing in use of coolants or other cutting oils for this reason.

Your small shop-helpers won't be getting heavy industrial use, unless you're making some article in production, so most of them can be made of bar aluminum rather than tool steel. They won't take much time to shape up, and if you make one wrong, you haven't lost much in either time or material. Just make another. Then you'll save a lot of time and maybe even material in the future! ●

Section 2

STOCKS

AS WAS INDICATED in *Rifle* No. 88, the intent of this article is to present information on dimensional stability of wood gunstock materials. The changes in atmospheric moisture conditions (relative humidity) from one season of the year to another, along with different locations, have an effect on the physical dimensions of wood. Just make a mental note of how the wood "fits" on the butt plate or recoil pad of your favorite rifle or shotgun. Sometime during the year you may observe that it does not match the wood very well. And yes, you know full well it originally did. The wood has swelled or shrunk.

As a brief review consider that the wood in gunstocks is a cellulosic material and by its very nature will absorb water. When a tree is first cut the green wood contains a significant amount of water. The major portion of this water is free water present in the wood cells. The other type of water in wood is "bound water," which is found within the cell walls. When wood dries, free water is removed first. Then, at about 30 percent moisture content, the wood starts to shrink as bound water evaporates from the cell walls.

Dimensional Stability

With most species, wood shrinks approximately twice as much in the tangential direction of the growth rings as opposed to the radial direction perpendicular to the rings. Once the wood has dried to an equilibrium condition, however, it can absorb water as atmospheric moisture increases and the wood then swells.

The shrinking and swelling of wood during the normal seasonal changes affects wood's physical dimensions (Figure 1). Those woods that show only slight changes are considered to be more dimensionally stable. They "stay in place." Many species are well known for their ability to be reasonably free of movement due to changing moisture conditions.

Specific examples of tangential and radial movement for some wood species are shown by the data in the tables. The "dimensional change coefficient" (DCC) data for thirty-four domestic and imported woods are listed. The DCC is defined in *Wood Handbook No. 72* as "the change in (physical) dimension within the moisture content limits of 6 to 14 percent . . . based on the dimension

at 10 percent moisture content. The actual coefficient values as given in Table II represent the dimension variation for each one percent change in moisture content.

The DCC Ratio (T/R) is simply the radial coefficient divided into the tangential coefficient and illustrates a degree of stability for a given species. For example black walnut has a DCC Ratio of 1.4 while silver maple has a higher ratio of 2.5. This ratio combined with the DCC values represent the dimensional stability of a wood species.

To further explain, the dimensional stability of a given wood species is influenced by its:

• Volumetric shrinkage — i.e., green condition to 6 percent moisture content — black walnut is 10.2 percent.

• Ratio of radial to tangential shrinkage — DCC Ratio (T/R) as previously defined — i.e., black walnut is 1.4 (Table II).

• Grain direction, i.e., the straightness in the forearm of a rifle stock.

It should also be stated that each of

DIMENSIONAL STABILITY OF STOCK WOOD

David Webb

Cross-sectional view of a tree trunk illustrating the effects of shrinkage on the annual growth rings. Tangential shrinkage is about twice that of radial shrinkage.

the above three factors influence the dimensional stability of wood. These three factors can be understood and controlled by:

• Selecting a wood species that has a high degree of stability.

• Bulking the wood fibers with a treatment using polyethylene glycol 1000 (PEG).

• Laminating several or many pieces of wood to reduce the effect of grain direction.

I may be putting the "cart before the horse," but the reader should refer to the data given in Tables I and II while reviewing the following discussion.

With regard to selection of wood species for gun stocking, there may be no choice due to personal preference. If you only like walnut for your rifle stocks, that's your choice. However, it is of interest to see why walnut is such an excellent wood for stocking a rifle or shotgun. It simply is that the walnut species are stable woods.

Other shooters, who want maximum stability from their solid wood stocks for target purposes, may wish to consider another wood species.

Dimensional Stability Index (DSI)

Using volumetric shrinkage and the ratio of radial to tangential shrinkage, DCC Ratio (T/R), and information for various woods, one should be able to determine how the different woods perform with changes in relative humidity. However, the author often found it difficult to "juggle" the numbers and make the comparison between the woods. Thus, the idea of a "Dimensional Stability Index" (DSI). This concept makes it quite easy to compare the stability of the different species. It is determined by the following procedure:

(1) Use only the first two significant figures for the DCC data as given in Table II;

(2) thus, for black walnut convert the DCC tangential value of .00274 to 27 and the DCC radial value of .00190 to 19;

(3) add these two values together (27 plus 19 to equal 46), then take the DCC ratio of 1.4 and convert it to 14;

(4) use this converted value of 14

Three-ply stock of Hawaiian curly mango treated with PEG.

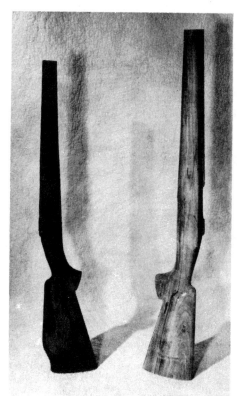

Shaped and inletted blanks treated with polyethylene glycol-1000 (PEG) to increase dimensional stability of the wood.

TABLE I

Most dimensional stable woods*

ranking	wood species	dimensional stability index
1	Eastern Red Cedar	57
2	Khaya	62
3	Teak	65
4	Catalpa	65
5	Walnut, old world	67
6	Sassafras	67
7	Mahogany	69
8	Honeylocust	69
9	Butternut	72
10	Locust, black	73
11	Walnut, black	74

* As determined by the Dimensional Stability Index (DSI)

DSI for black walnut is determined by dropping decimal points and using first two significant digits as follows:

$$DSI = DCC\text{-Tang.} + DCC\text{-Radial} + 2\,(DCC\ Ratio)$$
$$= 27 + 19 + 2\,(14)$$
$$= 74$$

twice and add it to the previous value of 46 to equal 74 — the DSI value for black walnut.

The DSI concept is purely arbitrary; however, it can be a useful tool in comparing the dimensional stability of the many wood species that are used for gunstocks. It is particularly interesting to note that (as shown in Table II) Eastern red cedar "leads the pack" in stability of all the woods listed. This answers the question as to why I have seen several laminated benchrest rifles stocked with this species.

Even though red cedar has a DSI value of 57 and black walnut has a value of 74, it does not infer that walnut is a poor gunstock wood. On the contrary it only suggests that red cedar is somewhat more stable. The excellent reputation that walnut has developed in over 200 years of use as a stock wood is completely justified. The function of the DSI concept is to put into perspective where other lesser known wood species stand in comparison.

TABLE II

Dimensional Change of Some Domestic and Imported Woods

nomenclature		Dimensional Stability Index [1]	Dimensional Change Coefficient (DCC)[2]		DCC Ratio T/R [3]
common name	scientific name		tangential	radial	
hardwoods					
Apple	Malus pumila	96	.00376	.00205	1.9
Beech	Fagus grandifolia	108	.00431	.00190	2.3
Birch: River	Betula nigra	89	.00327	.00162	2.0
Yellow	Betula alleghaniensis	85	.00338	.00256	1.3
Butternut	Juglans cinerea	72	.00223	.00116	1.9
Catalpa	Catalpa bignonioides	65	.00169	.00085	2.0
Cherry, black	Prunus seratina	77	.00248	.00126	2.0
Elm: American	Ulmus americana	94	.00338	.00144	2.3
Slippery	Ulmus rubra	86	.00315	.00169	1.9
Hickory, pecan	Carya illinoensis	86	.00315	.00169	1.9
Honeylocust	Gleditsia triacanthos	69	.00230	.00144	1.6
Locust, black	Robinia pseudoacacia	73	.00252	.00158	1.6
Madrone, Pacific	Arbutus menziesii	111	.00451	.00194	2.3
Maple: bigleaf	Acer macrophyllum	77	.00248	.00126	2.0
red	Acer rubrum	85	.00289	.00137	2.1
silver	Acer saccharinum	85	.00252	.00102	2.5
sugar	Acer saccharum	94	.00353	.00165	2.1
Persimmon	Diospyros virginiana	98	.00403	.00278	1.5
Sassafras	Sassafras albidum	67	.00216	.00137	1.6
Sweetgum	Liquidambar styraciflua	95	.00365	.00183	2.0
Sycamore	Platanus occidentalis	81	.00296	.00172	1.7
Walnut, black	Juglans nigra	74	.00274	.00190	1.4
softwoods					
Cedar: Alaska	Chamaecyparis noothatensis	74	.00208	.00095	2.2
Eastern red	Juniperus virginiana	57	.00162	.00106	1.5
Douglas fir (coast type)	Pseudotsuga menziesii	76	.00267	.00165	1.6
Redwood [4]	Sequoia sempervirens	79	.00229	.00101	2.3
Tamarack	Larix laricina	81	.00259	.00126	2.1
imported woods					
Khaya (African mahogany)	Khaya spp.	62	.00201	.00141	1.4
Lauans*: dark red	Shorea negrosensis	80	.00267	.00133	2.0
light red	Pentacme conforta	75	.00241	.00126	1.9
Mahogany, Central American [4]	Swietenia macrophylla	69	.00238	.00172	1.4
Teak [4]	Tectona grandis	65	.00186	.00101	1.8
Walnut: old world	Juglans regia	67	.00223	.00148	1.5
South American (Nogal) [4]	Juglans neotropica	79	.00258	.00129	2.0

* Philippine mahogany

[1] As defined in Table I.

[2] Per 1 percent change in moisture content, based on dimension at 10 percent M.C. and a straight line relationship between moisture content at which shrinkage starts and total shrinkage. (Shrinkage assumed to start at 30 percent M.C. for all species except those indicated by footnote [4].)

[3] Most wood species shrink approximately twice as much tangentially as in the radial direction. The T/R ratio shows the dimensional change relationship between tangential and radial grain structure.

[4] Shrinkage assumed to start at 22 percent M.C.

It also is interesting to note the DSI difference between the two walnut woods, native black — DSI value of 74 — and old world (French, English or Circassian if you prefer) — DSI value of 67.

Fiber Bulking

Enough has been written at this point about selection of wood species. Let's turn to the subject of how to improve the dimensional stability of a solid wood stock by some other means. There have been, over the years, a number of research efforts by various universities and government laboratories directed toward dimensional stabilization of wood. The only process that has been somewhat successful from a commercial standpoint has been a treatment using PEG.

We have established that wood will shrink and swell according to changes in the relative humidity. Recognizing this fact the U.S. Forest Products Laboratory during the early 1960s developed a treatment that gives a high degree of stability to wood gunstocks. PEG imparts dimensional stability to wood by diffusing into and replacing water in the structure of the wood fibers. This gives a bulking action which restrains the cell walls from shrinking during drying. Highly figured woods, because of their interlocked grain, usually shrink and swell more than straight-grained pieces of the same species. Thus, they have a greater tendency to warp and split during drying.

Stocks can first be shaped and inletted from green wood before treating with PEG. After treatment, the stocks can be either air or kiln dried with equally good results, or green lumber can be treated, dried, glued and turned into a stock blank. The PEG treated stock blank can then be fitted to a barreled action as is normally done with untreated wood.

The most important advantage of PEG treatment to the rifleman is dimensional stability of the critical areas, including the barrel channel and action (recoil lug and rear tang). Another advantage is the elimination of seasoning degrade, because the polyethylene glycol-treated blanks will not have seasoning checks, splits or honeycomb. Shrinkage is reduced to 90 percent of the original green wood dimensions. The wood does not swell appreciably when subsequently exposed to high moisture conditions. To be effective, however, the PEG treatment must be used on green wood. It is not recommended for stock blanks which have been exposed to any type of initial drying. Treated stocks cut well with normal woodworking tools due to the PEG bulking the wood fibers.

It is not the intent of this article to describe in complete detail PEG treated gunstocks. If you are interested in using this treatment for dimensional stabilization of wood stocks, it is suggested that you consult one of the cited references. Also the U.S. Forest Products Laboratory, Madison WI 53705 is a good source for additional information. PEG treated material, semi-inletted and shaped stocks are commercially available from the Crane Creek Company, PO Box 5553, Madison WI 53705. They also have several types of hunting and target stocks, furnished in a three-ply laminate to give maximum stability.

Laminated Stock Material

And this now brings us to the final area of discussion — laminated gunstocks. Essentially, the laminated stock gives more stability than a non-laminated stock. The following reason for increased stability is given to support this statement: *"If a stock blank were made of several different pieces of wood, stability would be improved over a single piece of wood because the influence of grain structure would be significantly reduced."* This point needs elaboration. For example, if the grain direction in the forearm of a solid stock blank was at a 30-degree angle with the line of bore changes in atmospheric moisture would cause the stock to put pressure on the barrel and change the point of bullet impact on the target. If, however, that blank would be cut in half lengthwise and face-laminated back-to-back, the effect of grain direction in the forearm would be reduced. The wood grain pressure forces that pushed on the barrel would tend to be negated in the glueline of the stock laminae.

It thus follows that the more laminae, the greater overall stability the stock will have. There is undoubtedly a practical limit to the number of laminae. With an increased number of laminae and correspondingly larger number of gluelines, the large amount of glue would increase the total weight of the stock.

The laminated stock is generally not considered a thing of beauty. In fact, one could probably say it is downright ugly. It is recognized, of course, that this depends on one's taste. Those who use a laminated stock on a target or varmint rifle feel that it gives better accuracy than a solid wood stock, and it probably does.

Conclusions

I have briefly discussed three general types of wood stocks — solid, PEG treated and laminated — and their effect on the dimensional stability of the wood in a gunstock. It is hoped that by suggesting the DSI concept, shooters and those working with wood stocks will have a better understanding of the material — wood. PEG treated solid along with treated and untreated laminated wood stocks offer another approach to riflemen and target shooters who strive to improve the dimensional stability and performance of wood as a stock material. There has been no attempt to compare wood stock materials with epoxy or polyester fiberglass. There are advantages and disadvantages to both materials and it is a comparative subject worthy of investigation and critical review.

REFERENCES

Hoadley, R.B. 1979. PEG for the Woodworker. *Fine Woodworking*, No. 19 (November/December 1979), pp. 68-71. Newton CT.

Hoadley, R.B. *Understanding Wood*. (The Taunton Press, Inc., 1980), Newton CT.

Mitchell, H.L. *How PEG Helps the Hobbyist Who Works with Wood*. (U.S.D.A. Forest Products Laboratory, Madison WI, 1972).

Webb. D.A. Lamination Increases Gunstock Stability. *The American Rifleman*, Vol. 123 (January 1975), p. 53. Washington D.C.

Webb. D.A. 1975. PEG That Gunstock. *The American Rifleman*, Vol. 123 (November 1975), p. 36. Washington D.C.

Wood Handbook: Wood as an Engineering Material, Revised U.S.D.A. Agr. Handbook No. 72, (U.S.D.A. Forest Products Laboratory, Madison WI, 1974). ●

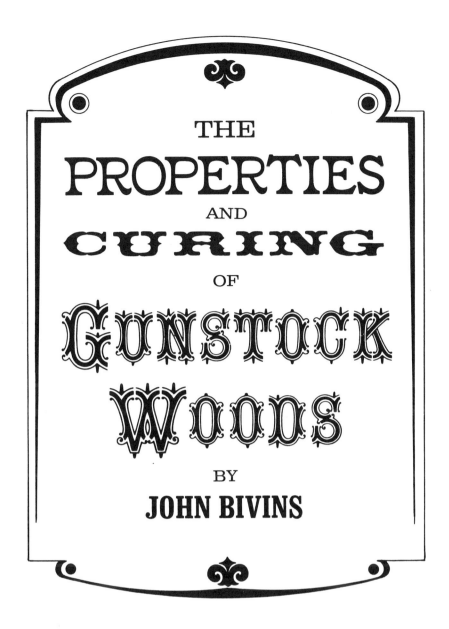

THE
PROPERTIES
AND
CURING
OF
Gunstock
Woods

BY
JOHN BIVINS

ONE OF THE heaviest variables a gunmaker has to deal with is wood, because of all the nasty tendencies that much-revered material has to move about in unwanted directions at unwanted times. Last winter, a beautiful Griffin & Howe Mauser-actioned sporter came into the shop, an early one, made before 1930. The stock architecture and checkering were flawless, the piece was tastefully engraved, and the lustrous rust-blue was a hundred-percent intact. It was a truly elegant rifle, except for the fact there were gaps in the inletting around the action, particularly at the magazine mortise, that you could damned near shove a finger into. Sloppy work on the part of the stocker? No. Deviousness on the part of Ms. Nature. That stock had spread open like the blooming of some noxious flower *after* it had left the G&H shop long ago, and probably with no fault of the makers. Of course, a good deal less was known about proper methods for curing stock woods in the late Twenties than we know now, but the fact of the matter is that the gunstocker is still at

the mercy of the innate properties of hardwoods, and though we may do our best to select stable blanks with correct grain structure, we may still occasionally find ourselves in trouble. Nothing is more sickening than to spend endless hours in achieving perfect inletting, only to have a seasonal moisture shift leave yawning gaps — and such gaps to a good stocker may be no more than 0.005 inch to be really hideous. Of course, this sort of thing usually happens after the piece is in the hands of a good customer who has laid out a goodly bundle of change for what he had expected to be work of perfection. It behooves us, then, to understand just what proper stock woods are, what their properties are, and how they should be treated. Though this is slanted toward the muzzleloading stocker, it has to do with any stock wood.

Quite a bit has been written over the years about just what are appropriate woods for the gunstock, even to the extent of publishing interesting tabular data about hardness and density tests, specific gravities,

and so forth. In the centerfire trade, it wasn't too long ago that gunstockers and their customers were all warm and moist over wild tropical woods such as monkeypod, bubinga, rosewood, and the like. Some sought out woods that appeared to offer the most challenge in terms of difficulty to work, such as screwbean mesquite. Happy to say, most of that wood craze has now gone by the board, and people are happy with the more conservative — and more stable — walnuts that have long been considered the best stock woods.

Muzzleloading-rifle stockmakers actually don't have a really wide selection of woods available *if* they are concerned about staying within their historical disciplines. American longrifles, for example, were stocked for the most part in fiddleback or, as most would have it, curly maple. Also used was plain maple, black walnut, cherry, birch, and apple, though the last-mentioned is rare on rifles. Many birch stocks have been mistaken for apple; apple is difficult to find free of wind-shake and checks, and though it works well, is not really a commercially available product. Birch is a sound wood, and dense, but has nothing to recommend it particularly in regard to interesting cosmetic features such as coloration and figure. Other woods, such as ash, persimmon, and so forth, are occasionally encountered on longrifles, but such things are the extreme exception to the rule.

The maples used in this country were sugar maple and red maple; both could be found with curly figure, and so could silver maple, though the latter is generally too soft for gunstocks. Red maple can also be very soft, depending upon the environment in which it grew. "Sugar-tree" can also be soft, for that matter, though I believe there is more soft red maple around than there is sugar. In fact, one of the reasons we cite for the relative lack of early Southern longrifles in existence is that most were likely stocked in softer red maple, since sugar maple does not grow in most of the piedmont South.

Curly maple was also plentiful in Europe, which may help to explain why it came into use so quickly in this country. Fiddleback-maple stocks are not uncommon on European pistols and fowlers, though they are seldom seen on rifles, for some reason. Before the Rococo period, the maple preferred by European stockers was either burl or root wood — exotic stuff,

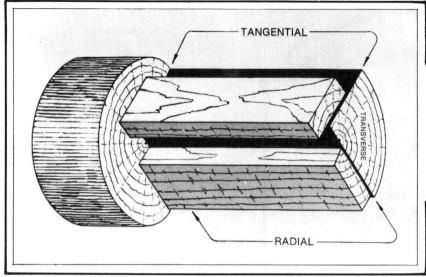

This section of a sawlog illustrates the grain structure exposed by both radial (quartersawn) and tangential (slab-sawn) cuts. Quartersawing is seldom practiced commercially but offers better stability and enhances figure of blanks.

exceedingly difficult to season, it tended toward instability even after thorough drying. It was seldom available in pieces of any size, for obvious reasons, and it is common to see even Baroque pistol stocks glued-up in more than one piece. For that matter, wood from the stump or roots of a tree, or from the cancer-like burls, is filled with flaws of all sorts — ingrown bark (flock-heads, as some call them), checks, dirt, and knotty growths — and European stockmakers thought nothing of gluing patches into such flaws, even on top-grade work. That's something you simply must accept if the muses drive you to using stuff from the lower part of a tree. That is the one place where modern epoxies shine, repairing small flaws thoughtfully left by Ma Nature. The early stocker had to be content with hide glue for plugs, and while that ancient adhesive has the excellent attribute of being reversible (you can unstick it with alcohol), it doesn't do as well with rapid changes in moisture, which stocks are frequently subject to.

Stump-wood, in fact, was always preferred to longwood by early Continental stockers, I suspect because it was almost free of long fibers and therefore took both inletting and carving better. This was true in both maple and walnut. Longwood, incidentally, is all the upper part of the tree above the bole. It is generally more stable than stump or root wood, but the lower wood invariably has more figure and often a great deal more color from mineral staining.

Europeans also used both cherry and plain maple for stocks; both are indistinguishable from our native woods, and these woods were for the large part used during those parts of the sixteenth and seventeenth centuries when lavish engraved bone inlays and overlays were in fashion. Pear was used during the same period and was occasionally ebonized with dyes; this was preferred to leaving pear its natural white or light tan. Pear carves more finely

than most woods, because of its density and short pores. It's a fine stock wood if you can deal with the color.

Also used across the briny deep were other fruitwoods such as lime, lemon, and the like, and hardwoods such as ash, beech, and even yew are encountered, though not on fine-quality arms. The favored stockwood for most purposes, though, was *Juglans regia*, which still reigns royally as the world's premier stockwood. This wood has been hung with any number of dubious appellations, largely by woodsellers, such as French walnut, English walnut, Grenoble, Circassian, and so forth *ad nauseum*. Though where a tree grows can be important to the quality of it, the species, unless it is a grafted hybrid, is best known simply as European walnut. Regardless of its habitat, it is distinctly different from its American cousin, *Juglans nigra*; it tends to have greater density and weight, shorter pores, prominent mineral streaking even in the longwood, lighter color, and greater shear and tensile strength. I doubt that it is more stable than black walnut, but it is one helluva lot nicer to work. Longrifle stockers will never know that, of course, since European walnut wasn't planted on our soil to any degree before the mid-nineteenth century, and then largely on the west coast — a region, in fact, where a large market in that wood exists today.

If you're after stocking-up a truly fine *stutzen* ("jäger") English fowler, or the like, nothing will do but European walnut. The problem is, no one cuts blanks in this country big enough for the purpose, say three to three and a half inches thick, from forty-eight to sixty-five inches long. The reason for it is that supply and demand in the *Juglans regia* market have turned quite a number of woodsellers into shifty-eyed diamond merchants, quite unabashedly asking five hundred dollars and up for fine centerfire sporter blanks at this writing. Cutting one big blank for a muzzleloader

can do away with two or even three short stocks cut from the same flitch, and on top of this, stocks for centerfires seldom require blanks much over two and a half inches thick. What can we do about it? Try to get wood out of Europe, which is fraught with problems of language barrier, transportation, and duty. Or we can remonstrate with our west-coast woodsellers; they'll cut if there's enough demand, and if we'll pay the horrible tariff. I see the time very soon in my red-eyed crystal ball when we'll be paying well over a thousand dollars for a stick.

In regard to European-style guns, other solutions such as using maple or cherry may be resorted to, but I don't think those are good solutions. Black walnut, unless it is largely butt wood and has tight, short pores, is unsuitable. California-grown black walnut, usually referred to as claro, *can* be used; its coloration is occasionally similar to European, and it generally has short pores and can be carved. However, it tends to be softer than European and can even be broomy and weak, and it often has coloration and figure entirely too brilliant and flashy for the purpose. However, I would prefer a dense and hard piece of claro over either maple or cherry for European-style stocks — that is, if I could find no suitable European. Good European walnut, when it has dark color, with dark-brown to black streaking and marbling, often makes other stock woods seem like junk by comparison — *believe* it. The only thing I don't like about it aside from the price I have to pay is that it is more difficult to see while you are working on it. Inletting cuts are harder to see, and penciled lines tend to disappear on its dark surface. Maple is much easier to work with in that regard.

Let's go back to maple for a bit, since it's so important to the creation of longrifles.

Sugar maple is preferred over red, since it is usually harder and denser, as we have noted, but there is nothing wrong with using red maple *if* indeed it is hard. My own built-in hardness tester is simply my thumbnail; if I can mark a board of stock blank significantly, I reject it out of hand. All maple will of course mark, but if your

One great problem for the stocker is seasonal change in dimensions of the wood, even in reasonably stable, dry blanks. The gap around this buttplate developed when a rifle stocked in Florida in late summer lost moisture in owner's northern home during the winter. Blank had been cured to eight percent moisture.

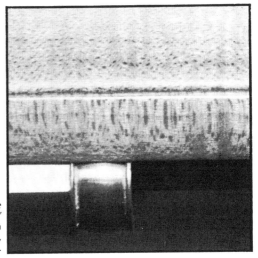

Quartersawing often exposes the ends of rays, revealing "robins' marks" in maple and other woods. These can cause brash areas in a stock, difficult to carve clean lines in.

thumbnail sinks right in and leaves a bold mark, forget it — *especially* if it has a lot of figure, for there is no greater hell on earth than working soft maple with heavy curl; there's too much contrast in hardness between curls, and it will vomit forth large ragged chips as you work it. Another good test is to take a small, sharp gouge and cut a blank across the grain. If the tool cuts without tearing and leaves a burnished, somewhat shiny cut, brother, buy that piece of wood.

I have found that the best maple is often a dark color, ranging from a pinkish-brown almost to orange, and when it is really hard, it even has a different feel — almost like stone, with a "colder" sensation to the touch on a dressed surface. Maple that is a brilliant white is often soft, brash, and broomy, and equally often is much lighter. These are not hard and fast rules, of course; a tree is the product of its environment. Altitude, temperature, the degree of water runoff, amount of sunlight, type and quantity of nutrients and minerals at the root source, and so forth, affect the coloration and working characteristics.

No one really knows just what causes the fiddleback figure in maple (or other types of figure, for that matter). Other woods have it, too, of course; it's seen fairly often in the walnuts, in ash and hickory and the fruitwoods, and I've even seen it in yellow pine. Physically, the figure is a result of undulating growth of the cellular structure of a tree — some cells growing faster than others and creating intrusions into the centers of neighboring cells, resulting in lateral displacement of the tree's tissues and a "folded" appearance. The figure is a function of the *radial* planes of a tree trunk, since cellular displacement takes place there, and the appearance of curl is caused by difference in light absorption and reflection between folded fiber ends that have been cut, as compared with uncut neighboring "valleys" in the undulating fiber structure. Since the walls of the distorted fibers are all curved, they give a different appearance with each shift in light source, hence the almost kaleidoscopic appearance of fiddleback when you rock it back and forth. The figure seems to move.

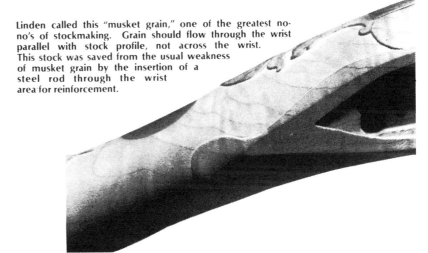

Linden called this "musket grain," one of the greatest no-no's of stockmaking. Grain should flow through the wrist parallel with stock profile, not across the wrist. This stock was saved from the usual weakness of musket grain by the insertion of a steel rod through the wrist area for reinforcement.

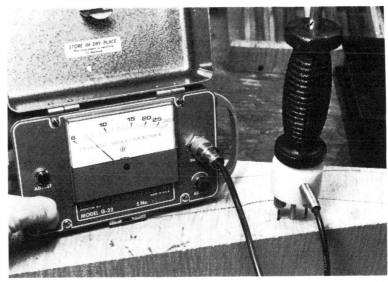

This resistance-type moisture meter registers 7.5 percent moisture with electrodes driven in part-way. With electrodes fully inserted, it registered 8.5 percent moisture near the center of the blank. This instrument measures moisture level in terms of the electrical resistance between the two electrodes (small pins). The more moisture, the greater the conductivity and the higher the reading.

Since the bent fibers occur in the radial planes of the trunk, at right angles to the growth rings of the tree, it is only natural that the best figure is visible on quartersawn wood, which is also oriented at right angles to the rings. "Ghosts" of the figure appear on the slab-sawn sides of a board, where cuts are made *tangentially* across a trunk irrespective of ring arrangement. But the figure is seldom as prominent on the slab or plain-sawn side. There are other advantages to quartersawing. A stock so sawn is easier to lay out accurately in terms of grain flow through the wrist, and if the stock warps, it will do so longitudinally. In other words, a forestock will warp up or down if quartersawn, while a slab-sawn board will have the tendency to dish if it warps, sometimes resulting in inletting gaps around a barrel when a blank normalizes. This can happen shortly after inletting or even just after a stock is fully shaped out, as stresses in the wood are lessened or redirected by the removal of material.

On the negative side, quartersawn wood exhibits tiny flecking that is in reality ray ends that have been sheared off. I've heard these flecks, which can be very prominent depending upon the exact angle of the cut, called "robin's marks," though I have no idea where that term comes from. A surface that is heavily marked with these flecks tends to be brash in working, even if the wood is hard. Even on a slab-sawn stock, if you'll notice, the robin's marks occur on the top and bottom of the stock in the quartering areas of grain, and consequently one usually finds that one side or the other of the stock, at the tailpipe, for example, is difficult to carve cleanly.

The working quality of wood is far and away a more important attribute than any of Ma Nature's neon displays of figure, if clean inlets, strength, and durability are to be counted important in a stock. Sure, I like curls too, on girls and gunstocks both, but I won't buy a piece of wood that I can't inlet and relief-carve cleanly. With dense, cleancutting wood, you can make a rifle that is so good that knowledgeable gun people will not even notice when there is *no* figure.

I much prefer maple to either black walnut or cherry for longrifles, since it carves so much better. It is possible to find both black walnut and cherry that is dense and hard enough even in the longwood to carve well, but believe me, that is the exception to the rule. If you find a source, call me! Of the three woods for longrifles, maple, walnut and cherry, cherry can be the most miserable to work. It often has poor shear strength and can be very difficult to inlet cleanly; pieces of it break out. However, both cherry and walnut are faster-shaping than maple and work better with a drawknife for good speed.

Since walnut and cherry blanks for longrifles often have no figure to speak of, they are usually best slab-sawn to add a bit of visual interest from grain flow. The fact

is, sawmills these days are not *about* to quartersaw hardwoods anyway, since so much wood is lost in the process, so for the most part, don't expect to find a dealer with a pile of quartersawn maple. Slab-sawing a tree of course produces some stocks that are quartersawn, since the cuts through the heart area of the trunk are at right angles to the growth rings. In a big tree, say three feet in diameter at the stump and yielding a straight log sixteen feet long, you could have as many as thirty stocks that have quartering cuts. Boards cut from either side of the heart, of course, are at a tangent to the rings and show slab-sawn grain flow. The heart of a tree, however, can be problematical. That area can be stressed, surrounded with wind "shakes" and cracks; it can have brashy and open pith in it, and it can be badly discolored by mineral streaking, though the latter is sometimes an attribute. Big cherry trees are particularly subject to deep checking around the heart, largely because of excessive stressing by the wind. Mineral staining in maple, which can also be caused by insect damage and other trauma entering through the cortex, causes no real problems in using a blank, though a maple stick so stained is often ugly to look at, *until* it is stained in finishing.

If you have a log that you want to have quartersawn, make sure it is a big one. I wouldn't bother to quartersaw anything much smaller than twenty-eight to thirty inches in diameter.

In purchasing stockwood, you are often better off if you can buy it in the board so that you can lay it out the way that you want. You really can't buy European walnut this way, of course, and it's difficult to even get maple in the board unless you deal with a sawmill. Stockwood dealers make more money by selling blanks rather than boards, but you have the option of going out and looking for your own trees, if hardwoods are native to your area. That's a good way to save money, but it takes a good deal of energy and time, and in the case of maple, not too many landowners smile benignly upon your skinning the bark off their trees to look for curl, even when the cut is properly tarred to keep out insects.

So, you're likely stuck with buying blanks, which isn't so bad if you play it smart. Be certain *always* that the blanks you're perusing are oversize and thick enough to take whatever pattern you have in mind. Also, you are better off ordering blanks from a reputable and well-known dealer, if you can't see the wood first-hand, so that you wind up with something that is properly laid out. One of the greatest curses of a gunstock is to have what Al Linden called "musket grain" in the wrist, that is, grain running out at an angle rather than flowing parallel to the upper and lower wrist lines. To make the wrist grain straight, a stock must be laid out at an angle on the board in most cases, which of course is a nasty waste of fine wood that some less scrupulous wood dealers are loath to bear.

Won't make any difference, they say. No? I have a friend who has *twice* broken his fine flintlock through the wrist just by trying to seat balls in a dirty bore — and now a three-eighths-inch steel rod rests through the middle of those breaks and all that grain runout. Stocks that have runout both on the sides *and* the top are particularly weak. If you're stuck with one, and it's too fine to throw away, then you can drill all the way through the wrist area longitudinally after you have the barrel inletted and the butt shaped, and epoxy-in a steel rod. The drill is run in from the breech inlet. If nothing smaller than three-eighths-inch rod is used, then the stock won't break regardless of the musket-grain. I've done this a couple of times, but I sure as hell don't like it. Buy a stock that has good grain flow to start with, and forget about the bloody rod unless you plan to use your rifle as a lever for tightening barbed-wire fencing.

I've always considered it kind of wood merchants to face off both sides of their stock blanks. It's not really necessary to see the figure, since really good fiddleback will show right through circular-saw marks. However, saw kerfs hold dirt, and a blank can be better examined if it's planed off, especially if it's walnut. A clean, planed surface shows you the grain flow clearly, and also any flaws, such as minute knots or checks, and insect entry or exit holes. Beware of such bug holes, for you don't know just how convoluted their path is inside the blank, and probing with a piece of wire doesn't always tell you. What you don't want is to be finish-shaping a stock and cut into an ugly, meandering trench right in the middle of the cheekpiece, say. You can probe surface checks fairly successfully with shim stock to determine approximate depth, but stay away from end-checks at the butt, since they can easily lengthen a great deal. End checks are usually the result of laying a blank out too close to the end of a seasoning board.

If you're cutting blanks from a board, also try to have the board planed for the same reasons enumerated above. Planing trues up things, too, making it a good deal easier to lay out the finished stock lines accurately. For laying out oversize blanks on a board, I use a clear Plexiglas pattern so that I can read grain flow and in some cases determine where the blank should fall for maximum figure. Incidentally, some folks use the term "figure" and "grain" to mean the same thing, but they aren't. As we've seen in the case of maple, figure is *bent* fibers that are at right angles to the growth rings; it's the rings themselves that we see as longitudinal grain, and the distorted cells we see as figure. Figure of course can be caused by other things, such as limb growth (crotch). The grain, as we see it, is really the *winter* wood of a tree, that narrow band in the growth rings that occurs during the cold season while the tree has virtually stopped growing. In maple, the winter wood occurs as darker lines, and when the stock is slab-sawn, the winter wood is much more prominent. It has the unfortunate characteristic of not taking stain well and can be on the hideous side where it is boldly exposed on tangential cuts.

If you're satisfied with the hardness, density, grain layout, and figure of a blank, don't just buy it right off. Look the dealer straight in the eye and ask in a flat and hard tone if the wood is dry; see if his left eye twitches or his feet shuffle a little. If he's a respectable chap, he'll tell you the truth. The problem is, many dealers don't have any control over the seasoning of wood. The most reputable dealers buy wood in the log or board and see to the seasoning by means they are sure of. Most stockwood is kiln-dried these days, which is no anathema to the stockmaker *if* the wood has been properly handled in the kiln and cycled over a reasonable length of time. What, you might well ask, is dry? Well, that depends. Airdried wood seldom drops below nine percent moisture inside, and even eleven is acceptable, while dry-kilns usually take hardwood right down to eight percent or less. The moisture level of a stock can be measured accurately by cutting off a sample, weighing it, then baking it in an oven and reweighing, but I prefer not to fool with such nonsense when good moisture meters are available. We have a good little instrument here, a Delmhorst G-22, and we use with this detector Delhorst's 26E electrode, which has two one-inch pins that penetrate deep enough to accurately measure wood up to three and a half inch thick. Since the electrodes have to be driven in parallel to the grain for a valid reading, you have to take care that the blank isn't penetrated in some place where you could cut into a hole — which fact, no doubt, would cause some dealers to suggest that you put your moisture detector in a warm, dark place where the sun don't shine, rather than poke holes in *their* wood. But it surely gives you peace of mind when you *know* a blank is ready to use.

The old boys had problems in getting enough dry wood for stocks. Sure, they air-dried it a year per inch of thickness, which was fine, but what happened when they were setting up shop and couldn't buy dry wood, or when they ran slap out of it? Well, sometimes they used greenish stuff, to the ultimate detriment of the rifle. We recently restored an otherwise fine Peter Gonter rifle of circa 1800, which had checks and fractures all over it, and over a quarter inch of shrinkage at the buttplate. And what happens when green wood pulls down tight on each side of an unyielding barrel? Right. Cracked all the way up the ramrod groove from forecastle to poop. And that's certainly not the *only* such example I've seen. Since seasoning is so important to a stable stock, let's have a little closer look at the process before you plunk down your bucks for wood someone else has been fooling with. They may have done you no favors.

The cells of green wood contain two types of moisture, free water and bound water. The former is found in the cell cavities and can move from cell to cell by capillary action, while bound water is held in the cell walls, moving by diffusion. In the drying process, free water empties out of the cells like pouring water from a gourd, without changing the dimensions of the cells. When bound water is released from the cell wall, however, the whole business comes down like a bear stomping a beehive, and the wood shrinks. In thick hardwood boards such as we are wont to cut stocks from, the wood dries from the surface toward the center; while bound water is evaporating at the surface, free water is still percolating up from the center. The result is moisture gradients in the wood, causing *considerable* stress as the outside cell layers shrink around cells still swollen with water inside. Warpage, splits, checks, and spring-like tension are the ugly heritage of drying too fast, which is why you don't put a load of dead-green wood into Granny's 150-degree attic on the Fourth of July. Put that wood in the garage to start, and have some of Granny's lemonade instead.

Green wood must be stacked carefully, the boards separated by at least 3/4-inch-thick "stickers" of uniform thickness, such as pine scraps from a building site. They should be placed on sixteen to twenty-four-inch centers along the board and aligned vertically through a stack, and the ends of the boards should be supported as well. Much of an overhang will surely result in warpage. The end grain of the boards should be liberally coated with an oil-base paint to slow moisture loss at the ends. Capillary action pulls water longitudinally like a soda straw, and you want to slow this action down and balance it with water loss across the cells to the sides and flats of a board. If you don't, the board will develop deep checks at the ends that will have to be sawn away later. Waste not, want not.

Now, the argument has long raged as to which is better, air-dried or kiln-dried wood. Some people are fiercely adamant about it, claiming that they wouldn't let their dog pee on a kiln-dried board even if it were in flames. I don't go along with that. Although a great deal of wood is in fact hurt by speed-'em-up, heavy-handed and greedy kiln operators, proper kiln seasoning is just as good and maybe better than air-drying. Henry Pohl at Bishop's, a fellow who knows a thing or two about drying wood, tells me that kiln-drying can actually result in a *harder* blank, for reasons that we don't know. Carefully done, a kiln-dried blank can have less stress than an air-dried one, from manipulation of the seasoning cycle to best suit the changing moisture level of the wood. Temperature, humidity of the surrounding air, and air movement through the pile are exceedingly important details.

Temperature must be handled with delicacy. While wood dries quickly at high heat, the problems mentioned above rear

their misshapen visages and can further reduce the strength of wood, making it brittle.

Green wood is started in a kiln at something a bit over a hundred degrees and held there until the free water is driven out; the kiln temperature can then be raised to pull out the bound water, which is more difficult to break loose from its molecular bond. Some kilns prefer to air-dry for a year to rid the wood of most of its free water, but this isn't necessary if things are taken slowly in the kiln and the pile constantly monitored with meters to check moisture levels. A good kiln operator adjusts both temperature *and* humidity in the kiln to prevent board surfaces from losing water too fast. That is why seasoning of thick lumber is more critical, and why you can't effectively dry four-quarter (one-inch) boards in the same kiln as twelve-quarter (three inches). If the unit is adjusted for drying the thin stuff, the thick boards will damn near have exploded by the time the one-inchers are ready to be used. But some try it anyway.

Air circulation in the kiln is important to carry evaporated moisture away from wood surfaces. Some kilns circulate the damp air around the pile, while others vent it out and depend on steam generators to moisturize the kiln if it is becoming too dry. This is why air-drying is *not* always what it is held up to be. The ideal situation is to have the wood start out in a schedule with high humidity and low temperature, with the humidity dropping and the mercury rising as the wood cycles along. At the end of a drying cycle, wood will normally have a certain amount of drying stress on the surface. A kiln can effect "stress-relieving" by suddenly raising the humidity; moisture enters the surface fibers to soften and relax them.

If you buy a green stock blank, that's fine, but take care that the end-grain is well coated, and such blanks are best *hung* rather than stacked, as some of us have found. Put a screw-eye in the small end of the blank and hang it from the ceiling, and don't let the wet wood stay in temperature over a hundred degrees until it's down to thirty-percent moisture; it can then be raised to a hundred and twenty degrees, and even higher below twenty percent. For that matter, I think it a good idea to hang all blanks, whether they are wet or dry; it tends to avoid stressing, and circulation is better. Be aware that green blanks should cost *less* than dry ones, not only because you are tying up your investment while the wood seasons, but also because there is always the risk of funny things happening while curing, even with the greatest of care. Highly figured woods of all sorts are often wound up like coil springs, and loss of bound water can make them turn into pretzels. I have had to straighten warped blanks a number of times by soaking and clamping. Don't be afraid to try a straightening job, but once it is straight, get it shaped out *fast* to relieve stresses, or you may wind up with a rifle that'll shoot around corners or blow your toes off.

How fast should a stock be dried? That depends on the type and thickness of the wood, what the moisture content is when it enters the kiln, and so forth. If someone tells you that they kiln dry 2 1/2-inch maple from the green state in three weeks, quietly suggest to the chap that he sell his product to someone interested in making tongue depressors for harelips. And go somewhere else. Fine hardwoods, especially figured stuff, that thick should take from eighty days to six *months* if you want unstressed and check-free wood.

The bottom line of Murphy's renowned law, though, reads "Mother Nature is a bitch." Well, I love the old gal, but sometimes it is hard to put up with her vagaries. Every piece of wood is a tale unto itself, with a mind and soul of its own. Like a human, wood, even "dead," dried stuff, reacts to its surroundings, particularly to quick changes in humidity. Violent dimensional changes can take place in even extremely hard and dense wood that is at a reasonable equilibrium in regard to moisture; that's why the extreme-accuracy centerfire boys have gone to plastics and epoxies to avoid atmospheric variables. One thing that does have some benefit for stabilization of wood is the "PEG" seasoning process, wherein green wood is soaked for a period of — from a few days up to several weeks — in a water and polyethylene glycol heated to a hundred and forty degrees. The PEG penetrates the cells, providing a chemical and mechanical bond that reduces drying stresses and shrinkage, and tends to provide stabilization in the wood later.

After soaking, the stock is seasoned normally. The only problem with this system is that a stock finished from the PEG-treated lumber won't take any finish except one of the urethane varnishes. If you're interested, though, contact The U.S. Department of Agriculture, Forest Service; Division of Wood Quality; Box 5130; Madison, Wisconsin 53705. They have a pamphlet that gives you all the necessary info.

Even with such technological advances, however, all of us — gunstockers and their patrons alike — must respect the fact that if we're going to continue to use hardwoods for gunstocks, we'll have to live with the bad alongside the good and forbear seasonal changes in dimension in critical areas. As for me, I'll put up with the problems, and the Lord willing, the day will never come when I'm on the phone to some supplier asking for a nicely marbled piece of acrylic for a stock blank. ●

SELECTING STOCK FINISHES

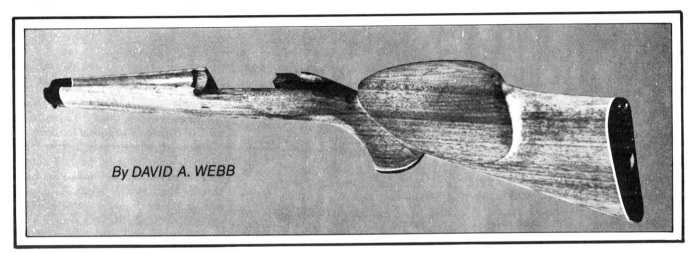

By DAVID A. WEBB

Table I — Properties of Finishes

Finishing Material	Abrasion Resistance	Film Hardness	Solvent Resistance	Water Resistance	Clarity (1)	Build (2)	Processing Ease
Solvent Evaporating (Lacquers)							
Acrylic	4	4	2	4	10	4	8
Cellulose Acetate Butyrate	2	2	1	4	10	3	8
Nitrocellulose	2	2	1	4	7	2	8
Vinyl	4	4	2	5	7	4	8
Drying Oil (Varnishes)							
Alkyd	4	5	5	6	8	7	10
Oil Modified Urethane	7	9	7	7	1	7	10
Phenolic Modified	6	7	6	7	1	7	10
Styrenated Soya Alkyd	6	5	5	6	8	6	10
Catalytic ("Plastics")							
Alkyd-Vinyl-Urea	8	7	8	8	10	7	5
Epoxy	10	10	10	10	8	10	5
Polyester	10	10	10	10	7	10	2
Urethane	10	10	10	10	2	10	4

Rating — 10 is best, numerically rated downward. With all finishing materials, ratings can be improved within their type through formulating techniques. Since coating technology principally consists of blending ingredients to achieve a desired result, a specific property can be improved, though generally at the expense of some other property. Therefore, the ratings above are relative and only an indication of the film properties. Data obtained from references 1 and 4.
(1) Color and non-yellowing property of the film. (2) Relative ease of "building" resin solids with each application.

*W*HAT IS A GOOD stock finish? That's an often-heard question, but the answer depends upon some other questions: For whom? For what? To be applied how? There was a time when the stockmaker's choice was severely limited, oil being about the only choice. But the traditional oil finish needn't be continued in this day of more modern, more serviceable, and equally beautiful finishes.

Just as it would be shame to insult a fine piece of wood with a finish which would hide its beauty, it is ridiculous to emphasize beauty over serviceability on a stock for a gun that's going to see hard use. Many different types of finishes are commercially available, and each might be suitable for a given application, so when custom stockmakers, gunsmiths, hunters, competitive shooters and others interested in wood get together, the principle topics of conversation are usually: handrubbed oil vs. synthetic or plastic finishes, the durability characteristics of different coatings, their color and appearance, and their practicality.

H. L. Woltman writes in his article, "Professional Approach to Stock Finishing" in the Jan. - Feb. 1970 *Rifle,* that there are specific uses for both the dull "London Oil" finish and the plastic finishes. I agree; however, more emphasis must be placed on the fact that the oil finish does not give adequate protection against the elements — no one will argue against its appearance. Nor will anyone argue against the excellent appearance characteristics of lacquer finishes — many fine pieces of furniture have been finished with lacquers. But in my opinion both the "oil finish" and lacquer belong on the stock of a show-piece firearm. The heavy use given the hunting rifle, and even more so the target rifle, makes a strong point in favor of quality synthetic finishing material. If one does not care for glossy appearance, a little elbow grease will soften it.

There are two primary reasons for finishing a gunstock. Primarily, the application of a finishing material should provide moisture, scratch and abrasion resistance. The wood of a stock needs protection from inclement weather and the "bumps and bruises" of hunting. Secondly, the finish should accent the natural beauty of wood. A film-forming synthetic resin will give the best possible protection to a gunstock with no ifs, ands, or buts.

The synthetic finish or plastic — if you prefer that nomenclature — dries and cures by evaporation and polymerization — chemical irreversible reaction — forming a durable protective coating. Historically, linseed oil and waxes such as beeswax have been rubbed into the wood. These "non-rigid" materials do enhance the appearance of a stock, however, as a protective barrier against physical abrasion and transfer of moisture they leave much to be desired (See Table II). Linseed oil never does completely dry; its ability to retard the movement of moisture in and out of a stock is very poor. True, the damaged portion of oil or wax finished stock can be sanded and quickly refinished, but the wood itself has been damaged. How much wood depends on the extent of "injury." With a harder synthetic finishing resin the scratch is predominately in the coating, thus affording more protection to the wood surface. Further, a good synthetic coating, through the use of an additive, has the property of "slip," which significantly improves the abrasion resistance of the cured coating.

Basically, there are three types of synthetic coatings, each with significant differences in properties and characteristics. Examples of several different finishes, in each of the three types, are listed in Table I, along with their ratings as to abrasion resistance, hardness, resistance to solvents, resistance to moisture, clarity, ease of building a significant coating of resin solids with each application, and ease of application. Each of these characteristics should be considered in selecting the finish most desirable for a particular stock.

Solvent evaporation coatings (lacquers) are low solids (15-25%) and are fast drying. These materials are essentially almost "water white" in appearance. They often have poor resistance to organic solvents — such as gun cleaning solvents. Moisture resistance also is not as good as the other synthetic resins. The most outstanding feature, however, is the clear, "water white" non-yellowing property of lacquers. Because of this feature the true beauty — color and grain patterns (figure) — of the wood is transmitted through the coating. The wood hues are not distorted by a yellowish film. For a show piece rifle there is not a better finishing system available than lacquer.

Drying oil resins — often referred to as varnishes — are usually in the range

Table II
Moisture — Excluding Effectiveness of Coatings

Material	Effectiveness
Linseed Oil	20%
Nitrocellulose	75%
Phenolic Modified Synthetic	75%

Data from Wood Handbook No. 72. Coated (3 applications) wood samples (11% moisture content) exposed to nearly moisture saturated air. Complete protection represented by 100%; no protection, as with uncoated wood, by 0.

Table III Abrasive Papers and Comparative Grit Sizes

Grain Types	Silicon Carbide	Aluminum Oxide	Garnet
Super Fine	600 500 400	400 10/0	400 10/0
Extra Fine	360 320	320 9/0	320 9/0
Very Fine	280 240 220	280 240 220 8/0 7/0 6/0	280 240 220 8/0 7/0 6/0
Fine	180 150 120	180 150 120 5/0 4/0 3/0	180 150 120 5/0 4/0 3/0
Medium	100 80 60	100 80 60 2/0 0 ½	100 80 60 2/0 0 ½
Coarse	50 40	50 40 1½ 1	50 40 1½ 1
Very Coarse	36 30 24	36 30 24 2 2½ 3	36 30 24 2 2½ 3
Extra Coarse	20 16 12	20 16 3½ 4	20 16 3½ 4

of 40-50 percent solids; thus, they can achieve a higher resin "build." Fewer applications will develop sufficient film thickness for rubbing. This type of film-former is more resistant to organic solvents than lacquers; as a moisture barrier they are also more satisfactory. However, varnishes are slower drying. Brushing is an easy method of application. As to color of the resin and the cured film, it can be literally the worst. For example a phenolic modified alkyd resin — spar varnish — is a dark yellowish brown. Open a quart can of this varnish and observe whether or not you are able to see the bottom of the can. If one desires to sacrifice wood color, a coating more durable than lacquer and oil type finishes will be obtained.

Catalytic thermosetting coatings are the most highly cross-linked (polymerized) of the synthetic resinous materials and develop the most durable finishes for a gunstock. Disadvantage of these resins is that they are generally two-component. After adding the catalyst to the resin portion, application life or "pot-life" is limited. Resin solids usually range from 40 to 50 percent, with the exception of vinyls, which are 25-35 percent, and polyesters, 65-75 percent. Color of the resin is often rather good. Most resins are a light yellow with some approaching water white.

In summarizing the three basic types of coating systems, there are a couple reasons why it is important to "select with care" when choosing a gunstock finish. Durability of the coating is extremely important in providing the best possible protection to the wood. The catalytic coatings are the most durable and a much-used target rifle will benefit from the use of this coating system. Color of the resin affects the final appearance of the finished stock. Dark yellow resins do not allow the actual wood appearance to be transmitted through the coating.

The final topcoat is not the only finishing operation that contributes to the ultimate appearance of a stock. Conditioning of wood, surface preparation, application of stains, fillers and sealers and topcoat rubbing and polishing all emphasize the wood figure.

Conditioning of the wood to a moisture content level of 6-10 percent is very important, not only from the standpoint of dimensional stability of the inletted stock blank, but to insure proper curing of the coating materials to give maximum adhesion to the wood.

By definition, moisture content is determined according to the oven-dry weight of wood. To calculate the moisture content (%), subtract the oven-dry weight from the original weight of the sample; divide the difference by the oven-dry weight.

Oven-dry weight is found by drying a wood sample at 105 degrees centigrade until the sample has reached a constant weight. If your "better half" does not object to your "cooking" wood, use her oven. The temperature-indicating dial is usually in degrees Fahrenheit rather than Centigrade so set the oven for 215 to 220 F and you are ready to make moisture determinations. Cut a sample (no more than one to two cubic inches) of wood from the butt or forearm tip area. These areas should have been sealed in the first place, so there will be no preferential loss of moisture because of end-grain. Using your reloading balance, weigh the sample to the nearest grain. Dry the wood. After two hours re-weigh the sample. Record the weight in grains and weigh at one hour intervals until a constant weight is obtained. Using the above formula you can find the percentage of moisture content for the blank — 8 to 12 percent is just about right.

Of all operations to ready the wood for finishing, surface preparation by "sanding" with abrasive papers is the most important. After obtaining the desired lines and shape of a stock with the various hand tools, start with coarse paper, 60 or 80 grit, working through medium grades, 180 or 220, to the extra-fine papers. Always avoid use of flint paper. The more suitable abrasive papers are silicon carbide, aluminum oxide and garnet. Given in Table III are a list of abrasive papers that can generally be obtained at the local hardware store.

After surface preparation is completed, stains and/or fillers can be brushed on the stock before the final topcoats. Staining is done to obtain even color contrast between sap and heartwood and to darken light-colored woods, such as maple. Porous woods similar to American walnut and mahogany are filled to obtain a smoother surface for applying the final finish. By the use of a color contrasting filler, the wood pores are accentuated. Maximum filling is achieved by wiping with a cross-grained stroke.

The topcoating synthetic resin is generally applied by either brushing or

spraying. If the coating is to be hand-rubbed, a minimum of three applications for a medium solids resin (40-50 percent) is required. Once the coating has hardened it can be rubbed using the following technique. White oil and mineral spirits (50/50 by volume) are mixed together. Liberal amounts of the liquid are put on the stock; using a fine grade abrasive paper (220) on a felt-wood sanding block the finish is rubbed. Rubbing continues with the finer grades of abrasive papers. Any of the super-fine papers (400, 500 or 600) will give the desired effect to the finished surface. When a uniform eggshell lustrous surface has been obtained rubbing is completed.

Final step in finishing is the use of a solid or liquid buffing wax, self-polishing wax or cream polish. The wax or polish helps to protect the finish from scratches and moisture, while the finish protects the wood.

The paint and coating technologists have made significant advances in the past few decades, but most amateur stockmakers haven't taken advantage of these developments. This isn't true of many professional stockmakers; in fact, some of the best-known and most-respected custom gunsmith and stockers are using "plastic" finishes, rubbing them with a technique similar to that described above, then rubbing a thin film of oil over the surface. The result is a stock with the appearance of a hand-rubbed oil finish, but done in a fraction of the total time, and much more resistant to knocks, scratches and moisture.

Referring back to Tables I and II it's obvious that the modern synthetic finishes are equal, or far superior, to traditional finishes in every respect; it should be equally obvious that if we care for our guns, their appearance and performance, we should be putting those new finishes to good use.

Jenuleson, W. R. "Modern Furniture and Panel Finishing Materials" Forest Products Journal *Vol. 16, pp. 53-57, 1966.*

Webb, D. A. "Gunstock Finishing" The American Rifleman *Vol. 113, No. 11, pp. 60-61, 1965.*

Woltman, H. L. "Professional Approach to Stock Finishing" The Rifle *Vol. 1, No. 7, p. 22, 1970.*

Wood Handbook. U. S. Dept. of Agr. Handbook No. 72, Forest Products Laboratory, Madison, Wisconsin, 1955. ●

Moisture in

David A Webb

The stock blank on the right must be dry (EMC for wood) before it is inletted and shaped; the accuracy of any wood-stocked rifle depends upon the way moisture affects its stock wood.

fact that it contains some amount of water.

In *Rifle* 79, Lynn Crook's article "Water in the Wood" covered some basic concepts of wood as gun-stock material, the relationships of moisture (water) and wood, and the drying problems that occur during the seasoning or drying of such woods as walnut for stocks. The purpose of my article is to explain further and to define some of the wood-and-moisture relationships, including factors that influence the drying of wood, the two methods of drying wood (air-drying and kiln-drying), and a discussion of climate and its effect on the equilibrium moisture content (EMC) of wood.

Wood must be dried before it can be satisfactorily used as a material for gun stocks. Removal of moisture from the wood (drying) has been a controversial subject. Volumes of information have been written and published on the subject, from both technical and nontechnical points of view. The drying of gun-stock blanks has been a constant source of discussion, with a wide variety of opinions expressed by knowledgeable individuals. For example: is kiln-drying or air-drying the best way to dry stock woods? Is there any difference in the stability of the wood, between the two methods of drying?

From a purely technical point of view, drying the wood is necessary to preserve it. Drying also results in a relatively more stable wood in com-

GUN STOCKS are reminiscent of the old soap commercial that advertised its product as "ninety-nine and forty-four one-hundredths percent pure;" the majority of the stocks put onto commercial sporting arms are pure wood. Substitute materials have not significantly threatened the supremacy of wood as the gun-stock material for factory-made rifles. Certain Savage arms were for a time supplied with stocks of Tenite plastic, and Remington's Model 66 autoloading .22 rifle made use of Nylon in its stock and other parts.

The index of advertisers in *Rifle* regularly includes a well known maker of polyester-fiberglass stocks, which are available from other makers as well, in a variety of styles and shapes for both hunting and target rifles. The use of these stocks has steadily increased among the highly competitive benchrest and silhouette shooters.

Still, wood is the reigning material for custom-made stocks as well as factory-made ones. Whatever may be the superiority of certain man-made or synthetic materials in terms of weight, durability, and stability, the beauty and traditional use of wood appear to guarantee that it will continue to be the chief gun-stock material for the foreseeable future. To be even marginally useful, wood that is to be used in rifle stocks must be carefully and properly prepared for such use — a use for which wood has certain drawbacks arising chiefly from the

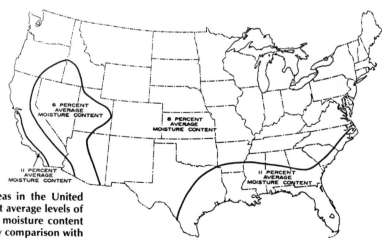

Since the climates of different areas in the United States are characterized by different average levels of atmospheric moisture, the average moisture content is likewise different in any region by comparison with that of another region.

Stock Blanks

parison with green or moist wood. Proper drying must precede the inletting and finishing of the stock. The grain and figure are never the same in two pieces of wood. To get the best out of a piece of wood, the user — in this case, the stockmaker or the shooter — must make sure that it is dry first.

Over the past few years, ten to fifteen domestic species of wood have been offered as material for gun stocks: birch, wild cherry, Pacific madrone, several maples, myrtle, flatpod and screw-bean mesquite, pecan, sycamore, and several varieties of the walnuts, for example.

Different woods vary widely in their physical characteristics. For example, the maples, myrtle, and birch are classed as nonporous woods, while the walnuts and wild cherry are typically classed as semiring porous woods. The mesquites are ring porous. The cross section of a tree grown in a temperate climate shows well defined concentric layers of wood — yearly growth increments or annual rings. Earlywood, often termed *springwood*, is formed during the beginning of each growing season. Cells of earlywood are usually larger and thinner-walled than those that are formed later in the year; hence, earlywood is softer, weaker, and usually lighter in color than the latewood or summerwood growth. Some species of wood, such as mesquite, have more-porous earlywood than other species such as myrtle.

Some of these stock woods are considerably denser or heavier than others. At twelve percent moisture content, pecan weighs forty-six pounds per cubic foot, while butternut weighs twenty-seven pounds. At the same time, weight varies substantially from one sample to another within a single species; walnut ranges from thirty-four to forty-two pounds per cubic foot.

Wood-shrinkage data (volumetric, from green to six percent moisture content) for different stock woods vary also — 4.5 percent for mesquite, for example, against 14.5 percent for Pacific madrone. The stump green moisture content of a wood species also varies; the heartwood of walnut

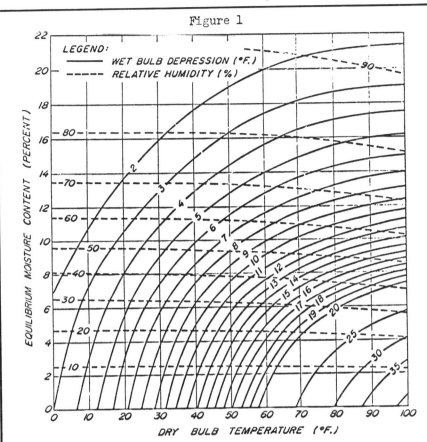

Figure 1

The equilibrium moisture content of wood is directly related to the dry-bulb temperature of the surrounding air and the wet-bulb depression — which is more familiarly known as the relative humidity of the air, usually expressed as the percentage of saturation for air at the given temperature.

some properties of stock woods

common name	scientific name	moisture content, green wood[1] (percent)	volumetric shrinkage[2] (percent)
birch	Betula allegheniensis	73	13.4
cherry	Prunus serotina	58[3]	9.2
madrone	Arbutus menziesi	81	14.5
sugar maple	Acer saccharum	68	11.9
Oregon maple	Acer macrophyllum	78	9.3
Oregon-myrtle	Umbellaria californica	65	9.9
flatpod mesquite	Prosopis juliflora	- - -	4.7
screwbean mesquite	Prosopis pubescens	- - -	- - -
osage-orange	Maclura pomifera	31	7.4
pecan	Carya illinoiensis	80[3]	10.9
persimmon	Diosporus virginiana	58	15.4
sycamore	Plantanus occidentalis	114[3]	11.4
black walnut	Juglans nigra	90[3]	10.2
white walnut (butternut)	Juglans cinerea	104	8.5
English walnut	Juglans regia	- - -	8.5

[1] average of heartwood and sapwood

[2] green to six percent moisture

[3] heartwood only

averages around ninety percent, while wild cherry is sixty percent.

These and other properties of wood influence the seasoning or drying of green wood to a satisfactory, usable moisture content of eight to twelve percent for stock blanks. The moisture or sap of freshly cut timber is primarily water. Within the wood, water exists in two forms: *free* water in the cell cavities and *bound* water held within the walls of the cells.

All wood gains or loses moisture as it approaches a balance with its surroundings in use or storage. This equilibrium or balance depends upon the atmospheric conditions of temperature and relative humidity of the air that surrounds the wood. Figure one shows the relationship between dry-bulb and wet-bulb temperatures (percent relative humidity) and the resulting equilibrium moisture content (percent) of wood. To further illustrate with respect to the United States geographical area, figure two shows the relative average moisture content of wood at equilibrium with the surrounding air in various parts of the country.

Contrary to a popular belief, the amount of water within green wood does not change with the seasons of the year. It has often been stated that trees should not be cut "while the sap is running," because the cross-cut section would severely check and split. This excessive checking, however, is not the result of sap movement but of the fact that the months of April through September are the period of the most active drying. If a log is cut during the winter, on the other hand, the wood dries more slowly and uniformly — thus the wood does not split as badly as the wood in logs cut during the summer.

Two methods of drying are generally used with wood intended for use as stock blanks: air-drying and kiln-drying. The primary objective is to remove the excess moisture. Both methods are entirely satisfactory and produce the same results. However, kiln-drying can reduce degradation of the wood, and it takes considerably less total drying time to dry the wood to the same moisture content as air-drying. The strength and stability of the wood are the same, whether the wood has been air-dried or kiln-dried.

Kiln-drying is an important method of drying stock blanks in a commercial operation and is important because it is the primary method of drying stock blanks for the firearms manufacturers. There are also a few companies that kiln-dry stock blanks for custom gunmakers. Kiln-drying is the drying of lumber in a closed chamber, in which the temperature and relative humidity of the circulated air are *controlled*. It is important to note, however, that properly kiln-dried material (including stock blanks) can be more satisfactory than air-dried wood. Control of the drying conditions reduces the degradation of the wood that occurs with seasoning. This is the advantage of drying wood in a kiln.

In both methods of drying, the movement of the moisture in the wood is similar. In wood, water tends to move from areas of high water concentration to areas with lower concentrations of moisture, with the tendency of the moisture to reach equilibrium throughout the block of wood. Moisture moves from the interior of a green blank to the drier surface areas. As the wood dries, several moisture-driving forces operate to lower the total moisture content. Free water moves through the cavities of wood cells by capillary action. Differences in relative humidity or vapor pressure cause some movement of moisture, also. The temperatures to which a wet stock blank is subjected are also involved. These factors explain why the air-drying rate is faster during the summer than it is during the winter. They also indicate why less time is required for the kiln-drying process with temperatures of 120 to 180 degrees Fahrenheit.

As I've already stated, moisture in the cell cavity is termed *free water;* moisture held in the cell wall is called *bound water*. When all of the water has left the cell cavity during the process of drying, but the cell wall remains full of water, the wood is at its *fiber-saturation point* (FSP). In most species of wood, the FSP is considered to be about thirty percent moisture content. This point is critical in the drying of wood. Movement of moisture from the cell walls begins at FSP, and the wood begins to shrink. The table shows the amount of water in a piece of green wood and the amount of shrinkage that takes place. Included are specific data on the shrinkage of fifteen woods that have been used as gun-stock material.

How rapidly a stock blank air-dries depends upon the species of the wood, the size or thickness of the blank, where it is stored for drying, and the climate in that region of the country. Some stock blanks air-dry very rapidly, others more slowly. A general rule of thumb has been that for every inch of thickness, one year of air-drying is necessary to bring a blank's moisture content down to around ten percent. It has been my experience that this rule of thumb is undoubtedly correct for *walnut* blanks; however, blanks of other woods such as wild cherry and the mesquites dry more rapidly than walnut does. In part, this is a result of their lower initial moisture content. In my own stock work, I have observed that black locust, elm, osage orange, and sassafras air-dry in about a year. All of these blanks were stump-green and processed from round log sections into blanks two and a half to three inches thick. At intervals of one month, the weights of the blanks were recorded until there was no further weight loss.

The storage location and climate are important. The best location is a covered outdoor area where there is a satisfactory movement of air. Neither a damp cellar nor a hot attic is a good drying area. Blanks dry faster in the arid Southwest, more slowly in places like the Olympic Peninsula of Washington. In all cases, it is a must that the ends of the blank be sealed against excessive loss of moisture from the green wood. Hot paraffin wax provides a satisfactory coating on the ends of a stock blank.

A beautifully figured stock on a handsome custom sporting rifle started with a man's cutting of the tree with a chain saw, a tree with a great deal of moisture in its cells. The water had to be removed before the wood could be considered suitable for such use. In a later article, I will present the shrink-swell characteristics of stock woods and the changes in relative humidity that affect the stability of gun stocks. ●

PROFESSIONAL APPROACH TO

STOCK FINISHING

By HENRY L. WOLTMAN

*F*OR MANY YEARS there has been considerable controversy on the subject of oil vs. varnish finishes; and the fight isn't over yet. Many very fine gunstocks are still done both ways—and the system of finishing described herein is simply the distillation of my experience with both.

The gunstock finish I choose depends on how I intend to use the finished stock. Since I am a target shooter and have literally worn through factory finishes to the bare wood, I use a plastic finish for target stocks. First, a target stock gets a lot of use. It probably is handled in practice and competition a hundred times more often than a fine big game sporter. Second, it is used in the rain and the heat. Heat alone is not a factor, but oily, salty perspiration and rubbing from whiskers are common hot weather by-products which can cause a thin, anemic stock finish to give up in one afternoon. And those of us who have fired in the wet, humid climate of Camp Perry have heard the wails of owners whose stocks have warped from that Lake Erie environment.

Ergo, the plastic (formerly varnish) finish. It has good appearance and excellent durability, showing off the texture of the wood while protecting it against the elements of water, abrasion and general abuse. The plastic has much better physical properties—especially resistance to abrasion and moisture permeability—than linseed oil. And it should have: it is a product of modern industrial R & D, not something that has been pressed out of the flax since Caesar.

On the other hand, the plastic finish is glossy and, by and large, a shiny, glossy surface detracts from a fine gun. The dull "London oil" finish, as this classic finish has been called, has the merit of restrained elegance and good taste. But it takes the right kind of gun. For the casual, less frequently used gun, oil is an excellent finish and is the type I normally use on non-target guns like varmint rifles, plinkers and shotguns. Actually, in analyzing the stocks I've made, I have found oil unsatisfactory only on some rather nicely figured American and claro walnut plus the target stocks mentioned. On these woods it just did not bring out the depth of color and figure the way the plastic finish can, so when I found it to be a disappointment, I refinished the

stock with plastic. On French and English walnut and some of the plainer American walnut, the dull oil finish is most beautiful and, if not subject to the rigors of water and perspiration, does a thoroughly satisfactory job.

So the choice of finish depends on the wood, the "visual effect" you want to achieve, and the use or abuse to which it may be put. In case "visual effect" is unclear, consider the typical California sporter with inlays, Monte Carlo comb, diagonal fore-end tip, zooty pin-striped butt plate, etc., *without* a glossy finish. Or consider the classic English-built double shotgun with straight grip, splinter fore-end, and no recoil pad *with* a glossy finish. Both are out of character. So as the architect of the job, you have the pleasure of deciding just what to do about finishing the wood.

A previous article, "Professional Approach To Stock Sanding" (Sept. - Oct. 1969), detailed procedures for sanding the wood, raising the grain and bringing the stock to the point where the finishing could begin. Before elaborating on the finishing operations, reading the summary of steps required in both finishing systems will help to clarify the procedure and enable you to size up the job. Before going further I should also warn that in my experience the plastic finish is definitely more time consuming and difficult to apply well. This is another subtle reason for favoring oil.

If the presence of sapwood necessitates staining, this must precede any finishing, and if the stained surface is cut down by sandpaper, it must be restained to maintain the color. Besides fixing sapwood, I like to darken and add some redness to English and French walnut. This can be done in the final stages of oil finishing by using oil that has been doctored up with stain.

A great variety of colors for staining can be made up using Du Pont water

soluble dyes. These are available from Brownell's, Inc., and the set of five dyes is $4.00. They may be mixed for various colors using your powder scale as shown in the accompanying table. (Cut down for smaller amounts if desired). After mixing, it's a good idea to stain some maple pieces and put them away for future use in color matching. Over the years since I first mixed these stains, I have found the Resorcin brown 5-C, and formula numbers 1 and 5 to be the most useful.

Another stain used by Bob Owen, the late, great stockmaker from Port Clinton, Ohio, is useful in bringing a rich red-brown color to French and English walnut. It is prepared by boiling alkanet root in boiled linseed oil. The alkanet root, which has the texture of common excelsior, must be obtained from a well-stocked pharmacy. The roots should first be compacted in a two-pound coffee can to the half-full level. Pour in a quart of boiled linseed oil and place on a stove, preferably electric. Bring to a boil and be ready to grab off said stove with a pair of pliers at the moment of boiling.

I was thoroughly cautioned on this point by Mr. Owen personally and didn't take him seriously enough—nearly forcing my wife to summon the fire department. I thought if a little boiling is good, more must be better. It instantly boiled over and, just as Bob said, smoked to high heaven. The root gives the oil a red wine color which is useful in the last stages of oil finishing. The colored oil is put away to cool with the root in it and may be stored this way in a wide mouth jar. A quart so treated will last nearly as long as the water stains—or practically for life. Other oil stains are available from every paint store and there is no specific caution except to *test every damn one on scraps or on the side of the rough blank before application to the stock.*

Should a streak of sapwood be present, test the stain on a scrap of the

same wood, varying the color to match the heartwood. Apply with a cloth and have another cloth wet with clean water handy to blend in the area where the overlap occurs. With care, a streak of white sapwood can be hidden completely. On one stock, I achieved an improved over-all color of a very nice piece of American crotch walnut by applying formula No. 1 to the entire stock.

While staining may or may not be required, filling the wood pores is necessary regardless of the type of finish chosen. For this purpose, plain old-fashioned spar varnish is used. Check the can label to make sure it is not a urethane varnish. Spar varnish is a mixture of the fatty oils, linseed and/or tung oil, plus phenolic resin. These are cooked together and a solvent such as mineral spirits added to adjust to brushing viscosity.

Other wood fillers such as paste fillers are sometimes used but I have found they tend to back out of the pores after perspiration and handling, leaving the surface slightly bumpy. Neither alkyd or urethane varnishes are

well suited to filling pores—alkyds tend to shrink with age leaving slight depressions long after the job is completed; urethanes are just too hard and much more work is required for removal of surplus.

After obtaining the real article, considerable thinnning will be necessary since spar varnish is packaged at about the viscosity of No. 10 or 20 motor oil, which is too thick for good penetration. Add turpentine or other commercial thinner to about 25 percent of volume to reduce it to approximately coffee cream consistency. You will have to be the judge. Brush strokes should flow together smoothly within a few seconds. Excessively thin material will require more coats to do the same job.

With the stock perfectly clean and dry, brush on the thinned spar varnish with a 1-inch brush. The grip cap and butt plate may be left in place but should be masked off. Brush the inletting first, keeping varnish off the glass-bedded areas. This will help seal the interior surface against oil and moisture penetration. Apply a full coat to the exterior and let dry for at least

SUMMARY OF FINISHING PROCEDURES.

Dull Oil Finish	Plastic Finish
1. Stain if required	1. Same.
2. Varnish 3 to 6 coats to fill pores.	2. Same.
3. Buff off surplus varnish.	3. Same.
4. Sand--400 grit.	4. Same.
5. Checker stock or recut if refinishing.	5. Same.
6. Finish checkering.	6. Same.
7. Sand--600 grit.	7. Mask off checkering.
8. Oil.	8. Apply plastic finish.
9. Polish with rottenstone.	9. Wet sand--400 grit.
10. Oil.	10. Apply plastic finish.
11. Oil.	11. Wet sand--400 grit.
12. Oil.	12. Apply plastic finish.
13. Wax (optional).	13. Wet sand--600 grit.
	14. Steel wool--000 grade.
	15. Polish with rubbing compound.
	16. Unmask checkering, clean up borders.

24 hours. Almost all varnish should soak into the wood except where wood fibers are running parallel to the surface. At this point you will wish you had some kind of handle by which to hold the wet stock and support it while drying. Actually a handle is required, but it is best to wait for several more coats before attaching it.

Between coats you have a chance to admire your product, for the application of varnish gives you your first real preview of the finished character of the wood. Meanwhile the brush can be left in a small can of solvent to soak. Cover the top with aluminum foil to prevent evaporation.

For the next coat wipe out the brush and apply more thinned varnish, both inside and out. After finishing this step, check the inletting carefully to verify that all is soaking in, particularly at corners. In areas of glass bedding or where wet puddles seem to appear, carefully blot up any excess with a corner of rag. The objective is to thoroughly seal areas of inletting against moisture without affecting the fit of metal parts with excessive finish.

After drying for at least 24 hours another coat can be applied. I have found about three coats of spar varnish sufficient to fill the pores of eastern maple, and on walnut about five coats seems to do the job, but it depends on both the amount of thinner and the porosity of the wood. About three coats in the inletting is usually adequate to seal the wood.

If you have attached a genuine ebony fore-end tip you will likely make the unpleasant observation (after coat No. 1) that it has not dried. Ebony contains an oil which prevents varnish from drying. I have remedied this by leaching the oil out with a solvent such as lacquer thinner, white gasoline, or even lighter fluid. Saturate a small cloth with solvent, rub down the fore-end tip dissolving the soft varnish and thoroughly wetting the ebony. Then dry promptly with a cloth. Change rags and repeat. You will notice a brown residue on the cloth which is the oil leached from the ebony. Dry thoroughly and brush on the varnish. It should now harden satisfactorily.

After several such coats the stock will have a pinhole appearance where glossy

The wood dictated the finish on these stocks. The top rifle, a Heeren .243 Winchester mountain carbine, has a stock of California-grown English walnut which looks well with the classic oil finish plus a coat of wax. The wax simply adds gloss. The Remington 40X gallery rifle at center is stocked in the same kind of wood, just not as fancy. It has the classic oil finish but is left dull -- "London oil" style. The Winchester 70 .30-06 at bottom, is of California claro walnut with much end grain showing in the butt. The figure comes through best with the plastic urethane finish, which also offers the most protection.

varnish has penetrated the pores more than the surrounding wood. Examine the pores and end grain areas carefully with a glass to verify that pores are filled up to the wood surface. We are going to cut the varnish back to the wood surface leaving all holes filled so that minor areas as yet unfilled must be varnished again or holes will be apparent in the final finish.

To cut off the varnish, use a *new, clean* cotton muslin buffing wheel and your little old bench grinder. As a safety precaution for the stock, remove the wheel guard and tool rest normally used for grinding, and clear the deck for action. You will want your safety glasses, hat and apron. Carefully buff the stock surface buffing crosswise to the grain. The buff will tear off the varnish in short order, leaving you approximately where you started but with the pores now filled. Buff rapidly and with fairly firm pressure rotating the stock against the wheel to leave the surface as clean as possible. Avoid heating the surface and also avoid the sharp edges of the inletting and cheekpiece. The buff obviously cannot get into all areas and corners and these will require sanding with 320 or 400 "Wet-Or-Dry" to clean up. Some furrows of varnish may remain and the entire stock will look somewhat grubby, but this is fixed readily by sanding wet with 400 "Wet-Or-Dry." If desired, you may wet sand with mineral spirits or turpentine if the smell is particulary attractive or you have some concern about wetting the stock; but I have found water to be harmless as long as it is blotted dry when the local area is finished. For this operation an old piece of carpet covered with newspapers is handy for covering the bench top.

After sanding, careful inspection should reveal a perfectly smooth surface—no pores, no minor blemishes. Do not hesitate to repair small spots with coarser paper or varnish again should they reveal faults. If water stain was used to color sapwood it is now reapplied where sanding may have worn it through.

At this point the filled stock is ready for checkering. Checkering will occupy your attention for quite a few hours but the stock is at least in condition for handling and other work. If you are refinishing a stock the checkering should be masked before varnish filler is applied. After the filler has been buffed off and sanded, the masking tape should

STAIN FORMULAS

Du Pont Dye Color	(Figures are weight in grains)					
	No. 1	No. 2	No. 3	No. 4	No. 5	No. 6
Orange Concentrate II	---	---	---	15	15	24
Resorcin Brown 5-C	270	30	---	60	80	90
Nigrosine WSB Concentrate	30	180	120	180	180	150
Scarlet NS Concentrate	---	---	300	60	30	---
Tartrazine Concentrate	30	30	---	---	---	---
Water - Quarts	2	1½	2	1½	1½	1 3/4

RESULTING SHADES ON MAPLE

Dye Color	Color
Orange Concentrate II	Brilliant Orange.
Resorcin Brown 5-C	Orange-brown.
Nigrosine WSB Concentrate	Black.
Scarlet NS Concentrate	Bright red.
Tartrazine Concentrate	Yellow.
Stain Formula	
Number 1.	Light brown maple.
Number 2.	Black-brown, very dark.
Number 3.	Dark red. (Half way between Scarlet NS and No. 4).
Number 4.	Red-brown mahogany. (More red than No. 5).
Number 5.	Brown mahogany walnut.
Number 6.	Dark walnut. (Less red than No. 5).

FILLERS AND FINISHES

Material	Approximate Essential Contents	Use and Comments
Spar Varnish	Linseed oil and/or tung oil, cooked together with phenolic resin. Solvent added (mineral spirits or similar) to adjust viscosity.	Excellent material to fill pores. Fair as a stock finish.
Alkyd Varnish	A polyester resin combined with linseed oil, coconut oil or tung oil, in solvent.	Alkyds are the base of many paints and varnishes.
Alkyd Melamine	A polyester resin combined with formaldehyde resin in solvent.	Suitable for stock finish but not up to urethane types.
Alkyd Phenolic	A polyester resin and phenolic resin in solvent.	Suitable for stock finish but not up to urethane types.
Alaphatic Urethane	Requires 2% catalyst of dibutyl tin dilaurate.	Quite expensive and unnessarily complicated for our purposes.
Moisture Cured Urethane	Aeromatic Isocyanite. Requires over 50% R. H. to cure.	Quite expensive and unnessarily complicated for our purposes.
Aeromatic Urethane	A urethane resin modified by safflower oil.	Excellent. High abrasion resistance. No pot life problem.
Lacquer	Nitrocellulose. Frequently modified with alkyd or castor oil for finishing furniture.	A production furniture finish for factory methods
Acrylic Lacquer	Polymethylmethacrylate resin in solvent.	Usually require spray application. For metal and plastic finishing.
Vinyl, Butyrate, Etc. Lacquers	Vinyl or Butyrate plastics dissolved in solvents.	Usually require spray application. For metal and plastic finishing.

be removed and the checkering recut.

For either new checkering or recutting, a cradle is very desirable. If you do not have a cradle the next best bet is to reassemble the stock and grab the barrel in a padded bench vise. For padding I use an old mail order catalog or a thick magazine with ½ to ¾-inch of paper to pad the jaws. To recut the checkering use a single Dem Bart cutter and go over each line from both directions sharpening the diamonds and going right to the bottom of the valleys. The border areas must be approached carefully and the borders done last. Carefully go around these. I cannot emphasize enough the need for care in this operation. Keep both hands on the tool. Hold the stock solidly. Approach borders with the hands firmly against the stock so the tool point is under complete control and does not slip past the border creating a run-over. (If necessary pull the tool out of its handle, shorten it up about 1½-inch and re-insert in the handle so that you get close to the cutting head.) For final border work some professionals reverse the cutter pulling it toward the center of the design. Any port in a storm!

With the checkering complete, it too requires finishing and there is one simple way to do it—thank God something is simple. Obtain some flat varnish from your friends at the paint store—it should be marked "Flat" or "Dull", not "Semi-Gloss." This is brushed into the checkering with a toothbrush. Do this to all panels and allow 24 hours to dry. Reapply a second coat. Usually two or three coats are required. The varnish may be thinned slightly, but this is usually unnecessary since the toothbrush has enough stiffness to move the varnish around. As it dries, observe whether it is uniformly wet and glossy, or if it has soaked into certain parts. The second coat may be sufficient. Do not apply any more than appears necessary. Two or three coats should do it. Areas adjacent to the checkering should be wiped free of the flat varnish before it dries.

Should the checkering extend into stained areas these will also require careful and very modest stain application. Use a rag barely dampened to start with, as excess stain will be absorbed very quickly by the extensive surface area presented by the diamonds. Finish with flat varnish after the right color is achieved.

The flat varnish is the most satisfactory finish for checkering. Glossy varnish is plainly gookey looking, while no finish at all leaves the wood dull, lifeless, and vulnerable to water. Finished as recommended, the panels will blend in perfectly with adjacent areas, and the diamonds will be protected and strengthened by impregnation with varnish so perspiration or rain will not cause damage.

From this point on, the two finishes, oil or plastic, differ. Let's discuss oil, the easier of the two, first. After the checkering is dry, the stock to be oil-finished should be sanded with 600 "Wet-Or-Dry." This will be faster if some solvent or water is used; however, any mess should be blotted up quickly to keep the checkering clean. Start by sanding the areas around the cheekpiece, then move to the areas adjacent to sharp corners and edges. After sanding the stock should have a uniformly dull gloss.

Next, apply a thin coat of alkanet root boiled linseed oil to which a small amount of thinner has been added. (No need to mix up any great quantity—about a teaspoon of oil plus an eyedropper full of solvent does the job.) Wipe over the entire stock using a cleaning patch saturated with oil and allow to stand, then re-wet any areas where oil has soaked in. Finally, wipe dry with a clean cloth and put aside for a few days.

Now, obtain some rottenstone and a piece of heavy, hard felt about ¼-inch thick. Tack the felt to a block if desired but save a piece about 3 by 6 for freehand use over curved areas. (If you tack felt to a block, tack it into the end grain so that no nail heads suddenly demolish your fine finish just as you are on the home stretch.) Dip the felt into the rottenstone, transferring a small amount to the stock. I use it dry—saves mess. Polish lengthwise all over including corners around the cheekpiece. When finished, dust out the inletting and checkering with a brush and wipe away the surplus rottenstone with a cloth. Apply some of our special colored and thinned linseed oil again. Use it sparingly, just wetting the surface. Let stand and repeat if any areas seem to be absorbing oil. Then after an hour or so, wipe dry and put aside for several more days. Repeat until no more oil is absorbed, the gloss is

fairly nice (but not shiny), and the job appears to be almost done.

If you like you can continue to put on a drop or two of the alkanet-boiled linseed, rubbing briskly with a wood cloth or the hand. Avoid leaving the stock with a sticky film, and don't make an application over a sticky film. This will eventually dry but will lead to a shiny surface where a film of visible thickness has been built up. This can be evened up quickly with rottenstone or one swipe of 000 steel wool. Them that likes an oil finish with that glossy-wet just-oiled look, must understand that this is achieved with a built-up film of oil. If this is what you want, continue to rub on the oil *very sparingly.* I have found our oil slow, but superior to other prepared oils that dry faster. By this method the stock will take on more and more gloss with each application. Stop whenever the appearance suits you.

To finish the job, I prefer wax and therefore stop oiling before a visible thickness or film is built up. Shop around for some silicone wax or carnauba wax. Try it out on a well-polished piece of furniture. It should add gloss, but have practically no visible film. A number of such preparations are on the market and are sold in gunshops. A furniture wax is also satisfactory, but avoid those appearing to contain plastics, varnishes, etc., as a polish is what is wanted, not a film. Waxes bragging about a high proportion of carnauba wax in paste form are usually OK. One such excellent wax I am now using is Lundmark's "Clear Paste Wax," which says on the label, "Pure Carnauba Wax in Turpentine." The one pound can was $1.49.

Before waxing, the finish will have an eggshell gloss; that is, a slightly dull semi-gloss appearance, not completely flat and not glossy-wet. After waxing the gloss will change to a high luster. If extensive perspiration or rain dulls or spots the surface, don't worry—no permanent damage has occurred. Simply go over with oil, rub dry and wax if desired. Waxes are not permanent and will wear away with use and handling, but they are easily renewed. I prefer this finish to a built-up thickness of linseed oil. It has great dignity, is completely satisfactory for light-to-medium service, and is easily freshened up to renew its good looks because the finish is entirely *in* the wood.

If you feel you must have a protective film *on* the wood that is what the high-grade plastic finishes are for. They offer much more resistance to moisture, abrasion, perspiration and scratching than waxes or linseed oil. So if you wish real protection and long, no-monkey-business-service from he finish, apply the plastic. It is much superior to a built-up film of linseed oil, waxed or not.

A number of very fine plastic finishes are available and I have used a sampling of many, but by no means all. My best recommendation is to go to your favorite paint store and buy a polyurethane or urethane varnish. My two favorites are: "Super Satinwood" (polyurethane) "Rez" by Rez Wood-Tones, Inc., and Pratt and Lambert's "Varmor Clear Finish Gloss." Many others would be perfectly satisfactory. In any case, the key word to find on the label is "polyurethane" or just plain "urethane." The "Rez" brand comes at the right viscosity for brushing; the "Varmor" needs a slight amount of thinner.

These finishes dry quite rapidly, dry throughout, and leave a film that is hard, wear resistant and insoluble even in lacquer thinner. They are too tough to use for filling pores, however, as they cannot be buffed off, but rather must be sanded to remove the built-up surplus.

A fairly fast-evaporating thinner such as VM & P (Varnish Makers and Painters) naphtha or heptane should be added if the material does not appear to flow out evenly to produce a uniformly smooth film. Thinner permits the wet film to level out before evaporating. Then oxidation takes place to crosslink or polymerize and harden the film. Heptane, VM & P naphtha and xylol evaporate relatively quickly—mineral spirits and turpentine, more slowly. Commercial proprietary thinners are generally unidentified mixtures and are good, but usually evaporate more slowly than heptane or VM & P.

In addition you should obtain a package of tack rag— a varnish-impregnated sticky cloth designed to pick up lint, fuzz and dust from the stock—and a soft brush 1¼ to 1½-inch wide, ordinarily used for lacquering or applying gilt finish and usually made of soft natural bristles or a mixture of natural bristles and ox hair, not nylon. You will also need masking tape and 400 and 600 "Wet-Or-Dry"

sandpaper. From this point on, *absolute cleanliness is necessary* to avoid imperfections and dirt in the final finish.

Start by masking off the checkering. Apply masking tape over the checkered design and press into the borders with the thumbnail. Then cut the surplus tape away carefully with a pen knife. Mask off all inletting and the mortise for the guard. Mask the butt plate and grip cap. Be careful to adhere all edges of the tape very firmly so that finish does not creep under the tape.

Next you will need a handle with which to hold the stock when applying the finish. Use a piece of 5/8-inch dowel rod or broomstick if the barrel channel will permit. The rod should extend from the recoil lug area to at least one foot beyond the fore-end tip. This last bit at the end is drilled with a hole and a wire loop inserted so the wet stock can be hung up conveniently to dry. Attach the dowel with a wood screw through the front guard screw hole and install a second wood screw at the front sling swivel hole, or if no swivel is present, run a screw from the dowel down into the barrel channel.

Wipe off the stock completely with the tack rag. Wash out the brush with solvent and dry carefully on a clean rag, checking for loose bristles. If any appear, give them all a tug. Then set up your wife's hair dryer so that it can be directed against the stock; or, if it is a warm summer day, be prepared to take the stock outside. We want to apply a full wet coat without having any sags or runs develop during the drying process.

With the clear urethane thinned as necessary, apply an even wet coat all over the stock. Work from the fore-end tip back to the pistol grip, then the opposite side, then the butt stock—first the off side, then the cheekpiece side. All lights should be adjusted to illuminate the stock adequately so that skips and faults can be spotted and corrected immediately with the brush. I like to dip the bristles fully up to the metal ferrule then squeeze out most of the clear. In this way you carry sufficient clear to the stock, but not enough to develop a puddle as soon as the brush touches the surface. Work quickly and keep rotating the stock so that runs or sags do not start. If they do, smooth out the area with the brush.

When the finish has all been applied, inspect by rotating the stock with the handle. Do not hesitate to rebrush an

area which has developed a sag or remove a bristle that has come out of the brush. The work should be done indoors where a cool, absolutely still, clean environment is available. If all looks well, switch on the hair dryer and rotate the stock barbecue fashion horizontally in the hot air. This will make short work of the solvent. The stock may also be carried out into the sunshine and warm air. After about 15 minutes most of the solvent should be gone and, if you were careful in laying on the clear, no runs or sags should be visible. Hang up in a dust free area and allow at least 24 hours to dry. Avoid basement drying in the summer months as basements are usually quite damp unless dehumidified. If the finish tends to fingerprint it will require two or three times more dry time.

When dry, wet sand using 400 or 500 "Wet-Or-Dry." The sanding is simply to even up the surface and remove paint nibs and dust particles. Check the finish for evenness, and sand out any sags or runs using a rubber or padded wood block to back up the sandpaper.

Apply a second coat the same way. Tack rag first, apply a thin even coat, and dry with the hair dryer or in the summer sun. Hold the stock horizontally and rotate slowly until the solvent is gone, then allow to dry thoroughly. Again sand with 400 or 500 "Wet-Or-Dry."

We are now very close to the end and it will probably dawn on you that a spray gun would be the best system to apply the last coat or two. Correct! If you have access to one, by all means use it. If not, continue with your brush. One or two more coats, sanded lightly between each coat will be necessary.

However, with a spray gun you can shoot a second coat about 30 minutes after the first, while the first coat is still wet but after much of the solvent has flashed off. Practice, dexterity and some knowledge of the equipment is necessary for proper spray application, but it provides a much more uniform coating than any other application system. Even the best brushing technique must rely on careful repeat applications of thin coats with sanding to correct imperfections between coats. Allow the last coat to dry for several days.

After the surface is thoroughly dry it should show no major

imperfections—no sags, runs or major blemishes. A few resin seeds or dust specks may be allowed, but if you have a major sag or run, sand out the blemish until it is all gone. Another "final" coat may again be necessary, but let's hope it isn't. If only a few dust specks are present, sand the final coat with 600 "Wet-Or-Dry" using water. After the stock feels absolutely smooth, go over the entire surface with 000 or 0000 steel wool, using light pressure at sharp edges so as not to wear through the finish. The steel wool will unify the gloss whereas sandpaper just cuts off the high spots.

The stock should have an over-all dull look with no gloss, but the urethane resin will be two to four thousandths of an inch in thickness. Just exactly what we want. Next, to bring up the gloss, obtain some automobile rubbing compound.

Rubbing compound should be available at any self-respecting auto shop that handles seat covers and mag wheels. Rub the stock briskly with a rag using polishing compound until the desired gloss is obtained. If the surface appears orange peeled or slightly textured give it a lick with steel wool and repolish. With the desired gloss achieved—and you get dull gloss by using an excess of rubbing compound, high gloss by simply more rubbing with less compound—the stock and checkering can be unmasked and the gun reassembled. Clean the checkering borders of the remains of rubbing compound and finish by going around the border with the single row tool. This freshly cleaned edge can be blended back in with a corner of rag saturated with linseed oil.

This then is the plastic finish. Admire to your heart's content, but when putting the gun away for the first week,

simply stand it in the corner so that the fresh finish does not get a surface impression from a case or other point of contact. After the novelty of having the stock all done has worn off, remove the steel butt plate, grip cap and other parts that require blueing and have this done. When reassembled, your pride and joy will be ready with the most durable hard-use finish obtainable.

The chart should help you make an intelligent selection at the local paint shop. This will give you the satisfaction of knowing what it is you are putting on, and that you can get the best job with it. Intentionally, not much has been said about all the miracle stock finishes on the shelf at the gun shop. These emollients are for the quickie finish, and at a dollar or more per ounce they are more expensive than bar whiskey. ●

NEW TECHNIQUES FOR FINE STOCK FINISHING

New finishing materials — and new techniques — can result in an "old" look, while giving a more serviceable finish. This stock was finished with four coats of low luster polyurethane finish, then rubbed with Brownell's stock rubbing compound.

By HOWARD MASTERSON

PUTTING A FINISH on a rifle or shotgun stock, simple as it seems, has traditionally been the big stumbling block when it comes to turning out a really nice piece of work.

Here in my home in Wisconsin I've had an opportunity to know and talk with great stockmakers such as Leonard Mews and the late Alvin Linden. I put in many fondly remembered hours discussing stockmaking with "Old Scratch" as he liked to call himself. He was a kind person in a gruff sort of way and a willing instructor, but when the talk got around to stock finishes his usually forthright opinion gave way to sincere apologies. "So far as I know" he once told me, "there is no known way to put a finish on a gunstock."

But anyone who has ever seen the deep rich luster of a Linden stock knows that he had some mighty good ideas about how to finish a stock, regardless of his private opinions. It seemed to me that he tried a new finishing technique on almost every stock he made. Or at least tried a different technique. "Each stock is different" he'd say, "something like a woman, you have to keep messing around until you find out what works."

The shelves in his shop were lined with different compounds and formulas he'd tried, none of which had ever given the results he was seeking. There is no doubt that he went to his grave without finding the finish that suited his exacting demands.

Leonard Mews, like every stock-

Here a built-up polyurethane finish is sanded level, using unorthodox circular motions of the sanding pad. The scratches will be filled by the final finish material.

maker I've known also keeps looking for the "perfect" finish. The perfect finish in nearly everyone's opinion would be a cheap compound, easy to apply, capable of drying in minutes to a dead level, rock hard surface, which would never shrink into the grain and would be perfectly waterproof.

So far there is no finish that comes close to any of these criteria, but we're a lot closer than we were in Al Linden's day. At my regular job as a high school instructor I have lots of time to mess around with various finishes and observe others doing the same. One of the most important factors I've thus learned is that the method of application is nearly as important as the finishing material itself. I think this is why some craftsmen get good results with a certain type of finish and others don't. I've observed this in my shop classes over many years. Some students will get good results finishing their projects — gunstocks are favorite items — while others seem to make a mess of things. These latter students, however, may get excellent results with another finish. Also, despite the instructions that may accompany a given finishing product one more or less has to "feel" his way along.

Talented wood finishers seem to have a sixth sense about what finish and what technique to use on a given piece of furniture or gunstock. Likewise some stockmakers seem to have the fortitude to "stay with" a stock until they get the desired results. I knew of Al Linden trying three different techniques on a single stock before getting what he wanted. In fact some of our top stockmakers say they never *really* get the finish like they want it, but just give up when they can do no better.

Be all this as it may, I have, by talking with good stockmakers, and trying

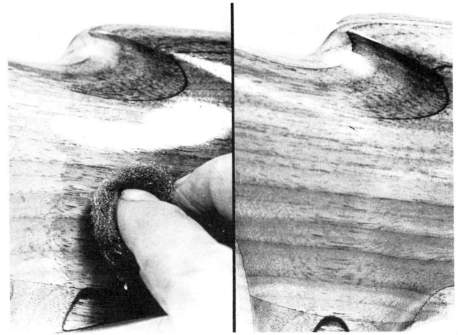

Above, the sanded polyurethane is being polished with fine steel wool and linseed oil. The final result of this method is a stock with the appearance of a hand-rubbed oil finish, but far more waterproof and more durable.

about everything personally, come up with a few finishes and techniques that can be relied on to give good to excellent results in most all cases. The final proof of the pudding, as I call it, is to have my shop students repeat the process. If they can duplicate my success then I consider the technique pretty much sure-fire.

First of all I'll go on record as stating that the so called "rubbed linseed oil" finish is very likely the worst of all possible gunstock finishes. In connection with other finishes, say, oil rubbed over a varnish filler, it adds a nice, soft, but temporary sheen. Used by itself however, the only thing linseed oil, boiled, raw, or otherwise, can do is ruin an otherwise good piece of wood.

If you doubt what I say, look at the "handrubbed linseed oil" finishes on the stocks of the otherwise fine English

doubles. I've seen Purdeys and Holland and Holland shotguns costing upwards of $5,000 that had ugly splotchy finishes that had utterly ruined otherwise beautiful wood. If any of my students turned in a piece of work like that I'd flunk him straightaway.

The best all-around finishes I've run across in the past two decades are the new polyurethane varnishes. These are tough, proof against moisture to a high degree, and resistant to about all liquids. Also they resist shrinking into the wood grain quite well. I've been watching such a finish on a stock for about two years now. There is a slight specking noticeable now at the grain pores but by contrast a regular spar type or "Bartop" varnish shrinks badly within six months. That is unless there it considerable build-up of the finish upon application. But of course this would be unsatisfactory for stocks. I have found the afore-mentioned polyurethane finishes to respond well to two types of application.

First: the brush-on: The first coat is thinned to a mixture of about one third part thinner. This thinner mix penetrates the wood better and gets a better "hold" on the grain structure. If the wood is open-pored a second or even a third coat might be needed.

With a good rubbing compound, the polyurethane finish can be rubbed to a soft brightness.

This brilliantly finished stock is the result of several "wiped off" coats of Linspeed, without any sanding between coats, or a final rubbing. Note the unusual smoothness.

Application is with a soft camel hair brush about an inch wide. Get the best grade you can find so there will be no worry about the hairs coming out. Upwards of three dollars is not too much to pay if you can find a really good one. Artists' supply shops are the best place to look.

While you are using the thinned finish give the inletting a good soaking and let the end grain under the buttplate absorb all it will take. The thinned finish will not build up in the inletting and ruin a good fit. After the first thinned coat, or coats, are applied and thoroughly dry, switch to the regular mix. Use long, lengthwise strokes and don't apply too heavily. If you do you'll get runs. When you have an even coat over the whole stock hang it up to dry.

The drying time of these finishes varies from four to twenty-four hours. Usually the drying time is about right to apply a coat in the morning and one in the evening. Also, for this type of finishing technique, don't attempt to sand or rub down with steel wool between coats. Just let it build up to a thick layer.

By the time about six coats have been applied the layer will be quite heavy. But don't worry about this, the main thing is to keep applying the finish until the "dimples" are gone. When a coat of finish is first brushed on it looks smooth and flat. As it

Using Linspeed, and similar commercial products, for a "wiped off" finish essentially consists of brushing on a thick coat of finishing material, then wiping it off with a soft, lint-free cloth so the surface appears almost dry. Although this method requires some practice it is relatively fast and easy, and gives good results.

dries however, some of the finish sinks into the grain pores and causes dimples. This is the idea of applying so much finish — to fill the grain up even with the surface, and then some.

When all the finish is stacked up on the stock it looks like a lot of work is in store just rubbing it down. It's not all that bad, though. Years ago when I used standard varnish finishes it seemed like it took forever to rub it down. These polyurethane varnishes sand remarkably well. By using the Durite no-clog "white" sandpaper the job goes plenty fast and about one sheet of paper will be sufficient for the whole job. The polyurethane sands into a fine white dust and the surface is easy to keep level. Use a small felt-padded block and sand in tight circles of about three inches diameter. This, I know, is a rather unorthodox sanding technique but is a good technique nonetheless.

Don't strive to cut the finish down to the wood, instead try to get the overall surface flat and level. Finally give the whole surface a final smoothing up with 280-grit Durite or a brisk rubdown with 0000 grade steel wool. At this time the entire finish has a white, chalky look, but don't worry about it. This is just the result of the myriad scratches left by the sanding.

If you happen to sand through the finish into the bare wood just brush on a few overlapping coats of finish until the bare spot is again well-covered. The trick of this finish is not to sand down to the wood, as you might have heard or read, but to leave a coat on the surface of the wood. Don't worry about it having the glazed appearance of some of the "space age" finishes advertised on some factory guns. It won't.

With the finish at this stage you have a variety of ways to go. If you want a low luster sheen just dip small patches of super fine steel wool in linseed oil and lightly scrub the finish. This takes out the chalky look and leaves the appearance of polished wood.

Another course is to rub down the stock with Brownell's stock rubbing compound. This is a fairly coarse grit as rubbing compounds go but the polyurethane is extremely tough and requires a robust compound. A good rubbing with small pads will leave the finish dead slick and mirror bright. Actually, however, much of the brightness of the finish depends on the grade of polyurethane. You can get high gloss grades or low to medium luster. For gunstocks I prefer the low luster. With this the stock will appear beautifully polished but not so bright as to knock your eye out.

Another application technique applies to other varnishes and commercial stock finishes as well as polyurethane. Most commercial stock finishes, such as Birchwood-Casey and Linspeed, supposedly are to be wiped on with the fingertips. Yet flaws are almost certain to result from this technique unless a considerable bit of sanding or rubbing is done too.

I use a technique with either Linspeed or B-C that leaves a beautifully smooth finish with no sanding or rubbing whatever. This is the "wiping" method. In all honesty it takes a bit of practice to master, but if it doesn't do right the first time nothing is ruined.

Simplified, "wiping" is nothing more than brushing on a coat of finish and then wiping it off with a soft, absolute-ly lint-free cloth or paper towel. This leaves a thin but dead smooth layer of finish. I've seen wiped-on varnish finishes so glossy that they appeared to have been rubbed with oil and rottenstone then highly waxed. When this technique is mastered, it not only is the best looking but also about the easiest.

Some masters of this art claim that different types of finishing material require a specific waiting period between the time the finish is applied and when it should be wiped off. I have found that this is not too critical. One does want to wipe the finish off before it gets tacky and wants to "grab" the wiping cloth. My personal standard procedure for all wiped stock finishes is to get a coat of finish on all of the stock and then come back and immediately start wiping it off. I prefer to use long steady wipes with moderate pressure. Wipe the stock so that it looks almost dry. Actually the wiping isn't too critical at all. Just be sure to wipe out all streaks and *don't* use any sort of cloth that will leave lint.

After a few coats have been wiped on, say two coats a day for three days, the finish will be done. In my opinion, the "wiped off" finish will, after the technique has become better known, become the standard finishing procedure for fine gunstocks.

So there you have it: two methods of finishing that work. Of the two, the wiping method involves less work, once mastered, but the polyurethane finish is harder and more waterproof, therefore it is preferable for guns which will see harder service. If my shop students can do it, so can you. ●

Care and Feeding of Gunstocks

David Webb

For an oil finish, use either tung or linseed oil — or a combination of the two. A coat of pastewax, applied over the finished stock, will help protect it.

O VER THE YEARS, so much has been written about gunstock finishing that one might wonder if anything new and different could possibly come down the pike. The fact is, there are only a few radically new stock finishing materials, but there are new concepts and fresh approaches worth reviewing. For example, there is increasing use of tung-linseed oil blends, tung oil-alkyd varnish resin blends and synthetic finishes to achieve the hand-rubbed, glowing oil finishes so highly desired by custom stockmakers. Then there's the shift to oils or resin blends when resistance to cracks and splits is the objective. In addition, there are several new synthetic gunstock finishing materials which are easy to work with, fast drying, flexible, non-yellowing and can be hand-rubbed to achieve a soft sheen.

Gunstocks are "finished" for protection and embellishment. The wood needs to be protected from scrapes and dents, and must be resistant to moisture. An equally important reason for stock finishes is to enhance and accent the natural beauty of wood.

A primary reference book in this field, *Gunstock Finishing and Care*, was authored by A. Donald Newell in 1949 and recently reprinted. In the November-December 1982 issue of *Fine Woodworking* magazine, Newell wrote a short piece entitled, "The Aesthetics of Clear Finishes." A quote from this article is germane.

"Consider a fine walnut gunstock. Historically, gunstocks have been finished with rubbed-in linseed oil, a material of countless shortcomings and only two possible virtues; it is easy to apply, and it is capable of producing a soft, pleasing luster if rubbed often and long enough. This soft sheen is generally believed to be a clue to a gun's quality, a perception that the gun is better made than one whose stock is not handrubbed. Ironically, for durability and moisture resistance, linseed oil is not a good finish for a gunstock. Tung oil, the popular Danish oils and certain penetrating varnishes can be made to look about the same as rubbed oil, and are far more durable. Yet even today, with these other materials available, a genuine, handrubbed linseed oil finish still sells guns."

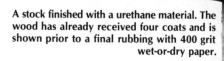

A stock finished with a urethane material. The wood has already received four coats and is shown prior to a final rubbing with 400 grit wet-or-dry paper.

A lustrous example of a "close to the wood" oil finish.

Bivins Express Oil finishes were formulated around urethane resins and were designed specifically for gunstocks.

The current trend in sporting rifle stock design follows the classic style. Gun Digest editor emeritus John Amber and the late Jack O'Connor were influential in developing the interest of the American shooter (and finally the manufacturer) in the classic rifle — straight comb, no monte carlo. Ruger obtained the services of the late Len Brownell to design the stock of the Model 77 Sporter. Both Winchester and Remington now offer classic stocks as options on their hunting rifles. Many custom gun makers prefer to work exclusively with the classic stock when building a rifle.

The appearance of a hand-rubbed, oil finish is synonymous with the classic rifle. Note I said the "appearance." There are several ways to obtain that look.

As Newell stated, the soft sheen of the linseed oil finish has been the ultimate goal for which those producing high quality guns have been striving. There was a time when the stock finisher had only the one choice — linseed oil. Today that is not the case. One can thumb through various trade journals and sporting magazines and discover numerous advertisements of-

fering various types of finishing materials for wood stocks. They range from the traditional linseed oil to those modified with alkyd resins, and synthetic materials such as polyurethane and epoxy.

For years, raw (unprocessed) and boiled linseed oil were used as stock finishes. This "non-rigid" material does enhance the appearance of wood but as a protective barrier against physical abrasion and transfer of moisture, it leaves much to be desired. Linseed oil never dries completely. Its ability to retard the movement of moisture in and out of a wood stock is very poor. True, the damaged portion of an oil-finished stock can be sanded and quickly refinished, but the wood itself may have suffered permanent damage. With a more durable, harder finish, the scratch should be predominantly in the coating,

thus affording more protection to the wood itself.

Boiled linseed oil is not generally recommended for stock finishing. Raw (unprocessed) linseed oil should *never* be used as a finishing material. The manufacturers of boiled linseed oil add "driers" and heat the oil which helps promote the drying of the oil when it is applied in a thin film. Linseed oil, as a finish, does not dry to the same degree that an alkyd resin or polyurethane finishing material will. The oil will remain soft and somewhat tacky.

With respect to boiled linseed oil, it is important to consider the poor moisture resistance property that this finish gives the wood. The U.S. Forest Products Laboratory in Madison, Wisconsin, has conducted tests on clear finishes for their "moisture excluding

Two commercially prepared finishes formulated with tung oil, resins, driers and solvents. Both can be employed to work up a "close to the wood" finish and offer greater moisture resistance than the oils can themselves.

Top, a scratched stock after sanding. Below, the same stock after refinishing.

effectiveness." Complete resistance of a film to moisture was rated at 100 percent, while no protection was 0 percent for uncoated wood. Data were reported in the USDA Wood Handbook No. 72. The moisture barrier resistance of boiled linseed oil was 20 percent. An oil-modified polyurethane's moisture resistance was rated at 75 percent. Boiled linseed oil is just not an effective moisture barrier.

Now you know why gunstocks should not be finished with boiled linseed oil. There is a case however, for an *oil finish*.

In the arid sections of our country, gunstocks need a different type of protection. The type of weather resistance required is not against moisture, but to help prevent the wood from becoming parched and brittle. For those sporting arms that are going to be used predominantly in dry areas, two types of oil-blend finishes can be used to resist dehydration: (1) a 50/50 (by volume) blend of pure tung oil and boiled linseed oil and (2) a 10 to 20-part addition of pure tung oil to an alkyd varnish resin.

With those blends, there are a few points that need emphasizing. First, prepare only the amount needed for one finishing session — the material will jell if prepared ahead of time and allowed to sit too long. Remember that boiled linseed oil has been prepared by the manufacturer. Do *not* buy raw linseed oil, then put it on your stove and boil it. To repeat, raw linseed oil should never be used as a wood finishing material. Above all, never heat any finishing material. Thin them with solvents if you want to lower their viscosity to improve their ability to penetrate into the wood.

The addition of tung oil to linseed oil increases the finish's hardness and speeds its drying. Blending tung oil with an alkyd varnish also shortens its drying time. If you desire to use an *all* oil finish, the best choice would be a 50/50 blend of tung and boiled linseed oil.

The tung and linseed mix, as well as the alkyd varnish/tung oil combination, penetrate into and remain fluid in the wood. That helps prevent the stock from checking and splitting. These finishes do not build a film on the wood surface and therefore can more easily be repaired if the stock is scratched during use. Oil finishes have traditionally been called "close-to-the-wood" finishes and known for their ease of repair. Nevertheless, techniques have been developed which will also make the newer polyurethane finishes into a "close-to-the-wood" penetrating finish.

The technologists who develop new finishing materials for the furniture and other related industries have made improvements in the types currently offered. One of the most useful is a modified polyurethane finish developed by a professional stockmaker, John Bivins. This material was formulated by Rich Schrieber for use specifically on wooden stocks.

There are several excellent synthetic stock finishes which endow wood with maximum moisture resistance. In addition, they are easy to apply, fast drying, flexible and non-yellowing. Those the author has found to be satisfactory include Bivins Express Oil Urethane and Minwax Spar Urethane.

Bivins Express Oil Filler and Sealer polyurethane finishing materials have captured the close-to-the-wood technique. These finishing materials should be applied exactly as the instructions indicate. Express Oil was undoubtedly formulated to achieve this desirable feature as John, being a gun craftsman, knows the value of this type of finishing system. Its ease of repair and low maintenance plus the added features of improved moisture and scratch resistance are definite plus factors for the Express Oil materials.

Minwax Spar Urethane was formulated specifically to build a finish on the surface of wood. When using it, I thin the finishing material with mineral spirits, 50/50 by volume. This lower viscosity finish will penetrate the wood

more readily and makes it possible to achieve the appearance of a hand-rubbed oil finish. Successive coats of the thinned urethane are applied until the wood pores are filled. Between applications and after the finish has dried, the surface should be rubbed with fine steel wool. After the third or fourth coat, the process is complete and a final rub with rottenstone and pumice completes the task.

Whether you finish your own stocks, have custom rifles built for you or purchase factory-made sporting arms, a *very* important procedure should be followed: Apply a wax to the finished wood surface. The wax protects the finish from both moisture and abrasion while the finishing material guards the wood. The use of waxes also protects against extremely dry conditions. After a rifle or shotgun has been afield for a season the stock should receive a good application of wax before storing it.

The best waxes to use are those that give a low luster. The paste types usually provide that. Minwax also makes a liquid wax that gives a satisfactory appearance. Of the paste waxes, Johnson's has always given excellent results. Another paste wax which gives more than satisfactory performance is Behlen's Blue Label which contains a mixture of carnauba waxes. Waxes formulated with carnauba are usually more heat resistant as they have higher melting points.

Improved clear finishing materials can lend the soft glow of a hand-rubbed oil finish to a wood stock — a must for a classic-style rifle. That kind of finish can be achieved in a fraction of the total time required for the old linseed oil finish. The newer finishes are more resistant to moisture and abrasion. Moreover, the oil blends described will prevent dehydration, so common in super-dry climates.

One must always guard against the effects of abrasion from dirt, dust, sand, etc. If a wax is applied after each season's use in the field, the stock's finish may last a lifetime. ●

Professional Approach to Stock Sanding

By HENRY L. WOLTMAN

*N*OTHING IS MORE PLEASING to a shooter building his own custom sporter than getting to the sanding and finishing steps of a stock making job. A goal is in sight. And here, remarkably few amateurs have much method in their madness other than getting it over with so they can take it out to the range. But lack of care in the final stages can ruin the looks of a stock which is internally perfect.

First of all we'll assume you have a custom stock completed, as far as inletting and shape are concerned--then we'll consider re-finishing a well-used stock. All metal parts are on the stock you've laboriously whittled, and the grip cap, butt plate, fore-end tip and sling swivels are installed. The vitals should all be down beneath the surface of the wood, unless they have edges which can be filed, like the butt plate or the grip cap. All contours in the stock are firmly established: the width and roundness of the forearm, the contour of the wood at the rear of the trigger guard, the fussy edges around the cheekpiece, and the undercut flutes at the nose of the comb. About the only other part of finishing which affects the lines of the stock will be the checkering design.

If you have been quite careful about keeping the edges of the cheekpiece sharp during your shaping, now is *not* the time to dub them off. The mark of good workmanship is sharp lines, the result of clean intersections where two surfaces meet, plus clean, flat, straight surfaces--which are mighty hard to come by in wavy, curly, burled-up wood. To a man who really likes fine guns wood figure is a beautiful sight, but it is a serious problem to finish well.

Before starting the job, consider the theory of sanding. When you sandpaper anything for the purpose of smoothing, the technique is to remove all imperfections in the surface as quickly as possible. Doing it quickly calls for coarse, sharp sandpaper, and it leaves its own scratches in the surface. But the only imperfections left are scratches from the coarse abrasive only, for all the dents and marks of filing are gone. Let's call this the first sanding operation.

The second sanding is done with a finer grade of paper, making smaller scratches. This second sanding removes the scratches left by the first sanding operation, but theoretically does not cut the surface down any lower. The scratches left by the second sanding should, in theory, only go to the same depth as the deepest scratches left by the first. And so, if all the chisel and file marks were completely eliminated in the first sanding, we won't have to remove any wood in the second save enough to eliminate the scratches from the first cut. The second cut should be sufficiently coarse to cut off the old marks quickly, then you stop. Don't waste time going any further with it.

The third sanding just eliminates the marks of the second cut and again removes only enough wood to do that. Sound easy? It is. This continues until the cut taken is so fine that scratches become invisible to the eye. The stock is then smooth -- the job done!

At this point two things are becoming obvious: (1) the first cut is all important because it dictates for the last time just how the surface is going to be shaped; that is, full of waves and ripples or straight and true, and is certainly the cut requiring the greatest care because the surfaces will be set; and (2) the number of stages of finer and finer abrasive can get to be tedium ad tedium unless we select four or five grit sizes of the most efficient cutting ability.

Modern sandpaper long ago quit having sand on it and is properly and accurately called coated abrasive paper. The minerals used on the abrasive paper can be flint (pale, almost white color), garnet (red color), aluminum oxide (brown), or silicon carbide (nearly black). For sanding gunstocks the aluminum oxide is the fastest, although the local hardware store might claim garnet or silicon carbide is just as good -- which is about right. The garnet isn't as sharp or fast cutting, and the silicon carbide is more expensive and, in finer grits, tends to clog a little faster. The paper should be "open coat" which is a slightly less dense deposit of mineral per square inch than something like the silicon carbide waterproof autobody refinishing paper which is not intended for use on wood. Here the slivers of wood don't have any place to go between the dense population of abrasive grains, therefore just clog.

One type of open coat abrasive paper is "Production Finishing Paper." You can buy other types of sandpaper, with cloth or very heavy paper backings at a ten-cent store, but stick with the quality hardware and paint stores. And don't let anyone try to sell you flint paper. It is just the ticket for sanding the siding on your house before a paint job -- but not gunstocks.

Sandpaper companies obligingly designate the grit of the mineral they

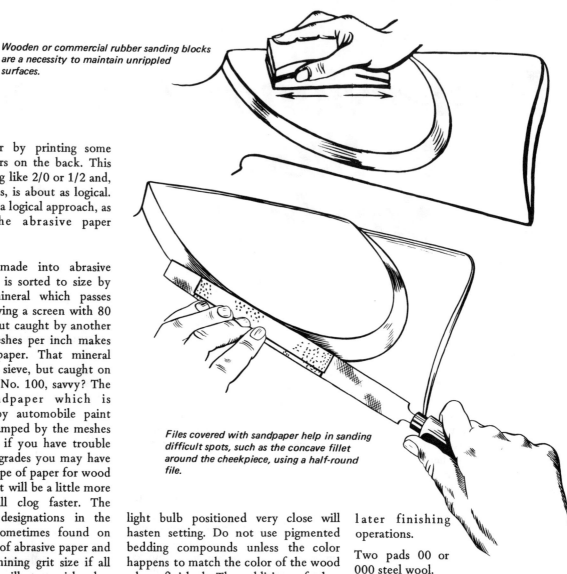

put on the paper by printing some mysterious numbers on the back. This will look something like 2/0 or 1/2 and, like shotgun gauges, is about as logical. But they also have a logical approach, as explained in the abrasive paper designation table.

Before being made into abrasive paper the mineral is sorted to size by screening. The mineral which passes through a sieve having a screen with 80 meshes per inch, but caught by another sieve with 100 meshes per inch makes 1/0 or No. 80 paper. That mineral passed by the 100 sieve, but caught on the 120, is 2/0 or No. 100, savvy? The waterproof sandpaper which is commonly used by automobile paint shops is usually stamped by the meshes per inch size, and if you have trouble locating the finer grades you may have to resort to this type of paper for wood sanding, although it will be a little more expensive and will clog faster. The coarse and fine designations in the above table are sometimes found on household packets of abrasive paper and may aid in determining grit size if all else fails. But we will start with what the sandpaper companies call medium and finish up with something they would have to call very, very, very, very fine.

Suppose we start sanding a stock we've just finished shaping. First there is a little matter of filling serious checks and cracks in the wood which we have uncovered in the whittling process. Most good wood with crotch figure can be counted on for a few checks. In the past, stick shellac was sold in a variety of wood colors and, when melted, run into the hole. This done, the surplus was filed off and sanded in the usual manner. But in this day of epoxy resins and glass bedding compounds, this much stronger resin is genuinely superior.

Mix sawdust from your stock with epoxy resin to form a paste, catalyze with your second component and, following thorough mixing, push into the check leaving the check upright to prevent the resin from running out. A

Files covered with sandpaper help in sanding difficult spots, such as the concave fillet around the cheekpiece, using a half-round file.

light bulb positioned very close will hasten setting. Do not use pigmented bedding compounds unless the color happens to match the color of the wood when finished. The addition of glass fiber is unnecessary, for sawdust from the stock will do unless a sizeable patch requires an actual transplant of walnut. If this last is required, care should dictate that the wood matches as exactly as possible and that the grain run parallel to the surrounding wood. Repairs of this sort are filed flush to the surface then sanded with the rest of the stock.

Materials we'll need for sanding make a pretty simple list:

Sandpaper
1 sheet 1/0 (80)
3 sheets 2/0 (100)
3 sheets 5/0 (180)
3 sheets 7/0 (240)
3 sheets 9/0 (320)

Miscellaneous
Small blocks for sanding.

Commercial all-rubber sanding block for two finest cuts and

later finishing operations.

Two pads 00 or 000 steel wool.

Right now this stock is mighty rough. The last tool that got a lick at it was a second cut bastard half-round file. There are a few flats along the forearm about 1/8 to 1/16-inch wide from draw filing. To get these out we'll take a half-sheet of 2/0 or 100 Production

ABRASIVE PAPER DESIGNATIONS		
Number Size	Sieve Size (meshes per inch)	Commercial Designation
1	50	coarse
1/2	60	
1/0 or 0	80	medium
2/0 or 00	100	
3/0 or 000 etc.	120	
4/0	150	fine
5/0	180	
6/0	220	very fine
7/0	240	
8/0	280	
9/0	320	
	360	
10/0	400	
	500	
	600	

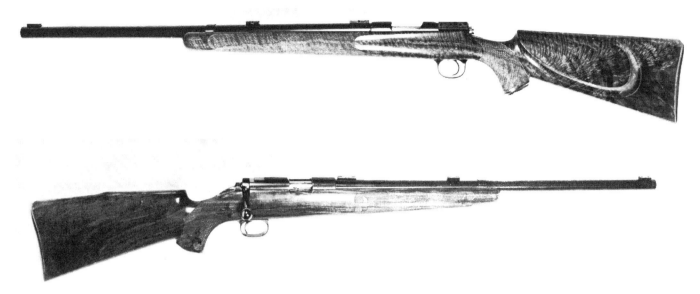

Shown are two samples of the author's work, using the difficult cheekpiece design discussed in the article.

Finishing paper and use it, shoeshine fashion, all around the forearm. Hold the stock in a heavily padded vise by the butt end and shine the heck out of the top, sides and bottom. Using a half-sheet cut lengthwise there is just enough to grab on to at the ends. By sanding cross-grain we quickly dispose of the flats and round up the forearm.

Go easy over the top of the inletting. You should be inletted beyond half-diameter of the barrel; even so, cut the surface down just enough to smooth it, no more. You can get carried away with this 2/0 and wind up with a pile of dust on the basement floor if you don't pay attention. A pal of mine, fascinated with the ease at which he was making sawdust, actually shoeshined past half-diameter and was well on his way to erasing the whole forearm except that his arms got tired first.

Cut the 2/0 sheet into 1-inch wide strips and shoeshine around the pistol grip and the curved area leading into the trigger guard. If it tends to tear, you can reinforce it, plus add handles by sticking it to a piece of adhesive tape or masking tape. You will find that even narrower strips -- 1/2-inch wide -- are sometimes helpful, especially when going through the trigger guard to smooth the surfaces adjacent to it. If you are afraid of cutting too much wood away with the embarrassment of leaving the guard edges sticking up above the wood, shim the guard out of its mortice with a couple thicknesses of paper. Leave them in until the last sanding before removing the shims. The wood will end up very slightly above the metal. Your shooting partner will think a real pro did the job.

To do a first class job you will have to ignore the blue finish, for if it hasn't

already suffered at the hands of various files, it is going to catch holy Ned in the next few hours. You will have to settle for a second best job if you don't want to injure the bluing. It is usually a simple matter to reblue just the rear tang and the trigger guard. Just figure you are going to booger-up the metal finish and get on with it.

The shoeshine technique is readily applicable to the butt end too. Just be careful on the bottom of the stock. Here you can accidentally scratch off the lower edge of the cheekpiece if you don't consciously hold one end out of the way. The area immediately under the cheekpiece is one of the most difficult spots to work because it is in a dead end. The pistol grip limits your motion back and forth, the cheekpiece limits your scrubbing crosswise. Here put the 2/0 on a narrow wood block about 1" x 1" x 5". I like to attach sandpaper to the ends of a block using a staple gun.

To the rear of the cheekpiece use a wider sanding block scrubbing crosswise first. Once the contour is established and the file marks removed, sand lengthwise up to the cheekpiece to eliminate the crosswise marks. Always use the block. For particularly deep scratches, places where the file chattered and compacted the fibers, a quick swipe with the 1/0 will make such contusions disappear. I keep a piece handy for just such spots.

On the off-side a shoeshine technique works well, but to make certain the surface is true lengthwise and crosswise, use the sanding block and scrub lengthwise up into the pistol grip area. Don't cut off any wood around the

undercut flutes at the nose of the comb just yet, however. On both sides of the stock, cut the wood down until it is flush with the butt plate all around. Use the sandpaper over a block when working near the butt plate. Check for straightness with a straight edge.

As yet I've said nothing about the cheekpiece, which will be of the design shown in the photographs. Here the main requisite when we're finished is the usual smooth finish, but with clean sharp edges all around. The same goes for the undercut flutes in the comb. The easiest way to insure sharp edges is to do everything which would tend to dub off the corners first, then later on do everything which would tend to sharpen them up. Most beginners would want to tackle the cheekpiece first, finish it up and put on a gallon of linseed oil before even rasping out the rest of the stock. They're so anxious to see how it's going to look when finished that they get the cart ahead of the horse.

The cheekpiece is actually easiest to shape up last. Forget about how rough it is on your chin just now. We want sharp corners and the procedure here is to finish up the fillet around the cheekpiece first, then cut the cheekpiece down with our sanding block. So break out the half-round file and wrap some of the 2/0 around it. Carefully go around this fillet so as not to skid over onto the top of the cheekpiece – breaking that edge. Change to smaller files with a wrap of 2/0 around them, and end up with a round rat tail up on the top of the stock where the fillet runs out. The radius around the bottom of the cheekpiece should be rather large, getting smaller rather than shallower as the cheekpiece fades into the stock at the top and at the nose of the comb. After sanding thoroughly with the 2/0 here, switch to the 5/0 and do it again. Remove all the old marks left by the 2/0. Then switch to the 7/0. This should make the fillet quite smooth and rather well finished so that we can forget about it for quite a while.

The same procedure holds true for the undercut on the comb. Sand this ditch out with paper over a half-round file. As with the cheekpiece, start with 2/0 and work it up to about the 7/0. Then proceed to cut down the adjacent areas of the stock with the 2/0 and finer grades, working always with the sandpaper over a block.

The outside of the cheekpiece is managed in the same way: Over a block so that the edges will come up sharp and remain sharp. The surface of the cheekpiece will cut off with gratifyingly high speed. I use a block about 3" x 6" here. Now, it didn't take long to get around that cheekpiece, did it?

There will be other troublesome areas to sand, areas that don't lend themselves to shoeshining, or sanding blocks. Mostly these are small areas just ahead of the cheekpiece and some small spots around the rear of the grip cap. Cut off a couple of strips of 1/2 and 1-inch wide 2/0. If you are right handed, hold one end in the right hand, lay the sandpaper over the spot to be sanded, put your left thumb on the back of the paper at that spot and yank the sandpaper out from under. Pressure from the thumb will make the wood under it disappear. This technique goes rather rapidly and is the only easy way to get some of the dead ends smoothed up.

If you have been conscientious about sanding with the sanding block, the surfaces are still straight and true, or properly curved. What would have happened if you had sanded by clutching the paper in your hot little fist and gone at it "with the grain" as they invariably advise in the handicraft books? The fancy wood, gnarled by fiddle back and feather crotch, is a mass of alternating hard and soft wood. And when you scrub it with sandpaper over a resilient backing like the palm of your hand, you put equal pressure everywhere and first thing you know, the hard spots are slightly higher than

the soft spots, which cut out faster. You think: "More sanding will fix that," and you perspire some more with the soft resilient backing now heating up behind the sandpaper. The result is worse than a hot palm – worse waves. At this point the sanding block is the only answer. It will cut down the high spots *only* until they are level with the low spots and then will take them both down evenly.

It is the only way to level and true a surface lengthwise. It is the only way to sand figured wood with the coarse papers where the cut is rapid. (Except for shoeshining or using it over the half-round files, of course.) In fact, you will find that we will do little or no sanding with the paper clutched in a mere hand.

After complete sanding with the 2/0 we are ready for the finer grades. Check back to the list of grit sizes. After starting with the 2/0 we can safely jump up two to three grit sizes -- from 2/0 to 4/0 or 5/0. From 5/0 we go to 7/0 and from 7/0 to 9/0. Thus in four jumps we have sanded the stock. There will be finer papers later when the finish is being applied, but we are sanding wood just now.

The 5/0 will only remove the scratches left by the 2/0. It is still a fast cutting paper so use it over a block. Use the 1 x 1 x 5 block and be quite careful around the mortise at the trigger guard. Shoeshine first through the guard and over the ends, then remove the guard and, with the sanding block, do the areas missed where the bow joins the upper part of the base. Wood will be high and unsanded here. The butt end is sanded the same as before except the fillet around the cheekpiece is already done, likewise the undercut portion of the comb. Smooth the butt down everywhere else.

On our fancy stock there is also a little step around the cheekpiece about 1/16-inch. high. We didn't do anything with the 2/0 here, but now that we've pulled the 5/0 out of the quiver we can use it. We could let it wait until the 7/0 was in use too, for that matter. It is another of those corners we want to keep sharp so it is one of the last things to get sanded. By sanding it last we don't run the risk of dubbing off a sharp edge while working somewhere else.

To sand this corner wrap a piece of 5/0 or 7/0 over the bottom edge of the 1 x 1 x 5 sanding block. Lay the block flat on the surrounding surface and grind the step all around. By working

with 7/0 here, you won't leave deep scratches in the butt stock below the step. I like to use the next finer grade of paper around this corner than on the rest of the stock. The next grade will then be the same as the scratches left around the cheekpiece and will therefore present no removal problem.

Sand this corner until the edge is sharp as well as the corner at the bottom. If you have trouble with the bottom corner, clean it up with a small, smooth flat file. Grind the end of the file off square and sharp, and scrape the corner out with the file point. Work carefully and use light pressure here. After cleaning it out, go over it with the 7/0 on a sharp cornered block.

The next grade, the 7/0, or 240, may be about as fine a grade as you can find in a hardware store. Exhaust the paint and hardware stores before you settle for something else. If you can't find 7/0 in a production paper, you can substitute the waterproof silicon carbide paper, called by one maker "Wetordry".

Some of this audience has waited patiently for the sawdust to settle and now have their hands up. The man in the blue shirt wishes to remove old finish, get rid of some dents, etc. All right, here and now is the proper place to discuss that. It is usually inappropriate to use the coarser grades unless some more serious repairs are contemplated. First off, remove any plastic or rubber butt plates, grip caps, unless cemented on. If a fore-end tip or inlay is plastic it must be masked off. We are going to dissolve the old finish with a liquid stripper that will dissolve not only the finish but the rubber or plastic right along with it. Any non-removable plastic must therefore be masked out, preferably with aluminum foil tape. Regular masking tape permits some solvent penetration so keep strippers off such masking.

Obtain from your friends at the paint shop some "cold stripper" for removing paint. This is a thickened methylene chloride solvent and is sold under names like "Strypeese," "Electro Cold Stripper," "Quick Strip," etc. The material is brushed on with a cheap natural bristle brush. (It will dissolve nylon bristles.) Its action is to blister and soften the old finish so that it can be scraped off with a stiff piece of cardboard. Follow the maker's directions. About a quart will be more than ample. Do your work outdoors or in an open garage as solvents are toxic and flammable. The brush can be cleaned after use or tossed out. Usually these materials are flushed off with water. Use water sparingly, keep it on the surface being stripped and don't give the inletting a bath.

Checkering is most easily cleaned at the same time by first applying stripper, then wiping clean with old wet towels, then final cleaning with a nail brush and soapy water used sparingly. Blot things dry promptly.

A second application of cold stripper may be needed. It depends on the make and the age of the stripper. Strippers do not keep particularly well, unlike good whiskey. Another observation I have made about such strippers is that they will do their work if you are patient. Keep the surface wetted with stripper and allow 15 to 30 minutes for the action to take place.

With the stock thoroughly clean and dry, inspect for necessary repairs. Dents may have to be raised, cracks may require some epoxy adhesive, and now is the time to install a new rubber pad, if required. Usually a cleaned up stock can go to the 7/0 sanding step. However, depending on the surface condition, you may want to back up one grade to 5/0 or go to 9/0. A little experimentation will tell. Most likely certain areas will require a coarser grade for dents and deep scratches (use a block, don't forget), while the remainder can be sanded with 7/0 or 9/0. This brings the re-finish job to the same point where we left the new stock.

The 7/0 should again be used over a block, however if your piece of wood is of rather plain figure you could safely use it (except on the cheekpiece) on a felt padded or rubber sanding block. For fiddle-back wood the wood block can be padded with one or two thicknesses of sandpaper. The padding will eliminate the tendency for the finer grades to clog and will let it sand faster. Notice now, when the cheekpiece and the nose of the comb get a workout with the sanding block, how sharp the edges remain.

At this point we have sanded the fillet around the cheekpiece and the undercut part of the comb of the new stock with the 7/0. Here and now let's finish these parts. Get out the half-round file and wrap it with strips of masking tape. Then put the 9/0 or finer paper over it. Masking tape will prevent the file teeth from wearing through the thin abrasive paper to start this whole job anew. Work quite carefully with both hands on the file and the stock firmly clamped in the vise. We don't want any accidental running over.

Bob Owen, the great stockmaker of Port Clinton, Ohio said this cheekpiece edge shouldn't be sharp, but should be ever so slightly rounded, as a sharp corner in later use will show dents and scratches more. Frankly, I am from The-Sharper-You-Can-Get-It-The-Better school and submit that you can make up your mind after you have it sharp, but not the other way around. So let's keep it square and clean and sharp until we get finished.

For the final cut, proceed over the whole stock again with 9/0 paper. If this is unavailable use waterproof paper in a similar mesh size or in the next finer grade, which will be number 360. Sand out all previous marks. You may find that this final rubdown will disclose minor scratches from previous sandings as yet unremoved. Treat these local areas to a taste of 5/0 and work up quickly to the 9/0. The fillet around the cheekpiece and the fillet at the nose of the comb are all done, of course. Merely sand out the 7/0 marks and, while you're at it, leave the minute scratches from the 9/0 running parallel to the grain.

The step around the cheekpiece must be sharpened again with the square-edged sanding block. Don't pad this block. You can use a sheet of paper or one thickness of cellophane tape over the abrasive that faces down so as not to scratch the butt stock. All we want to do is clean up the step and sharpen it.

There is one last operation before sanding is complete. The edges of the barrel channel have not come in for any cleaning up or particular attention. Here is where they get theirs. Using the 9/0 sanding block, but without padding, lay the block over the action mortise and barrel channel and scrub with the stock. By straddling both sides, a slight flat will be left along the edges next to the metal work. If the inletting was tight this will clean up any edges worn round by careless handling of sandpaper. Like the little step around the cheekpiece, this operation is held for the last when it is easy to get a clean edge.

Sanding the stock will cause wood fibers to be bent down, closing off pores in the wood. These will show themselves as a mass of whiskers unless we "raise the grain." The grain raised, such slivers are then cut off with the steel wool.

Wet a cloth or sponge with water and wring out fairly well. With the front burner of the stove, an electric hot plate or some source of heat percolating, wipe about one-quarter of the stock surface and immediately dry it by holding it at a safe distance over the hot burner. The heat is simply to evaporate the water as rapidly as possible. Do the surface a second time, then proceed to another area. The entire stock is done in this fashion. The stock will now feel quite whiskery and slivery -- the raised grain. This is best cut off with 00 grade (or finer 000 grade) steel wool. The 9/0 sandpaper works best for stubborn slivers that may resist steel wool. You may also discover a couple of rasp marks – rude of them to appear now -- and these will require minor local sanding. The grain-raising process should be repeated once more for good measure. The top of the stock at the inletting, edges of the cheekpiece, and comb flutes are all sensitive to rounding off with the steel wool, so keep the steel wool clear of these spots and use only 9/0 sandpaper.

Many authorities recommend cutting off whiskers with sandpaper, but I have found steel wool cuts them off, whereas sandpaper tends to push them down again requiring repeated dewhiskering for equal results. This treatment will leave the wood nearly dead smooth and clean, ready for finishing.

Now the stock is done so far as wood sanding is concerned. There will be more with waterproof sandpaper in even finer grades when the finish goes on, but it will take a mere fraction of the work expended so far.

Actually, sanding is one of the most pleasant part of making your stock. It is one of the rare stages where I find I can relax, turn up the hi-fi, and take my time. And, it is actually a good deal easier than I have made it sound, for it is simply a system that is methodical and thorough. No enthusiastic mad scratching, but we have smoothed up our stock, kept the surfaces straight and true, yet done it with a minimum of fuss and labor.

All this work shouldn't take you over a couple of evenings or one good devoted Saturday afternoon. We wanted a fine stock since it has cost us dearly in terms of inletting and shaping and we are one healthy step closer! ●

Hand-Sanding Hard Maple

Steven Dodd Hughes

THE VAST MAJORITY of gunstocks are made of one variety of walnut or another. Sanding and finishing walnut has been perfected to a science with excellent articles appearing in *Rifle* as well as the popular gunsmithing tomes. Your first maple gunstock might give you quite a surprise.

As a muzzleloading gunmaker, most of my work is with maple stockwood. If any of you are contemplating stocking a longrifle or possibly restocking one of those "newfangled" bolt actions in hard maple, this article should relieve you of some of the surprises. Although the techniques I'm about to describe are directed primarily to the longrifle maker, they apply to all gunstocks of hard maple. I am sure you can relate to scratches showing up in a finished stock. Sporter stocks are the same as muzzleloaders — just generally shorter with less complicated inletting.

Sugar maple *(Acer saccharum)* is hard. I mean *really* hard. Gunstock suppliers tell me red maple can also be very hard wood. The other maples marketed for gunstocks, silver and our western big leaf, just won't approach this hardness. Western maple often has beautiful fiddleback of flame grain but the wood is generally quite soft.

There are virtues to very hard stock wood. Although sugar maple is more subject to seasonal variation than some walnut species, it is much less likely to suffer the dings and dents of talus

slopes and car doors. Darkly stained and well sealed fiddleback will make an outstanding sporter stock with the ability to withstand hard usage. Besides, it is so representative of early American gunmaking. The tight, dense grain and extra hardness allow fine relief carving or ultrafine checkering, neither of which is likely to be readily damaged.

When finished with polyurethane, hard maple provides the toughest wood surface I've ever seen. Cheekpieces and comb noses can be shaped to knife-sharp edges. It's almost like filing mild steel. The hard lines blended with soft contours add pleasing character to all firearms. Maintaining crisp edges and scratchless curves can be achieved with a correct sanding technique.

Minute scratches and tool marks won't show on white wood, or even stained wood, until the first coat of oil dries. By then it's really too late to do much about such imperfections. The following method will get the scratches out before the finish shows them off.

Garnet sandpaper (orange in color) is preferred in the coarser grits. Some folks like aluminum oxide (tan) paper. Flint paper is worthless. When sanding 220 grit and finer, waterproof silicon carbide (about the color of a good rust blue) has more uniform grit, folds better, and lasts longer with less clogging.

Maple wears out sandpaper rapidly. Throw it away when clogged or worn

out. The idea is to employ a sharp cutting action, not to grind away at the surface. The sandpaper must be backed, at all times, with a hard or semi-hard supporting surface. Some antique guns show pronounced surface waves in the fiddleback. Such stocks were probably scraped rather than sanded. Sharkskin (shagreen) and sand grit glued to leather was also used in the eighteenth century. I'll opt for flat uniform surfaces as many early makers chose. They must have used a block backing the sharkskin.

A Norton brand or similar hard rubber sanding block is needed. That will back the paper for most of the work except the fine details and around relief carving.

Sixty-grit can be used for leveling flat surfaces on hard maple. I find it particularly useful for leveling the sides of the forestock on a fullstock, before contour shaping. Be careful. Sixty-grit will really remove lots of wood and has no place being near walnut. Final shaping and leveling of all surfaces is done with 80-grit. All surface areas are then progressively sanded with 120, 150 and 220-grit paper. Finer sanding of hard maple tends to leave more scratches than it removes.

Rasps and files tear wood fibers and compress them into the grain. The torn fibers are raised by wetting and rapidly drying the stock surfaces. Wet the stock with a damp rag. Then, without singeing or scorching, dry with a pro-

Items needed to sand hard maple: sanding block, scraps of grit paper, half-round file, pin punch, two hard rubber erasers, and a short length of gas line tubing.

pane torch. Holding the stock over an electric burner will also work. I use a hair dryer as the fan helps dry the wood and will blow away dust at the same time. The feathers will stand upright and can be cut off with new, sharp grit paper. Raise the grain between each sanding and as many times as needed.

Feathering serves two purposes: it shows wood trauma, and with just a touch, you can tell what hasn't been sanded. Neglect that step, and the first coat of oil will make the stock feel like your chin after a few days in a hunting camp.

As mentioned before, the paper must at all times be backed by a hard surface. A sanding block, hard rubber erasers, round and half-round files or pin punches can be used. The tools selected for delicate shaping are often the best for backing the paper when the same detail is sanded. Hard rubber gas line tubing is just the ticket for coved cheekpieces.

All sanding should take place with an incandescent light placed close to the work area. Mark Silver, who has great experience with both maple and walnut stockmaking, suggests a 150-watt bulb in a flexible fixture. The same shadows that aid good checkering will show scratches as well as hard lines and soft highlights. The lines and highlights show character in the finished gunstock in any light and particularly in photography. It is interesting to note that while Mark and I are from quite different gunmaking backgrounds, we use basically the same sanding methods.

With all types of firearms, leave as much of the metal in place on the stock as possible (bottom metal, buttplate, etc.). That will prevent sanding below inlet levels and rounding off inletted edges. Leave the barrel or barreled action in the stock as much as possible, especially if it's a fullstock, to strengthen the unit. The entry thimble, on a longrifle, should be in when sanding the short forestock and out the rest of the time.

A common area for scratches to show up is around those metal parts. If you don't think you have all the tool marks out of a particular area, rub in a little spit and let it dry from a light bulb's heat. That should reveal any scratches that remain.

Take extra care inletting slightly below the finished surface so the wood can be brought down to proper inletting depth. Periodically check inlet depths of parts which must be removed for sanding. Depth of the sideplate and lockplate are particularly critical. Lock panels and inlets are the first thing people look at when handling a finished muzzleloader. I usually start with 120-grit and have perfect depth at the first 220 sanding. If the wood is left high, there will be a shadow around the inlet. If the wood is too low, the plate will protrude above the surface and look terrible. Keep the lock panels flat with sharp edges; they show off your inletting.

Sand with the grain whenever possible. Cross-polishing (shoeshining) works with metal polishing but will only cause problems with wood. There is so much surface area on a fullstock longrifle that a rigid order of sanding procedure is necessary to ensure complete and uniform scratch removal. Having completed shaping with 80-grit and raised the grain, here is my procedure:

With the barrel out of the fullstock, and 80-grit on the block, sand the top line (edges of the barrel channel) and upper third of the forestock lightly. Sand the muzzle area if wood is exposed, and the quarter flats at the breech — but not the sides of the breech tang. That is done while holding the stock in your lap or on a padded bench. Install the barrel and sand the short forestock. That area will be held in the leather-padded jaws of the bench vise. Do as much work as possible while the stock is clamped in the vise.

With the stock bottom up, sand the ramrod channel, short forestock with

Torn fibers caused by filing are raised by wetting the stock with a damp rag, then quickly drying. The "whiskers" will stand straight up, and can be cut off with sharp new grit paper.

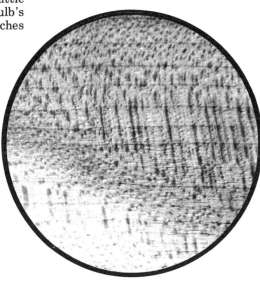

entry thimble in place, toe line, and the entire bottom surface. Use a dowel to back the paper while sanding the ramrod channel. Take care at the guard inlets, and if you are using a flat to the wrist guard, leave it in place.

Turn the left side up in the vise and sand all the detail work around the lock panel, cheekpiece, etc., using scraps of paper from the block and appropriate backing tools. Proceed to all the flat areas using the block.

Turn the top side up and get the sides of the tang, top of the wrist, comb nose and comb. On to the right side, patch-box in place, work details first then the larger areas. If you skip around and don't follow a regimented procedure, you are sure to miss something. Lightly brush the stock with your fingertips, feeling for whiskers, to make sure you have sanded everything.

One of these days I'm going to keep a score card to find out how many times a barrel goes in and out of a stock during construction. To reduce that number, remove the barrel and sand the area surrounding it last. Raise the grain with the barrel out and sand those areas *first* with the next grit. Replace the barrel and continue. That may not seem important but with three of four pins, a tang bolt and 40 inches or so of barrel to remove, it is a time saver.

The 80-grit sanding should remove all tool marks and surface wood trauma. Eighty-grit is powerful paper so go easy at the delicate spots. Take care to refine lines and define sharp edges with this and each progressive sanding. Proceed with the same steps twice with 120-grit, once with 150-grit, and twice (more, if necessary) with 220-grit, feathering between each sanding. That is a lot of work but it is the only way I've found to ensure removal of all scratches. Because of its dense grain, hard maple

When sanding the quarter flats of the stock breech, the sandpaper should be backed with hard rubber gas line tubing.

A pin punch is used as a backing for the sandpaper when smoothing up the lock panels.

should start to take on a marblelike appearance after the second 120-grit sanding. The last time over with 220-grit should leave the stock looking almost like polished bone.

After the stock is finish-sanded, it is time to add relief carving, forestock moldings and the like. That will leave you free to concentrate on just cleaning up the carved areas, knowing the rest of the stock is finish-sanded. When the carving is done and the adjacent areas sanded, I often employ a trick to make sure all the scratches are erased.

Lightly and evenly stain the entire stock. Be sure to use non-grain-raising stain. Water-based stain will just bring the whiskers back around the carving. A third careful sanding with 220 will show stain in the scratches. That staining will also enhance the fiddleback grain in maple.

It takes me about six hours and nearly five full sheets of grit paper to finish-sand a maple longrifle stock. Take your time. The finest inletting, shaping and finishing can only be complemented by complete, careful sanding. Sharp lines and distinct highlights can be emphasized or destroyed by the sanding techniques used. ●

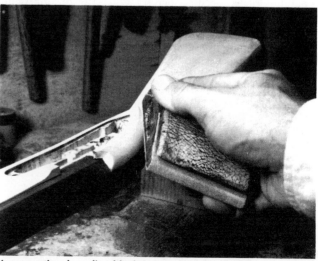

Author uses a hard rubber eraser as a sanding block when working on the comb nose.

A conventional sanding block is just right for finishing the large areas around the lock panels.

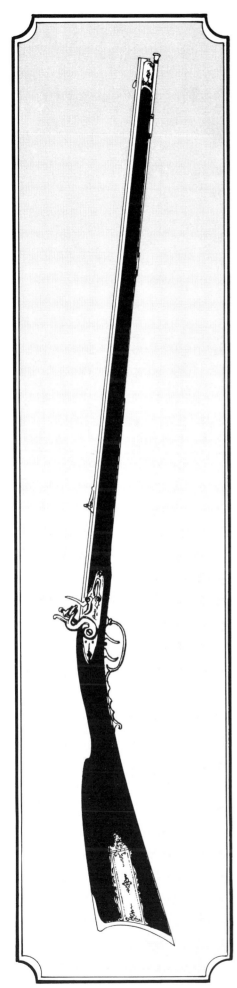

Inletting a MUZZLE LOADER

with Simple Power Tools

By JIM CARMICHEL

*B*LACK POWDER burning, more than any other type shooting, is the domain of the dedicated do-it-yourselfer. Why this is true I'm not exactly sure but it must be linked to the individualistic personalities to whom muzzle loading arms most appeal. Everybody, it seems, wants his long rifle to be one of a kind and the best way to accomplish this is simply to build it himself.

In all the muzzle loading matches I can remember attending, at least 75 percent of the shooters had built, or at least built on to their rifles. Granted, some of the work was pretty shoddy and some was even worse, but regardless of the quality of his workmanship, the shooter who had built his own was unmistakably proud of what he had wrought.

Having learned the trade of the long rifle from none other than the late Hacker Martin, the dean of twen-

tieth century riflesmiths, and having worked with the late Lester Smith, probably the greatest Kentucky rifle craftsman who ever lived, I can well sympathize with anyone who embarks on a do-it-yourself muzzle loading rifle project. In fact I worked my way through college making long rifles so I feel especially well qualified to commiserate with anyone who is faced with the prospect of inletting a four-foot barrel in a chunk of hard maple.

During my tenure as apprentice to Lester Smith I frequently had the "opportunity," if you want to call it that, to inlet the barrels for our rifles. It always seemed to me that the easy way to inlet an eight-sided barrel was simply to cut the walls at either side of the barrel channel to a fair depth then scoop out the bottom with a rounded chisel. This sounds like cheating a bit, but I did, in fact, have tradition on my side for many of the

The tools used by Carmichel for a complete power inletting job include a Dremel Moto-Tool with router attachment, Black & Decker router with edge guide accessory, three router bits; straight, round and 45 degree, and machinist's rule. Though cost of this equipment, especially that of the larger router, may be considered a rather heavy investment for the casual hobbyist who makes few muzzle loading rifles a club can share the equipment at a very small cost per member.

originals we repaired and restored had been thus inletted by the old masters!

Tradition notwithstanding, Lester Smith insisted that since our customers were kind enough to pay us upwards of three hundred dollars for a rifle (ten years later these rifles were bringing at least two thousand dollars), we should make every effort to cut a perfect five-sided barrel channel. Now bear in mind that this involved nearly two days work with mallet and chisel — and gaps between barrel and wood or any splintered edges, simply were not tolerated.

The memory of these days is well impressed on my person in the form of a scar where a barrel inletting chisel got out of control and field dressed my left thumb. Another less than happy memory of those bygone days is the selection of stock wood from which we had to choose. Oh, there was plenty of fine maple, all right, with a fine flaming curl that would bless the hearts of the most critical. The only trouble was that it was still in the *log* and the only thing we had to get it out of the log with was a two handled crosscut saw. So we sawed stock lumber off the logs in great *lengthwise* slabs. This chore was accompanied by much sweating, cussing and frequent trips to the water bucket.

Needless to say, by the time we had sawed a three-inch by three-foot by eight-foot plank out of a maple log that had been seasoning for ten years, the prospect of then having to inlet that band was less than appealing. So I began casting about for some easier way of getting the barrel in the wood. The only advice I could get from the local woodworkers was to grind a special cutter for a power shaper. This, however, would involve a different cutter for every barrel size. Too, this technique didn't offer the degree of flexibility I wanted — I was planning ahead for the application of power equipment in other areas of rifle building.

It had been pointed out that a router offered the flexibility I needed, but that the available router bits would not give the cut we needed for barrel inletting. Thinking this over I came up with the idea that perhaps a *combination* of router bits would do the job. After all, a barrel channel was only a series of vertical, horizontal, and 45-degree cuts. So why

not use a plain quarter-inch bit for the sides and bottom, then use a bit with a 45-degree cut for the two corner flats? Too, as I was delighted to discover, there were bits available which would be perfect for cutting the ramrod groove (another job I hated with a passion).

So, making the down payment on a Black and Decker router, three bits and a straight edge guide, I considered myself to really be in the barrel inletting business. Naturally, I assumed Lester would be delighted with my newfound technique for inletting the long barrels. He wasn't. Such machinery, he said, was treacherous and that I'd ruin more stocks than we could pay for.

I assured him that my method would be foolproof and that I was, right then and there, going to inlet a four-foot barrel in 30 minutes. Furthermore, I proclaimed, the fit would be absolutely perfect. Actually, I sounded more convinced than I was because I made a point of testing my new router on a plain walnut blank rather than one of our fine "hand sawed" maple blanks.

Lester said it wouldn't work and he was absolutely right, about halfway through the job, with everything going perfect, I relaxed my grip on the router and in an instant the bit chewed its way right through the side of the stock.

Despite ruining the first stock, I had demonstrated, to myself at least, that the router was the answer to my prayers. Also, that slip had really been a valuable lesson. So, I picked up a piece of prime maple and proceeded to do a perfect inletting job. Even Lester had to admit this was the only way to go.

As stated above, the only tools needed are a router, an edge guide and two bits, one 1/4-inch straight edge and a 3/8-inch V-groove bit. To be sure, routers are fairly expensive, especially if you intend to make only one rifle. The ideal arrangement in such cases would be multiple ownership. A muzzle loading club, for example, could share a commonly owned router. Or perhaps your neighborhood has a rental shop where you can rent a router for an hour or two.

The first step is to bandsaw your

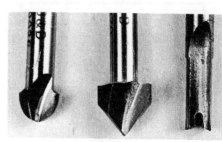

These three bits are all that will be needed for inletting any octagonal muzzle loading barrel regardless of size, as well as cutting the ramrod groove. From left 3/8-inch half-round bit for ramrod groove, 3/8-inch 45-degree channel cutter for lower sides of barrel channel and 1/4-inch straight edge bit for cutting outer sides and bottom of channel.

Here the Black & Decker router has been used to cut the two outer edges of the channel. Note how the tool is set up so that the edge guide is on the left side while the right side of the channel is being routed, which eliminates the hazard of cutting outside the line. Though the channel is being cut off center in the blank it is not off nearly so much as recommended in the text. In this case the channel was positioned to eliminate a flaw in the wood.

This illustration shows how the 45-degree groove cutter fits in the channel when it cuts the sloping lower sides. For larger barrels with flats wider than 3/8-inch the sides are cut in two stages.

These two views of the finished channel show the exact dimensions and close fit that are possible with the router. Total time for the complete operations is something like a half hour. Too, the high speed bits buzz their way through the hardest and kinkiest of maple without the nicks and gaps usually associated with amateur hand work.

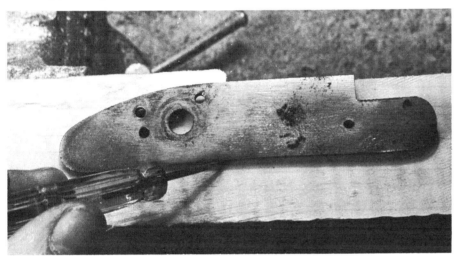

The first step in lockplate inletting is marking the outline with a sharp scribe. A pencil mark is too wide for this job because of the hairline tolerances required for an exact fit.

Here the Dremel Moto-Tool with router attachment begins opening up the lock recess. This light, easy to handle tool offers excellent visibility of work area for very close-up-to-the-line inletting.

stock blank to profile. Be sure the top and bottom edges of the fore-end are straight *and* parallel. It is a good idea to have the top and the sides planed smooth. The router and the edge guide will move more easily if they are smooth.

There is some dilemma in sawing the top edge of the fore-end because one has to choose between sawing to the *finished* stock line or cutting only on a false line where the *top* of the barrel will be. The dilemma is created by the "hump" or rise in the stock just aft of the breech. If the top of the fore-end is cut to *finished* dimensions, the channel cannot be routed to full depth because the router's base plate will stop against this hump at the rear of the channel. Thus the last four inches must be inletted by hand. This of course is not much of a job.

If the stock blank is profiled so that the top line is straight all the way back, the barrel channel can be cut to absolute length. But then you have to go back and saw, or cut by some means, the fore-end down so that the barrel will lay half depth in the stock. This latter method is a bit speedier if you have a bandsaw or table saw close at hand, but you run the risk of splintering the edges of the inletting somewhat. The decision is yours. . . .

Quite frequently, drying stock blanks will take on a considerable amount of warpage with the full length of the blank being out of line an inch or more. Obviously, since the router guide follows the edge of the wood, the routed channel will be ahead and cut the channel to the correct barrel size. When the fore-end is worked down to the final shape it will be flexible enough to be held straight by the barrel.

Also there is the matter of where to locate the channel in respect to the center of the blank. The answer to this is to simply allow the thickness of the lockplate along the right side of the stock between the edge of wood and the barrel channel. The top edge of the lockplate is usually something like a quarter inch or so. The beauty of this technique is that since the lock is to be inletted flush against the barrel, the surface of the lockplate and the side of the stock will already be level and require no additional work. Too, and of even more importance, offsetting the barrel this way allows additional wood on the left side for the cheekpiece! Now how about that? Of course if you're left-handed and using a left-handed lock, just reverse the process.

Begin in the routing by cutting the vertical sides of the channel. Cut only to the depth of the corners of the side flats. Don't try to cut it all at once, just take a cut the router can handle easily. Too, and this is important, when you cut the *left* side of the channel set the router up so that the edge is on the *right* side! Then reverse the position when cutting the other side of the channel. There is a very good reason for this: if the router "jumps" it can only jump into the channel area where the miss-cut can do no harm. I learned this trick when I ruined the first stock I routed.

Also, to play it extra safe, you might cut the sides of the channel 1/64-inch or so undersize. Later you can use the router to shave this open bit by bit until the barrel fit is absolutely perfect.

With the sides cut to full depth, the next step is to cut the 45-degree flats running inward to the bottom of the channel. The bit I use cuts this strip about 3/8-inch wide. If the flats on the barrel require a wider surface, set the router in and down a little until the bit lines up with the surface and make another pass. Getting this overlap to line up perfectly is best done by stopping the router — and unplugging it — and "eyeballing" the bit just where you want it.

Now, with the two sides and the inside flats cut to shape, all that's left is a ridge running up the center. This is quickly sliced away with the straight sided bit. So there you have it, the job is finished and the job is perfect.

Always, and I mean *always*, play it safe when using a router or any other piece of power equipment. Always be sure that the tool is *unplugged* when changing bits or making adjustments.

Now, moving on to the ramrod groove, fit a 1/4 or 3/8-inch half-round bit in the cutter and set the guide so the groove will be directly under the bottom flat. The thickness of the web between the channel and the groove is a matter of personal

As illustrated here, the inner area is roughed out before working up to the scribed outline. Note even depth of cut allowable with the router.

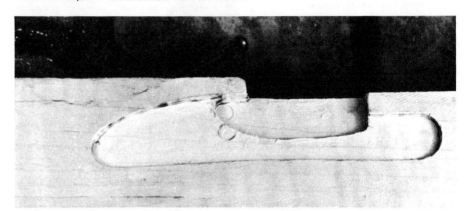

In this illustration the lock recess has been routed right up to the final outline. The "two-story" inletting allows for the flange at upper edge of lockplate.

Here the lockplate is fully inletted and as you can see the fit is hairline close. Absolutely no hand tools were used for this job—only the Dremel router by "free-hand" technique. Though a little practice is needed before attempting this method it is actually quite easy and much faster than hand tools.

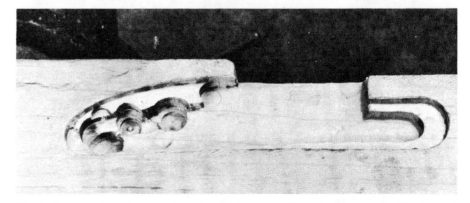

The lock recess after final inletting of springs, sear, bridle and other parts. This is much neater than the usual "hogged out" method and stronger too since more wood is left in the stock at a rather weak area. Total time for this operation was about 20 minutes.

taste, but for those really slim, graceful fore-end lines this web has to be pretty thin. About a quarter-inch is the most you'll want. Actually all you need is enough room for the barrel loops.

There are other applications for the router such as cutting the recess for the patch box and even inletting the lock. The torque of a big router makes it pretty tricky for free hand work when you get close to the line, but they are fine for hogging out most of the inletting.

For really fine, detailed inletting, the little Dremel Mototool with routing kit is about perfect. The light weight and low torque of this tool plus the excellent visibility makes it

possible to make right-up-to-the-line cuts for a perfect metal to wood fit.

If you really want to do yourself proud try this technique: Completely disassemble the lock and position the lockplate exactly where it is to be inletted. Now mark the outline of the plate with a sharp scribe, a pencil mark is too wide. Now rout the plate to its final depth. Cut the inside area out first then work cautiously up to the scribed line.

When the lockplate is fitted begin adding the "gut" parts, bridle, sear, springs, tumbler, etc., one by one and inletting them to their various and individual shapes and depths. The effect of this technique is to give the inletting a very professional look and

even though it can't be seen there is great personal satisfaction in knowing it is done right. "Grave digging," the technique of hogging out a big cavity for the lock, isn't all that much quicker and weakens the stock in a critical area.

After the lock and action parts are fully inletted, check all the moving parts to make sure that there is room for free operation. The sear arm and tumbler require special attention in this respect.

With the barrel and lock inletted and ramrod groove cut, you are ready to move on to the more creative and pleasant tasks of shaping the stock so from here on out you're on your own. . . . ●

THE "EXPRESS"

THE GREATEST enemy of the hand-craftsman, particularly the gunstocker and gunsmith, is time. The reputation of the artisan is based upon the quality of his work, from the smallest inletting cuts to the last detail of finish, and in order to maintain quality, many of the functions of gunstocking must of necessity be carried out slowly. Hurry is not exactly a key word in the gunstocker's vocabulary, yet if he is working full-time at the trade, he has no time to waste. When a job has been quoted, eighty hours spent finishing the project instead of an estimated sixty does nothing to put beans on the table.

One area of stock work where time can be saved without sacrificing an iota of quality or final appearance is in finishing. Much-vaunted in the trade is the oil finish, in which linseed oil is used for the final surface, with the intention of giving either a semi-gloss or flat finish — the so-called "Dull London Oil Finish," the mere mention of which brings forth nostalgic sighs and lofty comments regarding the great skill needed to apply it. Fortunately, that is today a lot of hogwash. We no longer have the need to laboriously apply raw or boiled linseed oil to wood over a period of weeks — or even months — to achieve the warm, lustrous appearance of the traditional oil finish. In fact, thanks to modern technology, we can do it now in less than four days, and have a better product at the end.

In my shop, hard maple makes up the bulk of stock woods used. Maple is one of the easiest woods to finish, since it has pores which are quite small and easily filled. Walnut, on the other hand, is open-pored, and takes considerably more finish to provide an integral surface. We'll be discussing both woods here, though what prompted this article were several inquiries from fellows who have been working with maple sporter stocks and longrifles.

Speed, in combination with quality, is a great necessity in my shop, since Monte Mandarino and myself regularly finish three or even four gunstocks each month. When the stock work is done, we can't afford to wait around for two weeks to send work out, which would almost certainly be the case if we adhered to earlier stock finishing practices. Instead, we regularly finish gunstocks in little more than one-and-a-half working days, and with a finish that I am satisfied will withstand both the elements and the most critical eye of the gun's new owner. I've been using this finish for twelve years, and have never had a complaint about it. Our finish is a true oil finish in that the final finish is actually linseed rather than modern synthetic resins or polymers, which satisfies a certain nagging feeling that it wouldn't be right to use a synthetic finish on something as traditional as a flintlock rifle. Actually, that bit of a romantic notion is purely academic. The purpose intended is to provide the appearance of an oil finish, and there are other finishes which will do the same thing, as I'll discuss later. The finish we use, in any event, is fast, water-repellant, non-gumming, easily repairable, and ridiculously easy to use. I admit the latter with trepidation, since I'm sure my customers would prefer to think of our sitting around for hours hand-rubbing a finish. But we don't.

Linseed oil and shellac are about the last generally available finishes that were common in the last century and before. Modern lacquer and varnish do not even remotely resemble what those terms described in the eighteenth century. Lacquer is now a complex structure of organic chemistry, while varnish contains synthetic resins and driers unknown before this century. "Varnish" a hundred years ago described a finish compounded by a natural resin dissolved in alcohol, which was about the only commonly available solvent in great-granddad's day. Because of the alcohol solvent, such natural-resin finishes are often referred to as "spirit varnish." Copal and damar were resins particularly favored by early stockers, since they were fast-drying and gave a hard and fairly water-resistant finish, yet could easily be rubbed out to a lustrous sheen. In fact, despite the tradition that early longrifle makers confined their finishing materials to raw linseed, I have examined a good number of specimens which were originally finished with a spirit varnish, often with a colorant such as alkanet root added to the varnish for a toner. The use of toners in spirit varnishes was particularly important to arms companies producing fine sporting and target rifles at the end of the last century. Both copal and damar varnishes are still available from art-supply manufacturers, primarily in-

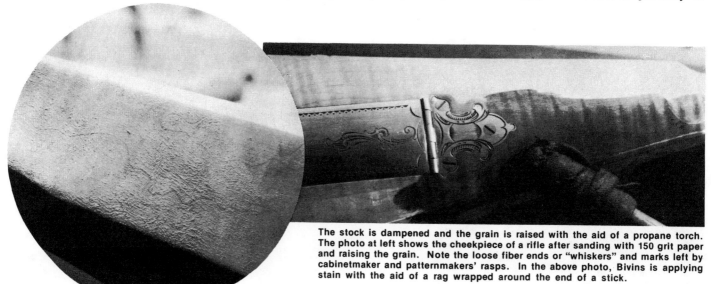

The stock is dampened and the grain is raised with the aid of a propane torch. The photo at left shows the cheekpiece of a rifle after sanding with 150 grit paper and raising the grain. Note the loose fiber ends or "whiskers" and marks left by cabinetmaker and patternmakers' rasps. In the above photo, Bivins is applying stain with the aid of a rag wrapped around the end of a stick.

OIL FINISH

By JOHN BIVINS

tended for a protective film on oil paintings. They are quite expensive, however, and have no advantage over more modern finishes.

Linseed oil was favored by custom gunstockers of the early part of this century. It was used in both the raw, unrefined version and "boiled." Actually, refined linseed is never boiled, but rather saponified with caustic soda to remove non-drying fats and oils, refrigerated to separate out natural waxes, bleached, and heated while adding a certain amount of driers. Boiling accomplishes nothing except to prematurely oxidize the oil and make it more viscous. Refined oil dries hard by a process of oxidation in about 72 hours, while raw oil oxidizes only incompletely over a period of a week or more. Sometimes *much* more — so there is really no good use for raw linseed in gunstock finishing.

Finishing a stock completely with linseed oil called for saturating the stock with oil, allowing it to harden for a week, and then applying subsequent coats, rubbed in hard enough to generate heat, over a period of succeeding weeks. Such a finish provided a not-to-be-equaled sheen and warm color, and could easily be touched up if the stock was scratched. Strong disadvantages, however, were the time spent in finishing, the necessity of having to use a secondary filler, the tendency to gum if applied too fast, and also a tendency to turn dark over a long period of time due to continued polymerization and the collection of dirt — creating a patina which is beautiful on a longrifle stock, but does nothing for a sporter stock, particularly if the figure is hidden. Most importantly, linseed oil passes moisture like a sieve, contrary to the popular notion. No finish totally seals water out of a stock, perhaps with the exception of epoxy, but linseed is at the bottom of the heap in regard to waterproofing. Linseed, however, can be used for its most important attribute of color and sheen as a light *final* finish, as we shall see.

Regardless of the type of finish to be used, a gunstock must be properly prepared unless you want a surface that looks like a plowed field the first time it is out in the rain. After roughing out a stock — we use gouges, drawknives, Stanley Surforms, and 10-inch pattern-makers' rasps, the latter after a recommendation from stockmaker Jerry Fisher — we sand with 100 and 150 grit garnet paper. The tearing action of toothed shaping tools, however, creates a certain "trauma" well below the surface of the wood. Using 150 grit paper will leave a smooth finish which tells nothing of the ugliness which lies below the surface, particularly where quartering cuts have been made, such as in the comb fluting and across a cheekpiece. Also, tools compress loose fibers on the surface, and if you don't believe grain-ends will come through a stock finish with grisly regularity, then omit the next step, which is of course grain-raising. All woods commonly used in stockmaking should have the grain raised, even the hardest and densest of sugar maples. The process is simple; just wet the stock with plain water, and dry it rapidly with a propane torch, preferably with a broad flame. Of course, keep the torch moving rapidly to avoid scorching the stock anywhere. Maple generally requires three such wettings and dryings, walnut, particularly black walnut, may require more. Remove the whiskers from the stock with 220 grit paper, and keep changing the paper so that you are using a sharp, new surface at all times, or you will simply be compressing the grain again. The idea is to lightly shear off the whiskers. After the stock surface is "dead" and shows no more tendency to raise fibers or to reveal tool marks, go over the entire stock with 220 a bit more heavily to completely level the surface. Sand no more than is necessary for good smoothness, however, since cutting down further may cause additional wood fibers to loosen.

Good quality walnut should require no addition of colorants before finishing, unless you are trying to duplicate an old Winchester, Stevens, or Ballard finish, which I'll mention later. Maple, however, is an abomination — at least to me — if the color is left in its natural state. "Natural" maple stocks remind me of the

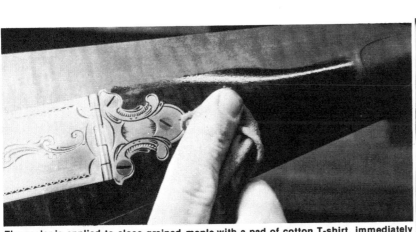

The sealer is applied to close-grained maple with a pad of cotton T-shirt, immediately above, and is brushed into the inletting, right. The first coat should be heavy, then steel-wooled, upper right.

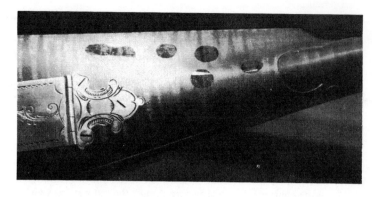

The first application of G-B Linspeed is "dotted" around the stock and then blended with the heel of the hand.

old "Moderne" furniture of the early 1950's. In any event, if you wish to stain, there are really only two generic types which are useful, water-base and spirit-base. Oil-based stains generally use earth colors such as burnt umber to impart color; they penetrate very little and have a muddy appearance due, of course, to the fact that the pigments are really refined and finely ground minerals — mud, by any other name. The pigment particles are simply carried in suspension in the oil, and cannot effectively penetrate the surface. On the other hand, water-based stains pigmented with aniline dyes such as those sold by Brownell's penetrate exceedingly well since the dye chemical is *dissolved* in the water. Such stains are probably the best in that they do not bleed and are non-fugitive to a high degree. In other words, they don't fade in strong light. Water-based stains can also be used during the grain-raising process if you want to avoid wetting the

stock too much, though wetting really does no harm since water does not remain trapped in the stock.

A trifle more fugitive, though not objectionally so, are spirit-based stains, usually carried in a vessel of toluene, methanol, or a combination of the two, and commonly called "NGR" stains in the trade, for "non-grain-raising." I much prefer these stains, since I raise the grain on my stocks before relief-carving, and I don't want to fuzz up the carving with water any more than necessary. Excellent spirit stains are available from Albert Constantine in New York; Sherwin-Williams used to market such a stain under the trade name "Artistain," which unfortunately has not been available for some six years or so. One of the colors available from S-W was "American Walnut," which imparted a beautiful deep golden-brown color to maple, duplicating the traditional nitric

acid stain favored by early gunstockers. Incidentally, I no longer use any of the acid-type water stains, since they have no advantages over aniline or NGR stains, but numerous disadvantages — such as the necessity of having to "kill" the acid with soda.

After the Sherwin-Williams "American Walnut" went off the market, I asked a good friend, George Welch, to duplicate the stain for me. His firm, Wampler Chemical Company (Harrisonburg, Virginia 22801) has this available under the name "Superstain Walnut No. 55"; a minimum order is one gallon, at approximately $9.00; order it UPS collect. If you need to add some redness to the stain, particularly with maple that has little natural color, order as well some of their "Superstain Red Mahogany No. 45" and add a bit to the No. 55. Both stains are alcohol-based, with 25 percent toluene added.

In using spirit stains, maple generally needs quite a bit of colorant added if the final product is to have a rich hue. We usually apply from six to ten coats of stain with a large swab, flooding it on the stock, continuing until the wood is *quite* dark. Don't let the darkness bother you, since it will lighten while rubbing the finish out. Spirit stains penetrate so well that we frequently find it has completely passed through the fore-end in places. After staining, put the stock aside for three hours to allow all the solvents and aromatics to escape from the stain, or you may retard the drying of subsequent finish applied to the stock. After drying, rub down the stock hard with 4/0 steel wool, which will polish the wood and remove stain left on the surface.

For production work, you are best equipped with a drying cabinet. Monte and I have a 3/4 plywood cabinet 20

The sealed and surface-finished maple stock with a dull oil finish is shown above, while the same stock with a semi-gloss finish is shown at right. Bivins prefers the semi-gloss finish on longrifle stocks since it resembles earlier finishes. The dull finish is more suitable for modern sporters.

Unlike the maple stock, sealer is applied to the open-grained walnut stock with a brush. Walnut must also be sanded between filling coats, rather than steel wooled, since wool tends to pull out filler.

inches wide by 20 inches deep, 70 inches tall, for this purpose. Obviously, longrifle stocks require a much taller cabinet than sporter stocks, so a smaller cabinet can be used for the "shorties." We stand the stocks in the cabinet on an angled, leather-covered piece of 2x4 nailed in the bottom; sporter stocks are most easily hung. Heat is provided in our cabinet by a single 40-watt bulb, which keeps the cabinet air at a uniform 78 degrees. We found that more than 80 to 85 degrees of heat will tend to introduce shrinkage, particularly during the summer when stock wood here in North Carolina can reach a water content as high as 11 or 12 percent. For even quicker drying of both stains and finishes, install a small "muffin" fan on one side of the cabinet near the bottom to circulate air. The light bulb should also be close to the bottom, since heat rises and you want to avoid a "cold" spot near the bottom. Incidentally, bolt your cabinet to the wall, since you don't want someone brushing against it and knocking down stocks inside.

Now comes the "secret" of the "express" oil finish: the sealer. We use a Sherwin-Williams product which has the improbable product name of "Beauty-Lok Clear Seal." Ignore that bit of advertising trivia, and ask for code number A66 V3 sealer. You won't find this product an easy one to come by, since it is essentially a commercial product and not stocked by many, if not most, of the Sherwin-Williams stores. However, if you introduce the correct tremor into your voice, and imply that your family will

starve if you don't get it, the store manager will usually order it for you. If you have trouble in getting it, give me a call and I'll try to help out. Order it in pint cans, for unless you use good quantities of the stuff, it has a low shelf life after the lid is opened. If you must buy larger cans, have it decanted into pints.

A66 V3 sealer is nothing more than a light amber-colored alkyd varnish sealer with special driers added. It is as thin as water, penetrates wood as if your stock were a sponge, and has all the water-shedding properties of varnish, which runs a close second to the epoxies in keeping moisture out. I know of no other commercial product which I prefer as well; Pittsburgh used to have a similar product called "Rez," but this was taken off the market years ago. This sealer provides a dense and hard base for linseed, though it is compatible with both

linseed and the spirit stains, and it also can be used as an excellent filler.

In finishing maple, first take a 1-inch brush and "drown" all of your inletting with the sealer, including the butt end grain. Wipe up what runs out. Then take some all-cotton T-shirt material — the best lint-free rag going — cut it into a 6-inch square, and then fold it over into a square about 3 inches by 3 inches. Dip it into the A66 V3, and sop it onto the stock. We usually go over a stock twice, since the wood will really drink up that first coat. Set the stock in the drying cabinet for twenty minutes, and then wipe off all the sealer remaining on the surface with a dry rag. Put the stock in the cabinet and let it stand for six hours to insure that the finish has oxidized all the way through. A good tip in using *any* finish is to dab a piece of clean glass with the finish and put it in the cabinet as well; the glass will enable you to tell quickly with a fingernail if the finish is hard clear through. Some finishers may harden on the surface and remain soft

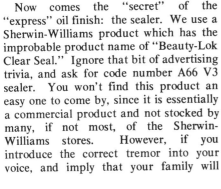
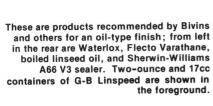

These are products recommended by Bivins and others for an oil-type finish; from left in the rear are Waterlox, Flecto Varathane, boiled linseed oil, and Sherwin-Williams A66 V3 sealer. Two-ounce and 17cc containers of G-B Linspeed are shown in the foreground.

below, and it is *disastrous* to add more finish if this condition exists.

After this first drying, take the stock and rub it down hard all over, but not in the inletting, with 3/0 steel wool, taking care that no patches of slight roughness are left. Dust off the stock thoroughly — an air gun is useful — to remove all of the steel wool fibers. Then brush a *thin* coat of sealer into all the inletting, and just dampen the outside surfaces with a T-shirt pad as before. This time, however, you don't want to flood it on. Take particular care from this point on that you don't leave any appreciable amount of finish around such cuts as relief carving or in the shadow-line of a cheekpiece. If you do, the finish will be impossible to rub out, and you will be left with a garish, shiny place where the finish has pooled.

After applying this light coat of sealer, put the stock back in the drying cabinet for two to four hours, and then wool the stock with 4/0 steel wool. Try to avoid rubbing color off any "corners" of the stock. If you do, however, the Wampler stain can be applied to light areas with a Q-tip, and it will actually penetrate the finish due to the presence of toluene. The maple stock, if it is hard wood, is now sealed. Very soft wood, which you shouldn't use anyway, might require a third light coat on the outside, but that is rare. Virtually all of the second coat of sealer should be standing on the surface when it has hardened, and the purpose of the wooling is to remove all the sealer from the surface.

Walnut, due to its open grain, must be treated differently than maple. Maple is easily filled with very little finish, while walnut requires more finish just to fill the large pores. I might comment here that carved walnut stocks are difficult to finish, since the filler must be kept out of the carving.

In using A66 V3 on walnut, brush on a heavy coat inside and out, and put the stock in the cabinet for six hours as with the maple. After drying, wool out with 3/0 wool; after this, steel wool should not touch a walnut stock until the final finishing steps, since wool tends to pull sealer out of the pores. After the wooling, brush on another coat of sealer, working across the grain, and brush a *thin* coat into the inletting; this completes the sealing of the interior surfaces. After two to four hours, take the stock out and brush another coat on the surface. After that coat is dry, sand both coats down to the wood with 280 wet-or-dry paper, using the paper dry. Back the paper with a block or a piece of thick felt, and fold the paper for stiffness when sanding radiused areas such as under the cheekpiece, so that you round no edges that should remain sharp. Dust off the stock with a

tack rag, which you can find at any hardware store, and apply three more successive coats of sealer, allowing two to four hours drying after each coat. Sand down to the wood again, this time using 400 grit wet-or-dry paper. The work will go a bit faster if you dampen the paper with the sealer, or with water. The stock should now be largely filled, particularly in the case of European walnut. Brush on another thin coat of sealer, and sand down with 600 grit wet-or-dry; if you can still see a glint of finish in any of the pores after the sealer is hard, give the stock another dose of sealer and rub out again with 600. I prefer to use the 600 dry, though it clogs rapidly. The walnut stock is now both sealed and filled.

For surface finishing, we prefer G-B Linspeed Oil, which is boiled linseed oil refined to a somewhat more viscous state than normal oils, and with additional driers added. The driers add gloss to the oil, so it must be used with caution. In fact, with all due respect to the manufacturer of this excellent product (George Brothers, Great Barrington, Mass. 01230), if G-B is used according to the factory instructions, you will in some cases wind up with a mess. For instance, they recommend that you do *not* use it over a sealer, and that you not raise the grain! Further, the standard 2-ounce jar of the stuff is identified as the "six-stocks" size, while the tiny 17CC bottle (which we much prefer) is supposedly the right quantity for one stock. If you used as much G-B as this implies, you would wind up with a stock that would rival a 1957 Cadillac grille for glitter, for, make no mistake, G-B is a *shiny* finish and must be used with considerable moderation to create a classic oil finish. In fact, one of the 17CC bottles will actually finish nearly *nine* stocks in our shop! The larger jar simply gums and cruds over long before even half of it is used.

For surface finishing your maple stock, pour a very small quantity of G-B into a saucer and proceed to give the stock a polka-dotting of light dabs of oil. Work on one section of the stock at a time, and blend all of these "polkadots" very uniformly with the palm of your hand. There is no need to sit there and rub it in; that won't do anything but make you feel as if you really are working. Rubbing stocks is sort of sexual, I suppose. Keep the oil out of cracks! Put the stock in the cabinet, and let it dry four hours; use your glass test piece to check hardness. Wool out the stock down to the wood with 4/0 wool, dust thoroughly, and then apply a second coat by dabbing some oil into the palm of your left hand; using your hand as a "palette," lightly oil your right fingers, and rub on an even and *thin* coat. Dry, and wool it all off with 4/0. Dust, and apply a third coat of G-B with the

same procedure as on the second coat, but this time rub the devil out of the thing, until the stock feels almost dry due to so little finish on the surface — not much more than a molecule thick. You now have a fine, lustrous semi-gloss oil finish on maple, with a total elapsed time of both sealing and surface finishing of 26 hours; call it 1 1/2 working days. If you want that hallowed Dull London Oil finish instead of the lustre, just grab a worn piece of 4/0 wool, rub the stock down again, and polish with a clean piece of T-shirt. There 'tis!

Oil finishes such as this benefit from an occasional rubbing out with oil, particularly after a hard junket in the field. To avoid building up excessive gloss, I would recommend adding to the finish with plain boiled linseed rather than G-B. Use the linseed very sparingly, with both hands only moist with it, and rub it in thoroughly. Of course, the gun will have to sit on the rack for several days after such a rubbing with linseed, unless you want to fingerprint it. A treatment like that twice a year keeps a stock lustrous, and builds a light and fine patina.

Surface finishing walnut, after it has been filled, is similar to maple. Dot on and spread out the first coat of G-B as with maple, wool to the wood with 4/0 as before. Rub on a second thin coat, and wool down again. Stop at this point if you want a dull finish; if you want some lustre, rub on a third *atom thick* coat and stop right there. Your walnut stock is now sealed, filled, and surface finished, with a total elapsed time of 46 hours, say, three and a half working days. You will find as with *all* finishes (except some epoxies) where the finish is a self-filler, the finish will shrink into the pores very slightly after some months; this can be brought back up with the judicious use of G-B if you wish, but I don't find it offensive to leave it as is. James Purdey himself would marvel at it, and call you a lying bounder if you told him how long it took.

If you are stocking (or refinishing) a piece in which you want to duplicate what the arms factories used on walnut in the last century, use the following procedure. Mix up a 50-50 walnut and red mahogany mixture of the spirit stain mentioned before; try it on a sample of similar wood before applying to the stock to ascertain that the color is what you want, and adjust if necessary. Apply one coat of stain to the walnut, and then proceed to seal and fill as outlined above. Apply a coat of stain after each three coats of sealer has been sanded down, and then apply a final, very light coat of stain before the final light coat of G-B is applied. After this, put on one or two more coats of G-B to provide a good gloss in imitation of the factory varnish finishes. The color, like the originals, will be quite translucent and give the appearance of toners added to the varnish. When using G-B for such a gloss finish, take care that you use a tack rag carefully between coats, and see that your drying cabinet is free of dust so that particles will not become imbedded in the surface.

Two other products deserve strong mention for those who seek a fine oil-type finish. One of these, "Waterlox" (Waterlox Chemical and Coatings Corp., Cleveland, Ohio 44105), is prepared from tung oil, one of the family of drying oils known by the Chinese for centuries. Tung oil is infinitely more water-resistant than linseed, and dries harder, but has the undesirable characteristic of hardening to a minutely wrinkled, perfectly flat finish with absolutely no lustre. The Waterlox folks have modified refined tung oil by the addition of varying amounts of boiled linseed, ester gum, and copal resin to both increase its "plasticity" and increase sheen. The most useful of their preparations is "Transparent," which hardens to a medium sheen; "Heavy Body" dries to a high gloss and "Satin Luster" does what its name implies. Waterlox may be used in exactly the same method as Sherwin-Williams A66 V3,

though drying time is extended to some eight hours between each coat. I have not tried it as a filler, though the more viscous "Satin Luster" grade may work very well for this in walnut. Due to its constituents. I don't believe that Waterlox would be as impermeable as A66 V3, however.

Another finish which is basically an organic construction of modern synthetic esters is "Varathane," made by the Flecto Company, Inc., (1000 45th St., Oakland, California 96408). Varathane is used extensively by such fine stockers as Jerry Fisher, Dale Goens, and Joe Balickie, and obviously with fine results. I haven't tried it, but a recommendation from such fellows is enough for me. Jerry Fisher says that in using it on walnut, three to five coats should be applied at first, with only two coats going into the inletting. Jerry then sands to the wood with 240 wet-or-dry, using Varathane as a cutting agent. He then wipes and hangs up the stock for 24 hours, then applies two more coats, drying 24 hours between, then sands to the wood using 400 wet-or-dry, again using Varathane as a cutting oil. He again wipes down the stock, and allows it to hang a day, then applies one more coat, which is sanded out with 600 wet-or-dry paper, again using Varathane to dampen the paper. He then wipes the stock down, allows it to hang twenty

minutes, wipes it down again, and lets it hang for several days. Although Varathane takes considerably longer than the A66 V3 treatment, it is an exceedingly durable and easily repairable finish, and seems to shrink a little less in the pores. The appearance is the same as linseed, yet no linseed need be used. Jerry uses Plastic Oil and Sealer for sealing and filling; if a customer wants a semi-gloss finish, he uses No. 91 Satin Crystal Clear Liquid Plastic over two coats of Plastic Oil. After the Plastic Oil has hardened, he brushes on several coats of the No. 91, allowing a day between coats, and then dry sands with Behr Manning Durite 280 grit paper, repeating the process with No. 91 until he has built up eight or ten coats.

With any of the finishes, if the stock is to be checkered, rub some finish into the checkering after it is completed — G-B into a stock finished with A66 V3 or Waterlox, and more Varathane into a stock finished with that product.

So, there are a few workable insights into an "express" oil finish, which, thanks to modern chemistry and manufacturing methods, is a damned sight better, in almost every way, than anything firearms fanciers drooled over in London salons seventy-five years ago. ●

First Put It On Paper

From Blank To Beautiful

PICTURE THE BEAUTIFUL stock blank—it has feathers and fiddle back, color and contrast, curved grain and straight. In its own right it is beautiful. You are going to make a stock of it. Friend, your obligation is clear: somewhere down inside that blank is a magnificent gunstock, and it is up to you to get it out.

Getting it out may seem like one of the most difficult tasks of the gunmaker. But like all seemingly difficult tasks, it is a process that is really composed of a series of relatively simple operations which someone with patience and basic manual skills can accomplish. Working from a blank also has its advantages, not the least of which is great satisfaction on the completion of the job. But the principle advantage, it seems to me, is that you can truly design your own stock and not be intimidated by the outlines and shapes of a pre-carved blank.

The job is begun like any engineering project. Proper drawings are needed which require in their preparation a complete thinking through of all the minor details. Once complete, the drawings will pave the way for an organized and confident attack on the final shape. Like other stock-making operations, the process of designing your own stock is a series of simple steps. But be warned in advance—if you cannot draw it on paper, you likely cannot whittle it either.

The drawing will be full size of the left side of the stock (assuming you are right handed, for we will draw the cheekpiece side). A top view or bottom view is not necessary; but if you believe it would be helpful, by all means draw it. We are going to need to know some basic facts as we go along which will make for interesting research. And the final objective is to have a full-size drawing of a sleek, handsome gunstock which looks right to you and which you may then duplicate in wood.

Procure a large piece of heavy plain paper 48 by 18 inches. This may be wrapping paper or drafting paper. You should have your barreled action, trigger guard, grip cap, butt plate and other hardware, including sights. Sights should be mounted and bore sighted. Drafting instruments necessary are a 24-inch or longer straight edge, draftsman's triangle, French curve, compass, medium or No. 2 pencil (HB or softer drafting pencil) and artgum eraser. Tape the paper to a bench or desk top using masking tape at the corners.

Wipe the metal parts free of oil and grease so the drawing and hands don't get dirty. Remove the bolt, and place the barreled action on the paper, muzzle to the left, trigger toward you, so that the muzzle is about an inch from the left of the paper. On the right side you should have 13 inches or more behind the rear tang. With a sharp pencil carefully draw around all parts so that the *exact shape* of each part is transferred to the paper in correct relationship to each other. You will have to angle the pencil at various places to obtain accuracy.

Be certain to draw in the telescope or

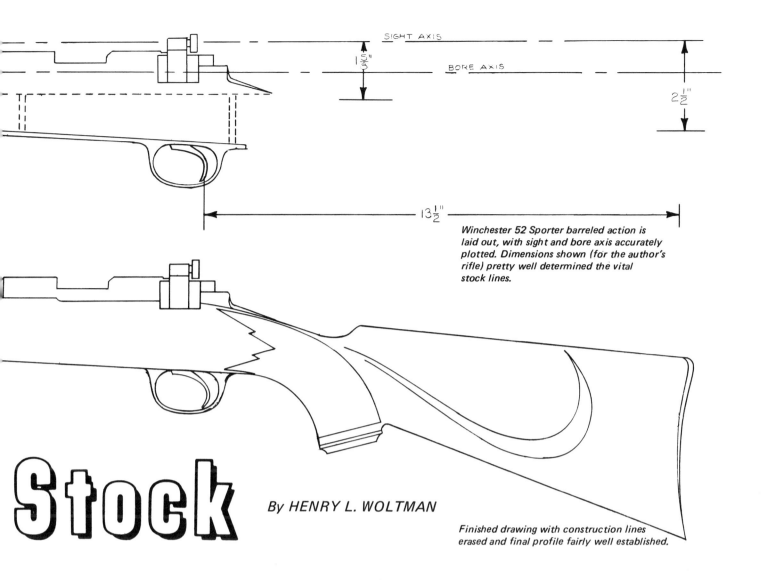

Winchester 52 Sporter barreled action is laid out, with sight and bore axis accurately plotted. Dimensions shown (for the author's rifle) pretty well determined the vital stock lines.

Stock

By HENRY L. WOLTMAN

Finished drawing with construction lines erased and final profile fairly well established.

other sight axis as well as bore axis. Check the diameters of the barrel, receiver ring and scope tube with a caliper to verify the accuracy and also to establish the centerline of the bore and scope axis. Also make certain that the trigger guard, magazine and guard screws are all correctly drawn in the right place.

Now with the bolt in and all the way to the rear, draw in the bottom line of the bolt. To draw this line, representing the path of the sear nose, the drawing may have to be turned around upside down with the bolt handle over the edge of the bench to permit the sear nose and its line of travel to be positioned accurately. The comb of the stock comes up to this line, but can come no higher. This line is extended to the rear along with the bore axis and line of sight or scope axis. This drawing of the metal parts should be cleaned up and those lines that will appear above the wood (at the bore axis) should be drawn in heavily.

The stock is next drawn. Details here will vary depending on the ultimate

purpose: a sporter generally is sleek and small, a target rifle heavy and bulky, and a varmint rifle in-between. It is best to take up each portion of the stock separately as it relates to the over-all design. Working from left to right, we will begin with the forearm.

There is no desire to make the forearm particularly long or especially short; just get it to look right. My suggestion is to have 12 inches of barrel showing between the forearm tip and the muzzle. This is generally a safe rule for any sporter or varmint rifle, whatever the barrel or action length. For target rifles the forearm can terminate at half the barrel length if an overly long barrel makes the forearm look a little too long at the 12-inch mark.

If an ebony or horn tip is planned, this can be 1¾ to 1 7/8 inches in length, and despite all the exotic materials sold for fore-end tips—I prefer plain old ebony cut off square, with no tip at all running a close second. Angled zebra

wood, rosewood schnables, and, worst of all—ram's heads of carved ivory—are out of character on a rifle of such restrained elegance as ours will be. You can see I lean to the "classic" styling.

Where to put the fore-end swivel? For target rifles you put the swivel where it is comfortable for prone shooting, or you install one of the adjustable stops. Personally, I dislike these and prefer a permanent swivel of simple, rugged design. Unfortunately, there are few of these around, simple rugged swivels having given way to complex detachable stuff made of discarded wire coat hangers. I'm cynical, but with cause. Lean into one of these and they may break, like mine did at the second shot in a string of rapid fire at the Camp Perry National Matches, causing numerous misses, cussing, etc. And even more profanity when I remembered I could have refired had I the presence of mind to stop shooting and call for the referee.

As to the adjustable hand stop, unless you need to move the base hither

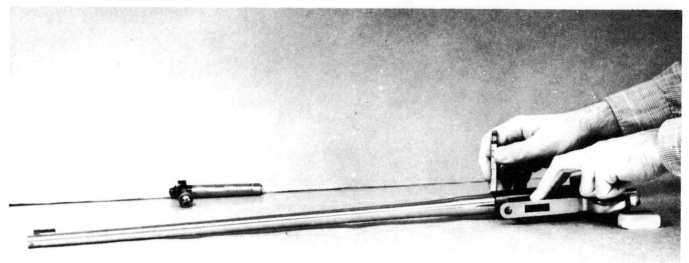

If you can't draw what you want, you probably can't whittle it either, says the author who begins a stock by demonstrating the "art" of stock design. Drawing around vitals starts the job.

and yon, the purpose of the custom stock is to put stuff like the swivel exactly where it suits *you*. Doing some research on this subject, I discovered that swivel placement 29 inches ahead of the butt plate was most comfortable for prone—28½ inches for sitting. On my match guns I compromise at 28¾ inches. This dimension is best measured from the butt plate as stock length may be different for target rifles for different uses. I emphasize that this is the correct dimension for me, at six feet and 180 pounds. If you are built like the Jolly Green Giant, you will need to add some inches. You must determine the distance for yourself. The sporter swivel should be located with similar interest in shooting comfort—or on the barrel if for a rifle of heavy recoil, since the base can bump the hand in an unfriendly way; otherwise just a quarter inch behind the ebony tip is usually satisfactory.

The depth of the forearm should be about 1 1/8 to 1¼ inches at the tip and the line from the trigger forward should be straight. If the extension of this bottom line doesn't end up at the fore-end depth that suits you, a slight break in the line at the front of the magazine can be made with little notice. One of these interesting aberrations occurs on the older Model 70 Target rifle. It has the same magazine depth as the sporter and therefore if a straight line were plotted out to the end of the fore-end tip the sporter and target models would have the same profile. But they don't. The target rifle has a far heavier forearm and close examination of this state of affairs reveals a decided

break in the bottom line of the forearm at the front guard screw.

Now, on the 70 custom target rifle you can straighten this out by not inletting the front of the floorplate as deeply as the factory intended, while inletting the rear of the trigger guard more deeply. This rotation of the guard and floor plate is easily done and allows an appropriately full forearm with straight lines.

The forearm depth of the target rifle runs 1 3/8 to 1½ inches. For sporters, the width of the forearm at the center of the tip is nearly the same as its depth—1¼ to 1 5/16. I find about 2¼-inch width about right for my hands for target rifles and have made forearms up to 2-7/16 for a pair of high power rifles. This greater width permits positive control of the forearm which is necessary in rapid fire and where the finger tips cannot comfortably touch the hot barrel. But for small bore rifles and for position shooting, the 2¼-inch width is entirely satisfactory for me.

Once the length, depth of the fore-end, length of the fore-end tip and swivel location are determined, the bottom line of the stock is drawn in, the corners rounded off the fore-end tip, and the top line of the stock extended back along bore axis to the rear of the receiver. Presto! You have the forearm designed.

The butt end is nearly as simple. First locate the butt plate position. For me, 13½ inches is the right length from trigger to the center of the plate. On match rifles it is a quarter inch less owing to padding for the shooting coat, need to operate the bolt handle in rapid fire, etc. But for a small bore prone stock it would be longer and for a free rifle stock it would be shorter. It depends on the end use. Here it is important to check your favorite rifle out and verify the length from the firing position with your hunting clothing or shooting coat on.

Once length is known mark it on the drawing and proceed to find the upper

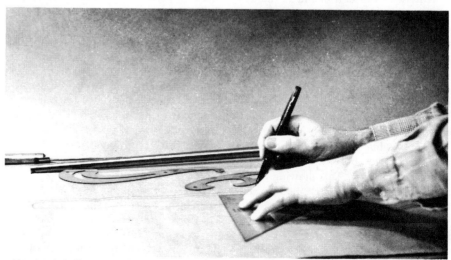

Usual artistic license can be employed only after vital dimensions are accurately determined.

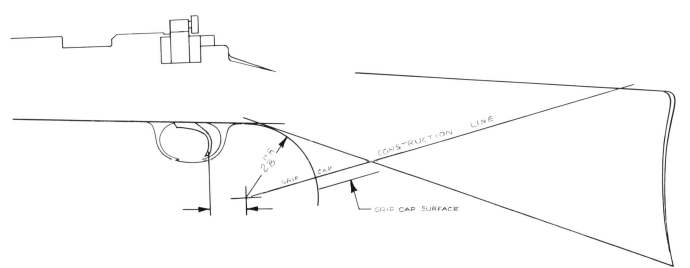

A vertical line one inch behind the trigger is used to draw the pistol grip curve. Another construction line from the center point is angled up toward the heel. Pistol grip cap is parallel to this line. Upper comb line of stock is merely a connection of points found earlier. Lower "belly" line of stock is adjustable up or down at the front, but cannot be much lower than the position shown.

line of the comb. The nose of the comb should be 1 5/8 to 1¾ inches below the line of sight. Chances are it won't be if this is a scope sighted rifle because the line of sight will already be about two inches above the line we drew for the sear nose. The nose of the comb can't go higher than that. What we are admitting is that the comb is not as high as desirable. On sporter stocks this fit to the face isn't really critical as the chin can be rested against the lower comb and still steady the head. But this paradox—comb a quarter inch lower than it ought to be—makes you wonder why anyone bothers at all with elaborate cheek pieces on sporter rifles.

The real necessity for proper fit is with the target stock where the rifleman must perch his face for many minutes at a time for a string of slow fire, and from the prone position yet, where the weight of the head must be totally supported by the comb without the normal support of the spine. From personal experience I try to avoid a drop of more than 1 5/8 by mounting

the lowest scope bases on the barrel rather than the receiver ring, using the lower choice of iron sight base, etc. Incidentally, most ¾-inch tube target telescopes will have their axis one inch above the barrel or receiver surface on which a base is placed. These sights are impossible to get too low.

The nose of the comb must be located horizontally as well as vertically. For the prone stock the comb must be adequately long as well as high. On a strictly prone rifle I find 10½ inches from the heel of the butt to the nose of the comb necessary to support the cheekbone. Again, for prone, the head is extended and I get a tremor in my neck muscles if I must draw my head back to compensate for a stock or comb that is too short. Check this out yourself. A compromise of 10 inches is used on a match rifle where standing and sitting courses are fired with the same rifle. For the sporter, a length of 9½ from heel to the nose of the comb is minimum. The heel of the butt should be straight back, that is, no drop at the heel, for high

power target rifles, prone stocks, and hippo killers like the .375 or .458 where straight back recoil is preferred to uppercuts and other Sunday punches. For the sporter, up to 2½ inch drop at the heel from the line of sight can be used. One-half inch below the nose of the comb is another rule which is safe, particularly if you are able to get the comb 1 5/8 below the sight axis. This makes the drop at the heel 2 1/8, which will fit most shooters well.

With the nose of the comb at 1 5/8 inches or at the sear nose line and 9½ to 10½ inches ahead of the butt plate, depending on the intended use, you have established one end of the comb; the other end is about a half-inch below it, so draw it in with your straight edge. Next draw the butt plate, angling it approximately at right angles to the comb line and through the 13½-inch mark where we plotted the stock length. The Niedner butt plate is 5 1/16 long by 1 5/8 wide and for my money is the model of proper proportions. The angle of the butt plate thus drawn will yield a down pitch of approximately two inches. Up to four inches down pitch can be used and I have a couple of rifles with nearly zero down pitch. Approximately four inch pitch is desirable on a lever gun where the butt may slide off the shoulder while operating the lever. But for most sporters and target rifles two to four, respectively, is approximately correct. Down pitch, unlike bore diameter, is an inexact quantity having its determination made by measuring from the muzzle to the wall while the piece is standing with the butt plate flat on the floor and the receiver bridge touching the wall. The measurement does not consider the barrel, the action, or the over-all length which will dismay most

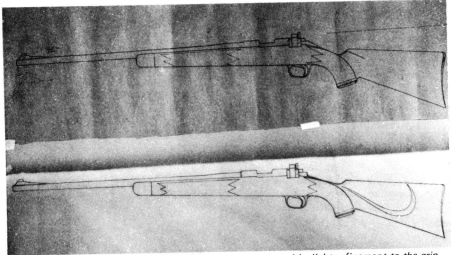

The master drawing at the top led to the second drawing with slight refinement to the grip.

of the subscribing scientists.

Next connect the toe of the butt with a bottom line from the forearm extended back to a point two inches behind the trigger. The line thus drawn will be a guide line which is subject to some adjustment depending on the way the grip works out. For sporters, a lean light little stock will suggest a line which is higher in front, that is, one closer to the nose of the comb. For target stocks, a fuller profile may be desired to the point where this bottom line intersects with the rear guard screw. In any case the butt stock essentials are now drawn in and the pistol grip and top of the grip lines are next.

To draw the bottom line of the pistol grip construct a curve with your compass. Exactly how to construct the curve will have to be worked out by trial and error, but two examples will help. For a target rifle the curve turned out to be 2 1/8-inch radius with the center of the arc 2 1/8 inches below the bottom line of the forearm on a vertical line an inch behind the trigger. On another rifle - a sporter - the radius was the same and the center line was 1½ inches behind the trigger. In both cases the arc drawn was less than 90 degrees. Next draw a straight construction line from the center point of the grip radius to a point about two or three inches ahead of the heel of the stock. The grip cap will be parallel to this construction line. On the target rifle the grip cap was 5/8-inch below this line. On the above mentioned sporter it was 3/8-inch below the line.

The Niedner grip cap is 1 13/16 long by 1 5/16 wide and a slightly larger target stock may have a grip cap size proportionately larger—up to two inches long by 1 7/16 wide. The grip cap is next drawn in and a small fillet of about 1/8-inch radius drawn to connect the grip cap to the lower line of the stock. Adjustment of the lower line may be necessary and adjustment of the grip cap angle may be required. Also in this process of adjustment it should be noted that the grip cap is generally centered under the nose of the comb.

Bear in mind that the above are given as starting points and the usual artistic license must be used to connect and adjust these lines to a pleasing outline. Don't be afraid to use your eraser. But one of the most critical points is yet to come. It is the top of the grip.

Extend a straight line from the rear of the receiver along the top surface of the tang straight back to a point about ¾-inch below the nose of the comb. The straight line should then be hooked up to the nose of the comb with a ¾-inch radius curve. This top line may require further adjustment. The small of the grip—"Wrist" say the English—should have a profile width of 1½ inches plus or minus 1/8. If it is 1 3/8, the minimum, the grip will feel quite small, whereas 1 5/8 is about maximum for comfort. The top line may be angled down to reduce the grip profile or the grip curve moved rearward to accomplish the same thing from the bottom side. In any case, the top line should be kept straight from the rear of the receiver through the tang past the small of the wrist until the radius leading up to the nose of the comb is reached.

Stocks with an "S" curve here are quite common on the amateur's first attempt. Mausers have an especially high tang which makes for a lump at the top of the grip and resulting "S" curve. The Mauser tang can be filed down quite a bit to straighten out this line. The Winchester 52 receiver is abruptly angled off at the rear and really has no tang as such; this may be reshaped to a much lower profile and improved appearance. On the Winchester Model 70, the tang can be considerably thinned in width which tends to improve the side aspect. The objective is to get smoothly flowing lines from the grip up into the mid-section of the stock. I know of no better way to learn an appreciation of this than to carefully examine all the custom guns shown on the pages of *The Rifle, Gun Digest,* and *American Rifleman,* etc.

But I digress - we have more designing to do. Two of the great frauds in custom stocks are Monte Carlo combs and cheekpieces. Both are institutions built up by the great and small stockmaker alike, even yours truly. A third one, almost, is the pistol grip. No doubt we would all feel like the cuffs had been torn off our trousers if we didn't have a pistol grip. Question: How have the British gunmakers managed from the days of Joe Manton (that's since George III) to the present without pistol grips, Monte Carlo combs and cheekpieces? The answer, I suspect, is that they know such stuff is unnecessary and frequently unsightly and therefore charge a hell of a lot more

for these options.

Before we draw this ornament on our gunstock be aware that the cheekpiece is quite easily made too large. If you are a stock crawler, as I am, the forward part of the comb is really the important part. Place your head in position on your favorite rifle and carefully note the relatively small area in contact. Go ahead—do this before a mirror. For me the rear half and lower third of the cheekpiece are superfluous. Thus armed with the knowledge of where the cheekpiece ought to be born, you may proceed to draw it in where it pleases you.

The cheekpiece is most easily drawn in lightly freehand with later correction using a French curve. If in doubt about how to go about this, lift the vital proportions from an illustration. For a target rifle for serious prone use, consider the rolled over cheekpiece. Some like it, some put it in a class with the Monte Carlo comb—a good example of bad taste, poor design, and a low state of morality in general. But it provides a good broad surface for the face to rest on. Properly done, it will fool some of your friends into thinking the cheekpiece was "laid on" after the job was all done. I like the rolled over cheekpiece for the target rifle. It is comfortable and, properly done, can look well.

The little step around the cheekpiece, which Al Linden called a "nuisance job," permits the cheekpiece to look larger than it really is. Many cheekpieces are larger than necessary for good appearance, to say nothing of being of questionable utility. The step, a small detail, makes the cheekpiece look larger than it actually is, which in a single stroke suggests a way to make the cheekpiece of a smaller, more practical size, yet retain the appearance of correct scale. The step is the optical outline of the cheekpiece—the cheekpiece itself is then made about a half-inch smaller.

While we are discussing the cheekpiece we should also discuss the undercut flute of the nose of the comb. This is designed to accommodate the base of the thumb and give clearance to the shooting hand. This thumb cut under the nose of the comb should not, in my opinion, grace the cheekpiece side of the stock. After all, if you are convinced you want the cheekpiece where your face is, the trigger hand must go on the opposite side, and that is the side for the undercut comb. On a stock without a cheekpiece it is okay on both sides for the sake of symmetry and for peace in the family.

The Monte Carlo comb is really designed for the shooter with a stiff neck, one who must shoot with the head quite erect. It is possible to provide great drop at the heel with this break in the upper line of the comb, and this feature is useful in certain trap guns where some shooters keep their head erect and rather far back on the comb. It is also useful for getting a high comb on the Winchester Single Shot where the upper and lower tangs make a severe angle with the receiver giving the butt plate inherently great drop at the heel. Such special conditions justify the Monte Carlo, but its wide proliferation on present-day sporters is neither necessary nor esthetically pleasing. The straight plain unbroken lines are preferred to humps and curves which makes many a contemporary stock look as crooked as a Scottish walking stick.

Minor details which make the difference between a great stock and a merely good one are numerous. The wood cut out at the opening of the right side of the action can be done leaving a sculptured flat, or the wood may be smoothly curved. But the wood should come up somewhat on the rear bridge to avoid giving the action the appearance it is hanging out of the stock.

On the opposite side of the action wood should generally come up to half diameter all the way back. The transition from the top of the grip to this line is aided by the bolt stop, in the case of the Mauser and Sako actions. Here the wood at the front of the bolt stop is at bore axis height, behind it wood height is at the top of the grip line. The bolt stop provides a nice way to change the line without an obvious step. Sometimes, as on the Model 70 Winchester where there is no receiver sight, this step must be made at the back of the receiver, or the wood cut down as it is on the factory stock. My advice is to leave the wood high. Most custom stockers do.

On the Remington 37, a fine old, but now discontinued, target rifle, the action should be inletted deeper than half diameter in order to bring the wood safely over a locking lug cut-out on the left side of the receiver and to bring the wood up to the loading port.

Final items: The lower sling swivel is generally positioned between three and 3½ inches ahead of the toe of the butt plate. And to complete the picture draw in a checkering pattern so that the fore-end and pistol grip appear adequately finished. Only an outline is needed. The pattern begins about at the rear of the trigger guard bow and extends to within a quarter inch of the bottom edge of the pistol grip. The forearm pattern begins ½ to ¾-inch behind the ebony fore-end tip and goes to the vicinity of the barrel-receiver junction. There you have it.

Tape the final drawing up on the wall of the shop where you can view it and compare this drawing with illustrations of some favorites. This is the way I do it. Occasionally the drawing comes down and the pistol grip is redrawn. This is my Achilles heel—the pistol grip—very hard to get it just right. But a satisfactory drawing is the only way to begin. Those who say they can't draw it, can't whittle it either. ●

Stocking The Ruger No. 1

By JIM CARMICHEL

The inletting of the Fajen semi-finished stock is almost complete, with just enough wood remaining to insure a close fit. The "ears" at the forward edge fit into action recesses (below) and keep inletting from opening up.

Prussian blue or other marking material will not detect high points reliably on slip-fit surfaces, so should not be used. Pressure points can be accurately detected by watching for and scraping away bright spots where steel parts bear against the wood, as indicated below.

FEW RIFLES INTRODUCED in recent years have had an impact equal to Ruger's re-introduction of the classic single shot, for its graceful lines immediately captured the fancy of a generation of shooters which had cut its teeth on relatively bulky repeaters. One of the greatest attractions of the single shot action is the unlimited variety of stock styles which may be used—ranging from the straight lines of the military rolling blocks and Martinis to the rococo scrolls and schnobbles of the *schuetzen* rifles to the handsome utility of the Stevens, Winchesters and Ballards of the first part of this century.

Thus, when the Ruger people announced that the Number One Single Shot was to be made available without stocks this writer, for one, began having dreamlike visions of the beautiful possibilities which now presented themselves. The Number One action, in addition to being a superbly engineered and crafted mechanism, possesses beautiful lines which will adapt harmoniously to almost any stock style one might imagine.

Shortly thereafter Reinhart Fajen announced that he was supplying semi-inletted and finished butts and forearms for the Number One in a variety of styles which included the standard or "Field" style, the "Classic" style and the "Aristocrat," with its modernistic rollover cheekpiece and deeply curved grip. Current catalog prices for the two-piece stock set run from $15.50 for the cheapest grade of wood up to $58.50 for the extra fancy grade of walnut. In other words you can buy yourself a Ruger barreled action ($140.00), the best grade of wood in the Fajen catalog ($58.50) and have $66.50 left over from what the

Ruger's handsome Number One single shot can assume a wide variety of styles—whatever the stocker's heart desires. Here is the handsome custom sporter which Carmichel stocked in the classic style.

Once the stock is inletted, a rasp should be used to work the wood down to near the action—take it easy or you'll need a blue job.

factory-stocked Number One will cost. Now how does that grab you?

Of course you have to do some work, but for the dyed-in-the-wool gun buff this is where the fun comes in. All that is needed are a few simple tools; a cabinet rasp, a couple of chisels (one straight edged and one curved) and a few sheets of sandpaper.

The inletting of the Fajen stock is so nearly completed that only minor final fitting is required. This final fitting,

79

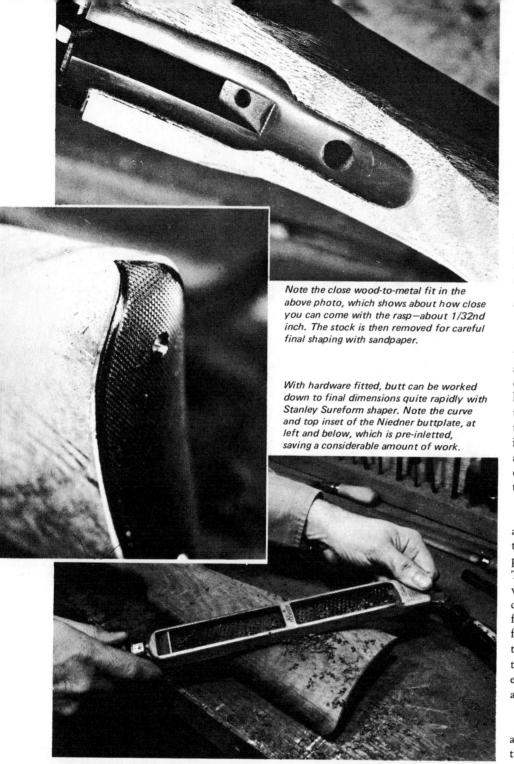

Note the close wood-to-metal fit in the above photo, which shows about how close you can come with the rasp—about 1/32nd inch. The stock is then removed for careful final shaping with sandpaper.

With hardware fitted, butt can be worked down to final dimensions quite rapidly with Stanley Sureform shaper. Note the curve and top inset of the Niedner buttplate, at left and below, which is pre-inletted, saving a considerable amount of work.

however, should be done with considerable care if you want a close wood to metal fit. Too, you should take time to examine the recoil surfaces of the action and consider how the force of recoil will be distributed against the wood.

You will, no doubt, be amazed at the remarkably large total area of the recoil surfaces (compared to most bolt actions) and rigidity of the fit. Too, the "ears" at the forward extension of the inletting which fit into special recesses in the action prevent any future spreading or opening up of the fit such as you've probably seen happen to some double-barreled shotgun buttstocks. This is very good engineering!

Though the stock can be fitted without removing the works from the action it's a good idea to strip everything out completely. The safety, lever, trigger guard and trigger will get in the way during the outside shaping and, too, sooner or later you'd have to take it apart to clean out all the wood dust anyway. The Ruger instructions on disassembly are very complete and easy to follow.

The entire fitting of the butt can be accomplished with such obvious ease that there is no need here for a play-by-play account of the process. There are, however, a few "don'ts" which should be observed. Due to the close inletting of the stock as it comes from Fajen one may be tempted to force-fit the wood by pounding it onto the metal or simply tightening the thru-bolt. Such procedure will put excessive outward pressure on the wood and will cause it to split or crack.

It is wiser to slip the stock on a little at a time and scrape away wood along the upper and lower tang channels wherever there are signs of hard contact. Spotting agents such as inletting black or lampblack don't work on these parallel fit areas. They mark everywhere but don't show where the tightness is excessive. Simply keep the metal clean and dry. Tight areas will appear as shiny spots on the wood where the fibers are compressed. Just shave these away bit by bit. Of course, inletting black is a good bet for spotting-in and equalizing

Proper gripcap fitting, at left, is a matter of getting the surface perfectly flat and the cap aligned with the centerline of the stock. The initialed Pachmayr cap on the completed rifle adds a distinctive touch.

contact on recoil surfaces and around the curved surfaces at the rear of the tangs.

With the inletting of the buttstock complete and the thru-bolt drawn up tight, the next step is fitting the buttplate that is if you intend to use a curved steel buttplate such as the Niedner. A special feature of the Fajen Classic style stock is that it can be ordered pre-cut and inletted for the Niedner buttplate. With this work very nearly completed all that remains to be done is a final bit of spotting-in and smoothing up for a perfect fit. And make sure it is a perfect fit, too, or the whole neighborhood will be gossiping about your poor workmanship, not to mention all the moisture that will seep in. Of course if you order one of the other style stocks a plastic buttplate comes already fitted.

So now we can fit the gripcap. Here again you can order a stock with a gripcap already fitted or you may prefer one of Fajen's fancy contrasting wood grips which come pre-attached. Our own preferences in gripcaps is the ultra stylish Pachmayr cap. The Pachmayr cap features a metal inlay available in gold, silver, steel, etc. which covers the screw and makes a mighty handsome looking fitting with your initials engraved on the plate.

The trick to properly fitting a gripcap is making sure that the wood beneath the cap is perfectly level and smooth. So take a little extra effort here to get it right. With the buttplate and gripcap in place and the stock fitted to the action, all that remains is working the outside down to final form.

As the stock is very nearly finished, about all the outside shaping amounts to is reducing the wood with the rasp until it is flush with the buttplate, gripcap and action. Shaping up the

The flat immediately behind the receiver, above and below, should be shaped with a rounded rasp, then filed flush with receiver flat as final step to insure a sharp edge to the design.

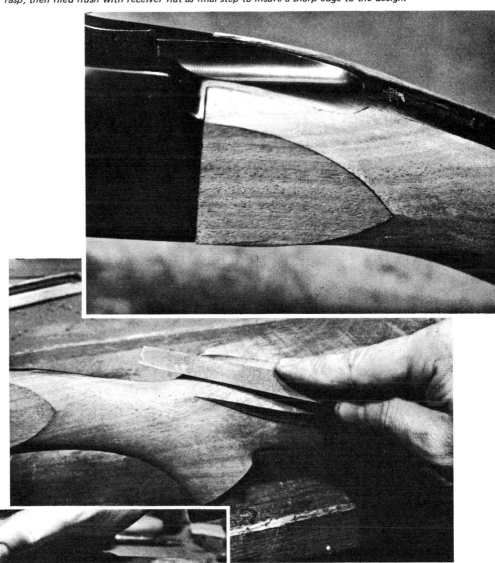

Detail work, such as the graceful flutes which flow the pistol grip into the main portion of the stock are cut with the rasp. It isn't having a lot of tools that is important, just knowing how to use them. A sanding block is essential for keeping areas flat and straight. Note the sharp edges of cheekpiece and undercut, the mark of a professional-quality stock.

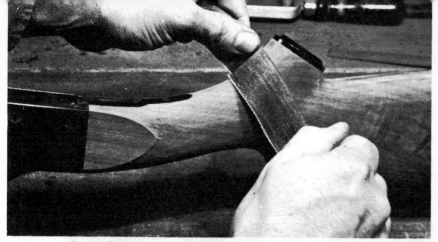

Strips of cloth-backed sandpaper make short work of concave areas under the wrist and behind the grip cap, above and below. Sandpaper wrapped around a dowel or the rasp used to cut the flutes will make the job easier and better-looking.

The fore-end requires little inletting for a close fit, and is shaped to final dimensions using the same techniques employed on the butt. To reduce the risk of minor marks on the blue, a couple of layers of masking tape can be used to provide some protection.

panel behind the action may be something new for those of you who are experienced only in rifle stocking, but is old hat for those who have made stocks for double barrel shotguns.

To be sure, this *is* a striking feature and offers an excellent opportunity to add some really nice custom features. The panel on Ruger factory stocks is a classic curve. The stock shown on these pages has the panel brought to a point at the rear. This point could be embellished with a beavertail carving like fine English shotguns or if you want to be extra fancy try a relief carved *fleur-de-lis.*

Working the wood down flush with the action surfaces is a pretty tricky proposition as the barreled action comes with a nice blue. One miss-lick and you've bought yourself a new blue job. The best technique here is to work the wood down as close as you dare with the rasp—giving the metal some protection with a couple of thicknesses of masking tape—then remove the wood for final sanding.

A wise man once said "sanding is a miserable job" and I've never heard this effectively disputed. However, proper sanding technique is so important to the finished product that sanding can well be called an art. In fact the difference between a $500 stock by a master stockmaker and a $50 plug by your local cobbler is largely skill with the sanding block. Therefore it behooves you to give this important step all due attention rather than just an unpleasant task to be done with as quickly as possible.

If the rasp marks are pretty deep start off with 80 grit paper and work the wood smooth and flat. Naturally you want to use a sanding block to keep the surface flat and ripple free and by all means sand with the grain! Sanding in tight spots such as behind the grip cap and curved surfaces such as the pistol grip can be handled quickly and easily by using strips of cloth-backed sandpaper and laying it on with a brisk shoe shine motion.

When all the rasp marks are gone switch to 120 or 180 grit paper and continue the slicking-up operation. A mark of good workmanship is sharp clean edges around the cheekpiece and in the case of the Number One stock, around the panel outline. A good way to make sure that these edges finish up sharp is to sand the curved surfaces such as the underslope of the cheekpiece first. This tends to round the edges somewhat but then you can come along with the sanding block on the flat surfaces and sharpen the edges up again.

Continue with 220 then 320 grit finishing paper until the wood is dead smooth and you're ready for the finish. You probably will want to wait until the forearm is finished before applying finish but now is a good time to apply a sealer to the inletted surfaces. With all the nooks and crannies of the buttstock, applying a thorough coating of sealer could be a problem. The simplest and best way out is to use a spray type finish such as Birchwood-Casey's spray-on stock finish. The spray gets in everywhere and gives the end grain a good soaking.

Actually, fitting the fore-end is such a simple task that little needs to be said. The wood is held in place by a screw which angles rearward at a 45-degree angle. Thus, when tightened, it has the effect of jamming the wood both upward and tightly against the action. (More good Ruger engineering.)

To insure good accuracy, fit the wood to the action extension as tightly as possible. A tight fit here will keep the wood from possibly rocking around and applying uneven pressure on the barrel. Our technique for fitting the wood around the barrel was to fit the wood to a light contact without any pressure points. Thus we hoped for a hairline fit without affecting accuracy. Of course, this left the way open to completely free-float the barrel in case performance indicated a change was needed.

As it turned out, accuracy was outstanding from the very first so this method of fitting the fore-end is highly recommended. With the fore-end fitted, all you need to do is work it down a bit, sand and you're ready to rub on some finish.

Despite all the old wives' tales you've probably heard about how much work is involved in getting a really good,

A bit of checkering—provided you're experienced in such matters—and a thinned coat of finish brushed into the diamonds completes the job, resulting in a custom sporter that will add grace to any rack.

Final finishing should begin by sealing inletting with a thin coat, a difficult task in close-fitting areas made easy by the use of Birchwood Casey Tru-Oil spray. Tru-Oil or another good finish with the desired characteristics is then applied to the exterior.

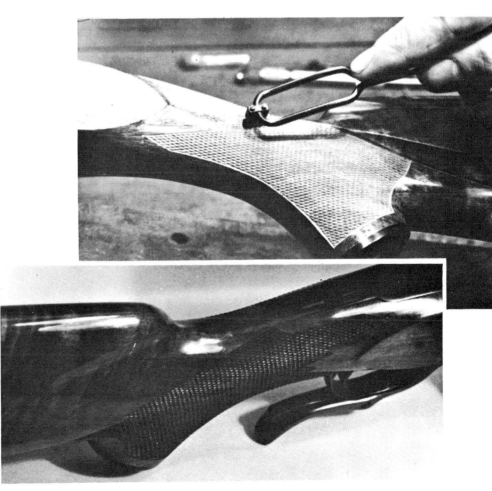

durable finish. The truth of the matter is that the modern commercial stock finishes are quick, easy to apply and a hell of a lot better in all respects than the old "secret" recipes brewed up by the "old masters." The finish on our Number One involved rubbing on three coats of Birchwood-Casey's True Oil, rubbing it to the wood with fine steel wool then rubbing on two more coats. A final buffing with Casey's stock conditioner brought the finish to a bright, mirror slick gloss. I'm sorry to disappoint you old-timers, but it just isn't very hard to do.

Something that *is* pretty hard to do is checkering, and frankly, the sparkling new stocks on your Number One isn't a good place to start if you're thinking about learning the art. Checkering adds a lot of class—make no mistake about it—but only if it is *good* checkering.

So if you can handle a checkering tool go ahead and do your best. Otherwise beg or hire it done. You saved enough money by making your own stocks to buy some pretty professional checkering. Or why not think on it for a while, you might not want it checkered anyway.

The next move is to run out to the range and show your efforts to everyone. Chances are no one has seen a custom-stocked Number One, so the ooh's and ah's are bound to fall in abundance. ●

Quality Stockmaking is a matter of careful

LAYOUT, INLETTING, FITTING

By HENRY L. WOLTMAN

*T*HERE IS MUCH temptation for the amateur to solve his stockmaking problems by sending off for an inletted blank on which the bulk of the inletting and shaping appears to be done. In many models available the hardware, such as it is, is attached Some selection of shapes and wood is available; but that is about it. It is a cop-out for the aficionado.

The better way, in my humble opinion, is to shop for three or four blanks which you can keep on hand to properly cure in your home while awaiting your own individual design and conversion to the stock. Put the $25 into finer quality wood, or better hardware, a superior barrel, or whatever. In addition to this exchange you get far more liberty to design it the way you want, but it takes more work, more courage and more tools. In the end if

you have the patience, the stomach for it, and have successfully laid out your design on paper as described in issue No. 12 of *The Rifle*, there is no more pleasant way to invest spare time for greater returns in satisfaction.

The tools and equipment used are not particularly expensive, and they serve for many other gunsmithing and household chores. I have visited full time professionals and the tools they use are sometimes simpler, sometimes more exotic, depending on the smith

and how fast he wishes to turn out the work. But all can do the job with extremely simple tools given the time.

The finished drawing of the stock is first transferred roughly to the blank. Ideally this is done with a piece of transparent plastic by tracing the outline of the stock on the plastic with a wax pencil or crayon. The template is then moved around on the wood of the blank first on one side then the other. The objective is to get the best out of the blank by having the grain running

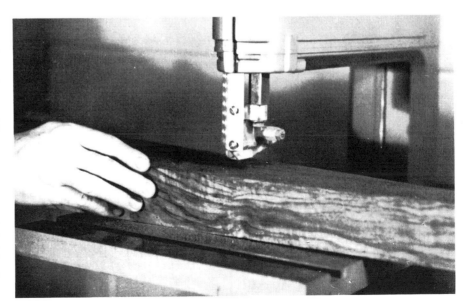

Start inletting the blank by first locating bore axis. The surplus wood is then cut off with the band saw and the top surface carefully squared with the left side.

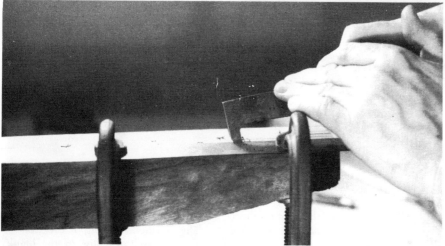

The inletting is laid out. After scribing a centerline, stations are measured fore and aft of the receiver ring, and the barrel dimensions and resulting contours transferred to the surface of the wood.

A hook cutter is now brought up for an assault on the barrel channel. The purpose is to cut the channel outline without running outside the scribed contour lines. It's simple with a steel straight edge clamped on the boundary.

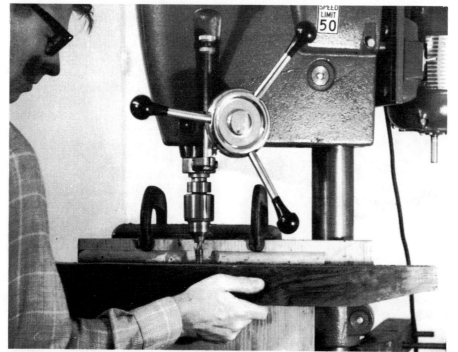

The stock is held against the accessory table and quarter round fence while passed under the router bit. The clamp on the column supports the table for sidewise adjustment when the cut must be set over.

in the proper direction through the pistol grip and by arranging the outline to encompass the best of the figure.

Always check with the template as far forward as the blank allows and in the upside down position, just in case the grain works out better this way. The guy that sawed out the blank in the first place didn't know exactly what you know, and furthermore, didn't have the blank planed off smoothly to see the figure as well as you. On one or two of mine I have moved the outline all the way to the front of the blank, tossing away about five or six inches of the butt to avoid light colored sap wood or poorer figure. In one or two cases I have turned the blank upside down. The figure was better that way.

The best of the figure should be arranged to fall in the back ten inches of the stock, and on the right hand side of the butt. Forward of this, the checkering pattern will obscure the wood; and, since the plain side is the right side—assuming the stock will have a cheekpiece—it can stand more decoration by way of better figure than the cheekpiece side. If the stock has no cheekpiece, then I prefer to put the better figure on the left side, which side is up as the stock is held for normal examination. For maximum strength the grain should run parallel to the top line of the pistol grip and in a generally uphill direction through the forearm. To the rear of the grip the stock is not stressed very much and the grain can be permitted to go in any direction.

Once the layout is arranged, draw in the top line (bore axis) of the stock on the blank using the template to locate the line. Then, with the straight edge draw in a sawing line 1/16 inches above this line. Step over to the bandsaw and cut, leaving the saw line. The 1/16-inch surplus should not be used in squaring up the blank, which is the next step. Hold the blank in the bench vise and plane the top surface flat and square with the left side of the blank. This is more easily done with a jointer, but an ordinary wood plane will do. Use the square frequently and take your time so that the whole top surface is the way you want it. If you have been careful with the saw and planing, the 1/16-inch will be available to inlet the barreled action down deeper in case a slight error takes place early in the layout or inletting.

The centerline is next scribed all

Spotting the action in determines high spots which are removed with the chisel. Much assistance is gained by using Jorgenson clamps shown, together with substantial persuasion from a 16 ounce machinist's hammer and wooden block. C-clamps support the stock walls to prevent splitting.

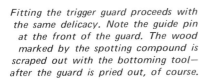

Fitting the trigger guard proceeds with the same delicacy. Note the guide pin at the front of the guard. The wood marked by the spotting compound is scraped out with the bottoming tool— after the guard is pried out, of course.

the way around the blank. If the full left side of the blank is flat and true, the conventional carpenter's adjustable scratch gauge is used. If the left side is not completely true, hold the left side against the top of a plate glass desk top (if you have one) and with a machinist's divider scribe a centerline with one leg of the divider against the glass top, the other set for the distance required. If you need the full width of the wood to make a wide target forearm you will have no choice but to put the centerline in the center of the blank. For an extremely full cheekpiece the centerline may be set over to the right side an extra ¼-inch. Either side may be favored if better quality wood figure appears to be lying close to one side.

In general, my advice is to put the centerline in the center if the blank is of normal thickness — 2½ inches.

Then, later on, cast off the butt plate about ¼-inch. This will leave very ample wood for the cheekpiece. I would favor one side or the other if better figure were available. Don't succumb to the temptation to saw off unneeded wood, which may seem to be a safe move to lighten the stock. The blank is left in full thickness for some time to come. The full thickness of the forearm is needed for holding in the vise and for strength during later operations when we will be attacking it with a heavy hammer and chisel giving birth to the cheekpiece. The full width of the forearm will be useful during inletting, so leave surplus wood until later.

With the centerline scribed, the next move is to lay out the entire receiver and barrel profile onto the top surface so that it is exactly bisected by the centerline. Start by replacing the

finished drawing of the stock on the blank with the bore axis line on the top of the stock representing the front of the receiver. The remainder of the barrel and action layout will be made from this line for the fore and aft dimensions and from the centerline for width.

Next, diameters of the barrel are transferred to the forearm surface. To do this, layout stations are first plotted at intervals forward of the receiver. The stations should be located at all points where the barrel changes contour. Mark off such stations on the barrel, measure their location forward of the receiver and mark a similar station on the centerline of the stock. Scribe a line across the stock at this point using a square.

Measure the diameter of the barrel

at each such location using a machinist's caliper. Write down this dimension, divide it in half (barrel radius) and reset the caliper to this dimension. Transfer this measurement to the station by putting one of the sharp points of the caliper on the centerline and marking the stock with the other. Do this on both sides of the centerline, then check the two dimples by measuring across the two with the caliper. The result should, of course, equal the barrel diameter. In this manner the barrel contour is accurately plotted so that it is bisected by the centerline. Connect the dimples with a scriber and a straight edge and recheck the dimensions of this outline against the barrel.

After the barrel has been laid out to the end of the forearm, proceed to do the same thing with the receiver. The receiver profile will generally be found to be narrower at the loading port owing to the fact that the loading port is cut down below the bore axis on the right side of the receiver. Be certain your scribed outline is brought in along the loading port. The rear tang should be laid out very slightly undersized. Connect the points with a scriber and straight edge as was done for the barrel. With the outline of the barreled action transferred to the stock, it should be apparent that if we cut out the wood at the lines scribed on the blank, the barreled action will go straight in.

The wood removal is begun by scoring a groove along the scribed lines with a scoring tool. The tool is made of a heavy duty scraper which is cut back with a grinding wheel to make a hook cutter. Scoring could also be done with a heavy duty pocket knife, but I prefer to remove exactly on the scribed line to a width of about 1/16-inch inside the scribed line. This allows some room for slight bobbling of the routing cutters and avoids running a router bit dangerously close to the edge.

Clamp a steel straight edge to the top of the stock between two stations. With a sharp pocket knife cut along the straight edge between the stations, then follow with the hook cutter. The pocket knife prevents tearing out wood behind the line. The hook cutter requires about a half dozen passes to cut out a groove which is about 1/8-inch in depth. After one section is cut, the straight edge is moved to the next station and the process repeated. A narrow chisel is used for cross-grain cuts such as at

the front corners of the receiver ring.

To get the wood out of the remaining section in the center I have adapted my drill press for use as a vertical milling machine by using a router bit and moving the blank against a rigid stop or fence. This permits close inspection and control of the routing. Good control over the depth of cut is achieved by adjusting the spindle to the desired depth and locking the quill. To set up the drill press for routing, the drill press table is turned 90° and an accessory table is C-clamped in place. This table has a quarter round at the top which serves as a fence against which the upper surface of the stock slides. The table and fence is adjusted to a right angle with the drill chuck.

If the drill chuck will be used to

hold router bits, it must be securely locked to the column. A chuck with just a taper fit will vibrate loose when side thrust is applied. An inexpensive set of router bits may be used but the best router bits are long end mills with spiral flutes having a smooth shank for holding in your drill press. These are about four or five times more expensive than common steel router bits for wood. They operate with less vibration and pressure, however, As with any such work, good lighting is necessary so you can see where you are plowing, and safety glasses should be worn.

Before routing, the location of the front guard screw hole is measured and located on the center line. Since the front guard screw is square with the bore axis, it is a good idea to drill this hole now as we still have a centerline

Above, the true centerline is visible and aids in positioning the butt plate for the desired amount of cast off. Material remaining on the left side is very ample for cheekpiece, but is in the way this far back, so it may be slabbed off.

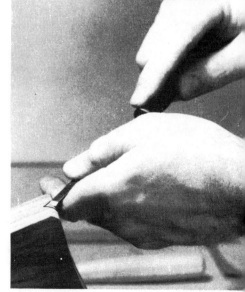

At right, a small pie shaped cut for the heel starts the Neidner butt plate fitting. Note that the curve of the plate has been cut with the band saw.

Glass bedding the barreled action first requires extensive masking or plugging of the action cuts, plus ample use of release compound. Author favors wide strips of "Scotch" brand No. 853 polyester tape for masking due to its thinness and toughness.

Above, with the barreled action removed, the hardened bedding compound will show perfect support. The action is a Winchester Model 52.

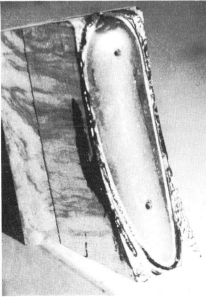

At left, butt plate bedding seals end against moisture plus supporting it perfectly. To assure a tight fit with the wood, rap the edges of the plate down with the mallet while the bedding compound is still soft.

and a squared-up blank. Clamp the stock up tightly against the fence, line up the drill accurately on the guard screw location, and run the drill in to full depth.

Routing is accomplished by running the drill press at top speed and carefully pushing the stock back and forth under the bit. The bit used should be 1/2 to 5/8-inch diameter and is advanced about 1/16-inch per pass by simply cranking the chuck down and locking the spindle at the desired depth. To move the stock sidewise, place a clamp on the column under the table, loosen the table lock, and swing the table slightly to the side. Check your progress with a depth gauge and take out enough wood to permit the action to come down to full depth after cleaning up. At the fore-end tip I like to leave additional wood unless an ebony tip is to be fitted.

If you are the type that believes in glass bedding, the steps left by the router bit are simply cut out a little deeper and the corners rounded off later with a gouge during the spotting in process. If you wish to hand fit it closely without glass bedding, the final cuts with the router should be with round end bits. In any case, careful work with the router bits plus attention to the depth being cut will yield work which can be on a par with the better semi-inletted stock blanks. It can also be worse. It's up to you.

After routing for just the bare action and barrel is accomplished, check the alignment of everything by putting a guide pin in the front guard screw hole and push it down into the mortise. It will not enter, but by careful examination you can determine how the outline registers with the profile of the metal parts.

The procedure from here on is to spot the barreled action into the wood using spotting compound and barrel inletting scrapers, chisels, and bottoming tools. With these parts down to full depth, then such added action parts as the magazine, bolt stop, trigger parts may be added, the mortise cut, and the parts individually fitted. But do not try to tackle anything more than the stripped barreled action just now. If you have an action wrench and can remove the barrel, the action mortise should be fitted first, then the barrel replaced and fitted.

A good many products will do for

spotting compound—lipstick, printer's ink, Prussian blue, or smoke from an old oil lamp—but the fastest, something that applies with a small paint brush, is probably best. My technique at the first stages is to clamp the action into the mortise with husky Jorgenson clamps, adding some persuasion with a heavy hammer. The blank must be secured against splitting with C-clamps. The high spots are marked by the spotting compound and when the metal parts are removed are easily identified. These are cut out with a chisel or any other tool which will reach the spot.

Despite what may seem like a heavy-handed approach, plenty of caution is used around the upper edges of the inletting so as not to over-cut the action or barrel mortise where it will later show. That goes for leaning the chisel against the top edges of the mortise which is a powerful temptation while attempting something like the cutting out of some corners down under. Wood taken out down below which will be covered by bedding compound can be treated with a little less care.

After you have the barreled action three-fourths of the way in, be careful to apply the pressure with the clamps in the same general areas that the guard screws are located. This way, the barrel (which is easily bent if of sporter weight) will not be over-cut and later stick up out of the barrel channel after the guard screws are inserted. The vertical surfaces of the inletting will be covered with spotting compound if you have a good fit. Don't touch these unless you suspect they are pushing the works to one side or the other. Rather use a scraper and check the results quite carefully on the opposite side. The point is, these vertical surfaces will pick up spotting compound every time the barreled action goes in and out, suggesting that there is wood to be scraped off, but don't believe it—wood removed here will open up the inletting excessively, leaving a bad case of "gaposis" when the job is done.

Keep at the spotting-in process until the barreled action is slightly below bore axis. In the process leave as much wood under the action as various action cuts permit. On the M-70 Winchester action, for example, wood should come up fully into the action in the vicinity of the bolt handle; otherwise, when the bolt handle is lifted, it will be apparent that too much wood was removed. The barreled action should fit well enough

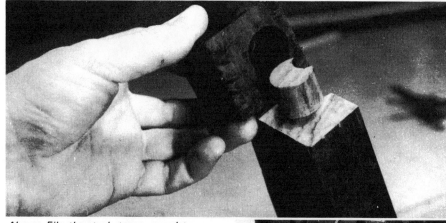

Above: File the stock tenon round to fit the hole in the ebony fore-end block.

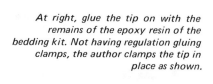

At right, glue the tip on with the remains of the epoxy resin of the bedding kit. Not having regulation gluing clamps, the author clamps the tip in place as shown.

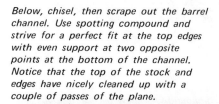

Below, chisel, then scrape out the barrel channel. Use spotting compound and strive for a perfect fit at the top edges with even support at two opposite points at the bottom of the channel. Notice that the top of the stock and edges have nicely cleaned up with a couple of passes of the plane.

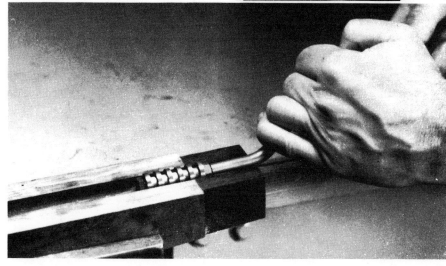

around the top of the mortise to require some pressure to start it out of its seat.

With the barreled action in the wood, the next step is to let in the magazine. (If this is an M-70, carefully trace through the action opening and, using the magazine box itself, determine the cut for the magazine.) The cut is started using some large bits on the drill press. Holes thus drilled are connected with the router bit or simply chiseled out. The final fitting of the magazine box is accomplished with a cabinet rasp to bring the mortise to proper width and length. If you have kept an eye on the squareness of the magazine walls with respect to the top surface, the magazine box, when attached to the receiver, should slide down and bottom just as though it was the barreled action alone. Other parts of the action may be attached and inletted after the magazine is in.

In all cases, be careful to remove no more wood than is necessary. For planning cuts for the action accessories the old factory stock is very helpful. The rear guard screw may generally be drilled through the existing threaded hole in the rear tang. This hole, naturally, must be square with the world and should be undersize. If it breaks out on the bottom line slightly out of position this can usually be corrected by filing the hole in the right direction with a rat-tail file first, then redrilling to full size.

We will discover that careful magazine inletting is absolutely necessary when fitting the floor plate and trigger guard, the next item on the agenda. If the magazine mortise is overcut, the floor plate may not cover the gap, as floor plates on some rifles have practically no overlap. This, naturally, is there to see before starting the job, so inspect it carefully.

On the Springfield and Mauser make a metal template of the exact magazine shape and use this in conjunction with the guide pins to arrange the floor plate mortise. The actual routing for this is done with the drill press table flat and the stock upside down. Determine the bottom line of the forearm by transferring measurements from the drawing and the assembled action to the blank. Saw the bottom line with the left side of the blank against the saw table to keep the bottom surface reasonably square. At the rear guard

screw, the cut should be angled sharply down from the pistol grip curve so that we do not accidentally cut into the grip area. As with the top line, I prefer to leave about 1/16 of an inch of wood—just in case—and plan the cut accordingly.

The actual mortising is handled in much the same way as the barreled action. Rout it to within 1/32-inch of the scribed outline and scrape from there. I prefer to use conventional bottoming tools and a small mill file with the end ground square and sharp to deepen and widen the mortise. Take your time and let the guard in by repeated spotting in and out until it is at the full depth and the guard screws enter and can be pulled up properly. At this point the action parts and the magazine enter and are functioning properly with the guard screws in place.

The last items on the program are the grip cap and butt plate. The correct contour for the pistol grip curve and grip cap surface should be sawed out. Don't cut off the surplus material at the bottom line of the stock just yet. For the pistol grip curve I like to make a cardboard template which closely fits the curve of the drawing. This is used to scribe the cutting line on the blank and for checking the curvature of of the grip later. By now fitting the grip cap should be child's play. File the surface smooth and square with the side, rescribe the center line of the stock and put the grip cap on the center line with the front edge of the cap just behind the curve of the grip.

For the Neidner butt plate which I normally use, I make a template which is used to scribe a line prior to cutting the butt off. The curve thus made is a close fit to the edges of the plate and fitting the plate then takes comparatively little time. After cutting the stock to the template shape, the centerline is rescribed. Now, if you wish to set the butt plate over on the extreme right side of the blank, arrange some cast off, or simply center it, you have the centerline to go by.

Mark the upper tip of the Neidner plate, cut this wedge out with a narrow chisel and spot the plate onto the surface. A light wooden mallet is helpful. After the heel of the plate is fitted draw the outline of the butt and band saw a slab off the stock just to the rear of the cheekpiece. This will make final fitting and filing of the

plate easier by eliminating some useless wood. At the final stages drill for the plate screws. These must be square with the adjacent surface of the plate.

With spotting compound to go by, about 75 percent of the plate edges should make contact all the way around the edge. Subsequent glass bedding of the plate will support the center of the plate and seal the end grain against moisture. But at this stage no gaps should be tolerated. After the butt plate is fitted, the wood hanging down below the toe of the plate to the grip cap can be cut off. Then cut off the wood from the top of the comb, leaving a little for clean up, so that the sear nose will just pass, or wherever you have planned to have the top line.

If this is to be a particularly light rifle you may wish to remove some weight from the butt end. Now is the time. Clamp the right side of the butt against the vertical table of the drill press and drill two one-inch holes to a depth of 5 or 6 inches. These are then plugged before bedding with corks. It may occur to you that weight can be added also. I have done this on several target rifles to better balance the heavy barrel. Lead shot mixed with glass bedding compound can be added or plumber's lead wool pounded in. These are subtle improvements the custom worker can sneak in with hardly any extra effort.

At this point the job is ready for glass bedding.

It is my good fortune to have the acquaintance of a number of excellent free rifle shooters and high power competitors, not a few of whom have had their smoke poles in my shop for glass bedding and other surgery. The value of such stuff, which has been scorned by the purists, has been made dramatically clear so far as I am concerned. Having done over several of the Schultz-Larsen free rifles, which in our club shot with superb accuracy, the following experience seemed to be pretty general: these rifles would shoot accurately as delivered, then lose gilt edge accuracy. This would be accompanied by six months of diddling with hand loads, bullets, etc., in the expectation of seeing accuracy return. At last the stock would be glass bedded. Lo! The old accuracy would be back.

The process was to bed the receiver and two inches of the barrel completely in glass. The guard screw holes would be reamed out so they would not bind the screws. The bushing around the guard screws would be removed and discarded so that these would not become pinched between the action and the floor plate, thus preventing the action from being pulled down hard into the seat formed by the bedding. This is substantially the way the successful target jobs get bedded even though they may be repeaters.

There is just no substitute for a very close fit around the recoil lug and even support of the bottom of the action. The bedding prevents oil soaking of the wood and moisture entry. It is significant that practically all the target stocks in use by the masters are bedded thusly. Carefully done, it need not show on the wood-to-metal joints of the rifle. Thus we have the best of both worlds—good bedding and good appearance.

Glass bedding resins are of two general types, epoxy and polyester. The epoxy materials are generally two-part mixtures the polyesters three-part mixtures. The advantage of the epoxy resins are that they have practically zero shrinkage, excellent adhesion and great strength. The polyesters of my acquaintance shrink slightly but otherwise appear to be satisfactory. I use the "Acraglas" kit epoxy produced by Bob Brownell's, Montezuma, Iowa. My own release compound is simply a mixture of paraffin wax and white gasoline. This is kept in a wide mouth jar and is liberally brushed all over the metal parts, the guard screws dipped in it, etc. I have had some difficulty with the release compounds supplied, mainly because I was too stingy. After mixing the "Acraglas" kit, I add even more fiberglass filler than supplied in the kit to bring the resin to about consistency of medium soft butter.

Before bedding rehearse each move. Lay out all the tools necessary, make certain every hole in the action is plugged with modeling clay, or parts covered with "Scotch" brand No. 853 Polyester tape, etc. I fill the mortises for the magazine and trigger mechanism with cork so they may be easily broken in and cleaned up. All butt plate and and grip cap surfaces are liberally covered with release compound inside and out. In other respects the instructions included in the kit are closely followed.

The guide pins and stockmaker's hand screws are used to get the job into the wood straight and to leave a relatively clean unplugged hole for the hand screws. These allow a firm grip when it comes time to remove them from the stock. *Mucho* release compound is used on these too. Only after all the work has been planned and newspapers placed strategically on the floor, is the resin mixed and put in place.

After the resin is in place and with the guide pins in the action, put the barreled action into the wood and "coax" it down into its normal depth with the pair of Jorgenson clamps. Turn it over, place the trigger guard in position, remove the guide pins and substitute the hand screws. Pull these up tight. Remove the clamps and check everything, making certain the barrel is down fully to its normal depth in the wood. It is quite easy to have the barrel sprung upwards at this point by entrapment of bedding mixture so it should be coaxed down with clamps, also.

We still have the butt plate and grip cap to go, so don't retire for a smoke yet. After the butt plate is in place, rap the edges of the plate down hard with the wood mallet to fully seat them against the end grain of the wood. Then pull the screws up tightly for the last time. Same thing with the grip cap. Now go back and scrape up the surplus resin. When this is done, retire for the evening.

The inletting job is not really finished until the action is again cleaned up, the mortises which were temporarily plugged, reopened, and the ebony forearm tip installed. Cleaning up the action after bedding is simple enough. Use paint thinner and scrape with pieces of hard wood or soft metal. Ample use of release compound will permit the bedding compound to come off of surfaces such as the inside of the action and the checkering of the butt plate. Take it from me, bedding will get on everything so be generous in the beginning with the release compound.

To fit the ebony tip we will drill a one-inch hole in it, file a round one-inch tenon on the end of the forearm and glue the two together. I have attached them with various screw arrangements and pins, however when this method of attachment is used the tip material will shrink, permitting the walnut to

stand out above the surface of the tip some months after the job is all done and the finish applied. When the tenon of the forearm extends into the tip any shrinkage will grip the tenon more tightly, and, because the tip is comparatively thin in wall thickness, no noticeable change results.

To prepare the tip hold it—end grain up—with the Jorgenson clamp so that it can be faced off under the router bit clean and square. The router bit is then removed and a one-inch bit run in to a depth of one inch. The hole should be placed slightly above center of the tip so plenty of material remains for the fullness of the forearm. Carefully plan the location of the tenon on the forearm with the aid of a plastic hole template. The hole drawn on the end of the forearm must be placed so that the edges lie below bore axis.

Draw this in. Extend perpendicular lines back an inch and carefully cut away the surplus wood with the bandsaw. Then file the tenon round and smooth up the joint so that it abuts the ebony tip smoothly without gaps. Then epoxy the two together with the remains of the glass bedding kit. The assembly is clamped up using the drill press as a clamp (I have no long regulation gluing clamps for the job) with a resilient rubber block to keep the joint under pressure. When hardened the fore-end tip is fitted to the barrel with the barrel rasp and scraper.

Variations of the inletting treatment will solve almost any stockmaking job. The important points are to plan the inletting as a series of steps; work from the barreled action to the squared-up blank to transfer accurate measurements. Then take your time and remove the wood carefully until the parts enter.

Having gotten this far quite a few times all by myself it is my impression that the toughest part of the job is over. The other parts of the stockmaking seem less difficult. But there are advantages to doing this part of the work myself rather than buying the inletted and preshaped blank from some factory.

Consider that we started with much higher quality wood, arranged to take the best wood out of the blank, left ample thickness for such items as a full cheekpiece, cast off, full forearm, and generally ended up with a more precise inletting job for the exact barreled action we had in mind. By so doing we made sure we didn't end up with just a plain old handle either.

●

BEDDING the BROWNING 78

By FRANK de HAAS

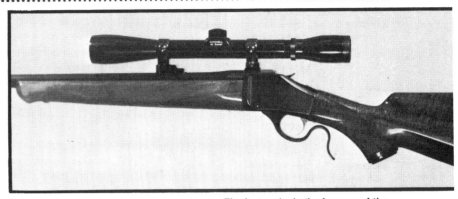

The factory beds the forearm of the Browning M-78 to exert considerable upward pressure upon the barrel, which, while usually aiding accuracy, means that the rifle will be more sensitive to shifts in zero due to humidity changes.

BOLT ACTION rifles have been bedded and re-bedded to such an extent that bedding techniques in these guns have been pretty well refined, whether for a bench gun or a sporting rifle to be carried into the woods. Single shot rifles require entirely different bedding systems, and like bolt action rifles, different models may require slight variations in bedding for the best accuracy.

The Browning 78 is no exception. Although the conventional two-piece stock has the fairly standard through-stock bolt in the buttstock, the M-78 forearm has an important role in regard to the accuracy of the rifle. Depending on how the fore-end is inletted and bedded, it can affect the accuracy, point of impact, and day-to-day zero of the rifle.

The M-78 Browning forearm is long and slim. It is attached to the rifle with two small screws which affix it to a forearm hanger: this hanger is an integral part of the receiver, projecting forward about six inches. The hanger, which is also the mounting for the automatic ejector system, tapers from rear to front and does not contact the barrel at any point. It takes up considerable space, especially the first four inches ahead of the receiver, and a lot of wood must be removed from the inside of the forearm for clearance. The hanger is steel, and despite its generous size, is not as rigid or as stiff as one might suppose. An adult with average strength in his fingers can easily move the end of the hanger a fraction of an inch either away from or towards the barrel.

The forearm of the M-78 is factory inletted and bedded so that when it is tightened in place by the two forearm screws, the front few inches of the forearm exerts considerable pressure against the barrel. The amount of pressure may vary from rifle to rifle, but on each of my two M-78's I estimated this pressure at around 15 pounds. The M-78 barrel, whether round or octagon, is of the heavy sporter weight, ideal for a combination varmint-sporter rifle which the M-78 is.

At the midway forearm pressure contact point with the barrel (at the front sling swivel base location), the round barrel is .915-inch in diameter. Even though the barrel from the breech to this point is heavy and stiff, the forearm tip exerts enough pressure against the barrel to affect it. This may be for the good as Browning intended it to be, and it is generally conducive to the best accuracy. However, the reverse could be true in individual M-78's. Another effect of this pressure is in the point of impact which can vary with the pressure on the barrel. This effect is easily demonstrated by a simple shooting test. For example, with my round-barreled M-78 in 6mm caliber, the 100-yard impact point drops from three to four inches with the same load when fired with the forearm removed or completely floating, compared to the factory-bedded forearm with pressure against the barrel.

On two M-78's that I experimented with, forearm pressure also produced a point of impact change to the side. This sideways change seemed to indicate that the forearm tip was exerting some side pressure. This later proved to be the case with both of these rifles. After checking the forearm channel inletting to find which side bore the heaviest against the barrel, I sanded it down until the uneven side pressure was removed. The point of impact then dropped straight down when the rifle was fired without the forearm — the sideways impact change had been eliminated.

Browning evidently found that the M-78 is generally most accurate with forearm tip pressure against the barrel. But wood is not always stable over a period of months, weeks or even days; the forearm of a M-78 can be affected by a change in temperature or humidity. Any slight change in the tip pressure due to slight warping, swelling or shrinkage of the wood, can, and usually does, affect the zero of the rifle. Not only does bedding affect accuracy, but with the pressure-against-barrel type of bedding in the forearm, changes in the way the rifle is held can also produce point of impact changes. For example, if the rifle is sighted in from a bench rest with the rifle resting on the forearm just to the rear of the sling swivel base, and afterward is fired with the forearm held or resting on a spot much farther to the rear, the chances are the point of impact will shift. If a sling is used to steady the rifle while shooting, sling tension on the forearm will also affect the forearm pressure and consequently the point of impact. The pressure-bedded factory forearm can also affect the accuracy and impact point as the barrel warms from repeated firing. The target shooter and the varmint hunter will want his M-78 to be as accurate as possible. The varmint hunter also wants his M-78 to stay zeroed from shot to shot and from month to month. The pressure-bedded forearm will probably give the best accuracy in most M-78's, but as mentioned, this method of bedding has its drawbacks. The thing to do, therefore, is to test your M-78 to find just how accurate it is with the factory pressure bedding and then follow up with one or more alternate forearm bedding methods to determine which one results in the best accuracy.

In these experiments, the accuracy testing should be done from a bench rest at a range of approximately 100 yards or more. All the testing should be done with the same ammunition, preferably a handload with bullet and powder that has proven accurate in that particular rifle. A minimum of at least four 5-shot groups should be fired with the rifle in each of the three bedding stages described below. The change from the factory bedding to the two alternate methods is simple and this allows all the firing to be done in one session at the range.

To prepare for this, take along a screwdriver that fits the forearm screws. A small washer about .075-inch thick is also needed to serve as a spacer between forearm and forearm hanger in one of the tests. This washer must be small enough, or its sides filed straight, so that it will fit into the forearm hanger inletting groove. For the round barreled M-78 take along a 6-inch piece of 3/4-inch dowel and a piece of medium grit sandpaper to fit over it. If the rifle has an octagon barrel, get yourself a piece of wood about six inches long and either 3/8-inch square or 3/8-inch thick and glue a couple of 3/8-inch wide strips of sandpaper to it. These sanding sticks are for smoothing and widening the forearm channel.

Lastly, to carry out test No. 3, drill and tap the forearm hanger to accept a socket-head setscrew and make a small pillow block to fit between this screw and the barrel. I used an 8x32 setscrew for this, drilling the hole for it about 3/8-inch to the rear of the front forearm screw hole. The support block is a .20-inch piece of 3/8-inch aluminum rod countersunk on one end for the end of the setscrew. If you don't mind having a small hole in the forearm of your rifle, drill a hole through it to align with the setscrew and in this way the screw can be turned, and barrel tension adjusted, without removing the forearm.

Bedding test No. 1 is with forearm-against-barrel pressure, as factory issued. This should be the first test, but it should follow preliminary testing to find an accurate load for the rifle. The rifle should also be properly sighted in to strike on point of aim. The test targets will then show the accuracy of the factory bedded rifle and the targets serve as reference index for the following tests.

Bedding test No. 2 is with the barrel "floating" or free of forearm pressure. This test can be done in two ways — with the forearm completely removed and the rifle fired by resting it on the forearm hanger, or the forearm rigged so that it is free of the barrel. This test is best done with the forearm removed. However, if

The forearm of the M-78 is mounted to the forearm hanger — a tapered arm which projects forward of the receiver. The two screws, shown in place, hold the forearm. The hanger is also the mounting for the rifle's automatic ejection system. Seemingly quite stiff, the end of the hanger can be pushed toward the barrel or pulled away with not too much effort.

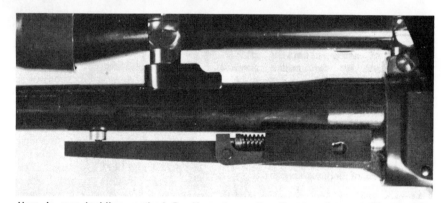

Here is one bedding method De Haas terms the "forearm hanger-against-barrel" pressure. This is accomplished by fitting a setscrew near the end of the hanger [arrow] and a pillar between the hanger and barrel for the setscrew to bear against. After sanding the barrel channel in the forearm a bit wider, the setscrew is turned tight enough so that with the forearm installed, it is just free of the barrel. With this method, steel-on-steel pressure is constant, unlike the rather unstable pressure of a wood forearm.

The correct way to test whether a barrel is floated or free of the forearm is by resting the rifle in a horizontal position on the forearm, and then use a strip of paper between barrel and forearm to check the clearance. Unless the paper can be easily passed between the two, the barrel is not fully floated. The main advantage of a floated barrel is a more constant zero in that the forearm cannot affect the barrel in any way; the disadvantage is that most relatively light barrels shoot more accurately if barrel vibrations are damped by forearm or similar pressure.

firing the rifle this way poses a problem for you, the same results can be obtained by placing a small washer about .075-inch thick over the front forearm screw between the forearm and the forearm hanger. With both forearm screws tightened, the washer will separate the forearm tip from the barrel and the rifle can then be fired in the normal way. However, before firing, and with the rifle resting on the forearm, make a test by attempting to slide a strip of thin target paper between the forearm and barrel. If this cannot be done then it will be necessary to sand the forearm channel smooth or a bit wider, or use a thicker washer, so that the forearm is completely free of the barrel. Fired either way, with forearm removed or propped away from the barrel, the groups will reveal whether the rifle being tested is more accurate, less accurate, or equally accurate with the

94

barrel free floated or with forearm pressure against the barrel as factory issued.

This test will also reveal the point of impact change that will occur when forearm pressure is removed. The vertical change need be of no concern, but if there is a horizontal change, it most likely indicates that the forearm tip is exerting some side pressure on the barrel as well as upward pressure. In this case, check to determine which side of the channel is bearing more heavily against the barrel and sand it down. This done, it is a good idea to repeat test No. 1 as this uneven side pressure might have affected the accuracy. At any rate, the forearm pressure bedding will likely produce better accuracy than the floated barrel and in this case an even all-around forearm pressure is less apt to disturb horizontal point of impact later. The forearm channel inletting is not very smooth, and in addition it is liberally and unevenly coated with stock finish. Just sanding the channel to smooth out the humps and ridges may be all that is needed to obtain even contact and pressure with the barrel.

Bedding test No. 3 consists of forearm hanger-against-barrel pressure. This is a bedding method which transfers barrel pressure duty from the forearm to the forearm hanger. The point of pressure contact is moved back several inches from the tip of the rather unstable forearm to the end of the much more stable forearm hanger. As described previously, the pressure is produced by the setscrew installed in the forearm hanger, with a pillar or support block fitted loosely between the hanger and the barrel over the setscrew: the screw can be adjusted to apply almost any amount of pressure to the barrel. Unlike the pressure supplied by the factory-fitted forearm, this hanger pressure method is stable, even and constant. Moreover, it's readily adjustable. In addition, it makes the forearm hanger as rigid as the barrel, which in turn provides a rigid mounting for the forearm either in contact with or entirely free of the barrel. With my

round-barreled M-78, after firing test No. 2 in which I had to smooth out the forearm channel to widen it a bit, I removed the spacer washer from between the forearm and the hanger, then inserted the pillow block and tightened the setscrew enough so that with the forearm installed it would have just enough clearance to slip a strip of paper freely between barrel and forearm. In a subsequent test I found no advantage whatsoever in having the forearm tip contacting the barrel.

In my forearm bedding experiments with two Browning M-78's, I fired 60 shots in each test with each rifle, and then repeated tests No. 1 and No. 3 to further verify the results with one of the rifles. This was a lot of shooting but actually I had the accuracy evidence after firing four 5-shot groups for each test. You can fire more groups if you want, but if you have good ammunition, are firing in good weather from a solid bench, and go about the testing properly, four carefully fired groups for each bedding test is all the information needed.

At home, with the targets marked and using a micrometer caliper, measure each group and figure the average for the groups in each test. If there is not much difference in the accuracy with the different bedding methods, then you may want to do the tests again, perhaps with a different load. Or you may find at the time you are firing the rifle that accuracy is noticeably better with one of the methods, and of course that's the bedding method that should be used for that particular rifle.

If there is no significant difference in the accuracy with the three different bedding methods, as was the case with my round barreled M-78 in 6mm caliber, then you have the choice of the three. You might prefer to retain the factory bedding, in which case just remove the pillar from under the hanger and attach the forearm again. However, you are still left with the rather unstable forearm bearing against the barrel and the likelihood of the zero changing with the first big change in the weather. To eliminate this possibility, choose one of

the other methods. In choosing between the completely floated barrel method and the forearm hanger-against-barrel pressure method, I would recommend the latter. The reason for this is that using the washer to keep the forearm away from the barrel is not a very good idea for a permanent arrangement, and to free float the barrel with the forearm attached in the normal manner, the barrel channel in the forearm has to be deepened and widened considerably, leaving a fairly big gap. Remember that a barrel is not free floated unless it remains free of the forearm no matter how the rifle is held or rested.

In my 6mm M-78 I chose to use the forearm hanger-against-barrel bedding method. As described before, the setscrew and pillar are used to supply upward pressure against the barrel which may help damp barrel vibrations. This arrangement serves more or less as a prop between the hanger and barrel, and actually pushes the front end of the hanger away from the barrel and holds it there rigidly. With the forearm attached in the normal manner and with the setscrew adjusted so the front of the forearm is free of the barrel, the original forearm channel does not have to be deepened to any extent and neither the forearm nor the hanger can give, no matter how the rifle is held when fired. A possible side advantage of this bedding method is that at any time the pillow block can be removed and the forearm reinstalled leaving the rifle bedded just as it originally was. Besides all this, the main advantage of this bedding method is that warpage or shrinkage of the forearm cannot affect or cause a change in the zero or point of impact of the rifle. There was no change in zero of this 6mm during a seven-month period, checking it on the range at least once a week. Also, this rifle showed no loss in accuracy as the barrel warmed from firing a long string of shots.

By the simple bedding tests and modifications described you may be able to significantly improve the accuracy potential and stability of your M-78 Browning, resulting in a much better "one-shot" hunting rifle. ●

By C. REED MOOR

**"Glued-in" barrels perform well
in light-recoiling bench rest guns;
would a big-cased 1,000-yard rifle
hold together and shoot as well
with the barrel epoxied to the stock?**

Building a Barrel-Bedded Magnum

THE RESEARCH and development branch of rifle accuracy is competition bench rest shooting, which has been the testing ground of many of most-significant contributions during the past couple of decades. While most of the competition bench rest developments have been adaptable — and many have been adapted — to other forms of competition rifles as well as hunting rifles, some aren't compatible, such as ultra-wide fore-ends and ultra-light three-lever triggers. In the past few years, the most radical development in bench competition has been barrels and actions "glued" into the stock; these have given excellent results, but this method of bedding has not, so far as I know, spread into other accuracy sports.

The purpose of both systems is to eliminate bedding problems, and to improve grouping ability by permanently affixing the barreled action to the stock with a vibration-free, theoretically unchanging bond of epoxy. As any accuracy competitor knows, bedding will change due to the effects of humidity upon the stock, which can bend the surface of conventional epoxy bedding, or it can change due to excessive or uneven torquing of action screws. No one knows precisely why bedding that misses a perfect fit by a couple of thousandths of an inch will so seriously affect accuracy, but it will. About four or five years ago, rifles with barrels glued to the stock, and the actions "floating," began showing up at NBRSA and IBS bench matches — and they won more than their share, due at least in part to the fact that they were being shot by extremely skilled competitors.

The most obvious disadvantage was that "barrel-bedded" guns had to be "un-glued," usually through the application of heat or cold, before they could be re-barreled (glued-in actions were developed primarily to allow simple barrel changing). A second disadvantage, removing the trigger for cleaning or repair, was solved by providing trigger pin access holes through the stock, and an enlarged trigger slot to allow it to be removed through the bottom of the stock. A major advantage, in theory at least, was that any flimsy action could be used, since it didn't have to be bedded to support itself, barrel and scope. While the Hot Stove League might argue forever about the merits of "glued-in jobs," there is one thing unarguable — those rifles *shoot;* while they are still a minority on the competition circuit, they have won titles and set records completely out of proportion to their numbers.

The question was: Would a barrel-bedded rifle for a magnum caliber stay glued together? And would it provide the accuracy advantages for 1,000-yard bench or prone shooting that the system has shown for 100 to 200-yard bench competition?

The occasion for the venture was the availability of a cheap used Remington Model 721 action fitted with a Hart barrel in 7mm Remington Magnum. The 28-inch tube was 1 1/4-inch in diameter, and the twist was one turn in nine inches. I had planned to stiffen the action, and provide additional bedding surface, by installing a sleeve (another development of bench competitors which has been adopted successfully for other games). But then I began looking at a Sporter Class bench gun which had been barrel-bedded by Remington's Jim Stekl, the originator, or at least one of the early practitioners, of the system. Jim had removed the recoil lug and excess wood around the action, then glued the barrel to the stock with a six-inch pad of epoxy just forward of the receiver. Would the same method work with the 1,000-yard gun?

A quick phone call to Jim brought plenty of information and lots of encouragement. Jim said that he had never tried this method with a magnum but the .308 Winchester offered no problems so he saw no reason why a magnum would not stay in the stock if the metal were adequately clean and the bedding compound mixed and applied properly. Jim had used Devcon for his work with good success but I felt that other materials might work as well. With that in mind several were tested; Bisonite was finally chosen primarily due to personal experience. Also, a letter from Bisonite indicated that more problems would be encountered in removing the barrel at a future date than would be anticipated by its shooting loose from recoil forces.

The usual procedure for removing a barrel-bedded barrel is to heat the barrel to about 350 to 400 degrees, at which time the epoxy bond will release and the barrel can be removed. The only time removal is necessary is when the barrel wears out or, if access through the stock is not provided, when the trigger fails. To install a new barrel, simply rough up the old bedding, clean the barrel and epoxy it back in place. This is simplicity at its finest and, to date, a rather successful method.

Wally Hart of R.W. Hart & Son, Nescopeck, Pa., provided an excellent heavy bench stock machine-inletted to my specifications, allowing clearance around both the barrel and action. All that had to be inletted was the rear of the action where the milling cutter didn't remove quite enough wood. It is better to stop a bit short than it is to have to try to add wood later. The stock was left unfinished for all of the work prior to the final bedding.

With all materials on hand the process began in earnest. The first job was to obtain shims or spacers to keep the barrel and action free, and equally spaced, above the stock wood. Chipboard was used for it was handy and about the desired thickness. The chipboard spacers were placed at each end of the action, at the forward end of the bedding area and at the fore-end tip.

After shimming, the trigger area was examined to be certain that it did not touch the stock. It was then discovered that the bolt stop would not function. Sufficient wood was removed from the stock to allow it to operate freely.

The area to be bedded was marked and the shims were given a coating of release agent to keep them from sticking to the bedding. It should be pointed out that I had planned to pre-bed this barrel by applying release agent to the barrel so it could be removed from the stock and the stock finished before the barrel was finally "glued in." Had I planned on doing a one-step job, the approach would have varied in that all operations would have been final — with no release agents on the barrel. Since this was my first attempt, I wanted to take it slow and allow room to correct an error if it appeared. Fortunately it did not and a few steps could have been eliminated had

the stock been finished prior to the bedding.

To keep things neat, a layer of masking tape was applied to the stock in all areas adjacent to the bedding. After the bedding became stiff, but not hard, the tape would allow the excess bedding to be removed neatly.

The bottom of the barrel was then coated with release agent so that the barrel could be removed for a check on progress when the bedding became hard. At this point the barrel had not been roughened in the bedding area.

Mixing the Bisonite according to instructions took little time and the solution was given about ten minutes to firm up a bit. Bisonite offers one distinct advantage in that the operator has about forty-five minutes of working time before the stuff becomes unworkable. It also has a thicker consistency — about like cold syrup — than a lot of other products, but it's "runnier" than paste-like Devcon.

Bisonite was poured into the bedding area, with the shims serving as dams. The barreled action was placed into the stock and held in position by a C-clamp placed above the center of the bedding area. When fastening the clamp, attention was directed to the trigger to see that it was centered in the trigger opening. This squaring up of the action assured the scope bases would be level. Once this check was made, the clamp was tightened only enough to hold the barrel firmly against the spacers. When the bedding compound hardened to a leathery-like toughness, the excess along the sides of the barrel was trimmed with a knife and the tape on the stock removed.

The next morning the barreled action was removed from the stock and the work inspected. The shims were removed, the stock was finished and a trigger guard was made from aluminum. The final gluing-in was to come shortly.

Prior to the final bedding the stock was taped to protect the finish and new shims were inserted at the forward end of the stock and at the rear of the action. These new shims were thicker than the originals by one strip of masking tape. This was to allow for a thin coat of bedding between the old bedding and the barrel so a better bond might result.

Attention was then given to the barrel bedding area. It was taped at each end and at each side of the bedding surface so that only a 180-degree area, six inches long would be exposed for roughing prior to final bedding. A file was used to make cross-channel marks and 50 grit paper was used to further rough-up the steel. This same grit paper was then used to rough-up the Bisonite in the stock. Making sure the release agent was completely removed was important.

With all preparations made for the

Prior to bedding, the area around the action must be relieved to prevent touching, and allow all parts to function, top. The Hart stock was machine-inletted to allow clearance around the 1 1/4-inch barrel and the 721 action in anticipation of barrel bedding, center. Shims to support the barreled action and confine the Bisonite were taped in place and coated with release agent prior to the preliminary bedding.

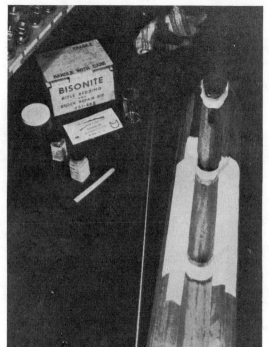

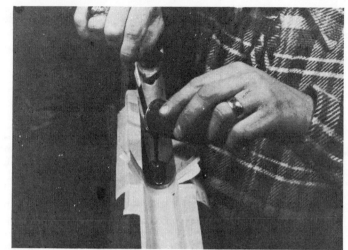

Bisonite is poured into the area to be bedded; the shims also act as dams to contain the liquid Bisonite. A coat of Bisonite was also applied to the underside of the barrel.

The stock was taped to prevent Bisonite adhering to the surrounding wood. The barrel and action support shims are shown in place.

bedding, with the exception of final cleaning, the Bisonite was mixed and allowed to stand and become a bit more firm. During this waiting time the barrel and bedding were cleaned. Carbon tetrachloride was used although Trichloethylene would have done a bit better job according to several sources, but I was unable to locate any in my area.

The Bisonite was applied to the stock bedding area. The barrel was wiped clean several times, just to be safe, and a small amount of Bisonite was wiped over the barrel area with a Q-tip. Some contend that a thin film of oxidation forms over steel in a few minutes, which might be detrimental to a good bond, so I cleaned and coated within a matter of a minute or so.

The barreled action then was lowered into the bedding area. A check was made to see if the trigger was located on center and just enough pressure was applied with the clamp to hold the parts together. Avoid excess pressure for it is possible to induce stress into this type of bedding. Remember that this is a bedding process which can be done improperly just as easily as any other bedding method. As soon as the bedding compound became firm, the excess was removed with a razor blade. I found that a light wipe with white gas smoothed the rough edges of the Bisonite yet had no effect on it. Lacquer thinner and similar solvents will dissolve the bedding material and should be avoided. The clamp was left in place overnight. The next morning there was a finished "barrel bedded" rifle on the bench with no screws to tighten and, hopefully, no tensions to worry about.

Any process must be judged by the success of the finished project, but the judgment day for this rifle had to wait for a week as the bolt handle had to be lengthened. While Wally Hart did this job I paced the floor in anticipation of the big day.

When that day arrived I loaded cases with 65 grains of IMR-4831 behind the Hornady 162-grain rebated boattail bullets and CCI BR-2 primers. The cases were Winchester. A box of cases with the same combination except for 64.5 grains of Norma-205 was also prepared.

Would it hold together? Some shooters using this type of bedding system place a non-bearing screw into either the guard screw or tang holes. This screw, which doesn't touch the stock, merely acts as a safety to hold the action to the stock in case the bond breaks loose. I didn't install the safety screw since I had confidence that if the rifle held for the first few shots there should be no problem. However, since this was a first-time thing for me the rifle was tested for togetherness by securely wrapping the barrel to the stock with furniture rubber bands. The scope was removed as a further precaution. I had no doubts as to the outcome but was taking no chances. A dozen shots later convinced me that all was well and the bands came off. Many additional shots have failed to break the bond.

Accuracy of the rifle at 100 yards is better than it is with either of my other 1,000-yard rifles. The first three groups at 100 yards printed in the .400-inch range which is almost bench rest accuracy. The 65 grains of IMR-4831 load showed a slight edge in grouping ability.

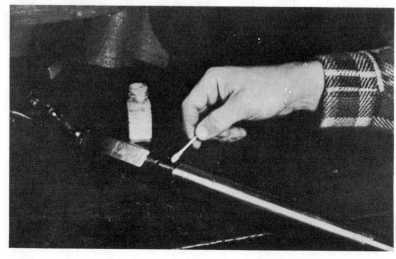

Release agent was applied to the barrel for the preliminary bedding. The shims were then removed and the barrel cleaned and roughed for the final bedding.

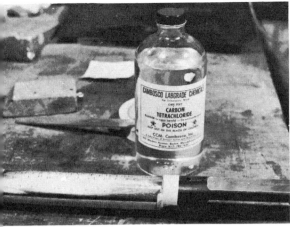

The roughened barrel section was cleaned immediately prior to final bedding to prevent any oxidation while the barrel awaits bedding.

After the preliminary bedding hardens, it is roughened with 50-grit paper. The surface is then cleaned with carbon tetrachloride or trichlorethylene prior to final bedding.

A C-clamp was used to hold the barreled action in position while the Bisonite hardened. The clamp was tightened just enough to secure the barrel; too much could bow it.

The next step was to check the rifle at 1,000 yards. The first job was to zero the rifle after the 100-yard readings were recorded. Usually 120 clicks of elevation on a Redfield 3200 scope will achieve the proper elevation. Today was different for the rear base was too low. Fortunately the impact was close enough to the target that a group could be located on paper by holding on a clump of brown earth peeking through the snow about five feet above the target center. It was with this aiming point that the initial testing was finished.

Starting with Winchester cases which had been once fired and neck turned, Federal 215 Magnum primers, Hornady 162-grain rebated-boattail bullets and 66 grains of IMR-4831, a ten-shot group was fired which measured 10.250 inches. The rifle was cleaned and allowed to cool while the target was pasted and prepared for the next group.

A second loading of new Winchester cases, Federal 215 primers, the same bullet as before and 64.5 grains of Norma-205 was tried. The conditions were getting worse with a wind blowing over the hill from the 1 o'clock position. This tends to push the impact down on the target. Care was taken to shoot when the flag appeared to be in the same position but this did not prove to indicate identical conditions as the target revealed two groups. One, a six-shot beauty which measured 7.937, revealed only 3.5-inch of vertical dispersion while the other, a few inches lower, measured 7.125 for four shots. The 10-shot group ran 15.625 which is respectable for many rifles in much better conditions at 1,000 yards. This load is so lacking in vertical problems that it will be tried again in better times.

A box of new cases with 65 grains of IMR-4831 was also fired in zeroing the rifle and plinking at various clumps of brown in the snow-covered backstop to gain a feel of the rifle. Though not fired on paper, the impact on the bank appeared to indicate that this load should be checked further.

Since that first trial the barrel-bedded rifle has performed well, considering the blustery conditions that prevailed, but it's too early to know whether this bedding system is an improvement over conventional methods. However, it's clear that if a rifle is assembled properly, the six-inch pad of epoxy is more than ample to hold things together at 7 magnum recoil levels. Tugging on the barrel shows no sign of separation. With heavier-recoiling guns, a non-bearing safety screw in the action might be advisable, but the strength of a proper bond is well above the recoil force of normal rifles.

In theory, the heavier-recoiling rifles used in 1,000-yard competition should benefit more from a vibration-free, "permanently" wedded barreled action and stock than the light-recoiling guns used in standard bench competition. I'm hoping that the theory will prove correct in this rifle. But from the results to date it appears that barrel-bedding has a lot to offer the shooter who hangs a long, heavy barrel on a relatively thin action, tries to hold it in a creepy stock with a pair of 1/4x28 screws, and expects miracles. ●

This 7mm Remington Magnum, which weighs about 30 pounds, is the first known barrel-bedded magnum-caliber rifle. It wears a 16X Redfield 3200 scope.

This system promises more~stable accuracy from magazine rifles

Installing an

ACTION BEDDING BLOCK

By NEAL KNOX

IN THE 1880's, when Peter Paul von Mauser, et al, designed the basic bolt action rifle, the action was attached to the stock on a fitted surface below the receiver ring and on a flat which mated with the tang. In almost a century of shooting that basic design and its derivitives, competitors and hunters have learned the importance of a close fit between the stock and rifle; but despite the fact that it's impossible to maintain a perfect fit at two points several inches apart, separated by narrow strips of wood alongside the trigger and magazine, factory rifles are still bedded the same as they were in Mauser's original designs.

It's no news to any rifleman that wood breathes, shrinks, expands, bends and warps with every change in the weather; neither is it news that the resultant changes in stock fit have a significant effect upon the rifle's point of impact as well as its grouping ability. While the importance of action bedding is well known, it's generally assumed that once an action is bedded properly, even in bare wood, it will tend to stay that way. It's almost an article of faith that once it's bedded with an epoxy compound, with a pad below the receiver ring, and another pad under the tang, the rifle will be a perfect fit to those two pads of epoxy from that day forward. But it simply isn't so.

The effects of humidity variations are most apparent around a fitted buttplate, which will project as much as 1/32-inch beyond the wood after prolonged exposure to a dry climate, or be considerably smaller than the stock after exposure to a wet climate. The most obvious effect upon accuracy is the change in impact, and sometimes grouping ability, which accompanies movement of the fore-end. If a rifle has a full-floated barrel, it will be noticed that the gap between the fore-end tip and the steel will change at different times of the year, even if the fore-end is a straight-grained piece of wood.

But few consider that the same type of movement is occurring in the action area. In a typical magazine rifle, there are large cutouts for the magazine and trigger, and on some models, additional wood is removed to provide clearance for a bolt release and side-mounted safety. While epoxy bedding pads will give a close fit to the steel part, the wood which supports them can move, and it undoubtedly will, for wood is never completely stable. Attempting to tie the front and rear

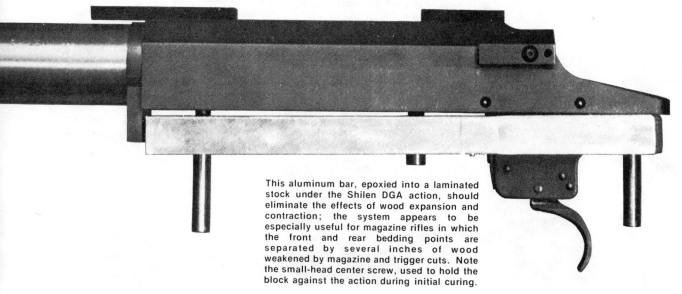

This aluminum bar, epoxied into a laminated stock under the Shilen DGA action, should eliminate the effects of wood expansion and contraction; the system appears to be especially useful for magazine rifles in which the front and rear bedding points are separated by several inches of wood weakened by magazine and trigger cuts. Note the small-head center screw, used to hold the block against the action during initial curing.

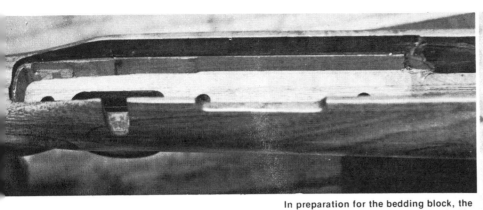

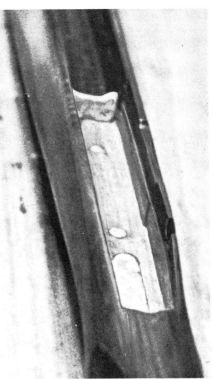

In preparation for the bedding block, the existing bedding was milled to depth, leaving a lip of original bedding surface to support the rifle while the block is epoxied into position. At right the trigger slot and action screw holes have been plugged with modeling clay and a clay dam built forward of the action recess to confine the Acraglas.

bedding points together by running rails of epoxy bedding material alongside the magazine box undoubtedly will help, but probably due more to removing wood than to any actual stiffening, for epoxy bedding will bend with the wood around it.

For some time I've been contemplating bedding a magazine rifle with an aluminum alloy bedding block, complete with cutouts for magazine and trigger. The block would be epoxied into the stock, then the bedding material applied to the aluminum. This may have been done, but I haven't seen any reports on it; it's not too unlike the highly successful Clerke rifle stock, which consists of a profile of aluminum, expanded in the magazine/trigger area, and sandwiched between two halves of wood.

But before trying a bedding block on magazine hunting rifles, I wanted to get some experience with bedding blocks on bench rest rifles — the testing ground for many of the best features on modern factory rifles. This past winter we have built three different competition rifles using variations of bedding blocks; it's still too early to say how well they will do.

In five years of active competition on the bench rest circuit I've received quite an education about the vagaries of wood stocks, with and without epoxy bedding. And like everything else in the graduate school of accuracy, the things learned about stocks are directly applicable to rifles used in other forms of competition and in hunting. Since a couple of things that I've said about bedding undoubtedly have raised some eyebrows, let's look at the experiences on which those opinions are based.

Most of you have "tuned" hunting rifles for maximum accuracy; and you've found that the typical lightweight hunting rifle barrel will shoot its best when the action is carefully inletted and the barrel vibrations are damped by a few pounds of upward pressure applied by the fore-end tip. By varying the amount of pressure by a pad of wood, or simply some thin shims under the barrel, some rifles will show a significant difference in their ability to

cluster all shots. But as barrel shims are varied, or the bearing points built up or reduced, it's apparent that not only does the grouping ability change, so does the point of impact. The same thing is going to happen when the wood in the fore-end moves, as it can be seen to do when the barrel is floated; that carefully applied ideal amount of pressure will vary with the weather, with equivalent changes in both group sizes and impact point. (Which is why I think hunting rifle barrels should be left free-floating, even if grouping ability is sacrificed somewhat!)

While the effects of a warping fore-end are well-known, the effects of the same type of wood movement in the action area aren't, probably because they're not so obvious. No one knows precisely why the action bedding must be an exact fit, but that's the way it must be if a rifle is to shoot its very best — as any bench shooter will attest. It's my opinion that bedding primarily affects the vibrations that race through the entire rifle during the moment of firing; I do not accept the explanation that improper bedding allows the action to shift between shots, which would seem plausible when a rifle is "double-grouping" — sending two or three shots into one hole, another two or three into another, with the shots jumping back and forth at random. But simple shifting within the stock, which would undoubtedly cause *beau coup* problems, can't be the cause when the action is bedded so that it cannot shift.

Anything which causes the action to be under even slight stress from bending can play havoc with normal accuracy. For instance, as related in several columns of about three years ago, my Remington 40XB-BR .222 Light Varmint rifle gave me fits until Master Gunsmith Dave Hall overhauled the bedding to prevent bending the action when the screws were

tightened. But that rifle was never shifting between shots.

Since this rifle had been bedded with a thick layer of Devcon Steel, most would assume that once-bedded, always bedded. Not so. Epoxy bedding materials are wonderful; they provide a more-perfect mating of action to stock than could ever be achieved by hand, but epoxy bedding is seldom as perfect as it looks. And even when it is perfect, there's no guarantee that it will stay that way, for even the strongest epoxy compounds will bend — the force presented by a warping or swelling piece of wood is tremendous. And epoxy bedding will *cause* the stock to warp!

Before branding me a heretic, consider that a sure-fire way to warp any wooden board is to paint one side, thereby partially sealing it and preventing it from "breathing" equally on both sides. No normal stock finish will seal wood absolutely air/water tight. But a thick layer of epoxy bedding material will. Result: the action area is sealed, the surrounding wood isn't, so there will be warping of wood around the bedding, and that warping will twist the bedding material itself without breaking its bond. When the bedding material is twisted, there goes your perfect action/stock fit.

The analogy of a board painted on only one side is an exact parallel to bedding the full-length of a barrel channel. While it's often done, particularly on Mannlicher-style stocks in order to reduce warping, it is certain to *induce* warping. Although epoxy-bedding a barrel channel will increase the strength of the stock

At left, the bedding area after the block was epoxied into position; the partial recoil lug support, thin seepage on the top of the block, and surplus hardened Acraglas around the walls were removed prior to an intended finish-bedding layer. At right, a C-clamp was used to hold the stock to the action while the barrel was clamped in a vise; although barely snug, the C-clamp apparently caused a low area in the center of the bedding, requiring an additional finish coat which cured while the stock was held to the action with a wrapping of surgical tubing.

somewhat, that layer of epoxy isn't enough to withstand the increased tendency of the wood to warp.

My 40X was unusually bad about changing bedding; in fact, it was probably one of the world's worst. But because it shot so well when the bedding was right — as well as any rifle I ever saw — and so terribly when it wasn't, that gun was a marvelous learning tool. On several occasions I corrected the bedding the night before a shoot by applying a "paint coat" of epoxy glue, and it would shoot beautifully; but within a few days the wood in the tang area would swell, shift or shrink, carrying the epoxy bedding with it — and bending the action! Proof, in addition to the fact that the gun's accuracy would turn sour, was the fact that a dial indicator mounted on the barrel, with the tip riding the fore-end, would show several thousandths movement when the rear screw was loosened. Since the same dial indicator setup had shown little or no movement at the time the screws had been tightened, the only explanation was that the warping wood had enough strength to bend both the bedding compound and the action steel.

The dial indicator would *always* tell whether the rifle would shoot well, by positioning it on the barrel or action, then reading the amount of movement between steel and wood when the screws were alternately tightened and loosened. For instance, with the indicator mounted on the barrel and reading off the fore-end, if the tang section was either high or low the indicator would show the barrel rising several thousandths out of the wood as the front screw was loosened. If the barrel rose when the center screw was inserted and tightened, with front and rear screws tight, it indicated that the center section of the bedding was low — usually caused by the tang section being high. If the bedding were bad enough to cause a substantial loss of accuracy, the movement of the barrel or tang could easily be felt, and sometimes seen. No movement at all indicated that the action was wedged in the stock, which can hide problems. Ideally, when reading off the fore-end there should be about a half-thousandth movement — usually it would be about a thousandth minimum — when any of the three screws were loosened. But if more than about .002 movement were apparent, accuracy would begin to suffer; .004 to .006 movement would make that quarter-inch rifle shoot three-quarter-inch groups.

In an effort to solve this problem we tried finishing the entire stock with clear epoxy resin from a fiberglass boat repair kit. It didn't work. But it did pinpoint the trouble: the epoxy resin refused to harden in the culprit area around the tang; apparently the wrist section of the stock was soaked during repeated cleanings with Hoppe's No. 9, which had penetrated the thin original oil finish and made the stock less stable.

The bedding of that rifle didn't stay put until Hall removed all the bedding with a chisel, and put in new support columns under the bedding area. I had already done the same thing, but the *way* Dave did it was what spelled success. I had drilled the holes for the Devcon in straight lines marching down the floor of the bedding area; Dave went much deeper into the wood and drilled the holes for columns in a zig-zag pattern in order to break the grain of the wood into short lengths, thereby reducing its warping strength. He also drilled into the wrist, to break the grain structure and provide reinforcement, then filled the cavities with Devcon Aluminum, since so much Devcon Steel would make the rifle overweight. Finally, he finished the bedding with a thin coat. That did it; the bedding hasn't moved for three years.

At the time all this was going on, and I was writing in my column about the bedding problems of the 40X, Ed Shilen delivered DGA No. 13 at the 1972 Tulsa Nationals. That rifle, a Heavy Varmint, was in an unfinished laminated stock, bedded in the wood by Doug Shilen. Ed joked that "If you glass-bed it, the warranty's off." Because of the DGA's flat bottom, and the laminated stock, I decided to leave it as it came, just to see how well it would work. After shaping the stock it was finished completely, including the bedding area, with two coats of polyurethane varnish and two coats of Trewax, an unusually durable carnuba wax.

The rifle shot well, with no significant changes in the bedding until the 1973 Nationals in Ohio; to avoid having to carry it on an airline, Skip Gordon kept it after the Speer Matches in Knoxville, delivering it at the Nationals, where it didn't seem to be shooting quite right (but I'm not blaming it for my poor performance there). I didn't think anything about it until Ed admonished me for having the action screws much too tight; he had checked the rifle at Dallas, a couple of weeks after the Nationals while another shooter was carrying it back to Arizona. Actually I had only snugged the screws before leaving Arizona; the rifle's lengthy stay in the humid East had swelled the stock enough that Ed had had to lean on the screws to get them loose.

That winter, back in Arizona, the stock shrank; by spring it was dry, but I had to spend several hours scraping the bedding before it was right. The 1974 NBRSA Varmint & Sporter Nationals were at Knoxville, held the week after the Unrestricted Nationals in Ohio, so the gun had been in humid country for two weeks prior to the shoot. The rainy morning of the Heavy Varmint competition I checked the screws and found that, although again they had only been snugged when I left home, the stock had swelled until they were so tight that I could barely get them out with an Allen-fitted screwdriver. But it obviously worked to my advantage, for the wood had apparently swelled into an exact fit with the action; with normal screw tension, it shot as it had never shot before, giving me the 100-yard and National championships. But this past winter the stock again shrank, the bedding went out, and accuracy soured. Rather than being faced with constantly

changing bedding, I decided to alter the bedding.

Some of my fellow shooters considered it sacrilege and insanity to tinker with such a rifle, and maybe they're right. Further, Ed Shilen, who knows more about rifle accuracy than I ever will, bluntly told me that all my fretting about bedding was nonsense, that I was getting different screw tension and apparent bedding unevenness primarily according to whether I had been yelling at the kids prior to tightening the screws. Maybe he's right; but I'm just as hard-headed as that proselyte Texan.

While a standard bedding job — a slab of epoxy strengthened with powdered fiberglass, aluminum or steel — might have solved the problem, this stock had already shown a tendency toward swelling due to humidity changes, and I didn't want to reproduce the troubles of the 40X. It seemed that the best course was to install an aluminum bedding block, which would be far stronger than any epoxy; the challenge would be in making the rifle shoot as well as it had when the wood bedding had been right: average groups well under a quarter-inch at 100 yards. After determining what is required to obtain such performance in a bench gun, it would be a simple matter to apply the same techniques to a magazine rifle.

Although I've had reports from bench shooters that some rifles will shoot well with a metal-to-metal contact of the action and bedding block, most who have experimented with this bedding system contend that there must be a buffer between the two — a layer of epoxy, paper, felt, rubber or other material. Initially, I planned to use an epoxy layer, since the other materials would tend to deteriorate with age.

Paul Marquart made the block for the Shilen, machining it slightly narrower and shorter than the action to allow positioning the action in the same location in the stock; a lip of the original wood bedding area on both sides of the action and at the rear was left for support. Paul allowed about a sixteenth-inch gap between the block and the recoil lug to provide a thick pad of epoxy behind the lug. A slot was milled out for the trigger, and holes drilled for the action screw. If a block were being made for a magazine rifle, it could be no wider than the action, in order to avoid cutting away surface wood at the upper stock/action line, but it could be no narrower than the magazine. Special care would be required in milling the magazine slot, for, depending on the rifle model, the lower section of the block might have to be enlarged to fit the magazine, or even replace a section of the magazine wall.

The inletting pins which Paul loaned me are worthy of special mention, for he had made them with a short section of 1/4 x 28 threads on an oversize shank. They are ideal for epoxy bedding, for after the epoxy has set up there is extra clearance around the action screws. Paul uses these guide pins each time he mounts the action in his bench rifle, providing added insurance that the action rests precisely in the same spot in the bedding.

Paul made a special screw for the center hole; the head was just large enough to hold the action block snugly against the action during installation, but small enough to remove through the stock hole after the epoxy had cured.

With the recess for the block milled in the stock, leaving about .030 to .060-inch clearance between the block and the surface of the stock, I closed the trigger slot on both the block and stock with modeling clay, fashioned a dam at the forward end and made short clay plugs in each of the three screw holes in the stock. The screw hole plugs would be pushed out when the action, with block attached, was seated; their sole purpose was to confine the epoxy.

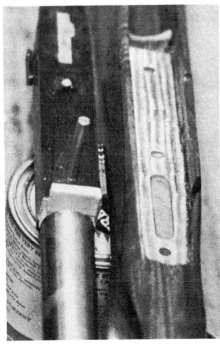

The stock and action are shown ready for the finish coat. The front, bottom, and sides of the recoil lug have been masked, holes filled with clay and the action waxed with release agent. The block has been cleaned and holes plugged with clay [the bolt slot was also closed after the photo was taken]. Note the scribe marks on the block, made to roughen the surface by "walking" a chisel down its length.

A dial indicator, held to the barrel by a magnetic base, and reading off the fore-end, will show how true the bedding is. An uneven fit will be reflected by barrel movement as the screws bend the action into low areas. More than about .002-inch of measured movement, which is magnified by the length of the fore-end, will cause a deterioration in grouping ability.

The action and guide pins were waxed thoroughly and the block cleaned with perchlorethylene (which can be obtained from chemical supply houses or dry cleaning establishments); the block was then attached to the action, using the guide pins and small-head center screw. The exterior of the stock around the action was also waxed to prevent epoxy drips from adhering to the finish.

Bob Brownell's Acraglas was selected for the bedding, for it has proved quite shrink-resistant, gives an excellent bond, allows ample working time, yet will set up hard in thin sheets, which some other epoxy materials will not do. For extra strength, I added some of the fiberglass floc from the kit, but left the Acraglas rather runny so it would flow up the narrow gap between the block and stock walls. With the barrel clamped horizontally in a vise, the stock was brought up to the action/block and lightly tightened with a C-clamp until the action rested against its old seat in the stock. A minimum of Acraglas seeped out the action screw holes.

The following morning I removed the center screw through the bottom of the stock, and removed the barreled action that night; it came out readily. The block was almost perfectly sealed in the stock, with only one gap between block and wood remaining to be joined. There was a slight flashing of Acraglas which had seeped between the top of the block and the action; this flashing was peeled off with a chisel, and a half-completed recoil lug support chopped away, along with surplus epoxy between the block and clay dam.

Everything was then readied for the second application of Acraglas. A layer of masking tape was applied to the forward face, sides and bottom of the recoil lug, the trigger slot and trigger pin holes in the action were plugged with clay, and the action and underside of the barrel coated with release wax. The top of the block was scribed with an old chisel,

providing a zig-zag pattern of cuts for the Acraglas to adhere to, and the wood bedding supports around the edge of the block scraped away. A fresh dam was fashioned and the stock's trigger slot, bolt cut and screw holes plugged with clay.

Another batch of Acraglas was mixed and spread around the block with a small wooden paddle to be sure there were no "holes" in the final layer. With the barreled action supported in a vise, the stock was again brought up to the action, supported by the guide pins and C-clamp; the clamp was turned almost tight, then backed off to provide a gap for the epoxy between the action and block. The reason I glass-bed with the barrel supported in a vise is because the stock is lighter than the barreled action, so there's less likelihood of the epoxy setting up while the action is under stress.

Others disagree; if an action is being bedded with barrel screwed in, they feel the stock should be supported, with any stressing of the action due to the barrel weight being the normal stress of the rifle in firing position. For the same reason, those from this school check their bedding with a dial indicator while the rifle is in a horizontal position, while I prefer to check it with the rifle vertical in order to eliminate the bending downward of the barrel caused by its weight.

Whoever is right about how to support the rifle while the epoxy is setting up, I goofed on this job, which I had intended to be the final bedding. Unlikely as it might seem, the slight stressing of the action caused by the C-clamp was apparently enough to cause a slight bow, with a resultant low spot in the center of the bedding — according to the dial indicator, which showed a thousandth or less movement when either the front or rear screw was tightened with the other tight, but about .003 when the center screw was inserted and tightened.

The only solution was to apply a "paint coat" such as is almost invariably needed

after a normal bedding job. The action was again taped, plugged and waxed, the bedding area cleaned and lightly roughed, and a small amount of Acraglas without floc mixed and smoothed over the top of the existing layer of epoxy, leaving a buffer about .012-inch thick. This time the stock was held to the action with a wrapping of surgical tubing, also obtained from Bob Brownell; the tubing distributes the holding force all along the action, rather than at one or two points. After curing, the cleanup included removing all epoxy which had flowed up the side of the action, leaving a few thousandths clearance which doesn't detract from the rifle's appearance, but which will allow the bedding block to shift a bit with the wood, if it has a mind to, without affecting the bedding one whit.

This last effort was apparently a success; the dial indicator showed no more than a thousandth movement when any of the screws was tightened or loosened. But I don't yet know whether this will be the final bedding for the rifle; I've only had the rifle at two matches since the action block was installed, and it was too blustery to tell how well the rifle was shooting. It did turn in some .5 and .6-inch 200-yard groups, which were a good sign, but it will take much better conditions than we've had this spring before I can tell if this bedding system will regularly produce the sub-quarter-minute groups of which the rifle is capable.

However, logic tells me that this system holds the key to both improved accuracy and ability to hold zero in a hunting or target magazine rifle. It can't help but help. It may be that the best results will be obtained with a softer, vibration-damping separater material, or with blocks which extend only from the front of the trigger to the receiver ring, leaving the tang floating; but the only way to know will be to experiment. Once I'm certain what works best with the bench guns I plan to see what it'll do with an accurate Remington 700V .22-250. ●

THE RIGID RUGER

INSTALLING A BEDDING BLOCK IN A MAGAZINE RIFLE

By BOB BRACKNEY

BEFORE FIBERGLASS stocks and glued-in actions came into widespread use, benchrest shooters used to spend a lot of time and effort worrying with the bedding in their rifles. Some of the tougher ranges around the country probably caused many perfectly good rifles to be torn apart and rebuilt simply because a bedding problem was the first thought most of us had whenever a rifle seemed to go sour. In fact, it wasn't uncommon to see a shooter hunkered down over his stock between relays, scratching away at a suspected high spot

(I've even seen Neal Knox doing this with a certain 40X-BR!). Since fiberglass stocks and glued-in actions are almost non-existent in the hunting fields, those problems that once plagued benchresters still plague hunters who prize accurate rifles.

While epoxy and fiberglass bedding compounds have been used for many years, they aren't the cure-all that some believe; the problem is in the wood stocks themselves. A rifle could be a real stinger at one point, and a few weeks later it would get sick as the stock responded to humidity changes — for warping wood

will bend epoxy bedding. One Arizona shooter I know hauled an excellent Heavy Varmint Rifle to a match in Ohio, only to discover that the epoxy bedding had begun oozing out around the action like toothpaste. This was apparently caused by the change in humidity from around 10% to around 90%, which caused the wood to swell.

An even greater problem is caused by the compression of the wood as the guard screws are tightened — whether or not a layer of epoxy is present. While most action designs give ample support in the receiver ring area, the bedding surface is often weak and inadequate under the rear tang. The difficulty is not so much with the action itself, but due to the cuts that have to be made in the stock to accommodate the trigger, bolt release, and safety mechanisms. Even in the best designs, there often is only a small pillar of support for the rear tang. More times than not, the bedding will go to pot simply because the stock is compressed slightly in that area. This allows the action to be warped as the guard screws are drawn up, and bad things usually begin to show up on the target.

A number of methods were used by benchresters to cope with this problem,

In choosing a Ruger 77 to illustrate the installation of a bedding block, Brackney probably picked the roughest of all actions, due to its many irregular features, and angled front action screw. It required much metal whittling, as this photo indicates.

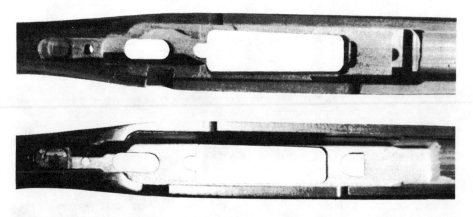

Benchrest shooters have learned that any wood stock is inherently unstable in the action area, and that action stressing — and resultant impairment of accuracy — will occur even if the action area has been "fiberglassed." One solution is to install an aluminum bedding block, as Bob Brackney has done on the Ruger stock on the opposite page. The upper photo, above, shows the original factory inletting, and the lower photo shows how little wood was left after the stock was milled to accept the bedding block.

usually involving a pillar of metal or bedding compound around each guard screw. These pillars went completely through the stock, and took the strain of the guard screws rather than the wood itself.

The big solution came with the creation of the full length, full depth aluminum bedding block. The wood was completely removed in the action area, leaving only a hollow outside shell. Then the wood was replaced with the bedding block and epoxy. This seemed to solve all the problems. The aluminum couldn't be compressed by the guard screws, and of course, it was unaffected by moisture and humidity changes. At first, some of us thought that temperature changes might cause difficulty, since aluminum has a relatively high coefficient of expansion. This didn't come to pass however, and my own rifles that use this system perform as

well in near freezing temperatures as they do in the summer heat.

With all these good attributes, it seems that the bedding block technique should also be applied to hunting rifles. While hunting rifles aren't expected to deliver anything approaching benchrest accuracy, they are subjected to all manner of weather conditions, and they have a whole array of accuracy-destroying, built-in problems. Chief among these are light-weight stocks with the action area almost completely cut away to accommodate the mechanism, and guard screws which are often put in tight enough to embarrass King Kong. As a result, the action is invariably warped into place when the rifle is assembled, and honest-to-goodness "minute of angle" accuracy becomes an elusive goal.

The bedding blocks used in benchrest rifles are simple affairs, with no magazine,

no floor plate, and usually no safety mechanism to cope with. The job is considerably more difficult with a hunting rifle, but if carefully done the results can be completely satisfactory, and there will be no visible change in the exterior of the rifle.

To demonstrate this technique, a brand new Ruger M-77 .270 was used — perhaps the toughest action to fit to a block. Some may feel that doing these things to a fine rifle like the Ruger is about as sacrilegious as installing a big-block Chevy in a Bentley. I guess the answer is "If the Chevy runs better, why not?" I'll admit though, the Ruger lay in pieces on my bench for several days while I psyched myself up for the job, and several times during the project I wondered if I shouldn't be placed in a "home."

The various Remington actions are the simplest to work with since they have a straight forward cylindrical shape. The Mauser, Model 70, and Ruger are much more complex and require a lot more measuring and fitting as you go along. The key is to work carefully and try to plan about three steps ahead so you don't cut something off that you will need later.

The block was machined from a 1 1/4 x 1 1/2 inch bar of 6061-T6 aluminum alloy, and is long enough to extend the full length of the action and project about an inch forward of the receiver ring to provide barrel support. After the bar was smoothed up on all four sides and coated with layout blue, a center line was scribed the full length of the top and bottom surfaces. A lot of mistakes can be eliminated by taking all basic measurements from only two or three reference points on the action. The points I used were the back surface of the recoil lug, the rear guard screw hole, and the flat on the underside of the action behind the recoil lug. Lines were scribed on the block marking these points, making no

In the top view of the block, just below, note the special recess around the top of the magazine area, which has been milled to accept the magazine box section. Note also, the miscellaneous other cuts to provide clearance for action parts.

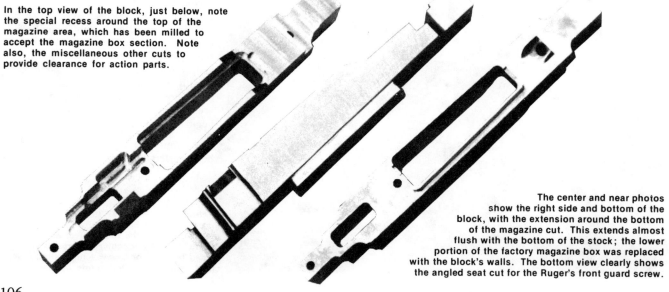

The center and near photos show the right side and bottom of the block, with the extension around the bottom of the magazine cut. This extends almost flush with the bottom of the stock; the lower portion of the factory magazine box was replaced with the block's walls. The bottom view clearly shows the angled seat cut for the Ruger's front guard screw.

allowance for the thickness of the bedding material which would be used between the action and the block. The bedding material will be compensated for later, through the use of shims; at this stage we are interested only in fitting the block to the action without the complication of leaving clearance here and there for the bedding.

Next, the slot for the recoil lug was milled and the hole was drilled for the rear guard screw using a No. 11 drill, which is just about body diameter of the 10x32 guard screw. This snug fit was used to help align everything and was also used later to keep the block straight while it was being glued into the stock. After the final bedding was completed, the hole was drilled out to allow proper clearance around the guard screw.

The top of the block was then milled to fit the receiver so the rear guard screw could be screwed in while the recoil lug was in firm contact with its bearing surface in the block. A line was scribed around the rear tang and the block was milled away about 1/16 inch inside this line so that, in a top view, the block was completely covered by the action, except for the extension in the front which would support the rear of the barrel.

The magazine problem was attacked next. In the Ruger action the top of the magazine box is curved inward to form two lips, which aid in proper alignment of the stacked cartridges to provide improved feeding. While it would be possible to mill a cavity in the block large enough for the entire magazine box to slip into (just like in the factory stock), I didn't do this for a couple of reasons. The magazine box should not touch the block or bedding at any point, and if the cavity in the block is made large enough to allow adequate clearance all around the box, then the block becomes quite thin on the sides, and the strength we are trying to build in is reduced. Besides, I think it looks neat to open the floor plate and see a polished aluminum interior rather than a piece of stamped metal. So, I compromised and used only the top 1/2-inch of the magazine box.

First, the cavity was milled completely through the block to an exact match of the inside dimensions of the box. The distance from the back of the recoil lug to the inside of the box was measured on the action, and the measurement was transferred to the block using the recoil lug bearing shoulder as a reference point. Then the outline of the cavity was scribed on both the top and bottom sides of the block, using the box itself as a pattern. Most of the metal was removed with drills, then the cavity was cleaned up right to the scribe line, using a long 1/4-inch milling cutter. A line was scribed around the outside of the box, and the cavity was opened up to about .020 inch beyond this

line, to a depth which would just allow the top section of the magazine box to drop in. After the rifle was completed, the magazine box section was permanently fastened in place in the receiver with epoxy; there is about .020 inch clearance between it and the block on all sides. Clearance at the bottom edge of the box section was provided by the shims which will be described next. The joint between the bottom of the magazine box section and the block itself is barely detectable and the magazine follower slides past it with no problems. As a result of all this, the inside of the rifle is pretty, the maximum possible strength has been

retained in the block, and the rifle feeds as flawlessly as ever.

The front guard screw hole on the Ruger is a little different since it goes through on a 30° angle, but locating it was no problem. Cardboard shims about 1/16-inch thick were made to fit between the block and the receiver at the rear guard screw and at the main bearing surface behind the recoil lug. This established clearance for the bedding material, and the finished relationship between the receiver and block.

Then the front guard screw was installed in the receiver and the receiver

The position of the Ruger's angled front guard screw is located on the bedding block by placing the receiver on the block.

The action, with the upper section of the magazine box fitted to it, is shown with the discarded lower portion of the magazine box.

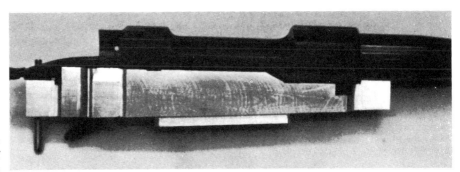

In preparation for epoxying the bedding block into the stock, the finished block is mounted to the receiver using the special guard screw. Note that Brackney has extended the forward section of the block to provide stable support for epoxy bedding below the barrel shank.

Before final bedding of the receiver against the block [which will already have been epoxied into the stock], masking tape is placed on the action to create necessary clearances, and modeling clay used to fill recesses.

107

was held in place against the top of the block, on the shims, with the screw extending along the side of the block. The recoil lug was held firmly against the shoulder on the block, and a line was scribed on each side of the guard screw. A center line was then scribed between these two, and extended around to the bottom side of the block. The block was clamped in the milling machine vise with these lines in a vertical position and the hole was drilled through.

The cutout for the trigger was milled next and the center guard screw hole was drilled. The factory trigger on the Ruger strikes me as being kind of a headache, so I used a Canjar and simply milled out enough material to allow minimum clearance around the trigger and safety mechanisms. Finally, the bolt handle relief was cut and the block was finished except for milling the bottom side to the proper depth to fit into the stock. This was not done until after the stock was opened up.

You will find out how firm your convictions really are when you clamp that handsome stock into the milling machine vise and get ready to remove all the factory inletting. The stock was held in the vise between cardboard pads, and was supported on each end with blocks placed between the stock and the milling machine table. The bottom side of the stock was placed flat against the bottom of the vise and a plywood template was made which was a snug fit in the bottom of the magazine cutout. This template provided some support for the sides of the stock as the vise was tightened; the stock is naturally weak at this point, and will get weaker as the milling progresses.

The milling must be done very carefully, with light cuts, since the stock can't be held very tightly. If you get carried away, the cutter may hang up and jerk the stock right out of the vise, and probably will just about cut it in half in the process. I used a long 1/2-inch two-flute cutter operated at a high spindle speed for most of the job, and then used 1/4-inch and 3/16-inch cutters to get into the corners. All wood was removed down to a depth that left a 1/16-inch web in the bottom of the trigger guard mortise, and the cavity was extended right to the top edge of the inletting in all areas. The idea is that the block should drop into place with about 1/16-inch clearance on all sides.

I also free floated the barrel, which may or may not be a good idea. The conventional wisdom is that a lightweight barrel will usually give the best accuracy with some up pressure at the fore-end tip. This may be true with many rifles using conventional bedding systems, but in this case, it doesn't make much sense to go to all this trouble to create a super stable

stock and then let the barrel bear on a long, skinny piece of wood. Also, it seems to me that consistent group placement is even more important in a hunting rifle than the absolute size of the group itself, and a pressure-bedded barrel can cause group placement to change over a period of time if the fore-end is not absolutely stable. Finally, whenever possible, I like to shoot sitting or prone with a tight sling, and the floating barrel is less affected by sling tension. Anyway, I did it and I'm glad!

The bottom of the block was then milled to an angle which matched the bottom line of the stock. To hold the block in place on the action while measuring for this operation, a special rear guard screw was turned on the lathe. The shank is 10x32, which is a snug fit in the hole in the block. The head is about 1 inch long, and was turned to a diameter that would just fit through the rear guard screw hole in the trigger guard. With the guard held in place with masking tape, the receiver and block assembly was dropped into the stock so the head of the guard screw protruded through the bottom of the stock and the hole in the guard. This located the block in the stock in proper relation to the receiver and the stock itself. Measurements were then taken to determine how much to cut off the bottom of the block and the proper angle of the cut so the finished block could rest on the remaining wood in the bottom of the cavity in the stock.

I decided to get fancy and milled an extension around the magazine cutout in the block which fits flush with the bottom line of the stock when the block is in position. This fills the gap which was formerly filled (more or less) by the bottom edge of the magazine box.

The final step on the block was to cut the angled seat for the front guard screw bearing plate, which was located using the existing hole in the bottom of the stock, and cut with a 5/8-inch milling cutter (this is just the right size and makes the cut with one pass). Then the recoil lug shoulder on the block was cut back about 1/16 inch to allow room for bedding material at that point.

The next step was to epoxy the block into the stock. After a thorough degreasing, the block was attached to the action, using the shims and special guard screw (with release agent applied) as previously described. Release agent was applied to the inside of the trigger and magazine cutouts, and the bottom of the block was coated with Duro Epoxy-Steel. A coat of epoxy was also applied to the bottom of the cavity in the stock and the barrelled action was set in place. The barrel was supported with paper shims between it and the fore-end tip and the action was checked carefully to make sure

it was in proper position, with the bottom of the block bearing against the wood at the bottom of the stock cavity. The excess was carefully removed from the exposed portions of the block around the trigger, magazine, and the front guard screw, and the epoxy was then allowed to cure. When the special guard screw was removed, the block remained firmly glued in place.

The gap between the sides of the block and the wood was filled with Brownell's Acraglas since something of thin consistency was needed to get into the small space. To get the Acraglas into the bottom of the gap, I bought a 50 cc plastic hypodermic syringe from the local veterinary supply store, with the biggest needle they had. Glass flock was added to the Acraglas to a consistency which could be easily forced through the needle, and the gap was filled to a point just below the bedding surfaces. Little dams were made from masking tape to keep the goo from flowing out of the bolt handle cut and into the recoil lug mortise. After the glass had cured, the rest of the hole was filled during the bedding process.

There are many theories floating around about rifle bedding, and there is no question that a number of different techniques can be successful. There are, however, several points which I think are generally agreed upon, and a brief description of these is necessary to explain the approach I took on the Ruger.

First, the receiver should not bind in the stock. This seems to be important since the receiver will flex to some degree each time the rifle is fired, and it should return to exactly the same position in the bedding after each shot. If it fits too tightly along the sides at any point, it may not return to the same bed each time, and accuracy will be affected. My own preference is to bed the rifle in such a manner that the barrelled action will literally fall out of the stock when the guard screws are removed. This means that a few thousandths of clearance must be provided around all the vertical surfaces, except for the back side of the recoil lug. I also check to see that the action can be moved fore and aft a barely perceptible amount when the screws are out to assure that none of the corners are binding. The alternative to all this is to bed the receiver tight enough so it can't move at all, which is exactly what is accomplished with a glue-in. While I've been able to make various Mausers, Model 70's, and similar designs shoot fairly well when bedded tight, I invariably get the best results the other way.

Second, the action must lie in its bed without any warping or stressing as the guard screws are drawn up. This can be checked with a dial indicator clamped to the barrel with the indicator leg bearing against the bottom side of the fore-end tip. As the guard screws are alternately loosened and tightened, the indicator should register no more than about .005-inch movement. Zero movement is bad because that indicates that the action is stuck in the bedding, and I consider .001 to .002-inch a "perfect" bedding job.

Third, actions that do not have considerable bedding area forward of the front guard screw usually require some support under the barrel for an inch or so ahead of the receiver.

Fourth, the downward pull exerted by the guard screws should be borne only by certain specific bedding areas on the bottom of the receiver, and not by all the miscellaneous little flats around the trigger, the safety, the bottom of the magazine box, etc. In the case of the Ruger, the bearing surfaces are the flat of the rear tang, the flats around the middle guard screw and along the sides of the magazine, the surface back of the recoil lug, and about one inch of the barrel. The bottom, sides, and front of the recoil lug do not touch.

Finally, be sure that clearance is provided all around the trigger and safety mechanisms, the magazine box, the guard screws and the bolt handle. If any of these places start acting like recoil lugs, anything can (and will) show up on the target.

The simplest way to provide the necessary clearances in the bedding is to tape the action as shown in the photographs. One layer of masking tape is about .004-inch thick and this is enough to do the job in most areas. A double thickness was used on the bottom and sides of the recoil lug.

After the taping was completed, the fit of the action in the stock was checked, and a little wood was scraped off here and there so the action could drop into place easily without hanging up on the tape. A sheet metal plate was cut to fit up into the magazine port in the receiver, and then the cavity was filled level with modeling clay, as were all the other holes in the bottom of the action. The action and guard screws were then coated with release agent.

The top of the block was thoroughly degreased and roughed up with coarse emery, and a coat of release agent was applied to the inside of the trigger and magazine cavities in the block. The cavities were then filled with wadded up paper.

When I reached for the Devcon F to do the bedding, I discovered the shelf was bare, so I substituted Micro-Bedding, which is a dark brown pure epoxy compound. This is actually a very good product, and some of my rifles which were bedded with it years ago still perform as well as ever. Because of the brown color, the material isn't noticeable around the edges, and the only place the bedding shows at all on the finished rifle is in some of the corners and along one side of the tang where the factory took some liberties with the inletting.

The barreled action was then placed in the bedding material and gradually worked down into position. The guard screws were started in their holes, but were used primarily to keep things straight and keep the holes open. The barrel was supported in place with paper shims at the fore-end tip, and when the action was down to the proper position the guard screws were still loose. This is particularly important in the case of the rear guard screw since it is very easy to warp the rear tang enough to cause the bedding to be low at that point. After the excess epoxy was cleaned off, the bedding was allowed to cure overnight. The important point here is that the action was simply lying in the bedding compound, completely unstressed by the guard screws, clamps, rubber bands, weights, or anything else.

When the bedding had cured, the barreled action was removed. This has to be done carefully when you are dealing with a lightweight barrel and stock, and particularly with a straight-sided receiver like the Ruger. The straight sides drag against the bedding and it takes a little more fooling around than is usually required with a round receiver like the Remington. Just have faith.

After the trigger and magazine cavities were opened up and the action cleaned, the rifle was assembled (minus trigger and magazine spring) to check the bedding with the dial indicator. We got lucky and the maximum reading obtained at the fore-end tip was just over .001-inch. Sometimes a second bedding job is required to get things right, but this usually doesn't happen with the bedding block. I think the reason is that clearance has been provided for in most areas, and the points that are in contact all contain a uniform thickness of bedding material, as established earlier by the cardboard shims. As a result, there is no problem with uneven shrinkage in critical areas.

After polishing the bolt, bolt lug ways, and the feed ramp at the front of the magazine, the magazine box section was epoxied into place and the rifle was ready for final assembly. The front guard screw was tightened to about 35 inch-pounds, and the center and rear screws were tightened to 20.

There hasn't been time for any real testing of the finished product, but the initial results have been interesting — the silly thing thinks it's a benchrest rifle. Five 3-shot groups were fired using 130-grain Sierra bullets and 59.5 grains H-450. The smallest was 3/8-inch, the largest was just over 5/8-inch, and the average was just over 1/2-inch, which I think is good enough for government work! These groups may be flukes, and I'm perfectly happy with any lightweight hunting rifle that will consistently shoot under an honest inch. Time will tell after I've had a chance to shoot it a little more.

The total job took between 25 and 30 hours, which would mean that it would be a pretty expensive project to turn over to your friendly neighborhood gunsmith, even if you could talk him into it. Since this was the first Ruger I had done, there was a lot of non-productive figuring, head scratching and pipe lighting going on, and the total time could probably be reduced considerably.

The whole point, however, is that most folks think there is nothing prettier than a wood stock, and by going to all this trouble the wood stock can be made as stable and reliable as the glass stock on your favorite target rifle. Whether it's worthwhile is an individual matter. ●

RUGER NUMBER 1

By FRANK de HAAS

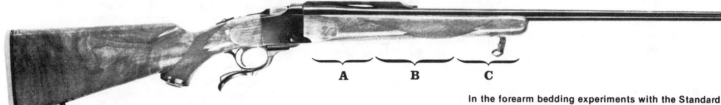

Bedding the fore-end to improve accuracy and zero retention

In the forearm bedding experiments with the Standard Model Ruger No. 1, it was found that the way the forearm was fitted and bedded, and what spot the forearm was rested on during firing, greatly affected the accuracy, point of impact and zero retention. Three forearm rest positions were used during the tests: [A] rear of forearm, [B] center of forearm, and [C] front of forearm. The test rifle always gave the best accuracy with the rifle resting on the rear end of the forearm. Sighted in with the forearm rested on its forward end, the point of impact would drop if the rifle were then fired from the center position, and drop still more if fired from the rear position.

THE RUGER NO. 1 falling block single shot rifle has a 2-piece stock and forearm. The butt stock is securely attached to the action with a through stock bolt, the best method. With the wood well mortised and fitted to the receiver, as is the case with the No. 1, and the stock bolt drawn up tight, the stock is about as secure as it can be made; accuracy and zero retention of the rifle is in no way affected. The separate forearm, however, and the way it is attached and bedded can, and often does, affect both accuracy and zero retention. This is especially true in regard to the Ruger No. 1.

While most Ruger No. 1 shooters are interested in getting the best accuracy from their rifles, those who use this rifle for hunting are just as interested in having the rifle stay in zero. One is as important as the other. By manipulation of the forearm on the No. 1, it is often possible to get the finest accuracy that the barrel is capable of delivering, and have the rifle stay perfectly sighted-in over a long period of time as well. But obtaining and maintaining both with the factory bedded forearm is often difficult, if not impossible.

A great amount of time and effort was spent in designing the Ruger No. 1 rifle, with special emphasis on the forearm and its attachment and bedding. Due to the design of the action, some of its parts had to be mounted in front of the receiver below the barrel. Not wishing to attach any of these parts to the barrel, the designers chose to make a projecting arm forward of the receiver on which to mount the parts, and making this arm a permanent part of the receiver. In so doing they made it long and heavy enough so that it could also double as a hanger for the forearm.

A single screw was used to attach the forearm to the hanger, but instead of putting the screw at a 90-degree angle through the forearm and into the hanger, Ruger drilled the hole at a rearward angle so that on tightening the screw the forearm would be drawn up against the hanger and back against the receiver. This fastening method positively prevents the forearm from moving forward due to recoil. On early No. 1 rifles the forearm screw was threaded directly into the hanger. Now the hanger is made deeper at its end, a hole drilled across it for a heavy pin, and this pin drilled and tapped for the forearm screw. This improved fastening arrangement allows torque-free tightening of the screw and some lateral

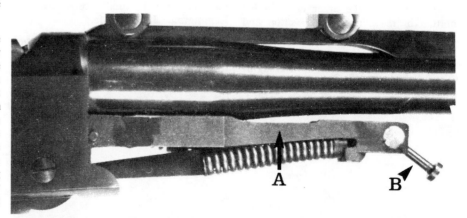

The Ruger No. 1 rifle has an arm [A] made integral with, and projecting forward of the receiver, with the forearm being attached to it by the single forearm screw [B]. The screw is positioned at a rearward angle as shown, and draws the forearm tight against the hanger and barrel, and against the receiver. This arm, which is generally referred to as the forearm hanger, also houses and holds some of the mainspring and ejector parts. Although appearing rigid, the end of this arm can be flexed by finger pressure.

110

Rifle 51 May/June 1977

movement so that the forearm tip automatically aligns itself with the barrel. By altering the bedding of the forearm against the hanger, the entire forearm could be made to be free of the barrel, contact the barrel its entire length, or just have the front part of the forearm contact the barrel with various amounts of pressure. Testing in the Ruger factory must have revealed that the best accuracy was usually obtained with the forearm bedded so that its tip contacted the barrel with considerable upward pressure, and this is the bedding method Ruger now employs on all No. 1 rifles.

Most Ruger No. 1 rifles are reasonably accurate with the forearms bedded in this manner, but accuracy and zero retention can usually be improved by experimenting with individual rifles, which the factory cannot economically do. However, some owners have reported experimenting with the forearms on their No. 1's and have found that better accuracy is often possible with a minor bedding change. We have also heard from shooters who are well satisfied with the accuracy they are getting from their No. 1's, but state that their rifles do not maintain zero.

Wood is a rather unstable material; if the forearm is bedded so that its tip exerts pressure against the barrel, any slight change in the forearm such as warpage, shrinkage or swelling is apt to have some effect on the barrel and consequently on the zero of the rifle. Varying the tension of the forearm screw, has the same effect. Further, in rest shooting, both point of impact and grouping ability is affected if

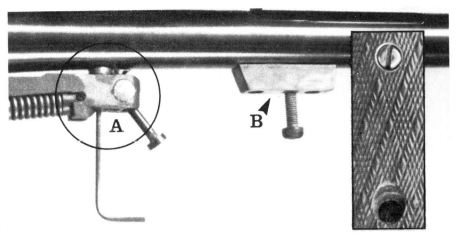

Bedding Method No. 3, shown here within the circle [A], consisted of a small setscrew [its location is indicated by the Allen wrench] installed in the end of the forearm hanger. Tightened against a small V block, this setscrew props the end of the hanger slightly away from the barrel, making the hanger very rigid to support the forearm free of the barrel. The anchor block and forearm screw is shown at point [B] which was installed for Bedding Method No. 4. The anchor block is attached to the barrel by two scope mounting screws and the forearm is inletted over it. De Haas recommends this method of forearm fastening on No. 1 rifles in calibers producing considerable recoil or if the sling swivel is attached to the forearm. The inset shows the anchor block forearm screw above, and the regular angled forearm screw in the forearm.

the rifle is not always fired with the forearm supported at the same point.

The Ruger No. 1 rifle we used for our forearm bedding experiments was the Standard Model in .22-250 caliber with 26-inch heavy sporter barrel. Frank stocked it with a Fajen semi-finished stock and forearm, making the forearm the same size and length as Ruger does on this model and bedded it the same way with the forearm tip exerting up to 12

pounds pressure against the barrel. All the test shooting was done from bench rest using a handload of 41.0 grains of 4831 powder behind the 53-grain Sierra match bullet. Four to ten 5-shot groups were fired for each test, sighting with a 10X scope, under ideal weather conditions. Some tests were repeated several times, and in most instances 20 shots (four 5-shot groups) comprised a test, starting with the barrel cold and the bore uncleaned since the previous firing, and

Forearm Bedding Test Results

RIFLE: Ruger No. 1, Standard Model, .22-250
RANGE: 100 yards, 5-shot groups
LOAD: 41.0 grains IMR-4831 with 53-grain Sierra HP Match bullet

		TIP REST		CENTER REST		REAR REST	
		Average Group Size, Inches	Point Of Impact, Inches	Average Group Size, Inches	Point Of Impact, Inches	Average Group Size, Inches	Point Of Impact, Inches
Bedding Method No. 1 (Factory bedding, forearm tip pressure against barrel)	Light pressure	1.115	-1.4			.750	-2.7
	*Medium pressure	1.275	0*			.540	-.9
	Heavy pressure	1.420	+1.0			1.305	-.6
Bedding Method No. 2 (Barrel floated, forearm free of barrel)		.693	-2.2			.678	-2.6
Bedding Method No. 3 (Hanger pressure against barrel, forearm free of barrel)		.929	-2.1	.925	-2.2	.673	+2.4
Bedding Method No. 4 (Forearm attached to barrel with anchor block & screw)	No pressure	1.265	-4.6			1.150	-5.2
	Light pressure			1.070	+.2		
	Heavy pressure	1.025	+.9			.630	+.4

*All point-of-impact figures are based on the rifle sighted-in to strike on point of aim and the forearm as factory bedded with medium tip pressure against the barrel.
Center rest figures not given can be calculated as being the average between the tip and rear rest position data.

ending with the barrel quite warm after firing at a rate of one shot per 60 to 90 seconds.

Frank worked out and installed the different bedding methods, as well as working out the testing routine in order to get the best possible test data. Before any test firing was done the rifle was carefully sighted-in to hit on point of aim at 100 yards with the forearm bedded by the factory method, and supported on the front third; no change was made in scope adjustment through all the subsequent test firing. The rifle was tested for point of impact changes with each bedding method over a period of several months. All of this required a test period of nearly two years.

After this groundwork of extended test firing was done, Mark took over the test shooting on his range, and in a planned and routine order over a period of several successive fine shooting days, repeated all of the test firings, shooting with utmost care and precision. He did all the firing in 10-shot (two 5-shot groups) relays, letting the rifle cool to about starting temperature, or up to one half hour or more, between relays. In the test shooting to determine the point of impact change from different forearm resting positions, he fired alternating shots on twin targets, alternating the forearm resting position with each shot. This resulted in the two groups being fired with an even temperature rise of the barrel while any variations in shooting conditions were equalized. With this method the point of impact change from one forearm rest position to another was instantly apparent.

Afterward, we also tested the rifle with the forearm resting on the center third, the normal holding and resting position. In all cases with the four different bedding methods tried, the center rest position group sizes and point of impact change was midway between those fired from the front and rear rest positions of the same bedding method. Following are the tests we conducted, with a description of the forearm bedding method employed in that test or tests. Bedding method No. 1 was the same as factory bedding, with forearm tip pressure against the barrel. Our test rifle was quite accurate bedded in this manner, certainly accurate enough for varmint shooting. Without changing the load, sight setting, shooting position or the tension of the forearm screw, our test rifle retained its zero and accuracy during the first months of the test period. Then the point of impact began to drop, enough so that after another three or four months the groups centered at least 1.5 inches lower than at the beginning. Checking the forearm to barrel pressure at the tip we found that the pressure had decreased so that now the forearm tip could be easily pulled away from the barrel. Apparently the forearm had warped or shrunk reducing tip pressure

and lowering the point of impact. With the lessening of the tip pressure came a slight increase in group size.

It was at this point that we made a demonstration as to the effect the forearm has on the point of impact and accuracy of the Ruger No. 1 rifle. Loosening the forearm, inserting a 3-layer strip of target paper between the forearm tip and barrel and retightening the forearm screw, pressure between tip and barrel was restored to approximately what it had been in the beginning. Doing this, the rifle returned to its former zero and accuracy. Repeating the test with the strip removed and again with it in place, the same results occurred.

More dramatic evidence of the effect the forearm has on the rifle is to carefully test fire several groups with the rifle as factory bedded, then follow it up after the rifle has cooled by firing the same number of groups with the barrel free floating. This is easily done by merely removing the forearm and firing the rifle with the tip of the forearm hanger supported. With our Number 1 this change resulted in approximately three inches drop in the point of impact.

Another easily made test which may show similar results, but less dramatically, is to test fire several groups with the rifle resting on the tip of the forearm as against the rifle rested on the rear part of the forearm. In this test the Ruger No. 1 Sporter Model is likely to show a greater change in the point of impact, and perhaps in accuracy as well, than the heavier barreled Standard Model, and the still heavier barreled Varmint Model. With the forearm of our test rifle bedded with fairly light tip pressure (estimated at about 5 to 10 pounds), with the rifle resting on the rear third of the forearm, the point of impact would drop 1.3 inches at 100 yards as compared to resting the rifle on the front third of the forearm. With the forearm bedded with fairly heavy tip pressure against the barrel (approximately 20 pounds), the point of impact at 100 yards was about 1.6 inches lower with the rear forearm support as compared to the front forearm support position. This last point of impact difference may seem insignificant at first glance, but to the varmint shooter it means that unless the rifle was rested on the same portion of the forearm as when the rifle was sighted-in, he would miss most shots at small varmints at ranges of 150 yards and over.

In the above tests we discovered that accuracy was also affected as to forearm resting position. Whether the forearm was bedded with light or heavy tip pressure against the barrel, the best accuracy was always obtained when the rifle was rested on the rear third of the forearm, although the rifle was more difficult to hold steady in this position. It

was most accurate with the heavy pressure bedding at the tip.

Even though our No. 1 Ruger rifle was quite accurate with the forearm bedded as the factory would have bedded it, we wanted to find out if there were not some other bedding method that perchance could make it a bit more accurate, and more importantly, eliminate changes in impact and group size due to the effect of the unstable wood forearm. Bedding method No. 2 consisted of the barrel free of contact with the forearm and hanger. Since the forearm hanger of the No. 1 Ruger is made free of the barrel, nothing had to be done with it in this bedding method and test. Two ways are open in test firing the rifle with this bedding method: (1) with the forearm removed and resting the rifle on the tip of the forearm hanger, or (2) with the forearm in place and either the channel sanded out or the forearm propped away from the hanger so that it is entirely free of the barrel while the rifle is supported on the forearm. We chose to use both methods, and with the forearm in place we chose to prop it away from the hanger rather than sand out the channel, since we may have wanted to repeat some of the other bedding tests with an unaltered forearm. To hold the forearm away from the barrel, we merely placed folded cardboard between the forearm and the tip of the forearm hanger.

While the forearm hanger of the No. 1 appears to be rigid, it is actually quite flexible. With the forearm removed it does not take much finger strength to flex the end of the hanger several thousandths of an inch, either by squeezing toward the barrel or pulling it away from the barrel. With the forearm attached and free of the barrel, the effect on the hanger is about the same as doubling its length, thus making it even more flexible. To us, this condition was intolerable, because with the rifle not resting on the forearm the gap between the forearm tip and barrel became considerable.

At any rate, test firing our rifle with the barrel floated, both with the forearm removed and with it in place, the rifle was fully as accurate as with any of the other bedding methods tried. To our surprise, however, there was a small, but noticeable lowering in the point of impact when resting the rifle on the rear of the forearm. We cannot explain this, nor do we care to put forth a theory for the cause. In any event, had our rifle proved decidedly more accurate with this bedding method, we could not have tolerated the forearm gap necessary to achieve a free floating barrel or the very limber forearm condition, and would have gladly chosen the second best bedding method instead.

Not unexpected, however, was that with this bedding method there was no change in the zero of the rifle over the entire period of our testing as we returned the rifle to this bedding at frequent intervals.

Bedding Method No. 3 we called "forearm hanger pressure against barrel," a method which we found worked best on our Browning M-78 single shot rifle, which also has a forearm hanger. This method is one in which a setscrew is used near the front end of the hanger to contact the barrel, and in which the forearm is attached in the normal manner but altered or otherwise adjusted to be free of the barrel. In other words, instead of having the tip of the forearm applying damping pressure to the barrel, the forearm hanger is made to do this instead. Since the steel hanger is far more stable than wood, the pressure will be more constant; theoretically there should be less point-of-aim and accuracy change than with any other type of forearm pressure. The question was whether accuracy would be equal to other methods.

To achieve this type of metal-to-metal bedding, we merely installed a setscrew near the end of the hanger and adjusted it so that the hanger was pushed slightly away from the barrel. We used a 1/4-inch long 8x32 cupped end setscrew for this, drilling the hold for it approximately .650-inch back from the end of the hanger, or just forward of the mainspring strut with the hammer in the fired position. Then we made a thin V block to fit loosely between the hanger and the barrel, positioning it over the setscrew to serve as a pillar between the screw and barrel. A 3/8-inch flat or round ended setscrew could be used, eliminating the need for the pillar block. After considerable experimenting and test shooting we found that the best performance was obtained with the setscrew tightened at least one full turn, which moves the tip of the hanger .031-inch away from the barrel (with 32 thread setscrew).

We tested the rifle both with the forearm removed, resting the rifle on the tip of the hanger, and with the forearm in place but with cardboard between the forearm and hanger tip so the forearm did not touch the barrel even when supporting the rifle. We found it much more convenient to fire the rifle with the forearm in place. Bedded this way there was no change in the zero of the rifle for a period of several months, and as long as the forearm does not touch the barrel when the rifle is fired, no zero change is expected over a much longer period. We found that our test rifle was much more accurate bedded in this manner than with the factory method, and just as accurate as the full floated barrel Method No. 2.

In addition, we had a forearm sufficiently stiffened and rigid enough so that a wide gap was not needed to keep the forearm tip free of the barrel. There still

was the point of impact change from the front to the rear forearm resting position, which we could not explain and which bothered us a bit. However, when shooting the rifle in the normal forearm rest position; that is, resting the center of the forearm on the sand bag, the accuracy delighted us. Further testing with the forearm resting just forward of the forearm screw and just to the rear of it, all within a five inch length of the center point of the forearm, accuracy and point of impact remained stable. This was exactly what we were looking and hoping for — rigid forearm, top accuracy, no point of impact change, all with a normal center-of-the-forearm hold or rest. What pleased us even more was the uniformity in accuracy and point of impact from the first shot fired from a cold and uncleaned barrel to the last shot fired after firing a string of 20 shots in four 5-shot groups.

Bedding Method No. 4 required that an anchor block be installed under the barrel, the forearm inletted over it and fastened to the barrel with a separate forearm screw through the forearm and threaded into the block. The block was made from a piece of 5/16-inch square rod about 1 1/4 inches long and attached to the barrel with two 6x48 scope mounting screws. The side that contacted the barrel was grooved to fit the barrel closely and the ends angled off as shown in the photo. It was attached about an inch forward of the hanger. Then a cavity somewhat larger than the block was chiseled into the forearm channel to allow the forearm to slip in place. A 10x32 forearm screw was then installed, along with a brass escutcheon in the forearm for the screw head. The forearm was then glass bedded over the block only, and both the factory and the new forearm screws used to hold the forearm in place while the bedding compound hardened. These screws were tightened so that the pressure between the forearm tip and barrel was approximately the same as the factory bedded forearm. After the compound had hardened and the forearm was removed, excess bedding compound in the forearm channel was sanded away leaving the channel exactly as factory made.

Reinstalled and fastened only by the new forearm screw, the forearm tip still exerted considerable upward pressure against the barrel. This was all done prior to the start of our experiments and all the prior testing was done with the block removed, which left the forearm as original except for the block cavity and forearm screw hole. Thus, we could proceed with the bedding experiments without disturbing any other part of the rifle which might have affected the zero. On testing the rifle with this forearm fastening and bedding method we found that the point of impact as compared to factory bedding changed little. Also, over

a period of several months of changing weather conditions, the zero changed less than it did with the factory bedded forearm under similar conditions.

All of this is perhaps due to the fact that the point of attachment of the forearm with this bedding method is closer to the pressure bearing forearm area of the tip, which resulted in a more solid and stable pressure contact between forearm tip and barrel. With this forearm attachment method the forearm was held rigidly in place, much more so than the factory attachment. Even if there were no accuracy improvement gained by the anchor block attachment method, this method would be the preferred one if the sling swivel is attached to the forearm and if the rifle is to be carried with a sling.

In regard to accuracy with the anchor block forearm attachment bedding method, we did this in two stages; first with the forearm tip exerting pressure on the barrel, and then with the forearm fitted free of contact with the barrel.

This last was done by merely placing a thick enough strip of cardboard between the bottom of the anchor block and forearm so that on tightening the forearm screw the forearm was just free of contact with the barrel; there was just enough free space so that a strip of target paper could be slipped between forearm and barrel with the rifle resting on the forearm. Also noted was that the point of impact changed but little from the first shot with the barrel cold and uncleaned, to the last shot with it warmed up, no more than that obtained with the rifle as factory bedded.

The anchor block forearm attachment method is a particular favorite of ours for use on full sized single shot rifles, and especially for hunting rifles chambered for a cartridge that produces considerable recoil. However, we have not found it a practical method to use on rifles having a forearm hanger such as with the Ruger No. 1 and Browning M-78 because we like to mount the block farther back than could be done in this particular instance. We believe the anchor block fastening method would prove to be better than the method Ruger now uses on heavy caliber rifles if the unused hanger tip (about .750-inch) were cut off and the block mounted .750-inch forward of the hanger, with the bottom of the block made with a forward lip to serve as an addition recoil lug.

After all the tests with the different forearm bedding and attachment methods on our Ruger No. 1 test rifle had been made, we spread the many targets that we had fired and made our evaluation as to which was the best forearm attachment-bedding method to use for that rifle. We wanted the best accuracy that the rifle was capable of producing, but we were just as much interested in zero retention. The targets and the notes we had made on them led us to the conclusion that with this particular rifle best performance was obtained with Bedding Method No. 3, the forearm hanger pressured against the barrel via the setscrew, with the forearm completely free of contact with the barrel.

•

Inletting the 'Swamped' Octagonal Barrel

**The classic
18th Century
'thin-waisted' tube
was tough to bed
— and still is**

A "swamped" barrel, which is thinner along its center than at either end, is shown clamped to the stock blank with the inletting jig rails lying on each side of the barrel. The barrel shown here is a bored and profiled blank, not yet rifled.

By JOHN BIVINS

URING THE EIGHTEENTH and early nineteenth centuries. . . and, in fact, for two centuries earlier than that. . .makers of rifle barrels commonly forged the exterior profiles of their finished barrels to a configuration which the early smiths referred to as "swamped." No longer a word in our modern vocabulary, this term meant something with a sunken surface, or a long object that has become thin. In a rifle, it refers to a barrel profile that tapers gradually from a relatively large breech to a small diameter a few inches from the muzzle, flaring abruptly at that point to result in a muzzle diameter as much as 1/8-inch larger than the smallest point. In such a barrel, the breech diameter may be as much as 5/32-inch larger than the muzzle. Generally speaking, rifle barrels of the seventeenth and eighteenth centuries tend to have a good bit more swamp than barrels made at the end of the eighteenth century and after. Wheellock and "jager" barrels have a particularly pronounced swamp due to their shortness. After the first quarter of the nineteenth century, rifle barrels tended to be relatively straight,

the swamped barrel having gone out of style with the advent of the percussion period.

Making a barrel with such a profile was no simple task in the eighteenth century, and it is not a great deal easier today, in terms of tooling. Early American gunsmiths, in producing longrifle barrels, not infrequently forged the barrel in two or three separate pieces, joining the short sections by "jump" welding them together. Such a method made it easier to make the longitudinal welds, since handling a short piece of work is more convenient, and it was also simpler to produce the considerable variation in barrel diameter that a swamped barrel would have. Today, the few barrel makers that do make swamped barrels simply mill the tapered-and-flared profile into a round blank. The set-up for such work, however, is rather complex, requiring a follower-mill and a cam cut to the desired profile of the barrel to be milled. Such work requires no small understanding of precision machining and engineering, which is why few barrel makers offer swamped muzzleloading

barrels, and why such barrels often cost twice what a constant-diameter or straight-taper octagonal barrel would.

Why did early smiths bother to make a barrel of such a pattern, when they were obviously more work to finish and to inlet? Theories on this are varied, and some of them aren't sound. The principal reason for the swamped barrel was to save weight. For example, if a hunting rifle of .50 caliber is to be built in the style of an American rifle of circa 1770, the minimum diameter of the breech should be approximately 1 1/16-inch. If the barrel were made 42 inches long, and the breech diameter of the barrel carried the full length, the barrel alone would weigh over 14¼ pounds, and the entire rifle perhaps 16½ pounds! A fine bench-gun weight, perhaps, but not just the thing to carry into a tree-stand after whitetails, unless you have the build of a Sumo wrestler. Taking the same .50 barrel, however, and tapering it to 3/4 or 13/16-inch six to ten inches from the muzzle, and allowing it to flare again to 7/8 or 15/16-inch, results in a weight loss of eight or nine pounds from the cumbersome straight tube. The resulting rifle will weigh perhaps eight pounds, yet the breech will remain substantial enough to support any conceivable charge of black powder.

The question remaining, however is why early rifle barrels are flared at the muzzle. Many, of course, were not. . .especially on eighteenth-century rifle barrels made in southeastern Pennsylvania, which were occasionally a simpler straight-taper. One modern theory proposed for the flared muzzle was that the added mass tended to damp barrel-whip in firing, which is possible. Although early gunsmiths had a less than perfect understanding of interior ballistics, they did understand to a surprising degree the relationship of barrel vibration to accuracy. Another theory embraced by some current longrifle philosophers is that the flare at the muzzle added weight at that point needed for steady offhand shooting, also a valid point. However, I strongly suspect that neither of these explanations comes as close to the truth as the fact that early smiths simply wanted to produce as beautiful a form as possible.

Art in the sixteenth and seventeenth centuries, when the rifled barrel was being brought to perfection, emphasized the curvilinear form. The swamped barrel with its flared muzzle answered this artistic requirement nicely, in addition to saving weight. Certainly a short and stiff wheellock barrel had little need of barrel damping with a heavy muzzle, nor would a flared muzzle have contributed significantly to shifting the balance point forward in such a gun. The latter would have been more significant in a longrifle barrel.

If early gunsmiths considered weight, balance, and a beautiful sweeping curve in a rifle barrel to be important features, why should we think otherwise when we endeavor to recreate muzzleloading rifles that seek in all other respects to emulate the art of the baroque and rococo periods? It is my own considered opinion, and I say this in full knowledge that wrath from several quarters will descend upon my bruised brow, that one cannot expect to make a *correct* American longrifle in the eighteenth-century style with a *straight* octagonal barrel with no taper or swamp. A swamped barrel affects the entire architecture of a flintlock's stock, from the form of the wrist to the size and delicacy of the forearm. The design of a fine gun is the result of a closely interrelated set of details joined harmoniously. . .whatever the period. . .and in an early longrifle, the loss of the visual impact and nice balance resulting from the use of a straight barrel rather than a swamped or tapered tube is quite significant.

In addition to the expense of a

The rails are shown clamped to the barrel. Note the closer spacing of the clamps nearest the muzzle. This is necessary in order for the rails to conform with the barrel's rapidly flaring profile at this point. The stock is then drilled for wood screw pilot holes; for No. 8 screws, use a No. 49 drill to insure a firm grip.

With wood screws installed and the clamps removed, the backsaw is used to cut the barrel profile into the blank. The saw blade should be pressed firmly against the inside of the rails, and long strokes taken. Note the use of the black tape as a depth gauge.

swamped barrel, however, we have another obstacle in our path toward constructing an ideal longrifle, and that is the inletting of the swamped barrel. Although straight barrels can be let in swiftly with several different efficient machines, the swamped barrel demands a considerable amount of tedious hand work, and has been considered difficult enough to discourage no small number of gunstockers from the task.

Here is where, however, we can learn from the art of the early gunstocker, who was forever searching for ways to save time in the use of hand tools. I take no credit for this discovery. The fellow that stumbled upon it, in fact, was my good friend Wallace Gusler, former master gunsmith at Colonial Williamsburg, who probably knows more about early firearms technology than anyone alive. In

Using a wide flat chisel, a triangular piece of wood is cut away from the inside of the saw kerf for the full length of both sides of the stock.

any case, Wallace noted one day that the barrel inlet of an early Virginia rifle in his shop for repair showed unmistakable evidence of saw kerfs along the sides of the inlet. Now, such saw kerfs may be found on an old stock with a straight barrel, since it was an easy matter to cut straight lines with a common rabbet saw. But this barrel inlet was *curved* to fit a heavily swamped barrel.

It occurred to Wallace that the stocker must have used some sort of jig to guide a short hand or back-saw in cutting a curved line to assist in the inletting. The system which he developed from this has proven to be efficient, and I have little doubt that it duplicates what early gunstockers used themselves. It certainly saves considerable time as well as preventing yawning gaps between the stock and barrel. While fiberglass is a perfectly acceptable method to bed a modern sporter action, it has no place as a gap-hider under the full length of a flintlock barrel, so we must use any method that we can to inlet a barrel tightly in the first place.

The "jig" used in this method is nothing more than a pair of cold-rolled 3/8-inch square mild steel rods, a bit longer than the length of your unbreeched barrel. To prepare these "rails" for use, they must be drilled full-length with a series of holes to take No. 1 — 8 round-head wood screws with a slip fit. They will be used to fasten the rails tightly to the stock blank. My rails have seventeen holes, most of them spaced three inches apart. Five holes nearest the muzzle end are spaced 1½ inches apart to adequately allow for better conformation where the barrel rapidly changes diameter near the muzzle.

In drilling the screw holes in the rails, the hole center must be placed as close to the outside edge of the rail as possible without the drill running through the "wall" of the rail. This should be done on a drill press. The reason for placing the screw holes to the outside as far as possible is to allow a sufficient amount of wood between the wood screw and the barrel inlet to finish-shape the stock. For this reason, take care also not to place a screw hole much closer than 3½ inches from the breech end of the rail, since a stock is a good bit thicker at the lock mortise, and with larger sizes of locks, not enough wood could be removed at that point to cut away a screw hole in the stock blank.

In using this inletting system, the upper part of your stock blank must be cut away and planed true, just as you would proceed for usual hand-inletting. Use a good-sized machinist's vise to hold your stock during inletting. Establish a centerline on top of the blank, allowing for cast-off unless you have a thick blank. Then chisel away enough wood at the

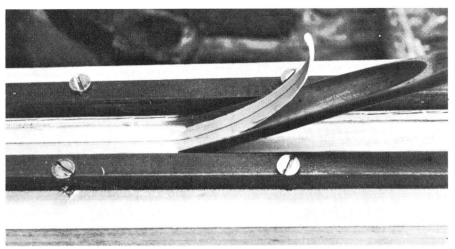

The bulk of the wood in the barrel channel is removed with a large gouge. The rails are left on the blank to avoid damaging the sharp edges of the inlet.

The barrel channel is shown gouged to within 1/16-inch of full depth, and the rails are removed. Note the penciled depth notations on the blank for periodic checking of the channel depth.

Bivins uses a rabbet plane modified into an octagon shape for planing to depth. For use in hardwoods, particularly figured maple, such planes should have a relatively steep angle to the iron, and the iron should be set for a fine cut.

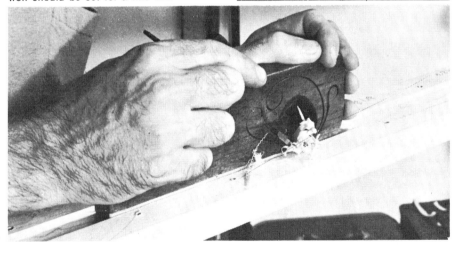

breech end of the blank for the barrel, when placed on top of the blank, to butt against the line which you consider to be the top of the recoil area. Remove the breech plug before making these initial cuts; it can be inletted after the barrel is in the wood to full depth.

The bottom barrel flat should have full contact with the top of the stock blank at the breech after this relieving cut is made. Align the barrel with your centerline, and clamp the barrel to the blank at the breech and muzzle with C-clamps. Don't clamp in the center of the barrel. . . swamped barrels need to be treated with a certain amount of respect in inletting, for they can be bent more easily than a

straight one. Most modern muzzle-loading barrels are made of free-machining screw-stock, and while quite resilient, should not be bent or levered an unreasonable amount unless you have some good reason for shooting round balls around corners.

With the barrel clamped to the stock blank, lay your 3/8-inch steel rails on each side of the barrel, with the screw hole on the side of the rail away from the barrel. The five holes with the 1 1/2-inch spacing should be at the muzzle. Using a half-dozen three-inch C-clamps, clamp the rails tightly to the barrel, making sure that the rails lie flat against the top of the stock blank. Space your clamps a bit

Bivins finishes the inlet with a straight chisel so that the inletting will conform with the barrel flats. Some gunmakers, like some old-time makers, "cheat" by leaving the bottom of the barrel channel round, but Bivins says that close inletting produces a solid sound when the stock is rapped and gives slightly more strength.

The barrel is shown here inletted to depth. Note the close inletting possible with this method.

These are the tools Bivins uses for inletting the swamped barrels. All cutting edges must be kept razor-sharp. One side of the saw blade is made "safe" to avoid undercutting the guide rails.

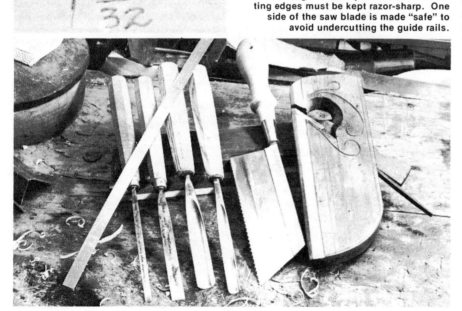

closer together around the muzzle area to make the rails conform to the abrupt flare at that point.

Make yourself a small center-punch that is a slip-fit in the rail holes. This may be easily done by turning down a piece of drill-rod with a file, turning the punch in an electric hand-drill. Slip the punch into each rail hole and give them a tap with the hammer, and then drill pilot holes into the stock blank through each of the rail holes. Pay no attention if you drill through the bottom of the stock. Wax your screw threads (unless your

stock blank is soft maple, walnut, or cherry), slip them into the rail holes, and turn them up tight. Remove all the C-clamps, pull the barrel from between the rails, and voila! You have an almost perfect profile of the swamped barrel contour. I say "almost perfect," since the rails will spring in very slightly when the barrel is pulled out, but not enough to be of consequence.

It may easily be seen from this why a 3/8-inch square rod is used for the jig rails. A larger rod would not spring and conform well to the barrel curves, while a

smaller rod would place the screw holes too close to the barrel inlet for comfort.

Take a common small back-saw and cut off about half of the blade, angling the cut back toward the handle if you like for better visibility. Take the bobbed saw down to your local saw-sharpener (if you don't have a saw-set) and have the fellow take *all of the set* off the teeth that are bent toward the right side of the blade. I guarantee that the honest mechanic who does this for you will think that you have bought a one-way pass to the funny-farm, but there is method in madness. If you did not remove the right-side set, the saw would undercut your jig rails.

Measure up from the points of the saw teeth 1/4-inch at two points and either scribe a line on the left side of the saw or tape the blade on that line to serve as a depth indicator. The tape is easier to see. Pressing the saw blade firmly against the inside of the right-hand rail (muzzle end facing you) with the left finger tips, make a light cut back-and-forth the full length of the rail from muzzle to breech. Continue cutting more or less full-length until you have reached the depth line of the saw. Avoid cutting short strokes in one point, since the saw will then tend to pack sawdust in the kerf ahead of the saw. After cutting the right side, turn the stock around in the vise and cut the other side, starting at the breech and working toward the muzzle.

After finishing your saw cuts inside both rails, take a large flat chisel and carver's mallet and make an angling-down cut perpendicular to the rails the full length of the inlet area, cutting away a triangular-shaped piece of wood. Take care not to drive the chisel much past the outside of the saw kerfs, since that will weaken the top edges of the finished forestock.

Leaving the rails screwed to the stock, use your big flat chisel to drive straight down into the stock blank inside the rails on both sides, the full length of the inlet. Don't undercut. This will correct the slightly angled cut made by the back-saw. With the set removed from the teeth of the saw on one side, the saw will angle toward the center of the stock in use.

At this point, I push the barrel back between the rails and make a pencil mark every two inches or so on the side flat of the barrel. Using fractional calipers, measure the diameter of the barrel at each pencil mark, subtract half the diameter, and add 3/8-inch for the height of your rails. Pencil a mark on the stock blank corresponding with each mark on the barrel, and pencil this half-diameter-plus-rail height on the stock blank. This will assist you in measuring for cutting the bottom of the inlet to depth; after removing the rails later for finishing cuts, subtract the 3/8-inch from the diameter figures, since you will then be measuring from the top of the stock blank.

Still with the rails in place, rough out the barrel channel with a 3/4-inch gouge, using a smaller gouge to cut the sides close to the rails, allowing the bevel of the gouge to ride along the rail to avoid actually cutting into the side of the inlet. Cut down to within 1/16 inch of the full depth of the diameters you have penciled on the stock.

Remove the rails, and make your finish cuts to the bottom of the inlet, measuring depth as you cut with a rule and straight edge at your pencil points. The finishing cuts may be made with 1/4 and 3/8-inch flat chisels, which is a little tedious, or you may use an octagonal barrel plane as most early stockers did. The plane must be slightly smaller than the smallest diameter of your barrel; I made mine from a mid-19th century rabbet plane, the sort which can still be found in antique shops for $5-6. Avoid rabbet planes with skewed blades, however, since it is exceedingly difficult to grind the iron to a correct octagonal shape.

Since such a plane cuts only one diameter of octagon, you will find that you will still need to do some roughing with chisels at the breech and muzzle. If you wish, you may "cheat" as perhaps 90 percent of early longrifle stockers did, and cut the barrel inlet round at the bottom except at the breech and muzzle. This, however, leaves only two corners of the bottom flat bearing in the inlet for most of the length of the barrel, so I prefer to inlet full-octagon for less wood removal and better strength, however marginal.

Set the barrel into the inlet, and with a light leather mallet, drive it into the inlet, taking care at the same time not to let the barrel cock or to spring excessively. You will probably find that the barrel won't seat on the first try. Lightly oil the bottom five flats of the barrel with linseed oil, or paint it with inletting black (I prefer the former, since it doesn't leave a mess), drive the barrel back in, taking care again not to cock it in the inlet. Pull the barrel, and using a coarse cut pillar file, slide the file back and forth along the inlet sides showing heaviest contact. The file is moved parallel with the inlet. After a few sessions with the file, the barrel should begin to bottom out. Re-coat with oil each time you pull the barrel from the stock, and remove high spots from the barrel inlet with chisels where the bottom three flats are beginning to touch. When the top flat of the barrel breech is flush with the breech area of the stock blank, the oil should indicate that the bottom flat of the barrel is bearing in the inlet full length. A little spottiness on the flats on each side of the bottom flat is forgiveable.

Inletting in this manner makes a barrel fit firmly in the stock, a situation which can be felt as much as seen. A finished rifle with a well-inletted barrel will have a vibrant "ring" to it when you rap on the forestock with your knuckles, while the forestock on a rifle with a poorly inletted barrel will have a dull, hollow sound when rapped.

Inlet the breechplug, taking care to have full bearing at both the barrel breech and the rear of the breechplug lug so that the stock will not split under recoil.

On a swamped barrel with a large bore (over .45 caliber), avoid cutting your barrel tenon dovetails more than .050 deep — less is desirable — since a barrel can swell slightly at the corners of too-deep dovetails with very heavy charges. Slot the tenons enough so that your barrel pins or wedges will have 1/16-inch or more of free travel fore and aft, to allow for seasonal movement of the stock wood. If you don't, your point of impact may change as much as four inches from winter to summer, depending upon the climate in your region.

Using this jig method, you should be able to let in your first barrel in less than eight hours, and after you have done two or three, four or five hours is not unreasonable. In shaping the exterior profile of the forearm, I first slab off excess wood to the depth of the rail screw holes with a handsaw, and then drawknife the forearm to shape, allowing the wood to follow the barrel contour a bit rather than being straight-sided.

Even with this efficient method, there is no question that the swamped octagonal barrel can be tedious to inlet, though any professional or amateur stocker capable of producing a decent-looking longrifle stock will have little trouble with it. The same method can, of course, be used for straight or straight-tapered barrels if you prefer to inlet them entirely by hand rather than with a router or table-saw.

The American longrifle is a subtle art form, just as the classic bolt-action sporter is. A straight line where a curved one should be, or vice-versa, can literally destroy the visual impact of the finished product. The barrel of a flintlock longrifle plays a critical role in the aesthetic makeup and balance of the piece; only a swamped barrel adequately serves the job. They are more trouble, certainly, but the result is more than worth the few extra hours at the bench if you want to own a rifle that really feels *alive* in your hands. ●

INLETTING the SIDELOCK

Whether antique or modern, the principles are the same

By JOHN BIVINS

U NTIL A LITTLE over a century ago, most hand-held guns of any description were fitted with side locks, beginning in the Fifteenth Century with matchlocks and ending with side lock breechloaders such as the Sharps, Peabody, and Springfield. The side lock was an efficient means of housing an ignition or striking mechanism in one compact unit, easily removed for inspection or repair. However, the advent of the breechloader quite naturally brought about the use of more efficient systems of concealed, self-cocking strikers, most of which could be suspended inside the frame or breechblock. Since 1900, side locks have been seen for the most part only on shotguns, the better grade of which have concealed hammers. Today, side locks are common enough again with the renewed interest in muzzleloading guns. A certain nostalgia, in addition to a strong push from the 1968 Gun Control Act, has caused many guns of the side lock type to again become popular among shooters. Such guns include a host of types from mid-eighteenth century military muskets to third quarter Nineteenth Century breechloaders, all burning black powder, and many requiring side locks for ignition. Those who contemplate stocking a Brown Bess musket or a Hawken rifle, sporterizing a "trap-door," or even building a .45-3¼ rifle on a salvaged 1858 Sharps action might well give consideration to how a side lock should be properly fitted in a stock blank.

A stockmaker's reputation is made on the quality of every aspect of his work, not simply on external appearances. It hardly seems appropriate, for instance, to stock a fine relief-carved longrifle, paying considerable attention to detail of finish and decoration, and yet inlet the lock in a manner that makes the lock mortise appear as if it had been chewed out by a trained rat. There are considerations other than those merely cosmetic. For instance, a longrifle, fowler, or musket stock is weakest at the area of the wrist where the tail of the lock is inletted; the same is true of a double shotgun. Failure to leave all the wood possible in a lock mortise is to invite possible fracture at that point. If a lock is properly inletted, no more wood is removed than is necessary for the action parts to have working clearance. Further, a lock should fit its mortise tightly, so that it cannot move under tension of the springs. It should fit tightly enough so that with the lock bolts removed, and the gun turned to the right, the lock will not fall out of the mortise when the stock is rapped smartly with the heel of the hand. Needless to say, if a lock is fitted this well, there will be no perceptible gaps between the lockplate and surrounding wood, and all non-working interior parts of the lock will have full bearing for good support.

A side lock can be tightly inletted with a router or vertical mill. In fact, precision

The lockplate lug is inletted first. A sharp scribe is used to scribe a line along the top and rear edges of the lockplate for a reference point. The inward-projecting lug is then painted with inletting black and its position marked while held in alignment with the scribed lines. Bivins uses a 3/8 flat chisel, driving straight down along the lug lines keeping the bevel of the chisel facing toward the inlet in cutting the lug profile.

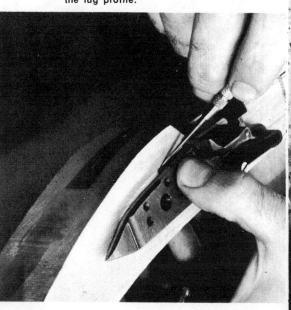
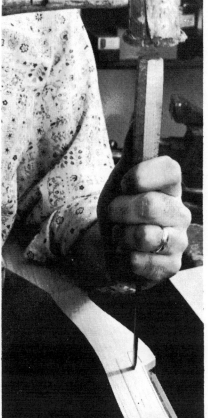

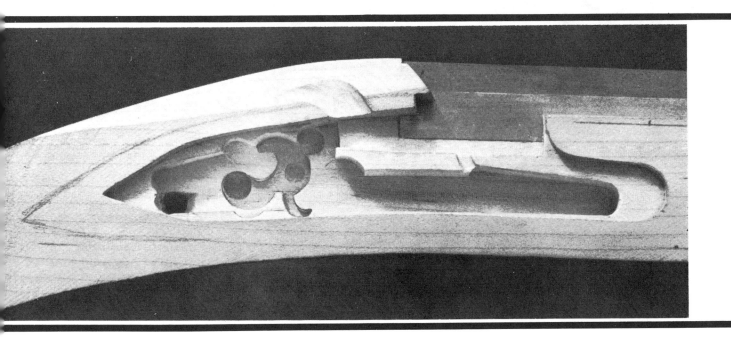

inletting with machines had been carried out in this country well before 1850, as any military musket of the period can attest. However, hand inletting is the usual method unless a great quantity of production is considered. Some stockers find good assistance in lock inletting through the use of high-speed hand grinders, such as those made by Dumore, Rockwell, or Dremel. These grinders can save time with some procedures, but a word of caution is in order. These small grinders operate at speeds of 15-20,000 rpm, and tend to fill the work area with fine sawdust, making it difficult to see where the tool is cutting. It is easy to make a slip with such a tool that will remove a considerable piece of wood just where you don't want to. I prefer hand tools for this reason, and also because I have never become used to working around the high-pitched shriek of such machines. My nerves aren't up to it, but more power to you if you can make use of a hand grinder. I would suggest the use of a flexible shaft if you do use one, to attain better control.

In starting the inlet, take care that your working surface on the stock blank is smooth and square. Leave little more wood on the stock blank than is necessary to fully inlet the thickest part of the lockplate; 1/16-inch of extra wood is more than enough.

In inletting a shotgun lock, or the back-action lock of a Sharps rifle, the position of the lock on the stock blank is determined by the frame cuts which receive the lock. On a muzzleloader, however, there is no totally fixed reference point to work from, with the exception of the fact that the lock must have the proper relationship to the vent on a flintlock, or the drum or bolster on a

caplock. Here we will discuss the inletting of a muzzleloader lock, which presents additional problems, but the techniques used are otherwise identical to those used for a breechloader, once the frame has been inletted.

Briefly, the frame of a breechloader, such as a double-barrel shotgun, is inletted in the same manner as will be discussed for the lockplate, scribing the tang outline and working downward and rearward. The initial cut of the tang mortise will be to the width of the tang,

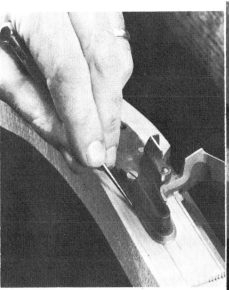

After the lockplate lug has been inletted, the lockplate outline is scribed on the stock and a groove approximately 3/32-inch deep is cut around the lock outline just inside the scribed line. This "gutter" relieves compression on the wood from the chisel when cutting the lock outline, preventing chisel marks being left along the edge of the inlet.

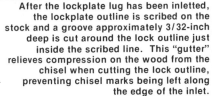

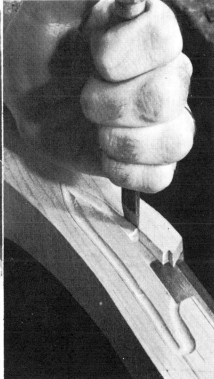

with a slightly long rough cut at the rear adequate to allow for setting back the frame as the forward edges of the buttstock are inletted. Care must be taken in alignment of the frame to avoid undesired cast-off or cast-on, and the recoil-bearing surfaces must be fitted as closely as possible. In most cases it is best to provide a few thousandths relief at the rear of the tang, carefully matching the rear radius to make it unnoticeable, for otherwise the slight normal setback of the wood due to recoil is likely to result in a

121

oriented in such a way that the hammer falls on the nipple correctly and not at an angle. Generally speaking, the throw of the hammer — the distance between the center of the tumbler square and the nose of the hammer — should equal the distance between the center of the tumbler and the center of the drum or bolster. Inletting a percussion lock is simplified a bit if the upper edge of the lock has been left blank, without a cut for the drum, as most are. The lock can be positioned fore and aft with the drum in place; when the hammer appears to be visually in line with the nipple, make several pencil marks on the stock blank to indicate the primary location of the plate. The lock is then more easily inletted with the drum removed from the barrel. The half-round notch for the drum can be filed in the plate after the lock has been fully inletted. Where a bolster is used rather than a drum, however, as on a "patent" breech, the lock must be cut in the beginning to fit the underside of the bolster. In either case, it may be necessary after fitting the lock to bend the hammer nose to one degree or another so

that it will meet the nipple correctly; this is best done with the hammer red-hot, since cold-working a steel casting is likely to result in a fracture.

Alignment of a flint lock is determined by the relationship of the pan to the vent area of the barrel breech. The vent should never be drilled until after the lock is inletted. Basically, the upper edge of the lug area of the lock plate should fall in the center of the side flat of the barrel, and the center line of the flashpan should be placed approximately 1/16-inch in front of the breechplug face. The lock can be set further to the rear if you wish to use gunstocker Don King's modified "Nock" system of coned breeching (see "Improved Breeching for Flintlocks," *Buckskin Report,* April, 1974, p. 23). Early stockers usually set the flint lock with the rear of the fence aligned with the rear edge of the barrel, but for quick ignition, it is more important to be certain that the pan is positioned in such a manner with the depth of the breechplug that the plug itself does not have to be grooved out to clear the vent, with the exception of the King breeching, where the breechplug face is opened up with a milled half-round cavity. In either case, and also with percussion locks, the lockplate should more or less parallel the barrel, rather than having the tail of the lock up or down, which will lend an awkward appearance to the finished gun.

After penciling position marks on the

chip or split at the rear of the tang. Depending upon the design, it may also be necessary to allow *slight* relief along the forward radii of the tang where it flares outward behind the breech; this area is also prone to chipping due to recoil setback since the grain of the wood usually flows roughly parallel to the barrel, while the wrist turns downward, resulting in short, therefore weak, grain at the upper edges of the wrist. Once the stripped frame is properly inletted, clearance can be provided for internal parts, taking care to remove no more wood than essential; some prefer not to make the internal cuts until the plates are inletted. With the frame inletted, inletting of the sideplates follows the same techniques as for the muzzleloader, except for the additional problems they entail.

The percussion lock, with its attendant "plumbing" fixed to the barrel, is somewhat more difficult to position than a flint lock, since the lock must be

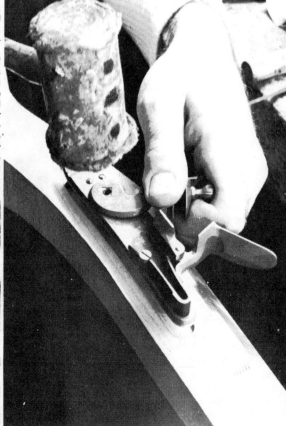

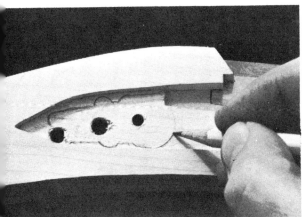
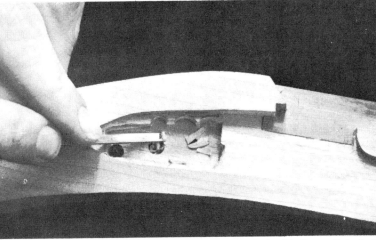

After the tumbler, sear spring and sear positions are marked with the mallet, their outlines are penciled in, combining these three parts in a continuous line which allows working clearance. These parts are then inletted to full depth.

stock blank, the lockplate should be stripped for inletting. The frizzen may be left on a flintlock to provide a "handle" for levering the lock out of the mortise while inletting. I know one gunsmith who inlets the entire lock without removing a single screw, and does the job well, but I have found it safer to inlet in stages.

The lockplate lug, which projects deeper than the plate, must be inletted first. With a sharp scribe, scribe a line along the top and rear edges of the lug for a reference point, and then coat the lug with inletting black. Carefully setting the lug on the reference lines, "print" an image of the lug surface by rocking the lockplate back and forth slightly. If a sharp impression does not result at every edge of the lug from this process, you can hold the lockplate carefully in position and strike it sharply with a leather mallet; the resulting slight dent made by the lug leaves a readable impression.

Drive straight down along the lug lines, using a 3/8 flat chisel and leather mallet, keeping the bevel of the chisel always facing in toward the inlet. Don't attempt to drive much more than 1/16-inch deep in such outlining work, since the chisel causes a wedging effect and could cause a split along the grain of the stock blank. Make a series of angling cuts in toward the outline of the lug, and then remove wood between the lines with a small gouge and the flat chisel. Generally, the gouge is safest for removing a quantity of wood in a hurry. Where possible, make such "hogging" cuts across the grain.

Continue this process of driving down along the lug inlet with a chisel and relieving wood inside until the side flat of the barrel is reached, taking care not to drive the chisel into the barrel. Inletting chisels should have a bevel of twenty degrees, and it is relatively easy to chip the working edge. For this reason, carving tools should never be used as a lever to break away pieces of wood in the inlet, unless they are quite small.

With the lug mortise cut to depth,

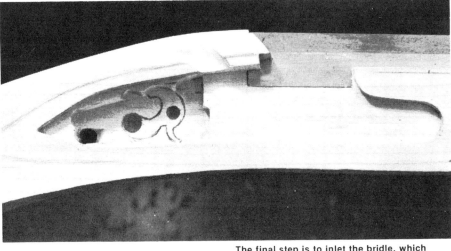

The final step is to inlet the bridle, which has already been marked in and the impression clarified with a pencil. The completely inletted stock is shown on the previous page.

place the lockplate in position and tap it down with a mallet. The mallet plays an important role in inletting; if a part is to fit tightly in the wood, it must be lightly driven in place. If resistance is felt, pull the plate and lightly chisel away areas of the inlet where the sharp edge of the lug is pushing up wood. While the lock should fit snugly, it should not be forced in place.

The lockplate now lies flush with the side of the stock blank. Using a sharp scribe — needle-sharp — strike a line carefully around the lockplate. If your lock is beveled inward at the inletting edge, try to strike a median between the inside and outside of the bevel. Flint locks usually don't have this inside bevel, though it is often used on percussion locks to facilitate close inletting.

Using a small gouge, cut a groove approximately 3/32-inch deep all the way around the inside of the scribed lines, keeping perhaps 1/16-inch from the lines. This "gutter" will assist in making the straight cuts around the lock outline, relieving the compression of the wood caused by the bevel of the chisel inside the plate line. The chisel's bevel tends to

drive the chisel *away* from the inlet area, compressing the wood along the inletting line. The sharp corners of the back of the chisel can leave dents in the inlet which are unsightly, to say the least.

After cutting straight down with the flat chisel around the lockplate line — use a very narrow chisel or gouge of proper radius to cut in the "nose" of the lock — relieve approximately half the thickness of the lockplate, using gouges. Since most of your cuts will run parallel with the lock inlet, take care that the gouge does not pick up a particularly hard portion of the grain and lift too large a curl. With fiddleback-grained hardwoods, it's often better to push the gouge with both hands rather than using a mallet, since it's easier to control the depth of cut with the hands.

After relieving a half-thickness of the plate, use the chisel again to drive straight down along the inlet line. Take care not to undercut at this point, since you will have as much as 1/16-3/32-inch extra wood to remove from the top surface of the inlet when finishing up. Using gouges again, and then flat chisels, cut the full thickness of the lockplate. Try the plate in the inlet, tapping with the mallet fore and aft. Some areas of the plate edges will be reluctant to enter the inlet; carefully trim excess wood at those points, *cutting straight down*. Always avoid making cuts with the chisel parallel to the inlet rather than at right angles. That invites trouble in a hurry. When the plate will enter the inlet stiffly, tap it down smartly with the mallet. The lock lug will now be within 1/16-inch or so of touching the barrel flat. Carefully pull the lock out of the inlet, using the frizzen as a lever, or levering between the lock lug and barrel with a thin screwdriver with file-rounded edges. With a percussion or breechloader sideplate it's often useful to screw the bridle screw into the lockplate from the outside to provide a handle, since a tightly-inletted lockplate should not pull out easily. With double-barrel sideplates, the mounting screw hole should be drilled through the stock to allow tapping out the plate from the opposite side.

Coat the backside of the lock with inletting black or linseed oil, tap the plate back in place for a "reading," and begin removing high spots in the inlet. After several sessions with this spotting-in, the lockplate lug should bottom out firmly against the barrel flat. Full contact between the lug and barrel is paramount, if the lock is not to leak fouling from priming or percussion caps inside the lock mortise and speed deterioration of the wood at that point.

If you started with a thickness of wood on the lock side of the stock blank slightly deeper than the thickness of the lock lug, the lockplate should now be slightly below the surface of the stock blank. With an early style flint lock with outside edges beveled, the lock will have a "buried" appearance. The finished inlet of a beveled lock will leave the entire bevel standing *above* the stock blank. With a percussion or shotgun lock, the entire plate will be flush with the stock. In either case, don't file the stock wood to finished dimension around the lock at this stage, since the extra wood may be needed to take subsequent minor dents or nicks which may appear on the sharp edge while inletting the lock's action.

While this technique will work as described for most sidelock rifles and some double-barrel shotguns, many side lock shotguns have a lip at the forward tip of the plate which slides into a recess in the frame. To properly inlet these plates, the surfaces of the stock must be almost flush with the frame — with just enough wood to take minor dents and dings. The plate can be eyeballed into position and the location marked with a soft, sharp pencil; then the relief channel is cut within the lines and the area inside the relief channel relieved almost to full depth. The plate is then inserted in the frame and the lip used as a fulcrum as the plate is inletted to full depth, slowly working from front to back, using a scribed line and inletting black to assure a proper fit. The side edges of such lockplates are usually square, but the rear is invariably beveled to allow the plate to be rocked into position without leaving a gap. By initially removing all but an eighth-inch or so around the edges, inletting is much faster.

With the sideplate, or plates, inletted to full depth, reassemble the lock, leaving off the mainspring. Before further inletting, the sear hole must be drilled. Stockmakers often make the sear hole twice the diameter it needs to be, but consider the fact that the sear hole penetrates nearly three-quarters the thickness of the stock at the wrist. Obviously, a small hole is desirable. Virtually all rifle-sized locks can be fitted with a 1/4-inch sear hole diameter, although muskets may require a slightly larger size. Holding the lock above the inlet, tap the tail of the lock with your mallet, leaving an impression of the tip of the sear in the lock inlet. Center punch this mark, and holding a 1/4-inch twist bit on the mark, see that the drill will cut almost to the bottom edge of the lockplate inlet, since the sear must drop considerably to engage the half-cock notch. However, don't drill *too* close to the edge of the inlet. Drill the entire depth of the sear, taking care to drill as straight as possible. Check your depth with a caliper or spare drill bit, and then drill the hole an extra 1/8-inch deep to give good clearance to the tip of the sear.

In softer stock woods, it's best to drill a pilot sear hole first, and then open up with the 1/4-inch bit, to avoid skewing away from your center punch mark.

In inletting the action of a lock, it is best to visualize the lock parts as being assembled on three levels. The primary level is, of course, the inside of the lockplate, while the secondary level might be considered the tumbler, sear spring, and the forward arm of the sear. A third level might be the bridle.

An easy way to inlet the action is to inlet these different levels separately. Remove the bridle, but replace the sear with its attendant sear screw. Placing the lock in the inlet, give the outside of the lock a solid smack with the mallet, leaving a good impression of the sear screw in the wood. Selecting a twist bit of a diameter very slightly larger than the head of the sear screw, first center punch the impression of the screw head, and then drill to the complete depth of the screw — the distance between the head of the screw and the inside of the lockplate. Similarly, set the lock back in the mortise, and tap in a mark for the tumbler axle, and then drill it to depth. A vernier caliper is helpful as a depth gauge. Placing the lock in the mortise once again, give the plate another solid thump, but take care now that the lock is level in the mortise, or the sharp edge of the plate may strike the plate inlet at some point and break the wood. By a few judicious blows, and perhaps a bit of spotting oil, you should have now an impression of the tumbler, sear spring and spring screw, and sear. Using a pencil, connect the outer edges of the impressions of these components together in a continuous line, and inlet them to their full depth, inletting closely above and behind the sear spring and below the sear. Then set the hammer or cock at full-cock, and holding the lock in the mortise, tap the lock again to indicate in the stock wood the full travel of both the tumbler and sear. Remove wood from your initial cuts so that these parts will just clear during movement. Working the hammer should result in positive clicks as the sear falls into the notches.

With this accomplished, re-install the bridle of the lock, and using the mallet treatment, make an impression of that part in the wood. Oil may again be necessary for a clear reading. Inlet the bridle as precisely as possible with a small flat chisel. The smaller tips of the bridle must at times be "worried" out with a rocking motion of the chisel. The bottom of the bridle inlet will be rough, despite your best efforts, but this can be cleaned up with small scrapers and by burnishing the wood with the tip of a pin punch with a slightly rounded nose. The bridle should bottom out against the stock wood, in addition to every possible area of the lockplate, to assure full support.

The mainspring may now be installed, and inletted in the same manner as the action components, using narrow chisels and small gouges. Remove no more wood above the lower arm of the spring than is necessary for full travel of the spring. When inletting a lock in a stock blank that is fitted with a large-breeched barrel, take care not to cut the mainspring mortise through into the barrel inlet. However, when both the mainspring and barrel are quite large, it will be necessary occasionally to actually remove metal from one of the bottom flats of the barrel so that the spring can clear. This is preferable to decreasing the width of the spring, and can be done easily with a cape chisel after marking and removing the barrel.

When inletting a flintlock, you will find that the cock begins to bottom against the upper edge of the plate inlet when the lock action is only half inletted. With the cock at rest, scribe around the cock, and cut a groove in the stock for the upper part of the cock to clear without binding on the wood.

With the components inletted, work the lock to make sure that nothing is binding. Add a slight amount of extra clearance around moving parts to insure that humidity changes don't bind the lock by swelling the wood. If parts do hang up a bit the sear and mainspring are usually the offenders — spot the parts with oil and remove wood where necessary. The extra wood which you left outside the lockplate inlet may now be taken off, filing flush for a percussion lock, or leaving the bevels standing on a flint lock of Germanic persuasion. Remove this wood with a new and sharp cabinet rasp, and avoid taking strokes at direct right angles to the lock inlet, to avoid crumbling wood on the inside surfaces.

Holes for the lock bolts, or "side nails" as our English cousins call them, are best drilled from the lock side. The safest method is to center punch the screw hole both in the lockplate and on the opposite side of the stock as well. Set a small center point vertically in a drill press vise, and align the point with the tip of a twist bit in the drill press chuck — use a pilot drill half the diameter of your tap drill — clamp the vise solidly to the drill press table, and then set the rifle stock over the table so that the center point rests in the punchmark on the left side of the stock. Proceed with your drilling slowly, and you will be assured that the drill will come out exactly where you want it to. After drilling the pilot holes, drill through with the tap drill, using a hand drill. Then remove the lock and drill the stock with the clearance drill, and you are ready to tap the lockplate for the thread of your lock bolts. In larger locks, a 10-24 thread is preferable to avoid stripping.

It's wise to drill your ramrod hole before drilling for the front lock bolt, if your lock is a flintlock (percussion locks seldom use two lock bolts). If your ramrod hole rises a little high, the front lock bolt can be positioned above the centerline of the plate, and the screw even notched slightly to clear the rod if necessary. If the ramrod hole rises above the centerline of the lock, however, you may have to leave off the front lock bolt, and possibly resort to a steel "hook" riveted inside the nose of the lock, engaging a mortise in the wood. Locks of double-barrel flintlock shotguns were commonly fitted in this manner, and no small number of single barrels were given the same treatment when the ramrod hole ran off too much to clear the front lock bolt.

The final inletting of a breechloader will, of course, differ from the muzzle loader we've described here, but only in detail. The same principles are applicable in all cases; for instance, a detachable trigger plate and lower tang, as found on some double-barreled guns, is inletted in precisely the same manner as the side lock for such guns, angling the piece into wood if it has a lip under the forward edge. The main thing is to study the design, do the inletting work in layers, and at no time remove any wood that doesn't have to be removed — this is most important on any thin-wristed muzzle-loader or modern double, but it can be absolutely critical when inletting a drilling, with its complex and sometimes cumbersome lock mechanism.

Inletting a lock by this meticulous method is far more time-consuming than simply hogging out an open cavity in the side of the stock, but the finished job will give you a feeling of pride from a job well done, even if no one ever sees it but you. And you can be assured that you have left maximum strength in your stock by not having removed a single splinter of wood unnecessarily. ●

Basic Gunstocking and the Flintlock Rifle

PART ONE

LAYOUT AND INLETTING

By JOHN BIVINS

A central premise to me in gunstocking is the desire to carry out every phase of the job as well as the next. A fellow should be just as proud to show off his barrel or lock inletting as he is fine carving or engraving. Decoration on a gunstock is the final icing, so to speak, and it's not too tasty an item if the cake is rotten inside. I've seen too many otherwise fine rifles that were "face" jobs to overlook this little editorial comment. Various states-of-mind bring about gnawed and cavernous lock mortises under gorgeous skins; I suppose some rush their work to get to the "goodie" part, while others just seem to live with the idea that it's fine if muzzleloaders are a little crude around the edges.

'Taint so, friends. Fine custom muzzleloaders cost every bit as much as fine custom centerfires, and if they are to be used, or even looked at, they should be equally as soundly made all the way through, or they aren't worth the powder it would take to blow them to that renowned section of the Nether World.

The beginning of our current game is the stock blank, from which we'll remove everything which doesn't look like a longrifle. You are better off if that stock blank is still in the board, for then you can lay out a stock to suit you. If you buy a piece already blanked out to an oversize pattern, either have a close look at it first hand or order it from a dealer who is reputable. Perhaps the greatest curse of the gunstock is to have what Al Linden called "musket grain" in the wrist. That is, grain running out at an angle rather than flowing parallel to the upper and lower wrist lines. In order to make the wrist grain straight, a stock must be laid out at an angle on the board in most cases, which of course is a nasty waste of fine wood that some less scrupulous wood

dealers are loath to bear. Won't make any difference, they say. No? I have a friend who has *twice* broken his fine flintlock through the wrist just by trying to seat tight balls in a dirty bore. . .and I suspect that a 1/2-inch steel rod now rests through the middle of those breaks and all that grain runout.

Don't be tempted to buy a soft piece of maple for a gunstock, no matter how fine the figure. If you can make a significant dent in the stuff with your thumbnail, leave it be, or you'll have to live with crumbling, broomy inlets and a miserable medium to have to carve. Good maple — preferably sugar, but red will do *if* it's hard — is dense and heavy, and the best wood usually has a good deal of color, often with a pink cast to it. Wood that is dead white is often soft and worthless. Black walnut and black cherry were also used for longrifle stocks, as was birch (often mistaken for apple), though less often. Birch is ugly, but works well; I don't use it, and I won't use black walnut unless it's all butt wood with tight, short pores and of considerable weight. The usual grade of black walnut, unlike its flossy European cousin, won't carve worth

One of the handiest tools in stockmaking is the Versa-Vise, which rotates on both horizontal and vertical axes. Bivins has fitted this one with maple jaws. [Editor's Note — We have not determined the purpose of the wineglass.]

Drilling for barrel pins, tang screws and lock bolt holes is done on centers, with the aid of a turned center, as shown, which bolts through the drill press table hole.

a toot, and some of it is lousy to inlet. Cherry has poor shear strength and shares the long, open pores of black walnut, and is even broomier to carve unless considerable figure or root wood is present. Since *juglans regia* is neither available nor appropriate for longrifle stocks, stick with hard maple.

In choosing a gunstock, always consider wood-working quality and density to be more important than any of Mother Nature's neon displays of fine fiddleback figure. Check a blank by cutting across the grain with a small gouge to see if the wood fibers tear rather than cutting cleanly. If the cut is clean, with a burnished appearance, you have the best stuff you can get — wood that will make a rifle so good that knowledgeable gun people will not even notice if there is *no* figure. Sure, I like pretty curls too, on girls and gunstocks both.

If you're fortunate enough to be able to cut your stocks from the board, work from a planed surface on both sides of the board so that minute surface imperfections, insect holes, and grain direction can all be easily spotted, and so the sawn blank will have squared sides. For best results, make an oversize stock pattern of Plexiglas, since this will allow you to see without question how the grain is running. Also, needless to say, when purchasing stock wood, look the dealer in the eye and ask in a flat and hard tone if the wood is dry; see if his left eye twitches or his feet shuffle a little. Wood is frequently kiln dried much too fast, which is another reason a board should be planed before layout. A rough-sawn surface can hide small surface checks caused by too-rapid drying.

We have no room here to discuss the vagaries of style in the longrifle stock; each gunsmithing school in the early days had its identifiable architecture, and these profiles are available in the books and occasionally even in blueprint, some of which are excellent. Whatever style you prefer, I'd suggest that you avoid any design which commits you to an exaggerated "Roman" nose or excessive drop at comb or heel, unless your specialty is muscular contortion and you particularly relish having your cheekbone viciously massaged every time you shoot. Many early designs will allow adjustment of buttstock dimensions to a usable set of figures. . .with the exception, perhaps, of Bedford rifles, which seem to have the plummeting stock drop of an ancient petronel. If you are locked in on a "school" design in both architecture and furniture, don't hesitate to take your brass buttplate and alter the pitch of the thing with a mallet to better suit shootable stock dimensions. And what are such figures? Well, unless a customer has a particular set of dimensions in mind, I make my longrifle stocks with 1

3/8 inches of drop at the comb, 3 to 3 1/8-inch at the heel, 3/16 to 1/4-inch castoff, depending upon thickness of the cheek. A pull of 13 5/8 to 13 3/4 inches is good, since muzzleloaders don't have a great deal of recoil, and I use a negative pitch at the butt which will position the muzzle some 13 inches away from a vertical surface against which the heel is resting. Except for the pitch, perhaps, these are good shotgun dimensions, and will instantly position the sighting plane at the eye when the piece is thrown up by most people. Except for a certain friend of mine who has a frog-like neck.

In locating barrel pin centers, the distance from the top flat of the barrel to the center of the tenon is measured with a vernier caliber, above, then transferred to the stock as shown at right, with the barrel clamped tightly in place.

Even though I have patterns, I often lay out a blank with nothing more than a tape measure, pencil and long straight edge. For the latter I use a stainless T-square from which the head has been "lost." You need something at least three feet long, and a yardstick won't do, since the edges aren't precise. After laying out a stock, I bandsaw the thing out 1/4-inch oversize all over except for the top of the stock where the barrel inlet is to go, and I don't bring the pattern right down to the line until after the barrel is inletted. This way you can absolutely verify your drop dimensions off the top flat of the barrel before inletting the buttplate.

Depending upon your stock style, and therefore thickness of cheek and amount of castoff, the barrel centerline may be placed on either side of the stock blank

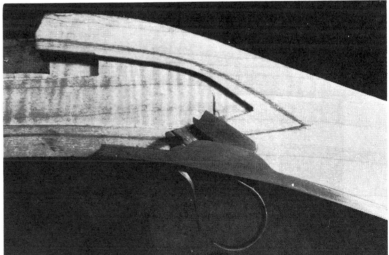

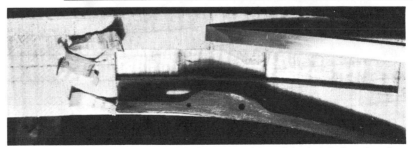

Triggers are aligned on the stock with the sear position of the lock before the trigger plate is inletted, as in the upper panel. [Note that this rifle is for a left-handed shooter.] The plate is then inletted, taking out no more wood than necessary to provide clearance for internal features.

127

center to suit you, if the blank is thicker than you need. If the blank is of marginal thickness, and you need castoff, the barrel may even be angled on the blank. In any event, establish a master centerline for the barrel, and from this centerlines for both upper and lower buttstock surfaces. If you are to have castoff, begin the cast with a line that begins about 2/3 back on the wrist, and extend the line to the point at the heel where the full cast occurs, say 1/4-inch (or whatever). Draw this new butt centerline in on both comb and lower side of the butt. Center your buttplate on the line to verify that you have ample wood left for a cheekpiece; this is

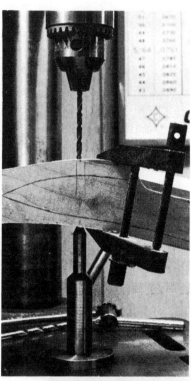

The tang screw hole is drilled with a tap drill, between centers, using the center post.

especially critical in an early style rifle that must be made from any blank that is less than 2 1/2 inches thick. It's best to start with enough wood in the first place.

Inlet the barrel as we discussed in *Rifle* 37, or if you are using a straight octagon barrel, the simplest thing to do is rout it in with Mr. Stanley's Finest. Many muzzleloading dealers offer blanks already routed for various sizes of straight barrels. I suggest that you don't buy one that also has the ramrod groove routed and the hole drilled, since that will tend to predetermine dimensions that you might not want to live with. Whatever you do, don't *ever* buy a blank with the ramrod hole routed out from inside the barrel channel; that weakens the stock and a rap on the thing sounds like a cheap cored door on a tract house. Ugh.

All right. Our procedure from here is as follows: inlet barrel and tang, install barrel tenons and pins (or wedges), inlet the lockplate, inlet trigger plate, install tang screw, inlet the buttplate, rough out the buttstock, inlet lock internals, and trigger internals. Cut ramrod groove, drill ramrod hole, rough out fore-end, install muzzle cap. If any of this order sounds perverse to you, you'll see as we go along why it's not.

Whether you use pins or wedges to hold your barrel in its inlet (we'll discuss pins here for brevity), you must use barrel tenons that are slotted, with at least 3/32 inch of slot on each side of the pin or wedge. These may be either folded from sheet brass or steel, or bought already

slotted. The reason for slotted tenons is that wood is subject to considerable longitudinal change with differing conditions of humidity, and often highly figured wood, especially fiddleback, is subject to rather extreme movement. I've had forestocks lengthen as much as 5/32-inch from winter to summer, which is admittedly an extreme amount, but if you don't allow for *some* movement, you'll wind up with seasonal changes in point of impact at least, and a bent barrel pin and buggered forestock at worst.

If you can find access to a drill press, drilling the forestock for pins or wedges is a simple matter, and virtually foolproof if you use the method of drilling on centers. I had a center turned up that I bolt to my drill press table from below. This device is set up with the point of the pin-diameter drill touching the tip of the center, and the center is then tightened down hard. A big nail held in a clamped-down drill press vise will do in a pinch. With a vernier, measure the distance between the center of the tenon slot and the top flat of the barrel, checking this distance for each tenon if the barrel is a swamped or tapered one. Rather than recording these measurements, you can simply prick them lightly onto a piece of cardboard with the points of the inside-measuring legs of the vernier, if you like, indicating which set of prickmarks is for which tenon.

Now mark the forestock at the top where the center of each tenon will fall when the barrel is in the stock, and using a square, pencil this mark vertically down both sides of the forestock. Return the barrel to the stock, and clamp it firmly next to the first tenon position you are to mark. With a precision-ground straightedge (I use the thick leg of a machinist's square) resting firmly on the top flat of the barrel, transfer your vernier measurement taken earlier to the stock by lightly pressing the point of the bottom inside-measurement leg into the wood. Make the same mark on the opposite side of the

The drop and comb line are verified before final trimming, with the aid of a T-square blade, which indicates the bore center line. The butt plate contour is then marked off, as at right.

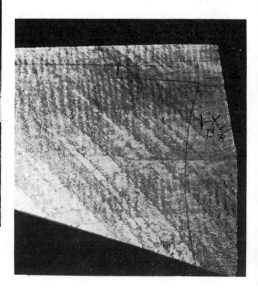

stock; both of the vernier marks are of course pressed onto the pencil line mentioned above. Center punch these light marks, and proceed to the other tenons, firmly clamping the barrel at each point.

The pin holes may now be drilled between centers by resting the point of the center in the centerpunch on one side of the stock, and drilling through the centermark on the other side. Set the drill press stop so that the drill does not quite contact the center point below, and finish out the hole with a hand drill. Always be sure that the stock is clamped for all such measuring and drilling, and you need not worry whether the drill will come out where you want it. The same method is used for drilling lock bolt holes and for the tang screw. A slightly different method must be used for round barrels, which I unfortunately haven't space to cover here.

For barrel pins, I use .079 round spring stock, and I drill the holes with a No. 47 drill, which provides a firm seat for the pin. I make the pins no longer than the diameter of the barrel, and file a slight taper on the end of each pin while turning it in a drill. Installed, such short pins are well shy of being flush with the finished surface of the stock, but they are excellent insurance that the pin holes won't ever be wallowed out.

With the barrel pinned in, excess wood on the sides of the forestock can now be sawn off. With a really thick piece, it's best to saw off the excess *before* the pinning operation, since you can drill only so deep with a small drill. I mark off the forestock with a pencil and simply bandsaw away all but 1/4-inch of wood on each side of the barrel, following the contour of the barrel if it's swamped. Saw all the way back into the lock area, angling the saw out when you reach the wrist area. This may be done with a sharp crosscut saw as well, with the barrel clamped in place and the stock held vertically in the vise.

I usually inlet the lockplate before installing the tang screw, since this provides a precise way of indicating the position of the sear, and therefore the trigger plate which the tang screw is to pierce. The lock is positioned so that the top of the pan falls on the centerline of the barrel's side flat; the center of the pan should fall 1/16-inch or slightly less in front of the breechplug face, since it's preferable not to have to notch the breechplug to clear the vent. This is why you should use a barrel that is breeched no more than 1/2-inch deep, or 5/8-inch at the most; having to notch the breechplug for the vent invites an uncleanable trap for all those gooey goodies left behind from burning black powder.

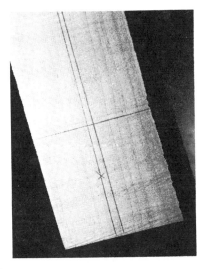

The stock centerline, and the castoff centerline [marked "X"] are drawn, and the front of the buttplate extension located. [This is a lefthand stock.]

After the buttplate contour has been cut, surplus wood around the edges is removed, then "inside" wood in the inlet is cut out to avoid having to fit the buttplate to a large area.

The buttplate extension pilot screw hole is located, above; the pilot hole in the stock will be drilled slightly forward to provide a "draw-bore" hole.

The buttplate edges are peened against the wood for a final "smash" fit — a technique Bivins adopted after noting peening marks which hadn't been completely filed away on an early rifle.

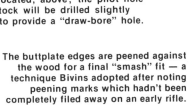

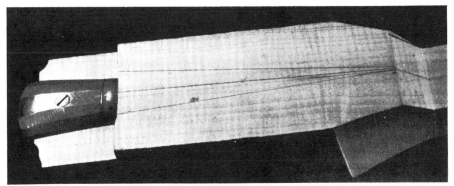

After the buttplate is completely inletted, the comb lines are drawn off in preparation for final shaping.

In positioning a lock, the tail may be angled downward slightly if needed, though care must be taken not to position the front of the lock too high when using a large diameter barrel (1 1/16 inch or more), since the front lock bolt needs to clear the barrel. You can, however, notch the bottom of the barrel for the front lock bolt if needed, though more than half the diameter of the bolt shank should seldom be necessary.

Before inletting the lockplate, take care that the side of the stock is square, and proceed with inletting as discussed in *Rifle* 38. After the plate is in, mark the position of the sear on the outside of the plate, and transfer this to the stock. Before proceeding, you'll need to verify your stock layout lines and saw off the rest of the stock to its final trim lines. With your straightedge resting on the top flat of the barrel, check the drop at comb and heel with a ruler, and adjust any buttstock lines necessary. Bandsaw off all the excess outside your trim lines on both buttstock and fore-end, and re-establish both centerlines and castoff lines top and bottom. Extend the bottom centerline entirely to the muzzle, since this is to provide a guide for the ramrod groove. In laying out a fore-end, incidentally, I allow for a fore-end height of no more than 13/16-inch, measuring from the center of the barrel flat to the bottom of the fore-end. This will often finish to 3/4-inch after final shaping.

Now extend the sear position to the bottom of the stock, and with this mark, and the sear mark in the lockplate mortise, locate the trigger so that when installed it will be bearing on the sear no more than 3/8-inch behind the shoe. For a decent pull and best mechanical advantage, a single trigger should be pinned in the wood rather than in the trigger plate. If the trigger pin is low and well in front of the sear, the pull will be heavy. For a double-lever double-set trigger, arrange the assembled unit so that both rear and front levers will reach the sear. Mark the position of the front of the trigger plate, transfer to the bottom of the stock, and lay off the trigger plate mortise with a flexible rule and scribe. I should note here that all components which are to be inlet into a gunstock should have the edges beveled to facilitate tight inletting, and that is especially true of a thick piece such as a trigger plate. The high supporting lugs of a set trigger should also be filed down on the sides.

The trigger plate is then inletted. One easy method to remove a set-trigger plate while inletting is to simply turn in the trigger spring screw from the outside, and the screw will push the plate out; this avoids endless prying with screwdrivers and the like. After the plate is inletted, position the tang screw on the side of the stock at an angle that will permit the

screw head to lie roughly parallel to the line of the tang; this will avoid the screw head ending up oval after it is filed flush. Center punch the top and bottom of the screw hole on the tang and trigger plate, clamp the whole affair together, and tap drill on centers as with the barrel pins. Also on centers, run the clearance drill through until you can feel the drill just touch the trigger plate, then tap the trigger plate while it is still in the stock to insure alignment of the threads. It's wise to also countersink for the tang screw on centers.

The lock bolts are installed in the stock in the same manner, though I suggest that you remove the barrel while drilling for these. One reason for this is that the rear lock bolt hole will usually fall in line with the rear lug of the breechplug, which usually has a slanted face, and the tap drill will tend to skid downward when it hits this surface. In using a barrel that is breeched 1/2-inch deep, and with a large Siler lock, I position the rear lock bolt hole 3/8-inch behind the barrel breech. I use 10-24 screws for both tang and lock bolts, since they aren't easily stripped.

Before beginning to shape the stock, the buttplate must be installed, since the buttplate has a great deal to do with the final shape of the buttstock. Since you now have cut the buttstock to its final trim lines, verify that your buttplate casting fits the pitch of your pattern; the top of the buttplate extension should align with the comb line with the buttplate toe falling where you want it. If this doesn't jibe, take a heavy leather mallet and bend the buttplate extension either up or down until it fits your pattern. Incidentally, a fair number of castings are twisted as they come from the foundry, so if the buttplate doesn't look quite true, chuck it in the vise and give it a twist with a big crescent wrench if needed. Now take a sharp mill file and clean up all the inside bearing surfaces of the buttplate; the edges of the casting should be razor-sharp all over when this job is finished, or you will end up with embarrassing little "walloons," as George Hoenig would call them, around the inletted buttplate.

Aligning the buttplate extension with the top of the stock, carefully trace off the profile of the buttplate onto the stock, taking care that it falls in the correct position to give the pull which you want. The top of the buttplate should drop 1/16-inch or less below the comb so that wood can be filed down to the buttplate, and you should leave 1/16-inch of wood at the front of the buttplate extension for safety's sake in inletting.

The buttplate inlet should be drawn on the right side of the stock for a right-handed rifle, and on the left for a southpaw piece, as shown on the rifle in progress, an iron-mounted piece for Buck

Buchanan. The reason for this is that the rear of the buttplate cut should be angled for castoff, and this is easily done by simply tilting the bandsaw table a bit. The amount of tilt needed is determined by drawing a line at right angles to your castoff center line on the comb, laying the stock on the bandsaw table, and tilting the table until the bandsaw blade aligns with this. A quarter-inch of cast usually requires about 1/16-inch of table tilt. Obviously, a stock is cast off to the right for a right-handed piece, and vice-versa. Carefully saw off the back of the buttplate inlet, and then the cut where the front of the extension falls. Return the saw table to zero, and saw off the "bed" of the buttplate extension. Mark a centerline on the buttplate extension, and keep it aligned with the castoff line on the comb while inletting.

I don't say dark incantations and haul out gallons of inletting black while inletting a buttplate, and I don't scrape and cuss for hours to get a perfect fit. I do get a perfect fit, but I use a hog-and-smash method to do it, and I just don't fool around with the job; time is precious. Forty-five minutes to an hour will usually do it.

The "hog" part comes with getting rid of all the areas of stock that slow down the inletting process. Lay the buttplate on the stock, pencil around it, and gouge away around the sides of the stock for a half-inch or so, leaving an eighth-inch margin around the plate. With a quarter-round gouge, concave the *inside* of the inlet somewhat, to within a quarter-inch of the plate edges. This gives you a much smaller bearing area to have to work with, which saves considerable time. Even on hard end-grain, a cabinet rasp may be used to remove most of the high spots during inletting.

Actual inletting begins with the buttplate extension, and I file, chisel, and scrape, spotting-in all the while until I have 100 percent bearing of the extension. Rather than using inletting black, I use linseed oil or just any clear oil handy, since I don't like inlets to look like a coal mine, and maple shows the imprint of a clear oil well enough. By the time your extension is bearing well, the buttplate should have begun to bear at the top rear and the toe. Proceed with the inletting until the toe is completely bearing for a distance of a half-inch up the buttplate. Now you are left with nearly a sixteenth-inch gap at several points around the center of the buttplate, right? You are supposed to keep scraping and spotting until these are all gone, right? Wrong. Now comes the smash part.

First, the buttplate extension must be fastened down. Centerpunch where you want the upper screw to go, and with the buttplate *off* the stock, drill through the extension with the correct pilot drill for the woodscrew you are using (I prefer 1 1/4-10's). Now put the buttplate back on the inlet, and insuring that its centerline matches that of the stock, drop the pilot drill into the hole, and with the buttplate pushed forward hard, tap the drill lightly with a hammer. Remove the drill and buttplate, and centerpunch a mark 1/32-inch in *front* of the mark left by the drill bit, and with the same bit, drill the pilot hole in the stock on that new center mark. This is the infamous draw-bore hole, and it will serve to make the woodscrew pull the buttplate extension tight against its forward inlet. *Don't* fail to do this, or you will have to go out and speak a few words to the mountains later. Clearance drill and countersink the extension, and screw the extension down tight. You should cut the countersink by trial-and-error until the screw slot comes within a quarter-turn of lining up with the centerline of the rifle; when the job is finished the slot can be turned all the way over.

As I mentioned above, the toe of the buttplate should have full bearing at this point. Now install the lower buttplate screw, with its center at least an inch and a half above the toe to avoid weakening the stock at that point. Ring the screw down tight. Now, you say, what about those hideous gaps still left? Don't I have hours of work left? No. Pick up your ball peen hammer, and proceed to peen the edges of the buttplate down to the wood,

giving the thing hefty but well-directed swats. A brass casting will pull right down with this method, leaving not even a hint of a gap anywhere. Don't, however, work too close to the toe with the hammer, and don't expect the "smash" method to work on soft wood; the wood will compress under your blows. This works equally well with steel castings or forgings, though requiring a bit more tapping, and we have found that it will work as well with a Neidner-type buttplate. On these, a punch can be used to avoid hitting the checkering with the hammer, and a curved riffler file used to file off the peen marks. In a longrifle buttplate, simply use a cabinet rasp to file off the evidence of the evil deed, and while you're about it, file those buttplate edges down thin. Thick edges on a buttplate look like thick ankles on a gal. If you're wondering how we came up with this method, I'll give you the straight facts. I found the remnants of some tiny peen marks on the buttplate of a carved Eighteenth Century American rifle. The stocker hadn't filed them all away.

Now you can pencil in lines for the sides of the comb and delineate the toe lines on the bottom of the stock. We'll take up stock shaping next issue.

We'll also go into tools a bit next time, but let me mention briefly here what I consider to be about the only really usable stocking vise available. It isn't by any means perfect, but it's ahead of the rest of

the pack until something better comes along, and I've been using one for ten years now. It's the Versa-Vise, sold by Brownell's (I haven't found it listed elsewhere). The advantage to a Versa-Vise is that it can be side-mounted on a shaft that will allow it to tilt forward and back; a camming action locks the vise in position when it is turned up tight. This tilting motion is of enormous value in stockwork, since it allows you to position a stock in relation to your working light so that shadows along the stock will reveal contours while you work. In order to have the tilting motion, you'll either need to buy the optional "flush" mount with the vise, or make a vertical piece with a shaft attached as shown on the unit we set up for my latest banjo-pickin' journeyman, Bobby Denton. The vise jaws should be drilled and tapped and hard maple blocks sawn with "V" cuts installed. These blocks should have at least 2 1/2 inches of flat area at the bottom for holding stocks still in the square; the "V's" readily hold a rounded-over fore-end, and belting leather should be glued inside the "V's" to avoid denting a stock.

Now, if some enterprising person would just make a vise like this, but heavier, and with jaws that would *swivel*, we'd really have something. Woodcraft, up in Woburn, Mass., has a swivel-jaw vise, but it doesn't tilt. I'd give a big box of French amber flints for one that would do *both*! ●

Basic Gunstocking and the Flintlock Rifle

By JOHN BIVINS

PART TWO

DESIGN and SHAPING

A well-designed drawknife is an excellent tool for rough initial shaping; the proper shearing cut is shown above. Immediately below, a gouge is used for other rough shaping. Note the three basic flats of initial cuts left by the drawknife and rasp (this is a lefthand stock). At bottom, a patternmaker's file is used for finishing the roughing cuts.

ONE OF THE fallacies brewed in the mind of the Twentieth Century gun buff is that early gunstockers and smiths worked with crude tools and under primitive conditions. As far as I can see, the Eighteenth Century gunstocker was at a *true* disadvantage only with his lighting, which couldn't be easily manipulated to fall where needed. Admittedly, some of his working materials were less convenient than those we can handily buy in the corner hardware, such as abrasives. The early smith had virtually all the grits we do, but largely in powdered form, and his sandpaper was exactly that, paper with sand glued to it. Wood finishing in the days before Norton and Behr-Manning called for plenty of scraping, rubbing with pumice-charged and leather-covered polishing sticks, and even using shagreen (shark skin), which was a pretty fair substitute for grit papers.

Any premise that the early gunsmiths' tools were crude, however, is preposterous. The fact is that early handworkers of all types often possessed many more specialized hand tools than we do today, and they were quite often better tools than those manufactured now, despite advances in metallurgy and the like. Tools in the Eighteenth Century, however, were a much larger overhead item to the smith than they are today, due to transportation and raw material costs. Common sense should tell us that early tools were good, even without having examined many examples of them, since the entire nature of the apprenticeship system instilled first and foremost a reverence for and understanding of tools. Too, the early gunstocker was faced just as we are with the need to finish his work as quickly as possible in order to earn a living, and since he was seldom able to

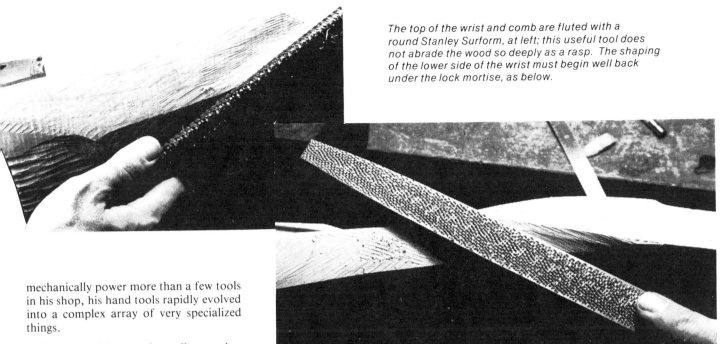

The top of the wrist and comb are fluted with a round Stanley Surform, at left; this useful tool does not abrade the wood so deeply as a rasp. The shaping of the lower side of the wrist must begin well back under the lock mortise, as below.

mechanically power more than a few tools in his shop, his hand tools rapidly evolved into a complex array of very specialized things.

We work with a much smaller number of hand tools today, tending to use such things as specially-shaped planes, spokeshaves, and the like very little. The modern tendency is toward one tool which will perform many functions, while the early artisan had many tools that performed single purposes, but usually faster and better. The problem now is that one is faced with the time it takes to make such tools, since many can't be bought. If, however, you'd like to feast yourself with a sumptuous array of woodworking tools that does approach in terms of quantity and quality woodworker's devices of the Eighteenth Century, send for a catalog from Woodcraft Supply (313 Montvale Ave., Woburn, Massachusetts 01801). The folks that run that business have done an incredible job of locating the finest imaginable collection of woodworking tools, and they aren't afraid to tell you just how well they'll work.

All the stock shaping tools basic to the work can't be bought at the discount mart unless you're willing to work more slowly and with clunky tools. I like to work fast and with good-feeling, springy tools that have a feeling of being alive. Take, for an example, the typical American drawknife. It's too big, often 10-12 inches across the blade; the handles are too long, and the blade is straight rather than being gently curved. The bevel is often too steep, and the thing feels about as vibrant in the hands as a rotten pine branch. On the other hand, Frank Mittermeier has a fine little German drawknife no more than 6 inches wide in the blade, with pear-shaped handles that fill your palms; its slightly curved, shallow-bevelled blade fairly zips through hard wood.

Incidentally, I've heard some folks say

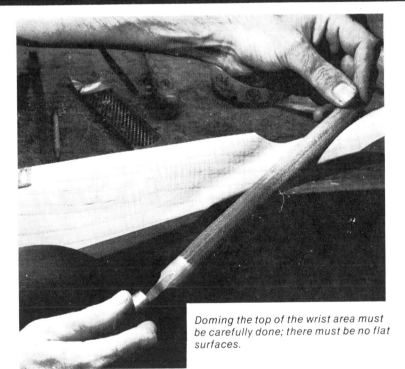

Doming the top of the wrist area must be carefully done; there must be no flat surfaces.

that you can't use a drawknife on curly maple, but that just isn't so. The trick is to pay attention to the grain structure, take light cuts, and be certain that your cuts are in an angular, shearing motion rather than just ploughing straight ahead. Also, the blade must be kept razor-sharp, as with all tools in gunstocking. Some blanks that are exceptionally brittle across the fiddleback figure often want to split in slabs rather than cutting, precluding the use of a drawknife in shaping a fore-end, but even then I use that tool on the buttstock for initial cuts where splitting

off large pieces can speed the work. It's not often that the drawknife isn't useful.

A hewing hatchet is also a useful tool for gross removal of buttstock wood; Al Linden used to use one, and so did Wallace Gusler while he was still in Colonial Williamsburg's gunshop.

Shaping a stock is one of the fun parts of gunbuilding to me. It's purely a sculptural sensation, since a gunstock truly must have the flowing lines and grace of fine sculpture to be successful. For this reason, I make considerable use

133

of a heavy ¾-inch half-round gouge and a 16-ounce lignum vitae carver's mallet for shaping. Though the gouge will effectively remove large quantities of surface in a hurry, the individual cuts are relatively narrow and allow you time to consider your work in a spatial sense while you proceed. The gouge is particularly useful on the cheek side of a stock. Another tool handy for the same purpose is a small-sized scrub plane, which has a convex iron that makes a smooth, hollow cut. Planes can't be worked into the convoluted areas of a stock that a gouge will reach, however.

Although the early stocker had available to him a large selection of files and rasps, made by such firms as W. Butcher in Sheffield, the expense of these items confined them somewhat more to metal work than wood. Spokeshaves and planes were used more often than rasps, and in fact cutting tools are often better than rasps in intermediate and final shaping in that they cause less trauma in underlying wood fibers, leaving few tool marks that rise to the surface later. Rasps, however, provide an easier control of shaping, and I use them extensively after the heaviest cuts are over. One of the finest such tools is the Nicholson No. 50 patternmaker's file, a tool recommended to me by stockmaker Jerry Fisher. Rather like the old farrier's rasp, the patternmaker's file has individual projecting teeth, but they're much shallower and are arranged in staggered ranks. The file is also light and flexible, and though it will remove great quantities of surface quickly, the cuts are smooth and shallow and don't leave telltale fiber

striations well below the surface as a farrier's rasp would do.

I also use half-round cabinetmaker's rasps in six, eight, and ten-inch lengths; I prefer a handle on all my files, though I often grasp a file well above the handle for fine shaping.

Tools of more "modern" concept in construction are the excellent "Surform" tools by Stanley; I use the large flat blade mounted on their rasp-style frame, and use a convex blade with no more handle than just duct tape wrapped around the ends, which allows the tool to be worked at a low angle to the stock. I also use the round "Surform" to a small extent, in conjunction with several sizes of standard rat-tail files. The round tools are particularly useful in comb-nose shaping and hollowing cheekpieces.

That's really about the extent of shaping tools I use, though I can think of others I'd like to have if I had the time or money. We'll discuss other necessary tools as we proceed.

The greatest understanding of the stock architecture of the flintlock rifle comes easiest from studying and handling

originals — not from any desire necessarily to copy the form of an old stock, but simply to understand just how the flowing lines and curves of a graceful stock meld into a flowing continuum of design. This is a difficult thing to grasp from halftones in books, which are basically one-dimensional even with excellent photography. Too many gently curved or rounded subtleties of the longrifle stock are lost in photographic translation, with the result that even the most willing neophyte gunstocker is left with flat and slabby areas where they shouldn't be. I don't know what the ultimate help for this is in areas where neither original rifles nor good contemporary work is available for study, though some of the published stockmaking elevation and section drawings are detailed enough to be really helpful.

The longrifle stock was actually a child of the Baroque style, derived from a Seventeenth Century concept of design which emphasized the flowing, swelling line, rounded, organic surfaces and a concept of decoration that was integral with the basic architecture of an object. Details such as carving and inlay, to the

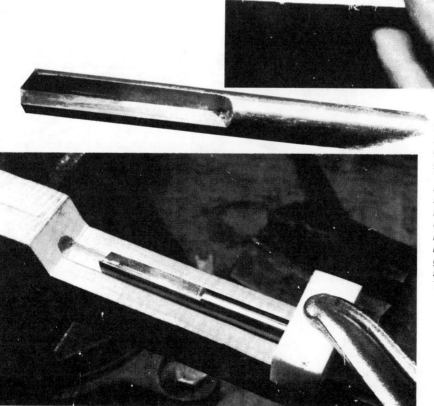

Gouging the ramrod groove, above, requires both uniform width and depth; note the center line and two guide lines pencilled on the stock. To drill ramrod holes without runout, make a single-flute deephole drill, similar in design to those used by barrelmakers. Note the pronounced clearance rake on the back edge. At lower left, the ramrod drill is ready to run, guided by the ramrod groove, and lightly clamped to the stock under a piece of grooved Teflon.

134

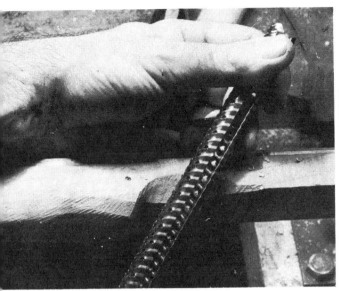

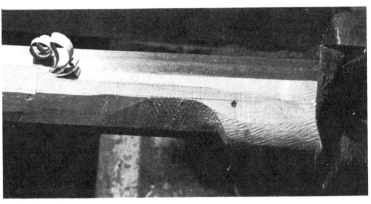

After making the beginning cuts for forestock shaping, as at left, the drawknife and rasp are used to shape the forestock into three basic flats for ease of finishing to a smooth, level surface.

Baroque mind, were to be extensions of the basic form rather than simply tack-on additions. For the whole to be successful, the basic form required perfection of line and symmetry, and the very development of the basic form invited enhancement with surface decoration, even to the extent of the mechanical portions. This is why the German rifle or the American longrifle can be decorated with easier success than a centerfire sporter. The modern sporter stock, even with its considerable grace, has evolved around architectural demands created by metalwork whose function has dictated form to a greater degree. The centerfire rifle can be, and is, decorated successfully with checkering, carving and engraving, but the very nature of the total design requires a greater consideration of details used than does a longrifle, unless the finished results are to turn out a visual disaster. That's not to say that the decoration of a longrifle stock is just a

simple matter of adding scrolls, but if the stock itself is architecturally correct the decoration can seem part of the total design rather than something squeezed from a tube.

With all centerlines established, stock shaping should begin with the buttstock. The position and shape of the lockplate and the form of the buttplate's sides and extension obviously play a considerable role in the form of the buttstock. However, in shaping a stock one should have a mental concept of the whole rather than concentrating on one small area and then proceeding to another, or things have a way of becoming disconnected. In order to define and keep track of the complex planes of a rifle stock, the angle of your work light is important; portions of the stock should always be in shadow rather than flattened with a "fill" light, and it's important to step away from your work frequently and have a look at the progression of things from a distance.

In stock shaping, although the finished

work is to represent an almost totally curvilinear form, the eye can perceive changing planes more readily if those planes are defined by a line. That's to say that if you want a rounded surface that is visually correct, it's easier to construct that surface from a series of *flats* than beginning with a continuous curve at the start. On the longrifle, this concept is particularly useful in developing the comb, wrist and forestock areas, though it can be applied to the entire stock if you're fussy enough. George Hoenig once told me of an old German stocker working for Gus Pachmayr who shaped all of his work in flats, constantly increasing the number of flats until the stock was round. That's going a bit far with it, since making a gunstock isn't necessarily just an exercise in geometric construction.

Most beginners begin to shape finished features too early in the shaping process. The cheekpiece, for instance, while definitely a projection from the stock, really doesn't rise considerably from the stock much less than three inches from the comb, and consequently the cheek side can be initially shaped almost as if there were no cheekpiece. Allowing for the total

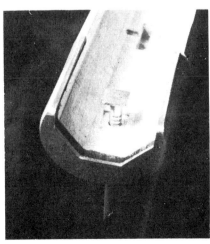

Bivins prefers a finished forestock shape as shown above, left, for strength and appearance; the triangular form becomes more rounded after running the forestock moldings. After the muzzle end of the stock has been contoured, center, the shoulder of the muzzle cap inlet is easily located with tape. After inletting, the muzzle cap is attached with a rivet, right, which is peened into a counter sink in the outside surface of the cap.

form of the cheek from the start slows the shaping; it's better to try and understand right at the first what doesn't *need* to be on the stock rather than what is to remain — or, as I said in Part I, think in terms of taking away everything that doesn't look like a longrifle stock. That seems like a hackneyed truism, but it's amazing just how difficult a thing it can be to grasp.

One thing you certainly don't want to allow for while shaping, with certain exceptions which I'll note, is relief carving. Beginning stockers tend to try to leave relief moldings around the lock mortise and the opposite stock flat while shaping, with the usual result of blobby moldings and slabby areas on the wrist. The only place I consciously leave extra wood standing for carving is at the rear of the cheek, and I seldom leave more than $3/32$-inch of wood above the buttplate at that point; more than that is unnecessary, even for carving with many overlaps. A sixteenth-inch is usually ample, since the stock tapers away from the buttplate. Other carving, including the lock moldings, are a matter of reducing areas of the *finished profile* of the surface to leave raised designs standing. If carving is treated that way, then it will follow the basic surface of the stock, seeming a part of it, rather than having the appearance of being stuck on.

I use the drawknife for initial shaping cuts since it is particularly fast for removing square corners from a blank. I usually prop my knee under the stock while shaping, with one foot resting on a round of my bench stool. A drawknife will only want to follow the grain, and will tear if pulled opposite the grain. With any tool, cuts across the grain are often the safest, and consequently the drawknife should be angled a bit while pulling through the wood. I reduce both sides of the stock to three basic flats with the drawknife, and then begin basic "feature" shaping with the gouge. This can be done with the Surforms or the pattern file, but the work is slower. I prefer to reduce the entire butt to its basic form with the gouge, leaving the rasp to bring the stock to its final rough form by having to do little more than removing the ridges of the gouge cuts. This is particularly useful on the "working" surface of the cheekpiece.

The cheekpiece line shouldn't be parallel to the toe line of the stock, but should lift a little at the rear, since the lines of a buttstock should be conceptualized as lines of differing angles converging somewhere in or above the lock mortise area. The lower edge of the cheek can be either finished off at right angles to the stock or left as a cove; I prefer the latter since it's a natural product of shaping with a gouge, and easier to finish. Also, the cheekpiece is one of those areas where the longrifle

draws directly from classical architectural design, and the cove molding is one of the standard elements of a classical entablature.

The "outboard" face of the cheekpiece doesn't need to be much longer than four inches on a longrifle, and it should set back from the comb nose at least $1\frac{1}{2}$ inch, and possibly more. This face is left as a tapering flat while shaping, though it will be cut with moldings later. This face should be closer to the stock surface at the front than the rear, giving a "wedge" appearance when viewed from above. Some old stocks don't have this feature, with their cheeks left parallel to the stock centerline, but I believe the "wedged" cheekpiece is prettier. Choose for yourself.

The upper section of the cheekpiece can either radius gently away from its outside edge or drop sharply in to a pronounced radius, depending upon the vagaries of style. To make a cheekpiece a useful appendage, I prefer to hollow it only enough to give it a graceful appearance. Many longrifle cheekpieces are little more than a vestigial decorative gesture, while the German "jager," with its thicker butt and wide comb, often has a full cheek that is essentially flat on the "working" surface, and these actually do work to position the face. On the longrifle, the face is often positioned more by the comb than the cheekpiece, and on early rifles with long "baluster" wrists running well back into the buttstock, the front of the cheekpiece is actually taken over by part of the wrist.

The rear of the cheekpiece is shaped as a cove rising as much as $\frac{1}{2}$-inch off the stock (seldom more than this), with its profile as a sweeping curve rising toward the corner of the buttplate. I prefer to drop this curve down rather than carrying it up at a high angle, since it is then easier to design a carving pattern that will flow naturally out of the cheekpiece profile.

In shaping the top of the comb, and while bringing the comb down flush with the buttplate, I prefer to leave the top of the comb in three flats until the sides of the butt are completely shaped out. The side edges of the comb are then readily apparent and easier to keep straight, and they may be rounded over in the final shaping. Lancaster rifles often have a domed "flat" as the *finished* comb, with definite "break" lines on each side of the comb, which is attractive. For that matter, early rifles are known with the comb left in three flats, which is also visually interesting, but when this is done the comb flats should be an extension of identical flats on the buttplate extension. In other words, the molding at the front of the buttplate should not be rounded if the comb is to be finished with flats. In any event, the comb line should follow the

line established by the top of the buttplate, and not run off at an angle either up or down. I much prefer a straight comb, and occasionally allow it to gently sink down toward the wrist, but then only in the last three inches of the comb.

The wrist of a longrifle often seems a troublesome area to the beginning stocker, and in fact it is perhaps the most complex area. I prefer to think of the wrist as being swallowed up by the buttstock; carved delineation of the wrist often gives the illusion when looking from above that the butt could almost be slid straight back off the wrist. Even on Federal period rifles, or "Golden Age" as some prefer it, the wrist should have good definition fairly well to the rear of the comb nose. On early rifles this definition is carried well back, with the upper wrist line actually tapering down toward the toe. Early German rifles, paradoxically, don't have much wrist definition; the longrifle very likely derives its baluster-wrist form from the fowler, particularly English and French pieces. Early American rifles tend to have a wrist slightly wider than high, though not always. A wrist that has this form, or is at least round in section, is the most graceful, while those that are higher than wide begin to gain a "thick" appearance pretty rapidly unless the stock is already a bulky one such as you would have with a large-diameter barrel, say $1\frac{1}{4}$-inch.

The width of the wrist in proportion to height is often determined by both the thickness of the lock lug and the diameter of the barrel at the breech. For the proper proportions and feel in the stock of a flint rifle, either a swamped or straight-tapered barrel is virtually essential. Some stockers using small-diameter (under $15/16$-inch) straight barrels overcome wrist-shaping problems by brazing a wedge-shaped piece to the lock lug, and welding up the pan cover of the frizzen so that the frizzen will still lie close to the barrel. This does throw the tail of the lock out, permitting a wide wrist with a low profile, but this is only a stopgap process since a straight barrel does nothing to add to the good balance of a rifle.

I try for a wrist that isn't a great deal more than $1\frac{1}{4}$ inches high by a bit less than $1\frac{1}{2}$ inches wide, usually $1\frac{3}{8}$-inch, measured at the smallest point; these dimensions are of course governed by the size of the barrel. I often shape a wrist as a rough, rounded diamond shape until I have it near the dimensions I want, then round the entire thing over with rasps. You don't want any flat places on a wrist. To make the wrist flow properly out of the comb fluting, I often rough shape most of the top of the wrist with a round rasp or Surform; I prefer the comb to come down to a knife edge where it meets the wrist, though the angles of this edge shouldn't extend too far back down the stock or you'll have a fragile comb nose. The idea is to radius the comb nose down to a knife edge.

The upper and lower lines of a wrist are not parallel, and in the case of an early rifle with a big barrel, where the stock is more than $1\frac{3}{4}$ inches in height, the wrist actually tapers rapidly toward the comb. Very early rifles, "jagers," and some schools of Pennsylvania stocking have virtually straight tangs, with the wrist humping down behind the tang. For better flow, I prefer to put a bit more curve in the tang, though this is a no-no on "jagers."

The underside of the wrist should be shaped from well forward underneath the lock mortise so the wrist makes a flowing transition into the lock area. There should be no abrupt change of planes at this point, and you need to file from front to rear at this point even if the grain is adverse. The area underneath the lock should be gently rounded on a longrifle, and really rounded on a "jager," and the top of the stock on each side of the tang should also be well domed over, even to the extent of rounding over the tang if necessary. Some Lehigh rifles were particularly flat on each side of the tang, but a stock can become unwontedly massive at this point if that is carried too far.

The toe flat of a longrifle stock is most graceful when it tapers from the buttplate forward. Depending upon the buttplate, of course, I try for a toe $\frac{15}{16}$ to 1-inch wide at the buttplate, tapering to $\frac{9}{16}$-$\frac{5}{8}$-inch under the wrist. After you have rasped the toe flat to its final level, don't be tempted to finish the trigger plate by drawfiling it while it is on the stock. If you do, you'll be left with a dip in the stock at the rear of the plate, due to the fact that steel is harder than wood, obviously. Remove the trigger plate and finish off the top surface with the thing chucked in the vise.

Before the forestock is shaped out, the ramrod groove must be established. Using the centerline drawn on the stock, run a shallow groove the length of the long part of the fore-end with a $\frac{3}{8}$-inch gouge. It's best to draw off three lines for the groove, one on each side of the centerline to establish the total width of the groove; work inside of these lines and your groove will remain straight. At this point, you should have the bottom of the long part of the fore-end cut down to its final dimension, the bottom line paralleling the bore centerline. The short part of the fore-end should also parallel the bore centerline, though it will be shaped out with a taper later. The bottom line of the forestock should allow a quarter-inch between the bottom of the stock and the bottom of the furthest-projecting barrel lug on a swamped barrel.

I cut the ramrod groove with three sizes of gouges, and finish shape with 100 grit paper wrapped around a piece of round cold-rolled stock. I frequently squint down the forestock to check alignment, and I strive to keep the groove a constant depth by checking with the depth gauge of a vernier. Most grooves need be no wider than $\frac{3}{8}$-inch, which is what I use on longrifles, even with a tapered ramrod (which all flint rifles should have). My rods are $\frac{5}{16}$-inch "inside the stock," $\frac{3}{8}$-inch for most of the rest of the length, with the business end swelling to $\frac{7}{16}$-inch. A rod should be as large as you can make it and still conveniently fit the bore, for obvious reasons. In any event, the ramrod groove on a graceful rifle should be considerably shallower than you might think; I like to finish mine out no more than $\frac{1}{8}$-inch deep for a $\frac{3}{8}$-inch rod, and $\frac{3}{16}$-inch deep for a $\frac{7}{16}$-inch rod. With less than half the diameter of the ramrod "buried," the forestock is much slimmer and the thimbles are easier to inlet; the thimbles, in fact, look much better with more exposure.

When you have completed the ramrod groove, you're faced with the hoary task of drilling the ramrod hole. The only way I've found of doing this with complete reliability is to use a drill bit that has the same configuration as a standard deep-hole drill. These are quickly made with the use of a mill to cut the single straight quarter-flute. The end of the drill is then simply ground away on a bevel to leave a single cutting edge which is at right angles to the axis of the shank; the cutting edge extends from the center of the bit to the outside. Make or have a machinist make one of these for you of drill rod, and heat-treat as you would a twist bit. Turn a shank on the opposite end, and using an appropriate diameter cold-rolled rod, lathe-drill a corresponding hole in a 46-inch length of the cold-rolled to accept the drill bit. I silver-solder the two together.

Most other types of bits, including the twist bit, will tend to follow stock grain when drilling, but the deep-hole drill, with its single half-diameter cutting edge, will bull its way straight through with virtually no run-out. That is, *if* you start the drill straight to begin with, which means that the ramrod groove must be even and straight, and of uniform depth. With the stock belly-up in the vise, I verify this by placing a long straightedge on the short part of the fore-end, and checking the distance between the bottom of the straightedge and the ramrod hole drill, with the drill lying in the ramrod groove. If this checks out, take a narrow flat chisel and cut a vertical flat face in the front of the short part of the fore-end where the ramrod groove terminates. This is done to insure that the drill will start straight with no influence from an angular surface.

Lightly clamp the drill down with a piece of grooved hardwood (I use a scrap of Teflon), avoiding binding or springing the drill, and drill the hole with an electric drill. The deep-hole drill can be run at full speed with no problem, though it should be pulled out every $\frac{1}{4}$-inch of cut with the drill still running to clear the chips or the flute will pack and cause run-out. Have someone stand beside the vise and rub a bit of beeswax on the hot bit each time it comes out to avoid binding.

You should wrap a piece of tape around the drill as a depth gauge so that you will know when to stop drilling. The tape should be near the drill chuck, positioned to signal "stop" when the tape is even with the muzzle. I drill the ramrod hole so that it will reach the position where the trigger guard pin tenon will go. This way, the rod will be plenty long, and will slip home into its hole with a nice metallic "snick" when the ramrod tip touches the guard tenon. If you're curious, incidentally, about the position of your ramrod hole (and who isn't), just drill a hole through the stock in a place where it will be covered by the guard extension, and use the drill bit as a depth gauge. This is useful to know when positioning the front lock screw.

At this point, I usually complete the inletting of all the lock internals, trigger, and fit the lock bolts, and usually inlet the sideplate as well. As mentioned in Part I, refer to *Rifle* No. 38 for lock inletting techniques.

Forestock shaping begins with the definition of the front of the lock mortise, which I find is most easily done with a gouge; I then proceed with the short part of the fore-end by chamfering off the upper edges with a drawknife, using *light* cuts and paying attention to the grain. You can avoid nicking the barrel side flat by simply stoning away the sharp points of the drawknife edge-ends. Drawknife away the bottom corners, or use a flat Surform, and finish the roughing with a rasp. This part of the fore-end should have a well-rounded surface, not flat on the sides or bottom. I generally plane or rasp the entire fore-end down to $\frac{1}{4}$-inch thickness or less before starting any shaping, and this should be a constant thickness, the fore-end following the swamped profile of the barrel. The short part of the fore-end, incidentally, should be no longer than 12 inches for best appearance.

The long part of the forearm is best started with a radiussed cut using a round Surform or a big rattail. I then shave away the length of the fore-end in a series of three flats, one at top, one at bottom, and leaving the sawn surface between. These three flats can then be easily straightened with a rasp, sighting down the stock occasionally until they are regular, and the entire thing rounded over. I shape a forestock with somewhat of a triangular shape rather than cutting down to a very thin, flatter shape. This adds considerable strength at a point where the stock is its flimsiest, and the forestock shows good highlights when finished. Even so, the sides of the forestock are no more than $^{11}/_{64}$-$^3/_{16}$-inch thick at the highest point. The stock loses most of its triangular shape when the forestock molding is relieved, so you needn't worry about leaving the fore-end flat near the bottom edge.

The muzzle end of the fore-end is then rounded over to receive the muzzle cap. I prefer this section to be 3½-4 inches long, though as much as 4½ inches won't hurt. If you are to use an ungrooved cap, rasp the stock right down to the bottom of the ramrod groove. For a grooved cap, some of the groove obviously must be left. I much prefer an ungrooved cap since they are far easier to make and look just as well. "Jager" tips are almost invariably grooved, but since they are made of horn the groove is easily cut in. We haven't the space here to go into the construction of a muzzle cap; the one illustrated here is investment-cast from one of my own patterns. Incidentally, don't be tempted to inlet the nosecap before the forestock is shaped, or undercutting and gaps will result.

The muzzle cap should be positioned at least $^1/_{16}$-inch behind the muzzle, and a little more won't hurt, since you must allow for seasonal growth of the fore-end, especially if the rifle is stocked during the winter. I locate the rear cut by placing the cap on the stock and then carefully wrapping a piece of tape around the stock. A flat chisel is then cut around the tape, a bevelling cut made, and excess wood rasped away with a patternmaker's file. One edge of the file should be ground "safe" for this purpose. When the cap will just begin to slip over the inlet, final fitting is done by spotting-in and paring with a flat chisel, or cutting down high spots with a coarse pillar file. Use a mallet to drive the thing on, and when it touches the rear of the inlet, spot it in until there is full bearing all the way around, paring lightly with a chisel as needed. The muzzle cap should fit tightly with no "rattle." When you have a good fit, remove the barrel and squeeze the top edges of the cap in so that they will be tight against the barrel. The cap is best riveted on, and I use a single rivet made from a copper roofing nail, the gripper marks filed off the sides and the head filed square for inletting into the stock. The inlet for the nail head should be no deeper than the thickness of the head, or the rivet won't pull down tight. With the muzzle cap off the stock, drill the rivet hole through the cap, and drill the hole through the wood $^1/_{32}$-inch *back* as with the "draw-bore" hole mentioned in Part I; when the rivet is inserted it will pull the cap tight against the shoulder of the inlet. The cap must of course be countersunk lightly on the outside; assemble the whole and clip off the rivet about $^1/_{16}$-inch above the surface of the cap. With the barrel pinned in the stock, peen the rivet down into the countersink with a small ball-peen hammer, and file it down flush.

With the barrel in the stock, and using a long straightedge, mark off the final top line of the forestock from one end to the other. The top of the stock at the breech end is governed by the top of the lock lug, but generally speaking the top forestock line should be at mid-point or $^1/_{32}$-inch below the center of the side flat the full length of the barrel, never above the centerline. If this line cuts into the top of the muzzle cap a significant amount, don't file off the entire top of the muzzle cap, but allow it to flare up. This is a nice accent which compliments a flared barrel. Rasp off the top of the stock down to your lines on each side, and round over the upper edge of the stock leaving no more than $^1/_{64}$-inch of "flat" next to the barrel. Much more than that is unsightly.

That completes the basic shaping of the stock, leaving inletting of the rest of the furniture, which we can't cover here lest our long-suffering editor be forced to unsheath his trusty red pen.

The hallmarks of a fine longrifle stock are its graceful, flowing lines and limber feel in the hands; while shaping one take every opportunity to step back and view the total picture. Try the stock constantly for feel, and sight down it for trueness of line. Above all, compare your stock mentally with the shape and feel of any original that you can get your hands on. If you have nothing but photographs to work from, carefully study the position of highlights in the picture, since they are a good indicator of where things must curve rather than becoming flat. ●

Relief Carving the Gunstock

By JOHN BIVINS

OF THE gunstocker's art, carved decoration is historically one of the most important artistic features used by the craftsman. Relief carving has fallen into disfavor in recent years, particularly since World War II, though as late as the early 1950's full relief-carved surrounds for checkering on pistol grips and forearms was still being regularly ordered from better carvers such as German-trained August Pachmayr and Reinhardt Fajen. American riflemen today prefer the relatively unadorned classic stock which has evolved in this country since the early 20th century; this form stresses purity and exactness of architecture, and is seldom embellished with anything more than fine, complex borderless checkering patterns. Europeans continue to order fine carving, however, often including extensive paneled game scenes in addition to foliate scrollwork, leafage, and other motifs. From the impact of American stock design on European stockers, however, it appears likely that the art will not long be practiced there on the scale which it is now. Too, carving is expensive work, though less so than engraving in most cases, and the basic cost of the guns themselves has caused many shooters ordering custom work to place more emphasis on technical aspects rather than decoration.

Unlike today, carving was basic to any fine arm in the seventeenth and eighteenth centuries, and it was considered a luxuriant extra touch well into this century, as one well might witness in the armsmaker's catalogues of seventy years ago. Relief carving attained its greatest artistic height in Paris during the seventeenth century, when the great baroque art of the French stockers literally influenced the hands of every stocker of merit from London to Tula in Russia. Published design books delineating carving and engraving constructions were inspired by the work of such Paris masters as Thuraine and Le Hollandois, and the larger European gunmaking establishments who could afford such expensive tomes purchased them for source material.

Relief carving reached a pinnacle of complexity during the rococo period, after 1720, when the stiff acanthus leaves and balanced symmetry of scrollwork of the baroque period gave way to a writhing, flowing assemblage of naturalistic floral motifs, ruffled and foliated scrolls, and stylized interpretations of sea-life, or *rocaille*, which lent its name to the art of the period. By the end of the 18th century, classical architecture had begun to cause a restrained, linear and formal influence upon carving, both on gunstocks, furniture, and building elements, though it was still France that proved the principal design center for the new classical taste. Boutet was the acknowledged master of the era in respect to gunstocks. After the first quarter of the 19th century, relief carving on gunstocks began to degenerate as a major artistic medium, and carvers began to revive in a rather florid manner motifs used in the two centuries past. The Victorian period, in fact, is singularly marked by an endless repetition of such revivals throughout the arts. The genius of the baroque and rococo periods has not been improved upon, and we can do no better today than to employ the art of these two great periods. . .if we are able.

The shooter of the 17th and 18th centuries was hardly satisfied with a gun that had no carving at all. It seems, in fact, that people of those times expected beauty in places where today we wouldn't take notice. Internal mainsprings of flintlocks, for instance, were often beautifully finished with filed decoration, even though the owner of the piece might not ever remove the lock himself. By the same token, even the meanest fowlers or rifles usually had some vestige of carved decoration, no matter how simple.

Away from the gunmaker centers, carving often became mannerist art, reflecting untutored folk-art woven throughout a general design influence from the cities. The carving on American longrifles is an example of this, for it seldom attains the technical excellence, for instance, of the very complex relief-carving on 18th-century furniture. American gunstock carving is interesting in its very naivete, however, for in it we find an often brilliant mixture of both baroque and rococo, modified by the experience and education of the carver himself. In order to study the greatest technical ability in gunstock carving, though, we must turn in most cases to fine-quality European guns, whose often exquisite work was more often than not the hand of a specialist carver. Such specialists in this country worked for cabinet makers in Philadelphia or Boston, however, and not for gunstockers in Allentown or Lancaster.

I won't discuss scene carving here for two reasons: it is not much used in this country, and when it is, it must be executed by a carver who is also an anatomical artist, or the work is usually a failure. Fine scrollwork can be carried out by anyone who is skilled with their hands and can draw a bit; the major point of understanding is to be able to visualize a harmonious, flowing continuum of design with each element relating to the next and contributing to the whole with meaning. The easiest method to obtain this understanding of design-flow is to study and draw carved designs executed by early masters on gunstocks, furniture, or any other medium. . .including relief plaster work and even tombstones. Good sources today abound in the republished French design books, monographs on furniture of the rococo period, and books on the longrifle. The student should set his sights high, however, and in studying the work of American gunsmiths, pay particular attention to the finer carvers such as Eister, Noll, and John Brooks. . . all of whom are represented in Kindig's *Thoughts On The Kentucky Rifle.*

The techniques which we will use here are basic to relief carving on any wooden surface, and may be used to execute carved decoration on a sporter stock as well as they may be used on a longrifle. The basic architecture of a longrifle, however, lends itself most readily to carving designs, since carving must appear to be a harmonious part of the stock design itself, not just some fussy appendage tacked on "for pretty." The curves of a sporter stock are more difficult to relate to a general carving pattern. In either event, a gunstock is far better left void of any decoration unless the work is carefully thought out and executed with precision, since the finest job of inletting and stock shaping in the world can be destroyed with mediocre carving. Carving is an art which one should feel committed to, not something which is done because there is a space to be filled.

Whatever the type of gunstock, only certain hardwoods are really suitable for

Designing the carving pattern begins with constructing the basic "skeleton" of the scrollwork, which must have good flow and spatial balance before the final details are added to the pattern. Each detail is drawn complete, though some of the design may be cut away during relieving or modeling.

Rough relieving of the ground is best done with gouges, cutting across the grain nearly full depth, to within 1/16-inch of the penciled pattern.

carving. For sporter stocks — or flintlock jaeger rifle stocks for that matter — the classic choice is always *juglans regia,* or one of the many forms of European walnut. This wood is dense, relatively hard, and, most importantly, has pores that are short in length. American walnut, or *juglans nigra,* by contrast, has long fibers with coarse pores, and is too brash or "broomy" for much detail, unless it has a good deal of figure. Figured wood always has the densest cell structure, and provides the best carving surface. Cherry suffers the same coarseness as black walnut, though an especially dense piece from a hillside-grown tree may take carving fairly well. Claro walnut, though not as hard as European, should take detail well if there is fairly abundant figure in the stock, just as black walnut does. All of the walnuts, and cherry, are more difficult to handle in finishing, however, since the grain tends to raise prominently. Sharp edges in carved detail can be lost by this if care is not taken.

Possibly the best gunstock wood for detailed carving is sugar maple, due to the natural denseness and lack of porosity of the wood. The best stocks for carving must be hard enough so that they can't be dented appreciably with a fingernail, especially if fiddleback figure is present. Soft maple with a great deal of figure is quite difficult to carve well due to pieces of wood splitting out of the less-dense sections of the figure. The best maple

often has a dark color with a pinkish cast, and a carving tool leaves a shiny cut in it, just as in European walnut of good quality. One good test of the carving quality of a stock blank is to make a cross-grained cut with a small gouge or parting tool, and note whether the tool cut is clean. If the tool tears the wood appreciably, you will experience difficulty in both cleaning up the carving ground and in modeling the carving with gouges.

Tools are basic to carving, and if you are serious about carving, this is no place to save money. Poorly ground and tempered tools might teach you some new vocabulary, but they won't help you do the job well. Thirty years ago quite a number of firms were in business which

140

The pattern is then outlined with the tools, cutting straight down on the penciled lines; for preciseness, using gouges for radiused cuts, flat chisels for straight and sweeping lines, and a small 1mm chisel for the smaller radiused cuts which can't be done with a gouge.

V-gouge, if your prefer) is needed, and a minimum of four sizes of straight No. 9 gouges: 2, 4, 6 and 10mm widths. Two No. 8 gouges, in 4 and 6mm, would be useful. Gouges are made in a host of radii, as you will note in the catalogues. One No. 5 quarter-round gouge in 8mm width should also be in a starter set of carving tools. For cutting around radii for which you have no gouge to fit, you should make yourself a tiny, flat, thin chisel with a 1mm blade, a tool useful also for inlaying silver wire, but that's another story.

Most of the carving knives on the market aren't especially useful in regard to shape. The spear-shaped pen blade of a quality pocket knife serves very well for the fast removal of carving ground. Pick a knife with a pen blade about 1 3/4 inches in length, and with a coarse stone, remove all of the edge from the blade except for 3/8-inch at the tip. This tip edge should be stoned with a very shallow angle to the cutting edge; the rest of the edge is left blunted since the thumb of your left hand is frequently used to stop the travel of the blade at that point.

made fine carving chisels, such as Addis in England, but many of these have either gone out of business or shifted production to other lines due to flagging demand. I have tried a number of both domestic and foreign brands of tools, and have found that the best quality commercial tools available here are those of David Strassman & Co., made in Wupperthal, Germany, and sold by Frank Mittermeier, Inc. (3577 E. Tremont Ave., Bronx, N.Y. 10465). A very close second are the fine Swiss tools sold by Woodcraft Supply Corp. (313 Montvale Ave., Woburn,

Mass. 01801). No other tools I have tried that are readily available have been able to withstand normal use. A flat chisel, for instance, ground with a 20-degree bevel, must be able to withstand being driven straight down in hard wood without developing a chipped or bent edge from either too little or too much temperature in drawing the blade. In purchasing carving tools, buy the larger professional size. They cost more, but you are making a lifetime investment.

Except for gouges, which few carvers ever have enough of, a basic set of carving tools need not ruin your bank account. Three sizes of No. 1, or flat chisels, are a good start, in 2, 4, and 6mm widths. A 3mm swept 60-degree parting tool (or

Stones are critical to proper use of carving tools. Needed are a four or six inch soft Arkansas, a hard Arkansas of the same size, and an India combination stone with a coarse grit on one side for shaping the bevel on new tools. Also needed is a hard Arkansas tapered point slip for honing the inside of gouges, and an Arkansas knife stone for use inside the parting tool. Stones should be kept in a covered box to keep dirt and sawdust off their surfaces, and they should be used with a good quality non-gumming honing oil, such as A.G. Russell's. There is not enough space here to discuss the sharpening and honing of carving tools;

The remaining ground is then broken up with chisel cuts at right angles to the pattern, allowing the knife blade to easily cut away the remaining fillet. Note the position of the fingers on the tools, where with the knife, the thumb is used continuously to position, guide, and brake the tool.

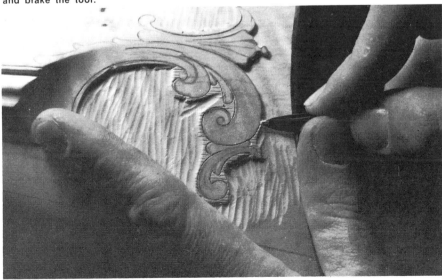

an excellent illustrated guide to the process may be found on page 10 of the Mittermeier catalog. Bevels on carving tools must be kept quite shallow, from 10 to 20 degrees angle depending upon the work. All of your tools must be kept *razor* sharp at all times.

A carving mallet is useful, but is not necessarily used continuously. Of the lignum vitae types, buy the lightest one you can find; the heavier ones are really for sculptors. I find that I more often than not have picked up my small rawhide mallet when the tool needs driving.

A toothbrush with stiff bristles — as stiff as you can find — serves very well to polish your carving after it is modeled, and will also clean away stray scraps of fiber that seem to cling tenaciously in various nooks and crannies.

Of all your tools, lighting is perhaps the most important. If you can't see the work properly, you won't be able to finish it well. A close friend recently brought one of his completed rifles to my shop. The rifle had extremely well-drawn and followed carving, but around the work small flakes of wood were missing. I asked my friend how he had overlooked the numerous tiny flaws, and he didn't know. . .until he admitted that the only light over his bench was a big fluorescent fixture. Fluorescent light is an excellent fill light, but what is needed in carving, just as with checkering, is a certain amount of *shade,* which fluorescent doesn't provide. I have an eight-foot fluorescent fixture over my bench, attached with a cord to the wall on the far side to angle the back side of the reflector up, bouncing light off the wall and keeping it out of my eyes. My "working" light is a 150-watt incandescent bulb mounted in an articulated-arm fixture, situated where I can throw light on the work from any angle desired. For best visibility, the carving surface should be in slight shadow at all times. . .not in direct light. This is vital to both modeling the work and to avoiding those "hickies."

Before starting a carving job, the stock should be fully shaped to final form and sanded with at least 220 grit garnet paper. Before carving a stock, I generally raise the grain three times or more on the entire stock to bring out the heavy rasp cuts and other tool marks buried in the wood. . .to do this after carving is to invite damage to your carved detail.

I prefer to simply sketch off the carving pattern right on the gunstock. Paper is fine for practice sketching, but is flat and won't tell you how the pattern will fit the curved surfaces and general architecture of the stock. A pattern may be transferred from paper with carbon paper, but that really doesn't work too well. Sketch it freehand, and if it doesn't

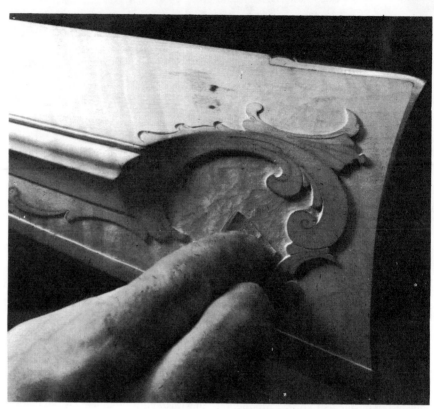

After the ground is cut as smoothly as possible with light cuts of the knife, and the entire surface is level, the remaining tool cuts are removed with 150, then 220 and 280 garnet paper. The ground must be free of tool cuts.

suit you, "erase" it with sandpaper. To achieve good balance and flow from one section of the stock to another, it is best to draw out all of the carving which you plan to use on the stock, including both straight and curved moldings, and while doing this step back frequently and take a longer view of the piece. On a longrifle, lock moldings are also drawn at this point. Many beginning carvers make an attempt to shape these moldings and finials while shaping the stock, but they must not be cut until the stock is finish-shaped for best results.

Good relief carving is seldom more than 3/32-inch in height, unless there is a great deal of overlapping elements, so there is little need to leave a lot of extra wood in areas which you want to carve. I generally leave no more than 1/16-inch standing above the buttplate on the cheek side of a stock; the natural angle of the stock gives you a bit more as you progress toward the cheekpiece. The section of the stock from the tang through the length of the wrist is treated as one piece of carving on a longrifle, so no extra wood is needed there. The entire surface is relieved.

In sketching a pattern, first establish the basic "skeleton" of the scrollwork to insure proper flow of the overall design. If your primary lines aren't correct to begin with, penciling in the balance of the detail won't make the pattern appear natural on the stock. When the basic lines satisfy you, draw in all of the detail you will be using, even though some of it will be cut away during groundwork and modeling, and will have to be re-drawn later. A

centerline is often needed on carving that must align with linear points, such as the axis between the point of the comb and the center of the breech tang.

Before making cuts for scrollwork, I often cut in all of the butt and lock moldings, though I don't relieve them at this point. Straight-line butt moldings are easily cut with a 60-degree "long jointer" single checkering tool; after making a light incised line, run the point of a thin-bladed knife down the groove to cut to full depth. Curved lock moldings are most easily cut with the parting tool, though take care in places where the tool must cut across the grain.

The preferred technique for relieving the carving pattern begins before a tool even touches the pattern itself. Called "bosting in" by English carvers, the process simply involves hogging wood away from around the design. It is best done with gouges and cuts running across the grain to avoid slips and splits. The knuckles of the left hand should be rested against the stock to help act as a brake for the tool, and at times a very slight twisting motion of the right hand will speed the cut. Make these relieving cuts to within 1/16-1/8-inch of the penciled pattern, but take care not to run over. Making these cuts before the actual pattern is cut in will relieve some of the pressure of the carving tools as they cut down.

The "secret" of precise and crisp carving is that the entire pattern must be "stabbed" in — chisels and gouges cutting straight down around the penciled lines. Carving may in fact be quickly outlined with a parting tool, but the resulting beveled cuts on every element rob the carving of the hard shadow-lines needed to provide sharp definition of the work. Use the parting tool for incised scrollwork and for outlining moldings, but limit its use in outlining scrolls that are to be relieved.

Gouges should be used as much as possible to make radiused cuts, such as the volute of a scroll. Angle the gouge away from the work so that the bevel is as perpendicular to the stock surface as possible, and tap the tool in with a mallet. Cuts much deeper than 1/16-inch are impractical since bevels tend to wedge and compress the wood, and may cause a fracture, particularly in curly maple. For long curves and straight lines, cut straight down with the flat chisels, always keeping the bevel facing away from the line being cut. Too much pressure on a flat chisel will leave nicks in the edges of the carving from the corners of the back of the blade; this may be remedied a bit by simply stoning away those back corners somewhat.

For cutting radii for which you have no gouge to fit, the small 1mm chisel mentioned earlier is the ticket. One may be made simply enough out of an old X-acto blade or any suitable piece of steel that is no more than 1/16-inch thick. This tool may be tapped in, or, if you prefer to push it down, make the handle long enough so that it may be grasped with the entire hand. I use both a small and large-handled version of this small-bladed chisel. Bevels are stoned equally from both sides of the blade, and the corners of the blade are relieved with the stone on both sides.

To make the chore of removing the rest of the ground around the carving a quicker one, cut straight down with a 4mm flat chisel at right angles to the pattern, all the way around. If you space these shallow cuts closely, the knife will cause small pieces of wood to break away easily around the carving.

Finish cuts on the ground are done largely with the knife, aided by both flat chisels and the quarter-round gouge. Some carvers prefer skew chisels for this work, but I have never found them particularly adaptable to my work methods. In using the knife, take care that the point does not stab the edges of the carving, and use your left thumb as a stop to prevent excessive travel. The blade is pushed with the index finger of the right hand or with the thumb of the left; a small bit of tape wound around the knife blade where these fingers contact makes the work more comfortable. Make light, shearing cuts, and continue cutting until the pattern is raised to the height desired, and all gouge cuts are removed. It is paramount that the ground be level from one section of the carving to another, so that the carving actually has the appearance of having been applied to the surface. If you should break out small chips with either knife or chisel, work the surfaces down with the cutting tools. Sandpaper simply won't remove such "walloons." If you should loosen a big chip. . .well, go sit out on the porch with a good glass of cold white wine for awhile, and then come back and re-draw the damned thing so you can cut away the break.

Your ground should show only the light chip-cuts of the knife blade at this point. I prefer to relieve all the carving on the gunstock before proceeding further, though one section at a time may be finished if preferred. The next procedure is to finish the ground. Start first with 150-grit garnet paper; anything finer will not serve to grind away surface irregularities. Sanding with the grain, level the entire ground. Hard-to-reach places may be sanded by folding the paper tightly several times and sanding with the edge of this "bundle," or, if you wish, glue the paper to some heavy veneer and cut it up with shears into shapes that you need, as my friend Bob Watts does. After leveling the surface with 150, switch to 220 and then 280 to make the surface as perfect as you possibly can. Finishing the ground before modeling the carving is necessary in order to avoid rounding edges which should remain sharp.

Now comes the fun part. . .modeling the design. Good carving is never flat, but is hollowed in such a way that the full three-dimensional qualities of your design are brought out. Good modeling should almost give the feeling that you can reach around *behind* a scroll or leaf. A study of the way a leaf twists in nature, showing

Modeling begins by reducing the pattern to its various flat planes and overlapping surfaces and continues with various sizes of gouges to sink the flutes and hollows, taking care that the tools are kept razor-sharp to avoid tearing the wood.

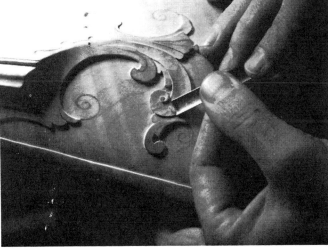

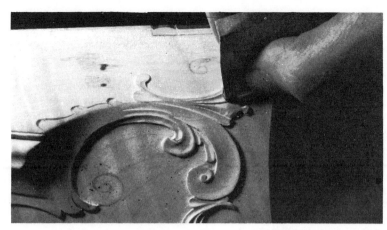

part of its bottom side, is helpful in understanding such an impression. In modeling, it's essential that the tools be kept as sharp as possible, since sandpaper cannot be used to finish every surface of carving without softening the design. With hard, dense wood and sharp tools, you will have a smooth cut in any event.

Begin your modeling by using the knife and chisels to bring out the different flat planes and surfaces of the design, and then proceed with the gouges to cut the hollows, always taking light cuts and paying particular attention to the grain structure. There is one direction in which the tool always cuts best, and take care that you are following that direction, even if you must change the direction of the tool several times while fluting a scroll or leaf. Don't hesitate to add a small hollow even to the outside of a scroll, for such techniques lend sharpness to the carving.

Edges which must be rounded may be done with either the knife or flat chisel; don't rely on sandpaper to do this, or your scrollwork will end up looking like a pile of bleached cow bones. When the modeling is completed, *carefully* clean up your surfaces with folded bits of 220 and 280 paper, taking pains to preserve the integrity of each sharp line. Flutes and hollows may be cleaned up with sandpaper rolled around a pin punch. Sandpaper should be used as little as possible, and don't be concerned with small tool marks in deep places in the carving, such as in the interstices of an acanthus leaf, since such tiny areas will be filled somewhat by the finish. Accessible surfaces, however, should look like carved marble, and finished off with a hard scrubbing with the toothbrush. The brush often loosens stray fibers and reveals places that need further finish work.

Early carvers used a good bit of chip-carved gougework to add detail and

add a further impression of depth. Drive a small gouge straight down, and then make an angling cut to remove the sliver. Don't overdo this, or you will cheapen the overall pattern. Incised-scrolled volutes which you have re-penciled onto the stock, must now be cut with gouges and knife. On this particular pattern, shown in the accompanying photos, I employed silver wire at these points rather than making an incised cut, in order to follow a customer's wishes. Wire may often be used to enhance carving, and we'll discuss techniques of inlaying it in a later issue.

With walnut, or a softer grade of maple, it's well to raise the grain around

the carving by dampening and heating before applying finish. Do not, however, dampen the carving itself unless you want to spend a good deal of time re-defining the carving. In finishing, I prefer to use either a methanol or toluene-based NGR (non-grain-raising) stain on maple, such as "Artistain," a Sherwin-Williams product, or one of the spirit stains marketed by Albert Constantine of New York. Water-based stains, particularly those containing either nitric or chromic acid, cause unnecessary work in re-polishing or even re-cutting the carving. NGR stains, however, despite their name, do raise the grain. When you have acquired the desired color, allow the stock to dry and then re-polish the carving with folded bits of 280 paper.

In using either a drying oil (linseed or tung) or one of the resin finishes, it's imperative not to load the carving with finish. Apply one heavy coat and allow it to soak in and dry. Resand your entire stock lightly with 280 and 320 paper, touching up the carving where needed, before applying more finish. After the

Detail may be added with restrained use of gouge-work, which lends depth to the carving.

first coat of finish, don't allow oil to collect in the carving cuts, or the resulting glitter in those places when dry will give a garish appearance to the work. The ground immediately surrounding the carving should be dull, with the highlights of the carving finished. Fluting of scrolls and leaves should not be filled with finish, either; if you put on too much, brush it out with a soft toothbrush. Walnut is more of a problem in finishing than maple, since the pores of the wood must be filled. Filler or sealer, however, must not be applied to the carving — you must take care to work around your designs, or the carving will be plugged, and detail lost. After the first coat of finish is applied, steel-wooling carving does no harm if the stock is of maple, but with walnut it's best to stick with 400 and 600 grit wet-or-dry paper in reducing the finish, to avoid pulling out sealer or snagging long fibers in the carving. Avoid the use of powdered pumice or rottenstone around the carving, since it will show white in places where it can't be brushed out. For those who prefer an antiqued look to a longrifle stock, you may moisten the stock very lightly with boiled linseed oil and then dust the carving with bone black (available from Brownell's). Take an old T-shirt and rub the carving down hard; this will leave the dusty black "patina" in the low areas of the carving. This is not a suitable process for walnut unless you have a very dark piece of wood to begin with.

Though relief carving is always at home on a flintlock longrifle, it is equally attractive on many other types of fine gunstocks, if used with taste and restraint. Carving is a dying trade today; even in Oberammergau, Germany, a world center of fine wooden sculpture, artisans are leaving their tools for less artistic but more lucrative work. It hardly seems appropriate that shifting trends in firearms fashion should allow the art to pass in this country. So buy yourself a set of tools, and give yourself and this ancient craft a boost. ●

Advanced Gun-Stock Carving PART I

STUDY AND TOOLS

John Bivins

SIX YEARS AGO, in *Rifle 44*, my article entitled "Relief-Carving the Gunstock" introduced the basics of carved decoration for rifle stocks. Of course, that's a subject that could well fill an entire volume. At a recent gunmaking seminar held by Western Kentucky University, we instructors attempted to present the art and history background along with discussion and demonstration of technique. I like to see things put into perspective that way, which prompts me once again to consider a few ways that we might court the muse of leaves and scrolls.

In my earlier article, I gave consideration to what sort of stocks might be appropriately carved. The answer to that, of course, lies almost entirely in the history of gunmaking and might well be considered confined mainly to a period from the middle of the nineteenth century back to the sixteenth century. Of course, stocks were carved both before and after that time, but the very best of it was done during a relatively brief period — from about 1660 to just past 1800, about a hundred fifty years. In the history of sporting firearms, which incredibly covers five hundred years or a little less, the period when stock carving was an important decoration really wasn't very long.

Shifts in both international styles and arms technology put stock carving into a very minor role after the middle of the nineteenth century. Breech-loading arms dictated new forms of gunstock architecture not as well suited to surface decoration, with a few exceptions. Germans, of course, have long been considered the high priests of relief carving, and the sort of genius that brought about the magnifi-

cent baroque church interiors of early eighteenth-century Bavaria certainly wasn't lost even in the early part of this century. One of the finest carved stocks that I've ever seen was executed by an anonymous carver for the prominent Munich gunmaker Carl Stiegele. The work covers the entire stock of a high-art *schuetzen* rifle made in 1908; a stock by the same carver is illustrated on pages 332 and 333 of Monty Kennedy's book, *Checkering and Carving of Gunstocks*. Of course, the stockwork of even the plainest *schuetzens* borrows not a little from the flowing, organic forms of the baroque, and that is the stylistic idiom where stock carving is a comfortable thing.

Twentieth-century bolt-action sporting rifles speak a different language, since the art of their stockwork must depend entirely upon a crisp and flaw-

less execution of stock architecture that is rather more linear than earlier styles. Areas of a modern classic stock that are appropriate for surface decoration lend themselves best to fine checkering patterns, and I must confess that my own tastes in such things run most to the light and delicate prewar English and German stocks nicely adorned with beautiful mullered (fluted) border point patterns. It's gratifying to see that some of our stockmakers are returning increasingly to those earlier classic forms.

Regarding the use of checkering, as a matter of fact, you may well be aware that checkering is not in the least modern. French gunmakers were using it, along with carving, before 1750 — and even the so-called skip-a-line patterns that are now generally out of fashion were common in France and England in the eighteenth century.

Such a long tradition of design is reason enough for us to consider the sources of gunstock ornamentation. Checkering, which is now both utilitarian and decorative, was originally derived from a technical means of covering broad areas of otherwise plain ground between carved designs. Really a sort of cross-hatching cut in a variety of styles, the work was incised or cut in low relief and in its earlier forms is referred-to as *diaperwork*.

That bit of information in itself might not seem terribly interesting to a stockmaker, but such things should be very important to us if we consider that the competent carver today is an artisan who has set out to understand and absorb a very complex vocabulary of stylistic details from a period in history whose artistic excellence almost defies description. We need to know the origins and development of such motifs if we care to build our own working styles. Of course, we may simply copy original work if we wish, which is certainly an excellent means of acquiring skill in design, but it seems to me that the serious stockmaker who wants to contribute to the art must ultimately make his own statement, whether in carving, subtleties of stock design, form of gun furniture, or whatever.

In using the term *historical*, I of course refer to the art that prevailed during a period of particular interest to the student of carving. This immediately brings to mind wheellock, flintlock, and early percussion rifles, fowlers, and pistols. Stockmakers who aspire to recreate the essence of a classic American long rifle of some given period rush to the pages of George Shumway's excellent *Longrifle Series* or perhaps one of the books sponsored by the Kentucky Rifle Association, all in a highly motivated desire to gain inspiration from early designs. Old firearms are, after all, documents of a sort, and a *fine* one is almost a book unto itself. Gunstockers who are interested in continental styles are a bit less fortunate in seeking comprehensive publications of fine stockmaking art. If we really want to understand the art of carving, though, why should we limit ourselves to studying early gunstocks? The art that graced those fine pieces, after all, was a manifestation of styles used in many media and on many different sorts of objects, and it was used by artisans across two continents.

To gain the ability to design fine decoration that fits historical styles and takes advantage of the finest possible detailing, the carver must learn to broaden his horizons and to be able to see exquisite art wherever it occurs. The acanthus leaf that adorns the knee of a rococo cabriole leg or the writhing and vibrant scrollwork of a baroque portrait frame should command our interest to the same degree that a good piece of stock carving does.

In Europe, of course, gunmaking was highly specialized, even in small urban areas. In the great gunmaking centers such as Paris and London, it was nothing for fifteen or twenty pairs of skilled hands to have executed a fine arm; one of these of course was in many instances a carver. A carver may have spent his entire career decorating gunstocks, but if he proved himself to be an artist adept in design, he more than likely applied his art to surfaces not associated with gun shops, including both furniture and architectural carving. The seventeenth-century artisan Jean Berain was apprenticed in gunmaking. Both his father and his grandfather had worked in the trade before him, but the young Berain proved to be most adept in design; in 1660, he published a set of engraved designs for arms decoration, and he later designed architectural decoration and elaborate furniture, the like of which graced the apartments of Louis XIV himself. Berain's designs and those of other artists and gunmakers like Thuraine, Simonin, de Lacollombe, and Marcou of Paris are still available to use today in published form.

The British were slower to publish design sources for decoration, but by shortly past the middle of the eighteenth century, a good number of architectural designs, furniture designs (such as Chippendale's famous *Director*), and collections of general motifs for use on any surface (such as

This baroque design (*right*) for acanthus tang carving is from the work of a Paris gunmaker and was engraved in the third quarter of the seventeenth century. From the same source is this design (*below*) possibly for forestock carving.

Monte Mandarino's jaeger stock in a baroque style similar to those above shows the integration of ornament with the architectural features that are essential to baroque work.

those issued by Henry Copeland) were available. Unlike the French design sources aimed at the arms trade, the British books were intended more for builders, cabinetmakers, and silversmiths, but you can bet your boots that some of these books were owned by the most fashionable London gunmakers as well. Just as we would study fine early carving on any surface that bears it, we should make every attempt to study all of the design sources that were available to those early stockmakers. Most of them have been reissued, and I'll include a list at the end of part two (in the next *Rifle*).

Whether our interest is in making a chiseled and carved Paris-styled fowler or a much simpler though elegant long rifle in the manner of the Lancaster school, we are dipping to some degree into that great swirling pool of seventeenth and eighteenth-century art that we now define as baroque and rococo. This is not the place for a long lesson in international art history, but it seems obvious that we'd want to know why Jacob Dickert's simple C-scroll carving has some stylistic connection with, say, the exquisite work of the Stockmar family in the Thuringian area of Germany. Was it because they were all Germans or because Dickert owned a set of published designs or had seen a Stockmar job? No, it was because they were all drawing from design trends that were common throughout the trades that decorated surfaces. To be sure, the Suhl carving was a great deal more sophisticated and detailed than Dickert's was, but even the larger American shops didn't achieve the European level of specialization until late, so we needn't chastise poor Dickert for showing less education in his decorative designs.

No matter who executed the work — or where it was done — with a bit of study, we find that we can see the elements of those great international styles in the way that the carving was designed and how it related to the surface that it decorated. Baroque art, which had its roots in the late Italian Renaissance mannerism at the beginning of the sixteenth century, had developed — by the late seventeenth century, particularly in France — into what might well be considered the most successful use of form and surface in the history of western material culture. Using pulsating, organic forms in combination with stylized "perfections" of natural flora and bizarre interpreta-

These designs for rococo stair panels (*A*) are from Abraham Swan's *The British Architect* of 1758. A relief-carved oak panel from Paris (c 1700-1710) is of classic baroque design (*B*) but shows beginnings of the rococo manner in the cross-hatching at the top. Copland's 1746 *New Book of Ornaments* includes these rococo ornamentations (*C*) for carvers or engravers. John copied this rococo carving (*D*) from original work in a house dating from about 1765-1770.

tions of quasihuman and animal figures, the baroque successfully combined those seemingly jangling motifs by observing the harmony and balance of Grecian classicism. The result, on either a gunstock or an armchair, was often a startling expression of illusion, where some curvilinear form spontaneously erupted into foliage and cavorting creatures that defy description.

Nowhere does the essence of the baroque display itself better than on a gunstock, where curving lines must compliment and blend with linear elements, and where decoration must be perceived as a natural enhancement of the basic form. The same is true of rococo art, which was really a first-quarter eighteenth-century whimsical maturation of the baroque, using the same naturalistic forms but with greater frenzy and spontaneity. Further artistic distillations of things in nature were added — such as the foamy curl of a wave. The style was relatively short-lived in urban centers, though; by the 1760s, the decorative arts had begun to reflect a more restrained and linear expression gained from new studies of classical ruins such as Herculaneum.

Why should the stock carver be concerned with all of this? Because the

This rococo carving (*left*) appears on the leg of a chair attributed to one Peter Scott of Williamsburg, Virginia, about 1750. John himself carved this bit of rococo (*below*); the wood hasn't been finished yet.

early artisans were. It was part of the "art and mystery" of their trade, as ancient apprentice indentures stated it. We should want to understand, as they did, how we may make a dramatic interpretation of natural forms that are harmonious extensions of the sculptural form of a gunstock. To think of the carving on a gunstock from any other viewpoint would defeat the purpose of the decoration entirely and lower it to the level of muddled twentieth-century concepts such as fake portholes on a 1956 Buick. We're not out to encrust a surface just because it's there. Instead, we want to accentuate and draw attention to the basic form of the gunstock, and that purpose at times requires more than a little restraint on the part of the carver.

In any event, the central message in this preachy preamble is that we all need to escape from our arms-related tunnel vision and see the basic art of the early period in *all* of its forms and media. We need to absorb it, to draw it, to build a reference file of sketches, photocopies, and rubbings, and we need to build our libraries with books that illustrate the art.

It should seem obvious that finely executed carving depends heavily upon a finely executed gunstock. If the stock has all the grace of a mud fence, then the world's finest carving won't rescue it. In fact, it would be virtually impossible to design fine carving to fit a stock with poor architecture. The stock must have its own inherent beauty without any surface decoration at all. Understanding that, let's turn to the materials that the stock should be made of, if we want to be able to adorn it with competent and well detailed relief carving.

Clean tool cuts and precise carving depend upon dense and hard wood, and that is the basic premise of any discussion of stock woods here. The European masters quite naturally preferred European walnut. Whether we call it European, French, English, or Circassian, and whether it comes from Grenoble or from northern California, it's all of the species *Juglans regia*. The *royal* in that Latin name is still a good one; a blank of European walnut is still the king of gunstock woods for almost every job that the gunstocker does on it, including carving. I have seen some that was brash and open-pored, the tree having grown too fast because of terrain or climate, or both. European walnut, of course, is really suitable only for stocking English and European guns — but I've been known to ignore that restriction myself. Early stock-

In the body of this article, John describes a round-nose gouge with a swept edge on top — here is how the thing looks.

The tools in this rack have the shapes that John describes as essential for carving wood.

makers preferred blanks cut from the lower bole of the tree, almost below the ground, for the greatest density and the best coloration, and they often had to deal with fairly serious flaws in the wood. It's not unusual to see a high-art carved fowler with plugs filling bark inclusions and fissures.

Longwood — the upper bole or trunk — is usually more open-pored and less dense, but of course few blanks are cut from low on the tree any more, since that requires more work, and the blanks are more difficult to season without developing surface checks. American black walnut is generally unsuitable for stock carving unless the blank is cut just at the ground, since the longwood of black walnut is relatively brash and open. There are exceptions to this, such as trees with fiddleback figure or areas of the tree where forks or large limbs yield crotch figure. Wood from such areas carves very well indeed, though if you make a study of such things, you'll find that early stockmakers generally didn't use crotch-figured wood. It came into fashion after the middle of the nineteenth century.

European stockmakers used plenty of maple in the seventeenth and eighteenth centuries. Baroque pieces were frequently stocked in burl maple, elaborately carved. By the first quarter of the eighteenth century, curly maple was used occasionally for pistols and fowlers, though I've never seen a rifle stocked in it, and the guns that were seldom showed much carving even though they may have had elaborate mounts. European maple is identical to ours, and stockmakers there preferred a tight curl, just as we now should. It's

obvious from this, of course, that there was plenty of precedent for the profusion of curly maple that was used in this country, and there was little hesitation to use that wood here for rifle stocks. I suspect that gunstockers arriving in this country found rather quickly that black walnut simply wasn't the equal of the European variety and turned to maple instead. The densest of that wood is of course eastern sugar maple, but some red maple can be plenty hard if it grew in the right place, such as high on the side of a hill. Most red maple is soft, though, and silver maple is out of the question in that regard. A maple blank suitable for carving is heavy, often dark, and you should barely be able to mark it with your thumbnail. The best test of what you can get out of a blank is make a few cross-grain cuts with a gouge. If the cuts show clean edges and a shiny appearance in the cut, run home with the blank. If the cut is a bit ragged and broomy, with loose fibers at the edges, leave it alone, even if it has figure beyond belief. I'd rather have a clean-cutting piece of plain wood than a soft stick that would shame the figuration on the back of Stradivarius's finest. Quarter-sawn wood shows the best figuration, of course, and yields the greatest stability in a stock, but virtually all wood is slab-sawn today. Even so, a certain portion of any slab-sawn tree yields a board or so near the heart that almost approaches quarter-sawing in the arrangement of the rays.

European stockers liked fruitwoods during the baroque era, particularly cherry and pear. You can carve anything on pearwood; it's incredible. But it usually has virtually no color or figure; and in Europe, it was usually

confined to such things as cheek-stock wheellocks intended to be heavily inlaid with engraved ivory or bone. Cherry is worse than black walnut as a carving wood unless the tree has grown in a harsh environment or the blank comes from low on the bole. Like black walnut, cherry blanks that are figured full-length are usually dense enough to carve, but cherry has little shear strength and can be a nuisance to inlet. Although I haven't been able to try it, I suspect that madrone — which is native to California — would be an excellent compromise if you'd like to carve a stock that looks like cherry. Madrone has a deep color like the best cherry but is very hard and dense, and if we could convince one of our west-coast wood merchants to cut some thick, long blanks, I think that the stuff would sell well even though it isn't a traditional stock wood. It might prove to be a good replacement for nonexistent or outrageously priced sticks of European walnut big enough for a muzzle-loader stock.

Another such possible substitute is claro walnut, which like madrone is quite inexpensive, but even the best of it seems to be rather soft and unsuitable for carving. Really dense pieces often have a riot of color, figure, and streaking — almost too much for good taste unless you want to stock a jaeger that looks as if it belonged to a Bavarian bawd.

That's pretty much the list of woods that are available and useful to the historical gunmaker. For those who would like to study the properties of stock woods in some detail, I recommend Bruce Hoadley's truly encyclopedic work *Understanding Wood*,

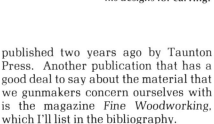

John made these tools — two of them from cut-down chisels — for stabbing-in his designs for carving.

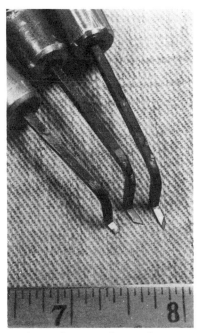

These three carving tools are grounding bottomers — a straight, a left-hand, and a right-hand.

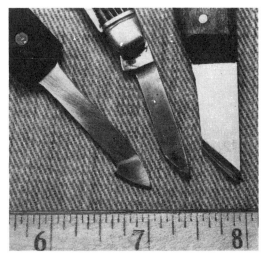

Three of John's carving knives include one (*left*) of his own design — his grounding and modeling knife.

published two years ago by Taunton Press. Another publication that has a good deal to say about the material that we gunmakers concern ourselves with is the magazine *Fine Woodworking*, which I'll list in the bibliography.

The tools of the carver of course deserve a good deal of thought. Most of us have our own ideas about what is proper as a workbench and what sort of vise suits us best, but one thing that isn't mentioned often enough is *lighting*. I covered this in *Rifle 44* but will do it again here and now. It should be obvious that one must be able to *see* the work clearly, and for the carver, that often means that light must be arranged in such a way that the work in progress looks as ugly as possible — not the design but the tool cuts. A raking light is needed to throw the work surface into slight shadow so that every cut is visible. Otherwise, you can see neither the surface flaws that need to be cut away nor the effect of modeling cuts as the carving is being completed.

Fluorescent lamps are fine for fill light, but they don't let you see the appearance of cuts on the surface of the wood. I have a double eight-foot fluorescent fixture with a reflector hanging four feet above my bench, but I have tied a string through a hole drilled in the rear of the reflector and to the wall, tilting the fixture up and slightly back toward the wall, giving me light bounced off the white wall. That cuts down on glare considerably. My principal work light, however, is a large Luxor articulated-arm lamp with

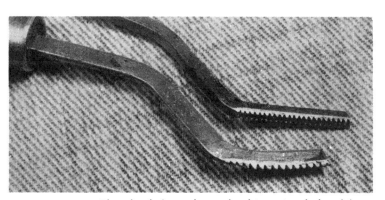

These bordering tools are a bead (*upper*) and a long jointer (*lower*) from Frank Mittermeier, used on gun-stock mouldings.

Anyone who uses tools that must be kept especially sharp has his favorite collection of stones, some of which he uses for special problems only, and some of which he hopes never to need at all. This is John's box of special stones.

a ceramic socket, so that I can use 150-watt bulbs in it without burning-up the switch. I have a series of three-eighths-inch holes drilled along the bench top near the front edge, and when I need to move the lamp, I simply plug the base stem of the arm into another of these holes. Keeping the lamp close to the work and low, I can see every cut that I make.

Carving tools are of course a major consideration to any gunmaker who wants to do fine work. Since all of the good ones are imported, they have unfortunately become quite expensive. Even so, tools are not the place to save money. Flat chisels, for example, must be able to make clean cuts in hard wood even though the bevel may be stoned to little more than five degrees, and that separates the sheep from the goats in a hurry. To put it straight on the line, most of the tools now available commercially are mediocre and worse. The only two brands that I can recommend with little or no reservation are the German ones sold by Frank Mittermeier. They are made by Strassman in Wupperthal and have a trade mark in the form of a woodscrew stamped on them. The other tools that I find suitable are the Swiss tools sold by Woodcraft Supply Company of Woburn, Massachusetts; these are finished better than Strassman's and are sent out with good octagonal ash handles, though the flat chisels have the abominable British double bevel; you have to grind the thing back if you want a bevel on one side only.

If you can find prewar tools by London and Birmingham makers such as Addis and Herring, don't hesitate to buy them, though I find that their legendary quality really is no better than modern tools by the two makers already listed. I have not found any modern English tools to be good, nor are other commercially available German tools any better — and I've tried all that I could get my hands on. There are small European toolmakers who don't export, and I have no doubt that some of them are excellent, but that doesn't do us much good here. Even the good tools are not what they could be; I'd like to see some enterprising cutler over here offer a line of tools made of something like D-2 steel, something that would hold up really well — but the price would probably gag even Bunker Hunt.

At last count, I found that I have something over forty carving tools in the shop. Many of those, of course, see a good deal more use in stockmaking and inletting than they do in carving, and in fact decent carving can be done with relatively few tools. The one thing that carvers need most is gouges;

there's always a radius or size that you seem to be missing, especially when the carving pattern is being outlined. In my earlier article on carving, I listed a basic set of eleven tools, including flats two, four, and six millimeters wide; number-nine gouges two, four, six, and ten millimeters wide; number-eight gouges four and six millimeters wide; an eight-millimeter number-five quarter-round; and a three-millimeter swept sixty-degree parting tool. That last item has to come from Mittermeier, since Woodcraft stocks only straight V tools, and I don't think that they are quite as controllable as the bent tools. I still stick by this basic set. Other shapes and sizes that you need become more apparent as you work and perfect your techniques.

It goes without saying that good sharpening techniques are important, both for the quality of the finished cuts in the carving and for the longevity of the tool. The best treatise on sharpening that I've seen is in a little book entitled *Woodcarving* by William Wheeler and Charles Hayward, issued in this country by Drake Publishers of New York. The book not only has a rather extensive examination of the shapes and uses of carving tools, as well as sharpening, but also has perhaps the best essay on the techniques of carving that I've seen among the host of carving books on the market. It can be obtained from Woodcraft Supply, and rather than take a lot of space here to discuss sharpening, I recommend the book highly.

One nonstandard sharpening technique that is particularly useful to the stock carver is the round-nose gouge; the edge may be stoned back at an angle from the top so that when the bevel is stoned-up, the resulting cutting edge is swept back and the nose rounded. A gouge so sharpened is pretty useless for such things as inletting; and for use in fluting and veining, it is a bit harder to control than a gouge with a ninety-degree face. Where it is very useful is in stabbing-in carving patterns, for the swept edge lets you fudge the tool around a radius in the pattern that the tool would not normally fit with standard stoning. If you can stand the tariff of buying a couple of extra gouges in the smallest sizes and giving them this treatment, you'll find them useful.

I house my stones in a fitted box with a lid to keep the dust off them. I use a double-sided india with a coarse and a medium side; I use the coarse side only for bringing a new tool to edge or if I drop something and break a chip out. Thankfully, that's bloody seldom, for I find that swearing inventively for a straight forty-five minutes tends to give

me a headache. I seldom use the coarse side of the india, and the medium side sees little use, for that matter. This combination stone is eight inches long; and beside it, I have a soft arkansas stone of the same length that does most of the basic sharpening on knives, flats, gouges, and quarter-rounds. I also have a six-inch black arkansas that I use only for final honing; these exceptionally hard stones remove very little metal.

Also needed are a selection of slip stones, and I find standard white arkansas stones fine for that. I use a tapered round, a half-round, and a knife-edge the most, though I have others. The edges of these stones can be reshaped by grinding them on the medium india if you need to make them fit a particular tool. For example, a knife slip can be rounded-over on its thinner edge for use as a hone for the inside of the smallest gouges. With all the stones, use a nongumming honing oil; and avoid grooving the surface of a flat stone by confining sharpening strokes to the center of the stone — instead, use the entire surface.

Also good is a strop; the one that I use is a piece of hard belting leather about three by ten inches, glued to a piece of pine, with one end of the pine backer shaped down into a handle. It's duck soup to put a mirror polish on your carving tools simply by squeezing-out a line of Simichrome polish on the leather, smearing it all over the surface, and allowing it to dry. Hollow tools can then be mirror-honed with a rocking motion, just in the manner that they are stoned in, and flats can be dragged backward down the strop. The high finish that results from this treatment shows in the cleanness of your tool cuts. Simichrome is sold by a number of gunsmith suppliers, and I'm told that motorcycle shops also stock it. I don't use my strop on carving knives; it's a bit too easy to round-over the bevel that way.

Of course your tools should be protected from banging against each other. I threw a bench rack together for the tools that I use the most; I kept the rest in canvas tool rolls, even though that's a bit of a nuisance, until recently. I solved my tool-storage problems in a manner befitting Grinling Gibbons himself when I acquired a pair of replicas of eighteenth-century knife boxes and fitted them with drilled mahogany blocks. I now have virtually all of my tools elegantly housed, standing edge-up so that I can see just what I'm after. Speaking of that, when I'm working at the bench, I keep the blades of all my tools facing toward me so that I can more quickly spot the tool that I need.

It's amazing how much time one can waste in looking for things on the bench, and I try to keep things uncluttered.

There are always tools that a carver winds-up making for himself because there's nothing exactly right available on the market. As I'll discuss in the second part of this treatise, a good deal of outlining can be done with small flat chisels. In doing that work, it's easier to control the tool if its blade is short. I've cut a couple down from regular flat chisels that had been poorly heat-treated and wouldn't hold an edge for cutting inletting. I ground them on a radius from all four sides, taking the tips of the tools down quite thin, then stoned them with a slight bevel. For use in stabbing-in, I also stone-off or break all four corners at the edge; that bit of clearance at the corners lets the tool make a cut on a radiused area of the pattern without showing prominent progression marks. The smallest of the tools is no more than a sixteenth of an inch wide at the tip; these tools can also be used for doing wire inlays. They're intended to be pushed in, not tapped.

While a carving knife isn't much use to a furniture or architectural carver, they are most useful to a stock carver. None of the commercial carving knives, however, is really any good for our purposes; they were designed for chip carving and whittling figurines, and their blades are light and flexible. They chatter and skip on a hard surface. Moreover, most of the blade shapes are about as useful for us as mammaries on a boar hog. Since the stock carver rarely uses more than a quarter of an inch of the tip of the blade, I drew myself a design for a knife some years ago with only three eighths of an inch of cutting edge. When I'm "grounding" the carving of a stock, my left thumb (your right, if you're a southpaw) is both a fulcrum and a stop, so I left the entire thickness of the blade stock behind the tip, which is three thirty-seconds, for stiffness. The bottom edge corners behind the point are dubbed-off with a stone to make it more comfortable. The tip of the knife was tapered a bit before the edge was stoned-on; and the handle was filed thin near the blade so that it would clear the workpiece when I make low-angled cuts. The blade is D-2 steel heat-treated to a Rockwell C of sixty-two — and man, does it hold an edge! A few of these were made commercially a few years ago, and another production run may soon be made by a commercial cutler.

You can approach the same effect by stoning-up the tip of a spear-point blade on a good penknife. All of the edge behind the tip can be dubbed-off with a stone. The thicker handle of a penknife, however, gets in the way at times, and most commercial pocket knifes don't hold an edge very well. A second type of knife that is useful for heavy hogging cuts on carving ground is a skew, which can be made from stock of the same thickness; but consider it a "magnum," not good for delicate detail and getting into tight spots.

Another specialized tool that is handy, though not entirely necessary, is the so-called bull-nose chisel, made like a diminutive version of the inletting bottomer, with a cutting edge three thirty-seconds of an inch or less wide. You can make these from spring-steel square stock, which holds up well enough for the purpose since the cuts made with it are light paring ones. A hardened blade should be drawn to about 425 degrees.

About the only commercial tools that I'd mention further are checkering border tools, which I use for running both lines and beads on butt stocks and fore-end mouldings. Mittermeier's standard sixty-degree "long jointer" works perfectly well for such things; so also does the beading tool sold by the same firm. I'll have more to say about their use in the next issue, when I get down to the actual drawing and cutting — the real business of advanced gunstock carving. ●

Advanced Gun-Stock Carving
PART II

THE FIRST HALF of this treatise explored something of the art-historical background of gunstock carving and had a go at providing a basis for understanding the tools that are appropriate for good work. In this concluding half, let's put those tools to work.

The first tool that concerns the carver is the pencil, which — unless he has a good understanding of flow and design — can be the downfall of his carving before he takes his first cut. I've long noted that treatises on engraving suggest that the neophyte spend many hours practicing *drawing*, though I've found that very much of that becomes irritating. As a consequence, I spent a good number of years drawing lackluster carving patterns on stocks. To create your own design, you must first be able to draw; and for that reason, practice work is certainly in order, even if the intent is to copy old work. The old saw about idle hands holds a certain truth, and nowadays if I find myself with nothing else to do — such as waiting for a lethargic waitress in a restaurant — I doodle whatever scrolls and leaves come to mind. No doubt, some of the napkins that I've left behind have branded me a bubble-brain to whomever cleared the tables, but I care not.

When it comes to drawing a design that is to be *cut*, I never resort to paper for the design. Paper is flat, but a gun stock is curved; and I have a devil of a time drawing a design a second time and making it come out as well as it did at first. *Well*, you might say, *transfer it with carbon paper!* You can do that; but I think it best to consider the stock a piece of sculpture, and designs drawn on paper then transferred don't always fit the curving lines of the stock as they should.

You should draw no design without sketching-in a basic skeletal framework first. Every carving design, no matter how elaborate, can be broken down into a few simple curves and lines, just as Hogarth perceived his S-curved "line of beauty" in virtually everything of organic form. I use a soft-lead pencil for the work, and I prefer Dixon's black number-2225 film-marking pencil — particularly for drawing on darker walnut. With a basic form in mind, I sketch the framework quickly, picking-up the curve of a cheekpiece where that is appropriate, and erase or sand-away the line frequently if it doesn't suit me.

Like the work of a water-color painter, such work is best done at arm's length, so to speak. Stand back and review these lines critically, to see that they complement both the stock architecture and themselves. When that framework flows as it should, *then* move in and begin filling-in detail, beginning with the larger elements and ending with the smaller. One of my illustrations here was the developmental skeleton for the stock pattern shown in one of the photographs; I drew the first lines on paper for the sake of illustration, but my original lines were on the stock.

I often draw all of the carving on both ends of a cheekpiece to see whether I've balanced both the amount

John usually makes his rough or preliminary drawings on the stock itself rather than on paper; but for this article, he sent these three sketches of the pattern that he carves in later photographs — first the "skeleton," then the same sketch with details roughed in, and finally the finished pattern (on the stock) with all the details drawn in, even though he may cut some away as he carves the pattern.

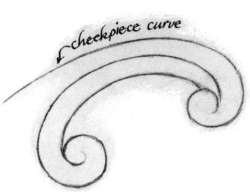

John Bivins

CARVING
and FINISHING

and the position of the main carving designs. I don't waste time with drawing but go about it like killing snakes, and I seldom spend as much as an hour even on an elaborate pattern for the cheekpiece side. Don't be discouraged, however, if the creation of a carving pattern takes you hours of pencil grinding; most of us go through that. Just don't become bogged-down with details, and learn to head for the back yard and yodel a bit before that red mist of frustration begins to arise over a leaf that doesn't fit or a scroll that remains clunky after seventy-three erasures. *Relax!*

With all of a carving pattern drawn-in, even the parts that you'll cut away in the process of modeling later, you're ready to start cutting. One thing that I should mention here — a little item that's basic to carving stocks — is leaving excess wood where it's needed for a raised design. Many beginning carvers are surprised to know that there is only *one* such place, and that is

right behind the cheekpiece. You must leave wood there, since you don't want to cut the butt plate away in the process of grounding. In all other areas, particularly around the wrist and lock mortise, carving is a matter of *sinking* the pattern below the lines of the completed stock. Trying to leave excess wood in those areas while you're shaping a stock would not only take all of the fun out of stock-making but would often result in clunky lines in one place or another.

Look at stock carving as rather like sculpting an irregular piece of marble whose inherent shape is desirable. In seeing the work from that point of view, you can readily understand that carving a stock is a process of removing material in such a fashion that you don't alter the lines of the stock in the process. If you change the flowing curves of a well designed stock by carving it, then like as not, the carving won't be successful.

The first matter at hand is ground-

ing, and although that work can be tedious, I rather like it. It's one of those things that you can do that doesn't require enormous concentration all the way through, so you can let your mind wander at times. But you'd best learn just *when* grounding isn't so critical, unless you want to lose the tip of a leaf. If you should have that happen, incidentally, don't reach for the glue. Instead, cut the offending thing away and *redraw* that part of the pattern, even if it takes a stiff jolt of Wild Turkey to help you do it.

The flattest area of a stock is behind the cheekpiece, and that's a distinct help in grounding what is usually the largest chunk of carving on the stock. If you have an elaborate pattern with many overlaps, you may have left as much as an eighth of an inch of stock standing proud of the butt plate at that point. I don't think that I've ever left much *more* than that, and most carving in fact needs less.

In any event, the idea is to remove as much wood as possible in the shortest time, for there's little point in messing with it. The safest and quickest method is to use a gouge, cutting across the grain where you can; cross-grain cuts are less likely to result in tears when you're working fast. Using a three-eighths gouge, I rapidly cut to within a thirty-second of an inch or so of where I want the finished surface to be. Now, this sort of thing requires a bit of hunkering down and squinting at what you're doing. Good carving has the attribute of appearing to have been laid over the ground. That is, the ground must be sunk on an even plane below the carving so that you're preserving the basic surfaces and lines of the stock, even as you lower them. Dropping lower on one side of a big

scroll than on the other removes some of the ability of the carving to appear as a flowing part of the whole. This isn't something that you should become hysterical about; simply let your eye move back and forth over the stock at times to pick up basic rough discrepancies in the plane of the ground. Keep the work in slight shadow while you're grounding, just as you should for virtually all carving work.

In cutting the rear cheekpiece carving, I prefer to rough-in the ground before outlining the carving, and I cut quite close to the drawn pattern. Cutting-in the pattern is actually a matter of vertical stabbing cuts; and if you've cut away most of the ground, a tool won't wedge in the wood so badly — since material outside the pattern is allowed to move slightly as you stab-in the line. Of course, there are other ways to outline carving, such as using a parting tool. Nice carving, though, has crisply defined edges that provide a good shadow line to the viewer — and some of that definition, along with other tricks such as undercutting, are best done by vertical cuts. That is not anything new; it has been the accepted way of doing clean relief carving for centuries.

Professional carvers who adorn fur-

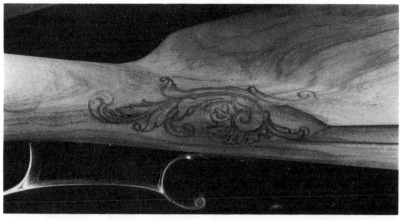

This pattern, drawn on the wood just ahead of the cheekpiece, is ready to be carved. Note the detail of the pattern and the width of its lines.

niture and interior architecture own more gouges than any kind of tool. Having many different radii and profiles of hollow tools makes outlining fast and efficient except for the time spent in looking for just the right tool to stab-in a curve. Most of us can't afford such an impressive array of gouges, so we must make do. I would certainly recommend that whenever you can adapt a radiused tool to your carving pattern, use it. There are times when the volute of a scroll can bear a little alteration if you find a tool that almost but not quite fits. To take measure of that, push the tool onto the pattern ever

so lightly, and then take a look to see what that curve is going to do. If it works, then push the tool in firmly. There's no need to tap a gouge with a mallet when you're outlining, even in hard wood, for there's a limit to how deep you can cut in any event. It's better to avoid burying the tool and to plan to deepen the cut later if necessary.

If none of your hollow tools fits a curve, then you must resort to stabbing-in with a straight tool. The smaller the radius, of course, the narrower the tool must be. In the first half of this treatise, I showed small shop-made flat chisels intended for stabbing-in. As I noted there, the corners of the blades were stoned away to avoid leaving notches in the edges of the carving. Like the gouge, these small flats are simply pushed in. Overlap their cuts as you follow a line. Though you may use wider tools to cut on a long, gradual curve, I prefer to stay with narrower

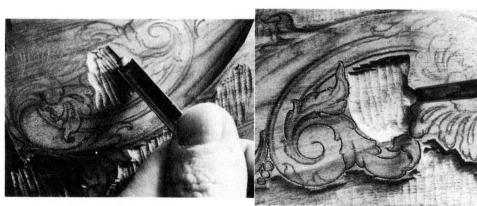

Carving begins with rough grounding, with a gouge (*above, left*). Stabbing the pattern's lines into the wood (*above, right*) is usually the work of a gouge, but small flat chisels can be used (*right*) when none of the gouges on hand fits the curve being stabbed-in.

tools since there is less tendency to wander off the line. It's really more difficult to cut-in a long, gradual curve than a small, tight one, and I often concentrate on those first to get them out of the way.

After stabbing-in, remove the rest of the ground. If the pattern is a high one, you will likely have to stab-in again before you reach the finished ground. To assist in grounding around deep carving, I often make a number of flat-chisel cuts around the pattern with a two-millimeter flat tool; this technique helps to loosen-up the ground in the more intricate areas of the pattern. Though you can use a variety of flat and quarter-round chisels for grounding, I find that the carving knife makes the quickest work of the job. In part one, I described the knife that I use. I control the blade precisely by using my left thumb as both a fulcrum and a brake, as I mentioned before. The intent is to make light cuts, leaving as clean a surface as possible. In curly maple, it's altogether too easy to pop wood out when you're following the folded grain that causes the curls.

Respect the grain flow of the wood and the way that it wants to be cut, and don't try hogging cuts. If a piece breaks away, sink the ground deeper. You can't really sand-away those little hickies, and they'll stand out like preppies at a hog killing if you don't excise them with the knife. Don't kid yourself; nice groundwork takes *time*. In working a really bitchy piece of wood, I've been able to hold an entire

day's work in the center of my palm — tiny flakes nibbled off the stock with surgical cleanness. As always, while you're grounding, keep your articulated-arm lamp low on the work so that each cut is distinctly outlined in soft shadow.

Really tight areas where the knife won't reach are another matter. To be blunt, I simply break the waste out of such places. After making cuts in the ground at right angles to the carving pattern, I simply use one of the little stabbing tools to pry out the thin flakes of wood left after the chisel's nasty work. You can then deepen and finish such areas by judiciously scraping with the grain.

Part of buttstock carving usually calls for running the lower butt moldings, which I first either pencil or scribe in and then cut with a sixty-degree long-jointer checkering tool. I often deepen that line by running a knife blade down the line made by the jointer — but if you have to do that, take bloody good care, since a sharp blade rather fancies the flow of the grain and may take off toward parts unknown. I sink moldings with a flat chisel, angling the tool very slightly so that the side of the blade bears lightly on the molding as it's cut. This slight angling prevents the corner of the cutting edge from burying itself in the molding and undercutting it — which you obviously must avoid as well when you use a knife to ground your carving. In any event, grounding around a molding is fast work with a flat chisel. Some stockmakers prefer a skew for that job, but I find the flat to be much faster.

I prefer to ground all of the carving on a buttstock before proceeding with other work, though of course you can ground one section at a time if you prefer. One part of carving that I don't care for particularly is sanding the ground, and I simply like to get the odious task out of the way all at once. If knifework is clean, and all of the gouge cuts have been removed around the rear carving (the gouge isn't used in grounding the wrist and other upper-stock areas), the sanding isn't too bad a job. You should use a gritpaper that grinds the tiny dips and ridges of the knife cuts flat rather than riding over them — on hard maple, this means 150-grit garnet paper.

For European walnut, I've found that 280-grit wet-or-dry paper usually works well enough, since walnut cuts more easily than maple does. I cut something like three-inch squares, fold them once, and have at it with vigor, taking care to sand closely around all of the carving and moldings. For tight spots that are difficult to reach with paper but too large to be scraped clean, I simply fold the piece of paper an extra time and sand with the edge of the crease. If you do that, you're better off with a lighter paper than the heavy C grades, which tend to break their adhesive films when they're bent sharply.

Another trick that is useful for crannies is to glue paper to pieces of veneer and cut it up with scissors, in the shapes that you need. While sanding, I constantly move the light to see that I'm leveling the surface perfectly smooth, and I frequently dust-off the work with a rag or toothbrush so that I'm not beguiled into believing that the ground is perfect when dust is actually masking hickies. Maple is especially bad about this.

On maple, I follow the 150-grit garnet paper with 220-grit and then dampen and whisker-off all of the ground as many times as needed. This avoids any possible complication in carrying-out that job after the carving has been given nicely detailed modeling — which doesn't take kindly to torch flames or being dubbed-over with gritpaper. I want that ground finished except for the last few touches with paper before I model the work.

Modeling tends to separate the sheep from the goats rather quickly. If you've drawn a relatively advanced pattern, it goes without saying that you must *understand* what you've drawn before cutting it — how a leaf must look if its

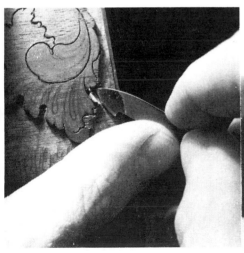

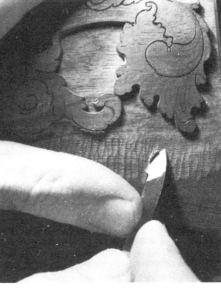

John takes the ground to final depth with the carving knife (*above*), using his left thumb as both fulcrum and brake, keeping his light (*right*) at a low angle across the cut so that gouge cuts are clearly visible and thus easily cut away.

Butt mouldings can be run readily with a long jointer, a checkering tool, then relieved with a flat chisel like this.

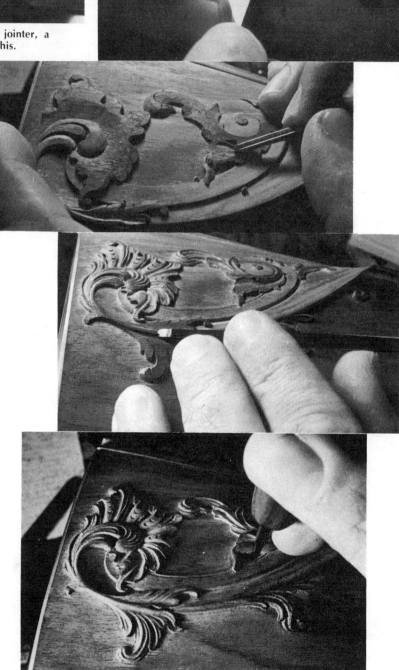

tip twists or curls, and how the fold of a leaf forms a sharp ridge and a little teardrop-shaped "eye" that must be slightly undercut on each side for effect. Gunstock carving is largely adapted from forms in nature, and there is little in nature that is represented by a straight line or a plane. Leaves undulate and curl at their edges. They may be lobate or spiny, almost to the point of appearing tattered, and they seem to writhe with a certain ordered asymmetry — which is the essence of baroque art. Carvers, sculptors, and engravers who are truly artists study these details in nature so that they can render them with vitality in their own translations.

We should learn something from that, but in my case, I am far more a historian of the decorative arts than an artist, and I have been content to study the techniques used by early carvers. Photographs in books and magazines are not as good as seeing three-dimensional objects, however, and the carver who wants to model with effective detail will take every opportunity to see original work "in the flesh."

It is a waste of time and energy to begin modeling with hollow tools. I start with what I call *flat* modeling — all the modeling that I can do with either the knife or flat chisels. If a leaf is to be hollow on both sides of a central vein, then I chamfer both sides of the leaf with the knife, cutting right down to the finished height of the carving. Similarly, I use the knife to relieve overlaps, to drop the edges of elements that are to curl, and to round the volutes of scrolls.

Dramatic carving, as far as I am concerned, shows very precise and well defined hollows and flutes, with sharp, crisp ridges. The flutes in

From the top: modeling begins with all of the "flat" cuts, using both the knife and chisels; next comes the use of gouges, in a variety of radii; then elements that must be chamfered or slightly rounded may be so treated with either the knife or the back of a flat chisel; finally, undercutting areas of high relief adds drama. This carving is shown here with both fluting and veining done, and small gouged chip cuts have been added to the ruffling of the main scroll.

158

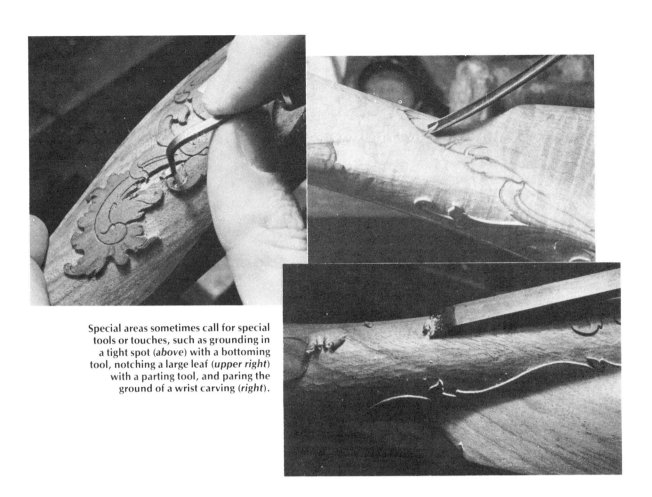

Special areas sometimes call for special tools or touches, such as grounding in a tight spot (*above*) with a bottoming tool, notching a large leaf (*upper right*) with a parting tool, and paring the ground of a wrist carving (*right*).

Voila! the finished carving

leaves and scrolls, however, are not cut just for the sake of having flutes; they should relate to the organic form of the element that is being modeled. Leaves don't necessarily have single big flutes to define them. Rather, they may have smaller flutes on both sides of a single ridge, or they may dip sharply on one side or the other, or the tip may undulate with a flute cut across the leaf. When I'm modeling the hollow areas of a carving, I choke-up closely on whatever gouge that I happen to be using. Care is necessary in running a gouge off the end of a leaf, for it's altogether too easy to snap off more of the edge of the leaf than you can stand to lose. When possible, make such cuts from the edge inward unless you're sure of the cutting quality of the wood.

Veining, which is done with the smallest gouges, is one of those techniques that gives movement and vitality to carved elements, though it can be overdone. Restrained use of the parting or V tool can complement the veiner nicely to identify individual lobes of a leaf and the like. The use of gouged chip carving, quickly done by stabbing a gouge straight down and then picking-out a second angling cut, is another technique that should be used with restraint.

Carving is often most effective when it isn't a solid whirling mass of detail but rather is broken into areas of *condensed* detail. Areas that must be rounded or chamfered — and there are really very few of those in good work — can be pared with a small flat chisel, cutting with the bevel up. Flats should have two to three degrees of bevel on the *back*, both to assist with such delicate paring cuts and to relieve cuts slightly when you're stabbing straight down.

On a relatively high pattern, undercutting is a subtle addition to the work that gives the appearance of even higher relief and adds a bit of illusion to the work, making elements seem to float above the surface. Using a tiny stabbing-in flat tool, I make angling cuts under leaves where appropriate and scrape-out the waste. No more than a sixteenth of an inch of undercutting can add quite a bit of three-dimensional illusion. I use a stiff toothbrush, bearing down hard, to clean loose fibers out of such places, and brush all over the carving vigorously to polish things up.

Good carving should be largely finished with tool cuts. If the carving tools are kept sharp, and the wood being worked is hard and dense, the hollowed areas of the modeling need no other treatment. Large flat areas usually need cleaning-up with gritpaper to remove knife cuts, though

judicious paring with flats or shallow quarter-rounds can often do the same job. When I have to sand such things, I generally use 280-grit wet-or-dry paper folded over and avoid like the very plague dubbing-over any sharp edges of leaves and other such elements. Such surfaces can also be scraped, which is likely what the old boys did. Professional carvers avoid sandpaper the way that a classic stockmaker shuns white-line spacers. If you have a broomy area of the stock that just doesn't allow clean flutes, however, wrap a bit of paper around some pin stock and clean the thing up. Clean tool cuts provide some of the life of a carving, so such cheating with gritpaper should be kept to a minimum.

The wrist area of a gunstock is one of the more tedious areas to carve, since there is so much ground to remove. The long "baluster" of the wrist can largely be taken down with the carving knife, though long paring cuts with a flat chisel add speed to the work. Though I stab-in the critical areas of lock moldings, such as the beavertails at the tips of that area, the long and gently curving areas of such moldings — particularly under the stock — can be outlined with a parting tool that is either pushed by hand or lightly tapped along with a mallet. I prefer to use a mallet, since it's faster and seems to provide a bit more control in following the line.

Similarly, the parting tool can be used to cut major notching in leaves; cut the notches before outlining the leaf, to prevent the parting tool from tearing a chunk off the leaf as it passes the edge. For such work, I use only sixty-degree tools, since the ninety-degree parting tools make a cut that is entirely too bold for most applications. In *really* hard wood, the parting tool may be used for both veining and shading leaves and scrolls, though that can be overdone. Fine shading in great profusion is more the mark of nice engraving than it is of relief carving. The parting tool, of course, is also used for incised carving, a technique that I seldom use except for accents. Relief carving can actually be enhanced somewhat by the occasional use of an incised leaf cut-in alongside the relief work and then fluted lightly. Such things can further add to the illusion of depth. Good carving, in fact, makes use of such illusion as much as possible. For carving a gunstock is not like ornamenting furniture — where the carver may have a dramatic depth of wood to cut.

The work is by no means done when you make the last modeling cuts. Finishing a carved gunstock is something of a baroque experience in

itself if you don't want to undo all that crisp art that you have so cunningly contrived. Walnut stocks are a particular problem, since the doggone things have to be filled. I can tell you from painful experience that it isn't worth the trouble of trying to fill with the finish alone. You must resort to mud — a pigmented filler, that is. Any high-quality reddish-brown commercial filler will do, particularly one that uses silica as a filler. I use an equivalent of the old Herter's French red for the purpose, and I daresay that it's no better than most anything else. It's all nasty stuff even though necessary.

Before using a pigmented filler, seal the stock thoroughly by slopping-on a thin varnish sealer until the wood takes no more, then wipe the excess off after twenty minutes or so. Use a toothbrush to get excess sealer out of the carving. After allowing the sealer to harden at least overnight, brush-on the filler cross-grain, even in the carving. After half an hour to forty-five minutes, wipe off all that you can, again cross-grain, and brush the goo out of all carving cuts — even if you see that the brush is pulling filler out of the pores as well. You don't want that junk in your carving cuts. I let filler stand for two days if I have the time, since it takes quite a bit of time for it to harden properly.

If it doesn't, you'll just pull it right out of the pores when you wet-sand. Before proceeding with anything else, I brush a second coat of sealer on the stock, taking care not to allow finish to pool in the carving. From this point on, you don't want finish left standing anywhere in the carving cuts or the ground next to raised areas, for you will not be able to get it out after it hardens. It will leave shiny places that look garish; which is why if you *do* allow finish to run into the carving, you must take a toothbrush and get it out before it hardens.

After the second coat of sealer — which is mostly lying on the surface — hardens, I begin wet-sanding. Since the dry stock was left with either a 220-grit or 280-grit finish before the sealing and filling, I wet-sand the first time with 320-grit. I prefer aluminum-oxide paper to carborundum when I can get it, particularly since the grit particles are more uniform and tend to leave fewer scratches. The 320-grit cuts fast when it's lubricated with sealer, and it doesn't tend to heat the surface enough through friction to cause any filler to loosen. Don't allow that paper to run over any of the carving, though!

After wiping the surface dry with paper towels as I work, I let the stock sit for a few hours, then brush-on another coat of sealer. I use a three-quarter-inch sable for all such brushwork. Finishing proceeds in a standard way after that: wet-sanding a second time with 400-grit wet-or-dry, sealing again, then wet-sanding with 600-grit, taking care all the while to keep finish out of the carving. Final finishing consists of hand-rubbing two light coats of sealer onto the surface to give the carving a bit of gloss in its highlights, while the hollows and ground immediately surrounding the carving are both dull.

If you want even more contrast, you can dust the carving with bone black and then rub the stock down briskly with an old T-shirt. I treat maple pretty much in the same fashion except for omitting the filler.

I am always delighted to talk gun-making if anyone has questions about any of the techniques that we publish here. I'd very much like to emphasize *talk*, however, since the time that I usually set aside for correspondence is from four to six in the morning, the fourth Tuesday of every third month, and I usually sleep through that, anyway. Call me evenings — 919-748-0275 — and I'll help in any way that I can.

sources for the gunstock carver:

Stephen V Grancsay, *Master French Gunsmiths Designs* (New York: Winchester Press, 1970).

Peter Ward-Jackson, *English Furniture Designs of the Eighteenth Century* (London: Her Majesty's Stationery Office, 1958).

Thomas Chippendale, *The Gentleman and Cabinet-Maker's Director*, third edition, 1762 (New York: Dover Publications, 1966).

Helena Hayward, *Thomas Johnson and English Rococo* (London: Alec Tiranti, 1964).

Bruce Hoadley, *Understanding Wood: a Craftsman's Guide to Wood Technology* (Newton, Connecticut: Taunton Press, 1980).

Pierre Verlet, *French Cabinetmakers of the Eighteenth Century* (New York: French and European Publications, Inc., 1965).

William Wheeler and Charles H Hayward, *Woodcarving* (New York: Drake Publishers, Inc. 1972).

carving tools:

Woodcraft Supply; 313 Montvale Avenue; Woburn, Massachusetts 01888

Frank Mittermeier, Inc; 3577 Tremont Avenue; Bronx, New York 10465 ●

Checkering

By JIM CARMICHEL

THE WEEKEND of the 1968 National Long Range Championships may well go down in history as the hottest ever recorded in the vicinity of Oak Ridge, Tennessee. Sweat flowed so freely that gripping a rifle's pistol grip was not unlike squeezing a wet bar of soap. My rifle, like the trophies which I eagerly sought, just seemed to slip out of my grasp and I suspect the same sensation was experienced by quite a few of my fellow competitors. A checkered grip, I decided, was the only answer.

Of the dozens upon dozens of magnificent target rifles which graced the firing line, the great majority were equipped with fine custom stocks. Yet only a handful bore any sort of checkering. Doubtlessly the reason for this is because very few shooters are willing to tackle the checkering operation. To be sure, the checkering of gunstocks is an exacting task and more than a few amateur craftsmen have come to grief when first taking checkering tool in hand.

The checkering on a sporting rifle must be of fairly fine line, layed out in closely matching, artistically designed panels and even the most minute flaws are sure to be frowned upon. The checkering on the grip of a target rifle, on the other hand, is rather coarse for

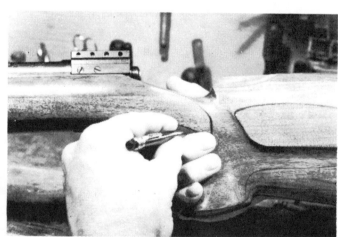

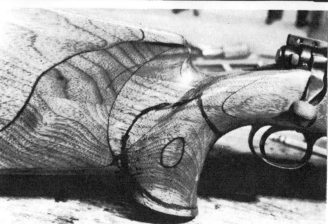

Function, not appearance, is the reason for checkering a target stock, so rough out the pattern by marking around your hand while gripping the gun, top left. The result, top right, looks a bit strange, so smooth out the pattern to make it compliment the lines of the stock.

Target Stocks

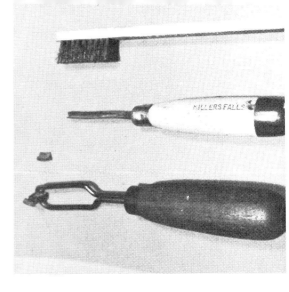

best effect, need follow no line other than the outline of the hand and since function, not appearance, is the only consideration there is no need to worry if the job is less than perfect.

To do a first class checkering job on your target rifle all you'll need is a checkering tool, a V-chisel and a grease pencil. A few other tools are helpful but aren't essential.

Begin work by placing the firing hand on the grip in the normal manner. Trace around the contacting areas with the grease pencil. This, of course, will result in a rather irregular outline but is, nonetheless, the basic pattern. Dress up and simplify the pattern by converting the irregular lines into more appealing border lines which compliment the design of the stock.

Using the V-chisel, cut the border into the wood about 1/16-inch deep.

This forms the permanent edge of the checkering pattern and should be carefully done. Just make sure the chisel is razor sharp and take your time. For the beginner, cutting such lines is more difficult than it may appear and this alone is good reason for keeping the design simple.

A slower, but easier way, in case the V-chisel makes you nervous, is to lightly scribe the border line with a stylus or

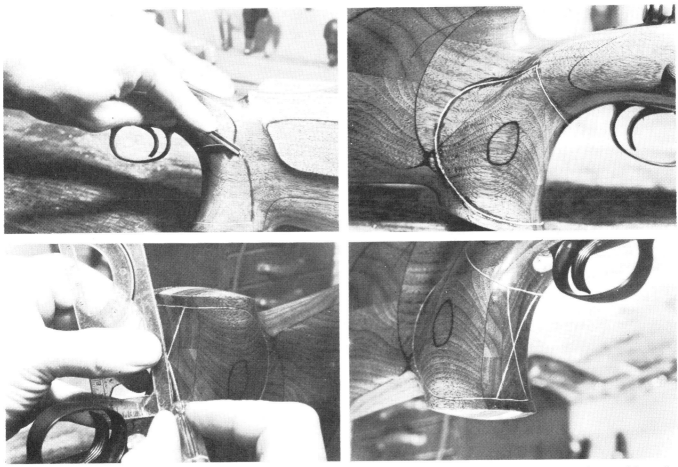

A good reason for making the pattern simple is to make difficult border cutting easier, as shown at top left where the V-chisel is used to make a smooth cut. After completing the border, top right, scribe the master lines, using a flexible straight-edge, lower left.

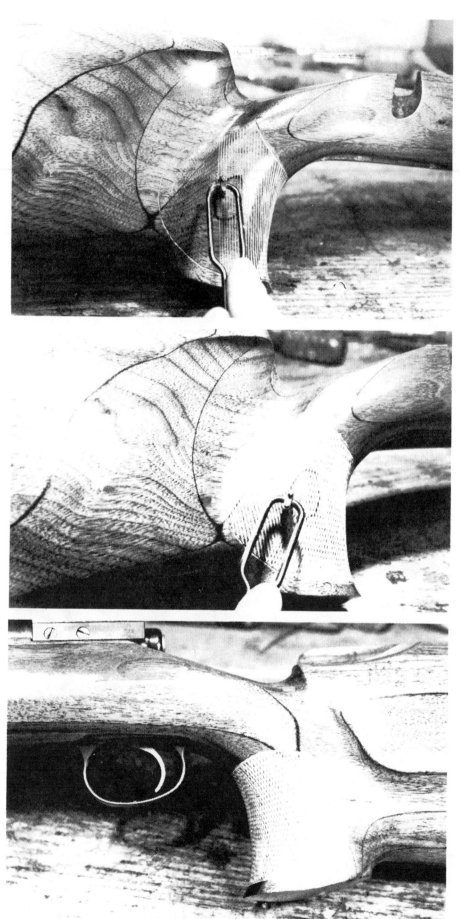

other tool, then erase the grease pencil mark, leaving a single narrow line as a guide. Checkerers who also dabble in leather tooling can use their swivel knife, which can be turned while applying even cutting pressure, to cut the border line guide. Beginners will often prefer to make such a knife cut, since it's easier to handle than the V-chisel. After a knife cut is made, it can be deepened with a bent needle file, "pointing-up" tool, or even the single line checkering tool. Whichever method of cutting the border is used, it is preferable to cant the tool slightly to make the outside edge of the cut almost vertical. Such a "wall" will help stop later slips of the checkering tool — sometimes.

One cannot then pick up the tool and start cutting, a bit of preliminary "figgerin' out" is required if there is to be any system to the pattern. Thus two intersecting master lines are cut to indicate the direction of the grooves. These master lines will determine the proportions of the diamonds as well as their directional arrangement.

The arrangement of checkering on sporting guns is usually such that the points of the diamonds tend to point along the line of the grip and fore-end. For a maximum non-slip effect on the grip of a target rifle the diamonds should run vertically. This looks strange at first, but the "grab" of such checkering is terrific.

For a checkering pattern which continues around and under the grip, the master lines must be layed out in the center of the forward (underside) of the grip as shown in the illustration. If the master lines were begun on either side the curvatures of the stock might cause the angle of the lines to shift considerably by the time you checkered around to the other side. Scribe the master lines lightly into the wood using a flexible straight edge as a guide; then cut them -- exactly straight -- with the single line cutter.

The angles of the master lines should be such as to result in diamonds which are about three times as long as they are wide. Too, for the best non-slip grip use a checkering tool which spaces the grooves about 16 or 18 to the inch. The checkering shown is 18 lines per inch. With the border and master lines in place all that remains is to fill in the space with checkering.

Checkering is nothing more than

Using a master line as a guide, make a fairly light, smooth parallel cut with the checkering tool, then use the new cut as a guide for another cut, and continue across the pattern, as in top photo. Then cut the intersecting lines, center photo, in the same manner. Note that initial cuts are shallow. After the diamonds have been laid out the lines should be deepened, lower photo, to bring the diamonds to a point.

cutting a series of straight, parallel V-shaped grooves from one side of the pattern to the other. A second series of grooves, angled to cross the first series, forms the diamonds. The checkering tool, in case you've never used one, is a simple tool with a double or triple row of cutting teeth. One row of teeth cuts a new groove while the other row follows the previously cut groove. This way the grooves are kept straight and evenly spaced.

The diamonds are made neat and sharp by progressively deepening the grooves until the tops of the diamonds become sharp. This should be done with the single line or "V" cutter, for the sole purpose of the multi-line tool is to insure even spacing. Usually about three separate passes are required to bring the grooves to full depth.

A few hints: Don't try to cut each groove to full depth before cutting the next groove; but do be sure that the line is cut smoothly, otherwise it won't serve as a good guide and the tool won't cut the next groove straight. Cut the crossing grooves after only a single pass on all the initial lines--otherwise it will be almost impossible to keep the crossing lines even. If the initial lines are cut too deeply, softer wood will tear when the crossing lines are attempted.

When the cutter slips -- and it will -- immediately straighten the line with the aid of the V-cutter or needle file and the flexible straight edge. If you don't, the bobble will be magnified in succeeding lines. In soft wood it will sometimes be necessary to use the file or V-cutter to smooth and straighten each groove to keep the guide teeth from cutting into the guide line, which will cause the tool to run amok.

The finish of the stock will serve as the best guide as to depth, for a smaller diamond of shining finish will remain on the original surface after each pass with the cutter. When deepening the grooves, make one cut on all lines running in one direction, then a single cut on all crossing lines; otherwise there will be a tendency to get some of the cuts too deep, causing the checkering diamonds to be uneven.

Although it is best to make all cuts from the same direction, the grain of the wood may, in places, tend to tear. In such areas -- you'll soon recognize them -- it may be better to carefully cut from the opposite direction. A final note: A stock can be checkered while

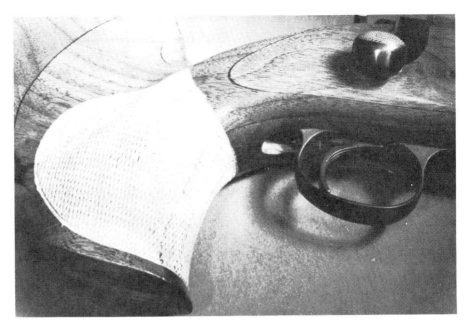

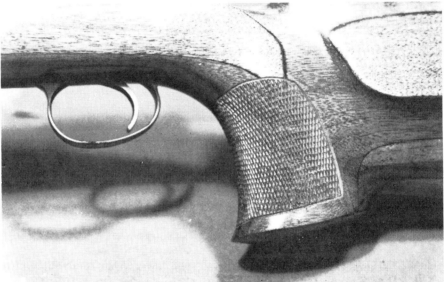

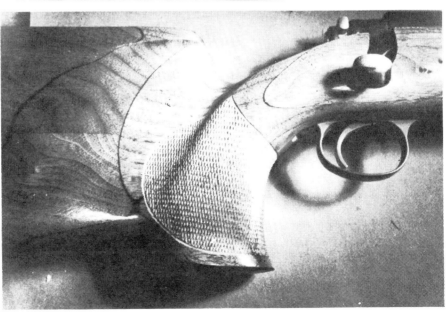

"Pointing-up," which should be done with a triangular bent needle file or single-line cutter, is accomplished by equal cutting of each line until each diamond center has a tiny speck of original finish, top photo. Remove all dust with a stiff brush, then apply a single coat of thinned stock finish with a toothbrush, brushing with the lines to remove all finish that did not soak in.

165

bouncing it on your knee, but it's many times easier if it is solidly supported in a checkering cradle.

By the time you finish "pointing up" the diamonds you may find yourself in need of one more tool – the border cutter. It consists of two rows of teeth spaced fairly wide and is designed to hide minor nicks and run-overs. In a pinch, a narrow border can be cut with the regular two-line cutter, but any border detracts from the looks of the finished job. However, as noted at the beginning, appearance is secondary to function in the checkering of a target rifle stock.

The checkering tool shown on these pages is the Brownell "Full View" tool which features removable cutting heads. Thus the spacing cutter, V-cutter and border cutter may be used on one handle. Other types of tools may require a separate tool for each operation. Take your pick -- they all work fine if used with care.

When the checkering is worked up to neat, sharp points give the job a good brushing with a toothbrush to remove sawdust then complete the project with a single coat of thin stock finish, using the toothbrush to spread the finish along the grooves in each direction. Brush out all the surplus or else you'll ruin the best of jobs by filling the grooves with finish.

If he takes plenty of time, even a novice can produce a handsome and functional checkering job with a minimum of tools. The job will likely be as good or better than average factory checkering, will result in better shooting and will give the shooter a real appreciation of the quality of fine checkering on custom guns. ●

PROFESSIONAL CHECKERING
for the amateur

By JIM CARMICHEL

By and large checkering is just checkering and the difference between an "easy" checkering pattern and a difficult one is usually the size of the area to be checkered.

As for the degree of checkering skill and experience required for this particular project, I'm going to hedge a bit further. The reason for this is that the natural talent and determination of some otherwise inexperienced individuals never ceases to amaze me. Good checkering, like everything else, is largely a matter of knowing what you want to do and then having the intestinal fortitude to see it through to completion.

And of course there are always those who question the purpose of so complex a pattern. They reason that checkering above and beyond that which is required for a non-slip grip is purely superfluous. If one is willing to accept this point of view one must also decline figured or well-colored wood for stocks, all engraving, well-finished surfaces and just about everything else of esthetic value. In my experience, however, the principal critics of ornate checkering are those who are unable to master the art themselves.

The work illustrated here was done on an "A" series Model 52 Winchester .22 rimfire which has been refitted with a sporter weight barrel. The nicely textured French walnut stock is the semi-finished Reinhart-Fajen "Classic" style with only slight modification.

The checkering pattern was copied, with some modifications, from an original Al Biesen rifle. The fleurs-de-lis, in fact, were traced from the Biesen pattern. I hasten to add that the modifications mentioned above were not an attempt to improve the original pattern but only to adapt it to this particular stock.

The checkering is 26 lines to the inch. Much has been said about the relative merits of coarse versus fine line checkering and I do not intend to continue the argument here. However, the neat delicate appearance of fine line checkering lends itself much better to decorative patterns such as this one. And, too, well-done fine line checkering is a nice showcase for the stockmaker's talents. It has been pointed out that fine line checkering of, say, 22 or more lines to the inch is not practical on a hunting rifle because it does take much abuse and general scuffing around. Again, I can't take sides in this argument for, though I have hunted with rifles having both fine and coarse checkering, I've made it a point *not* to abuse either.

First step is laying out the pattern. A soft lead pencil marks the unfinished wood easily and can be erased with a bit of steel wool. Draw and re-draw until the pattern is harmonious with the stock lines.

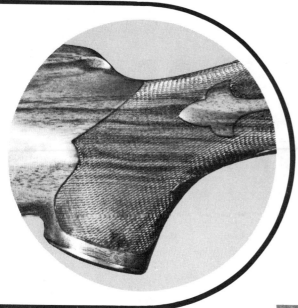

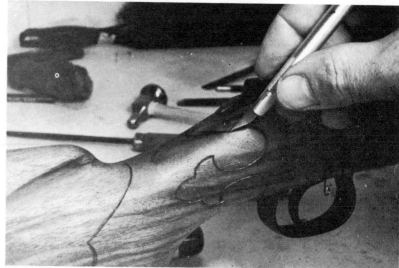

A thin-bladed knife such as used here is ideal for making the incising cut around the pattern. The cut should be about 1/32 inch deep.

I do know for a fact, however, that scuffed fine line checkering is easier to restore than coarse checkering. A few passes over the battered area with a V-tool (single line cutter) and the fine line checkering looks as good as new. Coarse checkering takes a lot more cutting to bring the diamonds up to point again and as a result, the pattern gets a "dug out" look.

True, it takes a bit longer to do fine line checkering and no doubt it's harder on the eyes. However, some of the extra time spent on the line spacing part of the project is made up for when it comes to cutting the rows to full depth. Fine checkering actually involves the removal of less wood than does coarse checkering.

The tools used on this job were the "Full-View" type made by W. E. Brownell, of Vista, California. I can't say that these tools are better than any other type, but they seem to suit my technique and, most important I suppose, I'm used to them. A person always seems to do his best work with familiar tools. Also, it is important to add that if you've been doing poor checkering with one brand of tools, don't expect a miraculous improvement by changing brands.

One of the principal features about this pattern is that it is slightly *inset*. Meaning that the pattern, even the tops of the diamonds, is about a 1/32 inch lower than the surrounding wood. This involves shaving, or relieving, the entire

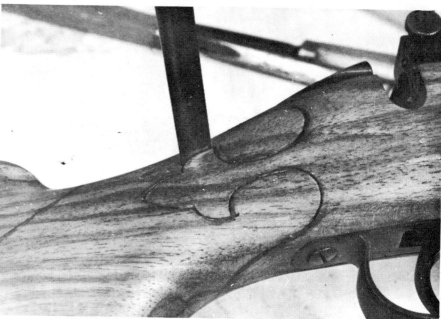

A curved chisel is used to cut the outlines of the fleur-de-lis. This technique makes possible a cleanly cut curve which can be exactly duplicated. Thus the "fleurs" are perfectly symmetrical and all are exactly identical.

Here the outline of the pattern to be recessed is fully incised and ready for the next step.

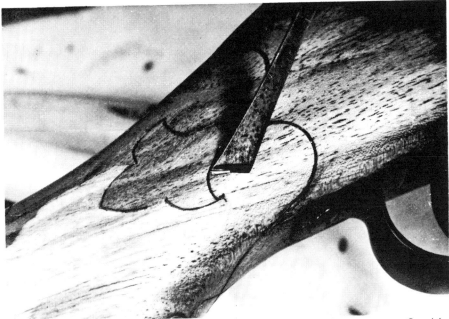

A razor sharp flat bladed chisel is used to shave the wood out of the pattern. Carmichel prefers to do the delicate edges first, then cut out the large central areas.

Here the recessing is completed and almost ready for the checkering to begin. Notice how smoothly the wood has been cut away. Very little additional finishing is required here.

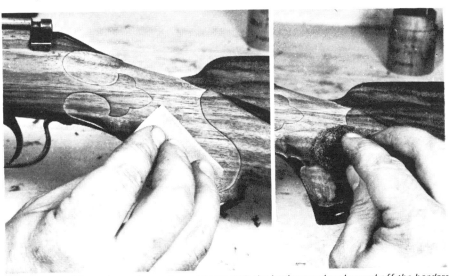

A small pad of fine grit sandpaper is used to smooth the background and round off the borders. Notice how the border of the fleur-de-lis has been rounded so it stands up in distinctive relief. A wad of fine steel wool adds the final polish.

surface of the area to be checkered before any checkering is done.

I can already hear the gasps of disbelief at the prospect of all this extra work. Actually it doesn't take all that much extra time and there are some very definite advantages and compensating factors. The first and foremost of these is the simple fact that it makes the job look a whole lot better. The higher level of wood has a framing effect that gives added emphasis to the pattern. The fleurs-de-lis, rather than appearing flat, stand up through the sea of checkering and have a distinctly sculptured effect.

From the standpoint of actual technique, it is much easier to avoid disastrous runovers because the "walls" at the edge of the pattern offer a fairly substantial and positive stop at the end of the line. This is not an invitation to give the edges a good battering, nor is it a sure-fire prevention against runovers, but it sure helps.

Begin work on the checkering layout after the final sanding is completed but *before* the finish is applied. Actually it won't make much difference if some of the filler coats have been applied but as we shall see later there is a good reason for applying the final finish after the border lines are cut and the relief cutting completed. One of these reasons is simply because it's easier to draw on bare wood. Laying out a pattern of this sort sometimes takes a bit of jockeying around, so if it doesn't suit you or come out where it ought to, it is a simple matter to scrub out the pencil mark with a bit of fine steel wool and try again.

Though it is convenient to trace a pattern onto the stock, most stockmakers usually improvise a bit in order to make the basic pattern more harmonious with the lines of a particular stock. For instance, the pattern may be shortened or extended to cover a flaw in the wood, or to better expose an especially nice streak of color or figure.

Too, it may come as a pleasant surprise to learn that curved border patterns such as this, where the lines and grooves of the checkering do not form any of the borders, actually take less "figgerin' out" than does a complex point pattern where all the lines and points have to come out exactly right.

Also you will discover that this pattern does not have any tight areas where there isn't enough room to work freely with a full sized checkering tool. The usually cramped area around and behind the fleur-de-lis, for example, has been eliminated by giving the "fleur" a longer stem than usual. It not only looks nice this way, but gives plenty of room to scratch around with your tools.

After the pattern has been laid out to your satisfaction, the next step is to trace the outline with a veining chisel (V-chisel) or a simple slender bladed knife. Bob Brownell's, Montezuma, Iowa 50171, offers a dandy little incising knife kit that sells for about $2.50 complete with extra blades of various shapes that is just about perfect for this sort of work.

For cutting sharp curves such as the outline of the fleur-de-lis, the best possible tool is a curved chisel which notches the curve. This way all you have to do is put the edge of the chisel on the wood, give it a press or a tap and there is your curved outline, as neat and perfect as can be. In fact, it's a good idea to take inventory of your curved chisels before doing your preliminary layout work. This way you can design the curves in your pattern to match the variously curved chisels you have on hand. Very clever.

During a recent visit to the *Rifle-Handloader* offices, Lenard Mews, the world-famous stockmaker, showed us a pair of chisels he'd made which were shaped like half a fleur-de-lis. When the tool chisels, or outline cutters, I guess they are, are held together, they form the complete outline. Two taps and the "fleur" is completely outlined on the wood. What's more, all are exactly alike. He didn't mention how long he worked on the tools, but my guess is quite a while. Like all of Mews' work they were perfect and beautifully made.

With the outline incising done, the next step is "insetting" or removing the 1/32 inch or so of wood in the pattern area. This is done with simple, flat bladed chisels. It doesn't make a lot of difference if you cut with, or at right angles to, the grain. In fact, you'll cut everywhichaway before the job is done. One thing you'll learn for sure is not to cut with the grain when it angles down into the stock. This tends to lead your knife deeper and finally causes a chipped out place in your otherwise smooth surface. Also, you'll learn right quick, if you don't already know, the value

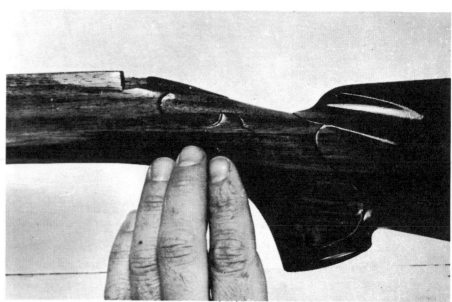

After recessing the pattern, but before checkering, the stock is finished as normal. Be sure to put plenty of finish in the recessed area as this will aid in checkering.

The trick, as shown here, to over-the-grip checkering patterns is starting the master lines at the top of the grip.

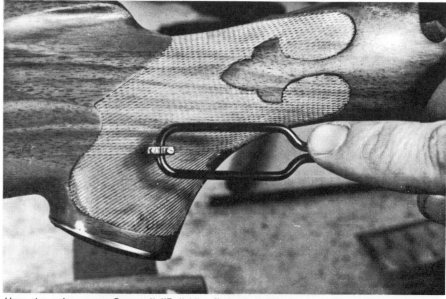

Here the writer uses a Brownell "Full View" checkering tool to space the 26-line checkering. Note the slightly battered borders — but lack of runovers.

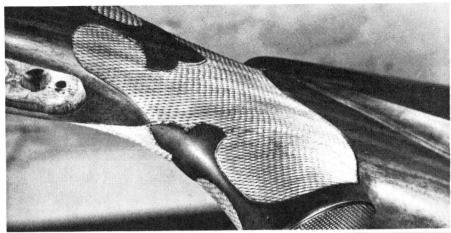

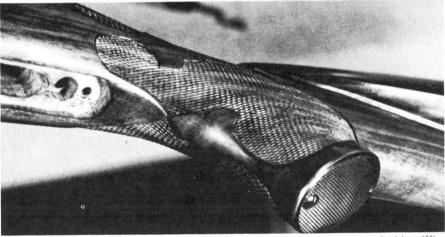

The top photo shows the finished checkering after the borders have been cleaned with a riffler. The lower photo shows the startling improvement after finish has been brushed in. Note how the inset technique gives the pattern a "framed" look.

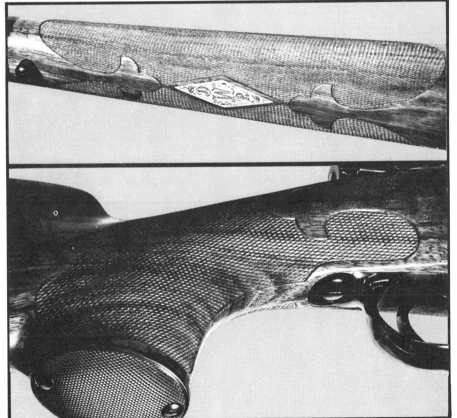

Detail of the superb checkering done by Al Biesen on a Biesen rifle owned by Dave Wolfe. The checkering pattern done by Carmichel for this article is a slightly modified copy of this original Biesen pattern.

and purpose of a razor sharp tool.

My technique is to do the area all around the borders first. One is usually fresher and has more enthusiasm for the job at the beginning and is less liable to make a boo-boo. So after the delicate border area is inset you can relax a bit and go after the open center areas in a reasonably free-wheeling style. For large areas such as the fore-end pattern I use an inch-wide chisel and make a single slice from one end of the pattern to the other — just like peeling a cucumber.

If you take long, smooth cuts there will be little need for additional smoothing up when you finish with the chisels. The surface doesn't have to be perfectly smooth because the checkering will level it out nicely. It should, however, be smooth enough that the checkering tool moves smoothly.

I smooth up the area with a small pad of 220-grit sandpaper but make no effort to get a dead flat surface; just enough to take out any humps, dips, or ridges left over from the insetting operation. During this sanding operation the sharp, square edges of the border are somewhat rounded and smoothed off. These borders should be sanded as nicely as the rest of the stock with a nice, uniform radius curve down into the recessed area. Remember, all of the border will show and is, in fact, the checkering's "frame." Any irregularities will stick out like a skunk in the strawberry patch. A final polishing with fine steel wool completes the job. Also, more than likely, the rest of the stock will, by this time, need a once-over-lightly with steel wool to get rid of the oily finger prints and smudges which have accumulated while you've been at work.

Now go ahead with your normal finishing routine and completely fill and finish the stock as you normally would. All of the recessed area is finished right along with the rest of the stock. One of the main reasons for doing the recess carving before applying the finish is so the inset area will be filled and finished before checkering. The stock finish penetrates the wood and makes it checker more cleanly. The diamonds are sharper, tougher and less likely to chip or break off while you're checkering or later in the field.

I will not go into the basics of checkering for the simple reason that those who will be most tempted to give this type project a try will more than likely have had some checkering experience.

Since this is an over-the-grip pattern, special instructions are in order. Rather than laying out the master lines at the side of the grip as is normally done, they must start at the *top* of the grip. This gets the rows of diamonds in proper order so that they will flow down either side of the grip in perfect order. If you get the master lines laid out evenly to start with, and don't get the lines too crooked along the way, you'll be pleasantly surprised at how neatly the rows come back together down under the grip. They won't rejoin perfectly so as to form a continuous pattern but the angles will converge neatly and look very, very professional.

The borders will look a trifle battered but with care and reasonable luck there should be no runovers. The battered look can be eliminated by tracing around the edge with a narrow checkering riffler (available from Brownell's) or even shaving a fine slice away with the incising knife. If the knife is razor sharp, the edges will be perfectly smooth and require no further work.

Now give the whole job a good going over with a toothbrush. Don't just brush away the sawdust and quit. Bear down and give it a good scrubbing. The stiff bristles tear away the loose fibers that make checkering look fuzzy. Also the bristles tend to burnish each diamond and gives the entire pattern a nicely polished look.

Now brush in a couple of coats of oil base stock finish and you're home free.   ●

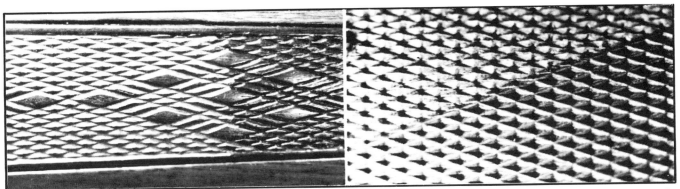

The two principal types of impressed checkering are "positive" (Winchester), left, and "negative" (Remington), both partially converted.

CONVERTING IMPRESSED CHECKERING

By JIM CARMICHEL

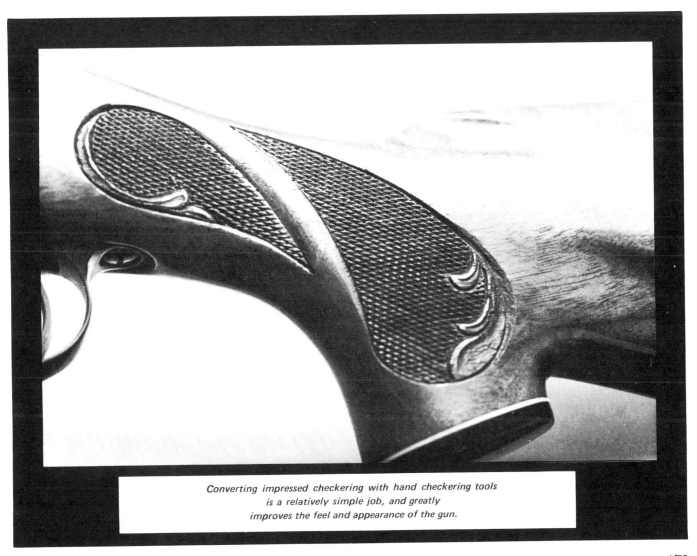

*Converting impressed checkering with hand checkering tools
is a relatively simple job, and greatly
improves the feel and appearance of the gun.*

$\mathcal{I}$MPRESSED CHECKERING, no matter how fancy the pattern, is still impressed checkering and quite a few of us "old-timers" are having more than a little difficulty learning to live with it.

I'm not implying that all impressed is ugly and all hand work beautiful; on the contrary, we've all seen skimpy, poorly done hand checkering, and impressed checkering that is surprisingly handsome—except in the eyes of die-hard traditionalists.

Back when all the manufacturers were producing guns with hand-checkered stocks, many shooters "cleaned up" the factory checkering to improve its looks. But most have been hesitant to attempt a similar operation on impressed checkering, primarily because it often looks as if it can't be done.

But all checkering types now offered by manufacturers can be converted to hand checkering—with excellent results and a minimum of tools and experience. In fact, the principal bugaboos of checkering (layout, pattern outlining and line spacing) are already done, which makes it an ideal project for the beginner; though experience has taught me never to say "foolproof."

Basically, there are two types of impressed checkering; the "positive" type such as found on the Browning Lever Rifle. "Positive" impressed checkering looks most like hand checkering; the diamonds are shaped more or less in the traditional form. However, they are not sharply pointed and the edges and corners tend to be rounded rather than perfectly formed.

The "negative" checkering used by Remington and Savage doesn't have projecting diamonds, but, rather, indentations in the wood that look like diamonds in reverse. Hence the name "negative."

Impressed checkering is accomplished by stamping or rolling the stock with a hot die that "impresses" a pattern on the wood. Though the die is quite hot, the process is completed so quickly that the wood does not burn or even scorch. The hot die or stamp literally melts the wood's lignin (nature's own plastic) and, in effect, moulds the wood under high pressure. Were it not for this technique, stamped checkering would look like a mass of crushed and bruised wood.

Reworking negative checkering simply requires cutting through the "walls" of the reversed diamonds with a single-line cutter such as this W. E. Brownell "Full-View." The initial series of grooves should be to half depth, otherwise the guides for the crossing cuts will be removed.

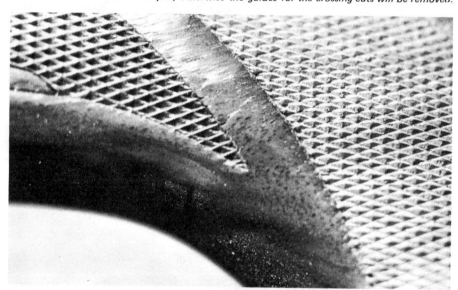

The finished panel, right, cannot be distinguished from an originally handworked stock. Note the evenness of the line spacing, which is aided by the impressed checkering grooves. The sharpness of the diamonds, unusual on such relatively soft wood, is made possible because of the compaction of the wood during the embossing process.

A short cutting head, such as this Dem-Bart S-1 tool, is easier to maneuver in close areas such as this rear panel on a circa 1967 Remington BDL grade. Multi-groove cutting heads may be used on wider areas, provided the spacing is the same, greatly speeding up the work, but requiring greater care and experience.

For our purposes this process is important because it compresses the wood into a dense, almost plastic-like formation that takes hand checkering as well as hard, close-grained walnut.

Basically, the only tool required for the conversion operation is a single-line checkering tool, preferably with fine teeth so the grooves are "filed" rather than cut. A tool with a rather long cutting head, such as the Brownell, tends to cut a straighter groove and "feels" its way along better. A shorter cutting head, however, such as the Dem-Bart S-1 tool is somewhat more flexible in that it allows working in tight, close areas and is maneuverable enough to follow fairly sharp curves. Such a tool is also handy for trimming up around the edges of the checkered panel. Either is adequate, especially for a beginner.

One other tool, the two or three-line spacing cutter, while not necessary, will considerably speed up the conversion operation. With it, one can open up two or three grooves at once. Using a multi-groove cutter, however, requires special care and the beginner will do well to stick to the single-line cutter. Of course, if a two or three-line spacing cutter is used it must match the groove spacing of the impressed checkering.

Since converting the positive-type impressed checkering is less difficult, let's discuss this first. Using a single-line checkering tool, trace each of the grooves in the panel. Two light passes over each set of grooves will sharpen up the edges of the diamonds and bring them to a point. A side benefit of this "touching up" operation is that while you're tracing out the checkering, you are also removing the finish from the checkered panel. Impressed checkering, as you'll notice, is stained the same color as the rest of the stock. By lightening the color of the checkering, it becomes more distinctive and contrasts well with the rest of the stock. Likewise, the shine of impressed checkering is gone, leaving the flat tone of authentic hand checkering. Best of all, however, is the "feel"—those sharp little diamonds bite into the fingers as only hand-cut checkering can.

Now, give the re-cut checkering a good brushing to get rid of sawdust, brush in a coat of stock finish and the job is all done.

The procedure for converting the negative-type checkering is nothing more than cutting into the already-existing grooves and removing the partitions which suggest the negatively formed diamonds. This will leave uninterrupted rows of grooves and sharp-topped ridges. When the operation is duplicated on the intersecting rows the ridges are divided into the diamond-shaped pyramids of true hand checkering.

The final step prior to finishing is cutting the border grooves, which will eliminate minor nicks and runovers. "Chasing" the impressions around fancier patterns will allow them to harmonize better with the hand-cut panels.

Though these grooves may easily be cut full depth on the first pass, it is very important that the first one-way series of grooves be cut only half way. Otherwise, the guide grooves for the second series, or crossing lines, will be completely obliterated. These crossing grooves may, however, be cut full depth without harm. Next, return to the half-cut grooves and complete to final depth.

With a single-line cutter you don't have to worry about an error being transmitted to all following lines, as with regular checkering, but any misalignment will show up in uneven diamonds when the job is completed. If you do cut a crooked line, immediately straighten it up with the edge of a flexible straight-edge. Finally, keep the

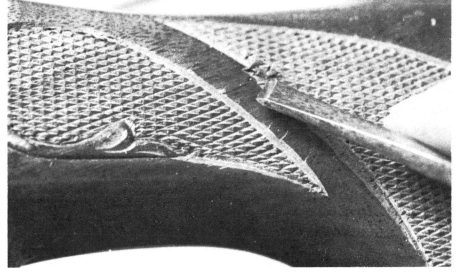

Stress cracks around the border can present a problem. Shaving the edges will sometimes help, but these cracks were still visible even after considerable wood was cut away.

tool head perpendicular to the surface so the diamonds aren't lop-sided.

Our first efforts at re-cutting the negative impressed checkering were done with a 90-degree single-line cutter. Though the results were highly satisfactory, we noticed that even after the diamonds had been brought to a sharp point, there were still some signs of the original stamping; a tiny pinprick mark remained in the grooves at the corner of each diamond. This, of course, is of no real consequence and can only be detected by close inspection. It is the only evidence that the stock had ever been impressed checkered. Switching to a Brownell 75-degree cutter we were able to remove this last vestige of the original stamping.

Impressed checkering is somewhat inset (i.e., below the surface of the surrounding wood) and the panel edges form a positive end-of-the-groove stop for the checkering tool, particularly if a single cut is made around the border to square the shoulder. Run-overs are almost entirely eliminated by this feature but by job's end, the borders may have a somewhat battered look, which is why finishing border cuts should be left until last. Here a short maneuverable cutter, traced lightly around the panel's edge, will remove most nicks and irregularities.

Upon discovering how well the checkering conversion works out you'll probably want, as we did, to do something about the borders on the fancier patterns. With straight-edged point patterns all you need to do is trace out the edging with the single-line cutter and you're home free.

But, with the more elaborate patterns, such as Remington rifles and shotguns, the problem is considerably more difficult. Not because of the curved borders—these are easily dealt with—but because of the moulded simulated carving and, worse yet, the crushed and cracked condition common to these mouldings.

Our efforts to eliminate, or at least hide, this condition were not altogether successful because the cracks simply run too deep in many cases. In the case of some older Remington 700 BDL rifle stock, for example, there is a ribbon about three-eighths of an inch wide running upward through the grip panel and dividing the checkering into two sections. The effect is handsome enough, to be sure, but our unsuccessful efforts

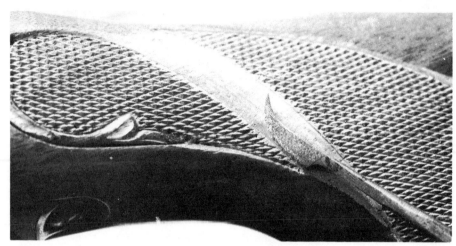

The border wood can be smoothed up nicely with a riffler or even a piece of fine sandpaper on a thin, shaped piece of wood or metal. If the border panels are cut or sanded, matching the finish can cause headaches.

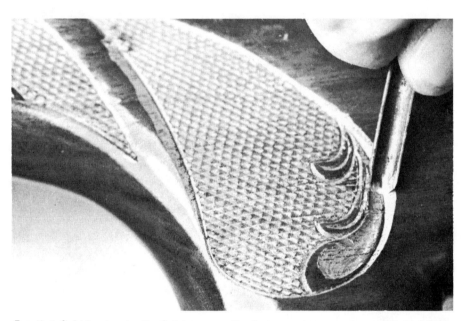

For that finishing touch, the flat leaves on Remington patterns can be carved, but due to the small cracks usually present in these areas, some chipping is likely. Carmichel advises against trying it unless experienced in carving.

to remove the slight cracks, caused by die crushing, involved relieving the wood a sixteenth of an inch. The fissures were still evident.

In another effort to improve the appearance of the moulded border, a veining tool and narrow gouge were used to carve detail and add dimensional character. This had the effect of giving the border a true hand-carved appearance but, again, the cracks and fissures caused some unsightly but unavoidable chipping.

About the only thing that can be done under these circumstances is to use razor-sharp tools, take it slow and easy and hope for the best. Of course, if you happen to have a stock without any of the above-mentioned flaws (we

deliberately selected a stock with pronounced flaws), there is no reason to expect anything but good results—discounting, of course, errors on your part.

All in all, the best advice we can offer, based on our own experience, is to leave the borders alone unless you are an experienced wood carver and/or the wood is in good condition.

Converting only the checkering is a tremendous improvement, and it looks quite good with the moulded border. In fact, it's difficult to describe just how much better an impressed-checkered stock does look—and feel—as a result of this relatively simple two-evening project. It goes a long way toward making a standard factory rifle look like a custom sporter! ●

Make a SKELETON Grip Cap

By Gary Hansen

A FEW YEARS ago the average shooter would not have had the slightest idea what a skeleton grip cap was. They were about as common as elephant hunters in Alaska, and even today skeleton grip caps are not exactly run of the mill. There are now, however, many custom gunsmiths incorporating them into their work and enough is being written about them that most shooters now know what they are.

Skeleton grip caps have become popular enough that they are now produced in quantity, in a rather limited selection, and are being offered to the trade by gunsmithing supply outlets. Unless a custom gunsmith has a well equipped shop or a wealthy customer, making a skeleton grip cap from scratch, instead of purchasing one, is not a financially rewarding experience. However, it is not always possible to adapt a commercial version to a particular design and it then becomes necessary to make one from scratch.

The purpose of a skeleton grip cap is to protect the edge of the pistol grip from chips and dents. Skeletonizing does reduce a small amount of weight, but its primary purpose is decorative. Rifle makers often use a custom-made skeleton grip cap as a ''showcase'' for their skill; thus skeleton caps are sometimes elaborately designed. However, the simple plain Jane types may also be attractive.

The skeleton grip cap in the accompanying photographs was chosen as an illustration because the design is about as intricate as commonly seen. Principles used in its fabrication are needed in virtually any other design, whether simpler or more complex. This particular design incorporates a coved border, two fleur-de-lis, two scallops, and a domed surface. To simplify inletting the back was milled out. The skeletonizing on the illustrated grip cap also has a 20 degree back taper to facilitate inletting. On a simpler design, a back taper is not absolutely necessary, but it is helpful.

The type of equipment available has a lot to do with selecting the proper material to use for a skeleton cap. In a shop with few tools it is best to make the cap out of plate steel or flat stock 1/8 to 1/4 inch thick, depending on the design. In a shop equipped with a power hacksaw, or a metal cutoff bandsaw, and other sophisticated machinery like a surface grinder, it may be easier to make the cap from round bar. A nearly finished grip cap blank can be formed by cutting 1-3/8-inch diameter bar stock at about a 45 degree angle. Since the grip cap is not critical to the safety or function of the firearm it is permissible to use a piece of scrap steel of unknown metallurgy if it is close to the proper dimensions and has good working qualities. Cold rolled steel is a good choice, but a free machining steel is preferable because of the amount of cutting, grinding, drilling and filing needed to complete the project.

If the grip cap blank is made from plate steel an ellipse must be accurately scribed on it to use as a guide for sawing, grinding, and filing. A 45 degree ellipse is most frequently used for grip caps and templates are available from drafting supply stores to ease drawing them. If the blank is made from bar stock the ellipse is formed by simply cutting at an angle. Since it is necessary to square up the ends of such a blank (if an exact 45 degree ellipse is desired) the blank must be cut at a slightly sharper angle to compensate for the stock that will be trimmed away.

The cove molding along the border of our example cap was formed by pin routing. This is an accurate and easy, but somewhat tedious, method. The grip cap is brought into contact with a ball end carbide burr in a drill press, by finger pressure. The burr should be running at about 2,500 revolutions per minute. A pin is positioned under the burr to be used as a stop. Where the pin is positioned in relation to the burr determines how far the grip cap can be pushed into the burr, and thus how much metal will be removed. To maintain accuracy, care must be taken during the routing process to keep the grip cap flush with the work surface.

There is another method of cutting a cove in the cap that is faster than pin routing, but requires considerably more care and skill. An accurate cove can be cut using equipment no more elaborate than an assortment of files. In order to file the cove it is necessary to scribe a line around the outside edge of the grip cap blank. This guideline should be at the precise bottom of the future cove.

To make the guidelines easy to see, first paint the blank with layout dye or cold blue. Place the grip cap on a surface plate, or any hard, flat surface such as a drill press or bandsaw table. If a surface gauge equipped with a scribe is available, use it. If not, use something to block a scribe up to the proper height and carefully scribe the line. Next, scribe an elliptical guideline around the top of the blank being careful to keep it the same distance from the edge as the first guideline.

The two guidelines are used as a reference to file a 45 degree chamfer around the perimeter of the grip cap. A flat mill bastard file works well for this job. After the chamfer is completed use a small three-square file to cut a groove around the grip cap in the center of the chamfer. This groove does not have to be very deep, as its only purpose is to help guide a parallel round file while it is used to cut the cove to full depth.

The majority of skeleton grip caps do not have a molding around the border. The outside edge is usually just rounded off. Sometimes the entire surface of the cap is domed or crowned. Scribing a guideline around the edge of the grip cap will make an accurate dome shape easier to obtain. In any case, it is best to leave the grip cap flat until the skeletonizing has been roughed out with a drill press or milling machine. Anyone who has ever tried to drill a hole in a precise location on a curved surface knows it can cause a headache.

One difficult problem is accurately laying out the pattern to cut out of the cap. A simple design may not pose much of a problem, but making sure a complex pattern is symmetrical and centered on the cap is a major undertaking. Some prefer to do only a rough layout which may not be precisely perfect, but is reasonably close. They ensure everything comes out right after roughing out the skeletonizing by skillful use of an exacting eye and frequent measurements with a vernier caliper and a steel rule. Working to an exact layout, however, is far easier for most craftsmen.

A layout can be applied to a polished surface of the cap by simply scribing with a scratch awl. The lines will show up much better of course, and be easier on the eyes if cold bluing or layout dye is applied to the cap first. On an intricately designed cap it is worthwhile to steal a trick from the firearm engravers. There is a white lacquer-like layout fluid available to the gun-smithing fraternity primarily for use in engraving. A grip cap blank painted with this fluid can be drawn on with a pencil and if a mistake is made, the line erased and redrawn. A carbon paper tracing can also be made on this layout medium. The layout should be scribed in only after it is perfected.

When there is a large open area, such as most simple skeleton cap designs have, a vertical milling machine can be used to good advantage to cut it out. On a more complex skeleton grip cap (like our example) some precision drilling is in order. Our sample cap was carefully center punched and then drilled with the appropriate size drills. Note in the illustration how the stems of the fleur-de-lis were formed by drilling 1/8-inch diameter holes. The scallops on the sample cap were also roughed in by drilling. A compound vice or a rotary indexing table is almost a necessity for this type of work. After the critical holes were drilled in the illustrated cap, other assorted and some overlapping holes were drilled just to remove stock.

Drill slowly when overlapping holes to avoid having the drill wander and break through into the neighboring hole. This is not the only drilling problem that may arise; there are many more! What can be done after noticing the hole that has just been started is not positioned exactly right? Make a deep center punch mark in the right position inside the started hole, then drill through with a 1/16-inch drill. Using the 1/16-inch diameter hole as a pilot, drill the hole out with progressively slightly larger drills until the proper size is reached. If a center punch dent is a hair off, move it to the right position before attempting to drill. Put the center punch back in the dent and point it toward the right position. Light tapping will "walk" the dent to the right spot. Once there, hammer the heck out of the punch to keep the drill from wandering.

Of course, lacking a vertical milling machine, a simple skeleton grip cap can also be roughed out with drills. A drill press is not really needed; a hand-held drill will work just fine. Simply drill a series of overlapping holes around the skeletonized layout. Knock out the center and the file work is ready to start.

For accuracy, the screw holes should be drilled and counterbored on a drill press or a milling machine, although it is possible to make do with the skillful use of a hand drill. If the screw holes do not line up on the center line of the grip cap, the mistake will stick out even to the untrained eye, so use care. Locate the fillister head screws to be used with the grip cap before drilling and counterboring to be certain of the correct size.

Good craftsmanship demands that the screw heads fit tight in the counterbores. This is best accomplished by machining the counterbores slightly smaller than the diameter of the screw heads, then filing the heads down to fit while the screw is turning in a drill or lathe. Screws designed especially for attaching grip caps are available from gunsmithing supply outlets. These screws have double thick heads so they can be reshaped to match the grip cap contours and the slots recut so they line up "north and south."

The back of the sample grip cap was milled out so the fleur-de-lis and the scallops were only 3/32 inch thick. This makes inletting them into the pistol grip much faster than if they were left a full 1/4 inch thick. Milling out the back also removes a lot of stock that would otherwise have to be removed with files later. Weight is another consideration; milling the fleur-de-lis and scallops to 3/32 only removes fractions of an ounce, but fractions add up in the overall weight of the finished rifle. A milling machine was not available to use on the sample grip cap so an end mill was used in a drill press to "drill" out the back of the cap.

After the skeletonizing has been roughed out and the back of the grip cap milled out, the file work can begin. A carbide burr mounted in a Foredom tool was used in areas of the sample grip cap where quite a bit of stock had to be removed. The lack of a Foredom, Dremel, or similar tool is not much of a handicap. A sharp, parallel round file will remove unwanted stock almost as fast and is easier to control. An assortment of needle files was used to finish up the skeletonizing in the sample grip cap. The majority of the shaping was done with a parallel round file that had a two-inch portion of the end ground to a half round configuration. The half round portion of the file with a ground "safe" edge came in handy for cutting the corners in the fleur-de-lis. If no other files had been available, this one file could have finished the job without much inconvenience. However, a small file with a curved side that matched the curve that was filed in the skeletonizing did make the job easier.

When finishing the skeletonizing remember to file in an approximate 20 degree back taper to simplify inletting. Filing a 20 degree draft in the skeletonizing may sound easy, but it can be quite tricky, especially in a complicated design like the sample. Closely examine it to make certain the relief angle is tapering the right way and at approximately the same angle all around the skeletonizing.

After the file work is completed the grip cap must be polished with abrasive paper backed by assorted files. This is best left until the grip cap has been inletted into the pistol grip, since scratches are sure to result from the inletting process. Also, it is best to work on the installed screw heads at the same time the rest of the cap is polished. During polishing, take care not to round over edges that should remain sharp and crisp. If the grip cap is to be rust blued or color case hardened, use progressively finer grits until a 320 or 400 grit surface finish is reached. If fire bluing or hot salt bluing is to be used, polish to a 600 grit finish.

Making a skeleton grip cap from scratch is a tedious and time-consuming project. The cap in the illustrations took almost twenty hours to complete. Once installed on a rifle, a well made custom skeleton grip cap will set that rifle apart from all others. A closely fitted skeleton grip cap on a fine firearm quietly transmits a message of quality. ●

A bench grinder is being used to square up the edges of a grip cap blank cut from bar stock.

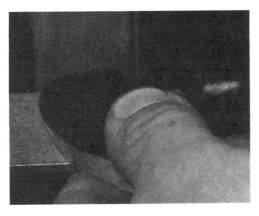 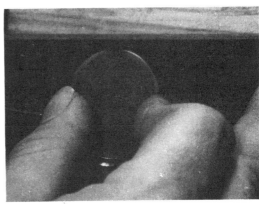

Far right, a technique useful in filing a truly square edge is to clamp a file in a vise against a square steel block. Then work the blank back and forth against the file.

Pin routing can be used to cut an accurate cove in the grip cap blank. The pin is used as a stop and its position in relation to the carbide burr determines how much metal is removed. Care must be taken to keep the grip cap flush with the work surface.

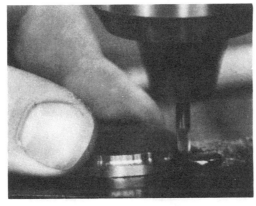 

Far right, a parallel round file is used to remove chatter marks left from pin routing.

A cross vise or rotary indexing table is almost a necessity for this type of precision drilling.

Far right, the skeletonizing in this grip cap blank has been roughed out with assorted drills. Note how the stems of the fleur-de-lis were formed by drilling. Also note blocking under cap.

Frequent measurements with a vernier caliper are made (below) to make sure everything ends up symmetrical and centered.

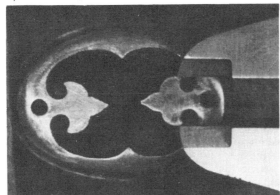 

Right, the back of the grip cap should be milled out to make inletting easier. In this case an end mill is used in a drill press to "drill" out the back.

179

GARY P. HANSEN:

Using an Electric

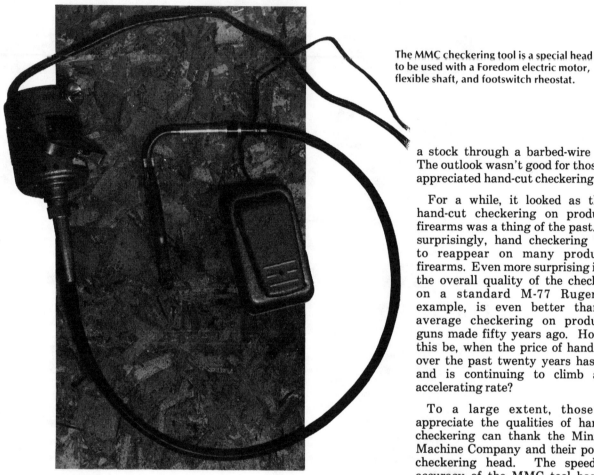

The MMC checkering tool is a special head to be used with a Foredom electric motor, flexible shaft, and footswitch rheostat.

A FEW YEARS back, the spiraling cost of hand labor and crasftsmanship forced Winchester to make changes in the design and manufacturing processes used in the Model 70 and Model 94 Winchester. The same skyrocketing costs for hand fitting caused Winchester to cease production of the standard Model 12 shotgun and replace it with the Model 1200. High hand-labor costs affected other companies besides Winchester. Many manufacturers were forced to modify time-honored firearm designs and to change manufacturing techniques.

One of the first things to go was hand-cut checkering. High labor costs made it financially impossible to pay someone half a day's wages to hand-checker a standard production stock and to recover that cost in the sale of the rifle. The absence of checkering on stocks became increasingly common. Then the firearms industry came out with several types of *impressed* checkering, which in the eyes of many firearm fanciers comes in a distant second behind scratches produced by pulling a stock through a barbed-wire fence. The outlook wasn't good for those who appreciated hand-cut checkering.

For a while, it looked as though hand-cut checkering on production firearms was a thing of the past. Then surprisingly, hand checkering began to reappear on many production firearms. Even more surprising is that the overall quality of the checkering on a standard M-77 Ruger, for example, is even better than the average checkering on production guns made fifty years ago. How can this be, when the price of hand labor over the past twenty years has risen and is continuing to climb at an accelerating rate?

To a large extent, those who appreciate the qualities of hand-cut checkering can thank the Miniature Machine Company and their powered checkering head. The speed and accuracy of the MMC tool has kept hand-cut checkering from becoming extinct on standard production firearms. Remington, Sturm Ruger, several subcontractors, and many custom stockmakers use the MMC checkering head. The MMC tool allows the craftsman to do in an hour what used to take half a day. If it were not for the Miniature Machine Company, elaborate hand-cut checkering would be out of the financial reach of many shooters who lack the skill to checker their own stocks.

Close examination of the MMC checkering head reveals that it is a well engineered and sturdily built precision instrument. The spacing guide can be adjusted so that the tool cuts from sixteen to twenty-two lines per inch with the standard carbide cutting wheel. Line spacing is adjusted by means of a micro-click adjustment knob similar to those found on some

Checkering Tool

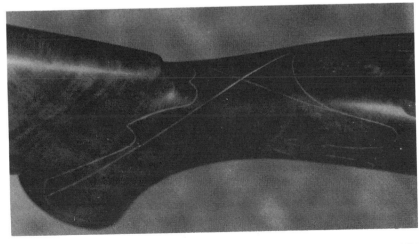

precision sights. With a special *narrow* carbide cutting wheel, the tool cuts from twenty-four to thirty-two lines per inch. The spacing guide is spring-activated, which helps prevent cutting in an unintended area. The depth of cut can be controlled by a depth-adjusting screw knob.

Checkering with the MMC checkering tool is quite similar to using conventional tools — but easier and much, much faster. It takes only one quarter as long to checker a stock with an MMC tool as it does with conventional hand tools, and that is a conservative estimate. With practice, and depending on the checkering pattern, the craftsman may be able to increase his speed considerably more. After some practice, a craftsman should be able to checker a stock at least as well as he can with hand tools, and probably a great deal better.

Both checkering patterns on the stock in the photographs illustrating this article were completed in ten hours using the MMC tool. This includes making and laying-out the pattern, cutting the borders, and applying the linseed-oil finish. It would have taken the same craftsmen forty hours or more to complete these moderately difficult patterns using standard hand tools. This checkering job was only the craftsman's second attempt with the MMC checkering tool. A minimum of hand work was needed to point up the diamonds next to the border in some areas, but the amount of hand work decreased as the operator became more experienced. The quality of the work is comparable to the checkering this craftsman produces with hand tools. Someone without any previous checkering experience but some aptitude could expect to produce top-quality work after checkering from three to five stocks.

Only one minor problem was encountered while checkering the patterns in the illustrations. The MMC tool cuts from right to left. This prevented checkering a small area on the left side of the pistol grip, where the comb of the stock interfered with the body of the tool. The stock was then turned around so the lines could be cut to full depth without the body of the tool interfering.

Many gunstock checkerers have never tried a pistol-grip pattern that completely encircles the stock. Possibly one of the reasons is that checkering the bottom of the pistol grip with conventional hand tools is difficult to say the least. It is possible to use the MMC checkering head at anywhere from about a ten-degree angle to a ninety-degree angle in relation to the work. This allows the tool to maneuver in tight areas such as the bottom of the pistol grip with ease.

As one might expect, the MMC checkering tool greatly speeds up the checkering of a broad semiflat pattern. A little more surprising is that it also accelerates checkering tight areas like those behind *fleur de lis* designs and the corners of point patterns. Checkering a tight area with a standard hand tool is difficult and tedious. Special checkering point-up tools are made for cutting short lines in tight areas where standard tools just will not go. However, they still cut by a reciprocating action, and it takes a lot of slow, careful work to prevent overruns. Since the MMC checkering head relies on a rotary blade and not reciprocating action to do the cutting, it is possible to cut lines as short as an eighth of an inch to full depth without problems.

The first few steps to checkering a stock using an MMC tool are exactly the same as when using hand tools. A

After the checkering pattern has been laid-out on the stock, master lines are cut with a standard hand tool in the conventional way.

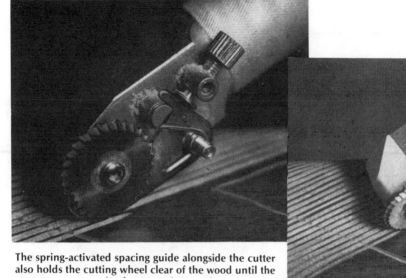

The spring-activated spacing guide alongside the cutter also holds the cutting wheel clear of the wood until the operator presses it down against spring pressure. Because the angle of the handle to the work surface can be as low as ten degrees or as high as ninety degrees, the MMC tool can be used to checker difficult areas — inside the curve of the grip, for example.

paper pattern is carefully positioned on the stock and secured with masking tape. A light line is then traced around the pattern with a scribe. The master lines are then laid out at any convenient angle from thirty to ninety degrees and cut to full depth with a hand tool.

After a pattern is laid out and the master lines are cut, the checkering is ready to be completed with the electric tool. The spacing guide is placed in a master line, and the cutter is revved up to a moderate speed by stepping on the foot-controlled rheostat. The spring-activated spacing guide keeps the cutter from coming in contact with the wood until the operator presses the tool down. The beginner should use a moderate speed at first and later progress to higher ones. Operating the machine too slowly could cause the cutter to chatter or exceed the manufacturer's design load.

The MMC tool cuts on either the push or the pull stroke. Most craftsmen find better control on the pull stroke. Therefore, at the end of a line, to avoid overruns, always cut *away* from the border. It is possible to cut right up to the border with only a minimum of hand work required to point-up the diamonds at the edge of the pattern. It is also possible to cut the lines to full depth with one stroke. The novice, however, may want to cut the lines only to partial depth and finish-up later with a hand tool.

Even the most expert gunstock checkerer has had a hand checkering tool jump a guide line on occasion. One might expect that the results of an electric checkering tool jumping the line would be disastrous. However, this is not the case. If the MMC tool should jump the line, the depth-adjustment screw on the spacing-guide blade prevents the tool from cutting to full depth. Carefully going over the damaged area with a hand tool usually removes all evidence of the mistake.

It is always advisable to lay out a checkering pattern to avoid having any knots inside the checkering. With standard hand tools, knots inside the pattern usually break off and leave an unsightly area without any diamonds. The MMC tool is designed to operate at up to twenty thousand revolutions per minute. At high speed and low torque, the cutting wheel often cuts through a knot without breaking or chipping it off. It is still advisable to avoid knots; but when it isn't possible to avoid including them, the MMC tool takes some of the worry out of cutting through them. The high speed of the cutter also prevents the tool from following the grain in fancy-figured stocks, as a standard hand tool does.

The company claims that the cutter may be expected to checker five or more stocks before it requires resharpening. Possibly, after elaborately checkering five stocks made from ebony or another extremely hard exotic wood, the cutting wheel might become dull. However, the carbide cutter should stay sharp for dozens of stocks made from even our hardest common gunstock woods like French walnut or cherry.

The MMC checkering head is used in conjunction with a Foredom electric motor, flexible shaft, and foot rheostat. The entire electric checkering setup is distributed by Brownells, Incorporated; Route 2, Box 1; Montezuma, Iowa 50171. The complete setup sells for just over four hundred dollars, which sounds like a lot of money until you take into account that a high-quality custom checkering job often costs two hundred dollars or more. Also consider that the Foredom motor and flexible shaft can be used to power small grinding wheels and rotary files, and it's easy to see that the setup is not all that expensive.

182

Several design changes have been made in the checkering head since MMC started production in 1960. Whenever possible, MMC has tried to limit changes so that the new design could be retrofitted to existing equipment. When an obsolete head is returned for maintenance, MMC updates it as much as possible by replacing old parts with those of newer design. MMC does not charge for updating old equipment, charging only for repairs. This type of service is almost unheard-of in this day and age.

The MMC checkering tool won't make an expert gunstock checkerer overnight out of someone who is all thumbs. It will, however, allow someone with a basic aptitude, patience, a steady hand, and an exacting eye to reach his full potential in the shortest time. Many home gunsmiths have bought the MMC checkering setup for checkering their stocks and the stocks of friends. For those who checker stocks for profit, it should be on their "must have" list. ●

Gunstock Inlays

Part One — Sheet, Composition, and Cast Inlay — by John Bivins

FOR SOME WHILE now, I've been receiving requests for information about methods of installing inlays, particularly silver-wire inlays So I've decided to cover the entire spectrum of things many of us use on the stocks of muzzleloaders. Though inlays *can* be used on centerfire rifles, I'm not one of those fond of seeing anything other than a simple initial plate under the toe line. On a nice classic rifle, anything more than that is like painting a flame job on your Porsche Turbo. Even on muzzleloaders, where inlay work comes into reasonable play, taste and restraint are appropriate.

Inlay is a challenging field to the gunmaker, since it extends the sense of early art beyond just the form of architecture. It delineates and even contrasts elements of the gunstock and its furniture, and it increases the immense pleasure one feels in finding intricate details to study, all representing the quirks of an artisan's mind and his grasp of artistic things. That is, it *should* provide that pleasure, but it must be done with sensitivity and understanding if it's to be successful. No gunstock should be used as an indiscriminate surface that has to be filled up with something, even If the piece is to be highly decorated. Inlay and engraving must have meaning in every feature and cut, and some relationship with the overall fabric of the piece, or it has no business being on the gun.

Take the American longrifle, for example. As the percussion era dawned, the artistic understanding of decorative elements left from the eighteenth century was rapidly slipping away, and suddenly American rifles had in some cases become glittering repositories of brightwork that didn't always show good design integration with the gunstock it was stuck in. This was particularly true after the early 1830s, when German silver came into widespread use. This alloy, which is a copper-nickel-zinc mixture, was actually in use in the form of *paktong* in China a number of centuries before its

> Sheet inlays were often used in conjunction with wire inlays during the baroque and rococo periods, as shown here on a new wheellock built in the style of about 1690. The lock-bolt escutcheon is held in place with nine silver nails. Daniel Goodwin is the artist who executed the engraving on this sheet inlay.

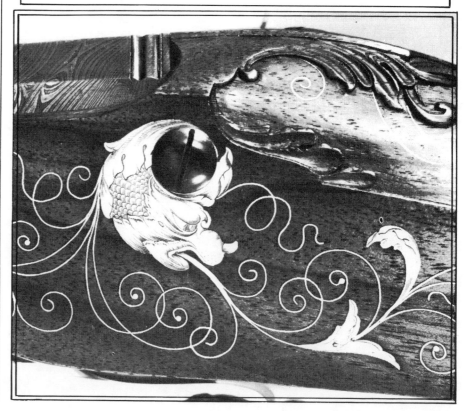

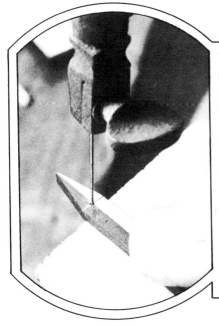

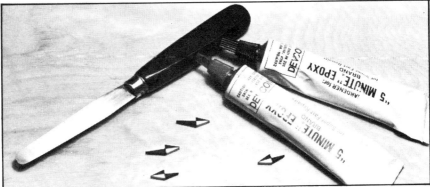

In making a composition inlay such as a variegated star with ebony and ivory, strips of the two materials are first made up and trued, then the points are cut off (left). Halves of the star points are assembled (right) on waxed paper to prevent the five-minute epoxy cement from bonding points to the table top.

general introduction here. Paktong has a higher zinc content than German silver, but is otherwise similar, and was used for gun furniture on the continent during the eighteenth century — but not here until later.

Whatever the alloy to be used for a sheet-metal inlay, I prefer sheet no less than 0.050 inch thick, and in many cases, I'd rather have material 1/16 inch thick. The heavier gauges may take a slight bit of extra time to inlet, but they're far less prone to distort, which means that you can tap them down fairly smartly while inletting. Further, heavy engraving cuts such as border work are less likely to cause problems on the heavier sheet.

The "secret" to decent sheet-inlay work is in providing a good draft or bevel on all edges of the inlay, so that the piece is wedged into its inlet. Without draft, you'll have gaps, I guarantee. Since most sheet inlays are sawn out with a scroll saw (jeweler's saw), the saw can be angled slightly to provide the draft naturally, or it can be provided by filing. I covered the use of the scroll saw way back in *Rifle* 51, where I dealt with making patchboxes; have a look at that again or dig out a copy of Meek's *Art of Engraving*.

Inlet outlines should always be scribed on the stock with a sharp scribe. A pencil isn't precise enough. Since you've provided draft on the inlay, the outline can be "stabbed in" straight down on the scribed lines without fear of cutting outside too far, since the scribe follows the *inside* of the draft on the metal. Narrow flat chisels

with a very shallow bevel, generally in 1mm to 3mm widths, are used for most of the work, and you'll likely find that you will have to make the narrower ones yourself, or else grind down wider ones. That's kosher if you can afford it. After stabbing-in the outline, make a beveled cut in the wood all the way around the inside of the inlet, and remove the bulk of the wood in the inlet with small gouges. Use flat chisels and scrapers to finish to depth, and it's best to spot-in inlays in the final fitting to avoid hollows that will allow the metal to be pushed down by a graver. I refer you again to *Rifle* 51 for illustrations of these techniques. Don't be afraid to tap the inlay down fairly smartly with a small hammer for a good "smash" fit, but at the same time, you must obviously avoid breaking wood or distorting the inlay. Keep the face of the hammer well polished for this work.

Like patchboxes, inlays must also be contoured quite often to fit a curving surface, and they're formed the same way. The inlay is placed on a block of lead and formed with a mandrel of suitable radius. Inlays should be left with a very small amount of metal standing "proud" of the stock, to be filed down, and as in the case of the patchbox, the inlay must be polished carefully so that the wood isn't worn away faster, leaving a lumpy feel to the surface. Obviously, you shouldn't be able to feel an inlay when you run your fingers across it, other than the change in surface material and the colder feel of metal.

Attaching inlays into wood is another matter. I don't see any completely justifiable reason for

cementing metal inlays into a piece of traditional work. Nails are the answer. Inlays *can* be set by filing a negative or dovetail draft on the metal, undercutting the inlet, and forming the inlay into place by lightly hammering it down. I've even seen a wrist inlay on an early longrifle done that way. The reason I knew that it was done that way, though, was that the wood had shrunk and the inlay had fallen out. That's reason enough to want a more secure means of attachment.

Inlays on old rifles were attached with nails made of various materials, including brass, copper, iron, and silver. On best-grade work, I feel that the nail holding the inlay should be of the same metal as the inlay, and it should be installed in such a way that it doesn't show at all when the inlay is dressed down and polished. When using silver inlays, that's very easy to do.

I noticed years ago, when using wire-type silver solder, that the solder had a tendency to form a little ball on the end when heated, which can be annoying while doing a soldering job. However, it's just the ticket for heading silver nails, because it's damnably difficult to *forge* up a head on a piece of soft stock and make it regular. For silver nails, I use 0.040-inch sterling wire. Holding a length of wire vertically, with the loose end pointing down, I heat the tip of the wire lightly with a propane torch until a little ball forms on it, then let it cool. I clip off the length of nail I need with side-cutters, making an angled cut across the wire to make a sharp point. For a head-forming swage, I drilled a 1/8-inch-thick piece of steel scrap with a number 60 drill and then

185

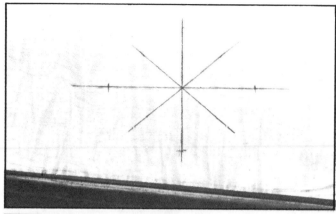

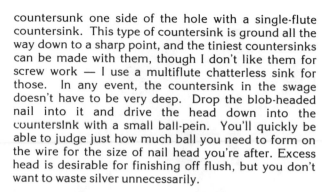

countersunk one side of the hole with a single-flute countersink. This type of countersink is ground all the way down to a sharp point, and the tiniest countersinks can be made with them, though I don't like them for screw work — I use a multiflute chatterless sink for those. In any event, the countersink in the swage doesn't have to be very deep. Drop the blob-headed nail into it and drive the head down into the countersink with a small ball-pein. You'll quickly be able to judge just how much ball you need to form on the wire for the size of nail head you're after. Excess head is desirable for finishing off flush, but you don't want to waste silver unnecessarily.

With the nail made and the inlay installed, drill the nail hole in the inlay with the same number 60 bit, taking care not to let the drill run into the wood any distance. Countersink the nail hole in the inlay with the uniflute countersink and drive the nail in; the head will be a perfect fit and invisible when you dress it off. Since silver bends easily, I often hold the nail in the hole with needlenose pliers while starting to tap it down so that it won't bend over, but in doing this, you'll have to take care not to strike the pliers, or the inlay or the stock (or both) will be marred. Also, if you know that you will be engraving over the nail, it's not a bad idea to anneal the head after you've swaged it so that it won't be harder than the inlay itself. Otherwise, the graver may want to catch the edge of the nail and tear out a little piece.

Tiny steel brads can have their heads formed in the same swage, though it's best to locate brads with shanks that closely fit the 0.040-inch hole of the swage. If you want to use smaller nails, you'll have to hunt for drills smaller than number 60, and they aren't always easy to find. Nails larger than 0.040 inch aren't really needed.

Brass nails can be made by chiseling off the edges of

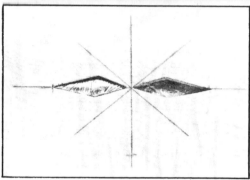

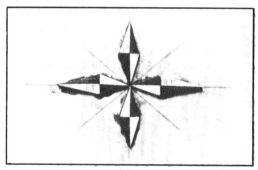

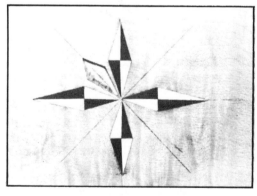

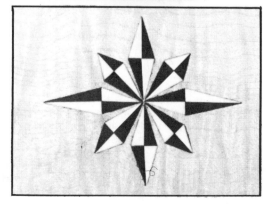

From the top down, here are the steps in making a variegated-star inlay: an accurate full-scale layout, precisely ruled on the stock, is a vital first step. Next, points are laid-out on the ruled lines, scribed, and cut in. Then, with a narrow chisel, wood in the inlet is chipped and removed. The first four points are epoxied in place before inlets can be safely cut for the remaining four points. When all eight points are inlaid, the inlay is dressed-down with files. In the photo at right above, a curved riffler was used because the stock surface was concave.

sheet stock, cutting off a piece with a little taper on it, and cutting at the same time a small T for the head. These devils have a way of flying across the room when you make the final cut that frees them from the sheet, so keep a close eye on it. The T is needed to rest on top of the head swage, just as you would leave a heavier section at the top of a piece of nail rod when forging a wrought or "rose-head" nail. Anneal the brass blank, tap it down into the swage, and proceed as above. Another way to provide fasteners for brass inlay is to install them with brass 1/4-3 wood screws, cutting the countersink to a depth that won't allow the screw to seat all the way down to the screw slot, and filing the excess head off. This isn't a traditional method at all, but it's one I'd much prefer over cement. Anneal the screw before installing it, for the reasons mentioned above.

Stock wood of course has a tendency to expel metal inlays as it moves around with changes in moisture. For that reason, you need enough nails to keep things anchored strongly. I never use nails shorter than 3/8 inch, but I don't make them longer than that, either. Regarding forestock inlays for federal rifles, these little scudders are notorious for loosening and falling out, especially when they are pierced for wedges or pins (I'd avoid putting inlays over pinholes altogether). To make certain they'll stay put, drive the nail all the way through the forestock side with the barrel in place. The nail will strike the lower oblique flat of the barrel, or the curving surface of a round barrel, and be nicely clinched over in the process. Make sure that your nail is long enough to provide at least 1/16 inch of clinch, though more than 1/8 inch isn't necessary.

A sufficient number of nails is cheap insurance that the inlay won't rise along one edge when you engrave it, so on a quarter-sized inlay, I normally use at least four nails and maybe more if the thing is very irregular.

Some years ago, I read a magazine article by a chap who thought that it would be a neat idea to make inlays of silver amalgam, such as dentists use, since that would require only that you cut an inlet and then undercut the edges a bit. Well, that's just peachy-keen, but I'd just as soon have a chrome-plated Dickert rifle. Let's face it, you can go only *so far* in trying to save yourself work without compromising good taste. Some other materials are legitimate, of course; inlays of contrasting wood and animal matter such as horn, bone, and ivory.

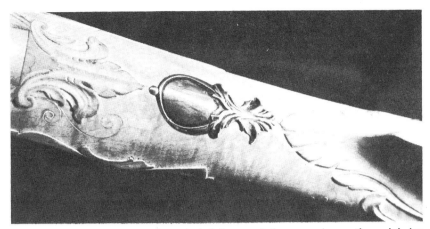

Relief inlays of nonferrous metals, particularly brass and silver, were frequently used during the eighteenth century. The pattern for this silver thumbpiece was first carved from pearwood; the inlay was cast with a stud on the back to receive a screw from below to hold it in place in the host wood. This was a standard technique.

Sideplates made as relief inlays are decorative as well as functional. This silver sideplate was investment-cast in two pieces by a dental laboratory, silver-soldered together, then inlaid into the stock. Firms specializing in the production of large jewelry can custom-cast pieces as large as this, easily and readily, John says.

Bone, antler, and ivory were used extensively on Germanic rifles from the end of the fifteenth century into the nineteenth century, particularly during the sixteenth and seventeenth centuries. Bone and particularly antler were used far more often than ivory because of the expense of ivory, even though it was available in Europe during the Renaissance. Antler was used for the extensive coverage of gunstocks, as figures and paneled veneering, both highly decorated with "engraving," which was really done in the same manner as scrimshaw. Both hunting scenes and classical allegories were popular subjects for this coverage, and so were religious scenes. Some rifles were even entirely veneered in staghorn, with the surface left in its natural state, which must have been exceedingly difficult. Bone and antler were also used for scrolled and straight-line strip inlay, much in the same way silver-wire work was done, requiring the piecing-in of many small segments to make a bend. A great deal of work in these materials, of course, was the work of specialists who

also worked with other surfaces to be decorated, such as elaborate coffers and even furniture.

One form of inlay popular on European sporting rifles from the late seventeenth century on was the variegated star, which was made up of two inlay materials. This star was more often than not a four-pointed affair, although eight-pointed ones were also used. Both of these, there's little doubt, provided a prototype for the eight-pointed silver star frequently used on the cheekpieces of American rifles by the 1770s and later. Variegated stars on European rifles usually are found either on the cheek or the butt-trap lid. More often than not, they're made of black cowhorn and antler, but ivory can also be encountered, and ebony was available in central Europe before the mid 1600s. Let's have a look at the construction of one of these things. The design here was actually borrowed from the fallboard of an American William & Mary desk made in the

Connecticut Valley about 1710, though it's not out of place on a gunstock.

An inlay such as this should begin with a full-scale drawing to provide a guide for size and position of the parts. This particular design uses double-ended points that come together in the center like a compass rose, so from the completed drawing, we see that we need a total of sixteen points, ten 5/16 inch long, four 3/16 inch long, and two 7/16 inch long. The job is begun by cutting out and gluing up several strips laminated of the two materials to be used, in this case ivory and ebony. Since I had a flat piece of ivory just a shade over 3/32 inch thick, that determined the thickness of the inlay. Strips of ivory and ebony were carefully bandsawed out, and the edges trued with a file, with the strips held lightly in the vise, almost flush with the top of the jaws. Only two edges needed to be trued. The two halves of each strip were then joined with twenty-four-hour epoxy, clamping them together. Ebony, incidentally, should be degreased with lacquer thinner and then alcohol for gluing operations, since it's an oily wood, as many tropical woods are.

After the strips have set up, both faces of the strips, which were now slightly over 3/16-inch wide, were faced off with an 80-grit belt on the belt sander to make them true and flush the full length. Care must be taken not to overheat ivory in such operations; this can be done equally well, but not as fast, with files, or better, laying the strips face down on 100-grit garnet paper laid flat on the workbench, and the surfaces leveled by pushing the strips back and forth. Points are then cut off the strips with a scroll saw, first cutting the angles and seeing that the point falls directly on the dividing line between the ebony and ivory. The point is then sawn off the strip, taking care that each point of a given size is the correct length for uniformity. In cutting the angles, I tilt the scroll saw slightly to provide a small amount of draft on the points for ease of inletting later. Incidentally, Bruce Meek points out an alternative way of using the scroll saw on page 162 of *Art of Engraving*. He cuts a slot in a piece of wood, the slot only slightly wider than the thickness of the saw blade, and clamps the piece of wood in the vise. He then mounts the saw blade with the teeth *toward* the handle, pushes the back of the blade against the back of the notch, and saws by pushing or pulling the workpiece into the blade. This no doubt is easier on those fragile saw blades.

With all the points cut out, the main points are then assembled, with a resulting double-ended point each made up of four separate pieces of material. Of course, with a four-pointed star, this wouldn't be necessary; you'd simply point both ends of a two-piece laminate. For gluing up these sections, I use five-minute epoxy, which doesn't have a great deal of strength but is adequate for this use, since all you have to do is hold the halves together until they're inletted. I glue them together on a board covered with waxed paper to prevent their sticking to the surface.

On this elaborate form of variegated star, you can't inlet for all the points at once, since the resulting thin slivers of wood between the points would break out. Instead, I inlet the north, south, east, and west points first, and before doing that, I lay out centerlines for *all* eight points on the stock with a pencil. In inletting the first four points, I plan for the points to be a press-fit in the cuts, leaving about 1/32 inch of inlay standing above the wood. You can't drive the points in with a hammer as you would metal inlays, or the brittle materials will break, especially the ivory. Number the points with light slashes of the file to indicate both their position and their orientation if they're the same length. Both the inlets and the points are then coated with twenty-four-hour epoxy, the points pressed in firmly, making sure that you don't trap too much epoxy under the point, and they are left for the cement to harden. Heated animal glue was used in the old days for this purpose, and can be used now if you prefer traditional materials. It would be best to warm the stock to prevent the glue from setting too quickly.

The next day, all four of these points are filed flush with the stock, and this is easiest done with a curved riffler as you can see in the halftone shown here. The centerlines for the remaining four points are reestablished if necessary, and those are then inletted, cemented in, and dressed flush, and the whole business finish-sanded. The inletting must be done precisely so that all of the points meet in the center, with none of the point centerlines straying off. The variegated star can then be further embellished with wire or silver-nail inlay if you wish.

Scrimshaw isn't an art that I've ventured into at this point, but if you want to try larger sheet-ivory inlay on a stock, I'd recommend Blackie Collins' book *How to Scrimshaw and Carve Ivory*. Those who have done it tell me that scrimshaw isn't necessarily difficult, and Blackie is a master at it.

Relief-decorated inlays, particularly for wrists and sideplates, but also used elsewhere such as the cheekpiece, were popular during the baroque and rococo periods in most countries. It is also found on American pieces, particularly pistols in the pre-Revolutionary period, though it was rarer here than in Europe. Wrist inlays often took the form of a large *cabochon,* or irregularly shaped device resembling a misshapen pearl, with a surround of scrollwork and leafage. Such inlays were both chiseled and cast, though the latter method was used more often.

Patterns for cast inlays can easily be made from a suitable hardwood with tight pores and good density. I like pearwood for the purpose, though box, lemon, and probably others like dogwood do just as well. After deciding the overall size of the inlay, since it must be fitted in the space available, I make a full-scale drawing of it and then transfer the outline to a flat piece of pearwood that's no more than 3/32 inch thick. I saw out the piece, closely following the outline, and then glue it to a piece of scrap hardwood using white glue with a piece of common sulfite-bond writing paper sandwiched between the wood pattern and the scrap of wood. This is done so that the finished pattern can be removed from the working base by dampening it with water. The paper laminated between soaks up the moisture more quickly and loosens the joint.

With the blank glued down, I trim the base block fairly close to the sides of the pattern so that the block doesn't interfere with modeling the edges of the pattern. From this point on, the job is simply a matter of relief carving, first sinking the center section in and then modeling the surround, in the case of a wrist inlay. Undercuts in the design must be avoided, or it won't be usable for a casting pattern unless it's used in a rubber mold. Cast inlay usually doesn't rise off the surface of the stock more than about 1/16 inch, so the design should be handled in such a way that it is in low relief yet with good detail. A conscious effort must be made to avoid letting details along the edge drop a great deal lower than the rest of the inlay, or you may have trouble inletting the piece. Some elements can wind up flush with the stock surface, with the rest of the inlay slightly raised.

After carving the inlay pattern, loosen it from the block by squeezing water around the inlay with a sponge. After five minutes or so, the blade of a palette knife can be slipped gingerly under the edge and the pattern lightly prized up. Clean the back off and let the pattern dry. If it warps slightly from the water, in most cases, it straightens with drying.

Such inlays are easily cast, and the people to do it for you can be found right at your local dental lab. Before taking the pattern to have it cast, put a light coat of varnish sealer on it for protection.

Dental labs are investment foundries in miniature — among other things, of course. Casting an inlay for you is a piece of cake compared with some of the other work they do. Many labs can't run a piece larger than 2-3/4 inches square because of the size of investment rings they use, which means that for a long piece like a sideplate, you may have to cast the part in two sections and silver-solder them together, which is no problem. In any event, you'll probably need to supply your own silver to the lab, along with the casting pattern. For a wrist inlay, ask them to stick a quarter-inch gate on the *back* of the wax duplicate of your wood pattern, with this gate as straight as possible and centered in the inlay. When the wax is invested and burned out, and the part run on the centrifuge, the casting is of course left with that gate. This leaves you a stud on the back of the inlay for attaching it to the stock, just as the old ones were done. For this inlay, drill a hole through the wrist after inletting the piece, and run a number 6 machine screw through the wrist, with the head countersunk inside the trigger-plate inlet. With the inlay stud drilled and tapped 6-32, the screw does a fine concealed job of holding the inlay down.

When you have such parts run at a lab, be certain to tell the technicians that you want the inlay as-cast, for you don't want any good-intentioned person polishing that thing for you. Polish it yourself, using round gravers for scraping out hollows. Various shapes of burnishers are also useful for finishing cast inlays, and one tool your collection should have in any case is a bent burnisher with slightly rounded surfaces, mounted in a graver handle. For wrist inlays, you'll have to find a piece of round stock of a diameter similar to the wrist where the inlay is to go, and drill a hole in the piece to take the inlay stud, so that the inlay can be set on the round stock and smacked down with a leather mallet to curve it.

Of course, other metals can also be run for cast inlays, such as brass. I wouldn't want to run these things in steel, though that would be no problem for a dental lab. Gun furniture in steel with relief decoration was always chiseled, not cast.   ●

Gunstock Inlays

Part Two — Silver Wire Inlay — by John Bivins

IN THE LAST issue, I covered sheet, composition, and cast inlays. Here, I'll treat wire inlay, an effective and relatively simple type of decoration that was in use from the earliest period of firearms right to the middle of the nineteenth century. Wire can be used to enhance sheet inlay and relief carving, and as an accent to gun furniture as border surrounds.

Silver-wire inlay really isn't *wire* at all, except for silver-nail decoration, which *is* wire but in a sense isn't inlay. Confused? Well, it'll all fall into place.

Techniques used for silver wire, of course, apply to brass as well, and to find brass thin enough to use for wire work, you'll have to buy sheets of shim stock. The reason that wire inlay isn't wire is that it's made of thin, flat strips rather than round stock or true wire. When such a ribbon is jammed into the stock, only the edge shows.

I use annealed sterling sheet in thicknesses of 0.007 and 0.010 inch.

Thicknesses less than 0.010 inch have to be specially rolled, since 30-gauge is the thinnest sheet commercially available as a stock item; T.B. Hagstoz and Son; 709 Sansom Street; Philadelphia is one of several firms that can roll special thicknesses. Jerry Kirklin uses a 0.005-inch-thick, highly polished cloisonne wire that works well for him. This commercially available stock has lightly rounded edges, which permit it to go into the cuts in the stock readily; a sample that Jerry sent me is 5/64 inch wide.

For wire inlay, I buy twenty-four-inch strips of silver two inches wide, annealed, and cut the wire off these strips. My procedure is to darken one side of a strip with cold blue, not to turn it black but to have it dark enough to clearly see a scribed line on the surface. Then, using a scribe and a precision straightedge, I lay out a 1/16-inch-wide strip to be cut off. No wider than this is really needed. Wire inlays in early pieces are seldom more than that and sometimes less. Wire that is too

Inlaid silver wire is particularly effective in enhancing relief carving, such as this knot of carving behind the cheekpiece of a new jaeger rifle. This kind of decoration is seldom or never seen on modern firearms but was frequently used in baroque and rococo periods.

Some of the tools used in wire-inlay work, left to right: small pin punch, small wire cutters, light ball-pein hammer, narrow stabbing-in chisels (here ground from larger chisels), and a six-inch smooth-cut half-round file. Closeup above shows tip of ground-down stabbing-in chisel; point may be less than a sixteenth of an inch wide, but not more than three thirty-seconds of an inch.

You'll have to stop several times and iron out kinks in the wire as you go.

Now you're ready to start inlaying. Sketch out your wire pattern on the stock. In designing wire layouts, I'd recommend studying illustrations of old wire work, particularly English and European examples. Though wire was used fairly frequently on American rifles, it usually didn't have the finesse of European work. A distinction must be made between baroque and rococo wire work, since the earlier designs have rounded, fairly constant scroll volutes, while rococo wire often has volutes that are flattened, and with a tighter decreasing radius as the volute is formed. Baroque work often used a small silver nail to form the final section of the volute, while this is rare in rococo work.

Although the engraved designs for wire inlay by early masters in decoration such as

wide is difficult to form over curved areas of the stock and has too much tendency to fold over when it's being inserted.

Before the narrow strip of wire is cut off the sheet, the edge is first prepared for inletting by filing a bevel on both sides of the sheet with a mill file. To do this without distorting the sheet, lay the sheet flat on a level surface, with the sheet hanging over the edge just enough to reach it with the file. What you want to do here is to provide a knife-edge on that little strip of silver so that it won't give you trouble going in. Some fellows cut off the strip of wire first and then draw it through scissors held in the vise to cut the knife-edge on it, but I've had better success filing the edge on.

Both the need for a narrow piece of wire and the beveled edge are reasons that the drawn strips sold by some suppliers aren't so good for wire inlay, with the exception of the cloisonne wire mentioned before. You're better off buying sheet and trimming out your wire stock yourself. I trim the wire with a large pair of shears. Large shears aren't needed to cut such thin stock, but the long blades help to keep the cut aligned, and that is very important. Place your light in a position that will allow you to see the scribed line clearly, and stay exactly on that line as you cut. The strip you are cutting off will roll up in a tight coil as you go.

Wood has the tendency to push wire out, so pieces could be lost eventually, especially those on curved surfaces. To minimize the possibility of this, I score the wire with full-length "teeth," a technique I learned from Wallace Gusler. To do this, pull the wire across the sharp edge of any smooth-cut file with double-cut teeth. I usually use a six-inch half-round file for the purpose. Hold the wire between the thumb and the file tightly, with the beveled edge facing away from you so that you won't get cut, and draw the entire strip across the edge of the file, both sides.

After the trim line for a ribbon of silver wire has been scribed on the sheet, the sheet is beveled on both sides with a file to provide a knife edge that allows the wire to enter its mortise in the wood.

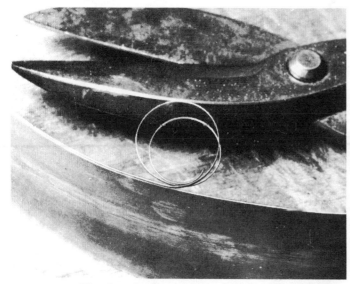

After the edge has been beveled, the scribed-off ribbon of silver is trimmed off the sheet with shears. Care is necessary; ribbon must be cut precisely along the scribed line to avoid irregularities in the top edge of the silver wire when it is inlaid. Next, the strip is drawn across the edge of a smooth-cut, double-cut file to score the sides of the strip longitudinally. This scoring provides a gripping surface for the fibers of the wood to retain the strip of silver. Smooth sides on the inlaid silver strip would allow it to work its way out of the wood in time.

Berain, de La Collombe, and Marteau show wire in graduated thicknesses, the wire used in most cases was all of one thickness. The illusion of various thicknesses was achieved by "bunching" the wire; that is, bringing a number of strands together side by side. On really elaborate work, you might find as many as six strands side by side, opening up into as many scrolls or flourishes farther out. This technique was done, of course, by laying one piece of wire at a time. A close study of old work reveals motifs in which bunching is appropriate, though in most cases, I'd advise that you avoid laying more than three of four strands together, or you'll risk the bunched ends coming out later. A bunch doesn't have the mechanical "foot" in the wood that a single strand does, especially in soft or open-grained woods — which is why wire isn't so good in such woods.

The slots for the wire are cut in with narrow chisels, and I use the same little chisels I use for setting-in carving, as illustrated here. Narrow points little more than 1/16-inch wide (or even less) are used for tight radii, and wider ones up to 3/32 inch wide are used for long curves and straight lines. These chisels can be as thick as 0.015 inch for setting wire, for what you're doing is separating the wood fibers more than you're cutting them, and the wood closes back up later. The slot cut must easily accept the wire, or the wire wants to fold over.

Stab-in your pattern, taking great pains to keep the curves and scrolls flowing properly, because clunky scrolls in wire work stand out like a neon sign. Cut-in and

The inlay begins (left) with a sketch of the pattern on the wood, then sinking the mortise with a narrow chisel. Keeping the tool at right angles to the surface of the wood is vital, to avoid having the wire fold over. Cut must be wide enough to accept the wire easily, and no deeper than a sixteenth of an inch. Pushing downward with the thumbnail (below) starts the wire into the cut prepared for it.

Once the silver wire has been started into the groove by thumbnail, the next step is to tap it into the wood lightly with a small hammer, avoiding heavy blows that upset the edge of the wire and make it thicker. Where the wire is not easily accessible to the hammer, such as near the edge of the cheekpiece, or inside a carved relief, the wire can be sunk safely with a punch, slightly convex on the face, and light taps with the hammer. Care is necessary to avoid denting the wood.

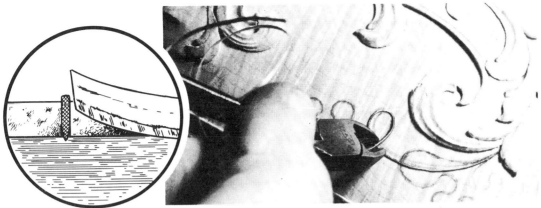

To inlay a loop, with the wire crossing itself, the wire is first pressed into place and led around to the point of crossing, where it is cut with side-cutters, making a mitered cut so that the top edge of the cut end overlaps the wire already seated in the wood.

install but one element at a time, because if you have two slots close together, you'll be cutting unsupported wood and will likely have a sliver loosen and fall out, and that surely does nothing for the finished work. To install the wire, I try to begin at the start of a scroll, say where the scroll emerges from a carving pattern, and I taper that starting end a little by flattening the wire with a small ball-pein hammer. I start that end in the slot by pushing down on the wire with my thumb nail, then gradually work the wire down into the rest of the slot, forming the wire to the curves as I go. On curved surfaces, you'll find that it's necessary at times to tap the starting end down a little with the hammer to prevent its pulling out when you cross the tightest parts of the radius of the stock surface. Don't overdo this, for you don't want to distort the wire or push it down flush at this point. When the entire segment is started into the slot, cut it off the main strip and lightly tap the thing down with the small ball-pein; it should go in easily, without your having to beat on it, or the top of the wire will be upset and thickened, which you don't want. Don't tap it down flush yet.

For tight joints in overlapping wire, the wire should be cut with a miter, and the overlapping or crossing piece started where it crosses another element already inlaid. This miter cut is simple, done just by snipping off the end of the wire at an "undercut" angle. That is, the point of the angle should be at the top of the strip. A very *slight* amount of this point is allowed to ride *over* the piece of wire already inlaid, so that the joint thus formed is tight.

Cutting wire is best done with the smallest pair of side-cutters that you can find. With my cutters, I stone the edges so that only 1/8-inch of the tip has the cutting edges closing together tightly, with no light showing, and the rest of the cutting edges slightly relieved. Once stoned-up this way, these cutters shouldn't be used for any other job.

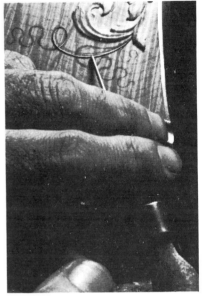

Bumps in the smooth curve of the wire can be tapped with hammer and punch until the curve is even and graceful. This is done when the wire is no more than two thirds of its width deep into the wood.

Final step is to dress the wire flush with the wood surface, using pillar file or small fine-cut rifflers. Coarse files must be avoided; they leave burrs on the edge of the wire, and these are very difficult to remove.

When the wire is tapped down with the hammer, you should leave 1/64 inch or so standing above the surface of the stock. The reason for this is that you may need to correct the flow of a curve before the wire is pushed down flush; this is easily done by using a small punch lightly driven in from the sides of the wire to iron out any "clunks." The wire can then be tapped down flush, ot as close to flush as you can get it, with the hammer. In areas that can't be reached with the hammer face, I use pin punches with the faces slightly domed over and polished, carefully tapping down on these with the hammer. After all the wire elements in a design are inlet in this manner, the wire is filed off flush with the stock using the eight inch number-four-cut pillar file. Avoid using anything coarser for filing, or you're likely to burr the wire, and that burr can't easily be removed. In places where the file won't reach, use a sharp penknife to trim the wire off flush. It cuts easily.

Now moisten a scrap of rag with water and wet the area where the wire is inlaid. Let it stand for a minute, then dry off the area with a propane torch if you want, though this isn't altogether necessary. The water swells the wood fibers and closes them up around the wire. The fibers lock into your score marks in the wire, and it is firmly anchored down, with little chance of being pushed out to any extent later. It *will* rise above the surface a slight amount, over the years, but that can't be avoided.

Incidentally, I've talked to some fellows who believe that some early wire work was deliberately left above the surface, but I don't agree. All of it was originally flush, and it worked out later and became slightly rounded-over on top from wear. If you build a rifle that's to have an aged

appearance, then the wire will have to be left standing a little, but you'd best make the strips wider if you plan to do that.

After wetting the wood, polish the wire off with 400 and 600-grit paper. When the stock finish is applied later, the sealer will provide an additional "lock" on the wire when the sealer hardens and "freezes" the fibers in place.

Silver-wire inlay is really very easy to do, and it is a nice enhancement of the stock if used in appropriate places. It's a good frame for carving, and it works well as a lid surround on a two-piece patchbox or around the lid of a wooden butt trap. Again, you should study old work as much as possible to see how it's most effectively used.

Silver nails driven into the wood in patterns, either in conjunction with the wire or whirling out of an inlay, can be effective. I make such nails out of the same 0.040-inch silver wire that nails for inlays are made from. For a dramatic effect, a curving line of nails spreading out from some feature on an inlay should be of diminishing diameter. This is easily done by cutting off 1/4-inch sections of wire and turning them down with a file while spinning the nail in the electric drill. Drive the nail in while holding it with needle-nose pliers, avoiding driving it down into the unturned section that was held by the drill chuck. Cut them off slightly above the

surface and file them down. Some European gunmakers such as the Stockmars in Suhl had special draw-plates for forming wire in star-shaped sections. When driven in, the end of the wire showed as a tiny star on the stock. It would be nice if some enterprising soul offered wire drawn in different patterns. If you're determined to have that, though, you can make your own draw-plate, forming the "eye" with a punch filed to the shape that you want and then hardening the plate.

If installed correctly, wire hasn't much tendency to rise in the stock over a period of time, but one nuisance about it is that it does of course tarnish. Removing the tarnish without harming stock finish can be difficult, particularly since stock finish often covers the blackened metal. Polishing solutions aren't the answer, particularly since many contain enough ammonia to damage a finish. A better remedy for darkened wire inlay is to polish it out with a good, stiff car wax. Most such waxes have a small quantity of abrasive such as pumice in them and polish wire nicely while bringing up the stock finish to a good gloss as well. Too-frequent applications, of course, grind a built-up stock finish back to the wood eventually, so take care with this. If you like, the wax can be melted, with a quantity of powdered boneblack added to darken the wax, which prevents white spots in crevices after the wax is dry. ●

Stock Options of the Synthetic Kind

by Gary Sloan

THERE'S LITTLE DOUBT left that synthetic stocks for sporting rifles are here to stay. Just scanning the ads in a current copy of *Rifle* or *Handloader* will give an idea about the number of custom shops specializing in glass-stocked rifles. Many firms manufacture their own stocks and offer them in various stages of finish for shooters who wish to perform the installation themselves. Among the sporting arms manufacturers, Weatherby, living up to its motto "Tomorrow's Rifles Today," has had the Fibermark version of the Mark V on the market since '83 and has since added the Fiberguard to the Vanguard line. Sako's Finnfiber, with its McMillan-made stock, came on the scene in '85. More recently, both Remington and Winchester have jumped on the synthetic bandwagon and rumor has it that Ruger will soon join the competition with either a synthetic or an epoxy-impregnated wood laminate stock similar to that of Alpha Arms.

Shooters tend to be a conservative lot when it comes to accepting firearms innovations. Nonetheless, it has become apparent to many who use their rifles under adverse field conditions, that manmade stock materials offer some real advantages.

The most important is stability. No matter whether it's hot and dry or wet and cold, synthetic stocks simply do not react as conventional wooden stocks do by shrinking, expanding and warping. A common solution to this problem has been to free-float the barrels. This has sometimes presented a dilemma because some rifles don't deliver their best accuracy with the barrels floated.

A family of synthetic-stocked Model 77 Rugers: (*1*) .243, (*2*) .270, (*3*) 7mm Magnum and (*4*) .338 Magnum. Note the lack of streaking in the .338's stock, the only one cured in a heat chamber.

Thus the choice is sometimes between less-than-optimum accuracy or risking a shift in bullet impact due to wood movement. With a synthetic stock, you can bed for best accuracy and not worry about effects of climate.

A second advantage is weight reduction. On an average, synthetic rifle stocks weigh about a pound less than their wooden counterparts, and this difference can be exploited in more than one way. Obviously, you can make your rifle a pound lighter, and lightweight rifles certainly seem to be the trend today. For those who don't care so much for the way light rifles hold — particularly in offhand shooting — there's the option of using a stiffer barrel without making the gun too heavy. Additionally, a glass-stocked rifle tends to put more weight on the forward shooting hand, produces less muzzle jump, and handles like a heavier gun. This phenomenon occurs because most of the weight reduction comes from the butt section, thus shifting the center of balance about an inch toward the muzzle. Best of all, if correctly designed, synthetic stocks reduce perceived recoil

by flexing in the grip and butt, thereby lengthening recoil time like a pad does.

Maintenance problems are minimal. Synthetic stocks are so strong and durable that not much ever happens to them which can't be repaired with a little paint or epoxy. Other than sling swivel studs tearing out (which I'll get into later), I've never experienced any trouble. I did repaint one stock that spent over 200 days afield — about half of that time in a damp saddle scabbard — but that was done more to check out the influence of a heat chamber on wrinkle paint than for any real need to refinish.

The commonly used synthetics in today's stocks are fiberglass, Kevlar and graphite. To offer anything like a brief comparison of those materials without oversimplification is next to impossible because each is available in various styles of weave, mesh, thickness, etc. A brochure put out by Hexel lists six variations of E glass, five of S glass, 10 of Kevlar and four of graphite. Comparison is further complicated by the fact that the various styles and

materials can be laminated together in almost any combination. Such lamination affects a stock's properties in different ways and degrees. A simple example: if you laminate two layers of the same material, say in the stock's forearm, it will end up twice as strong but *eight times* as rigid. Needless to say, a designer of synthetic stocks faces an almost infinite number of possibilities.

There are, however, some useful conclusions to be made about the three materials. The most common synthetic used in stocks is fiberglass, of which there are two types: E glass and S glass. In terms of desirable stock features, S glass is superior in every way. It is stronger, stiffer, more resistant to impact and slightly lighter than E glass. For the amount of glass cloth used in a stock, the cost of either type, about $5 per pound, is insignificant.

Typically, two or more layers of glass cloth surrounding a foam core are impregnated with an epoxy or polyester resin. This is set up in two-piece moulds which approximately duplicate the inletting requirements of a specific action while providing a generous barrel channel. To eliminate voids (places where resin impregnation is incomplete or

Bedding the forearm is the last step in the process. A pad of bedding compound is built up near the forend tip to support the barrel at that point.

A fiberglass stock with the inletting molded in. The white dot ahead of the recoil lug mortise shows where the foam core was injected.

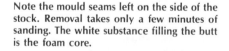

Note the mould seams left on the side of the stock. Removal takes only a few minutes of sanding. The white substance filling the butt is the foam core.

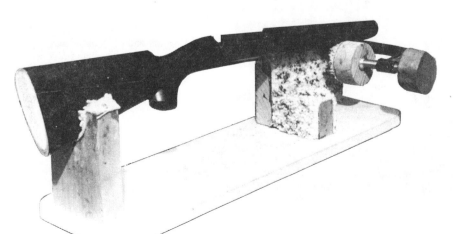

196

missing) some type of pressure or vacuum system may be used.

Many designs use solid epoxy in the action area, a most important feature if inletting has to be adjusted very much, because when layers of fiber are cut, they have to be patched, or else some weakening of the stock in this critical section will occur. What is produced is a stock which is moderately compression-resistant and fairly flexible laterally.

Those characteristics are beneficial in the grip and butt, since they help reduce perceived recoil. They are not so good in the action area, where you want the most rigidity possible. A stiff forearm is immaterial only if the barrel is to be floated. Otherwise, it should be as inflexible as possible especially when a sling or bipod may be used as a shooting aid. Fortunately, rigidity in a specific section is easy to build in by adding layers of glass or graphite.

Kevlar, the DuPont wonder material used in canoes and so-called "bulletproof" vests, is about twice as strong for its weight as S-glass, is somewhat stiffer and more impact resistant. Kevlar's basic cost is moderate (about $10 per pound, or twice as much as S-glass). On the minus side, it is extremely difficult to work with in hand lay-up applications, which require special tools and techniques, all of which increase costs considerably. Because a significant portion of the finished weight for either Kevlar or glass comes from the resins used, Kevlar's final weight advantage averages only about four or five ounces in a finished stock. Kevlar stocks run about $100 more than fiberglass, and Kevlar reinforcement adds about $30 to a stock's price.

The chief advantage of graphite is its property of rigidity — up to double that of Kevlar. Its strength is comparable to that of S glass (it's lighter than S glass but heavier than Kevlar) but its resistance to impact is relatively poor. This last feature, along with its high cost (up to $70 per pound), makes the use of graphite alone quite impractical. As a stiffening agent, however, graphite

has no equal. Laminations with graphite in butt-grip sections should be avoided because this construction dramatically increases perceived recoil. Graphite reinforcement usually runs about $30.

It has been my experience that stocks made from these various materials are similar in quality provided they're well-designed. The main advantage of Kevlar and graphite is weight reduction. One cheap way to reduce weight (up to half a pound in Mausers) is to replace the rifle's trigger guard and floorplate with a blind magazine. This conversion costs about $40, and as an added bonus you get a stock that is somewhat stiffer and stronger in the action area.

Because Kevlar/graphite is more expensive, and I'm not overly interested in ultimate weight reduction, my personal preference is usually for a plain, well-constructed fiberglass stock. If not familiar with the construction details of a particular stock, I like to call the stockmaker to find out before buying. Many of the brochures and catalogs don't give enough information for making good decisions. One notable exception is the catalog of Garrett Accur-Light, PO Box 8563, Fort Collins CO 80524. Cost is $2 and well worth it.

The cost for having someone else stock and bed your rifle in a synthetic has been in the $500 to $600 range. Expanding competition is beginning to force this price down considerably. You can do the job yourself for around $200 or a bit less. To do so is not particularly difficult but it is time consuming.

Should you choose to stock your own rifle, here are the sequences you'll need to follow and various options along the way. All cost estimates are my own; actual prices could be higher or lower.

First, you need to order a stock. Again, I strongly recommend doing this by phone so that the supplier can answer your questions and ask any he needs to know to ensure a good fit. You can specify length of pull at this time if you know the thickness of your recoil pad. This may save sawing off the butt later. In many cases you can order a buttplate or recoil pad already installed. Cost should be about $25, including pad. The basic stock should run around $115. Subtract a bit for an un-inletted

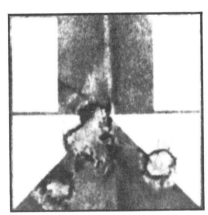

This five shot group was fired by a .338 Model 77 Ruger and spanned 1.3 inches — typical of the accuracy to be expected from a synthetic-stocked sporter.

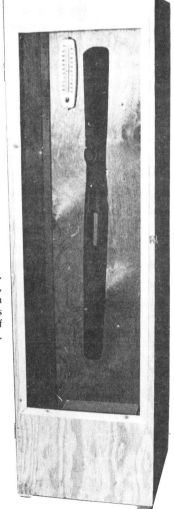

Right, Gary's easy-to-build heat chamber. It consists of a plywood box, a hotplate, a heat baffle, a thermometer and a Plexiglas door. Without its help, Gary says he could never match the quality of factory finishes.

The economy model — an inletted fiberglass stock with a solid epoxy core. Inletting will require several hours of painstaking labor and should be considered when weighing the stock's price.

197

model, add about $30 for Kevlar or graphite reinforcement and another $100 for a Kevlar stock. If you don't have the necessary supplies on hand, you may want to order a finishing kit at this time. Kits usually contain some glass cloth, bedding compounds, filler material and wrinkle paint.

The work begins by getting the rifle to drop cleanly into the stock. Make sure it's square and centered. Normally, this will require little more than minor sanding and scraping or perhaps realigning a screw hole. For that type of fitting, a Dremel tool is helpful but not a necessity. Should you be forced to cut through any fibers or do so accidentally, repair can be made by inlaying a piece of glass cloth and wetting it with epoxy resin. For very small cuts, a simple epoxy patch will do.

When satisfied with the stock-rifle fit, you're ready to glass bed the action. Commercial bedding compounds like Micro-bed or Acraglas are easy to use, work well and are provided with complete, easy-to-understand directions. I buy epoxy resin in bulk for this operation and control its viscosity with microfibers. Straight epoxy resin is too runny for any build up. **Caution:** Don't forget to apply a releasing agent to any metal that contacts the bedding compound or you're apt to get a permanent bond!

There's a lot of debate over bedding techniques. One that has always served me well is a four-point system: at the receiver tang, in front of and behind the recoil lug, and at the end of the forearm. In the first bedding I leave the forearm alone because it's too easy to spring the stock a little, even if you use shims. In addition, I like to see how well the rifle shoots with the barrel floated. After the compound has set up, recheck to make sure there are no high spots between tang and lug. If there are, remove them.

At that point, you may wish to fill between the barrel and its channel in the stock. Since this operation is mainly cosmetic, I just do the upper edges of the channel and leave the bottom alone. One way to accomplish that is to mix the compound thicker than usual and spread a slightly excessive amount around the top inside edge of the channel. Instead of treating the metal for release, I put a layer of wax paper between barrel and compound, wipe away the excess ooze, and let it set up. The wax paper will release easily and leave no more than a hairline gap.

The stock's surface is likely to be composed of an easy-to-sand epoxy compound, and you should sand out any mould marks. All pits, voids and low spots should be filled with epoxy or auto body filler and sanded smooth. Sixty-grit paper is about right for rough work; 220-grit is fine enough for a paint finish.

Glue on the recoil pad (last chance to adjust length of pull) and install the sling swivel studs. A flaw in some of the earlier stock designs was that no special provision was made for holding studs. Those that were merely screwed through layers of fiberglass soon ripped out, and about all you could do was fill the holes with epoxy, replace the studs and build a low epoxy mound around each stud on the stock's surface. Most stocks now use some type of metal insert to hold the studs in place or they provide thickened areas to receive the studs. In the latter case, installation is the same as for wooden stocks. You can have the studs installed at the factory for $10 or so.

Because oil and grease may have accumulated from handling, or wax may have been used in the resin for curing purposes, it's a good idea to wash down the stock with acetone prior to any painting. Paint the stock with auto body primer and let it dry thoroughly. I omitted this step on my first stock and spent several unpleasant hours using the back of a hacksaw blade to scrape off gooey wrinkle paint that refused to cure. For a factory filled, sanded and primed stock, add about $95. Cost seems to vary considerably, perhaps because different methods of manufacture result in more or less finish work.

The easiest final finish is to paint with an acrylic lacquer or a flat stove paint. Such finishes aren't pretty but they're practical — if you can put up with the slick feel, especially when the stock is wet. Most shooters seem to prefer the looks and grip of a non-glare, wrinkle finish. Factory wrinkle finishes run $50 to $65 ($50 or so more for camouflage).

Applying wrinkle paint can be an exasperating experience. Close attention must be paid to the directions on the can. The stuff is supposed to work at room temperature but I've found 68 degrees Fahrenheit too cold to produce an even texture. One hundred degrees is about right and will likely require the use of a heat chamber or heat lamps. In the summer, I've had good results hanging the stock to dry in a closed greenhouse.

To create the wrinkle effect, two coats are supposed to be applied, about three minutes apart. After three minutes, the first coat will still look wet and shiny, making it rather difficult to tell if the second coat is even or covers it completely. If not, the final finish will vary in texture, with shiny splotches showing where the second coat missed. A better technique, I've found, is to apply the first coat longitudinally. Wait three minutes, then apply the second coat laterally. Wait another three minutes and apply a *third* coat longitudinally.

Another solution is to use different colors for each coat. There's no blending of colors in this method. Gray will cover black or vice versa without either affecting the other.

Whatever method you use, it's important to mask off the internal parts of the stock to keep paint from messing up the precision of your bedding. The stock will feel dry in three or four hours but it really takes a couple of weeks for the paint to cure, and the stock should be handled gently during that time.

The final step is to bed the forearm. Since bedding at receiver tang and recoil lug is already completed, this is pretty simple. All I do is build a 1½-inch long pad of bedding compound under the barrel near the end of the forearm, tape off each end of the pad to keep the edges square, put a releasing agent on the barrel, drop the rifle into the stock, tighten the bedding screws, and let the compound set up. After everything is good and hard, the rifle is taken from the stock and the tape removed by cutting along its inside edge with a razor blade. If accuracy isn't better than it was in the floated mode, the barrel can be freed from its pad by a little sanding.

So far I've stocked seven rifles in the manner just described, with rewarding results. Using full-power loads, two .338 Magnums shoot 1½ and 1¼-inch groups at 100 yards; three 7mm Magnums all group around an inch; a .270 does about ¾ inch, and a .243 consistently shoots ½ inch or better. All those guns see long, hard use under harsh climatic conditions without problems — a reversal of their previous histories. I suspect the degrees of accuracy described here approach the limits imposed by the rifles' other components and could be achieved at least temporarily in conventional stocks. On the other hand, I can't see much sense in restocking any wooden-stocked rifle having a good track record of stock stability and season-to-season accuracy or one that really doesn't get much field use.

Restocking with a synthetic is moderately expensive. The cost can be reduced considerably if you do some or all the work yourself. One advantage in working with the manmade materials is that almost any mistake you make is easily corrected because, unlike wood, most shaping work calls for *adding* material rather than *removing* it. Thus, if you are moderately skilled and have the time, don't be afraid to tackle such a job. In all fairness, however, I must note that most of the glass-stocked rifles I've seen turned out by arms companies and custom shops reflect quality craftsmanship and fair prices considering the amount of work involved. ●

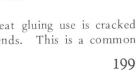

By L. S. Hacker, Jr.

The Many Uses of 'FIBERGLASS'

The epoxy resins of "glass bedding kits" have proved to be excellent for stock repairs when the fiberglass flocking is not added. This valuable Griffin & Howe stock was broken in half at the grip, but is now quite serviceable; the break line is barely visible, just within the rear point of the checkering.

IN ALMOST THIRTY YEARS as a gunsmith I've witnessed the introduction of quite a few significant aids to the gunmaker's art: low cost power tools, more efficient hand tools, high quality-low cost rifle barrels, compact welding units, the list goes on and on. But of all the innovations of modern science and manufacture, the one single item that most aids and upgrades my services are the various epoxy resin "fiberglass" compounds.

Back in the 1950's when epoxy resin/fiberglass compounds first entered the gunsmithing area they were hailed chiefly as the ultimate answer to rifle bedding problems. Some individuals, in fact, were so taken with the idea that they claimed long and loud that good rifles would be better and bad rifles would be good only if the actions were bedded in fiberglass.

As I recall, the introduction of fiberglass bedding compounds occured at a time when action bedding was a popular topic among rifle buffs. Since everyone was convinced that bedding played the major role in rifle accuracy (or lack of it) the idea of a "perfect" bedding system caught on big. To be honest I was not all that convinced

that "glass bedding" as it came to be called, could live up to all the claims made for it. But perhaps this was largely due to a case of professional jealousy. I had spent years perfecting my art of ultra-tight hand bedding and I didn't want my reputation (not to mention my livelihood) to be cast asunder in the wake of an "artificial" system that promised everything.

Thus for a few years I refused to do any glass bedding in my shop or even discuss it. However, when I finally discovered that there was no slackening in the demand for good hand inletting, I relaxed my guard and took a careful look at the pros of the fiberglass compounds. At any rate, by that time serious shooters had learned that glass bedding was not the cure-all they had predicted.

Nonetheless, some undeniable advantages of fiberglass had become abundantly clear. The resin compounds, for example, without the ground glass flock, are a super glue.

Since discovering this, my attitude toward broken stock repair, attaching

fore-end tips, grip caps and even attaching buttplates has completely changed.

When I was limited to ordinary glue I expected little and guaranteed nothing in the way of stock repair. Whenever a stock came in broken through the grip all I could do was insert a few dowels or pins, douse everything with glue and leave the repair clamped together for a few days. Even then, I was reasonably sure that as soon as the repair got wet, dried out, or got another blow it would come apart — and it usually did.

Likewise with fore-end tips. An ebony or rosewood tip would hold only until some uneven shrinkage of the mating woods came about. Then the glue would shatter and nothing would be left holding the fore-end tip in place but the pin or dowels and there was usually an unsightly crack between stock and fore-end.

Another great gluing use is cracked shotgun fore-ends. This is a common

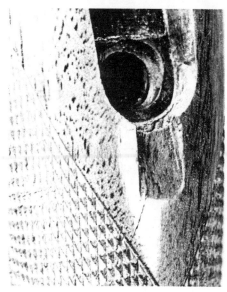

The small crack behind the
tang of this custom-stocked rifle
was arrested when the recoil lug and
tang area were fiberglass bedded.
Small cracks such as this one are almost
impossible to repair, but they can be
made less noticeable by filling
once further cracking has been stopped.

"bread and butter" item in gunshops. Recoil, abuse, age, and accidents create an abundance of grain separations which get worse and worse if not corrected.

My early technique was to go inside the fore-end, inlay a thin sheet of metal, draw the crack together, then glue and pin to the metal plate. This, of course, was time consuming and didn't always work. Now all I do is poke some resin in the crack, clamp it for 36 hours then return it to the owner with a guarantee that the crack won't open up again.

This is *not* to say that I've never had a failure — I have, especially with old, oil-soaked stocks. But the occurence is so rare that I can afford a guarantee without losing my shirt.

The strength that fiberglass lends to

wood is astounding, from the standpoint of arresting or preventing failures it works miracles. One of the inherently weakest gunstocks ever designed was the L.C. Smith. What with all the action and lock cuts there just isn't much wood left and as a result the buttstocks are notorious for splitting behind the tang and lock plates. Whenever a stock is brought to me with the beginnings of a split showing I simply fill it with bedding resin (without the glass) and put it in a clamp. So far as I know, none of these repairs have ever resulted in further splitting.

In this same category the fiberglass compounds are great for *preventive* medicine. For instance, whenever an L.C. Smith is brought into my shop for repairs I recommend that certain points in the action area be reinforced with fiberglass compound as a guarantee against splitting in the future. This, I think, is a great idea and should be recommended by all gunsmiths. It is interesting to note that when Marlin reintroduced the L.C. Smith all of the new guns left the factory with the stock reinforced with fiberglass just as described above.

The uses for fiberglass on shotguns are many indeed. Another use is coat-

A thin "paint coat" of epoxy glue applied on top of fiberglass bedding, such as in the bench rest rifle stock below, will improve any irregularities in fitting caused by uneven shrinkage of the bedding material. The paint coat was applied while the receiver was resting on strips of masking tape along the sides, near the upper edge of the stock, to eliminate any problems caused by "wedging" of the sides of the receiver. When fiberglassing heavy-recoiling rifles such as the .458 Magnum at right, the "glass" must be applied around, ahead of, and behind the recoil lug if the fiberglass is to distribute enough recoil stresses to do any good.

ing all of the wood areas which contact metal with compound. This, I suppose, is a glass bedding of sorts but has nothing to do with accuracy. Many shotgun mechanisms allow oil to drain down into the stock. This not only makes the wood look dark and dingy but also weakens it. Also the constant battering of wood against metal can cause the wood to chip and crack. By applying a thin coat of fiberglass compound to the wood where it will contact metal the grain is both effectively oil-proofed and significantly strengthened

Speaking of fiberglass compound on wood, one of the most waterproof stock finishes possible is the resin used in Brownell's Acraglas compound. A coat or two of this is not only good looking but remarkably durable. Also, when exotic wood inlays are used a fiberglass resin is the *only* sure way to keep them in place. And fiberglass compounds are great for filling checks,

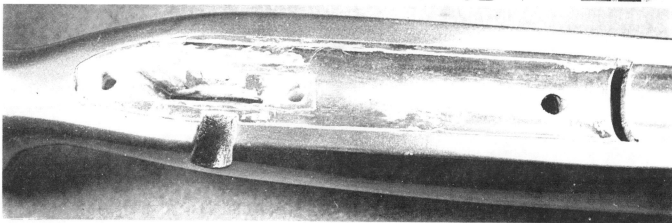

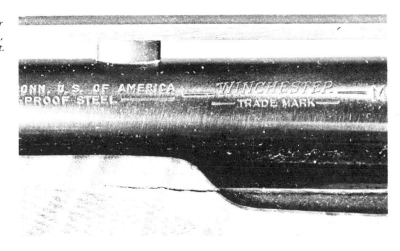

A fore-end crack such as this one on a Model 12 Winchester can be repaired by forcing epoxy resin into the crack, then taping the crack closed overnight.

holes, and other surface flaws. Not being able to match all types of wood coloring with the dye that comes in the bedding kits, I bought an assortment of watercolor dyes at an art shop. It worked great and now I can blend any color needed. In fact, I've even put different shades of compounds in a single fill for an absolutely perfect effect.

Fiberglass resins are also remarkable bonding agents for metal. In my time I've attached scope blocks to barrels and receivers, ventilated ribs to shotgun barrels, front sight ramps to pistol barrels and permanently anchored countless screws and pins that wanted to work loose. These resins are great when you don't want to apply the heat that is required for silver soldering. Also, since the resins leave no signs such as heat discoloration or solder smear there is no "clean-up" work required. Just wipe off the "squeeze out" and the job is done.

About six years ago I did my first repair job on a disconnected ventilated rib. It was a "temporary" job on a trap gun which I hoped would hold long enough to last through the remainder of an important tournament. That "temporary" job is still holding fast and strong after many thousands of rounds fired.

The secret to a good bond with the resin glues is getting the parts to be glued absolutely clean and dry. Trying to glue two oily pieces together is futile.

So how do you get a separation of a resin bond if necessary? Simple. Apply heat. Somewhere around 350 degrees or so the resins break down, and that's not enough heat to hurt anything.

I have also made a few repairs of rifle scopes which had lens loosened or completely out. The resins are perfect for a glass-to-metal bond. In fact, I understand that some optical manufacturers use these glues for permanent optical mounting.

Last, but not least, of course is the use of fiberglass compounds for stock inletting. Frankly, I abhor the idea of fiberglass being used as a substitute for careful hand inletting. In my opinion there is good inletting, and what isn't good is awful and no amount of fiberglass filler is going to make up the difference.

The great benefit of fiberglass is in the recoil lug area of the action inletting. The recoil will invariably batter the wood and set back somewhat. When this happens, gaps appear at the shoulder at the front of the action. Also, if the barreled action sets back far enough there may be some cracking and chipping of the wood at the tang area. Fiberglass, properly used, will eliminate this problem. By "properly used," I mean exactly that.

I've seen fiberglass used behind the recoil lug in such a manner that it could do no possible good. So small an amount was used, and that behind the lug only, that the recoil simply shoved the fiberglass into the wood and did as much harm as if no glass had been used at all. The idea is to have a fairly large mass of glass in the area so that it contacts a large area of wood, behind, alongside, and even in front of the lug. This way the recoil force is distributed over a wider area.

Bear in mind that any application of fiberglass must be to clean wood, for if applied over finish the compound

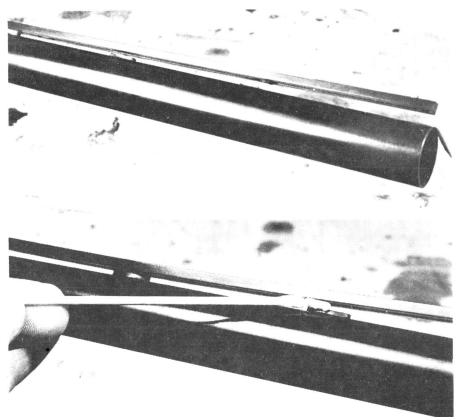

Separated shotgun ventilated ribs can be easily and permanently repaired by wedging the rib open, then applying epoxy resin to each post. Many times epoxy can be used for a repair that would be difficult with silver solder, and there is no chance for heat discoloration.

will adhere only to the finish, which will eventually crack loose. I've seen amateur bedding jobs where the fiberglass came out in chunks because it was applied over a thick factory finish (the stocks had been hollowed out around the recoil lug and tang, but the finish had been left untouched around the receiver walls and barrel).

When bedding for accuracy some users of fiberglass fail to take into account a slight shrinkage factor (around 1% to 3%). Thus what might look like a good fit isn't that good at all. The remedy for this is to brush a thin coat of resin (without the glass flocking) onto the hardened glass inletting and set the barreled action tightly in place again. This second coat makes for a super-close fit. Of course such precautions as this aren't necessary for hunting rifles but accuracy buffs find that it pays off.

Actually I don't think that glass bedding itself will improve accuracy over a proper hand bedding job. Its main advantage, however, is that the fiberglass bedding will *maintain* accuracy better in the face of moisture changes and temperature extremes and that's what's important in the long run.

In using fiberglass compounds, consider that they aren't all alike, and that some will do a particular job better than others. The type made available to professional and amateur gunsmiths usually requires a 50-50 mix, but some commercial epoxy mixes, such as used in automobile body work, require only a few drops of hardener for a fairly large quantity of material. As a rule, the latter type has few uses in a gunshop for it has to be applied in pretty thick layers in order to build up enough catalytic heat to insure complete hardening, and it shrinks more (around 6%) while curing than the 50-50 mixes.

The most obvious differences in the 50-50 mixes is the speed with which they set. Some of the bedding compounds set up so quickly — a matter of minutes — that you have to hurry to get the flocking stirred in and the mixture in place. These can be a pain if you're planning to apply the fiberglass to a large area, or to numerous places, such as the tang, recoil lug and along the barrel channel at one time, but they're ideal if you want to apply it to only one spot, as in a stock repair or only around the recoil lug and tang.

As a rule of thumb, or so I've been told by professional fiberglass workers, the faster a mixture sets up, the hotter it gets, and the greater the shrinkage. The slower-setting materials, while easier to use when applying the mixture to several areas, will also have less shrinkage. But when applying thin coats of such slow-setting materials, as when applying a "paint coat" to bedding or making a repair, I've noticed that they won't set up as reliably as the quick-setting types. The probable cause is insufficient catalytic heat, which can be helped by applying external heat from a heat lamp or large light bulb placed near the work. When applying such thin layers I often use the two-tube epoxy glue available from hardware stores, since it's designed to set up hard in a thin coat.

Even if I won't go along with the claim that epoxy resin/fiberglass mixtures can make expert stockmakers out of anyone with enough sense to read the mixing directions, I will admit that it has its uses — and as far as I'm concerned, its most important uses aren't even mentioned by its promoters. In fact, it's amazing just how useful the stuff is. ●

Bedding with

EPOXY

NEAL KNOX

Rusty's "trail worn" Remington 700 BDL (above left) had lost its accuracy potential; comparison range tests were done with Neal's rifle, also a 7mm Rem. Mag. Above right, properly epoxy-bedded stock shows primary bedding area to be around the recoil lug. Large cutouts for magazine, trigger and safety preclude any effective means of making the tang bedding more secure than the wood on which it rests.

I T WAS RUSTY'S favorite hunting rifle, not only because of the 7mm Rem. Mag's power and accuracy, but because the Remington 700BDL shot a variety of bullets to the same point of impact, and held its point-of-aim from year to year through several brutal Alaskan hunts. But after Rusty moved to North Carolina it had lost its edge — both in accuracy and as a hunting rifle's all-important ability to hold zero.

Those symptoms clearly indicated an action bedding problem, but considering what that rifle and its 3x-9x Leupold scope had gone through, I'm surprised that it still shot as well as it

did. Three-shot groups of Rusty's pet hunting load (63.0 H-4831/160 Nosler or Speer/Federal 210), which had consistently measured a minute of angle (MOA) for most of the rifle's life, had opened to two MOA (two inches at 100 yards, four inches at 200 yards, etc.).

Rusty, who is an Army officer and one of my brothers, had hunted all over Alaska with that rifle, alternately soaking it while hunting moose in constant rain, and freeze-drying it in 40-below Arctic cold. Not only had it made clean kills on caribou, wolf and an outstanding 42-inch curl sheep, it had also served as a walking stick as

he packed out the trophy and meat — protected only by a slip-on recoil pad.

The diagnosis of the problem as action bedding was easily confirmed by alternately tightening and loosening the action screws, and observing the way the barreled action had to "bend" to fit the stock. The bedding surfaces *looked* okay, with no gaps, obstructions or obviously beaten-down spots, but "looks can be deceiving."

If the rifle were to be restored to peak performance, the action would have to be rebedded, either by patiently scraping the high spots or substituting a bedding of epoxy. Of the two choices, epoxy bedding is infinitely easier, and is more likely to last longer;

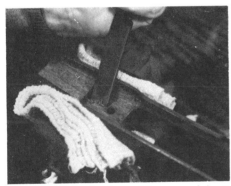

About 3/16th inch of wood is removed from the strongest section of the stock, behind the recoil lug, for primary bedding area. Finish has been removed from short section of barrel channel where epoxy pad will be located for additional support.

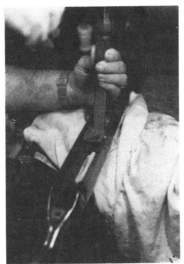

With the aid of a broad chisel and hammer, recoil shoulder is cut back and recoil lug slot deepened and widened.

An X-Acto knife is used to shape cuts for pad of epoxy. Note that epoxy will be below the stock line. No epoxy will be placed along the rails.

but considering the inherent instability of wood, neither is likely to be permanent.

Bedding a rifle in epoxy isn't difficult, only a little nerve-wracking as you wonder whether the thing will come out of the stock; of course, it will. But doing a *good* bedding job is another matter; just because every tool mark or inspector's stamp is reproduced in the epoxy doesn't mean that the action really fits the stock, or that it will continue to fit, or that the rifle will shoot its best.

The key is knowing what you want to achieve and why. The rest is mechanical.

When "glass bedding" kits first came on the market in the late 1950s, they seemed to be the answer to every shooter's prayer, for they held the promise of doing away with the well-recognized problem of poor accuracy due to poor action/stock fit. The epoxy kits did eventually fulfill that promise, but not without educating a lot of amateur, as well as professional, gunsmiths. There were plenty of mistakes, and there still are.

An acquaintance recently showed me his newly epoxy-bedded jewel, and like the artist in the TV wine commercial, proudly asked, "Would you believe I did it in only an hour?" Yes, I believed it. The stock was an excellent example of what not to do with epoxy bedding. The wood had been gouged out, none too neatly, for about an eighth-inch all around the action, with the resulting gap filled with glaringly obvious dyed-epoxy, smears

of which faintly glistened on the action and barrel. Since he hadn't left any of the original bedding in place, or otherwise supported the action during the curing, the tang had been pulled too far into the stock, causing the barrel to angle upward, so only a little over a third of the barrel was within the stock at the fore-end. And the epoxy had cured with the barrel angled off center-line. But that was no problem, for my friend had also filled the barrel channel with epoxy, "to seal it," he said knowingly; "making certain that it won't shift point of impact."

To show me how precisely everything fit, he pulled the action. The screws turned reluctantly, and stayed in the stock after they had disengaged from the action threads. Then it had to be pried and rocked out of the stock. "Now that's a tight fit," he beamed. I cringed.

As Rusty and I drove over to a gunshop to get an epoxy kit, I told him about that rifle, the probable reasons why it didn't shoot as well as my friend had hoped it would, and how it could be helped by judicious scraping and drilling. Almost everything that can be done wrong with epoxy had been done to that rifle. Almost. After all, this young lad did remember to coat the steel with release agent, which a friend of mine didn't on his first glass bedding job, presaging the bench shooters' glued-in actions by about fifteen years.

And he didn't do what I did on an early effort — failing to consider the deep inletting with which Bishop semi-inletted stock blanks were sold in the 1950 s; the well-dammed lake of epoxy oozed above the center line of

the barrel, resulting in a rock-hard semi-circle of epoxy that didn't break loose until my hammering and tugging split the fore-end.

But when it came to making his rifle look right and shoot right, my young friend had done it wrong, wrong, wrong!

The common tendency is to overdo the marvelous ability of epoxy to mould to a "perfect" fit, and to assume that if a little is good, a lot is better. A tight fit in all dimensions results in wedging, which doesn't result in best accuracy. The problem is multiplied if the action screws are also bedded in epoxy, as my young friend's rifle was, for most screws are bent slightly as a result of being pulled down too tightly with the normal slight misalignment of floorplate holes and action threads. Since the crooked screws are unlikely to be torqued to the same place twice, they exert a lateral force that tries to shift the action in its bed.

I confess to having bedded more than one barrel for the length of the fore-end, thinking that would add to the perfect fit and provide a stiffener to resist warpage; that was a mistake. Epoxy is waterproof, while all stock finishes are porous to some degree; by putting a coat of epoxy in the channel we produce an imbalance equal to painting one side of a board, which *induces* warping.

While we think of epoxy as rigid, due to its hardness, even brittleness, it is surprisingly flexible, as you can determine by observing how far some of your cured excess will bend before it breaks. Even a few thousandths of an

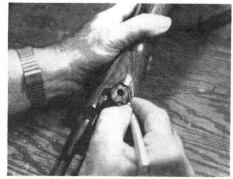

Tang pad is cut out slightly smaller than action tang to prevent epoxy from being visible on the completed job.

After the front of the magazine cut and rear of trigger cut are dammed with modeling clay, and rolled wax paper tubes are inserted in the screw holes, a thick coat of paste floor wax is rubbed on the stock to keep epoxy smears from adhering.

The action is prepared by filling cuts with modeling clay, placing longitudinal strips of masking tape just below the stock line of the action and barrel. Front, sides and bottom of the lug are taped to provide clearance from the epoxy.

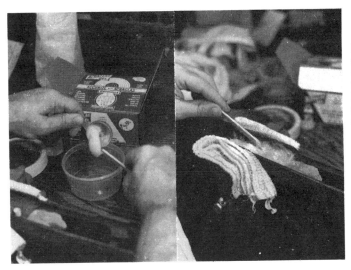

Brownell's Acraglas Gel (far left) is measured into mixing cup. Its thick consistency makes it extremely easy to work with. Gel mixed with hardener allows adequate time to smooth epoxy into all areas before it begins to harden (near left). Work epoxy into corners and against all surfaces to work out trapped air and assure adhesion.

After final assembly, tang was found to be a few thousandths "low," so surface of pad was roughed and a "paint coat" of epoxy applied. Trigger was protected with tape.

inch will amount to a lot of bend over the length of a fore-end.

There is no more certain way to start an argument among accuracy buffs than to make a dogmatic statement about what produces, or doesn't produce, an accurate rifle. Therefore, I'm a bit reluctant to give hard and fast rules for accuracy, for some rifles shoot well despite those rules. But from my own experience bedding and re-bedding many bench rest and hunting rifles, and more importantly, from talking with many of the leading riflesmiths in the country, I think there is near unanimity as to the basic principles of accuracy bedding.

If a rifle is to shoot its best, whether bedded in epoxy or wood, it must mate perfectly with the stock, without any stress-inducing bending to fit the bedding. In other words, with the front action screw tight, there should be no perceptible bowing or arching of the action when the rear screws are tightened, and vice versa; the action should have the same shape when out of the stock as when tightly buckled into the stock. The reason for this is debatable, but the effect isn't.

My theory is that while steel won't bend as much as wood, in the same thickness and shape, each will bend some to reach a compromise when an action is tightened into an ill-fitting stock. This compromise relationship is changed due to recoil or temperature variations from shot to shot, or after a few shots, resulting in a subtle shift in the bedding and a resultant shift in the point of impact, hence bigger groups. That's why rifles will shoot "snake eyes" — two or three shots together, followed by two or three shots together in a slightly different place. While such shifting or target-crawling is usually attributed to "the barrel warming up," I suspect it's really due to the action warming up,

and the elasticity changing, resulting in a change in the steel/wood bending compromise. (I think vibration patterns also play a major role, but let's not get into that.)

Since Rusty had removed the 700BDL's fore-end pressure point long before, allowing the barrel to completely float, it was easy to check for action stress. With the gun resting on its butt, I had loosened the front action screw while holding the barrel at the fore-end tip, with my fingers touching the wood. As little as .002-inch movement between the barrel and stock can be detected by this method — which is as much, or more, than will be allowed on a bench gun. Bear in mind that the movement at the tip is magnified by the length of the forearm, so the actual movement at the screw is far less.

In a properly bedded rifle, there should be a barely perceptible movement as the action breaks free during the first quarter-turn of the screw, then no more. (If the action doesn't move when the screws are loosened, it's wedged, and won't shoot as well.) But in Rusty's rifle, the barrel continued to spring outward for perhaps an eighth-inch, and would bow back and forth in harmony with the tightening and loosening of the screw. The action was bent over a hump, probably due to the recoil area or tang, or both, being beaten down or the wood compressed by the screws. Had there been a dip in the bedding, the barrel movement would have been less pronounced, but the barrel would have moved toward the tip as the pressure of the front screw was released. (If the rifle has a center screw, it should be removed for this test.)

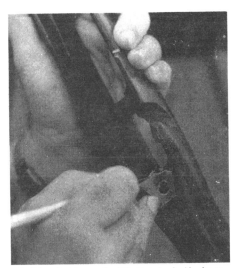

Tang is shown prior to clean-up. "Paint coat" was applied with front action screw pulled tight, tang "floating" in epoxy to assure stress-free bedding. Finish is protected with wax.

Flashing is trimmed with X-Acto knife from edge of tang. Epoxy pad will be concealed by the action.

The tip pressure usually found on light-barreled rifles, created by a pad of wood left "high" at the fore-end tip, will mask this test, since it's not possible to determine whether the bowing is coming from the action or the barrel. That may be the main reason tip pressure is used by some stockmakers — to hide imperfect bedding. Therefore, if the rifle isn't shooting as well as I think it should, I rasp out the fore-end pressure so I can properly check the bedding. Make sure you relieve enough to enable you to slide a dollar bill all the way down the barrel channel.

Although light barrels will often, or usually, shoot better with tip pressure, a subtle shift of the fore-end during a weather change is more likely to change point of impact. If your rifle shoots well without tip pressure, you're ahead to let it "float," as Rusty had.

Once you've decided to epoxy-bed the rifle, the question becomes: where do you want the bedding to be?

When Paul von Mauser set the pattern for stock screw location on bolt action rifles a century ago, he obviously had only one thing in mind: firmly securing a wooden handle on his gun. His fore and aft screw locations, with massive cutouts for the magazine and trigger, is sturdy, but it sure isn't conducive to stability or accuracy. One would think that after almost 100 years the firearms manufacturers would have come up with significant improvements.

From some lengthy experiments several years ago with a Remington 40X bench rifle, I became convinced that we'd be ahead of the game to put another large mounting screw just forward of the trigger of that solid-bottom action, and letting the tang "float" behind that destabilizing trigger cutout. But with a magazine rifle, there isn't all that much surface to bed, and there's no way for those two narrow panels of wood alongside the magazine and trigger wells to be sturdy enough to keep the tang area from wandering around with climatic changes. That little pad under the tang is going to drift about with any wooden stock, and we might as well accept it. Its saving grace is that it's easy to fix.

There is a misconception that running a layer of epoxy between the lug area and the tang will maintain the relationship between the two, and stiffen the stock. But a narrow rib down each side won't do it. Consider the relative flimsiness of an unsupported extension of epoxy in the same shape. Before the present dominance of fiberglass stocks, a lot of bench shooters permanently cured their bedding problems by hollowing out the entire action section of their stocks and installing an aluminum bedding block machined for the trigger cut. While the same thing could be done with a hunting rifle, machining an opening in the block to serve as a new

magazine box, few would be willing to go to so much trouble.

In any bedding job, the object is to get as large a bedding area as possible on properly supported surfaces; on a box magazine bolt gun, that effectively limits us to the recoil lug area. Since the main area behind the lug is so small, I prefer to extend the bedding pad forward under the barrel. But if you go more than three inches, you're getting too far away from the front screw. Some of my gunsmith friends don't like a pad under the chamber of the barrel, but it's worked for me.

Just because there's plenty of space for epoxy around the recoil lug area and rear of the barrel, don't forget to cut away the factory finish. A friend of mine's newly built Sporter Class rifle in a factory stock was really shooting hot in its first bench match a few years ago, but during the 200-yard stage his rifle suddenly went wild. He pulled it out of the stock and chunks of epoxy fell out, firmly adhered to the factory finish which had pulled loose from the wood.

The moral of this story is that wherever you put epoxy, be sure you've removed the finish. Since a thin coat of epoxy will do no more good than a thick coat of finish, hog out 1/8 to 1/4-inch of wood wherever you want the bedding pad to be, and plan to trim away all flashing of excess epoxy.

Chisel out about 3/16th-inch of wood at the rear of the recoil lug slot, and deepen and widen the slot to make a solid block of epoxy from the front of the magazine into the barrel channel. Don't increase the size of the action opening at the top of the stock, for epoxy in that area will do more harm than good, and there's no reason to allow any epoxy to show.

The tang area should be relieved, and the pad made as large as possible, but there's no advantage to making the pad wider at the surface than the steel it will support. You can undercut the tang, and even add to its rigidity by drilling from the tang pad into the wrist, but the holes should be carefully filled with epoxy and allowed to cure before doing the final bedding.

To prepare the action, strip it completely, unless you have a one-piece scope base, which should be left in place. No base fits precisely, so any slight bending that it imparts to the action should be bedded into the stock.

Fill the magazine, trigger and bolt handle cuts, and screw and pin holes with modeling clay. Then put a strip

of masking tape down each side of the action and chamber area, with the edge just below the stock line, which will prevent wedging in the finished bedding. Put three or four layers of neatly trimmed tape on the front, sides and bottom of the locking lug to provide clearance. Remember that a wrinkle in the tape, or a small gap at the top of the tape on the lug will make the action tough to get out of the stock after the epoxy cures.

Now coat the steel, tape and clay with the release agent supplied by the epoxy manufacturer. Also put a coat of paste floor wax all over the stock and barrel; you'll probably get some of the epoxy on your fingers, and where you touch, it'll stick. Certain car waxes can be used as a release agent, but some of the newer types can be absorbed by the epoxy, resulting in a glued-in action.

Now use the modeling clay on the stock, making dams in the magazine, bolt handle and trigger slots. Put a straw or tube into the action screw holes, large enough to accept the screws or, if you have them, the oversize guide pins. You can make a tube by rolling some fairly stiff wax paper. Leave the top of the tubes projecting into the bedding area; they will serve as a dam to keep epoxy from running through the holes, and will be pushed down by the action.

Now try the action in the stock, to see if everything lines up right. If it doesn't, shim it with more tape (such as several coils around the barrel and center of the action), insert brads or pins, or whatever will securely hold the action in exact alignment. (It should be supported at or near the recoil area and on the barrel, with the tang floating, but aligned with the stock wrist.) Make some witness marks on the tape to assure you obtain the same alignment when you've put it in the epoxy.

If you have headless action screws, use them as guides while holding the action in the stock with a few coils of *lightly* stretched surgical tubing, or a C-clamp. If you don't have the guide screws, use the regular stock screws, well coated with release agent, with the front screw doing the work: the rear screw should be lightly threaded into the action to assure lateral alignment.

After removing the action, make a final check to be sure release agent is on everything, take a deep breath, relax for a few minutes, then mix the epoxy — *exactly* like the manufacturer says. If it has some powdered dye to add for coloring, don't worry with it; the epoxy won't be seen anyway.

We used Bob Brownell's relatively new Acraglas Gel, which did an excellent job, and is infinitely easier to work with than standard Acraglas, or other syrup-consistency epoxies.

When you mix the epoxy and hardener, don't whip it, just fold it until thoroughly mixed. Whipping will cause bubbles, which will produce voids and cavities. When you put the epoxy into place, particularly if it is a gel or paste, work it against the wood and into corners to be sure that it will bond. With epoxy where you want it, but no more than will fill the space (the tendency is to fill the cavity, resulting in a messy flood over the top of the stock), ease the action into the stock and pull it down to the witness marks.

Unless there's a flood of surplus epoxy, I prefer to leave the ooze alone until it begins to set; when it's at a rubber-like stage it's a lot easier to cut off with a dull knife than it is to wipe off while wet, when you're almost certain to wipe it into stampings or checkering.

Now leave the rifle alone for several hours or overnight. While you're undoubtedly nervous about getting it out of the stock, having heard a lot of horror stories, it *will* come out. At worst, applying some heat with a torch, or putting the rifle in a freezer, will cause the epoxy to break loose — which is the way bench shooters get "glued-in" stocks off, and epoxied sleeves off actions. However, a gentle tug isn't going to separate the barrel and stock. Invert the rifle a few inches over a padded bench and give the barrel three or four smart raps with a mallet just forward of the fore-end. Once it cracks loose, you can worry it out, with the close fit around the taped lug being the only resistance.

More than likely there will be a few voids, or visible bubbles, but they aren't important unless they're large or in a critical area. In any event, they're easy to patch.

Remove the tape and clay from the stock, and using a sharp knife, clean away the flashing of excess epoxy. Depending upon the type of epoxy, it will probably be easy to trim, without the brittleness that will come after another day of curing. With everything cleaned up, put the action back in the stock, pull the screws snug, and check for movement at the fore-end by alternately tightening and loosening the screws. In theory, there shouldn't be any movement; in fact, there probably will be.

All epoxy shrinks as it cures, but while the early stuff shrunk by as much as five per cent the new materials only shrink about half of one percent. Although the amount of shrinkage is uniform, the thickness of the material won't be, resulting in slight dimensional variations. Most of the time, a bench rest gunsmith will put on a "paint coat" of thin epoxy, such as standard Acra-Glas, or even from a tube of five-minute household epoxy, after cleaning and roughing the bedding surface, putting fresh release agent on the action, and refurbishing the tape on the recoil lug — but with one less layer of tape so it goes in easily. They strive for no more than .001-inch movement at the fore-end tip after the screws break loose, but you're not likely to detect such little movement without a dial indicator mounted on the barrel and reading off the stock.

When we pulled the action out of Rusty's rifle, we found a void in the small tang pad, and a little fore-end movement due to the tang bedding being a little low (possibly due to putting a hair too much pressure on the rear screw while the epoxy was curing). It only took a few minutes to clean the pad, rough it, and put in a void-filling paint coat. This time, after curing the action seemed "dead" in the stock — no perceptible movement at the fore-end tip after the initial breaking free.

After cleaning up everything, and reassembling the rifle, Rusty let it sit for several days before taking it to the range. With three different bullets, 160-grain Speers, Sierras and Noslers, it gave three-shot groups averaging a hair over an inch (at 100 yards), to the same point of impact. A year later, Rusty and I tried the rifle during excellent conditions. It still held the same zero, with excellent accuracy: over an inch with that lot of Noslers, but three and five-shot groups with Sierras and Speers averaged in the .800's.

We had done the bedding job right. ●

Installation of a recoil pad on a fini.. stock is one of the most difficult jo. gunsmithing. Here length of pull i measured from marked tape whic. indicates location of trigger.

Gunsmithing YOU Can Do

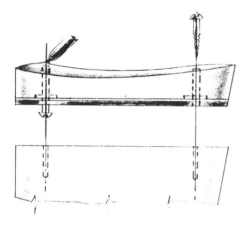

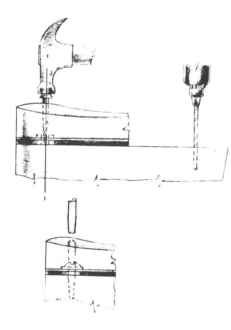

After stock has been cut off to pull and pitch desired, hole positions should be marked on face of pad, top left, by pushing a screw or dowel from below. A small slit may be cut, but no rubber should be removed, and screws lubricated with Vaseline pushed through to mark location of holes, which should be drilled (center). Screws should be seated with lubricated screwdriver with rounded bit. The author recommends that metal screws be used.

THIS ISSUE WE'LL GO INTO perhaps the commonest gun alteration there is, professional or amateur – the back of the buttstock, primarily installing a recoil pad or changing a buttplate. Also, shortening or lengthening the butt to gain the correct "pull length" for the owner, the distance from front edge of trigger to rear edge of center of buttplate. Which usually ain't correct for him unless he is six-foot-one, has medium-broad shoulders, a slightly short neck and orders his shirts with 32" sleeves. As Jack O'Connor once remarked to me about 20 years ago, "Everybody is trying to use rifle stocks too long for them and shotgun stocks too short."

This is very, very true. It is sometimes hard to convince an all-gun shooter that his rifle stocks should be at least one inch shorter than his shotgun butts and that the two are handled entirely differently. And that the different-purpose rifles need different pull lengths as well as high combs for high scopes and large fore-ends for target rifles. A rifle to be used for big game should have a quite short butt, since practically all shooting will be done standing or sitting and probably wearing several layers of clothing.

Many a man who found his super-whooper delightful to handle in the sporting goods store while wearing a summer sport shirt has been unpleasantly shocked a few months later when he finds the butt hung up in his armpit as the moose walks into the woods. We aren't running a gun-fit meeting, but how to fit pads -- just so you'll know why changes are so common.

The Rifle being concerned with

rifles, we'll happily ignore the shotgun butt problems since they are rougher than those found in installation of pads and plates on our chosen arm. Namely, assorted large holes in the butt which have to be filled with glued-in wooden plugs to take screws – a few lightweight rifles have these, but are seldom located where they will cause extra labor. Unless you are a basketball player type needing much added length, the stock has to be cut off from one to two inches for a standard top-grade recoil pad, which are from ¾ to 1 1/8-inch thick.

First of all you determine what pitch you want -- *pitch* is the relation of the line of bore to the line across the buttplate top to bottom, these lines roughly meeting to form a right angle, or about 90 degrees. There is no standardization of measurement in degrees of angle and everybody makes his own rules. If the angle is over 90 degrees, pitch can be called "positive," "plus" or "high;" if less, it is "negative" or "low." (Meaning it'll put the muzzle low when rifle is thrown to shoulder.)

The positive pitch is never used for rifles – it's the cure for a shotgun shooting low on fast shots. Rifles have varying degrees of negative pitch, factory-stocked target rifles having the most. Set your rifles on the floor with buttplate touching at both ends, put up against a wall -- even with scope eyepiece or receiver sight holding it well away you can see the barrel slanting out from the wall, and you'll see what I mean. The theory is that when an arm is fired, the pitch of plate tends to hold the muzzle down. However, in most cases only the top half or possibly two-thirds of the buttplate is contacting the shoulder or upper arm. So, my personal preference is no pitch --

RECOIL PAD INSTALLATION

By ROY DUNLAP

buttplate at 90 degrees to bore or line of sight, which means more buttplate against the shoulder, easier positioning against shoulder or arm, and no greater appreciable muzzle jump.

So, hold the rifle against the wall, determine what angle you want to cut and the relation to top or bottom of stock and mark for the desired pull length -- and put a pencil mark to show trigger position. Now you take the stock off the rifle, lay the pad or plate, on edge of course, on the stock and note the curvature since you must adjust by eye to fit to the prescribed pitch line, at the pull-length marking. Mark at the straight front edge of the pad for the cutting. Usually a straight scribed line 1½ inches long will be sufficient to guide you, but if desired you can use a flexible rule and mark all the way across the stock. Remove the old buttplate and swivel. Before cutting, check and recheck the pull length from trigger to rear edge of the new pad.

Now for the cutting-off business, which is much easier said than done. Literally every type of saw will break out tiny chips 1/16 to 1/8 inch back both ways from the cut on the far side so that working on a finished stock you can end up with a poor-looking job no matter what. Professional-size power (table) saws with sharp hardwood-cutoff blades do the least damage. Next best is the mitre-box hand saw -- I used one of these for years. Go visit your friend with the basement cabinet shop -- everybody's got a friend who is a do-it-yourself woodworking nut -- he'll probably be happy to advise and if he is any good you can no doubt con him into doing the job. Remember, you are getting rid of quite a lot of the back end, and have room for two or three

trial cuts, so you don't have to go for broke the first crack. Remember also that to saw at a right angle to the line of bore you'll have to prop up the stock at the grip. Otherwise you cut the butt at a right angle to the tapered side of the stock. It is easier to use a few layers of cardboard to prop up the grip area than to angle the saw blade as your woodworking friend will want to do -- just by sighting along the stock you can see whether or not it is within a degree or two of being correct. For target stocks I often purposely cut the buttplate this way -- for a heavy recoil-prone rifle you need as much buttplate surface against the shoulder as possible.

The varnish finishes and baked-dry wood of most factory stocks contributes greatly to the splintering-out mentioned above; oil-finished stocks aren't so bad, but still tear a little at the kerf. For a really fine stock there is the really hard way; you saw the stock 1/8 inch or so long, (actually as little as needed to clear the chipped edges, determined by trial sawing) then cut to the correct line by hand, using the cabinet-scraper, sometimes called spoke-shave -- which it ain't -- always cutting in from the edges, which of course leaves sharp clean outer surfaces. And a big hump in the middle to be removed by careful work with sharp gouges. Finally the stock is filed with a sharp metal-cutting mill file to level the surface so the pad base can seat flush at all points. And you file

Recoil pads are available in a variety of styles and types, as shown by these Pachmayr models. Each is designed for a particular type of gun or shooting activity.

209

carefully or the file will tear the far edge!

If the stock is in manufacture, unfinished, or to be refinished, all this matters not: you saw it off, level or square it -- I ram the sawed end against a 6-inch wide sander belt which leaves it flat fast.

Since 90 percent of the present stocks for rifles have cheekpieces, you will have to make shaped holding blocks so that the buttstock can be held in a vise for filing, drilling, fitting. This is easily done if you have access to a bandsaw -- just look down your stock from the rear and saw out a female profile on the blocks. Any approximation will do, for you'll need a piece of thick leather or semi-hard rubber between stock and block anyway. As the stock must be held vertically for most of the butt work you need a vise mounted close to the edge of your bench. A Versa-Vise with leather-faced wooden false jaws, easily made, is the handiest tool for stock work you can have. Not the best as it wiggles around some, but the handiest.

Attaching the plate or pad is done by simply holding it centered on the prepared butt end, marking through the pad holes, then center-punching and drilling the holes for the screws, which should be No. 8 1¼-inch sheet metal type. The standard wood screws usually furnished with pads are practically worthless. After holes are drilled with No. 31 or 32 bit, wax or soap one of the screws and wind it into each hole all the way, to tap it. If the stock is or is to be oil-finished, put oil on the butt end and let it soak in, put more on just before screwing down pad. With a varnish finish stock, use varnish.

The pad may have a warp or curve in the hard back plate -- a few minutes in a pan of reasonably hot water will render it quite flexible and it may be straightened. Bend it dry and you might crack the backing. Screw the pad down tightly, so there are no gaps at the edges anywhere. Next, wind masking tape around the butt, two layers, from 1/16 inch ahead of pad-butt joint forward for two to three inches. Omit this step on unsanded or unfinished stocks, of course.

Next, the dangerous part: there just isn't any way to cut a resilient pad down except with abrasive action -- by grinder, flat or disc sander. I have always used the rubber-backed sandpaper-disc sander, coarse discs to cut the pad to within 1/32-inch of the wood, then finishing with the fine disc. You work in a vertical plane so you can see at all times that the disc is cutting the pad, not the stock, and cutting the pad in line with the stock lines. And in the final stages cutting away the masking tape without cutting into the wood. This is damn near impossible, but only nearly so. The stock is always kept moving against the disc, each pass starting with the disc edge past the junction with the wood then brought across the line so pad is cut.

A little practice enables one to control the disc action quite well, providing there is no great vibration to the setup. You stop when the disc starts marking the masking tape next to the wood, take off the tape, blow the pad clean (the holes -- and you -- will be full of rubber dust!) put a one-layer band of masking tape back on the wood 1/16 inch ahead of the pad, then sand pad and tape with 6/0 garnet paper wrapped tightly around a file; you can work the edge of the pad down flush with the wood pretty quick. If there have been no slips, you're home free. However, the finished-stock pad job nearly always has a few places where the disc cut into the original finish and needs a little repair work. When the wood is natural, only a little sanding with very fine finishing paper and the addition of oil or spar varnish normally will return good appearance. When the wood has been stained and you cut through the stained surface it must be stained again -- for walnut, use burnt umber coloring direct from the tube, rubbing in with your finger tip, then the finish material. For other colors, get the required color by experimenting on the cut-off portion of the butt.

On an unfinished stock all this trouble is eliminated since you cut wood and pad together, going below the splintering at the edge of the cut to get a clean wood surface at the edges, for a perfect joining.

The two-piece stock with bolt through butt is handled a little differently in that you wait until the oil or varnish on the end is dry before attaching the pad. Bolts usually are recessed enough so that you can cut quite a bit of wood off before having to shorten the bolt and cut its counterbore deeper. You finish the pad job as for the one piece stock, then remove the pad and install the stock on the rifle. Screw the pad back on, but not tight -- edges will not be flush with wood at all points -- press with fingers to make the correct fit and hold while tightening the screws. There is enough tolerance in the screw holes through the pad to allow considerable movement of the pad on the butt. Holding the pad base and butt end with thumb and fingers while tightening will prevent off-side movement.

A good job of recoil-pad attachment to a finished rifle is one of the hardest operations in gunsmithing -- threading and chambering a barrel is far easier! All of you have seen horribly botched-up pad jobs, I am sure.

It is so easy to gouge the side of the stock with the grinder or sander that many shops protect the wood well and stay away from it, not attempting to make the flush fitting desired. The pad ends up .010-inch or so above the wood, which doesn't sound like much, but is quite visible and easily felt. If you aren't fussy, this way is OK, the job looks all right in general, and the wood is undamaged. The perfectly-smooth joining of pad and stock doesn't come easily.

This "pad" work includes of course the rubber, neoprene and similar material rifle buttplates which are also sometimes called pads. My old friend, Frank Pachmayr, invented practically all the types brought out in the past 35 years and has done more experimenting and made more pads than any firm in the world. Plain rubber is attacked by linseed oil and some other finishes, it also takes a set and goes out of shape; neoprene by itself is a little hard, etc. I don't really know what good modern pads are made of, but on a guess I would say it's pretty close to what comes on a good auto tire. I should have asked Frank for a little dope, but forgot. It's nice to know the details.

We aren't quite through, maybe . . . the butt swivel has to be put back in the stock, and if you cut much of the butt off, it may be too far back now. U. S. stocks usually have the rear swivel approximately 2½ inches from the tip of buttplate, foreign stocks up to 4 inches; so if your recoil pad is 1-1/8 inch thick and you shorten ½, the 2½-inch distance is reduced to 7/8, which not only places the swivel too far back, but may also interfere with the lower buttplate or pad screw. In which case, you plug it up all the way before installing pad. If you wish, you can make a plug from the wood cut off, for matching color. The new hole for the swivel screw is located, punched and drilled, first using a ¼-inch diameter or whatever is needed to accommodate the unthreaded part of the swivel next to the head -- this is only 3/16 inch or so deep.

Then drill the body diameter of the screw and wind it in. If the counterbore at top is left out, you'll force out a little chip at the forward edge of the hole. If drilling is done by hand, use a small gouge to cut this first large hole, or counterbore.

In the future this column will be more interesting to more people, I hope. The boss has taken the wraps off and wants all sorts of gunsmith coverage which helps me no end. Trying to limit operations to suit amateur gun fanciers' small facilities and yet be useful and interesting could be very trying in a short time. Most jobs can get pretty involved pretty fast!

We'll go into things such as making your rifle deliver the maximum accuracy of which the barrel is capable -- design of custom rifles for various purposes -- specialization is the today word -- and lots of things for the professional gun shops that'll interest most all readers, such as details on how to shorten rifle actions (this isn't nearly as much of a chore as you'd think, but making the stocks for them is!).   ●

Section 3

TUNING

'Shrink' Groups with Some Home Gunsmithing

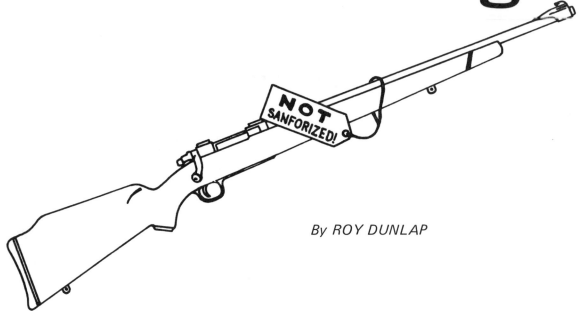

By ROY DUNLAP

*F*OR THE READER of *The Rifle,* accuracy is the important function. We are, fact is, a pretty narrow-minded lot. With us, a rifle just isn't much good unless it shoots very well indeed. No matter how flossy the stock or slick the action—nor even how the rifle handles—we cannot respect it if the accuracy isn't all that can be extracted from the cartr..'ge it chambers.

Unless your rifle came to you from a gunsmith specializing in building genuinely accurate rifles—I refer here to a man who range-tests every job—the odds are about four to one that you can improve on its accuracy. With the smaller cartridges like the .222, very often a straight factory rifle will produce beautiful groups, but among the larger calibers, an over-the-counter arm will seldom show its real accuracy potential without a little help.

"Ah," you exclaim, "Dunlap's going to talk about bedding again!" And I am, somewhat. The finest rifle in the world cannot attain optimum accuracy with a sloppy bedding job; it cannot do

this even with a pretty good job. Essentially, a bolt-action rifle is a combination of barrel, receiver and bolt/firing-pin assembly. All else involved with it—stock, sights, trigger—are there for the user's convenience in operation. These cannot add to the inherent accuracy of the rifle, but they can detract from it.

First, consider the stock: pressure against the barrel, either upward or from one side, can play hob with accuracy; the wood may vary with humidity and temperature changes to affect such pressure. Or uneven support of the receiver, or bedding that's high in the middle or low at the rear tang, or screws bearing against screw-holes, or inletting not squared so that the receiver is twisted a bit when the screws are drawn tight. Any of these conditions can make your barrel and receiver operate under a severe handicap.

There isn't a great deal to go awry with sights, beyond the obvious possible irregularities of parallax in the scope or loose screws in mounts or iron sights—

or perhaps backlash in adjustment screws in scope, mounts or metallic sights. However, at times the slightest strain in a mounting can affect accuracy. One customer brought me a rifle on which an inept gunsmith had improperly mounted a scope with a one-piece base across the receiver—failing to drill the rear holes in line. With some effort, the base could be tugged down tight onto the receiver. The strain was such that shooting had snapped off one screw. The unfortunate owner wanted me to weld up the bad holes and redrill. Since I was either too lazy or too busy to try this, I talked him into simply replacing the mount with a separate base arrangement—one base on the ring, the other on the bridge. It made virtually no difference that the rear base tilted a trifle; the setup left the owner with enough windage adjustment to get properly zeroed in. He came back happily advertising his 200-yard groups were just half what they had originally been.

The trigger comes next. Oh, you rise up on your hind legs and snap back, you *knew* you couldn't shoot well with a heavy or creepy trigger? Down, boy; now and then I cite things you might not know. We take for granted that we cannot shoot our best or the rifle's best with a poor pull, when we disturb aim with the trigger-hand. Even with a polished firing pin, all friction minimized and a perfect-seeming pull, your trigger can still get you in trouble. Almost all rifles fire by having the sear either pulled away or released. In either event, the cocking-piece or firing-pin head rides over the sear as it moves forward to ignite. If there is interference in its forward movement, for example by sear resistance against the bottom, accuracy is not being enhanced. In this, of course, I am classing the sear as part of the trigger.

We live with adjustable triggers now, for the most part; we like to adjust them so that the pull feels perfect in shop or den. We say unto one another, "Can't feel the movement when she lets go, can you, Sam? Got rid of all that over-travel, I think it's called, huh?" Unfortunately, you may have gotten rid of a little accuracy along with the over-travel. If a moving sear has to scrape its way down a secondary sear or a trigger-nose, it stands to reason that the cocking-piece has to push it down while it's moving forward. If the part isn't relieved below the point of engagement (and not all are, certainly), you may have increasing resistance to the sear.

Reason it this way: the firing assembly is going to move under the entire rifle a bit. Those interested in such mental maneuvers can try to figure what 1/100,000th of an inch in push can mean when transmitted to sight radius, metallic or scope-mount base-distance at a range like 200 yards or so. That fraction-of-an-inch of firing-pin fall magnifies any impropriety so much I am scared to think about it. It has done this to me ever since a day in the 1930s when I started to shoot low 4s at 600 yards and low misses at 1,000. The polished sharp edge of the sear on my National Match Springfield had crumbled; when the cocking-piece went over the sear, it wasn't a clean pass. The rifle was tilted or jarred enough to throw low shots on a very slow-trigger squeeze. A new sear cured the problem altogether, but it made me forever wary of sear-and-trigger function.

The release-sear or override systems such as are found in the Winchester Model 70 or the modern Remington 600 or 700 models requires the cocking-piece to be smooth and polished on the bottom—and straight (not any deeper at the rear than at the front). If you have an old, much-fired Model 70, it is better than even money the firing pin has become bent slightly at the safety cut at the front of the cocking-piece. This is curable by a mild belt with a lead hammer on the head, with the firing pin held in a vise. The pin moves forward under mild upward pressure from the sear, usually with no variation or increase in pressure beyond that begotten by compressing return springs. I'd rather not go into the matter of added side-pressure and irregular travel with a bent pin!

There are two ways to regard all this! We improve accuracy by doing things that help—or we remove factors which detract from it. With (frequently) the same results, gunsmiths often take the negative approach: they fix or change what can be found wrong, rather than trying to determine what can help the existing situation by improving it.

Bedding is the starting point. The rifle's receiver must be supported uniformly at a minimum of two points—front and rear, or front and center, in which case the rear must be free of pressure from the stock. Few magazine rifles allow as much bedding area as the Remington 700 series. Those illustrated are laminated walnut target stocks for the 700 short action as altered for .308 match-rifle use, machined for clip loading and with a heavy recoil lug. One illustration shows synthetic bedding material (in this instance, Bisonite); the other is with plain wood. Note the

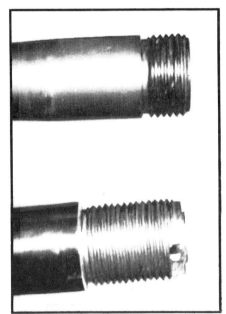

Top, a standard Mauser barrel shank, with a Finnish custom free-rifle barrel shank. The long-shank Finnish barrel will put less stress on the receiver. The short Mauser shank, if the barrel is to be free-floated, will require several inches of bedding just ahead of the receiver shoulder to help carry the barrel weight.

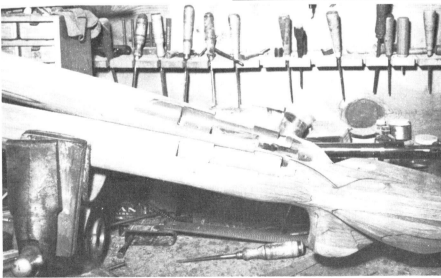

A pair of laminated walnut stocks for Model 700 match rifles. Large bedding areas are available with this action. The rear stock is Bisonite bedded, including two inches of barrel channel to support a heavy barrel.

great contact area possible.

Since this is a target rifle with a barrel weighing well over five pounds, the breech of the barrel is bedded: the idea is to support the great weight which would otherwise be upheld only by the barrel shank; that would put a great strain on the receiver. The barrel is wholly free of support forward of the bedded area shown. Almost never is it necessary to bed a sporter-rifle barrel this way, because with sporters the receiver is able to hold up the lighter weight of the barrel without harmful tension.

Nonetheless, I always do it so anyway, on the assumption it cannot hurt anything; I can scrape proper clearance should the rifle prove me wrong! If done, it is wise to scrape a few thousandths clearance on sides of the barrel bedding, leaving perhaps only a strip on the bottom perhaps an inch long. The light barrel of a typical sporter heats and expands rapidly, and if confined around half its diameter at the breech it can disrupt 10-shot groups.

Actions with huge trigger mechanisms, such as the Weatherby, the latest Fabrique Nationale and the Santa Barbara, are difficult to bed well because their trigger housings leave little of the receiver area open to support. And never, *never* bed the trigger housing! The narrow ledges of support must be of the strongest wood or bedding compound, and you must avoid leaning too heavily on the screwdriver when tightening the rear guard screw; too much pressure might pull the receiver right through the stock. Also, the bedding can be deformed, so make it tight but not ultra-tight.

Unless the wood is very soft or the inletting much oversize, it is not necessary to bed front and rear tangs of the trigger guard or the guard parts. No stock or bedding material should ever touch any part of a trigger system. The stock must always separate the receiver and guard parts so that screws hold the receiver against the bedding with tension; should a magazine box seat against both guard and receiver parts, you are in trouble. With one-piece guards such as those on the Springfield and standard Mauser, you should bed so there is visible clearance between the top of the box and the bottom of the receiver when the screws are pulled tight. This will feed all right; bullet noses will not be caught in even a 1/32-inch gap.

By removing or altering all elements which can detract from accuracy, you arrive at the nitty-gritty, the governing portion of the rifle—the barrel. If nothing is keeping it from its finest shooting performance, you will discover what the best genuinely is. You change bullets and loads and other elements and keep seeking to learn what the pipe prefers. Then, mercifully, if it still will not produce minute-of-angle groups or better the barrel can be replaced.

I use exactly the same bedding and mechanical checks and improvements on sporters that I do with heavy target and free rifles. For example, lighter triggers make shooting even easier. In the many heavy sporters barreled and tuned for Mexican silhouette (*silueta*) shooting, accuracy with rifles limited to eight and three-quarters pounds has equaled that of heavy match rifles—and I don't mean merely at 200 yards. *Silueta* rifles have produced groups under a minute of angle out to 500 meters, fired with 4 and 6-power scopes.

Sometimes, rather typically in fact, good barrels show marked ammunition idiocyncrasies. One of our top local shooters has a .308 built on a Remington Model 700 action which groups under four inches at 500 meters with National match ammo in this rifle. I put a Hart barrel on a Model 70 for a Mexican rifleman—and had to flute it to keep the weight within limits, even with a 24-inch tube; it shoots in an inch at 200 yards with three different bullets and loads. But if you mix the ammunition, you wind up with a 15-shot group the size and shape of the bottom of a cigarette pack.

Heavy sporter barrels yield nothing in comparison to longer, heavier target, varmint and bull barrels. Light and featherweight barrels can be just as accurate, but heat gets to them faster and precludes their being competitive in 10-shot groupings. However, within sensible confines the slender sporter barrels can be amazing. I have seen a short-barreled .22-250 produce a five-shot 100-yard group measuring .270—out of a barrel turned down to fly-rod dimensions, fired as a barreled action only from a simple mechanical rest. Five minutes were expended between each shot. It proves my point.

Many a rifle has excellent accuracy repressed or sidetracked by one or more of the factors I've mentioned here. I do not believe that more than five percent of the rifles in use today are delivering the accuracy within their capabilities. The solution? Simply eliminate the deterrents somewhat along the lines suggested here. And sit back and await the surprises. ●

TUNING-
BOLT ACTIONS

By BOB HAGEL

$\mathcal{M}$OST RIFLES BUILT TODAY, particularly bolt action rifles, shoot quite well just as they come from the packing box. In fact, most of them shoot better than the average once-a-year hunter can hold; but this does not mean that all rifles will give the accuracy the barrel is capable of producing. Of course, if the rifle does happen to have a sour barrel, there isn't much that can be done about it except

to have it replaced; but before this is done there are a few things that should be tried to make sure that the barrel is really bad.

Most hunters are not aware of problems that can often lead them to believe a barrel is bad when, actually, it may be very accurate under certain conditions. This is especially true when the shooter uses only factory

ammunition, and especially so if he uses only one make and one bullet weight and style.

Many rifles will not shoot one bullet weight worth a damn, yet will cut clover leaves with another weight of the same make. This is also often the case with two bullets of the same weight by the same maker, but of different designs; and it may be caused by the loading technique rather than by the bullet itself. Some factory loads are extremely accurate, some are not, and these can be in the same caliber and with the same weight bullets. Many times handloading the same bullet that is sour in the factory load will give fine accuracy.

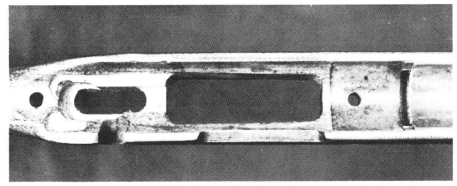

Receiver inletting should be checked to be sure that the guard screws, magazine box, trigger and safety, and even the bolt handle, do not make contact with the wood. Any of these "minor" items can cause accuracy problems.

When I tested the last of the pre-1964 Model 70 Winchesters for the then-new .300 Winchester Magnum cartridge, and the first of the 1964 rifles for the same cartridge, I found neither rifle shot well with the 180-grain Power Point bullets, but both of those rifles averaged 1¼ MOA (minute of angle) with Power Point 150-grain ammo. They both also gave groups hovering around the MOA mark with nearly any of the handloaders' bullets like Speer, Nosler or Hornady, and in nearly any weight including the 200 grain.

Then there was the Model 600 Remington 6.5 Magnum that shot wild with anything except the 120-grain Speer. This bullet, backed with anything from 52 to 55 grains of 4350 shot into an average of 1½-inch on the 100-yard target. I also remember a pair of rifles chambered for the .22-250 cartridge, one a Winchester M-70, the other a Remington M-700. Neither of these rifles would shoot either Remington or Winchester factory ammo with anything like varmint-class accuracy. Yet the Model 70 averaged near 1 MOA with

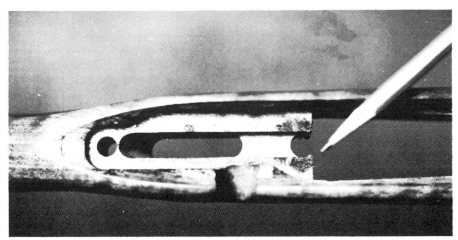

With rifles that have three guard screws, like this Winchester Model 70, be sure there is firm contact between the bottom of the receiver and the wood at the center screw position. Otherwise, there is a chance of springing the action. Actions with only two guard screws should not contact wood at this point.

several of the Speer and Hornady bullets in various weights. The Remington, however, refused to shoot anything we tried except the 50-grain Sierra backed by 36.5 grains of 4320. This load averaged below the 1-inch mark.

All this may be more important to rifle tuneup than appears at first glance. The reason is that if you have one of these finicky rifles with very definite likes and dislikes, it is often possible to tune it by changing its feed rather than by mechanical means. And this can often be done with factory ammo of a different make or bullet weight or design. For instance, I have seen few rifles chambered for the .222 Remington or .22-250 that shot Remington factory soft-point ammunition well enough to brag about, but I have seen fewer good rifles that did not shoot Remington Power-Lokt factory ammo with outstanding accuracy.

Another thing to consider regarding barrels—and this is true tuneup—is that many of them are a little on the rough side. If they do not shoot as well as you think they should when you first try them on paper, this may be the cause. If the groups aren't too bad, don't give up until you have fired 50 to 100 rounds through the tube—you may be surprised at how much groups improve.

To hurry the process along by the home-lapping method may give even better results. This doesn't mean the lapping process as done by barrel makers and gunsmiths. There is a product called J-B Non-Imbedding Cleaning Compound that is easy to use and will polish a rough barrel enough to improve accuracy in many cases.

Before using the compound it is a good plan to give the bore a good workout with a bronze brush and a good powder solvent like Hoppe's No. 9, then clean thoroughly with patches. Now give a patch a coat of J-B compound and scrub the bore with it. To do this it works best if you start at the chamber with short, three to four-inch strokes and, after a few strokes in each place, keep moving toward the muzzle, then work back. This method will keep the patch from jumping the lands so that the polishing action will act evenly on all parts of the bore. After the patch is set to the lands and grooves, you may give it a few full strokes from end to end. Be sure to give the throat plenty of action, as this is often the roughest area. It won't do any harm to repeat the process after the next firing session.

There is little doubt that poor bedding is the cause of more rifles shooting poorly than any other single reason, providing the barrel and ammunition are both capable of top rate accuracy. Poor stock fit is not always an original source of trouble, but may appear later, causing a very accurate rifle to go sour and give you fits. The reason for this can be a number of things; unstable wood, poor or total lack of inside sealing when the stock was finished, or the setback of the action under the pounding of repeated firing.

First, let's look at the method of bedding that *usually* produces the best accuracy. The italics point up the fact that not all barrels shoot their best with the same bedding method. A bedding method that may do wonders for the accuracy of one barrel may be poison to another, especially if the barrels differ in weight. There are, however, certain makes and styles of rifles that normally respond to a given bedding treatment.

Take the Winchester Model 70 as an example. The pre-1964 rifles had a screw on the barrel swell to apply tension to the forearm which gave up-pressure to the tip of the fore-end (also bend the barrel down in the center if you gave it too much). Usually the best accuracy came if this screw was backed off so that only moderate pressure was exerted. Many times I found that the best accuracy came when the screw was removed and the stock bedded so there was some up-pressure at the tip without the screw.

Then came the 1964 70 with a floating barrel. These rifles had hammer-forged barrels which were, in most cases, extremely accurate. I tried carefully shimming several of these rifles so there was up-pressure on the barrel near the fore-end tip to see what effect it had on accuracy, if any. In every case, and with every caliber, accuracy went down the drain. And this applied to the target grade with its heavy barrel as well as the sporter.

In 1968 Winchester again changed the stock on the 70, this time they went back to the pressure on the fore-end with their sporter barrels, but did not resume use of the barrel screw. In testing two rifles in caliber .22-250 and one in .30-06, I found accuracy was much better if the barrel were floated. In fact, group size with both .22-250's was cut nearly in half after the tube was floated.

When Remington brought out the 721-722 actions the barrels had very heavy up-pressure near the tip of the fore-end. Nearly all these rifles shot very well with this setup, but at times could

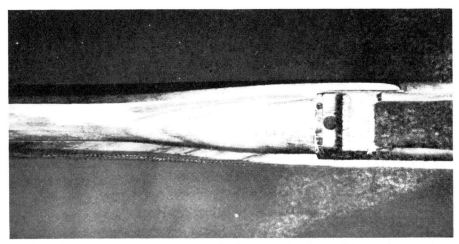

The face of the recoil abutment must be perfectly square with the recoil lug and bear evenly or accuracy will suffer. This Weatherby stock shows glass reinforcement in the center of the abutment to strengthen it for heavy recoil cartridges. Most gunsmiths bed the recoil lug directly against glass in the abutment.

be made to shoot better with less pressure, because the pressure was usually so heavy that it caused bullet impact to creep upward as the barrel heated up. This method of bedding was continued when the Model 700 replaced the 721, 722 and 725, but with somewhat less pressure. I have tried floating several M-700 sporters, but have never found one that shot its best that way. However, the Model 700 Varmint Special with its heavy barrel shoots much better with the barrel bedded tight for the first couple of inches, then full-floated from there.

The 1969 Model 700 sporter in 6.5 Remington Magnum has light up-pressure, but just what method of bedding will make it shoot best I do not know, not having had time to check it out. The Model 660 that replaced the 600 shoots very well with the barrel full floated.

Other makes of rifles also have their own styles of bedding, but most of them use some pressure near the fore-end on light barrels. Weatherby uses this method on his very light sporter barrels, and any Weatherby barrel I ever tried floating shot much larger groups than with pressure near the fore-end tip.

Contrary to popular belief, there is little difference in bedding methods when using glass or when bedding in the wood, except that it is a lot easier to do with glass and gives a more perfect fit than anyone can do in wood. Most shooters seem to believe that if they bed a barrel and action in glass, all they have to do is remove plenty of wood so the glass will fill in, clamp it in place, let dry, and the rifle will drive tacks. Maybe it will, but chances are it won't. The points that should make wood to metal contact when bedding in the wood

should also be used when bedding in glass, and the places where metal should not touch wood are better left so they do not touch the glass. The remark that is so often made that a stock is outstanding because of its "perfect wood to metal fit," is greatly overdone. It looks good and shows good workmanship, but if carried throughout the inletting, it may make a good rifle shoot about like a shotgun.

It is a good idea to bed with the top edge of the stock fairly tight to the metal of the receiver, and maybe the first couple of inches of the barrel, but from there on out along the barrel channel, be sure the wood does not touch the barrel except for the small section near the tip where pressure is exerted. This spot of contact will be just back of the fore-end tip, and is about ½-inch long. It may be made in two ways: One is to use the V method where a contact point about 1/8-inch wide by ½-inch long is left on both sides of the bottom of the barrel channel with about ¼-inch between them. This serves as a V-rest for the barrel and must bear evenly on both sides. If one side has more pressure than the other, the rifle may change point of impact as the barrel heats up. The second method is to leave the half-inch section about one fourth the diameter of the barrel with a perfect fit to the bottom of the barrel. This method works very well with glass bedding, but is very hard to execute in the wood.

If glass is used for bedding, relieve it by scraping or sanding from a point about two inches ahead of the receiver ring forward, except for the pressure spot. If the glass is left in full contact with the barrel, the rifle may or may not shoot well, and even if it does it will shift point of impact every time the stock wood moves from weather and moisture changes.

The amount of up-pressure required to make any individual barrel shoot its best must be determined by trial and error. This can be done by placing cardboard shims of various thicknesses under the barrel, trying a group, then doing the final bedding with wood or glass when the correct pressure is reached.

In bedding the action there should be firm contact from the magazine cut forward to the end of the receiver ring and again at the tang, but the receiver should not touch between these points

This stock for a Remington Model 70 heavy barrel varmint special has been bedded in glass around the receiver ring and for the first two inches of the barrel, then full-floated with no pressure on the barrel beyond that point. This method will give outstanding accuracy with nearly any rifle with a heavy barrel.

with actions having only two guard screws. If the action has the third screw like the Remington 700 ADL or the Winchester 70, be sure there is contact of wood and metal at the bottom of the receiver at this point. If there is none and the screw is tightened down the receiver will be sprung and accuracy may suffer.

Perhaps the most common reason for a new rifle not to shoot as well as it should, is that the wood along the barrel channel touches out near the fore-end or right at the very tip. This is usually brought on by the stock warping after being assembled. It may also be that metal and wood make contact somewhere else along the barrel, perhaps several places. The common result of this is horizontal stringing of the bullets as the barrel vibrates against the tight spots. The same horizontal stringing may occur if the recoil lug does not bear evenly on the recoil abutment, and is tighter on one side than the other.

If a rifle does not shoot as well as it should, take it down and coat *all* of the underside of the barrel and action to above the stock inletting with one of the blue or black preparations made for the purpose and sold by makers of semi-inletted stocks or gunsmith supply houses. Put it back in the stock, tighten down guard screws, remove, and check the marks on the wood where metal is bearing. Scrape or sand off the spots, and repeat until no marks appear except where the action and barrel should touch.

If the rifle still doesn't respond, try changing the pressure on the fore-end by use of the shim method. If you wish to check it with a floating barrel, put a shim under the receiver ring thick enough to lift the barrel away from the fore-end pressure point. If it works, remove the wood from the pressure point and you're set.

There are other things to check which can raise merry old hell with accuracy, and that are little known to most shooters. Be sure the guard screws do not touch the wood anywhere around the hole. If they do it will not only cause loss of accuracy, but may split the stock if pressure is on the back side. Check to make sure the bolt handle does not touch the wood, because, believe it or not, this, too, can cause trouble. It is also a good idea to make sure the magazine does not fit so tightly

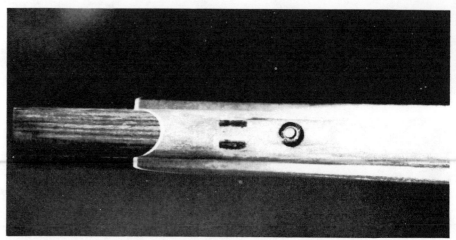

The "V" method of bedding a fore end is easiest to do in wood and works very well. It holds the barrel with even pressure from each side, yet does not change point of impact from minor changes in side pressure due to warping of the wood.

between the receiver and guard that it keeps the screws from clamping them securely to the wood. If this happens accuracy is invariably bad, and action and/or guard are sprung. Grind or file down the magazine box until there is visible clearance with screws tight.

All these things, with the exception of the magazine binding, often occur after a rifle has been used for some time, especially on a hunting trip in wet country. If the rifle goes sour on such a trip, either check the bedding or have it done as soon as you get home. If spots of stress are relieved then, it will not happen again under the same conditions.

All of this, of course, is assuming that guard screws are tight, and that scope mount bases and the rings are

tight; that the scope is also reliable under recoil and does not have excessive parallax. All these things should be thoroughly checked before any tuning is attempted.

There is a lot of know-how wrapped up in a good job of rifle tuning, especially if the rifle already shoots well and you are after that last small degree of accuracy. It is a job not everyone is capable of doing, or has the patience to execute properly. In most cases the best idea is to take the rifle to a good stockmaker and have it done. But for the guy who wants to do it himself, we have attempted to give an idea of what to look for when your rifle acts up in a certain way, and how to correct it. It takes time, perseverance, and no small amount of ammunition, but it yields a lot of personal satisfaction. ●

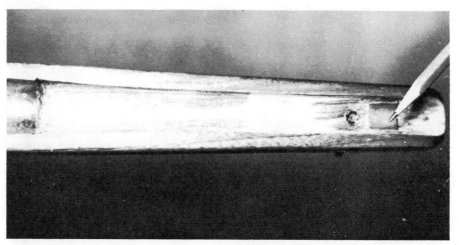

Another method of bedding the pressure point near the tip of the fore end is to lay a square of glass which bears uniformly against the barrel. It is very difficult to do in wood due to the necessity of getting a perfect fit with even pressures on each side.

Slicking the Savage 99

By ARTHUR REDMAN

Today's FACTORY rifles are some of the best ever built. Modern alloys, better barrel manufacturing processes and improved methods of mass production have resulted in average off-the-shelf rifle accuracy surpassing that of rifles built during any previous generation, and at a price most can afford.

However, due to the current cost of labor and the rate of production necessary to keep finished rifle costs down, finishing is left to machinery; for the most part, it does a pretty good job. However, the gun buff willing to spend a little extra time in smoothing and tuning his action can often increase its efficiency and smoothness. I found the late-production Savage M-99 responds well to such treatment. Adjusting the arc in the lever tip provides optimum lockup feel. Removing metal and wood under the lever loop maximizes locking surface area. Installing a trigger stop screw eliminates excess over-travel. Adding a pin to the lever trigger-recess notch, and relieving wood under the lever, creates a mechanical condition whereby 100% lockup must occur before the rifle will fire. These improvements, along with the normal smoothing of machine tooling rough spots result in a slicker, better-performing action.

These improvements are not at all that difficult for the serious gunsmith hobbyist. To gain access to the internal mechanism to perform these operations, first remove the butt plate (or recoil pad) and take out the stock bolt; a screwdriver having a clear blade length of about eight inches is needed, with a tip about 3/8-inch wide and thick enough to grip the screw slot solidly. This draw-bolt stock system contributes to the Savage's noted accuracy.

After the butt stock has been removed, the way the M-99 operates and locks can be clearly seen, but, in order to gain access for working on the necessary parts, the action must be stripped.

Stripping the action down is not difficult and no special tools are needed. A variety of screwdrivers which fit the screw heads properly, and a couple of small punches to drive out action pins are needed. However, two special tools will be needed for reassembly — a "spanner" screwdriver and a slave pin for the trigger spring.

The spanner screwdriver is used on the lock nut on the magazine-spool carrier screw — the screw horizontally placed in the rear of the sidewalls of the receiver. The screw threads into the receiver, but the lock nut is run up on the right end to "jam" it and insure that it does not loosen in firing — I found, on three rifles, that it was not necessary to loosen the lock nut first — the screw would back out of it, but you definitely should make and use the spanner screwdriver to reinstall and tighten the lock nut. An old, re-ground screwdriver can be made up for this, or buy an inexpensive one at a hardware store, and re-shape it. The slave pin can be made later — it is fitted to the trigger, best done when that part is out of the action. After the necessary tools are at hand, the action can be taken down. First, remove the "bolt stop," which is the small L-shaped piece attached by a screw at the rear of the lower tang. The large lever-pivot screw is then removed — note that the left side is unscrewed, the right being the body and main bearing portion. When you get the right part out, note that it has a small pin-like key under the head. This slips into a corresponding notch in the lever proper so that the whole pivot screw assembly moves with the lever as it is operated.

It might be a good idea at this point to look to the cartridge stop/ejector. That's the long piece which operates beside the breech block in the left receiver wall,

This photo illustrates the 99 action, locked and cocked. The basic locking system dates from the mid-1890's, but is still one of the simplest and strongest lever-action systems. The rifle shown is of recent production, and is well made and finished. However, it is possible to give this fine action a little extra gilt-edge of smoothness. The trigger system is the late type, and can be given a "tune up" that will produce a fine hunting pull.

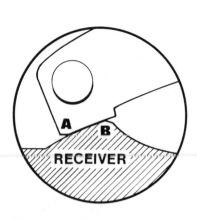

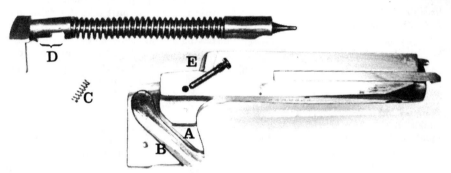

LOCKING SURFACES

The action is shown here stripped to the essentials, the lever and receiver, exposing the locking surfaces. This is where the greatest drag takes place in the locking function. Smoothing and adjusting this correctly will produce a lock-up that operates smoothly and is still safe and strong. The diagram at left shows easement bevels at "A" on the lever tip, and "B" on the floor hump, which ease the action into locked position. A certain amount of resistance will always be present in cocking, since the last part of the cocking stroke compresses the firing pin spring.

Shown here are the stripped breech block and components. The slot in the tail piece is where the lever tip stud runs. Only a minimum of metal should be removed from the slot surfaces at "A" or "B." Too much removed would produce a sloppy lock-up. The lower end of the slot is the "prop-up" area. The lever tip is interposed between this portion of the breech-block and the floor hump. Properly set up, the block is supported so that the face "E" is in a solid, straight-line thrust with the corresponding receiver abutment. The firing pin retractor spring "C" fits in the cut "D" on the pin. The firing pin retainer screw, lying on the breech block here, is actually threaded in from the opposite side.

magazine area. When the breech block is drawn farther back than normal, this piece and its spring will fall out. Better grab it now, before the spring gets lost.

Don't try to get the lever out yet, the trigger comes first. Using a suitable diameter punch that is at least long enough to go through the width of the frame, drive the pin out, but don't immediately withdraw the punch — get your finger over the hairpin spring visible in the trigger. Withdraw the punch carefully and you'll be able to retain the spring.

Slip the safety into its rearmost position — this gives clearance in the receiver slot to get the parts out (remember this when assembling or disassembling with the safety installed). The trigger can be wiggle-worked out of the receiver through the trigger guard area. Now the lever comes, breech-block back, so the stud on the lever-tip comes out of the tail slot in the block, then out of the widest part of the receiver slot. The breech block assembly comes out easily, perhaps requiring a slight twist to the left to clear the rear of the receiver; push the upper end of the sear forward to help clear. You might note at this stage the areas in the receiver which could be called the bolt runways; the Savage requires relatively little bearing areas to guide the breech-block in the receiver — noting this, and the simplicity of the lever/breech-block geometry, I believe your respect for Arthur Savage will increase.

What I call the sear carrier can be removed now. It is held at the forward end by the screw which holds the magazine spool carrier (rear support bracket). This screw can be removed, and the spool carrier, which is now loose, should drop out. The rear of the sear carrier is held in place by a short pin.

This must be driven out to the right. Note that its hole does not come all the way through the frame from the left as the other pins do. The small punch must be angled in the receiver to start the pin out — once out slightly, it can be removed with pliers. Note that the "outside" end of this short pin has indentations which spread it to wedge the pin in the receiver. Don't drive it all the way in during the fitting and adjusting period — no sense in over-working the wedge fit of the pin or the receiver. The sear carrier may require some prying to get it out of the receiver, but only the screw and pin hold it normally.

If you wish to work in the magazine area, you may remove the magazine spool entirely. The forearm must come off for this, by removing the screw halfway up on

Another spring which has a facility for falling out is the cartridge stop/ejector spring. This assembly is held in the receiver wall only as long as the breech-block is in place. The spring falls out easily, but can be made a bit more secure by opening the last coil so that it has a friction fit in the recess of the stop body.

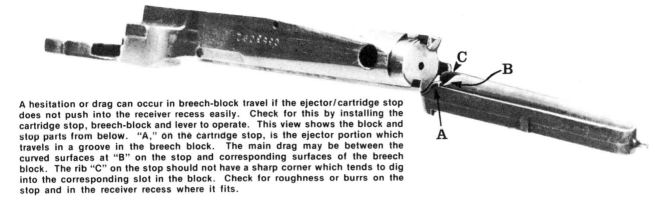

A hesitation or drag can occur in breech-block travel if the ejector/cartridge stop does not push into the receiver recess easily. Check for this by installing the cartridge stop, breech-block and lever to operate. This view shows the block and stop parts from below. "A," on the cartridge stop, is the ejector portion which travels in a groove in the breech block. The main drag may be between the curved surfaces at "B" on the stop and corresponding surfaces of the breech block. The rib "C" on the stop should not have a sharp corner which tends to dig into the corresponding slot in the block. Check for roughness or burrs on the stop and in the receiver recess where it fits.

the underside of the arm, which is then pulled down off the barrel stud, and forward out of the "socket" in the receiver. You can now see the front carrier of the spool. Take a scribe and make an indexing mark on the spool carrier and onto the receiver — it will help to re-establish location and spool tension on reassembly. The spool is removed by taking out the screw in the forward area of the left receiver wall. It is a headless screw with a long pin section which goes into corresponding cuts in the front spool carrier. When the spool assembly is out, you'll see that there are four cuts in the carrier into which the screw could go — one position gives the correct spool tension, and that index mark will help find it again.

You should now have access to all areas needing work. The breech blocks of all three 99s I worked on were "file soft" on all surfaces (except possibly the locking area of the block which I did not touch) so you can easily stone or file to get results. Check all areas where the breechblock comes into contact with other parts of the action and use a file, stone, emery cloth or Dremel tool to polish these areas. If you notice any burrs on the breech face, these can be lightly dressed down, which is especially easy if the extractor is out. Don't overdo this as it

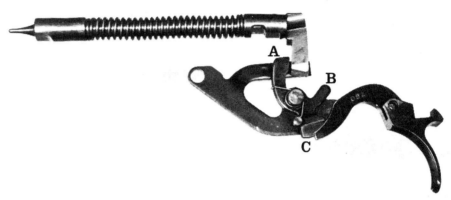

The trigger/sear/firing pin relationship is shown here. Unfortunately the trigger and sear engagement at point "C" is concealed in the receiver recess, so adjustment of the sear notch is something of a trial and error procedure. Arm "A" is the one holding the firing pin at cock — it does not slide off. When the trigger unblocks the sear at "C," the firing pin kicks the sear out of the way at "A." Arm "B" is reset — as the breech block drops back and down, the rear face of the firing pin rocks "B" back, insuring that the sear resets, engaging its notch "C" with the tip of the trigger.

will increase headspace if too much "smoothing" is attempted. If you note, from the burnishing of the rear locking surface, that your rifle isn't making "100%" contact, either leave it alone, or be prepared for a very involved corrective program. The locking surfaces of the block and receiver meet on a curving angle — a great deal of precise work would have to be done to maximize engagement, and would almost unques-

tionably mean that the barrel would have to be set back and re-chambered to get headspace correct. The only work on the block's *locking area* might be to stone a *very* small chamfer on the top edge to remove burrs or dings.

The "firing pin bore" in the block can also be cleaned up slightly by chucking an end-split dowel wrapped with 220 to 320-grit wet-or-dry paper into an electric drill. Do not over-work the sides of the lever-tip slot at the bottom (open) end, as this is the "lock-up" area. Too much metal removed will increase tolerances and make for a deficient propping-up effect between the block, lever and floor hump.

On one of the Savage rifles I detected a slight resistance between the block and the ejector/cartridge stop. As the block starts forward, the front left corner strikes the ejector on its concave surface and pushes the ejector aside. On this rifle the ejector didn't want to get out of the way. This was corrected by slightly radiusing the corresponding surface of the block; the ejector is a pretty hard investment cast piece, and reducing the steepness of its camming surface required a small diameter grinder in the Dremel tool, then polishing that surface with one of the

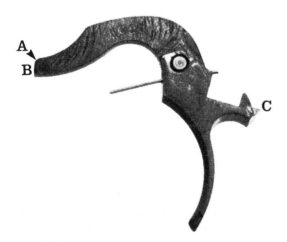

The trigger, shown with its spring in the correct place [loop up], is held in place by the slave pin for reinstallation. Surface "B" is the main sear contact, but note the release angle "A." Care should be taken in reducing the notch in the sear that it does not too closely approach bevel "A," creating a potential for the sear to jump off onto the bevel "A" rather than being held on surface "B." The projection "C" is the interlock which must drop into a cut in the lever before the rifle will fire.

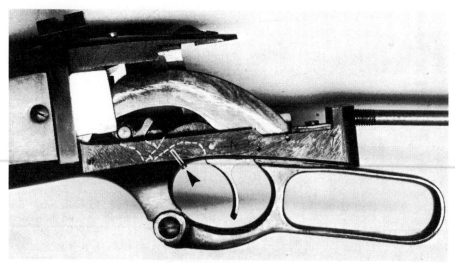

The dotted white lines on the side of the receiver show the relationship of the trigger and sear. The arrow indicates the overtravel screw head, threaded through the thickest part of the receiver to act as the stop on the underside of the arched tip of the trigger.

This is the interlock corrective pin in the lever arch, which insures that the lever is almost completely closed [and the action locked] before the trigger can be pulled. See the photo on the opposite page for the corresponding trigger part. This pin is difficult to install because of the hole location. Redman used a 6-inch aircraft drill to reach the difficult spot. However, most 99s probably don't require this modification.

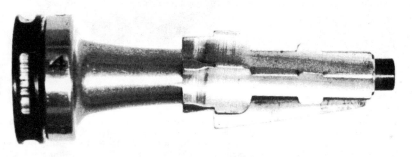

The ribs of the aluminum magazine spool may have small burrs which could scar the cartridges. Burrs are easily removed with rolled emery paper. Note that the front spool bearing has four grooves; all will accept the retaining screw which permits proper spool torsion setting according to the text. A special spanner screwdriver is needed to turn the spool, as well as tighten the jam nut on the rear bracket's screw.

abrasive-rubber wheels. You might also want to lightly grind the thin rib on the upper rear of the ejector so that it has no sharp edges to drag in the block.

While I am on the subject of the ejector, I was annoyed by the ease with which the ejector spring drops out. This I cured by using a needle-nose plier to radially open the last coil of the spring so that it self-retains when inserted into its socket in the ejector.

The only work done on the firing pin was polishing of the cocking piece portion.

The face on which the sear rides was smoothed and polished. Although the sear is not drawn down off the cocking piece to fire this model, it does have a sliding contact — when the block rises to lock, the cocking piece rises, sliding up on the sear. These surfaces, which are file-soft, were polished to minimize wear. Don't attempt to reduce the amount of engagement between the cocking piece and sear to get a crisper pull — it doesn't take place here (excessive reduction would cause the cocking piece to slide right on off the top of the sear to prematurely fire the rifle — possibly in an unlocked condition).

I polished both sides of the cocking piece, in case there was contact with either the lever or sear carrier. I don't think this is necessary, but some rifles might momentarily contact the side surface of the lever. (The top surface of the cocking piece pushes the cocking indicator up when the block is fully up and locked.)

This completes work on the breech block and its internal parts. I would suggest, at this point, that you reassemble it, but leave the retractor spring out — should you have occasion to take the firing pin out for sear work, you won't have to contend with that retractor spring.

Now the fitting of the lever can begin — the action should be stripped of the breech block and all trigger and sear parts, because we want to adjust only the lever to the receiver.

Replace the lever into the receiver, and reinsert at least the right portion of the lever pivot — since you'll be taking the lever in and out, the lever pivot screw won't be needed. Close the lever to full-lock position — note the feel as the tip rides over the hump. If the parts are clean, you've got some burrs or galling of the lock surfaces. The whole tip of the lever and its stud are hardened, so the roughness is probably on the floor hump. Before attempting to do anything about this, there are visual checks to make.

Take a look at the lever's finger loop where it contacts the receiver lower tang. Just how close a fit is it? I have found that a bit more metal could be removed on the lever, "closing it up" more to the receiver — and in the process, taking the lever tip further forward over the floor hump to give it (possibly) more locking contact area. I noticed on two of the rifles that the levers were slightly deformed in such a fashion that corrective bending would up-grade the lever/receiver fit.

Does your Savage lever look like it's case hardened? On the three I worked on, I've found the case hardening is purely a cosmetic touch — only the locking tip-end is hard — the remainder is a tough forging which can nevertheless be filed — and even bent.

Before doing any lever-bending, check the fit of the lever at the lower tang to see if it can be helped by filing the high spots to permit tighter lever closure, and, hence, greater locking surface in the lever tip/receiver hump area. This leaves the lever very "white," but by using touch-up blue, the bare spots won't look so horrible.

Now check the fit of the lever in the receiver as the tip rides over the hump. If the lock-up is too loose — or much too tight — this can be modified by bending the lever's arched section, with the aid of padded vise jaws, to increase or reduce contact pressure. Go slow here; the lever is very tough, it won't take all that much to correct it, but better to have to repeat the operation several times to bring it to "spec," rather than one huge "correction" that has to be "corrected back."

It would be nice to devise a simple method for determining (and obtaining) correct contact pressure — but I haven't figured it out. It's a trial and error system. Close the lever and whack the receiver top with the heel of your hand — if the lever flies open, it's too loose. If you have to really *pull* the lever open, it's too tight. How's that for "scientific methodology?"

Note whether the lever tip "tracks" down the center of the receiver floor hump — the thin arch can be bent a little to correct this alignment. Don't try to bend only the tip area — since it is the hardened part it could be broken or cracked. Obviously the foregoing lever-bending work is not for the faint-of-heart.

The locking surface of the lever tip can be checked for burrs and *lightly* stoned. The surfaces of the stud (which track in the breech block groove) should also be checked — but only *lightly* stoned. To ease the lever's tip over the floor hump, I stoned a very small bevel on the edge of the tip.

Having the magazine spool out helps to work on the floor hump — you can't work in through the magazine opening, but at least you can see what you're doing. Put the lever in the rifle, holding it with the pivot; work the lever several times to get the feel — it should go over the hump "snug," not hard. A heavy friction fit is not needed to assure locking. Back the lever off and note the surface of the hump. If the wear signs are concentrated on a very small area, you may want to stone for a better bearing. You could even try squaring the end of an ice-cream stick and wrapping emery paper on it. I also put a small bevel on the "lead edge" of the hump (file or stone nearly horizontal) — this, and the bevel on the lever makes for a smooth start for this lock-up, yet does not affect the security of it.

I also stoned the right side of the lever tip, where it passes beside the firing pin in closing the action. This may not be necessary, but check your rifle for roughness. You might also run a fine flat file in the sides of the slot in the receiver, just to knock off any burrs which will scrape the sides of the lever arch. (The hardened "nub" swaged into the right rear side of the lever arch is the piece which the safety engages on the new model Savage.)

Now you can reassemble what we might call the locking and breeching parts — lever, breech-block (assembled) and ejector/cartridge stop. The trigger and sear will be left out — they would, at this point, create disconcerting drag when all you want to check is the locking and breeching functions. Put the bolt stop back on the left rear of the frame.

Cycle the action — look and feel for unusual drag, momentary hesitation, etc., which might indicate that some part still needs some work. (It was at this stage that I detected resistance of the breech block to push aside the ejector on one rifle.) One of Arthur Savage's design virtues is that the breech block can work in the receiver with what appears to be downright sloppy fit — yet when the critical "close fit" is needed, it's all there at the right time. Work the action slowly and try to detect what part(s) are causing the problems. I suggest you have the mechanism scrupulously clean of grit *and* oil for this.

The trigger and sear now come to our attention. The "new system" trigger is an interesting device — it operates somewhat like a set-trigger in the sense that trigger movement does not physically pull a sear out of contact with the main striker system. This one "disengages" a sear — it unblocks the sear which is knocked aside as the striker falls. The original 99 trigger/sear is a conventional sear-pulled-out-of-engagement system; it is simpler, the parts very large and sturdy — but the "new system" permits finer adjustment.

The sear, sear-carrier, and sear "re-set" spring are an assembly not meant to be dismantled. Fortunately the work on it can be done without taking it apart. The sear carrier is not hard steel; taking it in and out of the receiver recess several times decided me to ease the fit a little — still snug, but not requiring prying to get it out. Each time you reinstall it, you want to put the spool carrier screw through to support the forward end, and the small pin in the frame at the rear to keep the carrier in the correct position each time. Don't drive the pin in each time; note the head is notched to retain it snugly, so repeated driving-in will just "wear out" the hole in the receiver.

Neither is the sear hardened — at least not so hard that it can't be filed. Release the little "re-set" spring on it so that it can be conveniently turned to perform smoothing operations. The upright arm of the sear engages the front surface of the striker. Notice that this sear is not "pulled down" the striker face — it just stands up there, in the way of the striker. The tip of the trigger sits in the notch of the lower arm of the sear; when it pivots down out of that sear notch, it "knocks the prop out" — the striker literally pushes the sear out of the way.

So the vertical face of the sear, bearing on the striker will not produce a drag you'll feel in the trigger. I smoothed the sear face there just so it wouldn't cause any drag as the striker knocked it aside. There's generous engagement here, but reducing it won't improve the trigger pull.

The length of the forward vertical arm must not be shortened — note its position in the "fired" striker condition.

(You can also see that the bottom surface of the striker must not be materially changed.)

The small round-end middle arm "serves no purpose," at least in regard to tuning. In fact, however, it is the "sear re-set" arm. Upon cocking the rifle, as the rear of the striker comes back and down, the striker backface pushes the sear back to re-set the trigger-notch arm into position for the next shot. It is this sear arm with its trigger-engagement notch which receives the main attention on trigger tuning. On one of the rifles, this notch was unfinished, still in the "as stamped-out" state, with only slight evidence of clean-up. This rifle had a somewhat rough trigger-pull, not as bad as might have been expected for its "unfinished" state. I would therefore think a bit of smoothing on any of these Savage sears would give a pull of positively virginal purity.

Unfortunately, the trigger/sear engagement is buried in the receiver recess, out of sight. You'll have to work it blind. Because it was not visible, I didn't attempt to materially reduce the amount of sear engagement — this thing could be more sensitive than I expected. The sear is soft enough to file, so adjustment was made entirely on it; the corresponding trigger surface was hard, and was stoned to give it mirror-smoothness — not "altered."

I would judge sear engagement this way: you will note that the trigger has a compound angle on its sear surface — the main part is roughly at "right angles to rotation," but there is a small "release angle" just as the trigger arm swings out of the sear notch. You certainly don't want to have the sear engagement in that release angle of the trigger. I elected to keep engagement deep (and safe); that means a little creep in the pull, but it's smooth. The angle of the notch in the sear was not well defined in the factory product; since it was not visible, I pretty much had to guess at making the face of the sear notch and the face of the trigger's arm parallel. Unless someone patents a small periscope to view this in the receiver, you'll have to go as I did. I gingerly reduced engagement to about a sixteenth of an inch, devoting more time to smoothing the sliding contact surfaces of the sear. Even if you don't want to reduce engagement, at least cut across the sear to insure that the edge of the notch is square *across* — the sear should release evenly across the width of the notch. Conceivably, some stamped sears are a little off in this regard. As a final touch, "break" the sharp edge of the notch, stoning just a tiny radius.

There are yet other things you can do to sweeten the disposition of your 99 trigger. I figured a way to install an over-travel screw; something of a nicety, as the triggers I worked on jumped like scalded cats after sear release. Maybe I'm overly picky about over-travel stops, but psychologically they seem to do a lot to "ordinary" triggers. I made up 4-40 Allen setscrews (headless) which angle up into the cut in the receiver where the trigger works. The photos show this better than I can describe. All this screw does is to limit movement of the sear-engaging arm of the trigger. I used 4-40 thread, but the width of the groove in the receiver will be the determining factor on screw diameter. I would guess a number six is maximum, and I would further suggest the finer thread pitch, 40 to 48. Note that this screw should be obviously "too long" — the inner end will be ground back to optimize the fit and so that it won't protrude too far into the trigger guard area as mentioned early in the article, a trigger slave-pin must now be made. Due to the nature of the trigger spring/trigger relationship this is necessary to get this "assembly" back into the receiver. The slave pin is simply a small steel pin, .125 diameter by .320 long. Length not critical — it goes into the trigger pivot-pin hole, so it should be the thickness of the trigger or a trifle less. Diameter can be a few thousandths more — it can be even a bit snug fitting in the trigger. The long leg of the spring goes forward, the spring loop is up. Slip the slave pin in and prepare to insert the trigger from the guard side. Start by "running" the long spring leg up the sloping cut in the receiver — once you get the trigger in approximate position, you'll have to hold it against spring tension. Slip the pivot pin in one side of the receiver — look into the other side's hole so you can visually align the trigger slave pin with the hole in the receiver. Then push or tap the pivot pin through, knocking the slave pin out ahead of it.

To make the over-travel screw preliminary adjustment, the action should be stripped to sear and carrier, and the trigger installed with spring in place. In particular, leave the lever off to permit turning the screw in. The trigger should have the tip in the sear notch as though it were cocked. Turn the over-travel screw in until it stops against the trigger. Now place your finger against the forward vertical sear arm, simulating the cocked striker pressure against it. Put finger pressure on the trigger — if you can manage this with the thumb on the sear, the forefinger of that hand on the trigger, the free hand can back the screw out gradually, allowing the trigger to release the sear. Then you can measure the excess length of the overtravel screw — remove it and cut off that amount *minus* about 1/32 of an inch. You will want it still a trifle too long so that a final "fine trim" can be made with the full mechanism — all action parts — assembled.

Now for the final adjustments of the trigger system. The action will be assembled — the following parts are not needed, and can be left out: ejector, magazine spool (the rear spool carrier screw supporting the sear carrier should be in place, however), and the safety. Clamp the rifle in a vise with padded jaws. If you are reassembling from scratch, the sear carrier goes in first, then the assembled breechblock. The lever is installed, working the stud up through the receiver slot, then into the slot of the breechblock tailpiece; install the lever pivot, and turn the lever pivot screw in just to keep this part from falling out. Now the trigger is installed, starting the spring leg in first, as described earlier. As it is nearly in place, it will be necessary to do a little juggling of "positions" to get the tip of the trigger in proper relation to the sear notch. If everything seems in place, install the breechblock stop. The overtravel screw can be turned in, but leave it out a little too far so that you can cycle the action and cock it — now turn the screw in fully. It should not be possible to fire the rifle. Back the screw out a fraction of a turn at a time until it will fire. Then cycle the action to be sure of your adjustment. Note how much screw protrudes. What you will now do is grind it down to just a few thousandths over-length — to compromise between being turned all the way in (least protrusion in the guard) and still being long enough to function properly as the stop. Proceed with caution.

After completing this operation and rechecking the fit, take the screw out and clean it and the tapped hole in the receiver thoroughly with solvent to remove all oil. Then dope it with Loc-Tite and reinstall. Make the adjustment for the final time, and when the Loc-Tite has set, the over travel will be "fixed." This screw does not affect future disassembly.

Another refinement which can be made is what I call for lack of a more imaginative name, the "trigger interlock." Determining the need for it is done as follows: Cycle the action, cocking it, but do not pull the trigger. Open the lever until the lever tip is just barely locking on the floor hump. Naturally, a trigger pull should not fire it at this stage. Close the lever a fraction of an inch at a time, pulling the trigger each time until it does fire. Note where the lever tip is on the floor hump — it should be fully on the hump, and the breechblock should therefore be fully "propped up" in locked position. But notice how far the lever-loop may still be from contact with the bottom of the receiver. It is possible to optimize this, thereby assuring you that there is no chance of firing a live round on an action not fully locked. I should like to state clearly that neither the design nor manufacturing standards of the Savage Arms Company would permit such a potentially dangerous situation to occur — but here is a method for detecting (and correcting) the situation should you find it in a used or altered 99. Again, if the lever tip has full bearing on the floor hump, the action should by fully locked and safe, even if the lever *appears* to be slightly open.

The interlock is a very simple design — note a small notch in the under curve of the lever arch — just above the finger loop. A corresponding projection on the back of the trigger must rock up into this cut to fire the rifle — if the lever is opened to the extent that the trigger projection strikes the un-notched part of the lever, trigger travel is limited and firing is prevented. Therefore, "adjustment" of this notch will modify the firing position. This might be done by building up weld on the lever or trigger and filing to get the adjustment. I chose to install a pin in the upper edge of the notch. This is something of a problem, as the hole has to be drilled with a 6-inch long aircraft drill — not a common item. This is because a drill has to go in a long way — the drill actually goes between the two lever bearings. You can see that any tapping operation would be near impossible due to the long reach needed. Even center-punching for the drill is tricky. I selected a drill size small enough that it would not weaken what would be thin walls of the lever arch — 1/16 or 5/64 would be okay. The hole need not be drilled deep — not over 3/16-inch. I then selected a piece of drill rod, a diameter about the thickness of the lever arch. The end was turned down to make a tight fit in the hole in the arch. The "big end" was cut off to about 1/4-inch to give a hammering length, and the small end driven into the hole. A bit tricky, as a long punch had to transmit hammer blows to this little stud. When driven home, it produced slight bulges in the arch walls — as can be seen in the photo. The protruding end was filed down to almost flush with the under-curve of the arch. Then, the stud was filed back, a little at a time, in effect adjusting the "leading edge" of the notch. By cocking the action and checking the trigger, filing the stud, I could get the trigger interlock to prevent firing until the lever was about an eighth of an inch from "closed" — surely safe enough.

This pretty well covers operations on the rear half of the receiver. The front of the receiver, the magazine area, has a few small modifications which can be done. Perhaps foremost of these is the polishing of the feed ramp to the chamber.

The magazine spool must be out to do this, and it would be best to have all other action parts out simply to protect them from grinding grit. Careful placement of rags into the rear of the receiver might keep most of the grit out. The ejector/cartridge stop must be removed also. A Dremel Moto-Tool is ideal for this; their new flexible-shaft tool would probably be even better. Take special care right at the chamber mouth — the wheels have a remarkable tendency to run on into the chamber.

The magazine spool is an alloy die-casting, the cartridge cuts machined in. Any slight burrs can be quickly removed — I rolled 240 or 280-grit emery paper into a cylinder and ran it in each cartridge channel.

On the cartridge-counter spools, you might wish to add a cosmetic touch by polishing the numbered area and filling the stamped numbers with black paint.

If the spool doesn't turn smoothly and seems to have gotten grit inside, it can be dismantled and cleaned. Clamp the small protruding rear end of the spindle, and remove the spanner nut on the front face of the spool. The spindle is soft, so be careful that you don't deform it by clamping. When you reassemble the spanner nut, lightly peen some metal into the spanner slots to prevent it from coming loose.

When reinstalling the magazine spool, it's a good idea to have the rest of the mechanism installed — at least the breech block and lever so that you can check feeding and magazine-spring tension by cycling dummy rounds through a couple of times.

The magazine spool assembly is reinstalled in this manner: you will note that by holding the spool proper, you can turn the front cup-shaped bearing either way and feel the torsion spring. But you want to replace it into the receiver with no torsion, so simply slip it in, being sure of two things: the large "stop" of the spool is on the left of the cartridge stop plate in the receiver (remember that the spool feeds from the left — this stop is for the last round coming from the magazine — from the left); the other point to watch for is that the end of the spool's spindle goes into the hole in the support bracket in the receiver.

Now, looking at the front of the magazine, you are ready to put the proper torsion on the spool. Using the specially prepared spanner screwdrivers, insert it into the small spanner nut on the bearing cup. Rotate it *one full turn* counterclockwise, and push the bearing retainer screw into the hole in the left receiver wall — you may have to "rock" the cup a little one way or the other, but it will be close to that adjustment. If you put an index mark on the cup and the receiver, they should line up. Put your finger in the receiver, onto the stop of the spool — rotate the spool to the left — it should have spring torsion rotating the spool stop against the stop plate in the receiver. If this is all correct, turn the spool bearing retainer screw into its receiver threads. Now you can check the feed with dummy rounds. I have increased spool torsion to 1 1/2 turns, but could detect no improvement.

The screw which supports the magazine spool rear bracket and the sear carrier screws in from the left; it should be installed with the head flush with the left wall. It will go farther, but should not be turned in more to "tighten" it. Turn in only flush, and put the spanner nut on the right end — *this* is the nut that is run up tight, acting as a jam nut.

Screws to check for tightness: the striker retainer screw — center-punch a little metal into the slot to prevent it from backing out. The breech block stop screw might require degreasing of the threads and application of Loc-Tite. If this comes out inside the stock you could really jam things up! The lever pivot screw may show a tendency to loosen from recoil; it should have the threads degreased and Loc-Tite applied. If any assembly pins are unduly loose, upset the ends a little to restore the wedging effect. Don't forget to reinstall that little striker retractor spring! ●

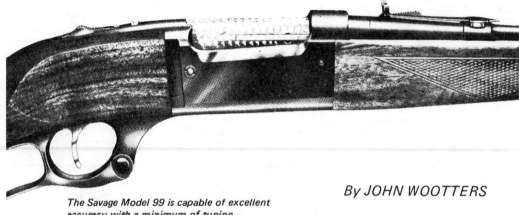

TUNING
THE

By JOHN WOOTTERS

The Savage Model 99 is capable of excellent accuracy with a minimum of tuning consisting primarily of close fit of the butt stock to the receiver, and either relieving the fit of the fore-end against the receiver or making the joint as perfect as possible to reduce uneven pressures.

Mᵞ SOMEWHAT STORMY love affair with the Winchester Model 88 rifle began on a rainy Sunday afternoon in Yong San, Republic of South Korea, in July, 1955. I was stretched out on my bunk in the barracks, trying to stay sane by reading--nay, practically memorizing--the June issue of *The American Rifleman*. There, in full color on the back cover, was a Winchester ad for a brand-new lever-action rifle, hammerless, with one-piece stock and a rotating, front-locking bolt head.

My attention could not have been more riveted had the picture been of a *Playboy* centerfold starlet; I had been a lever-action man (for deer-hunting purposes) all my life, and I'd passed

many an hour tinkering with Savage Model 99's, Winchester 92's and 94's, and Marlin 94's and 336's, trying to make my favorite action style shoot like a good bolt-action rifle. Here was a modern lever gun, well-suited to a handloader's purposes, and with obvious possibilities for accuracy tuning. I wrote my hometown gunsmith that day, ordering a Model 88 for delivery the following October, when my "figmo" chart told me I should be back in Houston, Texas, to receive it.

Four months later I walked into the gun shop, in mufti, and claimed my gleaming prize, Model 88 No. 5305, in caliber .308 WCF. It was said to be the first of its breed delivered to a private citizen in my part of the world. One

month later, I slew the first of many whitetail bucks taken with No. 5305 over the next ten years or so.

During those years I learned quite a bit, the hard way, about the care, feeding, and civilizing of this unique rifle. The design allows a good deal more tuning than the other lever action rifles, which may or may not be a good thing--depending upon how well you like to tinker. There is a school of thought which holds that the fewer items there are to "adjust," the fewer items there are to get out of adjustment. The Savage 99, for instance, requires a great deal less tuning due to its two-piece stock, which limits what can be done, and what needs to be done. But once tuned, it usually stays that way.

On the other hand, the various exposed-hammer lever rifles, such as the Winchester Model 94 and the several similar Marlin products, are pretty nearly untunable, in my experience. Some finagling with barrel bands and other gadgets attaching their tubular magazines to the barrels may, if stresses are being placed on the barrels, bring about some improvement in grouping. Chiefly, however, one simply keeps all screws tight and employs these wonderful old models for the moderate-range work for which they and their cartridges were designed, without losing sleep over that last iota of target grouping.

With the possible exception of the Finnish-made Sako "Finnwolf" lever-action rifle, the experiences to be described in tuning the 88 are not applicable to other flick-finger

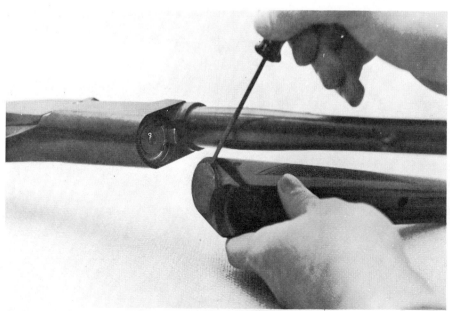

Model 99 Savage stocks of recent manufacture are usually inletted very precisely. Where tuning is indicated, the usual procedure involves relieving the rear surfaces of the forearm so no contact with the receiver occurs.

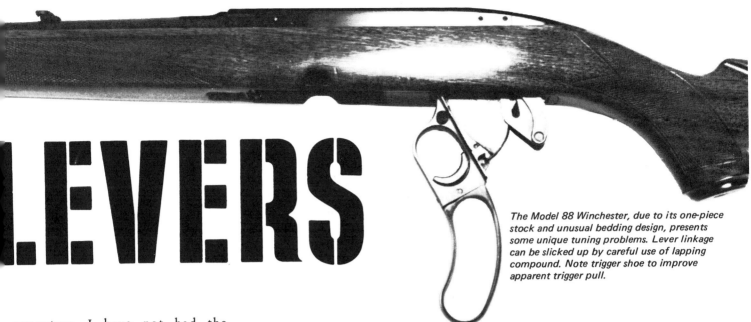

LEVERS

The Model 88 Winchester, due to its one-piece stock and unusual bedding design, presents some unique tuning problems. Lever linkage can be slicked up by careful use of lapping compound. Note trigger shoe to improve apparent trigger pull.

repeaters. I have not had the opportunity to break down a Finnwolf, but a study of construction diagrams suggests that at least some of he techniques useful with the Model 88 may be used to advantage in tuning the world's only European-made lever-action big game rifle.

However, the techniques of tuning an 88 may be applicable to some autoloading rifles, particularly the 88's cousin, the Model 100 Winchester. Two-piece stock rifles, either autoloaders or single shots, will often respond to the same treatment to be discussed for the Savage 99.

On No. 5035's first trip to the range for targeting I was pleased to see nice, tight three-shot groups form with factory ammunition...and then watched in fascinated horror as each succeeding

bullet marched steadfastly upward and to the right, at the rate of about one inch per round. Finally, when the barrel was thoroughly heated, grouping again became regular, but the center-of-impact was by then about eight inches at 2 o'clock from the first, cold-barrel round.

Out came the screwdrivers, and out of its stock came the barreled action. Almost immediately I learned the first lesson about this model: Never open the action when the rifle is unstocked! When the gun is assembled, the rear of the bolt is stopped in its rearward travel by contact with a steel block which is not a part of the receiver but remains in place in the stock when the barreled action is removed. Without that stop, the action can override its linkage if

opened smartly, and cannot then be closed again until disassembled and reassembled with the parts back in proper relationship.

The second distinctive feature of the 88's personality appeared almost simultaneously; the only means of attachment of the metal parts to the wood are the forearm screw and that aforementioned steel block (hereinafter called the "recoil block," since that is what it is, among other things) fastened in position in the rear of the stock's action mortise by a throughbolt through the buttstock. This block has a

Disassembled Model 88 shows recoil block, which must be perfectly aligned for accuracy. Note single tie-down screw dovetailed into underside of slim barrel, a key factor in bedding.

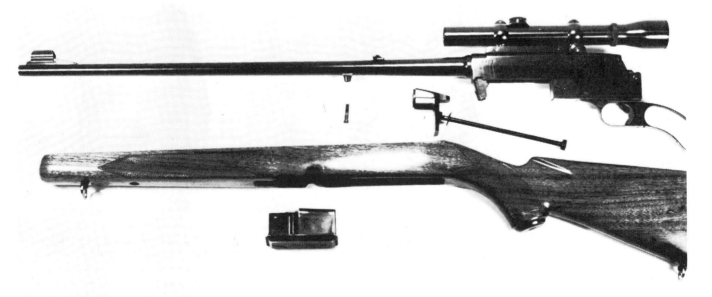

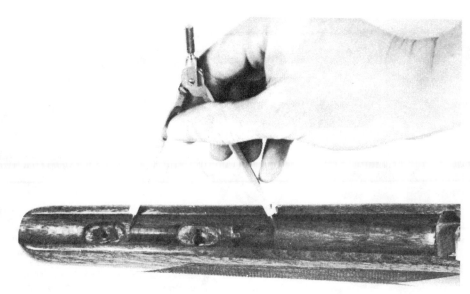

transverse slot which is engaged by a corresponding hook on the rear of the receiver, similar to the M1 Carbine. To place the barreled action in its stock, the muzzle is elevated, this hook is engaged, and then the steel parts are rotated downward into the inletting until the forearm screw can be engaged in a threaded hole in a lug which is dovetailed into the underside of the barrel.

To my knowledge the only sporter which ever bore any slight relationship to this system of bedding was the ill-fated Newton rifle of World War I vintage, which was a bolt-action gun.

Further study of the undressed rifle will reveal that the receiver itself receives no support from below unless what appears to be a recoil lug is allowed to bottom in its recess, a practice avoided in tuning Mauser-type actions. In the Model 88, however, this

is not a recoil lug at all (most of the recoil is transmitted from steel to wood via that recoil block behind the receiver), and it must be allowed to bottom firmly and evenly in its recess. The relationship of this surface and those supporting the barrel around the forearm screw, however, is critical. If this recess is too deep, tension on the forearm screw may warp the receiver itself; if it is too shallow, that same tension will surely place bending stresses on the barrel.

The rifle-tuner accustomed to thinking in terms of floating a sporter barrel, or using cunningly placed pressure points, will have to throw out all his previous conceptions when dealing with a Model 88. A little thought will reveal why it is necessary that the barrel of this lever-action be firmly bedded in its channel, at least in the vicinity of the stock screw. This screw, by the way, should be kept set

up as tightly as possible at all times, since any slack here results in looseness of the rifle in its stock.

At the same time, any uneven hard pressure between barrel and wood is likely, as in any other sporter, to cause poor grouping and a wandering zero. Which brings us back to old No. 5305 and her nasty habit of stringing bullets diagonally. The next step was application of a transfer color (I use my wife's old lipstick stubs smoothed and thinned with Vaseline) to the barrel, after which the rifle was reassembled and then broken down again. Quite a few irregular contact points were nicely printed in Frosty Spanish Melon (my wife was in her Spanish phase, at the time) on the wood. Out came the gouges, rasps, and sandpaper, and an hour's work removed all contact whatever except in the bottom of the channel around the forearm screw hole. At this point I paused and scratched my head.

It was obvious that the barrel had to rest firmly upon something in the barrel channel with no screw tension at all. Otherwise, tightening that screw would inevitably bend both stock and barrel. The system I eventually hit upon was a pair of raised beds, one each in front of and behind the forearm screw hole, centered in the exact middle of the barrel channel and about an inch long and a half inch wide. For perfect contact, I glass-bedded these two points. To repeat, it is essential that the barrel come fully to rest upon these beds, at exactly the same moment that the receiver lug bottoms in its recess, without any screw tension whatever. As a test, watch the relationship of barrel and forearm wood as tension on this screw is relieved. If there is the slightest springing-apart, something is wrong with the bedding.

While the machinery is out of the wood, clean up the mortise in the stock around the screw hole, into which the barrel lug fits when the rifle is assembled, making sure that the lug itself does not touch wood. Also, make certain that the front sling swivel nut, located in another mortise ahead of that one, cannot touch the barrel at any

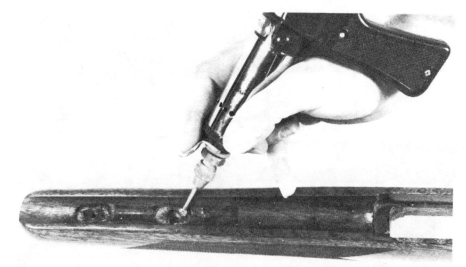

No contact should exist between barrel screw lug and its mortise in Model 88 forearm. Forward mortise is a recess for the front sling-swivel nut, which must not contact the barrel.

point, even after the cleaning-up job on the barrel channel.

Finally, it is even more essential in this model than in more conventional sporters that the entire inside of the inletting, including the barrel channel, be thoroughly sealed against moisture. With the barrel and forearm so intimately bound together by that infernal screw, any warpage in the wood is bound to cause the zero to stroll hither and thither through the woods.

All this accomplished, No. 5305 was put back together and hauled to the range. Her personality was notably sweeter; not only was the tendency to radical shot-stringing entirely gone, but the nice, round groups were smaller than before. The fundamentals of tuning the Model 88 had been accomplished.

Before we go on to the refinements, however, let us go back and take another look at that recoil block. As the photographs will show more clearly than these words, this unit is the key to the entire assembly system of the rifle. The precision of its alignment in all planes with the axis of the bore is crucial to everything else, since the receiver locks quite rigidly to it. If this block is installed crookedly in the vertical plane, the barrel will not center over the forearm screw hole, and tension on that screw will inevitably stress the barrel. If the recoil block's front vertical plane is angled upward, the tension on the front screw will bend the barrel, if not the receiver itself.

It happened that my Model 88 had its recoil block correctly aligned. I have seen a few specimens, however, in which this alignment was not perfect, and accuracy suffered. In some cases, a bit of judicious relieving of the wood behind this block allowed it to return to its correct position. In more extreme cases, it becomes necessary to relieve the wood extensively and to epoxy-bed the block, allowing the compound to harden while the rifle is fully assembled with all screws set up tightly.

Installation of this block, of course, is the key procedure in custom-stocking any Model 88. In passing, I may add that a custom stock of straighter butt pattern than the factory stock takes a lot of the bite out of the recoil of this rifle, especially in .308, .284, and .358 calibers.

Final tuning of an 88 (in addition to the usual process of developing custom handloads for each individual rifle) involves slicking up the action and trigger. First, it must be realized that the M88's action was engineered to be operated smartly. The lever linkage includes a pair of accelerators which change the rate of bolt travel constantly throughout the very short arc of the lever's throw. This system improves extraction and contributes to positive feed from the detachable clip magazine. It also has the effect of making an 88 seem rather stiff and rough when operated gingerly. Snappy operation will damage nothing; the mechanism is designed for it, and the rifle's smoothness should be judged only on the basis of such operation.

The best of them, however, will improve as the parts are broken in by normal wear. The process can be hastened by patient use of lapping or valve-grinding compound on the rubbing parts, plus a few hundred cycles of operation. Lapping-in of the three locking lugs should be accomplished as a separate operation, with care to see that it is not overdone. All traces of compound must be carefully removed and the parts oiled lightly, after which the action will have a feeling of icy slickness.

Finally, there is the trigger. One of the original design specifications for the Model 88 (established, I believe, even before World War II) was that the

Improper vertical alignment of the Model 88 recoil block, or a too-shallow receiver lug recess may be diagnosed by springing apart barrel and fore-end when forearm screw is backed out.

trigger must ride with the lever throughout the operating cycle. Anyone who has ever speared his finger on the end of the fixed trigger of any other lever action can appreciate Winchester's thoughtfullness; but any rifleman accustomed to the joys of a really good, crisp trigger will prefer that the engineers had not bothered.

The 88's trigger can only be described as long, mushy, creepy, and without "character," although it is

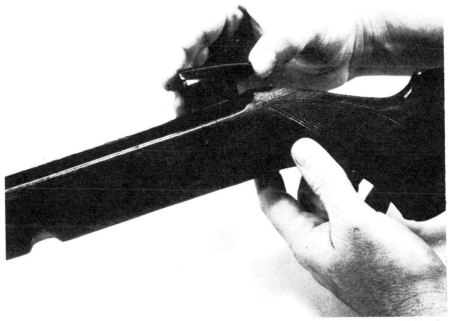

The Model 88's unique recoil block, which is similar to that of the M1 Carbine, is positioned at the rear of the receiver mortise. Any misalignment in either plane will result in bending of the barrel and/or receiver when forearm screw is tightened.

almost never too heavy. This is apparently caused by the necessity of disconnecting and reconnecting trigger and sear during the lever's stroke. The trigger's feel can be improved considerably by a capable gunsmith (not just anybody with a shingle hung out!) but it is no job for the amateur. Addition of a trigger shoe helps, and is about as far as the average Model 88 owner should go in this department.

Although 88's of recent vintage seem to have better triggers than the earlier specimens, I mourn the decision to sacrifice trigger-action quality in favor of largely theoretical convenience. I long ago learned to keep my trigger finger out of the way jacking a lever-action rifle, and never could break the habit with the 88.

How good is the Model 88, accuracy-wise, after all this effort? On the average, very good indeed--probably just about as good as the typical bolt-action sporter of similar price class. Especially in the .243 chambering, Model 88's are not uncommon which will hug one inch at 100 yards with good handloads. The tuning of No. 5305 cut group averages about in half with factory loadings, and handloads reduced groups to something like 1 3/8th inches, average. This means, of course, that the rifle delivered occasional sub-minute-of-angle clusters. Nothing spectacular, until you remember that I started with a gun capable of *nothing* better than three-inch groups, and damn few *that* small!

Best of all, the tuned rifle proved to be very steady in holding zero through all sorts of weather, with a hot barrel as well as a cold one. It killed a lot of game, did old No. 5305, and I was saddened to see its bore go sour after some 4,300 rounds of jacketed-bullet ammo had passed that way, plus thousands of rounds of alloy cast bullets.

My relationship with the Savage Model 99 began long before I saw that first Model 88 ad. Although the 99 is of similar vintage to the 94's and 336's, it was remarkably advanced in design for its day and is still quite modern. Its buttstock is attached, as it should be, by a throughbolt, which, of course should be kept tight. It is of "hammerless" pattern, and uses the spindle-type Mannlicher magazine to avoid hanging a long accuracy-spoiling tube under the barrel. And the 99 can be tuned, although the job isn't nearly as involved as the 88.

The forearm of this rifle is attached only to the barrel, by means of a screw-and-lug arrangement similar to that of the Model 88. The rear face of the forearm is inletted to fit the contours of the receiver front. The usual practice is to relieve this wooden surface so that no actual contact occurs between receiver and forearm, which can be accomplished, with proper care, without creating an unsightly gap between wood and metal. Another system sometimes used is glass-bedding the receiver and forearm for a *perfect* mating, with no stress being placed upon the barrel when the complete rifle is assembled. With any individual rifle, some experimenting may be necessary to squeeze groups, but a great many Model 99's can be made to deliver

bench rest groups which will distress certain bolt-action snobs!

The ideal solution to the forearm problem would be attachment, in some manner, of a hanger bar to the front of the receiver--similar to a Ruger single shot. The forearm would then be inletted to accept this bar, and the screw attaching barrel and forearm could be discarded. The rifle could then be treated as any other sporter, floating or pressure-bedding the barrel according to the owner's tastes.

It seems to me that I have read or heard of such an alteration, but I do not know how it can be done, nor do any of several gunsmiths I've asked about it. Perhaps a steel plate could be fitted to the front of the receiver with screws, so that it could be removed to get at the magazine parts located in the face of the receiver. This plate might have the hanger bar welded to it. It sounds like a good idea, but a lot of good theories harbor "bugs" when actually tried. It just might be, however, that a Model 99 with a target-grade custom barrel and such a forearm attachment could walk away with lever-action accuracy honors--and crowd even the best of bolt-action sporters in this department.

Until someone tries it, though, a well-tuned Winchester Model 88 must stand as the lever-action accuracy champion of the world.

The way I look at it, rifles--like gun dogs, saddle horses, and women--were born to be civilized by men . . . and the lever-action breed is one of the best of them all!

●

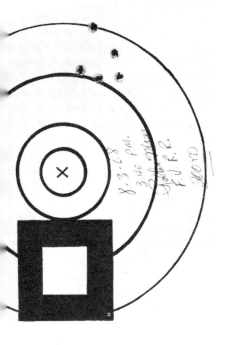

TUNING-
Ruger's Single Shot

By ROBERT REAGAN

Methodical mechanical and load tuning with a .243 Ruger No. 1 Single Shot resulted in several loads which will equal or better the 200-yard 1 3/16-inch group at left.

THE RUGER NUMBER ONE fills a blank spot in my gun rack that has been there since the boyhood days when that rack and the rifles in it were all a dream. Quite a number of Winchester Hi-Walls, Remington Hepburns and assorted Martinis have been tried in an effort to fill that spot. In the gun room there is an old cigar box three-quarters full of cartridges--three or four each of Improved Bee, 2R Lovell, Marcianti Blue Streak, Weatherby Rocket, 6mm Gipson Krag, two different Neidner .25 Krags, and many others I have used over the years. None of them did quite what I wanted it to do. Generally, if they

shot flat enough far enough, they did not shoot straight enough.

A number of our better bolt action rifles will fill our long range requirements, but if they have the long, chunky barrel that will take crows consistently at 200 yards they are too cumbersome for quick work at powder-burn range -- where the target may be a bounding whitetail. There are several cartridges capable of such extreme applications, but mighty few guns that will. The Ruger Number One Single Shot fills these requirements for me, and it meets my personal preferences, for it is compact, fast

handling and a work of art in the bargain. Most importantly, it can be made to shoot.

Reports on The Ruger Single Shot rifle indicate that some rifles shoot really well and some are subject to significant vertical stringing. One man I know has a .308 heavy barrel version with the Alex Henry fore-end that shoots 3/4-inch groups at 100 yards with 150-grain Winchester factory loads and, this, right out of the box. I have a heavy barrel, plain stock version in .243 Winchester that shoots consistent 1 1/4 to 1 3/8-inch groups at 200 yards with its favorite load after some tuning. Out

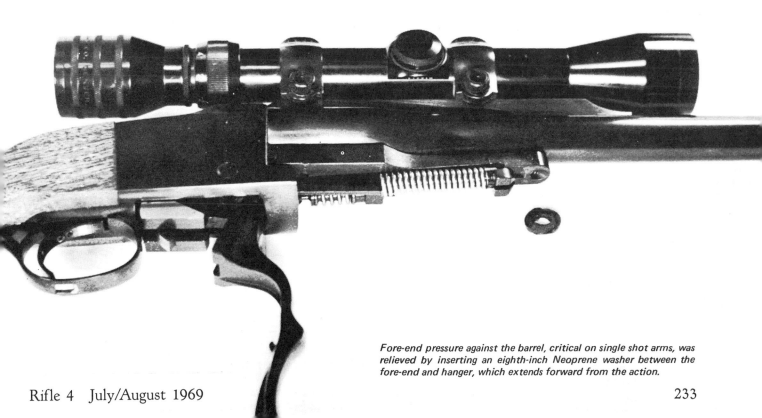

Fore-end pressure against the barrel, critical on single shot arms, was relieved by inserting an eighth-inch Neoprene washer between the fore-end and hanger, which extends forward from the action.

of the box, it shot 2 to 3-inch (horizontal) by 5 to 7-inch (vertical) groups with factory loads. But tuning the rifle reduced typical 80-grain Remington Power-Lokt factory ammo groups to about 2 7/8 inches by 3 1/4. A number of properly matched handloads will shoot 5-shot 1½-inch groups or better at 200 yards all day every day! And therein lies a tale.

Early experience with the Ruger, which was fitted with a Redfield 2-7X scope, was not encouraging. I had been reading about Remington's 80-grain varmint bullet and the premium factory round loaded with it. Five boxes of shells later, I decided neither this round nor the Remington 100-grain factory loads were the proper combination for the Ruger. Winchester's were very little better. Groups ran 3 inches by 5 to 7 inches at 200 yards, stringing up and down. Tuning and load development come faster for me at 200 yards than they do at 100. Changes in group size, for better or worse, are more dramatic and it seems to take less ammo to get development headed in the correct direction.

I had not shot much from the bench for several years and therefore discounted the fact that the groups kept shifting around on the paper. But poor groups, strung groups, and groups shifting around on the paper are standard signs of fore-end trouble. Of course, I had already made sure that all

scope and butt stock screws were tight. Usually, there isn't much that can be done with the butt section of a two-piece stock on a single shot, autoloader or lever action except to be certain that the wood solidly supports the metal. But the fit of the fore-end, and the pressure it applies to the barrel, is critical on almost all of these guns.

The fore-end on the Ruger is screwed to a hanger that extends forward from the action. My rifle had the fore-end bedded tightly against the action and the barrel. Single shot enthusiasts learned long before I was born to relieve the wood at the action, but I was not about to start carving on my pretty Ruger right then. So I tried for groups with the fore-end screw loose and at every half turn until it was again tight.

A moderate to light fore-end pressure on the barrel seemed best.

My notes made at the time read, "Best results with fore-end screw tightened all the way up, then backed off 2 1/4 to 1/2. Vertical stringing 4 to 5 inches. Increases with no fore-end pressure or a lot of it. High spot in the bedding, right side. Loosening fore-end lowers impact dramatically." This might have been acceptable had the range been 400 yards not 200! Further thought along these lines and a careful look at the fore-end and its hanger indicated a really loose fore-end screw created a sloppy, unstable condition up front. The fore-end screw does not go to the

LOADS FOR .243 WINCHESTER IN RUGER NUMBER ONE NO. 1315

Cases, Winchester Western

Primers, W-W 8 1/2-120

Bullet	Powder	Charge	200-Yard Accuracy
75-gr. Hornady and Sierra	4064	41	1 1/2 inches
75-gr. Hornady and Sierra	RL-21	42.5	1 1/2 inches
85-gr. Sierra BT	4064	40*	1 1/4 inches
85-gr. Sierra BT	Norma 204	45.5	1 3/8 inches
100-gr. Sierra	4064	38	1 3/4 inches
100-gr. Sierra	Norma 204	45	1 3/4 inches

*Best load

WARNING: This rifle is throated very long giving the pressure-reducing effect of either more powder space or freeboring. Approach these loads with extreme caution.

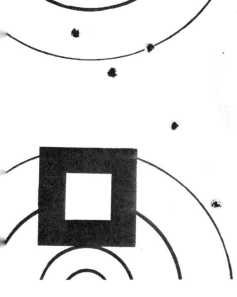

Even after mechanical tuning was complete, the Ruger gave vertical stringing at 200 yards with Remington factory loads.

but were still strung up and down three to four inches. The Neoprene washer is a temporary expedient. Taking some wood from the fore-end at the bearing points will do the same job.

This rifle may be amenable to even more mechanical tuning. Some shooters feel the telescope sight mounting rib, which is screwed to the barrel and bears on the action, should be relieved at the action. I may have this done, but so far I have done nothing to the rifle that is irreversible. Living with this rifle for seven months has given me a deep respect for the Ruger design and the execution of that design. There may be reasons for the fore-end bearing on the barrel and for the barrel rib bearing on the action. However, with groups going consistently to the same spot, I decided it was time to switch from mechanical tuning to load development.

When working for accuracy, we must remember that we are varying interrelated factors. Because the factors are interrelated, it is difficult for us to change a single variable at a time. I react to this set of factors by alternating

between rifle tuning and load development. I usually rough tune a rifle, develop a reasonably good load, then fine tune the rifle to that load. One could continue this process indefinitely. One could also wear out the barrel this way unless he finalizes development at a predetermined, reasonable level. I consider 1 1/2-inch groups at 200 yards going to the same spot on the paper month after month to be both excellent accuracy for varmint hunting and relatively easy to achieve in quality 6mm's.

Reloading the Remington cases brought two things to light: First, while I have had generally excellent results with Remington cases in recent years, these cases would seem to indicate that Remington does not care much if the .243 Winchester shoots or not. Primer pocket depth varies darn near a thirty-second of an inch. The short ones will not let CCI or even Remington primers seat flush with the case head even after cleaning the primer pockets out bright and shining. These cases occur at random, about one out of four, throughout what is probably three lots of brass. No load shoots well in these particular cases even after sorting into three lots by primer pocket depth. For now, the Remington cases have been set aside. Next winter, I expect to work on them until I get groups using at least some of them.

Second, my Ruger Number One is throated *long*. Hundred-grain Sierras and Noslers can be seated to just not touch the rifling with their bases slightly forward of the shoulder-case neck junction. Two Model 70 .243s and one Sako .243 in my experience have had about a quarter of an inch of any heavy bullet back in the powder space. The first *American Rifleman* article on loading the .243 stated that the bases of heavy bullets would be back in the powder space, but that their loads took that into account. The .243 case has less than a quarter-inch neck. Therefore, the long throat makes quite a difference. Seventy-five grain Hornady bullets seated 1/8-inch do not touch the rifling, but they can be made to shoot anyway. One wonders if bullets seated that shallow will stay straight in the case given normal, careful handling. Actually, the long throat is an advantage from my point of view. Long bullets buck the wind quite a bit better than the short ones, but long bullet trajectories can be held quite close to short bullet trajectories. On varmints, wind bothers

barrel and does not have to handle much barrel heat. So I put a roughly 1/8-inch Neoprene washer between the hanger and the fore-end. This stabilizes everything, yet keeps the fore-end completely clear of the barrel. This was particularly important to me for as an old target shooter, I use a sling some and do not like bedded fore-ends.

With the washer inserted, the width of groups came right down to better than two inches at 200 and they stopped drifting around on the paper,

Long throat of author's No. 1 Ruger allows bullets to be seated far forward, which probably explains why he had no pressure signs with loads which are too hot for most rifles. Bullets touch lands at depth shown with, from left, 100-grain Sierra, 89-grain Gardiner, 85-grain Sierra (must be seated deeper). At right is Remington 100-grain factory round with standard seating.

me more than small differences in trajectory. When the .243 Winchester first came out, I had trouble with ricochets with bullets over 75 grains. But recent experience has indicated reliable breakup of the 85-grain Sierra boat-tail bullets in near-maximum loads.

Using once-fired Winchester-Western cases with 8 1/2-120 primers, the Ruger Number One had just one more trick hidden up its chamber. It needs a case that really fills that chamber. This is another technique straight from old-time single shot practice. Most loading manuals point out that fitting the case to the chamber is one of the advantages of handloading. I had come to doubt this for three previous .243's, all bolt action, had seemed to shoot new unfired brass just as well as fire-formed cases. Light loads, as with lead bullets, may need a case that fits right, but full-power jacketed bullet loads fit the chamber long before the bullet gets very far down the barrel. I have killed dozens of crows and chucks while fireforming cases in cartridges all the way from K-Hornet to .25-06.

My Ruger wants formed and very lightly sized cases for tests at the shooting bench indicate that full-length sizing opens up groups. The falling block and lever system on the Ruger has a really powerful camming action, so chambering, extraction and ejection are positive and then some. In this sense, the Ruger is a real handloader's rifle. Any time the base of the case is forward of the face of the block it will go in and,

so far, come out. The effort required is minimal if applied at the end of the underlever. I usually neck size half of the neck with an RCBS Neck Sizer for three firings with stiff loads. About the fourth time around, I run the case far enough into an RCBS full length die so that light thumb pressure will move the case just forward of the face of the falling block, but heavy thumb pressure will not seat the case. Tests using some dirty oil for case lubrication indicated that I was sizing most of the neck and the forward half of the case body, but not touching the shoulder with the sizing die. These techniques should give me great case life for the cases are not being worked in the sizing die as much as they were in my bolt action .243's. An early indication of this factor has been a marked reduction in case stretching.

A number of loads made up in lightly sized cases with long bullet seating will shoot inside 1 1/2 inches at 200 yards—and three quarters of a minute accuracy in 6mm is the demanding standard I set. Actually, 3/4 of a minute is about my limit of sighting accuracy through the Redfield 2-7. This rifle is very consistent in its reaction to the various loading factors. Using carefully loaded handloads, unfired brass with normal seating for .243 (2.71 inches overall), it will shoot groups roughly 1 3/8 to 1 1/2 across and 3 to 4 1/2 inches up and down. Unfired brass with long bullets jammed into the rifling will shoot groups roughly 1 3/4 by 2 inches—all at 200 yards. The latter loads are plenty good enough for 250-yard

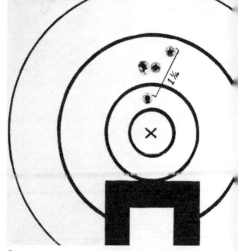

Best load with the Ruger is 40 grains of 4064 (above published maximums, but safe in author's rifle) behind 85-grain Sierra BT, Winchester-Western case, 8½-120 primer, neck-sized only. Group measures 1 1/16-inch, fired at 200 yards.

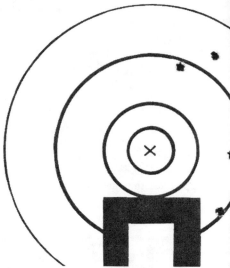

With the same load as above, but in new cases with standard bullet seating depth, Ruger gave vertical stringing similar to factory loads.

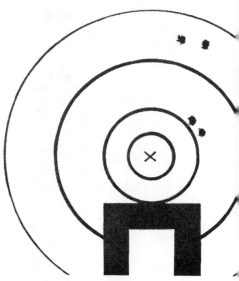

The same 40/4064/85 load with bullet seated long, but in new case, gives larger group than with fire-formed case. All targets fired at 200 yards. Photo-prints are one-half actual size.

Ready for testing, the Ruger fore-end is supported near hanger screw, butt supported by relatively large bag which is squeezed for minute sight corrections.

chuck shooting. With formed cases lightly sized and 85-grain Sierra boat-tails seated almost 2 7/8 inches overall, this rifle will shoot groups that will average one inch by 1 3/8 inches at 200 yards.

Adhering to these techniques, this rifle shoots tight groups with quite a number of bullets and powders. The best accuracy with each combination seems to fall in a range of powder weights a full grain and a half wide, just under maximum. Usually, groups open up just before pressure signs appear. These are normal patterns for quality varmint and target rifles. Often, a rifle that is accurate with only one powder and within a powder weight range only 1/2-grain wide is sensitive to temperature change.

Handloaders should view my powder charges with marked caution. Remember, I have more space in my case than most or I have considerable freeboring. Excellent accuracy can be obtained with IMR 4064, Reloder 21, and Norma 204. Both 4350 and 4831 have never given me gilt edge accuracy in .243 Winchester and did not work out in the Ruger. The only ball powders I have tried have been H380 and H450 and neither has done especially well. I expect to try H414 and if I can ever find any, I'll try the new 760BR ball powder.

My pet load uses IMR 4064 and it is *way over the maximum loads in the manuals*. The Ackley, Lyman, Pacific, Speer and Whelen books all show 38 to 39 grains of 4064 as a maximum load with 85 to 90-grain bullets. In Super-X cases with 8 1/2-120 primers, I use 40 grains of 4064 behind the 85-grain Sierra boat-tail bullet. I have tested up to 41 grains in this combination without signs of excessive pressure, but remember that my gun's chamber is not normal.

In a *Gun Digest* article years ago, Warren Page recommended 41 grains of 4064 and 85-grain bullets. At one time, I had a Sako Heavy Barrel with a tight chamber and a tight barrel. It would blow primers out of every other Norma 75-grain factory load. But the Sako also liked the 40-4064-85 Sierra BT load.

The *Du Pont Handloader's Guide To Powders* shows a 100-grain .2422 bullet and 38.5 grains of 4064 as giving 52,000 pounds pressure and 3,030 fps. My rifle likes 38 grains and a 100-grain Sierra. So far, I have settled on this one for a deer load. Nosler 100-grain bullets do not shoot well in this rifle and I have not been able to find any of the new 95-grain Noslers to buy and try. The 100-grain Sierras group one inch below the 85-grain Sierra varmint load at 200, giving me a single sight setting for the two loads.

The 85 and 100-grain Sierra bullets go to almost the same spot and into nice groups with 45.5 and 45 grains respectively of Norma 204. Norma 204 is quite dense, leaving a lot of unused powder space and, in these loadings, does not shoot quite as clean as 4064.

Although I do not expect to use them much, Hornady and Sierra 75-grain bullets group well with either 41 grains of 4064 or 42.5 grains of Reloder 21. This powder is less dense than some, it leaves very little unused space in the shell and shoots clean as a whistle. Light bullets group 3 to 4 inches lower at 200 than the heavier bullets.

Group centers with 85 and 100-grain Sierras and either 4064 or Norma 204 stay within 1 1/2 inches of each other. The first shot out of a cold, clean barrel goes 1 1/2 inches under the hot barrel group. Cold, dirty barrel shots split the difference between the two groups. Over six months now, zero on the Ruger Number One has not changed a particle.

The Ruger Number One in .243 Winchester will take game, short of big bear and big elk, at any reasonable range. It is beautiful. It handles fast and well. Given care in handloading loads it likes, it is finely accurate. What more could a man ask for in one rifle? ●

Tuning the New

Ruger No. 3
Savage/Anschutz 1432

The Hornet is ideal for use in the more settled communities. The low noise level isn't disturbing to landowners while the extremely fragile Hornet bullets are more prone to tear up on contact, rather than ricocheting.

I READ Jon Sundra's article on the two new Hornet rifles in the last issue of *Rifle* with great interest because I've been hung up on Hornets for many years. However, since Jon's article was aimed primarily at the guns' appearance and functioning performance, I felt that something more on the accuracy potential of these guns would be of interest. The tinkering I have done with the new Ruger No. 3 single shot and the Savage/ Anschutz Model 1432 has resulted in amazing performance from these high quality guns.

My fascination with accurizing Hornet

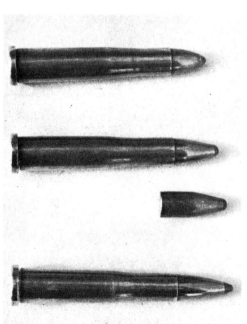

From top is a factory loaded .22 Hornet cartridge, a cartridge handloaded with the Hornady .224 Hornet bullet and a handloaded 50-grain Sierra spitzer. All makes of factory Hornet ammunition have the bullet seated so that it must jump considerably to reach the lands in most rifles. The Hornady spire point allows the bullet to be seated against the lands of the Savage/Anschutz and still work through the magazine while the spitzer bullet seated so that it touches the lands, will not work through the magazine.

rifles began long before either the No. 3 or the 1432. It started about 25 years ago when I acquired a battered Model 54 Winchester for the ridiculous sum of $40.00 — because the barrel was slightly bent, although you had to look hard to see it! Besides, I needed a varminter, and that's all I could afford. I must have tried every top load in every handloading book with discouraging results. One day an old-timer told me, "Son, you ain't never going to hit nuthin' unless you hit it!" That seemed to make a lot of sense to me so I asked how he managed an enviable record of 37 straight hits with a high sidewall Winchester Hornet on the gophers that infested his grazing pastures. "Slow 'em down," he said. "You can't make a Swift out of a Hornet so quit tryin'." He was right. He gave me one of the best tips that's made every Hornet I've owned shoot better than average groups.

I began to find out some facts for myself from then on: with careful handloading and rifle tuning, combined with good range and wind estimation, one can regularly connect out beyond the "accepted Hornet range." I've learned that this amazing little cartridge is just as good a varmint round at 200 yards-plus as a .222 or a .219 or any number of similar "middle class" .22 varminters. To say that the Hornet is a 150-yard rifle or the .222 is a 225-yard rifle is academic. That *is* the range if that's all your ability allows it to be. It could be even less. In other words, the Hornet's range on gophers and ground squirrels could be as far as you could hit, because a hit anywhere on game of this size with the fragile Hornet bullets will almost certainly result in the animal's quick demise. But in my

experience, in the case of woodchucks (which can weigh up to 12 pounds or more) the range had better be kept under 100 yards or wounded animals may result. The same applies to coyotes.

Proper bullet weight also aids in this long range potential of the Hornet. Most all factory rifles have had a rifling twist of one turn in 16 inches. (A lot of the old-time barrel makers cut 14-inch twists for custom jobs.) However, this 16-inch twist doesn't seem to stabilize bullets heavier than 45 grains at Hornet velocities. If you can get heavier weights to shoot well, they may be too tough-jacketed to break up reliably on impact, since they're primarily designed for .222-plus speeds. One exception to this is the Hornady SX bullet. I've never had one fail to expand at any range that I have been able to connect.

When Ruger announced the No. 3 single shot in .22 Hornet I'd already had a chance to examine the rifle in .45-70 caliber, the first caliber produced. My first impression was that the advertising photos had not done it justice. This was a very good looking and skillfully finished rifle, and being sold on Hornets, I promptly placed my order with my neighborhood gun shop.

When the rifle finally arrived, I was elated to see the barrel tapped for scope blocks; however, for which make, no one knew! But there's more than one way to mount a scope — I installed a Bushnell

Hornet Rifles

By BOB PETRO

custom D-M 3-9X scope with the Universal Mount system that utilizes two chrome-moly steel studs. By installing the high elevation collar and stud in the front tapped hole, and a low elevation collar in the rear, I was able to come up with as solid an installation as one could want. This mount put the center of the scope exactly 1½ inches above the bore. Unfortunately, Bushnell doesn't list this mount system in their latest catalog; perhaps they still have some in stock or, if not, it may be possible to locate one at a gun supply house.

Forearm bedding was then checked for unevenness. None was found even when the screw tension on the barrel band was varied. Particular attention was paid to how the recessed forearm screw pulled the stock back against the front walls of the action. It's important to accuracy that the rear of the forearm bear evenly and tight at this point. Also, the recessed screw must be tightened before the barrel band when replacing the forearm. On my rifle, the forearm channel made even contact against the barrel at the extreme tip, the rest of the channel being generously undercut.

The remainder of the pre-tune on the No. 3 Ruger consisted of nothing more than a tiny amount of molybdenum disulfide deposited on the sear before the buttstock was replaced, then the entire open action was lightly sprayed with a Du Pont No. 7 product called Slip Spray. This is a dry film lubricant which is also an excellent rust inhibitor. All of my guns receive the same treatment with a considerable smoothing up of the action in most cases. The workings of a lever or

single shot, where there is a lot of contact between adjacent surfaces of metal, seem to be especially improved with this treatment. The molybdenum is so fine a powder it actually penetrates the pores of the metal and is the next best thing to doing the job with polishing stones.

Just about the time I was getting ready to compare the shooting qualities of the Ruger against a superbly accurate pre-64 Model 70 I own — no, it isn't for sale — my neighborhood gun store owner called and said he had something I should see before someone else snapped it up. When I arrived (six minutes later) he just grinned and handed me one of the trimmest, sweetest feeling and best looking Hornet rifles I have seen since the fine little Winchester Model 43 was discontinued. It was the new Savage/Anschutz Model 1432 Sporter. I had difficulty keeping my emotions to myself, feeling like a 13-year-old boy at Christmas! The store owner had me hooked and he knew it. What followed was one of the most bizarre swap sessions I've ever been involved in. But after much name calling and dickering, with each of us feeling that we got the best of the other, I hurried home with my latest Hornet addition.

Jon Sundra covered the physical and aesthetic aspects of this fine rifle very well in his aforementioned article so it isn't

necessary to go into that here. Suffice it to say that the little woman promptly announced that when I got it shooting properly, it was to go in *her* gun rack!

I mounted a 6X Weaver with Weaver split ring mounts on the pre-drilled receiver and zeroed it on the Bushnell bore-sighter. The stock bedding was checked and it was found that the recoil lug was bearing evenly but lightly. The inletting around the tang was possibly a bit too close. I reassembled the rifle, leaving the action screws loose, and rapped the butt on the carpeted floor, which settled the action so that the recoil lug was then bearing properly. The rear guard screw was then tightened and the front screw was snugged up until no more downward movement of the barrel could be felt pulling into the stock. This left the forearm free-floating and the forward two inches of the barrel ahead of the recoil lug just settled onto the bottom of the barrel channel. That's the way it came from the factory and indicates the care that went into the assembly of this rifle. Did it shoot? You bet — but not without a little work.

None of the tune-up methods described here are new or guaranteed to be a cure-all for every rifle. They are merely a systematic approach that for years has been practiced by knowledgeable shooters and that has largely been initiated by the competitive bench shooters. I have found it just as interesting and challenging, and sometimes easier, to tailor a rifle to shoot well with a given load, rather than tailor the load to the rifle — providing, of course, that you have a carefully loaded

Striped areas show receiver and barrel contact points made to bear when Petro "pre-tunes" his bolt-action rifles. However, in the case of the Savage/Anschutz, the factory bedding was nearly perfect. By using electrician's tape to cradle the barrel in the fore-end channel, Petro controls the up-pressure on the barrel by varying the layers of tape on either side.

Petro's Ruger No. 3 carries a Bushnell Custom 3-9X scope. The short overall length of the No. 3 makes it a fast swinging rifle.

round with a good bullet to start with. Sometimes it doesn't work out this way and in the case of the Savage/Anschutz it turned out to be a combination of both.

All of the loads for these tests were prepared as follows: cases were once fired from new factory loads. (These produced 1½ to 2¼-inch groups without any tuning efforts but I wanted once fired brass and I have a lot of factory ammo on hand.) Case necks were sized only to the depth of the seated bullet. Primer pockets were then cleaned and primed with a Lee Priming Tool. All sizing and seating was done with RCBS dies in a C-H "H" press. Powder was weighed on an older Redding scale sans the oil damper. It takes longer to weigh the charges without the oil, but I feel it pays off in increased accuracy. The bullet was seated to just make contact with the rifling. With this loading technique and 9.7 grains of Hercules 2400 powder, my Model 70 will shoot consistent ½-inch 5-shot groups.

I have found that while assembling loads for the Hornet, care must be taken in keeping the variables as small as possible. Because of the smaller capacity of the case, errors and deviations are greatly magnified on the target. For example, a .1-grain error in a 10-grain powder charge is twice as great as a .1-grain error in a 20-grain charge. With some powders in the larger cases you can tolerate a plus or minus .1-grain error and not notice the difference in the group size. Some (most) bench shooters don't bother to weigh each individual powder charge and have good results, but I feel that carefully weighed charges for the Hornet can produce consistently smaller groups. Segregation of brass by plus or minus .5-grain differences — after the brass has been once fired and trimmed to the exact same length also helps. I also ream the inside of the case necks with a modified Lee Target Loader for the .222 and gauge flash holes for uniformity. I do not weigh bullets or spin them for concentricity; when loading for hunting, I'm satisfied with near ½-minute-of-angle accuracy for small varmints, and I believe that most factory bullets are capable of this. Bullets today are so much superior to those of 10 years ago that it's like picking fly specks out of the pepper trying to improve a group size that's already better than a shooter's capability in the field. The above procedures have helped get my varmint rifles shooting less than

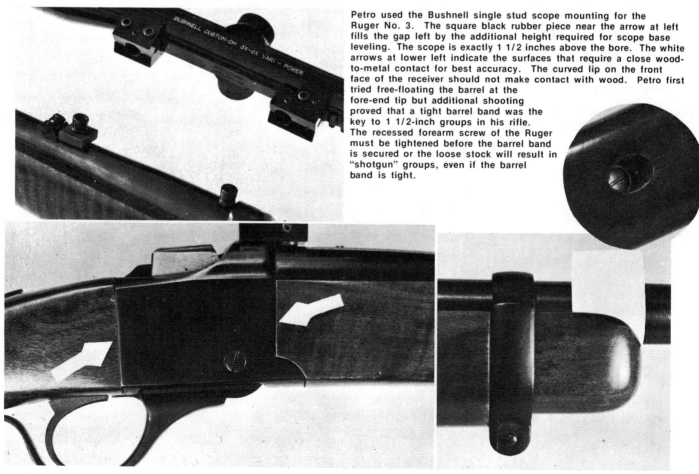

Petro used the Bushnell single stud scope mounting for the Ruger No. 3. The square black rubber piece near the arrow at left fills the gap left by the additional height required for scope base leveling. The scope is exactly 1 1/2 inches above the bore. The white arrows at lower left indicate the surfaces that require a close wood-to-metal contact for best accuracy. The curved lip on the front face of the receiver should not make contact with wood. Petro first tried free-floating the barrel at the fore-end tip but additional shooting proved that a tight barrel band was the key to 1 1/2-inch groups in his rifle. The recessed forearm screw of the Ruger must be tightened before the barrel band is secured or the loose stock will result in "shotgun" groups, even if the barrel band is tight.

This 100-yard target illustrates final tune-up results and indicates that quality rifles with tailored handloads can produce quality results.

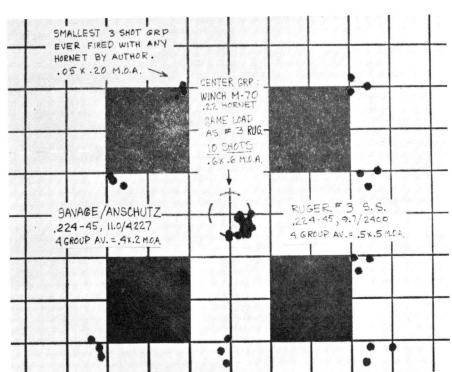

minute-of-angle groups with a minimum of effort at the loading bench.

The first shooting of the Ruger No. 3 was with my favorite Model 70 accuracy load mentioned, and was to determine what changes would result by loosening and tightening the forearm barrel band. Five-shot groups were tried with the band removed, allowing the barrel to free float, and resulted in round clusters with the best of the five-group series going to 1.1-inch. The worst was 1.4 — not bad at all but I felt the rifle was capable of better.

During all shooting, the recessed forearm screw was kept tight. The forearm band was replaced and after every two groups of five shots the band screw tightened ¼-turn. Groups opened up to 1½ inches at the first setting which made the band just snug enough to be finger tight. The screw was tightened another ¼-turn and a horizontal dispersion was apparent with a slight decrease in vertical size. The two groups measured 1 1/8 inches high by 1 1/2 inches wide and 1 inch by 1 1/2 inches wide. Another turn began to put a noticeable tension on the screw. That did it! Five groups went down to nice consistent clusters averaging .50 high by .56 wide. Then a series of 10 three-shot groups showed a predictable pattern beginning to be apparent. Four out of five of the first shots from a cold barrel went into a near two o'clock position from the center of the final group. Outside temperature was 42° and the thick beefy barrel wouldn't even get warm. The second shot of each group moved to 6 or 7 o'clock and in most cases the third shot would plop right into the 11 or 12 o'clock spot.

I should point out that the barrel was cleaned with a tight swab and Hoppe's No. 9 prior to each series of five group firings. Two fouling shots were then fired and the series commenced; then the barrel was allowed to cool. I was completely satisfied with the Ruger's performance at this point. Perhaps groups can be improved with other loads or more exacting forearm pressure and I'll attempt this in future tests. But for now any varmint shooter would be happy with these groupings.

The Savage/Anschutz was fired alternately with the Ruger during these tests. This allowed the heat of the slimmer Savage barrel to remain fairly constant. The trigger was perfect for my taste just as it came from the factory. Again, the disulfide powder and Du Pont Slip Spray

Ballistic Data, .22 Hornet

45 Grain (.224 Diameter) Hornady Hornet
Sectional density — .128, ballistic coefficient — .202
Scope mounted 1.50 inches above bore

Muzzle Velocity 2,600	100	150	200	250
Drop	2.91	6.87	13.05	22.20
Bullet Path	0	-1.75	-.5.73	-12.67
Mid Range Trajectory	.17	.77	3.66	6.40

Note: Data is from **Hornady Handbook of Cartridge Reloading.** Actual shooting results compare very close to the above but due to constantly changing atmospheric conditions of Petro's geographical location, it was felt that results from constant, carefully controlled laboratory conditions would be of more value to the reader.

Comparative Rifle Tune-up Results

Winchester M-70 and Savage/Anschutz — 24-inch barrel. Ruger No. 3 — 22-inch barrel.
Super X cases, weight 52 grains, Remington 6½ primers.
Instrumental velocity at 15 feet converted to muzzle velocity.
Temperature for Ruger & S.A. testing — 60°.

Rifle	Powder/ Charge	Velocity, fps	Average Group size, 100 Yds.	Notes
.224/50 Hornady SX				
Win. M-70	9.6/2400	2,490*	5 Shot, 1.1 MOA	Large varmint load to 150 yards, free floating.
.224/45 Hornady Hornet				
Win. M-70	9.7/2400	2,575*	5 Shot, .5 MOA	Small varmint to 200 +, free floating.
Ruger No. 3	9.7/2400	2,558**	5-5 Shot, 1.25 MOA	Band removed, free floating.
Ruger No. 3	9.7/2400	2,558**	2-5 Shot, 1.5 MOA	Light band tension, vertical dispersion.
Ruger No. 3	9.7/2400	2,558**	5-5 Shot, .56 Wide X .5	Heavy band tension
Sav./Anschutz	9.7/2400	2,558**	5 Shot, .75 Wide X 1.5	Free floating to any tension with fore-end pressure.
Sav./Anschutz	11.0/4227	2,585**	5 Shot, 1.0 MOA	Free floating, loose to tight guard screw.
Sav./Anschutz	11.0/4227	2,585**	10-3 Shot, .5 High X .38	Forearm pressure 3/4-turn on guard screw.

*Home built binary readout chronograph, certified accuracy by electronic lab calibration.
**Telepacific TPB-02 Chronograph.

were applied with the usual improvement in functioning. Firing this gun was pure pleasure. The man-sized stock provided a comfortable and secure feeling while shooting. The comb was just the right height for the scope, the pistol grip shape and bulge felt proper, and the reach to the trigger and trigger let-off was like a good bench rifle.

Factory ammo (45-grain SP) performed better than I expected. Some 5-shot groups were as small as 1½ inches, although the pattern was sporadic. When the front guard screw was tightened ½-turn from the starting point, one group went to barely over an inch indicating the rifle's potential. When enough fired cases were on hand for some serious reloading, the same favorite accuracy load was tried. The overall average wasn't much better than factory loads but a vertical stringing was showing up on the target, indicating some upward fore-end pressure might be tried to damp these vibrations.

Layers of electrician's tape were applied in the barrel channel at the fore-end tip. Two separate strips about ¼-inch wide and ½-inch long were laid to cradle the barrel evenly on each side at about a 60° angle. This is a good technique to use in the event further pressure may be needed only on one side, since several layers of tape can be used to increase pressure to the proper amount. However, it should be remembered that this tape isn't permanent, since its resiliency, and hence up-pressure, is affected by age, temperature and humidity changes. After determining the proper amount of pressure at each point, the tape can be replaced with glass bedding compound.

The forearm pressure on the barrel reduced the vertical stringing to about half with groups averaging ¾ inches high

and 1½ inches wide. Tension on the guard screw was increased, then backed off in ¼-turn increments with the only result being a shifting of groups on the target. It was apparent that this particular load had reached its full potential; therefore, a different combination was required if it were possible to shrink group size. A different powder could make the difference.

The Hornady manual lists a load with 11.3 grains of IMR-4227 powder giving 2,600 fps from their 22-inch test barrel. They also produced 2,500 fps with 10.7 grains. Interpolating, I came up with 2,550 fps if 11.0 grains were used. With the extra two inches of barrel length on the Savage/Anschutz, I reasoned that I may get about the same velocity as my accuracy load out of the Model 70. The Sierra loading manual shows 2,600 fps with 11.0 of 4227 from a 26-inch barrel. On the basis of this comparison, it indicated that my reasoning should be on the right track. Later chronographing proved this almost correct; velocities averaged 2,585 fps at muzzle.

The next series of tests with the new load started with the free-floating barrel. I prefer a slim barrel to shoot free floating if it will, especially when coupled with a slim forearm that is more susceptible to changes in humidity. The beefier stocks, as on the No. 3 Ruger, do not give as much problem this way because of their rigid nature.

Groups were again scattered but this time staying around an inch. Tightening the guard screw only shifted groups slightly, so forearm pressure was again tried. The tapes were replaced until contact was made with the barrel and the front guard screw — snug but not tight. Again a slight vertical dispersion

appeared but group size didn't increase. The next tightening produced what I was looking for; groups shrank to half size showing a slight vertical stringing. One quarter turn more proved to be the answer. The rifle would shoot the ½-minute-of-angle groups I consider necessary for serious, humane varmint shooting.

The first two shots from a cool barrel almost always touched. The third shot seldom would go further than 3/8-inch out but sometimes above and sometimes below the first two shots indicating that the forearm pressure could still be tinkered with. Group sizes for a series of 10 three-shot groups averaged .38 inches wide by .5 high. As far as I was concerned, the testing was over.

I felt lucky indeed to have gotten an accurate combination so easily. Some of my rifles still aren't tuned after months of trying and hundreds of rounds. But then if it were all this easy some of the glamour and satisfaction one derives from licking a really stubborn rifle would be gone. A less fussy shooter than I would probably be elated over one-inch groups with factory ammunition. Most good centerfires today can shoot near this if the shooter will spend the time to properly tune his rifle.

But with a little extra effort in handloading and getting to know that load's trajectory, a shooter can make a 200-yard-plus varmint rifle out of the Ruger No. 3 or the Savage/Anschutz .22 Hornet. And let's face it, this comprises about 90 percent of most varmint shooting opportunities. For that other 10 percent, I have a tack driving Ruger No. 1 single shot in .243 that I'm still "tuning up". ●

MAKING A GARAND SHOOT ACCURATELY

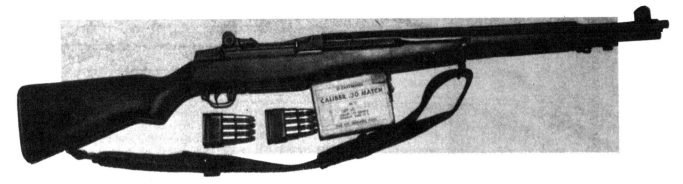

MAYBE THE TITLE should have read "Can anyone make a Garand shoot accurately?" because so much misinformation has been passed around about the rifle's scattergun accuracy. Even military National Match specifications will allow a Garand to pass if it can shoot 3½-inch groups at 100 yards. That did little to impress the general shooting public about the accuracy potential of the Garand, which followed the granddaddy of all match rifles — the M1903 Springfield.

Anyone who ever read a copy of General Julian Hatcher's book about the *Garand* or *Hatcher's Notebook*, remembers the section in which the general compared the scores of the 1939 and 1946 National Matches. The Garand was used in the 1946 matches and the Springfield in 1939. In the 1946 competition, the Garand bettered the scores that had been shot by the Springfield in 1939 by a pretty wide margin. That feat looks even more impressive when it's remembered that the shooters at the 1946 matches were forced to use standard GI Ball. National Match ammunition was used in 1939. The scores produced by the Garand in the early years after WW II pretty much sounded the death knell for the magnificent Springfield, although it lingered on in competition for at least another 20 years.

The 10-year period from the end of World War II to the development of the Army's National Match specifications for the Garand in 1956 saw the evolution of the Garand from a battle rifle to a match rifle supreme. The adoption of the M14 in 1957 initiated the demise of the Garand at the National Matches, but the old M1 continued to be the most used rifle at the matches well into the early sixties. The Garand was abandoned by most armed forces teams only after they were directed to use the NM M14 at the 1963 National Matches.

The process I have developed to convert an M1 to National Match specifications is a composite of those worked out by armories, shooters and other writers. It does not require the use of expensive equipment or the expenditure of money for special jigs and fixtures. The rifles I convert exceed the accuracy potential of the Army's NM specifications (3½-inch groups at 100 yards) by a considerable margin. Most will consistently shoot two MOA groups, even during the rapid fire stage. The approach I use also takes advantage of the techniques developed in the NM specification for the M14 by the Army's Marksmanship Training Unit where they can be applied to the Garand.

Locating a basic rifle is very similar to looking for a restorable Model T. Sometimes you can spend as much time searching as you do accurizing.

The major flaws in most Garands are: (1) pitted barrels caused from firing corrosive ammunition, (2) eroded throats caused by excessive rapid firing, (3) worn gas cylinders and pistons on the end of the operating rods, (4) excessive headspace, (5) worn bolts and receiver rails caused by firing without proper lubrication, (6) bent operating rods caused by firing reloads containing slow burning powders, (7) worn or damaged splines on barrels or the spline sections inside the front rings of the gas cylinders, (8) eroded gas ports or ports enlarged by a shade tree mechanic, (9) cracked or broken stocks, (10) bent or worn front or rear sights, and (11) worn sears or trigger hooks.

When buying any rifle, especially a Garand, it is very wise to disassemble it completely then put it back together. If you are not familiar with a Garand, don't attempt complete disassembly because it is not as easy as it looks. If you do know how to disassemble a Garand, tear it down and check each part for excessive wear, the way it fits other parts of the rifle (does it go back together normally or do you have to force it?), to see if parts are bent or damaged.

The disassembly should give some hint of the rifle's condition and the treatment it has received. It won't reveal its accuracy potential, though. Only a test at your local range can do that, but most dealers won't let you take it out and try it.

John Clarke modifies the M1 rifle to National Match specifications, employing methods used by the military armorers, with adaptations from the M14 NM models, and his own procedures.

The most important part of the Garand, the one which determines 99 percent of its accuracy potential, is the quality of the barrel — its straightness and the quality of the rifling at throat and muzzle. The critical areas of a bore are the first two inches and the last two. Everything in between is just along for the ride.

The muzzle of the barrel can be checked visually to see if the rifling is sharp and that there are no visible burrs or nicks caused by careless cleaning. Make sure the rifling isn't too worn. Excessive cleaning causes the gradual erosion of the rifling, especially in rifles that have to be cleaned from the muzzle, such as the Garand. If the rifling appears sharper in the middle of the barrel than it does at the muzzle, you can bet your bottom dollar the barrel will have to be replaced.

The throat tapers gradually from the end of the chamber to the beginning of the rifling (about .06 inch after the end of the chamber). In a well-used Garand, the rifling may become so eroded in the throat that a condition akin to free-boring may exist. the long, eroded throat will allow the bullet to accelerate for a distance (determined by the amount of erosion) before the bullet engages the rifling. This can cause the bullets to strip on the rifling due to the tremendous torquing forces.

As mentioned above, rifling usually begins about .06 inch after the end of the chamber, but I have seen Garands whose throats were eroded more than three times that much. Free-bored Garands usually produce substandard velocity and poor accuracy. The only cure is to rebarrel, which is an expensive process.

There is a special "Throat Erosion Gage" used by the government to check the condition of the throat, but I use a specially loaded dummy round. Two dummy rounds are needed: one of normal length (3.34 inches) and another containing the same bullet as used in the first round but seated out to an overall length of 3.42 inches.

To check the throat, insert the 3.34-inch round in the chamber and notice how far it protrudes from the bolt recess (the counterbored part of the barrel where the bolt fits in). Remove the 3.34-inch round and insert the 3.42-inch round. The longer cartridge should stick out further than the shorter round did. If it goes to the same depth, you can bet that the rifling in the throat is worn past serviceability. These are not exact tests, but they are good indicators of the length of free boring in the barrel. I have seen rifles that will swallow a round loaded to 3½ inches because of eroded rifling. This check is one of the critical ones in determining barrel serviceability.

The condition of the splines used to maintain the position of the gas cylinder is also critical. A visual inspection of their condition should reveal no deep peening or flattening. Measure the diameter of the spline section. The minimum acceptable diameter is .5995 inch. Examine the condition of the gas

port. Look for excessive erosion or evidence of it having been drilled out to a larger size.

The correct diameter of the gas port is .0805 inch, which is between a number 47 drill (.078 inch) and a number 46 drill (.0810). The gas port should accept the number 47 but usually will not accept a No. 46. If it will accept any drill larger than a 46, either the gas port has been drilled out to allow positive feeding with an undersized operating rod piston (or oversized gas cylinder) or it has eroded from years of use. Whatever the problem, such a barrel will have to be replaced.

Another part of the rifle which requires close examination is the operating rod. The part that must be measured is the small piston-like portion on the end which is about .125 inch long. Its diameter should be greater than .5255 inch. With an inside micrometer, check the inside diameter of the gas cylinder. No part of the gas cylinder's inner diameter should exceed .532 inches. If the piston's diameter is too small or the cylinder's interior too large, they will have to be replaced. Most new gas cylinders are .530 inch inside. Most unused pistons are .527 inch outside.

The operating rod should not touch the inside of the gas cylinder at any point. The wide rounded portion that engages the operating rod catch should barely touch the bottom of the barrel as the rod is worked forward and back. If you smear a little grease on the bottom of the thick part of the barrel (in front of the operating rod catch), the grease should smear lightly when the rod is worked back and forth.

Remove the follower rod and operating rod spring before checking the rod's fit in the gas cylinder or against the bottom of the barrel.

A normal operating rod should have two, *and only two*, bends in it. The bends have to be in the correct places or they will play havoc with the rifle's accuracy, cause accelerated wear to the inside of the gas cylinder and the out-

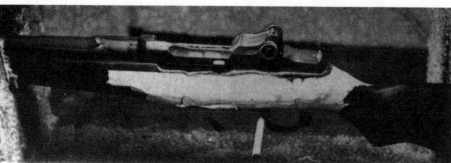

Left, John uses a drill to ream out the gas cylinder's rear ring. There must be enough clearance between the inside of the ring and barrel to prevent contact between them, even when the barrel heats up. Below, glass-bedding the M1 can be a messy operation. That's why John protects the outside of the stock with lots of tape. Note the unlocked trigger guard.

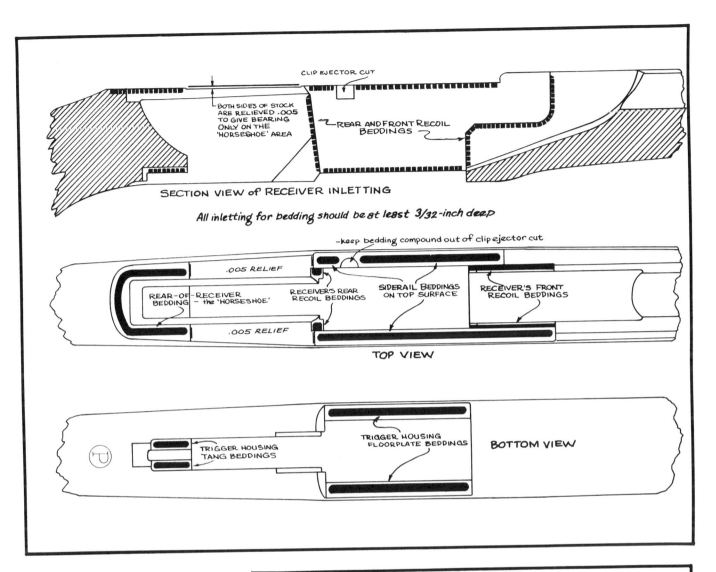

CLIP EJECTOR CUT

BOTH SIDES OF STOCK ARE RELIEVED .005 TO GIVE BEARING ONLY ON THE 'HORSESHOE' AREA

REAR AND FRONT RECOIL BEDDINGS

SECTION VIEW of RECEIVER INLETTING

All inletting for bedding should be at least 3/32-inch deep

-keep bedding compound out of clip ejector cut

.005 RELIEF

REAR-OF-RECEIVER BEDDING – the 'HORSESHOE'

RECEIVER'S REAR RECOIL BEDDINGS

SIDERAIL BEDDINGS ON TOP SURFACE

RECEIVER'S FRONT RECOIL BEDDINGS

.005 RELIEF

TOP VIEW

TRIGGER HOUSING TANG BEDDINGS

TRIGGER HOUSING FLOORPLATE BEDDINGS

BOTTOM VIEW

side of the gas piston. Bent operating rods will usually show up in the test described above.

Most armorers prefer the operating rod to lie to the left side of the opening in the stock ferrule, when the position of the operating rod is viewed with the rifle inverted. That is because the gas pressure will tend to straighten the operating rod during firing.

The operating rod's first bend is just forward of the thick portion that locks under the operating rod catch. The bend is bi-directional, in that the rod is bent up and slightly to the left when viewed from the top rear. The second bend begins about six inches from the end of the rod and aligns the last five inches of the rod with the inside of the gas cylinder.

There are special jigs needed to straighten bent operating rods. I use a small propane torch or a rosebud tip on an acetylene torch to heat the areas to be straightened. Once straightened the required amount, quickly quench the rod in cool water to keep from annealing the steel. Hydraulic presses and

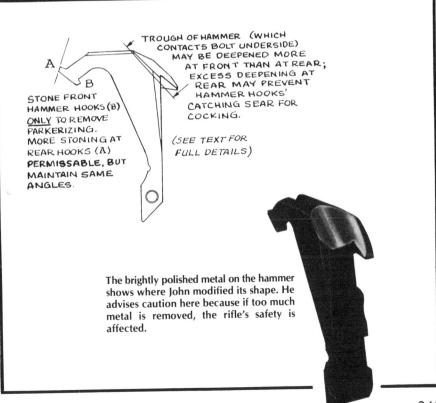

TROUGH OF HAMMER (WHICH CONTACTS BOLT UNDERSIDE) MAY BE DEEPENED MORE AT FRONT THAN AT REAR; EXCESS DEEPENING AT REAR MAY PREVENT HAMMER HOOKS' CATCHING SEAR FOR COCKING.

STONE FRONT HAMMER HOOKS (B) ONLY TO REMOVE PARKERIZING. MORE STONING AT REAR HOOKS (A) PERMISSABLE, BUT MAINTAIN SAME ANGLES.

(SEE TEXT FOR FULL DETAILS)

The brightly polished metal on the hammer shows where John modified its shape. He advises caution here because if too much metal is removed, the rifle's safety is affected.

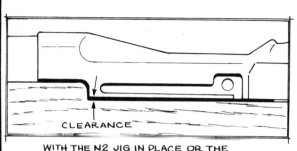

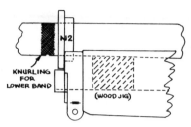

WOOD JIG MAY BE USED IN OPERATING·ROD CHANNEL INSTEAD OF N2 JIG

CLEARANCE

WITH THE N2 JIG IN PLACE OR THE WOOD JIG PROPERLY PLACED IN THE BARREL CHANNEL, THERE WILL BE CLEARANCE BETWEEN RECEIVER AND TOP OF STOCK — THIS MUST BE AT LEAST .030 TO GIVE CORRECT BEDDING TENSION. (THE GLASS BEDDING COMPOUND FILLS THIS GAP TO MAKE THE BEDDING SET·UP PERMANENT.)

LOCATION OF N2 OR WOOD JIG TO ESTABLISH CORRECT BEDDING PRESSURE AT RECEIVER.

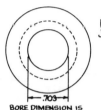

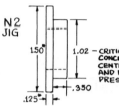

N2 JIG

BORE DIMENSION IS CRITICAL - IT MUST BE A SNUG FIT ON BARREL WHERE IT WILL REST ON STOCK FERRULE

1.02 — CRITICAL DIAMETER, AND MUST BE CONCENTRIC WITH JIG'S BORE TO CENTER BARREL IN STOCK CHANNEL AND PROVIDE CORRECT BEDDING PRESSURE AT RECEIVER

*FLANGE DIAMETER AND THICKNESS ARE NOT CRITICAL

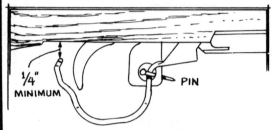

1/4" MINIMUM

PIN

TO CLAMP THE ACTION CORRECTLY DURING BEDDING, SET SAFETY FORWARD AND INSERT PIN OR NAIL AS SHOWN

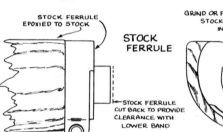

STOCK FERRULE EPOXIED TO STOCK

STOCK FERRULE

STOCK FERRULE CUT BACK TO PROVIDE CLEARANCE WITH LOWER BAND

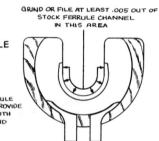

GRIND OR FILE AT LEAST .005 OUT OF STOCK FERRULE CHANNEL IN THIS AREA

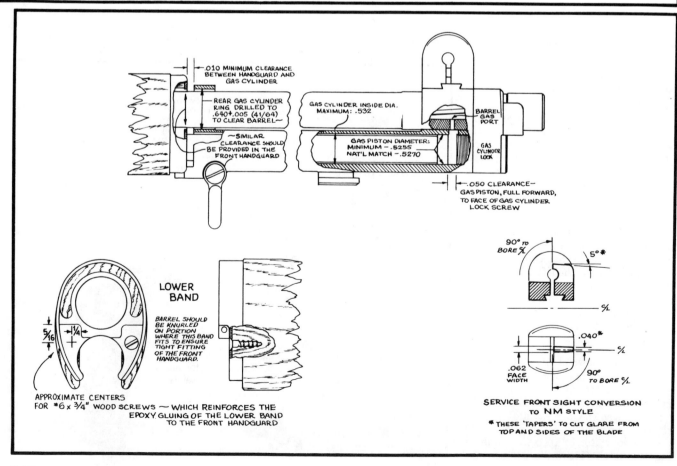

.010 MINIMUM CLEARANCE BETWEEN HANDGUARD AND GAS CYLINDER

REAR GAS CYLINDER RING DRILLED TO .640+.005 (41/64) TO CLEAR BARREL

SIMILAR CLEARANCE SHOULD BE PROVIDED IN THE FRONT HANDGUARD

GAS CYLINDER INSIDE DIA. MAXIMUM: .532

GAS PISTON DIAMETER: MINIMUM —.5255 NAT'L MATCH —.5270

BARREL GAS PORT

GAS CYLINDER LOCK

.050 CLEARANCE — GAS PISTON, FULL FORWARD, TO FACE OF GAS CYLINDER LOCK SCREW

LOWER BAND

BARREL SHOULD BE KNURLED ON PORTION WHERE THIS BAND FITS TO ENSURE TIGHT FITTING OF THE FRONT HANDGUARD.

5/16   1/4

APPROXIMATE CENTERS FOR #6 x 3/4" WOOD SCREWS — WHICH REINFORCES THE EPOXY GLUING OF THE LOWER BAND TO THE FRONT HANDGUARD

90° TO BORE ℄   5°*

℄

.040*

.062 FACE WIDTH   90° TO BORE ℄

SERVICE FRONT SIGHT CONVERSION TO NM STYLE

* THESE 'TAPERS' TO CUT GLARE FROM TOP AND SIDES OF THE BLADE

bending jigs do a better job of straightening rods, but this will do a good job if heat is limited to a minimum and the carbon is not burned out of the steel. It is a trial and error proposition and usually demands a great deal of patience.

Be very careful not to change the position of the handle end of the operating rod or it may bind in the track alongside the receiver during firing. After you are sure the operating rod is straight, put it in the receiver with the gas cylinder installed and see if the bolt will open and close as the rifle is tilted forward and back. The tip of the operating rod must not drag inside the gas cylinder at any point. The handle end of the operating rod must not move more than .03 inch away from the side of the receiver. When all else fails, buy a new operating rod.

It always requires the use of three hands to install the glass bedding compound to the stock prior to inserting the release-coated barreled action.

The first thing that must be done is to decide what glass bedding compound to use. I prefer Brownell's Acraglas Gel because it is easy to work and has sufficient rigidity to stay where it is placed. Brownell's regular Acraglas is good but it will run all over the place, even when mixed with the ''floc'' provided in the kit. Acraglas Gel is available from Brownell's, Montezuma, Iowa, and many other dealers, distributors and wholesalers, and the cost is reasonable. Each kit contains enough compound to bed at least two rifles.

Before working on the stock, look over the accompanying illustrations and note the areas that must be routed to accept the epoxy compound. Each area must be routed to allow a sufficient base for the compound, but not so much that the shrinkage of the bedding compound, which occurs normally, will affect the receiver's bedding.

The stock must be routed on the upper side and also on the lower. My procedure calls for router bits of two different diameters. I use a compound vise on a drill press to allow me to move the stock a round.

Depth of routing is controlled by the depth of the chuck, locked to that depth. I recommend routing to good wood (not oil soaked), but don't rout much deeper than .03 to .09 inch. Depths greater than that allow the bedding compound to shrink too much while drying.

Before routing, install the receiver in the stock and with a sharp knife, razor blade or pencil, trace the outline of the receiver and flat portion of the trigger

guard. That is done to restrict routing to the areas of the stock which serve as bearing surfaces and to keep as much of the bedding compound hidden under the supported areas of the action as possible. Nothing looks worse than dried bedding compound all over the top and bottom of a rifle.

After the receiver and trigger guard's outlines are traced, use a .125-inch diameter router to make a full deep cut inside the trace line to a depth of at least .09 (3/32 inch). This narrow cut will provide the bed for the compound. The cut should be in the center (as much as possible) of the bedded area. After the deep cuts are made, make shallow cuts over the whole area to be bedded. Cuts should be made deep enough to get to good wood which will provide the major support for the bedding. It's best to limit cuts to .030 (1/32 inch) to keep shrinkage to a minimum. All routing should be toward the inside of the stock. Do not rout outside the trace lines but up to them. Many articles have provided architectural drawings showing each cut as if it were destined to support the Golden Gate Bridge. These dimensions are just not that critical.

The idea is that the bedding should provide a perfect negative of the receiver and trigger housing in order to keep the receiver from assuming a different position in the stock after each shot. You may make routing cuts deeper and wider than those indicated with no ill effect on the accuracy of the finished product, but you must be careful not to cut too deep or bedding shrinkage may create a problem.

The hardest part of preparing the stock for the bedding compound is routing (or filing) out the interior parts of the stock to bed the recoil lugs and receiver tangs. I rout those portions of the stock a full .090 (3/32 inch) and the compound is used to build new bedding areas. This task will sometimes require the use of files, a Dremel tool, a carbide bit and chisels to remove enough wood for the new bedding surfaces.

There is one special jig which must be used when glass bedding the Garand. It is used to tilt the front of the receiver slightly upward when it is bedded. That angular mode is necessary to provide at least 20 to 40 pounds pressure between the lower band and stock ferrule. The pressure keeps the barrel from walking up the target as it warms up, bends and expands during firing.

I use a device similar to the N2 jig used to glass the receiver into position in the U.S. Army's specifications for the M14. It centers the barrel in the stock ferrule and raises it the required

amount to get correct pressure between the lower band and the stock ferrule when the rifle is reassembled after the glassing operation. The same amount of pressure can be obtained by placing a small wooden block .75 inch high, .50 inch wide and .75 inch long under the barrel just to the rear of the stock ferrule during glassing. The block won't center the barrel but it will set the same amount of tension at the lower band and stock ferrule as that provided by the N2 jig previously mentioned. When using the N2 jig, make sure it is up against the ferrule and its round body is laying in the ferrule.

Within the kit containing the bedding compound is a little bottle of release agent. It must be applied to all metal parts of the rifle so they can be freed from the stock once the compound sets up. *Put at least two coats* of the release agent on every part of the rifle which has a chance of coming into contact (either accidentally or on purpose) with the bedding compound. If you don't you will have a serious problem when you try to remove the barrel and receiver from the stock after the compound hardens. Fill every nook and cranny with the release agent, making sure that no part is left unprotected.

Read the directions included in the bedding compound kit and follow the instructions. Acraglas Gel is mixed in a 1:1 ratio. I mix the two parts in a small paper cup and stir them together with a tongue depressor. They must be mixed thoroughly.

Within the bedding kit is a small packet of tinting compound used to color the gel. It takes very little of this stuff to darken up the compound so mix it in gradually or you will end up with some really dark bedding. Try to match the color of the stock.

When installing the bedding compound, I use a large disposable hypodermic syringe (20 cc) that I get from a local veterinarian. I use the tongue depressor to push the compound down into the syringe and when it is full, I am ready to begin bedding.

Use masking tape to tape the sides of the stock adjacent to the areas to be bedded to keep the compound from contacting the wood. Since it is best to use more compound than actually needed, the masking tape provides a safety net to catch the surplus.

With the syringe (or other tool), place the compound on the top portion of the stock that has been routed out. Then put it on the areas within the stock that contain the recoil lugs and receiver tangs. Install the barrel and receiver after making sure the N2 jig (or stand-off block) is in position. Turn the barrel, receiver and stock over and fill in the routed areas on the bottom of the stock and then install the trigger guard.

The trigger guard, which will be installed during the operation, need not be complete but can be limited to four parts: trigger guard housing, trigger guard, hammer pin and safety. The rest of the assembly is not needed and only provides hiding places for surplus compound. Install the trigger guard on the trigger housing and pin it with the hammer pin. Put the safety lever into position within the trigger housing but remove the clip ejector spring.

With the trigger guard in the open-mode, install the assembly in the stock after it has been reinforced with bedding compound. Make sure the safety is in the off (forward) position and gradually close the trigger guard until you can inset a small nail in front of the trigger guard, through the hole in the safety lever. In that position, the trigger guard should be around ⅜ inch from the fully closed position. The nail will keep the trigger guard from opening and the pressure of the compound will keep it from closing.

Turn the rifle right side up, being careful not to let anything touch the trigger guard or the clearance between it and the trigger housing will be changed. Lay the rifle in a cradle while it dries; a warm light over the receiver will speed up the process.

The rifle can be removed from the stock when your fingernail won't make a deep mark in the bedding compound that oozed out as the receiver was snugged home by the trigger guard. Usually, drying takes two to two and a half hours (under a warm lamp); four hours if not left in a place with a temperature greater than 70 degrees F.

I never leave a barreled action in a stock for the recommended eight hours because it takes a lot of work to pry things apart if any of the bedding compound has found some spot inadvertently left unprotected by the release agent.

When you think the compound has set sufficiently, remove the nail and carefully open the trigger guard and pull it out of the stock. Clean off any excess compound from all parts of the trigger guard. That is a very delicate process and must be done carefully to keep from damaging the new bedding. With the rifle inverted, take a large brass drift or block of wood and stick it through the stock into the rear of the receiver. Using a good sized hammer, carefully drive the rear of the receiver

out of the stock. Try to drive it straight down, because that is the only way you will get it out of the stock without damaging the bedding.

With a sharp knife or razor blade, trim off all excess compound from the stock. Remove the masking tape from the sides of the stock because it will be harder to remove later. Clean off all excess compound and loose release agent from the rifle. Don't worry too much about the release agent because it can be removed later. Coat all metallic parts with oil, grease or wax and reassemble the rifle as it was during the drying process (exactly, nail and all). *Do not close the trigger guard completely.* Remember to reinstall the N2 jig (or stand-off block) in position. We want the assembled rifle to be exactly like it was during the setup process, but it will now be allowed to dry completely. Put it back in a cradle or rifle rack and allow it to dry at least 24 hours. Never fire a glass-bedded gun until the compound has cured at least 72 hours.

The front handguard and lower bands must be joined together. For the adhesive, I use Acraglas (not Acraglas Gel). It is reinforced by two No. 4 to No. 6 (½ inch long) wood screws.

The locations of the screw holes in the lower band are critical because of the lug on the lower band which contains the lower band pin. The locations indicated on the accompanying drawing are not exact, because each handguard is milled a bit differently. You will have to use some judgment when determining their exact locations.

The purpose of the screws is to hold the two parts together while the Acraglas is drying. They also help prevent vibration from upsetting the bond during firing. Other epoxy compounds may be substituted for Acraglas but make sure you always use the screws.

Countersinking the screw holes must be tackled with a very narrow tool because the clearance between the edges of the band and the lug for the lower band pin is so small. I use a 45-degree countersinking tool which was originally a carbide tipped router bit. It is about .375 inch wide. Anything wider won't countersink the holes without cutting up the lug and sides of the lower band. After the epoxy has dried, any part of the screws that protrude above the band surface should be dressed down.

The only other modification the lower band/front handguard assembly needs is to drill out the front end of the handguard and use a new, larger lower band pin. I use a standard ⁴¹⁄₆₄ drill to drill out the front end of the handguard from

.640 to .645 inch. Standard drill rod can be used to make the new lower band pin so it will make a tight fit in the hole of the lower band.

The rear handguard will have to be shortened at its aft end (adjacent to the receiver) to provide at least .03 inch clearance between it and the receiver. The bottoms of both sides will have to be filed to provide at least the same clearance between them and the stock. If these clearances are not provided, the rear handguard will exert pressure on the barrel as it heats up during firing and cause it to change point of impact. I also grind off the clips of the rear handguard band a little bit at a time until I can slip the band on the barrel with little difficulty. Don't grind too much off the clips or the handguard may slip back off the barrel.

The only modifications which must be made to the barrel are: knurling the area where the lower band is seated, and peening, ever so lightly, the splines to provide a tight fit for the front portion of the gas cylinder.

The part of the barrel upon which the lower band fits should be knurled until the lower band forms a tight fit on the barrel. The lower band must fit tight or it can affect accuracy and point of impact adversely. Care must be taken not to make the knurling too deep or it can damage the bore. Only knurl the barrel deep enough to provide a good tight fit of the lower band.

Before peening the splines, it is advisable to determine the location of the gas cylinder upon the barrel. Mr. Garand recommended that the gas cylinder be positioned so as to provide a gap between the operating rod and the gas cylinder lock screw at least .05 inch wide when the operating rod is completely forward and the lock screw is screwed down tight. With some barrels and gas cylinder locks, it is possible to close this gap to less than .05 inch, but that must be prevented because the gas reserve of the rifle will be affected adversely.

I use a No. 6 lead pellet to measure the gap. The shot pellet is inserted between the operating rod and gas cylinder lock screw and the bolt closed. The flattened piece of shot is measured, then the gas cylinder locked in place to provide a gap between the end of the operating rod and the gas cylinder lock screw of .05 inch. When the gas cylinder is installed in this manner, most tend to touch the front of the front handguard. The contacting surfaces must be relieved and care must be taken to ensure that the rear of the gas cylinder is square with its longitudinal axis.

Don't go crazy when peening the splines on the barrel because you can damage the interior of the bore. I make a scribe mark on the barrel after the location of the gas cylinder is determined, then remove the cylinder. The scribe mark, located to the rear of the front sight portion of the cylinder, indicates the most rearward areas of the splines that must be peened. The area just forward of the scribe mark is peened the heaviest. The peening is gradually decreased as you work forward. The cylinder is then installed and the gas cylinder lock is tightened down by bumping it with a plastic mallet until it is at six o'clock (lined up with the cylinder) and the front sight part is on the scribe mark. Do not tap the cylinder lock past the six o'clock position or you will move it forward when the lock screw is tightened down, and loosen it on the splines. Once the cylinder is installed, it is *never* removed from the barrel without re-peening the splines. You may remove the gas cylinder lock and gas cylinder lock screw for cleaning but don't mess with the gas cylinder unless you plan to tighten it again before putting the rifle back together. A loose gas cylinder will cause the front sight to assume a new position after each shot, which will wreak all sorts of havoc with grouping. I always put Locktite on the splines before assembly to ensure the cylinder stays in place. Do not put Locktite on the gas cylinder lock or lock screw unless you have a large screwdriver and hammer to remove them for cleaning once the Locktite has cured.

Other modifications to the gas cylinder include drilling out the rear ring to provide clearance between it and the barrel and removing enough metal from the rear end of the gas cylinder to provide at least .01 inch clearance between it and the front handguard when both are installed in their proper positions.

I also bevel the square lug on the rear of the gas cylinder to keep it from touching the sides of the front handguard. The lug has no functional purpose and it can just as easily be milled or filed off.

A word of caution about the gas cylinder. It is stainless steel and will not take Parkerizing or blueing. When I have to reblacken stainless steel, I use 1,600-degree paint (obtainable in most automotive parts stores) and put about two good coats of it on a degreasd gas cylinder. After the paint dries to the touch (about 30 minutes), it is put in a 600-degree (Fahrenheit) oven for about 30 minutes. After curing, the paint will be a flat black which does not go well

with the rest of the gun. To put a little sheen to it, coat the part in a good grease (any will work; I use light wheel bearing grease) and put it back into the oven at 400 degrees for about an hour. After the part cools, it will have the correct semi-gloss finish of the original gas cylinder, and that 1,600-degree paint won't come off, either.

One other part of the gas cylinder assembly needs to be carefully inspected before it is used on the finished rifle. The gas cylinder lock screw is made up of three parts: screw body, spring and valve. Occasionally the valve, which was installed because of the need to use the Garand to fire grenades, gets dirty around its seat in the case body and leaks gas. It is wise to depress the valve and clean the valve seat. That will help prevent gas leakage which can cause the rifle to short-cycle.

Unless the valve and valve seat are worn or corroded, this part doesn't have a great effect upon the functioning of the rifle. I recommend leaving it in, but keeping it clean and maintained. Occasionally, powder particles lodge under the valve and allow the escape of some gas but that can be checked by examining the cross-shaped hole on the front of the screw for traces of burned powder. If, after a thorough cleaning, the lock screw continues to leak, replace it with another valve type or try to find the original one-slot lock screw used on the early Garands.

There is not much work required to bring the trigger assembly up to National Match specifications but several parts do require some attention. Trigger action can be improved either by reducing trigger pull or smoothing out the convex portion of the hammer.

When reducing the pull, never touch the front hooks of the hammer except to smooth the Parkerizing finish and square up their surfaces with a small triangular-shaped oil stone. The rear hooks of the hammer are stoned to reduce the trigger pull. Try to maintain the angle on the hooks by stoning both hooks simultaneously. The final trigger pull is determined by the amount of pressure the sear requires to release the rear hammer hooks. The trigger pull of a Garand must exceed 4½ pounds. Lower pressures can cause the rifle to go full automatic if the engagement surfaces of the rear hammer hooks and sear are stoned too much. I usually set trigger pulls in the neighborhood of five pounds to allow for wear of the parts during firing.

The other part of the hammer that requires a few modifications is its convex portion. The angle of this groove is too

steep and causes undue wear on hammer and bolt. Study the acccompaning pictures and diagrams carefully to determine the correct modifications. Metal will have to be removed from the front of the groove, but remove as little from the rear of the groove as possible. Prussian blue can be used to coat the groove to indicate where bolt and hammer may be binding. As a rule, metal must be removed from the sides of the groove as well. That will widen the groove sufficiently to reduce friction between bolt and hammer. Remove as little metal from the rear surfaces of the hammer as possible because this affects the amount of engagement between hammer and trigger. Removing too much metal can prevent the hammer from cocking. Polish the new surface to a mirror finish to reduce friction to a minimum.

Ideally, the angle and width of the groove in the hammer should correspond exactly with the bottom surface of the bolt. Do not grind the spur on the left front side of the hammer (although metal may be removed from its right side, as viewed from above). It is a safety feature which pushes the hammer back from the firing pin during the first movement of the bolt.

There are many fine stock finishes that provide complete moisture protection to the wood stock if applied properly. Birchwood Casey's Tufsheen, a polyurethane varnish, provides excellent moisture protection in addition to a good tough abrasion resistant finish.

I usually sand and finish the stock prior to bedding but that chore can be undertaken after the bedding is completed, if you prefer. Sanding and raising the grain is done in the normal manner but make sure that there is no oil remaining on the stock. The finish won't adhere to an oily surface. Spray at least two coats everywhere, including the opening in the buttstock for the cleaning kit (two holes). If the rifle has already been bedded, keep the finish off the bedded areas. The outside of the stock should receive at least seven coats of Tufsheen. Sand it with 320 grit between every second coat. It is best to allow the first coat to dry at least 24 hours. If the weather permits, you can recoat it every 4 to 5 hours.

This is not the type of finish you try to make look like an oil finish. Don't sand it down to the bare wood after each coating, but let the layers build up, sanding just enough to allow good adhesion of succeeding coats and remove runs which constantly plague this kind of finish.

Care must be taken because the finish does not dry completely for 28 days. Polyurethanes and other finishes (lacquer excepted) dry from the outside in. When they are dry on the outside, they aren't necessarily so on the inside.

National Match sights are aftermarket items which are becoming quite rare. The rear sight base and windage knob for the Garand are a matched pair threaded with 64 threads to the inch. Standard bases and knobs for the M1 Garand and M14 are threaded 32 threads to the inch (tpi). Rear sight apertures for either the M1 or the M14 are threaded 32 to the inch. Rear sight apertures for either rifle will work with these sight bases.

If you are forced to use regular 32 tpi parts, the windage knob and receiver will have to be modified, a fairly easy operation. The windage knob will have to be ground with eight grooves (instead of the standard four) and a small .125-inch diameter hole will have to be drilled in the receiver to accept a small ball bearing to provide a detent surface for the new equally placed grooves. Instead of a 90-degree rotation for half-MOA windage adjustments (with the 64 tpi parts) it will take 45 degrees.

One final caution: if you find you must rebarrel the rifle, have a competent armorer or facility rebarrel it with a National Match barrel and have the headspace set between 1.940 and 1.942, and *specify that in writing*. Tight headspace will allow a slightly crush-fit to most cases and give years of shooting with no worries about incipient head separations. ●

Making Revolvers Shoot

Veral Smith

WHETHER USING JACKETED or cast bullets, attempting to develop revolver loads capable of precision accuracy is an effort in futility if the gun's critical dimensions are not given first consideration, and, if not right for best performance, corrected. Close tolerances are essential to any accuracy formula, and revolvers, with their complex lockwork and short bullets, require the ultimate in precision if accuracy is to be obtained. I no longer attempt to develop a load for a newly obtained revolver without first checking its critical dimensions and if necessary, correcting any flaws found.

As a general rule, you get what you pay for, and a revolver's dimensional tolerances and the quality of its bore will be proportionate to its purchase price when new. Bargain-priced six-shooters are usually strong and reliable but they seldom deliver 10-ring accuracy. Honed lockwork, lustrous finishes and quality barrels require more time and attention at the factory. Consequently, they bear higher price tags. Most mass-produced, rifled arms made today have mediocre bores which are too rough for top cast-bullet performance when new. Furthermore, bore diameter variations are common, especially in guns with barrel attachments forward of the chamber. Such variations can be due to imperfect machining but are most often caused by stresses created or released by work done on the barrel after the bore was rifled. Attaching a barrel to the receiver, or attaching something to a barrel by threads, welding or press fitting usually causes dimensional changes within the bore.

Small, tapped holes have little effect but machining a sight dovetail normally alters the bore diameter, especially if the barrel was button-rifled. Cold-working steel creates high internal stresses. Cutting a cold-formed piece of steel relieves stresses and causes it to bend. Cut rifling introduces few stresses and barrel blanks are almost always stress-relieved prior to machining. As a result, quality cut-rifled barrels tend to be more stable if they are subjected to any post-rifling machining.

Contouring barrels after button-rifling practically guarantees an increase in bore diameter proportional to the amount of external metal removed. In addition, the bores of almost all button-rifled sporter barrels are considerably larger at the muzzle than at the breech. Most revolver bores are choked where the barrel is screwed into the frame due to thread stresses, and frequently at the front sight, if it's welded or brazed on. Dan Wesson revolver bores are constricted about the same amount fore and aft, depending how tightly the barrel is torqued in. Contenders, with chambers shorter than the barrel's mounting lug, will have a smaller bore diameter in the lug area due to weld-caused shrinkage.

The most severe dimensional variations I've encountered have been in revolvers; the worst being a .0035-inch bore constriction where the breech was screwed into the frame. The least I've measured in that area was .001 inch.

In rifles, .0015 inch is the most I've encountered, while .001 is very common and to be expected in lower-priced models. Makers of the best target-grade barrels only guarantee a dimensional accuracy about .0002 in their premium barrels and as I recall, about .0005 inch in standard barrels. The best barrels I've measured are hammer-forged Remingtons.

Most revolvers can be made right in about one or two hours, while those which need cylinder throats enlarged may require three to four hours — a small price for the resultant improvement in performance.

I won't attempt to explain how to correct cylinder misalignment because few shooters have the required skill or equipment. It is a very common problem though. If you have a gun with a misaligned cylinder, don't give it up without a fight. The detrimental effects of misalignment can be partly overcome by carefully tuning a load, and if

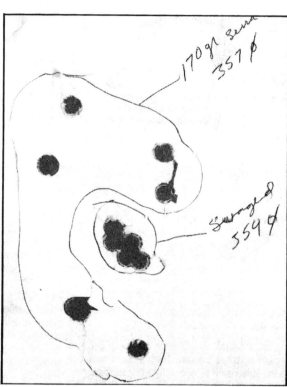

The four-inch pattern in the photograph was fired with .357-inch bullets in a bore which had been lapped to .3579 inch. The one-inch group was fired through the same barrel with custom-swaged .359-inch bullets.

shooting cast bullets, by using very hard alloys and a heavy-duty lubricant.

Avoiding the problem is much easier than trying to fix it, so let me explain how to check for misalignment before purchasing a revolver. Incidentally, cylinder alignment on both the test revolvers used for this article was checked prior to purchasing. Neither is perfect but their misalignment is barely visible, which is better than average.

Make certain the gun is unloaded, then with your back to the sun or a bright light and the barrel pointed straight at the light source, look down the bore. When the light source is where it should be, the light will shine down the barrel. If there is serious misalignment, it will illuminate one side of the cylinder's front edge. Repeat that with each chamber, keeping track of the direction and approximate amount of misalignment of each chamber.

If no chamber is visibly out of alignment, buy the gun! That kind will shoot almost any load accurately and all other potential problems you might encounter

can be corrected easily.

If varying amounts of misalignment, and misalignment in different directions, can be seen, bullet impact will shift relative to the direction and amount of misalignment. Look for another gun.

Having all chambers off the same amount in one direction normally doesn't cause the impact point to shift, but may either make tight groups impossible or a little harder to obtain, depending on the amount of misalignment.

I know of no simple or inexpensive solution for either vertical or varying lateral misalignment. If misalignment is lateral and all the error is on the same side, an experienced pistolsmith can retime the gun quite inexpensively.

If the gun has a considerable amount of lateral cylinder play and the chambers are out of line an equal amount on both sides, performance should be the same as for a gun which locks up tightly. Again, if misalignment is uniform laterally but lockup is loose,

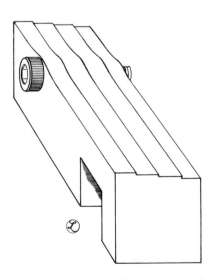

To demonstrate the effect of torquing a threaded screw home, Veral milled three steps (each .0002 inch lower than the other) on the top of a steel block, drilled and tapped a hole through it, then snugged a screw home. Next, he began lapping the steps away. The highest (that nearest the viewer) was almost completely removed when the lap began leveling the second step and just a bit of the third in the area above the screw. Hard to believe that seating a screw would cause the metal above it to bulge like that but Veral estimates the steel there rose about .0005 inch.

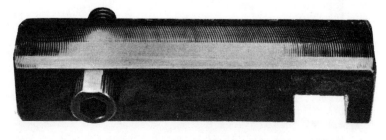

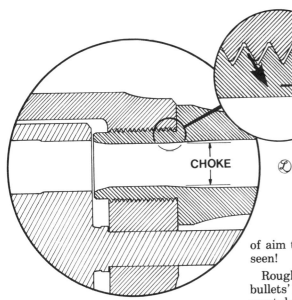

When a conventional revolver barrel's shoulder butts up against the frame, torque forces the mating thread surfaces to ride down in the direction of the longitudinal pull, creating a slight constriction in the bore over the length of the entire threaded area.

a pistolsmith can correct the problem easily.

Bore finish is of little concern when only jacketed bullets are used. At worst, a shooter will notice slightly increased jacket fouling for the first several hundred shots. For cast-bullet shooters who otherwise know how to make lead bullets work, rough bores are probably the most common cause of inaccuracy. Surprisingly, I don't recall ever reading about a good home cure or a method of ascertaining whether roughness is a problem or not. The most common advice for smoothing a rough bore is, "shoot jacketed bullets for a while," but that's only partly effective.

If barrel roughness, severe enough to affect lead bullet performance, were visible to the naked eye, life would be easier. Unfortunately, there are only two ways to identify it, by shooting and by feeling resistance when pushing a lead slug through the bore.

To detect a rough bore by shooting, one should start by checking the accuracy of a cylinderful of properly fitted, low-velocity, plain-based, lead bullet loads (under 800 fps). If accuracy is good, increase the powder charge a bit and shoot another cylinderful. Repeat that until maximum accurate velocity is determined. Start with soft bullets (8 to 12 Bhn). After their velocity limit is found, try hard, plain-based (20 Bhn or more), then hard, gas-checked bullets. Roughness is definitely a problem if plain-based lead bullets can only be stabilized at low velocities, sometimes as low as 800 fps. Instability is normally evidenced by slight bullet tipping (elliptical holes) in close range targets and by wild, tumbling bullets at longer ranges. At 50 or more yards, keyholing in the target is often evident. On a dirt bank 200 yards away, bullets fly several feet apart when pushed past their limit, frequently striking so far from the point

of aim that the impact point can't be seen!

Rough bores literally abrade the bullets' bearing surfaces away, with the most damaged area being between the bullet and the driving side of the lands. Hard alloys probably won't give an appreciable increase in accurate velocity over soft bullets but gas-checked bullets always give a dramatic improvement in both accuracy and maximum accurate velocity limit.

Magnum revolver bores in good condition will stabilize soft bullets when driven as fast as 1,200 to 1,400 fps and with good loads, should produce groups spanning three inches or less at 25 yards. Hard bullets will normally tighten groups appreciably at those velocities and probably shoot accurately at speeds up to 1,600 fps or the gun's limit for the bullet weight. In both cases, bore leading shouldn't be a problem if a high quality bullet lube is employed. Even so, bullet stability at long range should not be completely lost. Poor groups can be expected when a given bullet is driven beyond its alloy's capability but bullets should fly point-forward and be reasonably well stabilized. Gas-checked bullets with a hardness exceeding 14 Bhn should equal or surpass jacketed-bullet accuracy, while bettering jacketed-bullet velocity by at least 100 fps.

The presence of a rough bore isn't normally announced by severe leading when using loads that shoot with reasonable accuracy. A gray wash of lead is often the only visible hint of roughness within the bore. I have seen the driving side of rifling lands choked full of lead in several guns which had been fired perhaps a hundred times with wild-flying bullets. In one .45 Auto, ribbons of lead could be seen hanging from the leading edges of the rifling lands. If accuracy is so poor that bullets fly several feet wide at 100 yards or so, the bullet's entire outer surface is probably being stripped away to groove diameter by the rifling lands. If a revolver throws plain-based cast bullets wild at velocities below 1,200 fps or so, and you feel reasonably sure the bullets and lube

are good, the problem is almost certainly a rough bore. Lapping is the cure.

After continued shooting of plain-based bullets, visible lead buildup in the throat is normally caused by the lubricant's failure rather than bore roughness. A thin layer of lead confined to the grooves but leaving the lands clean, is evidence of undersized bullets which are too hard to obturate. A lead wash over the bore's full length, or at the muzzle, or a lead star decorating the crown, is evidence of lube breakdown. That last condition may be improved by lapping the bore if velocity of the problem load is under 1,400 fps and a high quality lube is used — providing the bullet design is good and pressures are reasonable, of course.

The following shows the most productive sequence for checking a gun's dimensions and fitting bullets.

Measure the bore diameter and check for bore constriction first. To do that, slug the bore by shooting a soft bullet through it with a squib load of about 1.5 grains of Bullseye or some other fast powder. Catch the bullet in a cardboard box of rags. Insert the recovered bullet into the muzzle, then use a rod or wooden dowel to push it back through the bore, feeling for resistance and variations in resistance. (Be sure the bore is clean, as fouling reduces bore diameter.)

It is almost impossible to find a top quality bore in a recently manufactured revolver if the barrel hasn't been lapped, or had a fairly large number of heavy jacketed loads fired through it. If a lead slug is forced through a good bore, it will offer even, smooth resistance all the way from muzzle to breech — or even better, be tightest at the muzzle. If you get so lucky, check each of the cylinder throats as explained later. If the gun has seen little use, the slug will probably slide loosely down the bore until it meets the almost inevitable bore constriction where the barrel is screwed into the frame. At that point, a noticeable increase in resistance will be felt. If the bore is rough, resistance will feel gritty.

Dan Wessons are normally tight at both ends of the barrel and loose in between, as they have the same sized threads and amount of tension at both ends. A few hundred fairly heavy loads with jacketed bullets wears the first choke away just a mite, leaving what is essentially a tapered bore to grip the bullet as it exits the muzzle. That

To measure chamber mouth diameters, Veral depends on a snap gauge (top) and a small-hole gauge (bottom).

Bullet-to-throat clearance can be checked by inserting a strip of aluminum foil between the bullet's side and the throat. It may take more than one thickness of foil to do the job. Once the gap between bullet and throat has been filled, the foil thickness(es) can be miked to determine the amount of clearance.

muzzle choke probably has more to do with the Dan Wesson accuracy reputation than the stretched barrel theory.

The remedy for constrictions and roughness is to lap the bore. When working with a Dan Wesson, I lap the barrel with the barrel nut tightened just enough to hold the barrel securely. After the bore is smooth and straight, I torque the nut to shooting tension and lap the forcing cone choke, leaving just a slight choke at the muzzle about .0005 inch.

A .357 Ruger Super Blackhawk had what I thought was an above-average bore. Initial slugging indicated a maximum groove diameter of .357 inch, constricted to slightly under .357 where the breech was threaded into the frame. The standard diameter bore was a pleasant surprise because 17 recently manufactured Rugers measured had bores from .001 to .003 inch oversize, with none at or less than standard jacketed bullet diameter. (The cited .357 is one of the discontinued 9mm/.357 conversion models.) Lapping its bore required less than an hour and yielded a final groove diameter of .3579. That was the greatest diameter increase of any bore I've lapped. Normally, the largest pre-lap diameter will become more than .0002 inch larger. Except for the constriction at the breech, very little metal removal is required to smooth the average bore. As a rule, only the high rough spots need to be leveled. A cutting tool (lap) does it quickly and with precise control. Smoothing a bore by shooting relatively non-abrasive jacketed bullets is a very slow, expensive process and offers no control as to where the wear will take place.

After making sure the bore has a smooth surface and a uniform diameter (visually, and by judging lap resistance), wipe the lap and bore clean, tighten the lap up in the bore as though lapping, then measure the lap to determine the final groove diameter.

After obtaining the bore's groove diameter, use a small-hole or snap gauge to measure the cylinder throats. Small-hole and snap gauges are sold by machine tool dealers for about $12 to $20, depending on brand name. Any

Above, jacketed softnoses modified for testing: (1) .357-inch 110-grain Nosler; (2) the same bullet bumped up to .3589 inch; (3) .357-inch 170-grain Sierra; (4) the Sierra bumped up to .3589 inch. Cast bullets can also be bumped up: (5) .357-inch, as-cast Lyman bullet from an unmodified mould; (6) the same bullet after the lower lubricating ring had been squared; (7) After the mould was modified to a truncated conical shape and the bullet was bumped to .3589, it looked like this.

In the right rear, a C-H finish-swaging die. It can be used to bump up bullets in a conventional loading press in addition to its primary role. If the desired bullet diameter is non-standard, C-H dies will have to be lapped or a set of custom dies, like those from Bullet Swaging Supply in the foreground, can be employed.

dealer or machinist will explain how to use them. They are simply gauges adjusted to fit whatever hole is to be measured. The gauge's diameter is then measured with a micrometer.

If small-hole gauges aren't available, or if the barrel has an uneven number of grooves, making measurement of the slug difficult, check the throats by inserting the bore slug in each cylinder throat. If it doesn't slip through each throat easily, the throats are undersized and should be enlarged by lapping.

Bullet-to-throat clearance can be

checked by inserting a strip of aluminum foil or some other sheet of known thickness alongside the bullet. Standard weight kitchen foil is usually .0005 inch thick, while heavy duty foil is .001 inch thick, making them excellent feeler gauges. Just cut strips of the foil and stack the assortment needed to obtain a tight fit. Measure the stack with a micrometer to determine the amount of clearance.

Although revolvers with throat diameters several thousandths of an inch larger than groove diameter may be encountered, and can perform well with properly fitted bullets, most throats will be fairly close to groove diameter, or slightly smaller. In my experience, ideal cylinder throat diameter for either cast or jacketed bullets is .002 over groove diameter, as it offers optimum latitude in bullet fitting.

For low-velocity, cast-bullet target guns with near-perfect cylinder alignment, cylinder throats .001 over groove diameter may give the best results. Throat wear will never be a problem and minimum bullet deformation should provide a slight accuracy edge. Minimum cylinder throat diameters demand very precise bullet fitting.

In magnum revolvers, or any revolver which will be used extensively with jacketed bullets, throat wear will be a problem after a few thousand rounds. To compensate for throat wear before it happens, lap cylinder throats two thousandths of an inch larger than the barrel's groove diameter if cast bullets will be used extensively. Lap them .001 inch larger if jacketed bullets will be used exclusively.

After ascertaining that a revolver's cylinder throats are larger than its groove diameter, bullets should be fitted so they just slide easily through the throats. A clearance of .0005 inch seems about right for most revolvers. If cylinder throats are at least .001 larger than groove diameter, I've never had bullets so fitted fail to perform well. A .001 inch bullet-to-throat clearance works as well with 20± Bhn cast bullets if throats are at least .002 over groove diameter.

On the other hand, revolvers having cylinder throats slightly larger than groove diameter are very sensitive to cast bullet diameters. Bullets which fit the throats tightly give inferior accuracy while hard bullets which are too small to fill the barrel's grooves cause bore leading and deliver poor accuracy. That explains my reasons for recommending throat diameters .002 inch over groove diameter.

Anyone who has read extensively about developing cast handgun loads knows the importance of obturation in controlling bore leading. Though leading by undersized (smaller than groove diameter) bullets can be effectively controlled by adjusting bullet hardness to give optimum obturation, I've never had them produce the accuracy of hard bullets which fill the grooves completely.

The reason soft, undersized bullets give inferior accuracy is because the bullet's forepart doesn't expand appreciably, its only guidance being that obtained from the rifling lands.

Guns with precise cylinder alignment can give phenomenal accuracy with soft, undersized bullets but the slightest cylinder misalignment will mash one side of the bullet's forward driving bands into the rifling until support is gained at the groove bottoms, leaving the opposite side of the bullet nose unsupported and the bullet's longitudinal axis out of line with the bore's.

A hard alloy bullet, slightly larger than bore diameter, is forced to center itself in the bore, even if cylinder misalignment is quite serious. Forcing cone angle and smoothness, bullet design and the lubricant's ability to make the bullet slip into proper alignment rather than abrade and deform also have a tremendous influence on accuracy. If your revolver's cylinder is out of line, and most are, give careful attention to the above details. Revolvers with visible cylinder misalignment derive much greater benefit from heavy duty lubricants than revolvers with well-aligned throats. Furthermore, the best bullet designs are the long bearing, cast bullets with relatively wide forward driving bands, an alloy hardness rating of at least 20 Bhn, and a diameter considerably larger than the groove's (with properly oversized throats, of course).

Jacketed bullets are tough and abrasion-resistant, making them more tolerant of poor fit than cast bullets are. Even so, optimum fit for jacketed bullets is essentially the same as it is for their cast counterparts — and just as critical. If the bore diameter is larger than the jacketed bullets' diameters, custom swaging offers the only answer. With a given bullet weight and powder charge, jacketed bullets which fit the bore tightly develop considerably higher pressures than do undersized bullets. If they are .001 to .003 smaller than groove diameter, they can be pushed to higher velocities due to reduced friction, yet will give acceptable accuracy.

If a revolver is to fire standard-diameter jacketed bullets exclusively, don't lap the bore larger than the bullet's diameter because bore roughness is far less detrimental to jacketed bullet performance than an oversized bore. Lap only if you're willing to swage or re-swage jacketed bullets or switch to cast bullets which can be easily fitted. To bump jacketed bullets up to proper size, inexpensive swaging dies for .38 and .44-caliber bullets can be obtained from C-H and enlarged to the needed diameter. They are of excellent quality and designed to work in heavy duty loading presses. If you'd like to swage bullets from raw material, their complete two-die set can be purchased for about $45, while jackets and lead core wire can be obtained from C-H or any of several other sources. Though C-H only lists the full set of two swage dies in their catalog, Tony Sailor informed me they'll sell only the finish swage die for half the two-die set price. That is the only die needed to re-swage factory bullets.

If you opt to swage from components, a canneluring tool and lead wire cutter will also be needed to round out the equipment. C-H sells only standard diameter dies and will not supply custom diameter dies, so you'll have to lap them to the correct diameter or order custom dies from another manufacturer.

If you prefer to purchase custom diameter swaging dies, Bullet Swaging Equipment will make dies to fit standard loading presses in any diameter or shape desired. They provided the excellent quality die I used to re-swage .44-caliber bullets. BSE dies require a special swaging press which can be obtained from either Bullet Swaging Supply or Corbin. I assume Corbin would also provide custom diameter dies for loading presses but I'm not certain as the catalog I received upon inquiry left me wondering.

Cast bullets, on the other hand, do not produce markedly higher pressures when fitted tightly but are capable of their highest velocity and accuracy. Furthermore, when optimum bullet hardness is coupled with a high quality lubricant and a smooth bore, maximum velocity of cast bullets in magnum revolvers can be as much as 300 fps higher than properly fitted jacketed bullets of the same weight, fired at equal pressures. Soft cast bullets protected by mediocre lubes, however, cannot match jacketed bullet velocities at equal pressures. ●

Smoothing

Lapping lugs and polishing guide surfaces can work wonders

OW OFTEN DO WE SEE a sparkling new custom rifle fitted with match grade barrel, super-fine trigger, beautifully bedded and finished stock but with no effort expended on improving the quality of the action? This, no doubt, is simply because most shooters assume that everything about a rifle action is as it should be and no refinements other than a nice blue job and perhaps a bolt jeweling is possible. "After all," the reasoning goes, "a modern turnbolt action is designed to hold pressures well in excess of 50,000 psi,

so it has to be right when it comes from the manufacturer — right?"

Wrong!

Though only a fraction of a percentage of modern actions fail under the pressure of test firing, the odds against a new two-lug bolt bearing evenly in the receiver are something like three to one. While one lug holds firmly, the other (or others) may be free of any contact by as much as .006-inch. This, of course, means that all is not well, because a single lug is holding the entire load.

This is more prevalent with *new* ac-

tions simply because in some older actions, especially if they are of rather soft steel, the condition will correct itself as the lug receiving the greater pressure sets back until the pressure is more or less equalized. This is not good either, because excessive headspace may have been created. It may take surprisingly few shots, by the way, for the lugs to "set back" in the rear wall of the lug recess of some actions — helping to make it difficult to open. Some of the otherwise beautifully made '98 Mausers shipped to the South American republics are so soft that the lug set back when the piece was testfired and had excessive headspace thereafter.

I've personally inspected a number of what appeared to be new and unused arms that had a distinct depression in the lug recess where one of the lugs set back. I suspect that these rifles were fired no more than twice: once by the German manufacturer and once again by the purchasing government. The soft receivers notwithstanding, there would surely have been less setback, or none at all, if the two lugs had borne evenly.

In the case of harder receivers, especially those of more recent American manufacture, the lugs probably won't set back at all and a single lug continues to hold all the pressure. I recently removed the barrel from a Model 70 Winchester of about 1960 manufacture

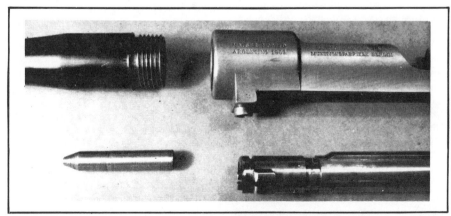

The basic requirements for lapping bolt locking lugs to a smooth fit are a stub of barrel, a dummy steel "cartridge" and a lapping compound. If done properly, the lugs will mate perfectly against the receiver, insuring distribution of firing stresses over the widest possible area, and improving accuracy and smoothness of operation.

256

Bolt Actions

By JIM CARMICHEL

in .264 Winchester Magnum chambering and found no sign of setback despite the fact that the "lazy" lug had never contacted the receiver.

From this one might assume that only one lug is needed anyway, so there is no need to worry about it. An action with two primary lugs was designed with the intent of both lugs bearing evenly and fully. Likewise, modern high-intensity cartridges are loaded to pressure levels which assume maximum holding efficiency from the rifle's action A bolt that is hanging on by only one lug certainly is not performing at the anticipated level.

Too, lugs which bear unevenly do not in any way contribute to top accuracy. This is why knowledgeable bench rest shooters insist on lapped locking lugs and top gunsmiths consider lug lapping, or at least an inspection

for proper bearing, an important part of fitting a barrel.

The importance of at least a lug inspection was made startlingly clear only recently when a routine lug check of a new action of excellent reputation disclosed that *neither* lug was in contact and the full load would be placed on the safety lug. If that action had fallen into the hands of a gunsmith who fitted barrels without checking the lugs, the results might have been unfortunate indeed. Fortunately, however, the gunsmith was Paul Marquart of A&M Rifle Company, where a lug contact inspection and correction (if needed) is standard operating procedure.

Paul also points out that in the case of rather roughly machined lugs and receivers lapping is advisable even when the contact is uniform. The tool marks should be lapped off so that two polished surfaces are joining. Likewise,

there are instances where the mating surfaces have galled somewhat and should be polished. This is especially prevalent in Remington rifles that have been fired extensively or without proper care to keep grit out of the lug cuts.

How does one go about checking the lug contact and lapping for an even fit? A check for relative contact is accomplished easily enough by simply coating the rear of the lugs with layout blue and then closing the bolt in the receiver. Some care, however, must be taken to make sure that the bolt is being pushed *straight* to the rear just as it would be by the rearward thrust of a cartridge at the instant of firing.

You can *not*, for example, duplicate this rearward pressure simply by exerting rearward pressure on the bolt handle nor will the mainspring's rearward pressure on the bolt when the piece is cocked suffice. The natural looseness in the receiver (some more than others) will allow the bolt to cock out of proper alignment and give a false reading. This false reading, by the way, will usually show that the lugs are bearing evenly.

The correct technique is to use a headspace gauge, dummy cartridge or even a cartridge case with the necessary thickness of shim material between the face of the bolt and the head of the case — after removing the cocking piece and extractor. The idea is to get a firm in-line pressure parallel to the axis of the bore. Thus, with the pressure distributed over the face of the bolt and thus holding it at a right angle to the axis of the bore, "cocking" out of true alignment will be largely eliminated and the lugs will bear on the receiver as they do when the rifle is fired.

If the layout blue is scraped from the rear of both lugs smoothly and fully, it

Applying layout blue to the lugs on a stripped bolt and applying pressure to a bolt face will show how evenly the lugs are bearing, and over how wide an area. The lug at right shows firm contact over about one-half of its surface — better than many. After a fine grit lapping compound is applied to the rear lugs, the steel dummy "cartridge" is inserted into the chamber and the receiver screwed on until the bolt will barely close. Rapidly cycling the bolt while maintaining firm pressure against the face will insure a perfect lapping job.

Bright wear streaks along, or around, bolts show the high-friction areas which are the cause of "stickiness." Diagonal wear streaks, center, are an indication of burrs or bumps which "bite" as the bolt is being locked.

means that both lugs are bearing evenly, and all is well. On the other hand if the blue is peeled from only one lug, it means that that lug is taking all the load. There are, of course, any number of conditions which will be indicated by the imprint on the blue. One lug, for example, may be found to bear fully while only a part of the other lug touches. Or, only a small part of both lugs will touch. Any of these conditions is just cause for lapping. You may wonder at this and question the need for lapping when both lugs are contacting equally if not fully.

If the lugs do not contact the receiver fully, it means that the full thrust, when transmitted to the receiver, is distributed over a relatively small area. This is more likely to result in setback and also tends to make the bolt harder to open.

The same principles which apply to checking the lug's contact also apply to the actual lapping operation. Namely that the firm, direct pressure must be applied to the face of the bolt. Perhaps the best and simplest method is that shown in the accompanying illustrations.

An old barrel is used in conjunction with a steel dummy of approximate cartridge dimensions. The dummy, however, is longer than a normal cartridge. For actions with difficult-to-remove extractors, such as the Remington 700, the head of the dummy should be less than normal case head size so the extractor can be left in place without bearing. With the barrel held fast in a vise, the action is screwed on and the dummy inserted in the chamber. Since the dummy is longer than a cartridge, the bolt will not close; so, with closing pressure held on the bolt handle, the receiver is backed off the barrel shank until the bolt will just close. This gives a firm rearward force to the bolt lugs

Roughness on the bolt body can be polished with a hard Arkansas stone. Bolt ways in the receiver are most easily polished with a piece of wood shaped to the approximate size, with 400-grit or finer finishing paper stapled or glued to it. Note that the action has been completely disassembled to avoid getting grit into delicate parts.

against the receiver. Lapping is accomplished by coating the lugs with a lapping compound and raising and lowering the bolt handle in rapid cycle. As the lapping advances there will be a corresponding lessening of pressure on the bolt handle. To increase the pressure, simply advance the receiver on the barrel shank.

I've heard it suggested that a spring-loaded dummy be fashioned which will keep a steady pressure on the face of the bolt during the lapping operation. This sort of a device, however, would not be good. It would aid in polishing the mating surfaces, to be sure, but the spring load would allow the lugs to ride over the high spots and at the same time apply pressure to the low spots. In other words, lap the "valleys" as well as the tops of the mountains. The advantage of the solid dummy is that pressure is applied only to the high spots.

It is possible to lap the lugs with the present barrel in place by using a carefully fitted dummy, headspace gauge or even a shimmed cartridge case. Of course, shims must be added as the lapping progresses. The wisdom of using a good headspace gauge for this work is questionable, simply because of its contact with an abrasive action. A maximum gauge may thus become a minimum gauge after a few jobs.

Another problem of lapping lugs with the fitted barrel in place is that you may create a condition of excessive headspace. On an average, a lapping operation will remove from .002 to .003 of metal, but in extreme cases as much as twice that may be removed. Thus, if you already have maximum headspace, the additional removal of metal could result in a critical situation. In this case the correct procedure would be to turn the barrel in a thread and rechamber — or else use only neck-sized handloads that have been fire-formed in that chamber.

The lapping medium can be Fine grinding compound or a fine abrasive flour (about 120 grit) mixed in light grease or petroleum jelly. Simply smear a bit of the lapping compound on the rear surfaces of the lugs and have at it. Be sure to keep the compound off the face of the bolt or you'll be lapping it, too. In fact, it's a good idea to put a dab of lubricant on the bolt face to reduce friction against the dummy or whatever you're using.

There are some "self-destructing" lapping compounds available which break down with use and offer no further abrasive action. The one tried, however, quit before the job was completed, requiring additional applications.

When the lugs are completely and properly lapped, the surfaces are well polished and it is easy enough to tell by looking that the bearing surfaces contact fully and evenly. Just out of curiosity, however, you may want to put on another coat of layout blue and check everything again. Now, wash the the lapping compound off and the job is done.

With the lugs now seating so well and working so smoothly, you'll probably want to get the rest of the action slicked up. What seems to be a rough, sticky bolt can often be made to run a lot slicker with a bit of touching up here and there.

One way to make a bolt run smoothly is to simply lay on the buffing wheel with a heavy hand and thus peel off a few thousandths. Actually, this may do more harm than good in that it makes the bolt loose and wobbly and just as likely to "grab" in the receiver. Bolts that run in and out with silky smoothness are usually rather closely fitted to the receiver but have no "catch" or "grab" points. Examples of this are Krag and Mannlicher actions which are extremely close-fitted yet are unmatched for smoothness.

After a bolt has been worked a bit, the points of maximum resistance will become apparent in the form of line-like worn spots. These lines may run the full length of the action but also can be found running radially or in an angled direction. This latter is caused by abrasive points on the downstroke.

First of all, match these lines up with the offending points in the receiver and see if there are any burrs resulting from the manufacturing process. If so, these should be polished out at once. Also, check for "puckers" where the receiver has been drilled and tapped for sights or scope mounts. It is even possible that sight mount screws are extending through the receiver walls and scraping against the bolt.

Perhaps the most common offenders, are the top, lower and outside surfaces of external claw-type extractors on Mausers, Springfields, Pre-'64 M-70's, etc. A quick glance will show where they are rubbing.

The situation can be corrected by stoning the scraped areas until contact

is reduced or eliminated. Friction between the bolt lugs and bolt ways is reduced by stoning the lugs with a hard Arkansas stone and polishing the ways with fine (400 grit or finer) finishing paper. A good technique here is to cut a piece of hardwood so that it approximately matches the inside cut of the receiver. Attach the finishing paper to the stick with glue or staples and proceed to polish the inside of the receiver to a fine brightness. Not only does this make the action work smoother, it looks a lot better. Most custom gun makers prefer to polish the inside of the receiver in this manner after the gun has been blued. This takes out any final roughness and the brightly polished inside looks mighty good against the blue exterior. Very professional.

A handy tool for "erasing" rough or high spots is the Dremel Moto-Tool with an abrasive impregnated rubber wheel. These wheels come in assorted sizes to match different contours. My personal experience with the Dremel tool is that the variable speed rheostat is very worthwhile in that the Moto-Tool's normal top operating speed causes the polishing wheel to skip and bounce. Reducing the speed makes it much easier to handle and the results are as good as fine hand polishing. So, for this reason I consider the Dremel Veriable Speed unit a very worthwhile investment. (You can use it on your other power tools, too.)

An Arkansas stone can also be used to polish the bolt at points of hard contact with the receiver. This sounds like work, but removing only a slight bit of roughness will sometimes work wonders. Remember, even if the inside

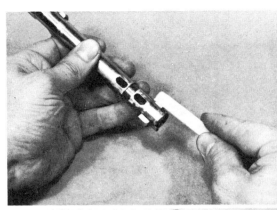

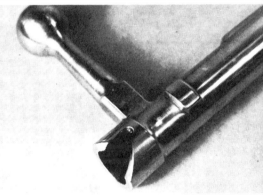

259

of the receiver and the bolt's surface are both rough, you only have to polish one or the other to make the contact comparatively friction-free. A rough surface rubbing over another rough surface causes lots of friction. A *slick* surface against a rough surface is nearly as good as two slick surfaces. If you doubt this, try running a piece of sandpaper over a piece of glass. This is why an action can be made to work so much more smoothly by simply having a few key contact points on the bolt.

One final thing, and I saved this for last so you won't forget: Be sure and remove the trigger assembly, sear or cocking piece and firing mechanism before attempting any lapping or polishing projects. Abrasives can and will play hell with a trigger mechanism and won't help the rest of the delicate parts either.

●

CORRECTING the REVOLVER'S CRITICAL DIMENSIONS

By VERAL SMITH

ROUGH BORES and the improper fit of bullet to gun are probably the two most common causes of unsatisfactory cast-bullet performance in revolvers. The gun's bore and throat finishes and diameters should be the cast shooter's primary concern. Second in importance is bullet fit. The most experienced cast-bullet shooter cannot get top performance if those factors are ignored. On the other hand, a beginner can get fair performance if bullet fit is correct and the bore is good. Since relatively few handgunners seem concerned about bore quality, I'll describe some of the problems I've encountered, identify their causes, then explain how to correct the most serious problems.

Most handgun purchasers base their selection on a pistol's cost, the way it looks, feels, and functions. Manufacturers know that and compete for the market accordingly. Reduction of bore quality is an extremely effective production cost cutter so if you didn't buy a gun with a decent barrel and want improved performance, it is going to cost you. Many competitors who depend on mass-produced guns have custom barrels installed. I choose to improve whatever comes on the gun if possible, and believe lapping will make most production barrels as good as the best custom target barrels of similar contour.

To improve cast-bullet performance in rough bores, many authorities recommend shooting several hundred jacketed-bullet loads through the bore, cleaning frequently to minimize the buildup of copper fouling. Because jacket material is abrasive, that approach works fairly well on bores which require only a small amount of smoothing. It can remove small constrictions in magnum revolver forcing cones, too. As methods go, however, that one is both expensive and time-consuming. Worst of all, it can't correct severe dimensional variations.

The easiest, least expensive and best method of smoothing a bore — and the only way I know to remove constrictions — is to lap it. The same techniques employed to lap bores can enlarge cast-bullet sizing dies and revolver cylinder throats. Then too, lap-cleaning a bore will frequently restore accuracy of both jacketed and cast bullets.

There are two common methods of lapping bores. The simplest is to fill the lube grooves of hard-cast bullets with

J-B bore cleaning paste and shoot them through the barrel at very low velocities. That will produce a mirror-finish with 100 or 200 shots if the bore wasn't too bad to begin with. In the revolvers I've worked with, it removes forcing cone constrictions at the rate of about .0005 inch per 200 shots. Stainless steel is tougher and will require more shooting. If one lacks tools or mechanical ability, that is the method to use.

Consider hand-lapping first, though, as it's quicker and more effective on rough guns. Resistance of the hand lap as it passes through a bore also provides a gauge by which to judge uniformity of bore diameter the full length of a barrel. If the lap offers uniform resistance from the muzzle all the way to the forcing cone, you can be assured that the bore diameter is consistent within .0001 inch — or twice as precise as premium barrels are guaranteed to be.

In the most dimensionally precise bores, the roughness which plagues cast bullets may require that no more than .0001 inch of the bore's finish be removed to obtain decent performance. Removing more than .0005 inch or so for the full length of a bore is rarely practical, or even desirable, as it enlarges the bore too much. In my experience, lapping the high spots away just enough to provide a smooth bore, will satisfy most shooters' requirements.

Without specialized equipment, measuring dimensional variations is limited to each end, and the smallest diameter, of the bore. Moreover, the only way for individual shooters to determine a bore's condition is to shoot the gun with properly fitted cast bullets, comparing performance to that of a barrel of known high quality and performance.

Inaccuracy at a low velocity/pressure level with no visible bore leading indicates the presence of a rough bore. If increasing the hardness of plain base bullets does not give a measurable increase in velocity and accuracy over the softer slugs, that can be taken as corroborative evidence. The use of gas-checked bullets in rough bores usually provides an immediate improvement in performance, often shrinking groups in half, even at velocities under 1,000 fps. If plain base bullets tend to keyhole and fly wild at velocities below maximum in magnum revolvers or below 1,600 fps or so in rifles, the bore's surface is probably so rough it is actually abrading the bullets' driving bands. (Bullet design might be a limiting factor, as well.) Damage can be so severe at times that ribbons of lead are left hanging from the

leading edges of the lands. Low velocity rounds such as the .45 Auto and .38 Special will benefit from top quality bores but are much more tolerant of rough bores than higher intensity cartridges like the 9mm Luger, magnum revolvers and most rifles.

If a bore is dimensionally correct and its finish smooth, the heavier plain base bullets should fly point forward and deliver reasonable accuracy at magnum handgun velocities and pressures, even if bore leading is quite extensive. There should be little difference in accuracy between gas-checked and plain base bullets at velocities up to 1,200 fps or so with most lubes, or 1,400 to 1,600 fps if LBT Blue is used. Rifles should accommodate 20+ BHN gas-checked bullets almost as well as jacketed hunting bullets at velocities to 2,400 fps and give good hunting accuracy from 2,800 to 2,900 fps with LBT Blue lube. If a gun does not meet those performance standards, lap the bore.

Lapping is a viable method for a shooter to enlarge cylinder throats because of the low cash outlay and because it doesn't require a custom reamer. It is time-consuming, though, and would be unduly expensive were one to hire the work done.

A sizing die can be enlarged by forcing bullets coated with an abrasive compound through it until an as-cast bullet

can be squeezed down to the desired diameter.

The operation is accomplished by removing the ejector plug from the die so that bullets can be pushed completely through it. Size several hard-cast bullets, coat them with an abrasive compound and force them through the die repeatedly until resistance to their passage disappears. Repeat with fresh, unsized bullets until the required diameter is established. To apply a highly polished finish, make 20 or 30 more passes with soft bullets and J-B paste.

Don't employ a coarse abrasive because too much pressure against the lubricator handle will be required to force the coated bullets through. Sizing dies, on the other hand, don't scratch easily, and cutting action is slow if very fine abrasives are used. A fine automotive valve grinding compound on a rotary lap is a good choice for roughing most of the material out. After that, the interior can be polished with a finer abrasive.

Before a person without machine shop experience attempts to lap a bore, it is important that he understand several things about cutting with abrasives, and the difference in metal finishes obtained with the aid of a given grit and different cutting pressure. Most importantly, one must understand

Below, the rotary lap itself must be made of softer metal than the part being lapped. Copper and aluminum make excellent choices. Right, cast bullets, sizing and swaging dies can be lapped the same way. A fine automotive valve grinding compound can be employed to rough-lap hardened steels but a less abrasive paste must be used when rough-lapping bores or cylinder throats. Easy does it — metal once removed can't be replaced!

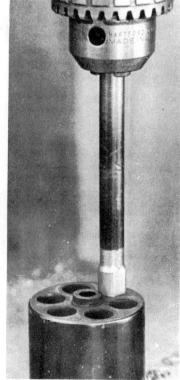

Above, a bore lapping skag lying beside a Ruger barrel, waiting for the lap to be cast. Right, after the skag is taped and inserted into the bore, molten lead is poured into the breech to form the lap. (On open-breech barrels, the lap should be cast at the muzzle.)

proper procedures and be fully cognizant of the consequences of doing something wrong.

There are several ways a barrel can be damaged by lapping: One is to allow the lap rod to rub against the rifling at the muzzle when working from the muzzle end. Everyone knows a dirty cleaning rod can damage a muzzle if allowed to rub against the rifling. When a rod is smeared with lapping compound, as it is bound to be eventually, it becomes absolutely mandatory to avoid dragging the rod against the rifling at the muzzle. Wrap the rod with electrician's tape. The tape's resilience reduces the cutting effect of any abrasive which might collect on it.

Working with a loose fitting lap will round lands and fail to scour the corners of the grooves. Because the rifling's grip of a lead bullet depends upon the condition of the rifling's leading edges, the lap should be tight at all times to make certain that area is left smooth.

A loose lap will offer considerable resistance because the rifling lands tend to create a drag until the lap plug becomes worn to bore diameter. To be sure the lap is cutting the bore's entire surface uniformly, tighten it periodically. Tightening is often required after each stroke of the lap for the first few strokes in a very rough bore. Keep the lap as tight as possible without letting it bind and it will cut evenly.

It is possible to lap a bore too much but that will not be a problem if lapping is limited to visible roughness. If the gun will be used primarily with jacketed bullets and its groove diameter is nominal or larger, I don't recommend lapping at all. An oversized bore is more detrimental to accuracy than a rough one. Cast bullets, on the other hand, can be fitted perfectly to an oversized bore

but they will never deliver optimum performance if its surface is too rough. If the barrel is intended for cast bullets, lap the bore smooth enough to obtain the desired performance level, regardless of final diameter.

Fortunately, bores are seldom as rough as they could be. Sometimes, removing as little as .0001 inch of metal is enough to smooth things out. The worst bore I've ever lapped only required an increase in diameter of .0005 inch. Bore constrictions can be completely removed and left free of all tool marks but be careful, short constrictions wear away very rapidly. Because so little metal needs to be removed, coarse abrasives, such as automotive valve grinding compounds, shouldn't be employed. It's best to choose an abrasive no coarser than 600 grit. Lapping compounds are available from abrasive suppliers, from Brownells, or a lap kit containing one container of LBT lap and J-B bore paste, along with complete instructions, is available from Lead Bullets Technology, Box 357, Cornville AZ 86325.

Due to the fear of bore damage, many gun owners avoid using abrasive compounds in their gun barrels. Bore damage is possible but the danger is no greater than it is when a bore is cleaned improperly.

An abrasive's cutting power is proportional to the force applied against it. For example, 600-grit abrasive is a polishing compound when used on a cloth buffer and will create a brilliant lustrous finish. On a very tight-fitting patch, it's slightly more abrasive to a bore than jacketed bullets, yet it will remove

softer lead, powder and jacket fouling and leave an unbelievably clean, bright finish. The abrasive crystals in J-B bore paste are only about a quarter the size of those in the LBT compound, making it an even finer polishing agent when used on a patch. A patch is flexible, applies relatively little pressure to individual abrasive crystals and slides over imperfections such as pits, scratches, forcing cone tapers, etc., leaving a smooth, rounded surface in its wake.

When those same compounds are used on a lead lap, their cutting power is greatly enhanced. Consequently, the finish they produce will be slightly rough. Furthermore, the lead retains its shape, fitting tight and cutting only in the smallest diameters of the bore, leveling off high spots but leaving low areas untouched.

Abrasives on a cleaning rod act just like they do on a lead lap, except that the operator has little or no control over them. For normal cleaning purposes, hard rods are often recommended; the idea being that dirt cannot embed itself in steel and act like an abrasive. Hard rods should never be used for lapping because the rod will be fairly well smeared with grit most of the time, even though it is wiped clean frequently. Abrasives should never be used on metal brushes either — or brushes wrapped with steel wool. Such hard but flexible surfaces encourage rapid, uncontrolled cutting and tend to round lands and deepen pits.

Lapping is far simpler to do than to explain, and the improvement in performance it provides is worth many times the effort expended. ●

Left, sawing the swollen end of the lap off so that it can be with drawn through the bore. Above, grooves resembling lube rings on a cast bullet should be filed around the lap's body. The grooves will be filled with lapping compound and act as reservoirs while the lap is being forced through the bore.

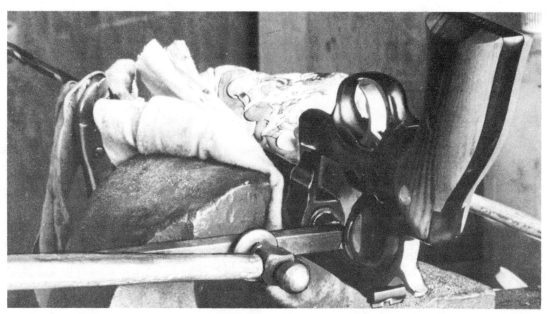

Tightening the lap is accomplished by bracing its face against a metal rod inserted through the muzzle. Another, shorter rod is pushed against the rear end of the lap from the breech. By holding a steel transfer bar against the base of the short rod and hammering against it gently, the lead lap is squeezed between the two rod ends and expands to fill the bore completely. The lap must be tightened periodically. A loose lap rounds the lands.

An undersized bore brush wrapped in cloth and smeared with a very fine abrasive paste like LBT or J-B makes an excellent polishing bob.

Section 4

BARRELS & CHAMBERING

BARREL

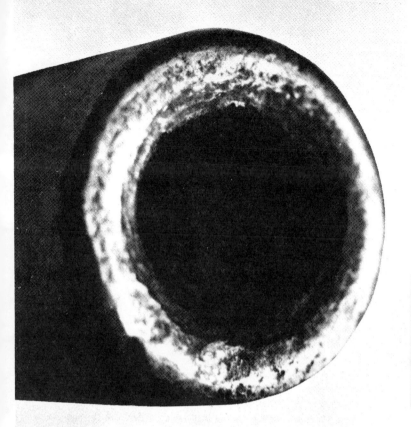

This M 08 Mauser muzzle, shown at left has been badly battered. On the left is a gouge and on the right a burr turned into the bore. Either or both will spoil accuracy and are easily removed by re-crowning or amputating the muzzle.

Gunsmith supply houses sell mounted brass balls for crowning muzzles, but a large-size, round-head brass screw will work just as well for an occasional job. Don't use a power drill. Chuck the screws or ball in a hand drill and rotate slowly, first in one direction, then the other, rocking the drill simultaneously. Use fine valve-grinding compound and oil between screw head and muzzle.

I SOMETIMES WONDER how many hundreds of thousands of guns sit idle in closets and attics, even barns, because the interior of their barrels has been shot out or ruined by neglect. An amazing number of guns are simply set aside and forgotten when they no longer shoot close to where they look. Often these are older models, and the owners simply can't see spending the money a new barrel will cost. Then, too, new barrels frequently aren't available except from custom makers--and that kicks the price up and adds to the difficulty of getting the job done. Trading such a gun in on a new model is often difficult unless the fellow has his mind made up to take whatever the local gun shop offers. Consequently, when "Ole Betsy" won't hit her mark anymore, she's just laid aside and forgotten.

No matter how bad the barrel looks, there are few circumstances under which it cannot be restored sufficiently to produce at least acceptable performance in its original or another caliber. There are several basic gunsmithing operations which can be performed to place these barrels back in service. Some are so simple and easy they can be accomplished with hand

tools by any reasonably dexterous shooter; others cost little at your neighborhood gunsmithy; and a few are relatively costly—but still more economical than fitting a complete new barrel.

Let's take a look at a few of the simpler jobs first. Out West I've encountered a number of rifles that were in perfect (apparently) condition inside, but had become badly battered externally from being constantly carried in the back of a pickup truck or the trunk of a car bouncing over open range and dirt roads. Occasionally owners have asked me why such a gun that had

performed satisfactorily for years suddenly developed an aversion to the target. Aside from sight damage, the most common cause turned out to be muzzle damage and, in one instance, a barrel bent by having a heavy snatch block tossed on it. No help for that one, but those with battered muzzles shot as well as ever after re-crowning.

REJUVENATION

By MAJ. GEORGE NONTE

In each case, impact with some hard, sharp object had carved a deep nick in the mouth of the muzzle or had turned a burr into the bore. These defects then deflected the bullet as it exited and spoiled accuracy. Most gunsmithing supply houses offer brass muzzle-crowning balls which are coated with valve-grinding compound and oil and rotated against the muzzle at low speed in a hand or electric drill. A ball can't take more metal off one side than another. In a pinch, a round-head brass wood screw of large size will serve for the job. In any event, it seldom takes more than 20 or 30 minutes to restore a muzzle to newness and accuracy. If the damage extends more than 1/32-inch into the barrel, time can be saved by sawing off an appropriate portion, filing the fresh muzzle square, then crowning it anew.

A gun whose owner is addicted to excessive and careless cleaning from the muzzle—usually with a bent and battered springy rod—may develop a belled muzzle which is ruinous to accuracy. This occurs most often with lever and pump-action guns which must be cleaned from the muzzle; and with older models whose barrels are made of relatively soft steel. This condition can usually be seen readily by examining the interior of the bore closely under good light right at the muzzle. Since this damage seldom extends more than an inch or two into the muzzle, amputation and re-crowning restores accuracy. The barrel should be carefully sawed off as squarely as possible, then filed exactly square, and properly crowned. Again, this is something you can do yourself in no more than an hour or two some idle evening. Hacksaw, file, and some means of crowning are all the tools you need. Where iron sights are

involved, this normally requires re-fitting the front sight, but that's no great chore.

Amputation is also the answer for some other forms of damage. To digress from rifles for a few moments, shotguns in particular are prone to burst muzzles. It's so very simple to unknowingly dip the muzzle of your scattergun in snow or mud, then take a fast shot with the obstruction still in place. At the very least, this will produce a bad bulge or split at the muzzle and can mean chunks of barrel wall blown completely clear. In a single-barrel gun, simply sawing off the damaged portion and fitting any of the adjustable or interchangeable choke devices on the market restores performance. In the case of a double, even though only one barrel is damaged, both must be cut off at the same point. This generally removes all or nearly all of the choke, which can be restored only by careful reaming and/or polishing by someone competent in this work. Though less likely, this type of muzzle damage can occur to

Lapping a rough barrel isn't as difficult as you might believe. Cast a lead lap in the bore around the end of a cleaning rod, then pass it part way out the muzzle to apply fine abrasive and oil. During lapping, don't let it protrude farther than this from the muzzle.

Squaring a cut-off muzzle can be a chore. Keep checking with a common adjustable square in this fashion until the same gap exists between the muzzle and the arm of the square from opposite sides. Lower end of the arm must touch the tapered barrel several inches behind the muzzle.

rifles—especially those of large caliber. Corrective action is the same but must include crowning as mentioned earlier.

Occasionally a bulge may be produced almost anywhere along the length of the barrel. In shotguns this is usually due to a wad left in the bore by a "blooper" shot. In rifles, a stuck bullet, stripped bullet jacket, lost cleaning patch, or any other obstruction is likely to be the cause. Often barrels will continue to deliver normal accuracy even when a readily visible bulge exists

This S&W M1917 .45 revolver barrel is bulged just behind the front sight, probably caused by being fired with a bullet stuck in the bore. It is easily restored by cutting it off behind the bulge, truing up the muzzle, then fitting a new front sight.

if it's back a way from the muzzle. In that case, there's no actual necessity for removing or reducing the bulge. A not-too-large bulge on a relatively thick rifle barrel can be draw-filed flush with the adjacent surfaces to restore original contours. This doesn't help the inside but, if the gun is delivering satisfactory accuracy, is an acceptable cosmetic repair. Shotgun tubes cannot be given this treatment because of their thin walls—however, shotgun specialists such as Simmons Gun Company, (500-510 East 18th Street, Kansas City, Missouri), can reduce such bulges and can also raise dents by means of their special tools. The cost is far less than replacing the barrel.

When the bulge occurs near the muzzle, the most practical solution is to cut off that section of the barrel and re-crown or, in the case of a shotgun, fit a choke device. In doing this, one must keep in mind that the minimum barrel length for rifles is 16 inches; 18 for shotguns. There is no minimum length for pistols and revolvers, so any amount of reduction necessary to remove the bulge can be tolerated. However, in the

case of automatic pistols whose slide surrounds the barrel, shortening is not possible. As a matter of fact, a barrel bulge in this type of gun will probably jam the slide tightly to the barrel.

Amputation also works at the breech end of the barrel. High-intensity cartridges working at tremendous heat and pressures of 50,000 psi and more will eventually erode the rifling completely away directly ahead of the chamber, even though the remainder of the barrel is in near-perfect condition. Of course, with anything except ultra-hot wildcat cartridges, it takes many thousands of rounds to produce erosion extensive enough to spoil the accuracy of hunting rifles. Eventually, though, erosion will reach the point where in passing through this roughened and enlarged portion of the bore the bullet is so damaged that it will not deliver satisfactory accuracy.

When that state is reached, the barrel may be removed from the action, shortened from the breech an amount equal to the length of the worst-eroded portion, then rethreaded and rechambered and fitted back to the action. Some bench rest and varmint shooters who fire unusually large amounts of ammunition often deliberately start with barrels two or three inches longer than necessary in order to have room for subsequent shortening as erosion develops. This is, of course, a gunsmithing operation and may cost upwards of $20. But, that is still significantly less than the cost of a new barrel—especially in a bench rest gun fitted with a $100 tube.

In some instances it is possible to eliminate some of the effects of erosion

This Lee-Enfield barrel has been factory relined to .22 rimfire caliber for use as a training rifle. The joint between barrel and liner is scarcely visible without magnification.

British WWI vintage S.M.L.E. rifle was factory relined to .22 rimfire caliber, fitted with new bolt head, firing pin and extractor. Many thousands of training rifles were produced in this manner under several designations. Rifle pictured is "No. 2, Mark IV" and is currently available from Century Arms, St. Albans, Vermont -- the only relined-barrel gun that can be purchased across the counter at this time.

by simply rechambering. For example, rechambering for a longer cartridge will sometimes clean up the worst of the erosion. A 7mm Mauser barrel can be rechambered to the .280 Remington or 7mm Remington Magnum. A .243 Winchester may be rechambered to any one of the 6mm wildcats based on the blown-out full-length .30-06 case.

An old artillery sergeant once brought me a virtually new 7mm Mauser sporter he had acquired in Europe. The gun would have cost several hundred dollars to duplicate in this country. In spite of its appearance, the gun was ruined by deep rust pitting in the chamber. The pits were so deep that fired cases could not be extracted normally. The problem could have been solved by shortening the barrel about 1/2 to 3/4-inch at the breech and refitting and rechambering it. However, this would have spoiled the wood-to-metal fit in the fore-end. Not wanting to do this, we looked about for a larger diameter 7mm cartridge and found it in the .284 Winchester.

A .284 finish reamer removed sufficient metal to entirely eliminate the pits. This left the new chamber with a neck and throat slightly longer than standard for the .284, but the rifle shot quite well. Since the owner was a handloader, he compensated for the long throat by seating bullets out to the same length as the original 7mm Mauser caliber. Rechambering for any one of the belted 7mm Magnums would have cleaned the chamber up completely, but this individual didn't want a belted magnum.

Even a bore that appears badly rusted and pitted can frequently be salvaged in one way or another. Many times it will not be as bad as it looks. A thorough scrubbing with solvent and

Many older guns such as this Winchester M1886 .40-65 are often found with ruined bores or cannot be used because ammunition hasn't been produced for decades. In either case, reboring the barrel to handle readily available .45-70 cartridges restores the gun to service.

steel wool packed tightly around a brass bore brush will remove all rust and accumulated fouling of the years and will also provide some smoothing action on the roughened rifling.

This operation should *always* be conducted from the breech, even if the barrel must be removed from the receiver to do so. In addition, some sort of stop should be attached to the rod to prevent the wad of steel wool from passing through the muzzle. This will prevent belling of the muzzle, and will also result in a slight amount of choke which often seems to improve accuracy. The steel wool should be replaced after each few strokes because it loses its cutting ability rather quickly. This treatment should not be extended past the point necessary to produce acceptable performance. If kept up too long, it can virtually destroy rifling. The best procedure is to fire a few test groups as soon as all rust and fouling has been scrubbed out. Once cleaned out and smoothed up a bit and perhaps recrowned, barrels that look rough inside will produce surprisingly good hunting accuracy.

Essentially the same thing can be accomplished far more precisely by lapping a rough bore. This is done by casting a pure lead lap about 3 inches long on the end of a cleaning rod inserted into the bore. The rod is inserted from the breech, and the lap cast in the muzzle. When cooled, the lap is passed part way out of the muzzle and coated with oil and very fine flour emery abrasive powder. It is then worked back and forth full length in the barrel, fresh emery and oil being applied as necessary. Here, too, the lap should not be allowed to protrude from the muzzle except for application of abrasive. As polishing progresses, a new lap should be cast. Even a badly pitted bore can be completely smoothed by lapping and still retain reasonably clear rifling. However, this can result in so much enlargement of the bore that standard diameter bullets will not shoot well in it. Lapping should not be carried

past the stage where a reasonable degree of accuracy is produced.

A bore so badly ruined that it cannot be salvaged by lapping or scouring may still be restored, through not in its original caliber. Reboring is the answer. This consists of drilling and/or reaming to completely remove the rifling and all roughness. The smooth hole thus produced is then reamed and rifled in the conventional manner in a larger caliber. The barrel is then rechambered and refitted to the action. This is, of course, a special job that can be accomplished only by those shops tooled up for it. Fortunately, a good many such shops exist, even though most of them are considerably behind in their work. Depending upon the particular gun and the caliber, a typical reboring and rechambering job may cost from $20 to $35. To be sure, some new barrels can be purchased for less, but

Typical of reboring jobs possible is opening up a ruined .308 Winchester (left) barrel and chamber to handle the .350 Remington Magnum.

they often will not fit the stock channel.

Reboring is a particularly good way to restore a gun while maintaining complete physical originality and authenticity of the gun. I once owned a .35 Whelen Springfield fitted with an integral-ribbed half-octagon barrel that would have cost nearly $150 to replace. I got the gun cheap because the bore was ruined through neglect and for the sum of $22 I was able to get it rebored to .400 Whelen caliber. In this instance, not only was the rifle's originality preserved, but also its integrity and association. We simply substituted one Whelen caliber for another.

Of course, reboring is only possible where a step-up in bore size can be tolerated. Barrels with unusually thin walls do not permit this to any large degree, nor is it possible to rebore a rifle for a caliber developing pressures beyond the capacity of the barrel and/or action. Certain limitations are also imposed by the size cartridges the action and magazine can handle. A .30-06, for example, can't be rebored to .375 Magnum unless the action is extensively modified. Generally speaking, the less increase in bore diameter resulting from reboring, the more likely the job is to be entirely satisfactorily. Drastic increases in caliber may produce or unleash undesirable stresses which can cause erratic shooting, especially when the barrel heats from sustained firing. Of course, the heavier the barrel, the less likely this is to happen. In sporting-weight barrels it is best to go up only one caliber step at a time—for example: .22 to .243; .243 to .25 or 6.5mm; 6.5mm or .270 to 7mm: etc. I have one heavy 6mm barrel which produces better accuracy since reboring to that caliber than it ever did as a .22.

Reboring has been conducted on a large scale. For example, large numbers of 7mm Mauser military rifles have been rebored to 7.62mm NATO caliber. At other times in history, 7mm and 7.65mm Mausers have been rebored to 7.92mm caliber. In many instances one may even continue to use the same cartridge case if handloading is acceptable—for example, numerous .303 Lee Enfields have been rebored to use

8mm (.323) bullets loaded directly into the old .303 British case. And so it goes.

It is also possible to re-line a barrel. This procedure is not generally considered satisfactory for high-intensity cartridges. It does, however, work quite well in rimfire and low-power centerfire calibers. It consists simply of drilling and reaming the barrel as for reboring, then fitting a thin-wall rifled tube of the proper caliber. This tube is then chambered for either the original or a new cartridge. Many fine old single-shot rifles have been restored in this manner by such specialists as V. M. Starr, (Eden, South Dakota), and Snapp's Gunshop, (214 N. Washington, Royal Oak, Michigan). It is obvious that re-lining can be accomplished only by those shops especially equipped and experienced in the processes. Probably the most widely known re-lining work is done by Parker-Hale Ltd., Birmingham, England. Many re-lining specialists in this country use Parker-Hale tubes for their work.

In the past, liners were usually soft-soldered in place. This requires special heating and tinning tools, not to mention a very careful fit of liner to barrel. Some 'smith's preferred a shrink fit obtained by chilling the liner in dry ice, heating the barrel, and then inserting the liner. At best, this is a chance method. Too much shrink may occur before the liner is fully seated, causing the liner to be jammed where it can neither be pulled out or fully seated. A German gunsmith once used the heat-shrink method to convert an old .455 Triple Lock S&W to .38 Special for me. He not only relined the badly pitted barrel, but installed chamber liners as well. It worked fine, even with hot .38-44 loads, for several years thereafter.

The latest method, though, is the use of epoxy adhesives to bond barrel and liner together. This permits careful fitting without the application of heat and may also be more easily controlled by allowing adjustments after seating but before the adhesive sets up. One outfit did, in fact, offer do-it-yourself relining kits consisting of a .22 rimfire chambered liner, drill and counterbore, and adhesive. All one needed was a power drill, a fixture to hold the

barrel—and patience and caution—to finish the job. While I've not used one of these kits, it would seem a careful workman with a little metal-working experience could expect to do a satisfactory job.

There are times when it is desired to alter the chamber of a barrel to accept a smaller cartridge of the same bullet diameter. An example that comes to mind was accomplished by a friend of mine with a Winchester single-shot rifle in .25-20 Single-Shot caliber. He could not obtain good brass for reloading in the original caliber, so he drilled and reamed a deep counterbore in the barrel breech to completely eliminate the original chamber.

He then carefully fitted a bushing made from a section of another .25 caliber barrel into this hole. By selecting a piece of barrel with identical rifling and then carefully indexing that rifling with that of the original barrel he was able to extend the rifling rearward so as to be able to cut a proper chamber and throat for the shorter .25-20 Winchester Repeater cartridge which is still available. The bushing was secured by low-temperature silver solder flowed into very shallow grooves cut in the outer surface of the bushing. Careful lapping of the bore where the rifling of the bushing met that of the barrel provided a smooth transition for the bullet. After this job, the rifle shot as well as ever and the owner's ammunition problems were solved for all time.

Other rather odd methods of salvaging a barrel will occur from time to time. I once acquired a brand-new premium-grade .30-06 barrel in medium target weight that had been "ruined" by the owner's attempts to install target-type scope blocks. He had goofed and drilled one hole through the bore. In high dudgeon he threw the barrel in his trash can from which I rescued it a few days later. The hole was threaded full length, then plugged with a very tight-fitting screw which was peened and filed flush with the surface. A lap was cast in the bore and used for a half-dozen strokes to remove slight burrs around the mouth of the hole. Care was taken, incidentally, to make certain the screw did not intrude into the bore.

After the first 50 or so rounds fired, which I assumed ironed out any unevenness around the hole, that barrel began producing minute-of-angle groups. Anyone looking through the bore got a shock when he saw the hole, but that $50 barrel was salvaged with a three-cent screw and a half-hour's work. If you question that a barrel with a hole in it will shoot well, keep in mind that National Match M1 and M14 rifles regularly shoot possibles at 600 and 1000 yards. Every one of them has a gas port drilled in the barrel.

When you're out swapping and trading, these various methods of barrel rejuvenation should be kept in mind. Now and then someone will be ready to unload a good model cheaply because of barrel damage or wear which can be corrected at little cost. And the salvage rights can be yours. ●

BARREL

Profiled receiver wrenches, which must be made for each action type, are necessary for removing barrels without gun damage. These are, from left Large Ring Mauser, Model 70 Winchester and 1917 Enfield.

BARREL-FITTING is a subject that could fill a king-size book, so I'll split things up and take off on one rifle, the pre-1964 Model 70 Winchester, that is, with serial number under 700,000 (above this number, some of the details are different). This is a medium-hard fitting job, harder than a Mauser or Remington, easier than a Springfield or Enfield. The thread is V type, pitch 16 per inch, a standard 60-degree, so it requires only the normal commercial threading tool. It must be sharp, with left side ground for clearance so you can bring the thread as close to the barrel shoulder as possible. I don't think I have to mention that you must use a thread-cutting lathe having three-jaw universal chuck, steady-rest, etc.

Unless working with a stripped action you naturally first have to remove the old barrel, and taking for granted you do have to get one out, you need a barrel vise, hardwood blocks fitted to the barrel and receiver wrench. The latter will be a true old-fashioned type, I hope, profiled inside to just fit the receiver over the recoil shoulder with clearance for a protecting bit of thin cardboard or heavy paper between wrench and receiver. Nobody sells them--you must make your own. And you need a separate one for each forged receiver you work with--the one for the 70 won't fit the Mauser or Springfield.

This type wrench does not injure a receiver. "Universal" wrenches, made to clamp around any receiver with screw-plates, etc., are for the birds, and the inside-receiver-strap wrenches should only be used on round receiver rifles such as Remington, Cooey, Savage, etc. And they should be made to just barely fit--no wiggle inside the runways or you'll put dents inside the receiver. They should not be used on Mauser-type actions, which include the 70, 1903 and 1917, that can have barrels fitted far tighter than the round receiver jobs, and which do not have the same metal distribution in the ring. I've seen one M70 receiver broken with an inside wrench, and many rifles with bent and dented runways.

With the old barrel off, clean out the receiver threads and locking-lug area with solvent and brush. Then check the lug seats--if one has more bearing than the other, work the stripped bolt in the receiver with lapping compound until both lugs have approximately the same contact area. Just hold the bolt hard to the rear while turning to lock and unlock. File or stone the front end of the receiver straight across in all directions to get rid of any burrs, and get it reasonably square if it isn't.

Next, the bolt face. Many have rings of pits in the center, opposite the edge of the primer pocket, due to years of accumulated miniscule leaks around primers--and not cleaning the bolt face after each day of use. If not numerous or deep, the pits won't matter, but if they are deep, set the bolt up in the lathe preferably on a threaded rod screwed into the back end with the bolt

Bolt face has been cleaned with tail of bolt in chuck and head supported in steady rest, as shown, for proper alignment.

FITTING

By ROY DUNLAP

handle knob against a lathe jaw to act as its own 'dog,' and steady-rest set just ahead of the extractor collar cut in the front end of the bolt body. You have to center on the firing-pin hole to set up, which is an interesting process since forged bolts are seldom even close to being straight, round, or having the firing-pin hole in the middle. However, you can come close enough for this job.

Use a sharp lathe bit with a very tiny radius stoned on tip. Start at firing-pin hole and come straight out to rim of the lips or counterbore. Little metal need be removed--seldom ever over .010-inch to clear out pits, though of course really bad ones can crop up. Ordinary tool bits work okay, though most Mauser bolts will require carbide. This same turning system is used to open up the standard-face bolt to magnum size. This cleaning up, or cutting back of the bolt face is, of course, increasing the basic headspace of the action, but since you are fitting and chambering to a particular action, not replacing a factory threaded and fully-chambered barrel, there is no problem.

The barrel should be pre-turned to desired size, left one inch or so longer than finished length at the muzzle, both ends squared off true, and clean centering cuts made. I always hold the barrel by the muzzle and do all fitting work back at the tailstock, both because my lathe doesn't have a large hole through the headstock and because I noticed early in the game that the characters who stick barrels through the head and turn, thread, chamber, etc. close up, turn out practically all the off-center and oversize chambers you run into. So, with the barrel between centers I turn down a section at the muzzle, 1/16-inch or so under diameter, 1/2-inch or so long, because when you turn the barrel around and put this "tenon-end" into the chuck you have a solid-shoulder against the jaws so the barrel cannot move into the chuck and away from the tail-stock support under the pressure of the turning and

threading work on shank. (Everyone who has ever fitted barrels has had this happen and knows how much trouble is caused, like cutting off the back end and starting all over!)

You can now hold the barrel solidly at muzzle and breech and turn down the shank. The M70 requires a 1-inch diameter shank .750-inch long (factory shanks vary from .735 to .745 as a rule). With a straight-edged tool, take a .010-inch cut approximately .750-inch forward from the breech end, run the shank under a flat file a few turns to clean it smooth and put the indicator on it to find out if the middle is in the middle. If the needle wobbles much, you now set up the steady-rest on the shank, take a truing cut across the back end of the barrel and use the center drill in the tailstock chuck again, to get a new center. Take the steady-rest off, put the center back in tailstock and barrel, again take a cut off the shank section, again check the shank with

Barrel shanks vary greatly, as shown by the standard Mauser 98, at left, and a barrel from a custom Finnish free rifle, which has the same thread as the Mauser, but more than twice the shank and a pronounced shoulder.

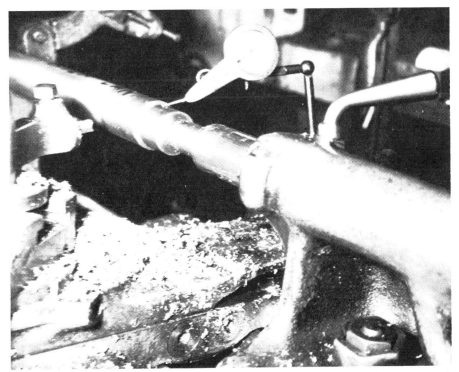

Using a .0001 indicator as a guide, the barrel blank can be centered so external cuts are exactly concentric with bore.

This sectioned case shows that the solid base is completely within the chamber, with thin sidewalls encased by steel. Extending the extractor cut into the chamber will leave the brass unsupported.

indicator....you go back and forth with this system until the needle barely quivers which means that the shank is now true, or concentric with bore.

It is surprising how easy it is to reach extreme accuracy here. I use a 1/1000-inch indicator, but with an extended tip that makes each graduation much less, about .0003-inch....and often get shanks trued so that the tip can hardly be seen to quiver, meaning that error has to be less

than 100,000th inch. So, threads cut on this shank will place the bore, and consequently the chamber, extremely close to dead center. This is important only if you want maximum accuracy, easy extraction, and long case life!

To be an absolute purist, you can now make a light lathe cut on the barrel cylinder ahead of the shank, which of course will make the cylinder true to center. Back to this later--now cut your shank down to 1.000-inch plus nothing, minus .002-inch diameter, .745 to .750-inch length. Put the steady-rest on the shank, centered perfectly, set the lathe-tool carriage to 40 degrees and cut the cone, working from the center out until you reach the edge, as smooth as you can cut it with a rounded cutter, then polish with abrasive cloth. With the cone finished, put the center drill in again for a new center--40 degrees ain't 60, what the center needs.

I have a precision live center, but stick with the old solid jobs for threading barrels. Remove the steady-rest, set up for threading and thread the shank, as close to the shoulder as possible, until the receiver can be screwed on all the way by hand, but not loosely. Receivers often have a tapered thread--that is, tighter at back than at front (not on purpose) and if the receiver goes on freely two-thirds of the way and gradually tightens, take the barrel out of the lathe and use the barrel vise and receiver wrench to see if it can be worked on without great effort.

Barrels should wind in freely by hand all the way to the receiver then take 1/8 to 3/16-inch drawup tightening with wrench. (You thought it should be a tight fit? No. It is no great chore to make a tight thread, but if the rifle should be fired fast enough on a hot day, the receiver may suddenly crack! Heat expansion. I know of it happening, not on any of my jobs, luckily. Tighten on the shoulder, not the threads.)

Now, take the bolt minus extractor--it's a good idea to have old extractors with front ends missing that can now be put on the bolt to hold the collar together and keep it from tying up the bolt in the receiver. Try the bolt--if it closes without marking the cone of barrel, the cone is deep enough. This is not a brilliant deduction, but if it won't close you must cut more cone, and you don't want any more than is absolutely necessary.

So, back in the lathe for chambering. Center up with the steady-rest on threads, or on the trued-up area of barrel ahead of shoulder. In theory, running on the threads is not as accurate; however, I can find no appreciable difference in the final results and like support right at the back end. You use the four-lip roughing reamer at medium speed in back gear, lots of cutting oil and push....I always leave the tailstock free to slide, with reamer held in tailstock drill chuck, and push in by hand. The pilot follows the bore and the reamer follows the pilot. And the chambers come out close to the size of the reamers. Tie down the tailstock and wind in the reamer with the mechanical feed and you end up with any size except small.

Run in the roughing reamer to the precise measuring point--like a notch ground in the back of one reamer flute, to line up with rear edge of cone by eyeball, 1/16" or so short of full depth. This was ascertained earlier by dropping reamer into an old barrel when you were trying to figure out where to grind the notch.

Clean out the chamber, get rid of chips--I use a lot of oil and a lot of air when chambering, blowing from breech end of course. Have always intended to make a long tube-nozzle for the air hose to make things easier, but never got around to it. Set in the chambering reamer, the finisher, slow down the lathe and repeat the chambering process

Dunlap uses this vertical mill setup with Woodruff cutter to make the extractor cut, taking care to cut no further than necessary for clearance. The job can be done with files.

but cleaning the reamer often and watching the index mark on reamer. With luck and experience you end up with the finished chamber .010 to .020 short and it is time to check.

I've seen all sorts of setups for final chambering, but made my own gadget early: a 1-inch micrometer-head set into a 10-inch steel bar which has two fixed pins slightly over 1-inch apart, inside edge measurement. Clean the chamber, put the minimum headspace gage ("GO") in, put the gadget on, pins through steady-rest arms solidly against barrel shoulder and run the mike against gage. Use a standard depth micrometer against bolt face through receiver to get distance from front of receiver to face with bolt held to rear limit of locked position. Check your two micrometers direct, against each other....begin to get the idea? You then know how far you must go, take light chamber cuts as needed.

Screw barrel in the receiver by hand first, trying gages—if the bolt will just barely close, tighten with wrench and you may be home free. If bolt doesn't begin to go down, you'll need the reamer again, either by hand or back in lathe—safer to go by hand with the extension through receiver until you get to proper headspace. On the other hand, if bolt handle flops down, and chamber is too deep (you may have had a shaving holding the gage back?) the barrel goes back to the lathe on center and you cut the shoulder forward a few thousandths so you can wind the barrel further back into receiver. Most of the time all these operations, including the last, are about as easy as they read, and don't take much more time. Unless you've read a mike a turn off, or otherwise goofed, and really booted the reamer in. Then you have to cut the shoulder forward so far the cone won't let the bolt close, which requires more work!

This shank work is why you need to thread full depth as close to the shoulder as possible, just for insurance. The M70 receiver is threaded almost to the front face and you need as much thread as you can get to reach the shoulder, even if it has to be moved forward .010-inch or even more, after the threading. It is no fun at all to have to pick up a thread to continue it a partial turn, though often necessary on re-fitting jobs, say where a man wants a .30-06 set back and rechambered to .308.

Eventually we have the barrel tight in

Gunsmith's name and cartridge for which the barrel is chambered should be stamped with one-piece stamps, otherwise individual letters or numbers will not be straight.

receiver, and correct headspace. Go through the receiver with a steel bar notched or with sharp corners (place a gage in the chamber to protect it) mark or scribe on the cone to locate the extractor cut, following the top and bottom of right side runway in receiver. You can at this time throat the barrel to take the type bullet to be used. My reamers are made to cut the chamber only, and do not have the common all-purpose throat section integral with finish reamers, so I need a separate throating reamer, used with an extension through the receiver. Throating can be done at any time after barrel is in, of course.

Remove receiver and polish the chamber, which it will probably need for good appearance, if not otherwise necessary. I use a hand grinder with a 2½-inch long arbor I made to take a little cross of fine abrasive cloth, 320 or 400 grit about 1¼-inch square, the arms of the cross about 3/8-inch. Run first into an old chamber to break down the grit a little, then oil; this setup puts a polish in a chamber fast, like in three seconds. The cross must be folded back and inserted in the chamber before the motor is started; the grinder is started and the mandrel with cross is moved back and forth in the chamber slowly for two to three seconds, motor is

Dunlap made this barrel polishing lathe attachment for final polishing while other work is being done. Note pan to catch grit.

switched off just as it is removed from the chamber. Centrifugal force on the cross of abrasive keeps the mandrel tip (tiny screw head) from ever touching the side of neck or chamber. Think my grinder runs 17,000 rpm, but I would assume that any high-speed job would be OK.

This system seems to remove no metal, can be used to clean up rough chambers in old rifles--it doesn't grind out rough spots and enlarge chamber, but seems to smooth things up so that extraction is free. Of course, with coarse, sharp cloth it can really chew out metal--I use a long 1/4-inch mandrel with rough cloth to polish insides of bolts. Anyway, I've used the system for 20 years on everything from .22's to .300 Magnums with good results.

You can now mill the extractor cut in what will be the right side of the shank, following the scribed markings, or do a lot of filing if you don't have a mill, and finish file to follow details of the extractor cut in an old 70 barrel. The inner edge of the cut should never break the edge of the chamber, but always just come to the edge. Polish with old abrasive cloth around a triangular file, use a triangular needle file to clean burrs from edges of threads, etc. When the barrel is installed in receiver for the last time, the extractor cut is your index. When you can close the bolt smoothly with the regular extractor in place, the barrel is in position.

Right now, you stamp the caliber, your name, and whatever else is to go on the barrel. Locate opposite and above the extractor cut, on the cylinder of barrel just ahead of shoulder. Individual one-at-a-time figures and letters never line up and always make a sad-looking job. It is expensive, but the best way to go is to obtain through Frank Mittermeier custom-made one-piece stamps for name and the principal calibers you barrel for. There can be some combinations of course--one "Remington," one "Winchester," one "Magnum" can combine for many calibers--6mm, .257, .280 or .225, .270, .300 etc. Figures and letters in 1/20-inch are about best size. Stamp the barrel, take a wide mill file, wrap well-worn 320 cloth over it and polish down the raised edges of stamping.

Now polish the barrel, preferably in the lathe with fine cloth and crocus, if a high finish is wanted. I made a motorized affair, a band-sander, springloaded pulleys carrying belts of abrasive cloth, that mounts on the lathe carriage and rides back and forth. Belts of 180, 240 and 320 grit, waxed, and used progressively, will clean up even quite rough-turned barrels painlessly. Smooth old belts will give a very fine finish--you are only limited by your patience in giving the lathe time. Target barrels I usually snatch off after a few passes, figuring a real polish is not only unnecessary, but usually unwanted. The stamping looks very good. (I haven't buffed a barrel in 15 years!) If you should decide to make up a barrel polisher, it needs power--use a 1/3 HP 3,600 rpm motor. Yes, it'll throw grit on the lathe ways, but most can be caught by paper or a thin metal shield placed just under the bolt, carried along by the carriage.

With the barrel polished, you can now cut off the front end, since it is no longer needed to hold the barrel in the chuck. In polishing I clamp by the shank, muzzle at tailstock where belts can run over the holding-shoulder cut, to clean up all the way. Saw off back of the cut just over the finished length and you are ready to crown. So, how do you hold a polished barrel without marking it? I have made a collection of steel rings, 1/16 to 1/8-inch wall thickness, inside diameters of various sizes, outside grooved to fit the steady-rest jaws. Take the nice bright barrel, wrap clean paper around it at muzzle and put on the ring that fits best with the least amount of paper, front edge of the ring preferably 1/8 to 1/4-inch back from the end of barrel.

Center on bore, with ring in steady-rest, and face off barrel. Then re-center and re-adjust steady-rest, do your crowning, counterboring or whatever muzzle detail you prefer. Gunsmithing books are full of details on muzzle-crowning balls, lapping, etc. If you can't get the barrel in a lathe, you do it this way, but with a lathe, why be stupid? A lathe carriage is steadier than any hand and a sharp tool can't help but cut rifling square! (Amazing how few barrels have the hole in the middle, ain't it?)

Anyhow, take the barrel out, pull off the paper and ring, wrap the breech section in clean paper to protect from marking by the hardwood barrel-vise blocks, clamp it and screw the receiver on for last time. Any cleanup work needed on the receiver should be done first, as the polished barrel must be handled with great care until blued. Literally anything it contacts will mark it. You even need to put cloth or Kleenex on wooden racks you rest it on or against. It can be held in wooden vise jaws, protected by leather and clean paper, for sight-mounting work should any be required.

I have tried not to digress too much from describing the straight work on a barrel fitting operation, feeling it not necessary to talk about stoning reamers, types of cutting oil, center lubes and other matters familiar to anyone involved in barrel work. In my shop we seldom do a single barrel at a time, but try never to get involved with more than eight or ten in a batch--beyond that you can get mixed up on parts, run out of room, etc. It is obvious that you can turn all the muzzles down with no change of tool or lathe accessories, the same with shanks, and so on, to save much machine time.

However, on a single job with all the changes described, either Tom Eason, my former apprentice, or I can do a complete job in two hours or less, not counting the polishing time, when the lathe polisher can be running up and down the barrel while we are on stocks or something else, only having to reverse the carriage direction every 15 minutes or so. I know there are many people who take less time for the same work, but their customers aren't like mine. If our rifles stay in one minute of angle, the owners don't think they are very accurate.

One memorable experience--a customer shot a 100-19V at 1,000 yards, followed with a 100-13V with metallic sights, then handed me the rifle on the firing line for a new barrel....not shooting good enough, worn out. So I put in a new barrel. Top-grade accuracy is the result of doing *every* operation in assembling the rifle just as close to perfection as possible. Every little bit of care helps. ●

PRECISION BARREL FITTING

By NEAL KNOX

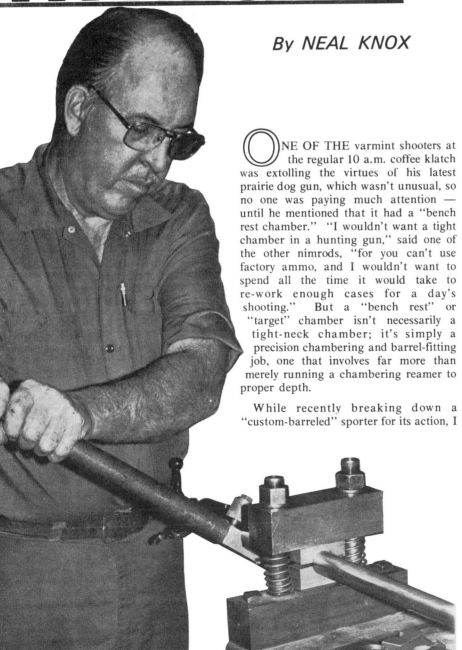

ONE OF THE varmint shooters at the regular 10 a.m. coffee klatch was extolling the virtues of his latest prairie dog gun, which wasn't unusual, so no one was paying much attention — until he mentioned that it had a "bench rest chamber." "I wouldn't want a tight chamber in a hunting gun," said one of the other nimrods, "for you can't use factory ammo, and I wouldn't want to spend all the time it would take to re-work enough cases for a day's shooting." But a "bench rest" or "target" chamber isn't necessarily a tight-neck chamber; it's simply a precision chambering and barrel-fitting job, one that involves far more than merely running a chambering reamer to proper depth.

While recently breaking down a "custom-barreled" sporter for its action, I had a good look at what *isn't* a precision fitting job. The cases that came with the rifle showed firing pin indents well off center, which *may* not hurt anything — but can't help accuracy. The right bolt lug bearing surface showed galling and scoring; the left lug still wore unblemished factory blue, indicating that it had never touched its support. When the barrel was unscrewed, it required more torque to break the joint than should have been necessary, but after an eighth of a turn the action was so wobbly on the threads that it almost rattled. The face of the receiver showed factory milling marks and there was a bright spot indicating a high point which had undoubtedly caused the barrel to be somewhat offset. The puzzling thing is that this rifle had shot reasonably well.

Each of these deficiencies will be missing on any bench rest rifle, high-grade target rifle, or even a hunting rifle assembled by a master gunsmith who takes pride in his work, and whose customers are willing to pay for the extra time that a precision barrel fitting and chambering job requires.

The techniques used will vary among different gunsmiths, but the results will be the same: barrels and actions assembled with maximum concentricity and minimum uneven stresses; chambers concentric with both the bore and bolt face. How much all this helps in terms of accuracy may be debated, and certainly cannot be exactly defined, but it will be a rare gun that fires a string of 100-yard groups averaging under a quarter-inch, or shoots possibles at 1,000 yards, that doesn't have a precision chambering and barrel-fitting job.

I'm neither a machinist nor a gunsmith, so I can't tell you *how* to do precision work, but from watching several fine gunsmiths do it, and from talking with many others, I do know *what* they do — and it makes me realize what a bargain precision gunsmithing is, for if equal time-consuming, close-tolerance work were ordered from a custom machine shop, the bill would be ferocious.

In *Rifle* No. 3, Roy Dunlap detailed how to fit a barrel to a Model 70 Winchester; in this article, I'll try to relate what goes into a barrel job on a Model 700-type Remington. I think you'll be as amazed as I was the first time I saw it done.

The first step is to re-work the bolt,

Barrel-maker Bill Atkinson of Atkinson Gun Co., Prescott, Ariz., buckles up a new barrel on a bench rest rifle. The massive barrel vise and cheater-equipped action wrench are necessary to take factory guns apart, but not to re-assemble them, for he uses well under 100 foot-pounds of torque.

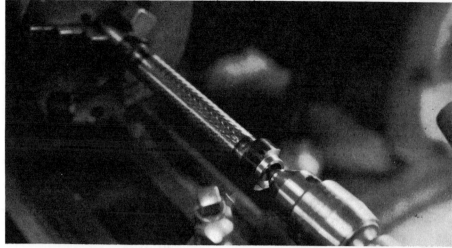

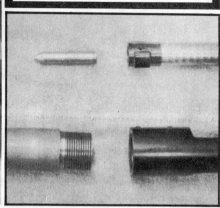

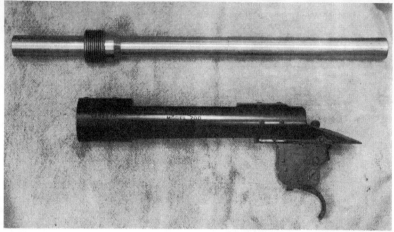

First step in working over an action is to screw a spud into the stripped bolt, above, center it on the firing pin hole [if initially fairly close to center], and turn the bolt nose and front face of the lugs, using either the live center or steady rest; the steady rest is then used while facing the end of the bolt and the bolt face, which can be done without removing the extractor. Lugs are lapped, top right, to assure even bearing by working the bolt up and down with non-imbedding grinding compound on the lugs while thrust is applied to the nose of the bolt by a steel ram that will fit the chamber of an old barrel. During the lapping operation, constant pressure is applied by turning the barrel into the threads. To cut the action face concentric, the mandrel, immediate right, is screwed into the action with the tapered cone behind the mandrel threads centering on the bolt hole. The mandrel is then chucked into the lathe and centered on the tail-stock.

which is stripped and screwed onto a stub which is in turn chucked into the lathe. The bolt is aligned by centering on the firing pin hole with the tail-stock, then supported in that position by a brass-jawed steady-rest located just behind the lugs, and the tail-stock moved away. In all probability, the bolt nose outside diameter will be a few thousandths eccentric from the firing pin hole, but by taking light cuts back to the lugs, the section forward of the lugs will be made concentric with the firing pin hole, which will mean that after the barrel has been properly fitted to the bolt, firing pin indents in primers will be virtually dead center. As a practical matter, in a typical hunting rifle, an off-center firing pin strike probably won't have any effect upon accuracy, for too many accuracy-destroying, or accuracy-lacking, factors are present. But in a competition gun, or a well-tuned varmint rifle, any imperfection can be critical — Ferris Pindell, an excellent gunsmith and *Rifle* Bench Rest Hall of Famer, swears that centered firing pin strikes are critical, and considering the type of shooting he does with his guns, I'll take his word for it.

One thing to bear in mind is that if a firing pin hole is not reasonably close to center to begin with, everything will be snarled up if the nose is turned concentric with the hole — so on some actions it simply isn't possible to get the firing pin

strike centered. Remington firing pin holes are usually quite close, and the various parts well-aligned, which is one reason this make is so popular among bench shooters.

Once the bolt nose has been turned clean, a light cut is made across the forward face of the lugs to square them, and provide a uniform surface for measurements during barrel fitting. Unless badly galled or scored, the critical rear faces of the lugs will not be cut, for they will be fitted to their recesses later by lapping.

Another critical area is case head support; if bolt fit is sloppy, or the bolt face anything other than absolutely square, the case will fire-form with a matching slight angle of the head. This angle will not be ironed out during reloading, for the head brass is much stronger than neck and wall brass; indeed, by tending to cock the case as it is pressed into a die, a non-square case head will tend to induce non-concentric sizing and bullet seating, which results in a bullet that is not aligned with the bore, cocked bullet entry into the rifling, and a resultant slight angle of the bullet base. If you don't think that affects accuracy, cut an angle with a file on the bases of a few bullets, shoot them and see what happens. Further, the cocked-head case is unlikely

to be positioned in the chamber the same on the next shot — the high spot may be supported by the high spot on the bolt face — resulting in even less support for the case head, renewed twisting and stretching of the brass.

The fix is a light cut across the face of the bolt, which will square it with the nose cut while also removing imperfections. New bolts are almost always burred around the firing pin and ejector holes; old bolts will have a ring due to gas cutting from primer leakage, or a radiused firing pin hole due to wear or too-enthusiastic removal of the original burr with a drill bit — and such a radius will cause "cratered" primers, or even perforations, at normal pressures.

With a properly shaped cutting tool, the face of the bolt can be cleaned with that dad-blamed riveted-in Model 700 extractor in place. However, if the extractor shows much wear, the gunsmith probably will have removed it while stripping the bolt; a special tool is required as an anvil while replacing the extractor rivet, making it exceedingly difficult to replace in the field or at a shoot, which is why I prefer the old snap-in Model 722/721 extractor.

Various other modifications can be done in order to improve an action, such

278

Cutting oil is brushed on as the barrel shank is cut to slightly over thread-cutting size. The final shoulder is cut during this operation, providing a reference for facing the barrel, chambering and cutting the recess for the bolt nose.

After the breech has been faced to the same dimension as the distance from the action face to the bolt lugs, plus the thickness of the recoil lug, plus .005-inch clearance, the bolt recess is cut to within .0015-.002 of bolt nose diameter. The depth of the countersink is the same as the bolt nose projection beyond the lugs. These close tolerances are held in order to support the nose of the bolt and as much of the case as possible, and to leave minimum space for gas flow in the event of a case rupture.

as installing a bushing near the rear of the bolt, and fitting it to the receiver; or taking various measures to improve bolt smoothness, wobble (which will improve trigger consistency), or "jump" during striker fall, but such things will rarely be done in conjunction with a routine barrel-fitting job.

After one last cut   across the face of the bolt nose, the projecting case support ring — the bolt is finished except for lapping the lugs into their action recesses. The latter operation probably has more effect upon accuracy than any of the other operations yet mentioned, for if the case head is not squarely and firmly supported, a rifle cannot shoot as well as it otherwise would.   Jim Carmichel of *Outdoor Life* recently told me of some tests conducted by a major firearms manufacturer in which lugs were lapped into an action, then one lug was ground back .001-inch at a time, with the rifle tested for accuracy at each stage.   The result was progressively worse vertical stringing, reaching a plateau when .006-inch, as I recall, had been removed; apparently the bolt used could spring almost .006 under firing stresses. The reason for vertical stringing should be obvious, for when a Mauser-style bolt is in the locked position, the lugs are straight up and down.

With a relatively new bolt, a glance at the lug face will indicate how much of each lug is bearing, and where.   But a more accurate check is to paint each lug surface with machinists' layout blue, then open and close the bolt while subjecting it to a *straight-back* thrust — which can be applied with a tight case, or a headspace gauge or a case to which thin brass shims have been "glued" with a dab of grease. Attempting to apply the rearward pressure by pulling the bolt handle won't work, for the thrust will be assymetrical, and will result in false results.

Lapping is quick and easy, if it's done properly. All it requires is applying a dab of a Fine-grade, non-imbedding grinding compound to the lug faces of a *stripped* bolt and working the handle up and down while a symmetrical load is applied to the bolt face.   The grinding compound used by most gunsmiths comes as a powder which is mixed with oil; in addition to not imbedding in the metal, where it would continue to cut, as common valve grinding compounds will do, it has the advantage of breaking down with use so that any residues inadvertently left in the action are not abrasive, or soon cease to be.

The thrust on the nose of the bolt is usually applied in one of two ways: with a spring-loaded plunger in a device which screws into the barrel threads, or with a stub of old barrel into which a steel driving rod like an over-length headspace gauge has been inserted. With the latter,

279

more common method, thrust is applied by screwing the barrel into the action and gradually turning it deeper as the locking lugs and recesses are ground and polished to a perfect fit. With a Model 700 such as we're discussing, or with any other action style in which the extractor cannot be removed easily, the driving rod face should be turned smaller than the case extraction groove to avoid the extractor. While a spring-loaded plunger has the advantage of applying constant pressure, some contend that it is too constant, applying cutting force to low spots as well as high.

By working against each other, the bolt lugs and their recesses are soon perfectly mated and highly polished. Periodic checks with layout blue show how the work is progressing.

Although we're talking about fitting a new barrel, where the new chamber will be headspaced to a worked-over action, the lugs of a completed rifle can be lapped without removing the barrel, with thrust applied by brass shims on a case. But bear in mind that headspace — the distance between the bolt face and the point where the cartridge is supported by the chamber — is certain to be increased, perhaps beyond safe limits for factory ammo. Usually, a lapping job will set back the bolt — thereby increasing headspace in the existing chamber — by at least .003, and .006 isn't unusual. Since .006 is the maximum allowable extra headspace for some cartridges, and the gun is unlikely to have minimum headspace before the work begins, the result of a do-it-yourself lapping job is likely to be excess headspace — allowing too much fore-and-aft movement of the cartridge, short case life due to the resultant stretching, and possible destructive release of gases due to a total head separation.

True, you can fire-form cases to the over-length chamber, then only neck-size them during loading, without any problem — so long as you, or someone else who is aware of the potential hazards, are the only ones who will load for it. But if you have a rifle that you're not ready to re-barrel, yet which has a non-bearing lug, the proper course is to lap the lugs until the offender begins to bear, check headspace, and if excessive, have the barrel set back one turn and re-chambered. You can live with a rifle of less-than-maximum accuracy, but you might not live — or be able to see — after trying to shoot a rifle with excessive headspace. Be safe by doing the job right.

One last step that some gunsmiths will do in re-working an action is facing off the forward face, where the barrel or separate recoil lug will bear. Probably the simplest method is a special mandrel, somewhat longer than the action,

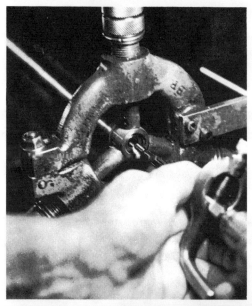

The barrel is chambered with a fast-cutting roughing reamer followed by a finish reamer, supported and driven by the tail-stock, but hand-held by the clamp in order to feel the cut. Depth is checked by measuring from the base of a "Go" or minimum headspace gauge to the barrel shoulder with a depth mike. When finished, that dimension will be the same as the distance from the action face to the bolt face, plus the recoil lug thickness. The final check will be by closing the bolt on the headspace gauge after the rifle is assembled.

With the barrel supported by the tail-stock, the threads are cut to almost full depth, then tried on the action. They will be gradually deepened until the barrel will screw all the way into the action by hand.

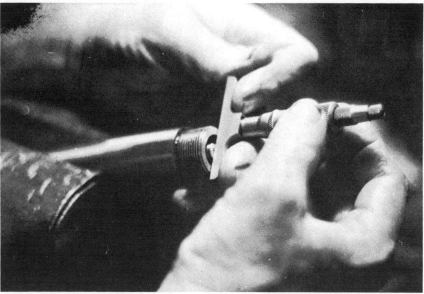

If a special throat is desired, a dummy round loaded with the bullet to be used, seated to desired overall length, is dropped into the finished chamber; the bullet striking the lands will keep the cartridge from seating fully. The length of throat to be cut with the throating reamer is determined by measuring from the base of the cartridge to the barrel shoulder, as with a headspace gauge.

threaded to fit the action and with a tapered cone behind the threads to center it in the bolt hole. After screwing it into the action, with the cone tightened against the bolt hole, the mandrel is chucked into the lathe on centers and the action faced off.

Now for the barrel. The sequence that is followed in chambering and fitting a barrel, as well as the type of set-ups used, will vary from one gunsmith to the next. Also, due to special circumstances a gunsmith may not follow his usual routine on a certain job. For example, if trying to make a certain total weight on a competition rifle, while removing no more metal than necessary from the barrel, the gunsmith may turn the shank and rough-chamber the barrel before turning the contour. The sequence and the set-ups outlined here approximate those usually followed by Bill Atkinson of Atkinson Rifle Company, Prescott, Ariz., whose barrels and gunsmithing skills have gotten me into the money at many bench matches.

Assuming the barrel blank has been turned to its final contour, the muzzle end is chucked into the lathe and the breech centered on the bore with the tail-stock. The to-be-threaded shank is turned to .010 oversize, forming the final shoulder — the point which will bear against the action, or in the case of a Remington, against the recoil lug. The steady-rest is then set up on this bore-concentric surface for most of the remaining work. Although the barrel could be threaded at this point, Bill prefers the greater steadiness allowed by running the steady rest on a smooth surface rather than threads; secondly, he prefers to cut the threads last, with the tail-stock supporting the barrel by the larger, finished chamber hole.

Returning to the action, a depth mike is used to measure the distance from the receiver face to the front of the bolt lug. The barrel shank is then faced off that distance plus the thickness of the recoil lug, plus about .005-inch — to provide bolt opening clearance when the barrel is heated due to firing, yet to allow as much of the bolt to be shrouded by the barrel as possible. (It's pretty easy to forget to allow for the recoil lug thickness, either here or during chamber reaming — at a bench match not long ago, one of the competitors was shooting his newly re-barreled 6x47 for the first time. The first fired case came from the gun with a grossly lengthened body and only a hint of neck. The gunsmith, who is no longer in business, swore he had test-fired the gun, of course.)

The next step is to rough out the chamber, although it makes little difference whether it or the bolt recess is cut first. Bill usually hogs out surplus metal from the chamber with a specially

sharpened drill bit .020 below cartridge shoulder size, to a depth about .100 less than the finished chamber, which saves time and wear on the roughing reamer, but he cautions that this can cause trouble since a normal drill bit won't exactly follow the hole.

The roughing reamer, supported and driven by the tail-stock, is then fed into the barrel — guided by a bore-diameter pilot — to within about .050 of final depth. Depth is determined by a "Go" headspace inserted into the developing chamber, and the distance from its base to the barrel shoulder measured with a depth mike. When the chamber is completed, that dimension will be the same as the distance from the receiver face to the bolt face, plus the thickness of the recoil lug.

The chamber quite likely will not be finished until a later operation, but to simplify the discussion, let's get it done now. The finish reamer is of approximately the same dimensions as the roughing reamer, but it has more flutes, cuts more slowly, and gives a better finish. Like the roughing reamer, the finish reamer is supported and driven by the tail-stock, while held by hand in a reamer tool. Thus the pilot and tail-stock provide alignment while the gunsmith can feel the rate of cut, controlling it with the tail-stock drive wheel. With either reamer, frequent stops are made to blow chips out of the chamber and dip the reamer in cutting oil. During the roughing stage, depth is controlled by cross-checking between the depth mike reading against the headspace gauge and the indications on the tail-stock ram, checking more often with the headspace gauge as full depth is neared.

With the chamber roughed to within about .050, a dial indicator is mounted on the tail-stock ram, reading off the steady-rest. The finish reamer is fed in until it begins to cut, then the dial indicator is zeroed and the amount to go determined with the headspace gauge and depth mike. The final amount is cut while watching the dial indicator, with stops to check with the gauge and micrometer.

The rate of feeding in the reamer is largely a matter of experience, for it will vary with the hardness of the barrel steel, the cartridge being cut, and the sharpness and design of the reamer. Too fast a rate and the reamer will chatter and gouge; too slow a rate and the tool will be dulled. In the job in the photos, Bill was feeding a .222 Remington Keith Francis finish reamer at about .002-inch per second.

Counterboring the barrel shank requires measuring the distance from the bolt nose to the lug face, which will be the depth of the counterbore — bolt opening clearance, and allowance for heat

expansion, was allowed when the shank was faced off .005-inch short of touching the lugs. The diameter of the counterbore is the diameter of the bolt nose plus .0015-.002 total clearance. These tolerances are much closer than factory standards both for manufacturing simplicity and for utility — one kernel of powder, or one bristle from a cleaning brush in the bolt recess and the bolt will close with reluctance. However, the close fit between the end of the bolt and the rear of the chamber gives maximum support for the case, but if a case or primer does let go, the gases must wend their way through a 90-degree turn in a passage considerably narrower than the thickness of one of the pages of this magazine. Secondly, since the bolt nose was turned concentric with the firing pin hole, and since the bolt nose will be closely supported by the barrel recess, which is concentric with the bore, the firing pin will fall within a thousandth of an inch or so of the center of the chamber — where the center of the primer will be.

Now the barrel is ready to be threaded. The tail-stock is run into the chamber hole, the steady rest removed, and a pass taken down the shank to finished thread size — 1.060-inch for a Remington. Setting up the lathe to cut 16 turns per inch, the threads are cut to almost full depth, the points broken with a file, and the fit of the action tested by removing the barrel from the lathe and screwing the action on. If it's too tight, another thread-cutting pass is made. This cut-and-try method continues until the barrel will screw all the way into the action by hand. Because of normal manufacturing tolerances, if threads are cut to standard depth the action may wobble on the barrel as on the previously mentioned hunting rifle. These custom-fitted threads may not fit another action of the same make and model, and they may require two or three extra trips in and out of the lathe, but the result is a stronger joint.

Of course, such close-tolerance fitting will also reveal any manufacturing errors such as tapered action threads. I know of a case where a well-known gunsmith fitted a barrel and commented to his customer that his Shilen DGA action had badly tapered threads. Naturally, the customer complained to Shilen, who broke it down and discovered that the gunsmith had threaded the shank to the standard Remington 16 threads per inch — but the Shilen action is cut with 18 threads. When the news of this event went around the bench rest circuit, there was considerable chortling, and some discussion of taking up contributions to buy a thread gauge for the distinguished, if somewhat red-faced gunsmith.

Another problem that may be encountered is misaligned action threads.

They can be straightened only by re-cutting, then matching the barrel threads to the over-size body. Some bench rest gunsmiths reportedly recut action threads concentric with the bolt hole as a matter of course. Without re-cutting the misaligned threads, the only solution is to cut the barrel threads relatively loose, relying upon the barrel shoulder and action face to line things up.

The rifle can now be assembled and headspace checked by closing the bolt on the gauge — it should just barely close, with some friction but without force. If the chamber needs to be deepened, it can be done while the barrel is throated. Factory-standard chamber reamers are ground with an integral throat, but most of the reamers used for target rifles have no throat section, requiring a separate throat reaming operation. The reasons are: some factory cartridge specifications call for a continuously tapering leade, rather than a cylindrical, groove-size throat followed by a leade, which is preferred by most competitors. Secondly, most competitors have preferences concerning throat length; a separate throating reamer makes it simple for the gunsmith to provide whatever the customer wants.

In the job in the photos, the owner wanted a throat which would allow his bullet to touch the lands when seated .125-inch into the neck; he had provided a dummy round loaded with the bullet to be used. The throating reamer was run into the barrel, which had been removed from the action, and given a couple of light twists to "break" the sharp edge on the lands, then the dummy cartridge was dropped into the chamber and measured like the headspace gauge to determine how deep the throat should be cut. Since the throating reamer will remove only the lands and about .0005-inch of the groove, the job can be done either by hand or in the lathe, although the latter makes it easier to control the depth, using the same setup as with the finish reamer. The final step on the chamber is to insert a fold of oiled Fine emery cloth on a dowel into the rotating chamber in order to polish it; if the reamer has cut well, the chamber will have a mirror finish in a few seconds.

The barrel is then reversed in the lathe, faced off and crowned according to the preference of the gunsmith — whose method of crowning is almost a trademark. Bill uses a spade-shaped tool to cut an 11-degree crown angled to within about .080 of the edge of the muzzle. He prefers it because it's an easy set-up, and because a study some years ago determined that gases exit from the muzzle at that angle. The crown is checked for burrs visually, and with a patch (fuzzy side out) on a cleaning rod. If it feels okay on the first pass, on the second the patch is stopped half out of the muzzle, and the rod withdrawn. If there are any minute burrs, traces of lint will catch around the muzzle.

I can understand the importance of a symmetrical crown, since any unevenness can cause uneven gas release behind the bullet, tending to upset it. But what I can't understand is why a much-shot barrel with apparently good crown will often be restored to its former glory simply by a fresh crowning job. It isn't reasonable, but it happens.

After a final polish of the barrel with a slack-belt sander, the barrel is screwed into the action and torqued to well under 100 foot-pounds. Factory barrels will be torqued to twice that, or more, which is probably why some gunsmiths screw in barrels like they were torquing head bolts on a diesel engine — with a three-foot wrench and a six-foot cheater bar. The many bench shooters who are firing marvelous aggregates with "combination guns," screwing in different barrels for different events with light, short-handled action wrenches and C-clamped barrel vises have proved that all that torque isn't necessary. Further, Bill says that it's easy for excess torque to form a stretch ring in a chamber at the point of the barrel shoulder. Such a ring cannot be seen, but it can be detected with layout blue and the finish reamer.

After test-firing, the rifle is ready for several thousand accurate rounds — made more accurate by the precision "bench rest" barrel-fitting and chambering job. There's a lot more to it than simply twisting in a reamer until the bolt will close on a factory round. ●

BORING
a rifle chamber

Unusual Case Designs
Don't Require a Reamer
If You Have a Good Lathe
— And Know How To Use It

By JAMES PARFET

Last summer I was asked to fit and chamber a barrel to an action in a wildcat caliber for which I did not have a set of reamers. The individual wanting this non-standard chamber was in somewhat of a hurry and did not wish to wait to have a set of reamers made up, nor did he want to stand the expense. Therefore after considerable thought, I came up with the idea of boring a chamber, using a single tool to cut the chamber with a lathe.

The idea intrigued me to the extent that I selected a piece of barstock suit-able for a set of sizing and seating dies as a means of inexpensive tryout. The results were a spectacular success, so much so that the barrel was tackled without apprehension. A test case was formed and loaded in the dies, the completed barrel-action assembly was placed in an old tire and fired with a long string. Careful inspection of the first case, and accuracy tests with the finished rifle, proved the job to be equal to my best efforts with purchased ream-ers.

Though the idea of cutting or boring a chamber shocks most gunsmiths, since they are so familiar with the reaming method, there is no reason why a good chamber cannot be cut by this method if careful attention is paid to setting up the job. While I do not know of any other gunsmiths using this method, some loading die makers use a similar technique on special high-production machines in which the cutting tool is guided by a template which is an over-sized duplicate of the internal profile. Though an individual gunsmith must guide the cutting solely with the lathe adjustments, proper attention to those adjustments and to the boring bar geometry will result in a smooth cham-ber of the proper dimensions.

This is such a fun way to produce a near-perfect rifle chamber that to date I have produced six of them, along with eleven sets of dies, without one failure or the need to cut the barrel back and deepen the chamber to remove chatter marks or a tear such as can be produced by a reamer.

A chamber can be produced in a

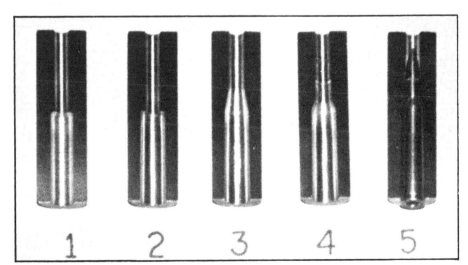

These sectioned views show the stages in boring a rifle chamber: (1) the rough cut, made with a twist drill; (2) the body taper, cut to the point of the shoulder with the boring tool and the taper attachment on the lathe; (3) the shoulder, cut with the same boring bar set-up and the compound slide; (4) the neck and throat, which can be cut with a boring bar or a reamer; and (5) the completed, polished chamber with a dummy case in position.

barrel in approximately 45 minutes, with a set of dies taking approximately one hour, after a little practice. This process would seem to hold great promise for the firearms experimenter and obsolete cartridge buff as well as anyone with requirements to produce a chamber for an odd cartridge. I do suggest a set of dies, or at least a piece of scrap bar stock for a starter in order to check out the process and build confidence.

A detailed, step-by-step description of the necessary operations for forming a chamber should start with setting the taper attachment to correspond to the body taper of the case. I use two dial indicators, one with 1/4-inch travel to measure the cross-slide travel, or taper, and one with one-inch travel to measure the length of axial travel. The one-inch indicator cannot measure the total length of the case body, but it can be used to set up the correct taper for a segment of the body, which is all that is necessary.

The dimensions to be checked by the indicators are calculated by taking the difference between the shoulder diameter and the base diameter, divided by four, and the length of the body divided by two, if the case body is less than two inches long. The reason for dividing the length by two is simply to bring the segment within the travel limitations of the one-inch indicator. The purpose of dividing the difference between the shoulder and head diameters by four is that we are looking for the amount of taper per side, which is the difference in diameters divided by two. Since we divided the length by two, we must also divide one-half the difference by two, which is the same as dividing the total difference by four. If the case body is more than two inches long, that length must be divided by three, and the difference between head and shoulder dimensions by six.

The calculated dimensions are used to set up the taper attachment, using a straight rod and the dial indicators. The shoulder angle is set with the compound slide (after the barrel shank has been threaded).

The second step is relatively simple, but extremely important: the *bore* must be indicated to absolute straightness and zero runout. I prefer to use a steady rest and a bushing with three set screws 120 degrees apart for this operation; this arrangement is much

The first step in preparing to bore the chamber is setting the taper attachment to cut the case body wall. It is adjusted using dial indicators to measure the amount of taper while running on a round, straight bar.

The bore must be indicated concentric and straight, either by indicating directly in the grooves (left photo) or with a slip-fit arbor. The face of the barrel is then cleaned (right photo) and the length of the shank measured in order to calculate the depth of the chamber.

The chamber body is roughed-in, using a twist drill which will leave about .020 stock per side at the shoulder. It should be run in to about .030-inch less than finished depth of the shoulder.

With the compound set to the proper shoulder angle to avoid changing the boring bar relationship later, run the boring bar in to the depth of the shoulder, measuring with the one-inch travel dial indicator. Zero the indicator at full depth. A second indicator is set from the cross-slide to the back side of the tool post and is used to return the compound to its original position when cutting the

shoulder angle. The body taper is then cut to full diameter, measuring at a point .060-inch within the mouth of the chamber. To cut the shoulder angle (right photo), the boring bar is backed out about .100 and a series of passes made with the compound slide until full depth is reached.

easier to adjust than a chuck on both ends of the spindle.

The straightness of the barrel set-up is roughed-in by selecting a distance as close to each end as is convenient to check with an outside micrometer and an indicator. Mark these two extreme ends, mike them for size and divide the difference by two, which is the taper per side. Set the indicator on the center line of the barrel and move the tool slide to either of the marks. Zero the indicator at this point and run the tool slide to the other mark; the taper is adjusted until the indicator reading equals the figure reached earlier by dividing the two mike readings by two. This should be done on both the side and top of the barrel.

If we could assume the bore were

perfectly centered in the barrel we could proceed, but I have as yet to find a case where this is true. Therefore I have used two methods of final adjustment for taper and concentricity. One method is to make an arbor about four inches long which is a snug slip-fit in the bore, then check for eccentricity over a one-inch interval. The second method is to indicate the bore itself. Taper and concentricity are both held to a plus-or-minus .0001 or less. If the bore isn't exactly true, the chamber will be eccentric, causing loss of accuracy.

The first work on the chamber itself is started after the barrel has been chucked straight and concentric, turned and threaded. Before cutting anything, however, the chamber body length — the distance from the barrel face to the chamber shoulder must be determined. First, measure the distance from the bolt face to the face of the receiver; from this dimension, subtract the distance from the barrel shoulder to the face of the barrel. Subtract the result from the cartridge body length (distance from cartridge head to shoul-

Though a boring tool can be used to cut the neck and throat of the chamber, it's simpler to make a double-diameter piloted reamer, as is being used here.

285

The final step in completing the chamber is polishing, done here with a small rubber wheel on a long arbor in an electric drill. The barrel is simultaneously rotated in the lathe, resulting in a high polish. Final checks can be made with a dummy cartridge or a headspace gage.

der, measured from a fired case or from a cartridge dimension drawing.)

For example, the distance from bolt face to receiver face on a Mauser is about .735, while the distance from the barrel shoulder to the end of the shank is about .625. The difference, in this example .110-inch, is the distance a headspace gauge or cartridge will protrude from the barrel. Subtracting this distance from the body length of the cartridge will give the depth the chamber body is to be cut.

Roughing the chamber is done with a standard twist drill. Keep in mind that it is easier to make an extra pass or two with the boring bar than to straighten up a mistake caused during this roughing operation, so take it easy. I select a drill that will leave about .020 per side at the shoulder, and feed it in

to a depth which leaves approximately .030-inch of stock to be bored out in forming the shoulder.

The finishing work is started by boring the body taper. First be sure that the compound has been set to the proper shoulder angle, which will allow using the original depth indicator setting for both the body taper depth and the shoulder angle starting depth. Take a "touch" cut across the face of the

barrel end to be certain the boring bar is flush with the end of the barrel shank.

With the one-inch travel indicator, set the depth of the boring bar to the chamber body length, as previously calculated. With the boring bar fed in to this depth, the indicator should be re-zeroed with less than one revolution of the needle passing zero, to eliminate errors in counting revolutions of the

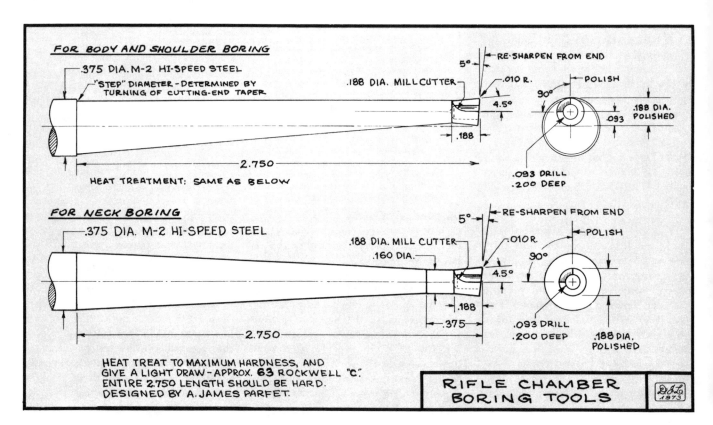

FOR BODY AND SHOULDER BORING

.375 DIA. M-2 HI-SPEED STEEL

"STEP" DIAMETER - DETERMINED BY TURNING OF CUTTING-END TAPER

.188 DIA. MILL CUTTER

5°
RE-SHARPEN FROM END
.010 R.
4.5°
.188
.188
90°
POLISH
.188 DIA. POLISHED
.093

2.750

HEAT TREATMENT: SAME AS BELOW

.093 DRILL
.200 DEEP

FOR NECK BORING

.375 DIA. M-2 HI-SPEED STEEL

.188 DIA. MILL CUTTER
.160 DIA.

5°
RE-SHARPEN FROM END
.010 R.
4.5°
.188
.375
90°
POLISH
.093 DRILL
.200 DEEP
.188 DIA. POLISHED

2.750

HEAT TREAT TO MAXIMUM HARDNESS, AND GIVE A LIGHT DRAW-APPROX. **63** ROCKWELL "C". ENTIRE 2.750 LENGTH SHOULD BE HARD. DESIGNED BY A. JAMES PARFET.

RIFLE CHAMBER BORING TOOLS

DJL 1973

needle. With this set-up, the one-inch indicator will pick up the movement of the boring bar during the final portion of its travel, early enough to prevent cutting too deep.

I also set an indicator from the cross-slide to the back side of the tool post, again with less than one revolution to zero. This indicator is used only for returning the compound to its original position when boring the shoulder angle, and will not be affected by the movement of the cross slide or main tool slide. Therefore, when the body diameter is reached with the tool slide, and the depth is reached with the main tool slide, the compound slide may be returned to zero with this indicator.

With this set-up, the chamber is bored until finish diameter is reached at a point .060-inch deep. With a proper set-up, this is the only dimension necessary to check at this time. The finish diameter at that point may be measured from a fired case, or may have been previously calculated while determining the taper of the case.

The same indicator set-up used on the last operation is now used to bore the shoulder angle. Back the boring bar out approximately .100-inch from zero and make the first pass with the compound slide, return the compound to zero on the indicator (bless that indicator), move the boring bar in .020 or so, and make another pass with the compound slide. Repeat this procedure until within approximately .005-inch of zero on the boring bar depth indicator, from where you must proceed slowly in order to achieve a very smooth finish on the shoulder. With a final pass at zero on the depth indicator, the body taper and shoulder angle are complete. If you are in doubt about

either the taper or shoulder operations, a headspace gage and depth mike can be used to check your work.

The neck clearance and throating is relatively simple and can be done with a double-diameter piloted reamer, or bored with the set-up used for the chamber after unlocking the taper attachment. Remember, if you are going to bore these diameters, that it's a deep small-diameter hole.

I have bored necks and throats in two barrels and it's quite satisfactory for chambers of .30 caliber and above, but it's tricky for smaller bores and probably easier to make a reamer. But please remember to make the reamer before you set up to bore the chamber; I didn't the first time, and it's aggravating to have to take the barrel out of the lathe, then set it up true again.

In making a reamer, I have found that the chamber neck diameter can be from .002 to .008 over the diameter of the neck of a loaded case without affecting accuracy. I make neck reamers to a diameter calculated from the bullet diameter, plus twice the maximum neck wall thickness, plus .003 for clearance. This is smaller than most factory necks, since they usually leave a generous amount to allow for brass with exceptionally thick necks, which can run up pressures in a tight-necked chamber. But by holding the clearance down, the neck brass is not worked any more than necessary, thereby prolonging case life.

A 45-degree angle is used at the end of the neck-forming portion of the reamer and is undercut into the throating diameter so as to leave a sharp transition angle. The throat-cutting portion is made to bullet diameter and made long enough to seat all bullet

lengths. I do not shoot for a long freebore. The angle used on the end of the throating portion of the reamer is made to a 3-degree angle. Naturally, if chamber dimensions are available, I use them.

The final step to a completed single-tooled chamber is the polishing. I use a small rubber wheel on a long arbor, chucked in an electric drill. By rotating the barrel in the lathe and the wheel in the drill, a very high polish can be achieved, and if the boring has been done with care, next to no stock need to be removed in order to get a burr free finish of 10 RMS; 400 grit emery paper on a wooden dowel can also be used. Keep in mind that this polishing operation is only to remove burrs and polish, *not to correct mistakes or remove stock.*

With any extractor cuts milled in and the barrel screwed tightly into the action, you are now ready to see how good a job has been done. Check the headspace with the proper gages and or a dummy loaded shell (less powder and primer).

If everything checks out here (I have yet to get this far and find a problem in the barrels I have chambered this way), you are now ready for the old tire and long string test fire. The care and accuracy of the boring job will determine the serviceability and accuracy of the rifle.

While boring a chamber might sound difficult, requiring both unusually good equipment and unusual skill, it isn't. I don't expect this technique to make reamers obsolete, but I do think it adds a challenging bit of fun. Even if you don't care to risk a barrel, you'll have to agree that this technique offers an inexpensive way to make special dies.

●

Fitting and Chambering Barrels, Benchrest Style

by Bob Brackney

FITTING AND chambering the rifle barrel is a fairly simple, straightforward process, and at the same time it is one of the key factors in determining whether the finished rifle will be a ho-hum affair or a real barn burner. Once the barrel is screwed into the receiver, it is difficult to tell whether a first-class job was done, and the fact that the price range for this work varies from about twenty up to sixty dollars or more doesn't help with the confusion. This article will first discuss the basic requirements for a quality chambering job and then outline in detail a procedure for accomplishing all these good things.

Like most phases of gunsmithing work, the difference between an outstanding fitting and chambering job and the other kind is determined not by what the gunsmith does but by the time and care he is willing to spend in doing it. Regardless of the quality of the work, the gunsmith will have to finish the outside of the rough-turned blank, thread the breech end so it will screw into the receiver, cut a chamber so the cartridge will go in (with safe headspace), and cut off and crown the muzzle. If he is charging twenty dollars for his trouble, he will obviously approach the problem differently than the fellow working for a benchrest shooter who is willing to part with sixty dollars (in addition to the cost of the barrel blank).

There is no one correct way to catch a fish, train a dog, or chamber a rifle. Every gunsmith has his own approach, and most have a lot of good reasons for feeling that their method is far superior to any other and that every other gun mechanic in the world is still groping around in the Dark Ages. This all makes good bull-session material, but the important thing is that in any quality job, certain things must be done, regardless of the details of the method used.

This bit of wisdom isn't any great breakthrough in solving the mystery of life, and it seems to me that the important characteristics of a good job are fairly obvious. First, the barrel threads must fit the receiver properly. This means that the receiver should screw onto the barrel smoothly, without appreciable looseness in the threads, and more important, without any interference from the threads themselves. The interference comes when the threads are too tight and the receiver can't be screwed on easily by hand. Consider how a thread works: the back side of each receiver thread pulls against the front side of the corresponding thread on the barrel, and this pull is exerted against the face of the receiver and the barrel shoulder. If the threads are too tight, the crest of one thread may be

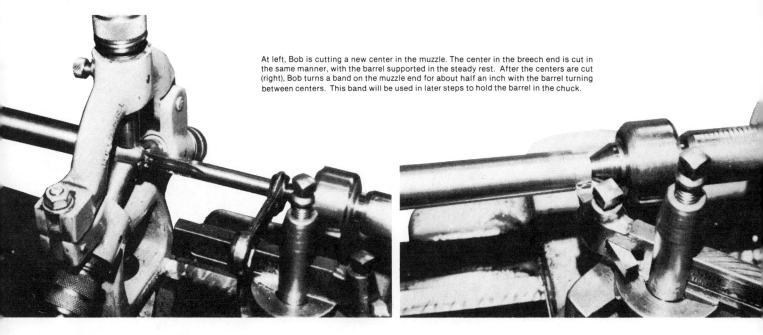

At left, Bob is cutting a new center in the muzzle. The center in the breech end is cut in the same manner, with the barrel supported in the steady rest. After the centers are cut (right), Bob turns a band on the muzzle end for about half an inch with the barrel turning between centers. This band will be used in later steps to hold the barrel in the chuck.

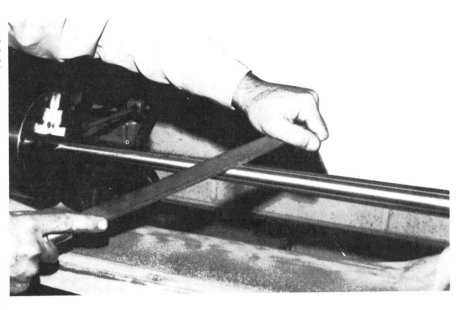

jammed into the root of the other, and the mating surfaces do not line up properly. Thus, we are concerned not only with the depth to which the threads are cut but also with the diameter to which the barrel shank is turned before threading.

Second, the barrel shoulder should square up with the face of the receiver so there is complete, even contact all around when the barrel is in place. This condition doesn't always exist, since the receiver threads are often slightly crooked in relation to the rest of the receiver and the receiver face. As a result, the receiver face and the barrel shoulder may not come together properly but make contact on one side with a visible gap on the other. This is bad news, and a method for correcting the problem is outlined in *Rifle* 51. Even if the receiver threads are straight, they are often very crude affairs (some Mauser threads are terrible), and a little clean-up may be required of the gunsmith.

In summary, as far as the threads are concerned, the receiver should screw on smoothly by hand all the way, until there is immediate, full contact between the barrel shoulder and receiver face. If everything fits properly, very little additional turning with the action wrench and barrel vise will be necessary after the parts have been "bumped" together by hand.

The third important feature of a good chambering job is a smooth, accurate chamber that is true with the bore. The chamber should be perfectly round, with no tool marks in the chamber wall, and with the throat absolutely concentric with the bore. The chamber should be on the minimum side, with the bolt just closing on a "go" headspace gauge. To some degree, this is all a function of the chambering reamer itself, and it is impossible to cut a top-quality chamber with a crummy reamer.

Finally, the muzzle must be square with the bore, and the crown must be free of burrs. The bullet will pop out of the muzzle at tremendous speed and under great pressure. If it is not released from barrel friction at the same instant on all sides, accuracy will obviously be affected.

Before we begin a discussion of the actual fitting and chambering, another obvious point should probably be mentioned. That is, you aren't going to help a poor barrel much by spending a lot of time on a first-class chambering job. If you are looking for a really accurate rifle,

the barrel blank is a poor place to try to save money — get a good one, or all your efforts will probably be pretty futile.

The chambering method I use is the one I learned about ten years ago from barrelmaker Pat McMillan. Like any procedure, it is only as good as the guy using it, but do it properly, and you can turn out a barrel job second to nobody's.

The barrel blank will come from the barrelmaker with a rough-turned exterior, anywhere from twenty-six to thirty inches long, and perhaps with a sixty-degree center of sorts in each end. Some barrelmakers trim off both ends after lapping the bore, and you can use any portion of the blank you want — it's all good. Others send you the whole thing, with a shallow saw cut a few inches from each end. This indicates that you are to use only the portion of the blank between the saw cuts, since the extreme ends were belled slightly during the lapping process. In any case, I usually end up cutting an inch or more off the breech end to get

down to the part of the barrel contour I want to use. If there is a sixty-degree center in the muzzle end, this is also cut off, so a new center can be established. The centers used by the barrelmaker have usually been wallowed out during the barrel-turning process, and in all cases, new centers should be cut for the fitting and chambering.

After you cut the ends of the barrel off, clamp the breech end in the lathe chuck and support the muzzle in a steady rest. Adjust the steady rest against the barrel with the tailstock center in the bore to hold the barrel blank in proper position. Then move the tailstock out of the way. Face the muzzle off square, and then cut the new sixty-degree center with a center

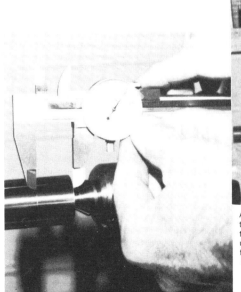

Above, Bob measures distance from front of receiver to front of locking lugs on bolt. Note that he includes the barrel bracket in this measurement, since it will be used on this particular rifle. At left, Bob is transferring this measurement to the barrel blank by scribing a line with the point of the dial calipers.

reamer. This reamer looks like a fat chambering reamer, but its sole purpose is to establish an accurate center. The center reamer is fitted with removable pilot bushings; select a pilot that gives a snug, sliding fit in the bore. Operate the lathe in slow backgear, and feed the reamer in using the tailstock handwheel. Support the rear of the reamer by the tailstock center, and hold it from turning with a small wrench (see photograph). Cut the center to give a bearing surface about a sixteenth of an inch wide.

Now move the steady rest out of the way and support the muzzle by a live tailstock center. Turn a cylindrical band on the muzzle end for about half an inch. The diameter of this cylindrical section doesn't matter, but the idea is to establish an untapered surface concentric with the bore for holding the muzzle end of the barrel in the chuck.

Now turn the barrel around, hold the muzzle end in the chuck, and support the breech end in the steady rest. Face-off the breech and cut a center just as in the muzzle.

The next step is to finish the exterior. Hold the barrel at the muzzle in the chuck (by the cylindrical band described above) and support the breech by the live tailstock center. With the lathe turning at fairly high speed, file the barrel using a mill smooth file about twelve inches long. If you hold the file at about a forty-five-degree angle to the barrel and move it smoothly the full length of the barrel with each stroke, the metal will come off the barrel like fine steel wool, and a very smooth finish will result. Keep the file cleaned out, or "pins" will accumulate in the teeth and you will do more harm than good.

After all the lathe marks are filed out, polish the barrel using progressively finer grits of emery cloth. I start with #180 and end up with #600 if the barrel is to be polished bright. A word of caution here — the polishing generates considerable heat in the barrel, and the barrel expands in length. Check the adjustment of the tailstock center frequently and back it off as necessary. The barrel can actually warp if you don't do this.

After the polishing is complete, it's time to turn the barrel shank to size and cut the threads, but first we have to make sure the receiver passes inspection. The locking lugs should be lapped, using the procedure outlined in *Rifle* 19. Then check the threads, for both smoothness and straightness, using a barrel stub, which is nothing more than a short piece of barrel threaded to fit the receiver in question. I have a 1 1/16-inch by 16-thread tap, ground 0.005-inch oversize, which I use on Remington receivers. I run this into the receiver threads to smooth them up and to remove small burrs and rough spots. Then I mount the receiver

on a tight-fitting mandrel between centers on the lathe, and take a light clean-up cut on the receiver face. Next, I screw a barrel stub into place to determine whether the receiver face and the shoulder of the barrel stub come together properly. If they do, the threads are OK, but if the threads are crooked, I straighten and recut them as outlined in *Rifle* 51. Most threads are straight enough as they are, and few gunsmiths go beyond cleaning up the threads and facing off the face of the action. If the threads are too crooked, the action should be set aside and used on something less demanding than a benchrest rifle. I happen to think that the shiny, recut threads are neat, but then I also like polished connecting rods in an engine, so what does that prove?

Now we can get back to the barrel-threading business. Mount the barrel between centers on the lathe, with the lathe dog on the muzzle end and the breech end supported by the live tailstock center. Place the bolt in the receiver and measure the distance from the receiver face to the front of the locking lugs, using a depth mike or a pair of dial calipers. If a barrel-bracket recoil lug is to be used, be sure to include it in the measurement. This measurement will give you the length of the barrel shank; transfer it onto the barrel, with a line scribed around the breech end at the proper point. The measurement should be a few thousandths long, and the breech will be faced-off later to establish proper bolt clearance.

The accompanying photographs show a Remington Model 700 receiver, and while some of the details covered apply only to the Remington action, the basic principles are the same for all types. The standard Remington barrel thread (sixteen per inch) calls for a barrel shank 1.062 inches in diameter. Even when I use the 0.005-inch-oversize tap in the receiver, I still use the standard barrel-shank diameter, which leaves a small flat on the crests of the barrel threads. I think this is a good idea, since the threads are less easily damaged than if they are cut to a sharp crest, and it also insures clearance between the crests of the barrel threads and the roots of the receiver threads.

This particular receiver had the threads recut and straightened, and the barrel shank was turned to 1.075 inches. The surface of the barrel shank should be smooth and should come to a sharp corner at the barrel shoulder. Pretty things always work better, so give it a light polish with #400.

There are two ways to remove the metal when cutting the barrel threads — you can slice it out smoothly, or you can tear it out in hunks. Given the realities of economics, it's easy to understand why most factory barrels look like they were threaded in about three passes. The thread surfaces are often rough and chewed up and look terrible.

The careful craftsman takes his time, and the completed threads have a smooth, almost polished appearance. The threading tool should be ground to exactly sixty degrees, with the edges honed, and the point should be set exactly on center. The type of cutting oil used has a great deal to do with the surface quality, and I've had excellent results with a product called Cool Tool. The stuff is expensive (about eight dollars a quart), but the results are worth it.

The thread should be cut as close to the shoulder as possible. I use a dial indicator against the carriage apron to mark the "kick-out" point, which is much easier than trying to watch the end of the thread come up, and reduces the chances of breaking the tool point. Set the compound rest at twenty-nine degrees, and for the first few passes, advance the compound handwheel about 0.007 inch each time. As the thread deepens, gradually reduce the cut to 0.002 inch per pass. These light cuts give a much better finish on the threads than heavier cuts would produce.

After the thread is cut nearly full depth, try it in the receiver. Remove the barrel from the lathe, wash the threads in solvent, and coat them with lubricant (I use STP). Also lubricate the receiver threads. On the first try, the receiver probably won't start on the threads at all. Put the barrel back in the lathe, take another light cut or two, and try again. After a little of this, the receiver will start on the threads, but it probably won't go all the way. Don't force it — if you do, the surfaces may gall together, and then you do have a problem. Keep taking light cuts until the receiver screws on smoothly all the way by hand. If you are not using the barrel-bracket recoil lug, and if the receiver threads haven't been counterbored back from the receiver face (first receiver thread removed), then the receiver will not go on all the way to the shoulder, but it should go on smoothly to the end of the thread. Then the barrel threads can be undercut at the shoulder so the receiver can screw on the rest of the way. Actually, I prefer to remove the first receiver thread — this seems to me to be a better approach than undercutting the barrel thread.

At this stage of the game, you should be able to take the barrel in one hand and the receiver in the other and screw them together all the way, with an abrupt, complete stop when the barrel shoulder and receiver come in contact. If the last half turn or so is tight and the barrel shoulder contacts the receiver with kind of a grinding halt, then there is interference somewhere that should be corrected.

Now put the barrel back in the lathe with the muzzle in the chuck and the threads running in the steady rest. If the threads are well lubricated (STP again) and the brass fingers of the steady rest are properly adjusted, the threads will not even lose their shine. Face off the breech end to leave about 0.010 inch clearance between the barrel and the front of the locking lugs, and in the case of the Remington action, counterbore the breech to accept the bolt nose. I always take a light cut on the bolt nose to clean it up and then fit it snugly to the breech counterbore, with about 0.010 inch clearance between the end of the bolt and the bottom of the counterbore. Finally, take a chamfering cut on the end of the barrel thread and the edge of the counterbore to remove the sharp corners, then clean up and temporarily put everything together. The stripped bolt should close easily, and there should be about 0.010 inch of end play.

Now it's time to make a chamber. Hold the barrel on the muzzle end with the chuck, and support it by the steady rest running on the barrel threads. The threads are concentric with the bore, since they were cut with the barrel turning between centers, and the bore should appear to sit dead still, with no runout, when the barrel is turning in the steady rest. Select a reamer pilot that will slide into the bore with no side play but loose enough that it can turn easily.

The chamber can be started with drill bits, and many top gunsmiths do this, but I prefer to do the whole thing with the reamers. Douse the resize (or roughing) reamer with Cool Tool and start it into the bore, with the tailstock center in the back end of the reamer and the reamer held by a wrench supported by the tool holder in the tool post. Run the lathe in slow back gear, and pull the reamer back far enough so it won't try to cut when the lathe is started (if the reamer is hard up against the barrel when the lathe is started, you may break a flute). Then slowly advance the reamer, using the tailstock handwheel. Use your other hand to hold the reamer back against the tailstock center as the cut is started to keep the reamer from slipping down on the center and getting out of alignment.

After cutting about 0.100 inch, pull the reamer out and remove the chips. If you hog the reamer flutes clear full of chips, you will probably cut some rings in the chamber. With most reamers, about 0.100 inch is plenty for each cut. Clean all the chips out of the chamber (they make rings, too) and repeat the whole process.

By holding the headspace gauge alongside the reamer, you can tell when you have gone about 0.100 inch less than the full depth of the chamber, just by eyeballing the reamer. When you have reached this stage, run the finish reamer in to the same depth, using the same procedure.

At this point, most of the gunsmithing books have you get out the depth mike, measure A and B, subtract from C, and come up with D (or is it E?). Forget it — there is a better way. Wash out the chamber and the barrel threads and hold the barrel in a padded vise. Put the headspace gauge in the chamber and screw the receiver onto the barrel about three quarters of the way. Then put the stripped bolt in the receiver and continue turning the receiver onto the barrel until the bolt just closes on the "go" headspace gauge. The gap between the barrel shoulder and the receiver face is now exactly equal to the amount that you must remove from the chamber end.

Let's say the gap, as measured with the dial calipers, is 0.080 inch. Put the barrel back in the lathe, stick the finish reamer all the way into the chamber, take the slack out of the tailstock handwheel, and set the handwheel scale at zero. Then slide the tailstock up until the center contacts the end of the reamer and lock the tailstock down. Back the reamer out a little until the lathe is started, and then slowly advance the tailstock handwheel. Watch the handwheel scale; the reamer should begin to cut as you pass the zero mark. Keep going until you have gone about 0.065 inch (always go short — the stuff is easier to take out than it is to put back in).

Now wash things up again and put the barrel and receiver together with the bolt and headspace gauge in place. This time, measure the gap with a feeler gauge. Go back to the lathe; this time, figure on going about 0.002 inch short. Check the gap again with the feeler gauge, and take out the last thousandth or two in the same manner — on the lathe. Many do the last bit holding and turning the reamer by hand, but it seems to me that it is better to finish up in the lathe so the reamer is firmly on center at all times.

During the entire reaming process, it is important to keep the chips cleaned out and to keep the chamber and reamer flooded with cutting oil.

Finally, cut a small chamfer on the chamber edge, to keep the case mouth from hanging up during cartridge feeding, and polish the chamber walls with #600 wet-or-dry wrapped around a split dowel. Don't try to polish beyond the shoulder, or you may mess up the throat.

The last step is to cut the muzzle off to length and crown the end. Hold the barrel in the chuck by the threads (carefully) and support the muzzle in the steady rest. For a standard target style crown, first face the muzzle off square, and then counterbore it 0.025 inch or so for about half the diameter of the muzzle. The lathe tool should be ground and stoned to cut a smooth surface, because it's not a good idea to try to polish around the crown with emery — you may damage the ends of the lands.

There are several ways to cut the actual crown or chamfer in the end of the bore. Many use a spherical stone, but I prefer a ball bearing about three-eighths of an inch in diameter (for .22 and 6mm bores), coated with #400 Clover Compound. The ball was annealed and drilled on one side so a short length of eighth-inch drill rod could be driven in for a handle. I cut the crown until the ball just begins to touch the edge of the groove. Then I reverse the lathe for a few revolutions to take off any wire edges that may have developed on the trailing edges of the lands. I remove any remaining wire edges by giving the barrel a good scrubbing with a bronze bore brush and Hoppe's. When I've finished, a dry tight patch should slide through the bore and come smoothly out the muzzle without any hint of snagging as it passes through the crown. After this, I put everything together, and the job is done.

A few odds and ends should be mentioned at this point. The feeler gauge can't be used when the action is sleeved and the receiver face isn't accessible. In that case, the simplest approach is to deliberately chamber about 0.010 inch short, based on measuring an old barrel, and then go in about 0.002 inch at a time until the bolt will just close on the "go" gauge.

Most reamers have an integral throater, so they cut the throat at the same time the rest of the chamber is done. Many gunsmiths, however, prefer to cut the throat separately, using a separate throating reamer. This tool is also used if a longer, nonstandard throat is required. This, of course, is done after the rest of the chamber is complete.

Finally, when you assemble the barrel and receiver for the final time, clean and lightly lubricate the threads (more STP). Tighten the receiver firmly, but don't overdo it — seventy-five to eighty foot-pounds is plenty, and many target rifles aren't even this tight. Some folks approach this like they're tightening the lug nuts on a Kenworth, but this isn't necessary at all.

So there you have it. Other methods may produce equal results, but I'm convinced there is no better approach; benchrest rifles chambered this way, by several gunsmiths, currently hold a bunch of world records.

However the job is done, keep in mind that the hidden craftsmanship represented by the bore, threads, and chamber is the heart of any rifle, as far as accuracy is concerned. A poor barrel or a lousy chambering job may not show, but the results will show where it counts — on the target. ●

Tools needed for polishing are flat and grooved blocks of wood, wet-or-dry sandpaper in a variety of grits, and a lubricant to keep the sandpaper clean and speed up process. A padded vise is a great help.

The polished and cleaned barrel is ready to be blued. The pad of steel wool and the small bowl are used in applying the blackening solution. A supply of steel-wool pads and paper towels should be kept handy.

Though not required, a fine wire brush (0.005-inch) can be useful. It leaves a very fine matte finish similar to that on rust-blued guns.

Beginning the blackening; do not worry about finger prints or streaks in the finish at this stage of the process.

FIREARMS COME in many shapes and sizes: rifles, handguns, and shotguns. Some are polished, some are engraved, and some are inlaid with precious metal. But the one thing most firearms have in common is a beautifully blued finish on the metal parts.

Firearm bluing and rebluing are important parts of the firearm industry. Without these processes, new arms would be beautiful pieces of wood with unsightly shiny pieces of steel attached. Those fine old guns that we value so highly would often be just faded, rusty remnants of the past.

Although the cost of professional rebluing often seems quite high, the gunsmith's hourly return, in terms of money, is often just the opposite. It is, however, this cost that often makes the difference between a shabby-looking gun and a great-looking gun. But this need not be the case for the careful, patient amateur gunsmith who is willing to get his hands dirty and spend a few hours working.

I have developed a method of cold (instant) steel coloring that is quite acceptable. It is also nearly foolproof. I use this method in my shop to refurbish the barrels of double-barrel shotguns. While the appearance is not quite as attractive as that of a hot-dip blue or a genuine rust blue, the color is acceptable and durable. I have had no complaints, and my repeat business is good.

No special equipment is required to do the job. A vise with padded jaws is helpful, but you can get by without it. The items required are two or three sheets each of number 100, 240, and 320 wet-or-dry auto-body sandpaper for polishing, 3/0 steel-wool pads for applying the blackening solution, and a bottle of Brownell's Dicropan IM blackening solution. (Other brands may not work using this method.)

The quality of any bluing depends upon the polish. So let's begin there. The polish *must* be done properly. The wet-or-dry sandpaper is used for polishing. The 100-grit paper is for removing heavy rust and pits. The 240-grit is used for removing the old blue and small blemishes. The 320-grit is used for the final polish. If the items to be colored are not pitted, you can begin with the 240-grit. The 320-grit is as fine as is needed, because the application of the blackening solution with 3/0 steel wool adds to the polish.

Polishing is best done so that the direction of each successive operation differs from the preceding stages by about forty-five degrees. For example, when polishing a pitted barrel, you would begin using the 100-grit paper at a right angle to the bore. The popular shoeshine method can be used for this step. The next stage, using the 240-grit paper, would be done at an angle of forty-five degrees to the bore. The final sanding, using 320-grit paper, would be parallel to the bore. The best polish usually comes from doing the final polishing with the grain of the metal. Long length-wise strokes should be used to prevent unsightly low spots.

For polishing barrels, particularly the final polish, use a grooved wood block behind the sandpaper. Flat wood blocks or files are used on flat parts. This is to protect corners and maintain the original contours. To speed the cutting action of the sandpaper, a lubricant such as a light oil or WD-40 can be used to keep the sandpaper clean. This reduces polishing time by about one third. Polishing *must* be well done and complete. There are, however, some areas to avoid when polishing. The mating surface between the action and barrel of a break-open shotgun is an example. Enscribed areas such as those bearing the maker's name, gauge, choke, *etc.*, should be only

After the first application of solution, barrel is wiped dry with paper towels before the second application.

The actual bluing is a dirty process, so expendable old clothes are "uniform of the day." Here, the blackening solution is applied with steel-wool pad.

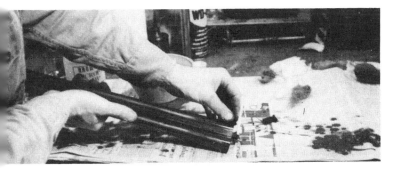

CLARK LAWRENCE
INSTANT BLUE

When the barrels are blued, a protective coating is applied — and rubbed into all grooves and crevices — with the fingers.

lightly polished. It is better to leave a few pits or scratches than to remove this information.

After polishing is complete, the parts are degreased (lacquer thinner works well for this), and the blackening solution is applied. If there is a secret to this type of coloring, here it is: the blackening solution is applied with steel wool. The 3/0 steel wool is torn into small pads about the diameter of a quarter, and this solution is rubbed on with these pads. You should make at least a dozen of these pads.

Now you're ready to blue. This is the dirty part of the job. Wear old clothes, and protect your tabletop with newspaper. The blackening solution will stain your hands, so rubber or plastic gloves might be in order.

Pour about half an ounce of the blackening solution into a small saucer, grasp one end of the barrel in one hand and one of the steel-wool pads in the other hand. Dip the steel wool into the blackening solution and vigorously rub it onto the barrel. Do not worry about the streaks or finger prints at this point.

Continue dipping and rubbing until

the barrel is completely blackened. As long as the steel wool is clean, the solution "bites" when applied to the steel. When it ceases to do this, use a fresh steel-wool pad. When the solution becomes very dirty, discard it. This is the reason for using only half an ounce at a time. Again, you need several steel wool pads.

With the first application complete, you have an uneven finish. Do not be concerned with this. The second application leaves the steel a uniform, very dark grey (almost black).

For the second application, wipe the barrel dry with a paper towel. Starting with clean blackening solution and clean steel-wool pads, repeat the whole process — with one exception. Dip the steel wool into the solution, and this time, squeeze it nearly dry before rubbing it on the barrel. Rub and rerub, changing steel wool and solution as needed (you'll develop a feel for this) until the finish appears dark and uniform. Remember, it will not be black but a very dark grey. Any light areas can be remedied by rubbing with clean solution and a clean steel-wool pad.

When you are satisfied that the color is uniform and as dark as it is going to be, you are finished. Wipe the

barrel dry and apply a coat of grease or STP. Rub this on with your fingers using heavy pressure. The finish should be allowed to age for two or three days before you consider using the firearm.

As I said before, I have had no complaints with barrels colored using this method. It could be because the charge for using this method is much less than the time-consuming rust-bluing method, but I think it is because it is satisfactory.

There is one other application for this method of coloring that may be just as important as the one just described. I have a few collector and trader customers who have a firearm that they want cleaned up and made to look better. For these arms, I clean and refurbish the wood (another story) and touch up the steel parts using the method described. This works quite satisfactorily, even on lightly rusted surfaces. No special preparation is required or even desired. The pieces are degreased (again no special pains), and the blackening solution is applied with the steel wool. It is applied all over and rubbed on using some pressure. Even heavily worn arms can be made to look quite decent. They seem to take on a "used but cared for" look.

●

The DAMP~BOX

for fine rust~browning or blueing

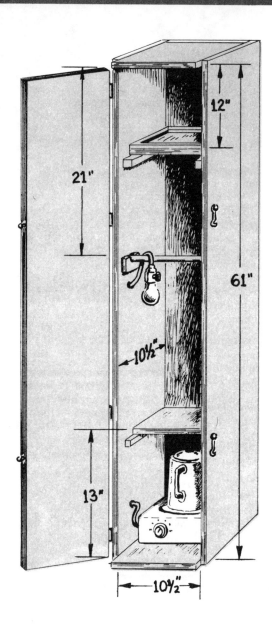

Bivins tried several different types of damp-box setups before finally settling on this one. This 3/4-inch plywood box, which includes a parts tray, 40-watt light bulb and a pot of water on a thermostatically controlled hot plate makes rust-blueing and browning operations independent of atmospheric conditions.

By JOHN BIVINS

ONE WINTER DAY some years ago, I sat in my room staring at my grandfather's old Smith double sixteen hanging on the wall, perched on its pegs until another nine months brought dove season around again. A fine, tight, though well-used piece, the shotgun showed considerable thinning of the blue, especially at the muzzles, from years of case wear. The old veteran was ready for a face-lift.

I had heard of an old man in the area who could "rust-blue" the barrels, so I prevailed upon my dad to drive me to the man's shop the next Saturday. After some twenty minutes of my shifting impatiently from foot to foot, and Dad having put his hand on the doorknob to leave, the gunsmith finally looked up from his lathe and peered tiredly at me over his spectacles. I explained in a rush that I had heard he would refinish double shotgun tubes, and wanted mine done, handing over the silvered Smith.

The old man put the gun on the counter, pushed up his glasses, and allowed as how he couldn't do it until summer. Having envisioned Old Betsy returning to her former glory instantaneously, I stammered out some form of impatient and frustrated query. The gunsmith, already turning back to his work, only said "Not enough damp to blue in January; come back in July." My further questions were cut off by the slapping belts of an ancient Atlas lathe.

I never understood the meaning of that terse statement from the grizzled old gunsmith until about twelve years ago, when I suddenly had occasion to brown longrifle barrels during the winter. In our section of the Southeast, a hot summer day will drip forth with enough humidity at times to mildew your boots, cause beards to grow in your rifle barrels, and generally turn any non-air-conditioned building into varying degrees of a sauna-like sweatbox. In this kind of weather, bare steel will darn near grow Spanish moss. Come October, however, the humidity plummets to an ambient 30 percent. Trying to brown or blue steel with chemicals in such a dry atmosphere is almost as successful as rusting 24-carat gold, unless you use a hot-brown and blue with one of the caustic salts methods; neither of which is the best for longrifle barrels or double shotgun tubes. No small number of gun tinkerers have this problem year-round, especially in the arid Southwest.

I struggled with this winter-season malady for years, trying such unorthodox techniques as hanging rifle barrels

density of the chemical-aided oxidation. While common iron oxide tends to be coarse-grained, the rust brought about by browning and blueing solutions is quite fine-grained, especially that of blueing. Chemical blueing wasn't used much before the mid-19th century, although it may have been known earlier. Firearms blueing in the 17th, 18th and early 19th centuries was done by tempering the highly polished metal over a low forge fire. This process required a highly skilled artisan to bring off successfully, but the deep luster of the fire-blued color can't be duplicated by any other method. It does not wear quite as well as the blue produced by chemically induced oxides (as opposed to heat-induced oxides), since the coating is a great deal thinner in most instances.

At some point, some poor fool like myself no doubt discovered by accident that his browning recipe would also produce a fine, if less lustrous blue, when the parts were introduced to water. Since that time, a great variety of salts have been experimented with, and our modern hot-salts tank solutions tend to produce a color that is closer to black than what was used even thirty years ago. Ease of application and speed has brought this about, though some of us cranks are still only completely satisfied with the "true blues" of slow-rust or "nitre" blueing. If you feel this way, then give Niedner's formula a try. As for browning, the same is true. . .the *best* finish simply can't be done in a rush. If you have a damp-box, though, the chore is considerably less tedious.

The box itself is nothing fancy. I built mine of 3/4-inch exterior-grade plywood, but 1/2-inch will likely do as well. Mine, as you can see in the illustration, is over sixty inches high inside to allow for room for a hot plate, pot, and as many as a half-dozen longrifle barrels. No great amount of depth or width is needed, unless you contemplate a considerable production. If so, simply enlarge the design and turn up the heat.

It is best to construct the box with either coated or sheet-rock nails, and glue the joints with a waterproof glue. Varnish the inside surfaces with two coats of a good grade of phenolic spar varnish, or a

in the bathroom and turning on the shower every half-hour or so. My wife loved that, and I couldn't even make a return dig at her, since she never hung stockings from the shower rod. In any case, when it came time to brown a barrel in almost any of the months with an "r", my disposition suddenly soured, and I found myself continually cussing under my breath. I had almost come to the point of seeking out some person versed in the Black Arts for some encantation that would cause the Muse of the Oxides to rise, when I finally read an article about A.O. Niedner's superlative finishing methods. Slow-blue was one of the trademarks of his shop, and his workmen did it beautifully, winter or summer, with the aid of a damp-box. With the size of the Niedner shop, it was probably more of a damp-room rather than a damp-box. In any event, my problem had been solved, at least in theory.

I first tried a narrow, long box lying horizontally on the floor, with a cheap hot plate and a saucepan of water to provide heat and humidity. I learned a great deal from this experiment. One end of the barrel was immediately browned a beautiful plum color, while the other end turned a sickening blotched blue-brown.

Most of the heat had remained in the hot plate end of the box, and the humidity reaching the far end, where the temperatures were lower, condensed on every surface, the atmosphere at that end having reached the dew-point. I decided that a vertical damp-box was the answer, since rising heat would tend to maintain the same atmosphere from top to bottom. The new arrangement was so successful in controlling metal finishing that I now use the damp-box exclusively, even in the summer.

Browning and slow or "rust" blueing solutions are sensitive to the amount of moisture they are subjected to during application. Browning solutions may be even more sensitive, since many will actually blue metal as well as brown it. In fact, if some of the slow-blueing recipes are used without boiling the parts between application, they will also brown metal. That browning can play a dual role was illustrated by my experimental failure. . .when the moisture in the box condensed in beads on the metal, the browning turned blue or black at those spots. In other words, too much humidity can cause as much trouble as too little. Trying to finish metal with chemical applications can be a total failure on a day when a rainstorm has cranked up the hygrometer to 100 percent, just as you can have little or no success when the humidity has dropped below 50 percent or so. The ideal is a moisture level between the extremes.

Both browning and blueing, whatever the method used, are one form or another of red or black iron oxide, not altogether dissimilar from common garden-variety rust. The difference lies in the speed and water-resistant polyurethane, to prevent or at least slow moisture absorption by the plywood, to prevent the plys eventually separating. The outside doesn't matter, though if it makes you feel good to cover it in fine crotch-walnut veneer, do it. . .then you can stand the thing in the living room rather than the basement.

The door is hung with four medium-sized butt hinges and held shut with two screen-door hook and eyes, though you can use a piano hinge and fancy catches if plain utility offends you. Two 3/8 x 1 x 9-inch strips of pine or hardwood are nailed to the inside surfaces of the sides of the box near the floor to receive a narrow (6-inch) removable plywood shelf to rest rifle barrels on. Shorter barrels or barreled actions can also be hung on a string looped over cup-hooks screwed to the bottom surface of the top shelf. This upper shelf, which is mounted in a removable fashion like the lower unit, is for small parts which must be finished. This shelf doubles as a tray, and to prevent screws and other small objects from rolling off when you remove the shelf to carry it to your bench, tack a 3/8-inch strip of pine all the way around the outer edge of the top surface. The top shelf should not be more than 8 1/2 inches deep, if you use the dimensions of my box, to allow the humid air to circulate around the parts.

I have at times found it necessary to raise the temperature of the box to slow the browning a bit. The easiest method to do this is to simply hang a lightbulb in a switched socket about two-thirds the height of the inside of the box. Keep the hole in the side for the lamp wire small to prevent humidity loss, and hang the lamp on a dowel supported by U-shaped wooden brackets nailed to each side of the box. This enables you to let the bulb and its support down and out of the way when you are putting in or taking out barrels or barreled actions. Both of the latter should hang or rest near the back of the box so that the light bulb does not overheat the metal where it is nearest the bulb. In a box of this size, I have found that a 40-watt bulb is ample for secondary heat; a 60-watt is too much.

One side of the box near the bottom is also drilled for a line cord, this time for the hot plate. When using such an electrical appliance closely surrounded by wood, it is best to cover the bottom and sides of the box for a distance of about 12 inches from the floor with sheet asbestos. That way you can turn on your hot plate, close the door of the box, and go to bed without worrying about the house burning down around your ears. If the box is larger, there would be little need of this precaution.

The hot plate, with a pot of water sitting on it, generates the moisture needed for slow-blueing or browning. I'll discuss just how much moisture is needed later. One very important thing is that you must have a thermostatically-controlled hot plate, and by all means buy the most expensive one you can find. Cheap hot plates won't maintain an even heat. A unit without a thermostat is useless, since it will simply boil the water in your pot. The water shouldn't even approach boiling temperature, unless you want a baroque mess to polish off your metal.

The water is best put in an aluminum or stainless coffee pot, and here you can save money by buying a cheap one. Mine stands seven inches high with the lid, and holds eight measured cups almost brimful. If you purchase a taller pot, you may have to move the lower shelf in the box up to clear.

After constructing your damp-box, it's best to give it a trial run before throwing all the parts to your pet squirrel rifle or offhand Schuetzen in and turning it on. Take some steel scraps of the same alloy as various parts of your gun, and draw-file them clean. There's no need to polish further for the test. Put a couple of these pieces. . .such as barrel-stubs. . .on the top shelf, and hang one on a string about midway down the box. Put another on the lower shelf. All these should be coated lightly with whatever potion you have concocted in the dark of the moon. . . or bought over the counter. . .to rust metal with. Switch on the hot plate to its *lowest* position, fill the pot with water hot from the kitchen tap, and put the pot on the burner. If you have a percolator pot, you might knock out the glass perking "window" at the top, or, if you have a plain pot, punch a few 1/4-inch holes in the lid before putting it on. Latch the door, and leave it for six to twelve hours, whatever length of time you are accustomed to using with your solution. After that period of time, your parts should have a thin, yellowish, fine-grained layer of rust. . .not a heavy, coarse coat. If no rusting has occurred, raise the thermostat on the hot plate a bit and give it another try. When you find the level that causes oxide to form quickly and yet with a fine grain, make a scratch-mark on the thermostat dial if it isn't graduated, and you're ready to brown anything that comes along at that setting. Each time that you open the box, see that the pot is filled with hot water. If too much evaporates and the level drops a few inches, the water will become overheated. Never allow the moisture level to rise to a point that the inside surfaces of the box feel wet or extremely damp to the touch. If moisture condenses near the top of the box, though the lower half is satisfactory, resort to the lightbulb mentioned earlier.

A perfectly acceptable level of moisture may be obtained by this "seat-of-the-pants" method. If you are fussy and want to know exactly what is happening, purchase a cooking thermometer to test your water temperature, and a wet-bulb thermometer for obtaining relative humidity inside the box.

In my damp-box, the most efficient water temperature appears to fall in the 140 to 160-degree (Fahrenheit) range. Checking the humidity and atmospheric temperature in my box over a five-day period with a Bristol recording Thermo-Humidigraph, the most efficient rusting occurred with the temperature in the 80 to 90-degree range, and the humidity 70 to 80 percent, with a 40-watt bulb burning. Opening the box for five-minute periods to card rust from and re-coat parts caused negative "spiking" on the graph equivalent to a 20 percent drop in humidity and a 15-degree drop in temperature inside the box. This was recorded in early March, when the relative humidity in my shop was steady at 35 percent for the entire test period. A piece of "control" metal left in the same room and coated with the same browning solution did not form any oxides during the period, whereas most of the parts in the damp-box were finished in 2 1/2 to 3 days, with applications of browning solution each 12 hours, just as the "control" sample was treated. These air and water temperatures and damp-box humidities will no doubt differ in your own box, due to variations in hot plates. The chemical make-up of your solution may also require a different atmosphere. Although it is interesting to know what these levels are, it's not necessary to get efficient use from a damp-box, whatever the season of the year.

There are dozens of fine browning and blueing solutions available for trying. . . have a look in Angier's *Firearms Blueing And Browning* for a host of recipes. After trying eight or ten different browning formulas over the years, I have settled on one that never fails to give me a fine plum-colored brown, regardless of the alloy of steel. Many formulas will not color some alloys well. The one I use, shown in the table, was introduced to me by a gunsmithing friend who had run across it in the course of researching and restoring American 19th century martial arms. The formula, couched in somewhat more archaic chemical terms, was published in the *U.S. Ordnance Manual of 1841.*

Look for a druggist that has been in business for a long time to make this up for you, since he will probably have the ingredients on hand. In this formula, the ethyl alcohol acts as a wetting agent, and the copper sulfate serves the purpose of a stain, so that you can readily see where the solution is being applied on bare metal. The rest of the concoction is just about as poisonous and corrosive as anything can be, so keep it in a locked closet in a dark brown bottle. As with any other browning or blueing solution to be used in the "swab on and wait" manner, your parts must be thoroughly degreased, though I do not bother to degrease sections of parts which will not be finished, like the inside of a lockplate.

Many scribes have recommended boiling browned parts after the desired color is obtained, in order to stop the salts from working. I don't recommend this. Even pouring boiling water repeatedly over browned parts can spoil the fine reddish color by turning the oxide permanently black. I prefer to simply wash the parts with hot, not boiling, soapy water and then rinse and wipe dry. When the parts are thoroughly dry, oil them, and leave them on the bench overnight. If any after-rust has occurred overnight under the oil, wipe it all off, and oil again. Seldom does after-rust occur again after this, at least with the 1841 Ordnance formula. Boiling, of course, does not harm a slow-blue.

If you want to try slow-rust blueing, Niedner's formula, which we have reprinted from Roy Dunlap's fine book, *Gunsmithing*, where complete instructions will be found, is one of the least finicky and most durable of the old formulas — more durable, in fact, than the thinner blue-blacks commonly used today. "Rust" blues such as Niedner's are the only appropriate finish for sporting and target arms of the late 19th

and early 20th centuries, and modern custom rifles benefit considerably from such a finish. Certainly this type of blue involves more work, but the result is more than worth the effort.

Not surprisingly, Niedner's formula is virtually identical to a browning solution well known at least as early as the 18th century. In any event, the acids should be mixed carefully outdoors, preferably in a stoneware crock due to the resultant heat caused by the reagents. The nails are added, and after they are dissolved, the distilled water. Keep the solution in a brown glass bottle.

The polished metal parts to be blued must be boiled in a degreasing solution such as Oakite; plug the barrel both at chamber and muzzle with wooden plugs, both to protect the bore and to provide "handles," since, as with browning, the clean parts must never be touched with your hands. After cleaning, the parts are swabbed with the blueing solution (use a piece of lint-free, clean scrap T-shirt tied on a dowel), placed in the damp-box, and left for three hours or less. The first coat may have little effect, and you may wish to apply another coat after only the first two hours or so. After no longer than five hours, you should have a fine yellowish "bloom" on the metal. Remove the parts from the damp-box and boil them for about 15 minutes in distilled water.

Remove the parts from the water, and card them with a degreased wire brush having wire diameters not over .004-inch. Remove the barrel plugs, allow the metal to cool to room temperature, drive in dry plugs, recoat the parts, and return them to the damp-box.

From this point on, the parts should not remain in the box for more than four hours at a time, which means that you cannot leave them in overnight. Seven to twelve coatings, rustings, boilings, and cardings may be required, depending upon the alloy being blued. Don't card the last coat, when the metal has reached the color you want; a light polishing with 4-0 steel wool is sufficient. If certain parts resist rusting in this process — case-hardened parts are especially bad about this — try etching them lightly with a 5 percent solution of nitric acid and distilled water.

With slow-rust blueing, the use of the damp-box is identical to that in browning, although you may find that you can work with slightly more humidity in blueing to speed the process.

Give the damp-box system a try. Once you have tried a damp-box, you won't care whether summer comes or not. . .at least when it comes to the task of finishing gun metal by traditional methods. ●

Building an
Action Sleeve

Text and machine work by Bob Brackney

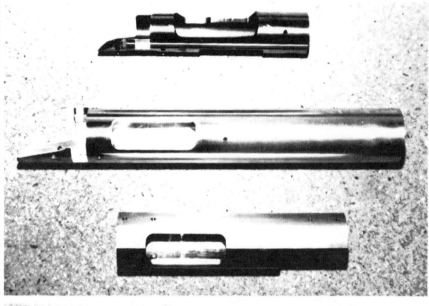

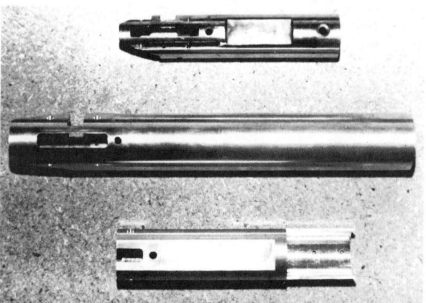

Both sleeves in the upper photo fit the Remington XP-100 action. The larger of the two is a full-length round sleeve for a Heavy Varmint rifle. The shorter sleeve covers the action from bolt handle forward, would be used on a Light Varmint or a Sporter rifle. Lower photo shows the great improvement in bedding area action sleeves provide, compared with the bedding area of the standard XP-100 action. Bottom sleeve has integral recoil lug at right end of flat area. Large round sleeve has no recoil lug — this one will be glued into the stock.

ONE OF THE MOST significant devices ever dreamed up by benchrest shooters in their search for ultimate accuracy is the action sleeve. These have been turned out in endless variety — long and short, round and square, aluminum and steel, epoxied on and soldered on — and all have their devotees, although no particular style has ever been clearly proven superior to the others. While the current widespread use of glued-in actions has decreased the number of action sleeves appearing on new rifles (the glue-ins seem to shoot just as well with an unsleeved action), the development of the action sleeve still represents an important contribution in the field of superaccurate rifles, and they still have their place on rifles bedded in the conventional manner.

The use of a sleeve should not necessarily be restricted to benchrest rifles, either. A properly designed sleeve could certainly be used on a varmint or hunting rifle, and a very significant accuracy improvement could result.

In its simplest form, a sleeve is nothing more than a tube covering all or part of the action, with a few holes cut in it to allow proper functioning. The tube is usually made of aluminum alloy and is cemented to the exterior of the action with epoxy. Some sleeves are the full length of the action, including the rear tang, while others start just forward of the bolt handle. Both types generally extend beyond the front of the receiver to provide a longer scope-mounting radius and increased bedding area.

There are two primary reasons for using a sleeve. Most commercial actions have a much larger ejection port than is needed on a benchrest rifle. If the action has a magazine, then we have a situation where most of the bottom, one side, and part of the top of the receiver have been cut away, greatly reducing its stiffness. When a heavy, free-floating target barrel is hung on such a receiver, the action is inclined to flex or bow, making a high level of accuracy difficult to achieve. Even a lightweight aluminum sleeve stiffens an action considerably.

The second purpose is to improve and enlarge the bedding area. The bottom side of most actions is pretty badly cluttered with unnecessary holes (from the benchrester's viewpoint), which complicate the bedding process. The ideal benchrest action is completely smooth on the bottom with only the guard-screw holes (if used) and a minimum opening for the trigger breaking the surface. This can be achieved with the sleeve, since everything else is covered up.

If the action is to be bedded full-length, the bearing surface in the tang area can be greatly improved by sleeving, since this is the real problem area with most action designs. When a short sleeve is used, the action is bedded only from the bolt handle forward, and the tang is free-floating.

Round bottom or flat bottom? This controversy still goes on, and each style has its "true believers." Round-bottom fans say that the action is positioned more perfectly in the bedding from shot to shot, since the curved bedding surface doesn't allow any lateral movement of the action — it has to settle to the same low point each time. Flat-bottom advocates say that the flat bedding surface holds up better and does not rely entirely on the guard screws to counteract the torque the action feels when the bullet is forced into the rifling twist.

The fact is, they both work fine — it's like arguing about Fords and Chevrolets. The lightweight sleeves I build are actually a combination of the two — there is a flat surface about 3/4 inch wide with a radius on each edge. That works fine too. In the case of a glue-in, of course, it doesn't matter, since the action can't move in the stock. The sleeve bottom could have a cross section like the ace of clubs and be O.K.

The sleeve shown in process in the photographs is a round, full-length job for a Heavy Varmint class rifle, being built on an XP-100 action with a Brown fiberglass stock. The procedures used

would apply to any style sleeve, with the lightweight types requiring additional milling to get the modified octagon shape. There is nothing sacred about the exterior shape of a sleeve anyway, and you can do almost anything you want to blend the outside surfaces of the sleeve into the rest of the rifle, as long as enough material is left to provide reasonable strength and good bedding surfaces.

At this point, it should be obvious that the best candidates for sleeving are the cylindrical actions like the Remington. While it would be possible to sleeve a Mauser or Model 70 for instance, it would be a real project, and it would be better to start with something else in the first place. In actual practice, very few sleeves appear on anything other than Remington actions, and when accuracy is the primary consideration, the Remington is hard to beat, anyway.

For raw material, I use 6061-T6 aluminum tubing, 1.75 inch outside diameter, with a 0.250-inch wall. This leaves a 1.25 inch inside diameter, while the Remington receivers have an outside diameter of about 1.360 inch, which is what you call an interference fit! To solve this problem, we have two ways to fly. Many sleeves are made with an inside diameter large enough to accept an unmodified receiver, and there is nothing wrong with this approach — the aluminum tubing is simply bored and reamed to the proper inside diameter.

I prefer, however, to turn the outside of the receiver down to a diameter of 1.320 inch. The aluminum tube is then reamed to an inside diameter of 1.325 inch, which leaves 0.005 inch for the

epoxy. Many receivers are not concentric in relation to the bolt bore and the outside diameter of the action. Turning the outside down takes care of this and makes everything line up better.

To accomplish all this, the tubing is mounted in the lathe with one end held in the chuck and the free end supported in a steady rest. After the ends are faced-off square, the inside is reamed to the required diameter. I use an ugly old reamer I borrowed several years ago from Pat McMillan (if he ever decides he wants it back, I'm in trouble). Before starting in with the reamer, the tube should be bored out to reamer diameter with a lathe tool about 1/4 inch. This gives the reamer a place to start and will eliminate reamer chatter as it starts into the hole. Keep the reamer flooded with cutting fluid (kerosene works fine in aluminum) to keep the chips from balling up in the reamer flutes, and clean the chips out of the hole occasionally so you can end up with a smooth surface. The lathe should be operated in slow back gear

The trigger-pin holes are drilled with a drill press and drill jig. Center guard screw holds action in alignment, inside.

On the XP-100 action (left), the web at the top of the ejection port is cut back to provide finger room for removal of the fired case. Photo at right shows the loading port being milled. Action is in place, inside the sleeve, and vise jaws are padded with paper towels to protect the sleeve.

and the reamer fed in slowly, using the tailstock handwheel.

After reaming, the tube is placed between pipe centers, and the outside is turned down to give a wall thickness of about 0.200 inch. Pipe centers are cups that go on over the regular centers to fill up the big hole in the tube. No lathe dog is used, and the tube is turned just by the friction of the centers against the ends of the tube. Only light cuts can be taken, but this way the entire length of the tube can be turned in each pass.

After the tube is turned and polished, the action is placed on a tight-fitting mandrel and mounted between centers. If a short sleeve is to be used, then of course, the action is turned only up to the front of the bolt handle. In this particular case, however, the sleeve is full-length, so the action was turned full-length also.

In the past, I have had no trouble turning actions with a regular high-speed cutter bit. This particular one was harder than normal, and the high-speed tool just couldn't hack it. I tried a carbide bit, but the interrupted cut as the tool passed over the various holes and cutouts in the action made short work of the carbide edge. Finally, I ended up grinding the outside down, using a toolpost grinder. As stated earlier, the action was ground to an outside diameter of 1.320 inch.

The next step is to devise a means for holding the receiver in the proper position in the tube while the cuts are made for the ejection port, the rear tang is shaped, and the trigger cutout and trigger-pin holes are located. There are several ways to do this, and the following procedure is probably as good as any. First, the existing guard-screw hole in the action just forward of the trigger is drilled and tapped 1/4 x 28. Then a corresponding hole is drilled in the tube with a number-three tap drill. The action is inserted into the tube, the holes are aligned, and a 1/4 x 28 tap is run through both holes *from the inside*. The idea is that the tap is engaged with the existing threads in the action when it starts cutting threads in the tube so the threads line up all the way through.

When the threads are completed, a short Allen-head setscrew can be run in, locking the tube and the action together, with the setscrew engaging the threads in both. This way, the action can be removed and replaced in the tube several times during the various milling steps and always returns to exactly the same place.

So how do you get a tap in from the inside when the top of the action is in the way? I cut about 3/4 inch off the end of a 1/4 x 28 plug tap (use an abrasive disc in a Dremel tool) and

ground a shank about 3/16 inch in diameter on what had been the front end. The end of the shank was squared off so it could be held in a tap wrench. The remaining full-threaded portion of the thing is only about 1/4 inch long. With the holes in the action and the tube aligned, this funny-looking gadget is dropped in from the inside, shank down, using a pair of tweezers. The squared-off end of the shank then sticks out through the hole in the tube, and the tap wrench is attached to the end. The tap is engaged with the existing threads in the action, and it is simply screwed right on through.

This threaded hole will be used for the center guard screw when the action is in place, and the screw will engage both the aluminum of the sleeve and the steel action. If conventional bedding is used, the same procedure can be used to locate and thread the front guard-screw hole.

The port in the tube (let's start calling it the sleeve) is cut next. I do this with the action in place inside the sleeve, and simply mill a hole right up to the edge of the existing port on the ends and at the bottom. The port opening is made just tall enough so you can get your finger in easily to remove the fired case.

The port in the XP-100 action has some funny angles at the ends, and I adjust the sleeve in the mill vise to match up to these, using the time-honored "eyeball technique." Just be careful not to bump into the receiver itself with the mill cutter, or you will have a refinishing and rebluing job to do to repair the damage. Also, the XP-100 has a web at the top of the port that extends out over part of the port opening. Unless you have very skinny fingers, this web will get in the way when you are picking out a fired case, so it's a good idea to mill the web back as shown in the photographs.

The rear of the sleeve is shaped next, again with the action in place. There is nothing cut and dried about the shape of things here, and the whole idea is to end up with a pleasing match to the existing contour of the action and the stock you plan to use. The angle of the rear tang on the sleeve shown is considerably lower than normal, since this is what matches up with the contour of the Brown benchrest stock being used. So, you can do whatever turns you on in this area, as long as adequate clearance for bolt handle functioning is provided.

The next problem is to locate and drill the holes for the trigger pins. This is best done with a simple drill jig as illustrated. First, the location of each hole is marked, using the jig, and a small flat spot is milled on each mark.

This is to allow the drill bit to start straight without being deflected by the round contour of the sleeve. Then the action, sleeve, and jig are assembled and mounted in the drill-press vise. The holes are drilled all the way through, using a 1/8-inch bit, which will pass completely through the existing holes in the action and out the bottom side of the sleeve.

The opening for the trigger is best done with the action removed from the sleeve and is simply machined to provide minimum clearance for the trigger mechanism. The gas vent on the right side of the receiver ring is located by careful measuring and drilled through. Many sleeves cover this vent over, but it's probably a good idea to drill a matching hole in the sleeve, just in case.

To replace the factory bolt stop, I drill and tap an 8 x 32 hole through the sleeve and the rearmost sight-mounting hole on the left side of the receiver bridge. An 8 x 32 thumbscrew is then used for the stop.

If the rifle is to have a magazine, again it is just a matter of opening up the bottom of the sleeve enough to let the magazine box slip through. I would do this with the action in place in the sleeve, and mill right up to the magazine cut in the receiver.

The scope-mounting holes are drilled and tapped next. These can be placed anywhere you want, to get the proper scope location. Just be careful to get the holes in a line that is true with the sleeve centerline so the scope will be pointing in the same direction as the gun. This can be done easily on the milling machine. The vise is first checked with a dial indicator to make sure it is exactly parallel with the table on the mill. Then the location of the first hole is marked, and the sleeve is clamped in the vise. The dial on the longitudinal table feed is set at zero, and the first hole is drilled and tapped, with the tap held in the mill chuck so it is perfectly aligned with the hole. Then the table is advanced an amount equal to the hole spacing (0.860 inch for the Weaver bases shown), and the second hole is drilled and tapped. You can drill as many pairs of holes as you want, to allow for different scope lengths. This procedure keeps everything straight, and the hole spacing can be controlled very accurately.

This completes the manufacture of the sleeve, and all that remains is the finishing. To remove the toolmarks from the milling cuts, I've had excellent results with 320-grit wet-or-dry paper, used wet with kerosene. The kerosene keeps the grit of the paper open, and the aluminum melts away. The little ridge around all the tapped holes is removed using a strip of wet-or-dry in a shoeshine fashion. From this point, you can use finer grits of paper and then polish the sleeve bright, or it can be glassbeaded for a flat, frosted appearance.

Since the original make, model, and serial-number stamping on the receiver will be covered by the sleeve, this information must be duplicated on an exposed part of the action or on the sleeve to comply with federal law. Most trophy houses will engrave the necessary data on the sleeve for about ten cents a letter, and this makes an attractive finished product. If you are proud of what you have done, you could even have your name engraved on it somewhere.

While the sleeve could now be used as it is, with no further finishing, it is a good idea to have it hard-anodized. The sleeve shown was glassbeaded, dyed black, and hard-anodized. In addition to improving the appearance, the hard anodizing gives the aluminum a very hard skin, so it is less susceptible to dings and scratches than the unprotected metal would be. Anodizing also gives you your choice of decorator colors, including green, pink, and purple (perish the thought!). Be sure to have the engraving done before the hard anodizing — when they say hard, they mean *hard*.

The next step is the nasty part — gluing the receiver into the sleeve. Thoroughly degrease the sleeve and the receiver with a solvent such as trichloroethane, and scratch up the inside of the sleeve with emery. Any guard-screw holes in the action that will not be used are plugged with a short piece of 1/4 x 28 bolt, and the small holes such as the scope-block mounting holes in the action are plugged from the inside with a dab of modeling clay. The front of the receiver is covered with masking tape, which is trimmed around the outside of the receiver ring with a razor blade. This is to keep the epoxy out of the receiver barrel threads.

The sleeve and the receiver are both placed in an oven or under a heat lamp until they are warm to the touch (this makes the epoxy spread better), and then a layer of epoxy is spread on the outside of the receiver and inside the sleeve. I use Duro Epoxy Steel for this. The receiver is then inserted into the sleeve, using a twisting motion to spread the epoxy evenly. As soon as the receiver is in proper position, the center guard screw is screwed in, through both the sleeve and the receiver, to keep things properly aligned (be sure to put some release agent on the screw!).

At this point, you have a terrible mess with epoxy all over the place. Clean the worst of it up with small sticks (popsicle sticks, with the ends ground square, work fine) and then finish up with cotton swabs and cleaning solvent. Be sure all the excess is removed before it begins to set up. Poke the masking-tape disc off the front of the receiver ring and be especially careful to clean up the face of the receiver where the barrel shoulder fits up. Clean out all the holes (such as the trigger-pin holes), give it a final check to make sure you haven't left any epoxy fingerprints behind, and set it aside until the epoxy is completely hard.

As a final finishing touch, I like to fill the gap between the sleeve and the receiver bridge. Since the receiver bridge is a flatter, lower contour than the rest of the receiver, a crescent-shaped space will remain between it and the sleeve at that point. A wad of cotton is packed into the center of this space using small dowels to poke it into place. Then the sleeved action is held in a vise with the tang up, and the back half of the space is filled with epoxy to a point that is level and smooth with the contour of the action and sleeve. After this has hardened, the sleeved action is turned over, and the front half of the space is filled. The epoxy can be shaped and smoothed with small cotton swabs wet with cleaning solvent, and any epoxy that gets on the sleeve or action is removed at the same time.

That completes the process. The

attachment is permanent, and the sleeve can be removed only with great difficulty. I've taken only one sleeve off and nearly destroyed the thing in the process. It can be done by heating the sleeved action to the point that the epoxy breaks down (450 to 500 degrees), and then the action is pounded out of the sleeve with a large wooden dowel and a big hammer. The action won't be hurt, but the sleeve will probably get a little dinged up. The other way is to simply mount the whole thing between centers in the lathe and cut the sleeve off.

If you want to buy a sleeve, there are a couple of ways to go. Excellent sleeves in a variety of styles are available from Al Davidson of Las Cruces, New Mexico, at prices starting around fifty dollars. These are intended for do-it-yourself installation and fit an unturned Remington receiver. Al also sells a neat magazine-port filler block and feed ramp for the various Remington magazine actions. Most sleeved actions are single-shots, and this block fills the hole in the bottom of the action. The action will then feed just by dropping the round in and closing the bolt. The price is right too — around six dollars.

If you get a sleeve built and installed by a benchrest gunsmith, the cost will vary but will probably be somewhere in the area of eighty dollars, depending on the type of sleeve and the gunsmith. Many of these gunsmiths are listed in the information kit now available from National Bench Rest Shooter's Association. This can be obtained by sending $2.50 to Mrs. Stella Buchtel; 5735 Sherwood Forest Drive; Akron, Ohio 44319.

Sleeves certainly have their place on benchrest rifles and could even be considered on a super varmint or hunting rifle. The bedding will definitely be improved, and this should show up in improved accuracy. As an added bonus, just as a Ferrari appears to be going a hundred miles an hour when it is parked at the curb, a sleeved action just plain looks accurate and is great for intimidating the troops at the local gun club. ●

301

Section 5

TRIGGERS

Pro Gunsmithing

TRIGGER

For proper functioning a trigger, whether like the simple direct trigger-hammer arrangement sketched above, or an elaborate system of levers and counterlevers, must have contact faces on a 90-degree angle from the pivot points.

Dunlap's favorite factory trigger is the Winchester Model 70, shown at left, which is of the override type. Only spring tension can be manually adjusted, but a gunsmith can "tune" it. Dunlap explains how.

𝒲HILE AT THE NATIONAL RIFLE championships at Camp Perry in August, Neal Knox wandered up and among other things casually mentioned that it might be nice to write an article on triggers sometime, perhaps not realizing what a bag of snakes he was opening up. To a gunsmith, there ain't no good triggers; some are just worse than others. This, of course, is not understood by the customers who expect a gunsmith to put a perfect pull on any kind of rifle they may have inherited, bought, or put together in the basement. There are lots of triggers, but only a few types, all operating on one of five principles. It is the material, fit of other parts and human stupidity that cause us trouble in trying to make them operate satisfactorily.

First, a trigger has to be reliable to be useable, naturally. A rifle must *not* be capable of firing unless the trigger is moved on purpose. We have long been familiar with rifles that go off when the bolt handle is touched, when the safety is released, when the stock is bumped, etc. Whether it is due to insufficient engagement, worn edges, loose-fitting bolt or sleeve, insufficient cam by safety or whatever, we have to fix it. The second measure of a trigger is the pull, which is about all the customer worries about, and the only real criterion is: can he fire the rifle without disturbing his aim when pulling the trigger?

I don't use the word "squeeze" much -- that's for basic training on the target range. Anyone who does much shooting in any form develops a pretty fast, controlled pull and senses exactly when the rifle will fire. When the shots don't go as expected, the rifle comes in for trigger work. Men vary of course -- some are insensitive, can use almost any trigger -- heavy, creepy, or what have you, and some of them shoot quite well. But most do not.

Military target shooters get used to 4½-pound pulls, and can handle them perfectly. They know exactly what they are doing. If the pull increases two ounces, they don't need weights to tell! The sportsman-shooter with his fine bolt actions very soon becomes hypercritical about triggers for through his scopes he sees rifle movement due to trigger manipulation. After shooting a bit he develops trigger control and is less critical; then in a few years he really becomes aware of triggers and starts over again. With a scope-sighted rifle for precision shooting a three-pound trigger gets heavy -- two to two and a half is desired (often less) which is hard to get and very hard to maintain on most rifles.

The basic figure on literally all triggers is 90 degrees: somewhere in the setup, whether direct trigger-to-hammer contact as on old single shots or on a complex double-sear mechanism, there

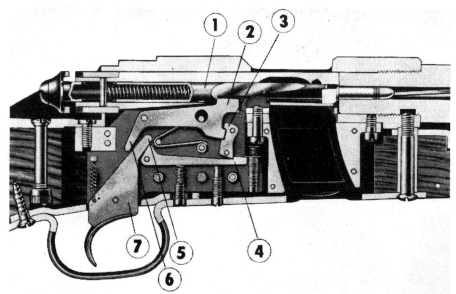

This complex trigger system is on the 1950-vintage Model 52 Winchester. When pulled, the trigger bears on the vertical arm of the "multiplying lever" (4) with the long horizontal arm of the lever disengaging the vertical secondary sear (3), which no longer supports the primary sear (2), releasing the striker (1). No one except a trigger specialist should attempt "tuning" this type of trigger.

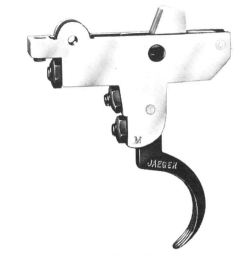

The Jaeger trigger is one of several commercial triggers on the market. Many shooters are prone to reduce engagement, visible through the hole in the housing, to below safe limits.

TUNING

By ROY DUNLAP

has to be a 90-degree angle on contact faces and therefore on lines figuratively drawn from them to the pivot points -- pins -- on which sears, hammers, triggers or connectors operate. If the angle is greater, the trigger cannot hold the sear or hammer safely without spring tension so great as to create very heavy pulls. If the angle is less, you have a hook situation giving a scrape-off action -- some cheap .22's have been made this way for added safety. And in eliminating the need for careful fitting of parts, pulls often are not good and not easy to correct. Only with a perfect 90-degree facing of trigger and sear can you achieve a good pull.

Engagement is of course the key to the pull. The less engagement, the less trigger movement required to disengage. This is the problem: to reduce engagement without reducing safety, and to retain that engagement every time the bolt or action is actuated. The more engagement, the more weight and creep on the trigger. Now for the types of triggers.

The basic bolt action Mauser trigger, including the Springfield, 1917, Krag, etc., has a direct sear to cocking-piece contact. The trigger is hinged in the sear with the top of the trigger machined to cam the sear down out of engagement. It employs double cams, the first close to the pin to give great leverage and move sear down to minimum engagement; the rear cam takes over for final pull and let-off. Designed for safety, there is great engagement; the trigger has a two-stage pull and the user knows that when he "takes up the slack" he has a short and reasonably crisp final pull.

In a tight action, where bolt or bolt sleeve or both fit the receiver well when the bolt is closed and won't wobble up and down with the first pull, it is possible to install very good second pulls -- we used to do it on National Match Springfields. On a real tight job you can even cut down the sear or

cocking piece, eliminate the take-up and reduce engagement so that a very decent single-stage pull can be achieved. (You're following me? A Mauser, etc., bolt sleeve built up on the bottom so it is tight in the receiver when the bolt is closed permits undue familiarities with grinding wheels on sears.)

However, most of our people wouldn't be caught dead with a military trigger, even it if were fixed up with a good three-pound pull, so we come to the patent triggers: Canjar, Timney, Jaeger, Dayton-Traister and others I can't remember at the moment. These are self-contained mechanisms incorporating sear and trigger, the needed springs, and adjusting screws to control engagement, limit movements, etc. They replace the original sear and trigger and are designed to give clean single-stage pulls, with some slight weight adjustment. They all have the same problems, the main one being the screwdriver in the rifleman's hand.

Users literally always expect too much from them, adjust to ultra-minimum engagement that puts two sharp edges against each other rather than one on top of the other, and minimum travel, which makes the two sharp edges just scrape past each other on release. I'll flatly state that 90 percent of the trouble with these triggers, particularly Canjar, is due to this screwdriver work -- then back to the store or factory with loud complaints.

The problem is pressure. I'll give some hypothetical figures, all of which I am sure are well on the positive side -- the true ones would probably scare me more than you. Say we have a .005-inch engagement of a .200-inch wide sear and trigger -- this figures out to 1/1000th square inch. We'll say the mainspring gives a 40-pound tension to the cocking piece. You want to figure out the pressure in the tiny 1/1,000 of a square inch, and spread out in a .005-inch strip at that? This terrific area-force is

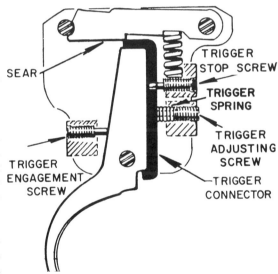

The Remington Model 700 trigger, above, is fully adjustable, but engagement between the trigger connector and sear should not be less than set by the factory.

constant when the rifle is cocked. When the rifleman slams the bolt forward he can double or triple the pressure momentarily.

So, the trigger-maker has to make his tiny parts hard enough not to wear rapidly and not hard enough to break under the bolt slam. It ain't easy. You can adjust the trigger to minimum safe engagement, leaving a little over-travel of trigger -- this is never felt when the rifle is fired, only when the guy holds it in his lap at home and snaps the rifle by the hour. If you can educate a man to leave the screws alone and not practice slamming the bolt back and forth as hard as he can with the rifle empty, the trigger should hold up quite awhile. It is

305

always best to have an empty case in the chamber when adjusting a trigger for it holds the bolt, and consequently the cocking piece, in the same position it will be in when the rifle is loaded and fired in the field.

About 400 years ago siege crossbows become a little difficult to fire -- steel bows with string-pulls of 1,000 to 1,200 pounds needed rugged trigger systems, and straight triggers got too heavy to control, so some Spanish or Swiss armourer invented the double-set trigger system, which was soon adopted by gunmakers and has been with us ever since. Up to about 100 years ago, almost every non-military rifle made in the United States had double or single-set triggers, the single being simpler and easier to make by almost any gunsmith. No rifleman worthy of the name would consider a rifle without a "hair" trigger. The Civil War brought breech-loaders, dozens of designs, mass production and hundreds of thousands of military-arm-trained men who were used to heavy single-stage triggers. Set triggers fell out of popular use, though available on order on most factory-made sporting rifles until World War I.

The double-set trigger, which has a separate light lock system developing enough power to knock a sear out of cocking-piece engagement, is a natural for all rifles with Mauser-type firing systems. It is much neglected in the U.S. today, mainly because the average rifle owner doesn't understand it -- he thinks it has to be used set down to a hair, firing on just a touch, and he can't control it. He doesn't realize that the trigger can be set up to hold a few ounces so the trigger finger can rest on the trigger like any other type, which allows perfectly controlled let-offs. True, the double-set has a time-lag so ignition is a millisecond or two slower than with a straight Mauser-type trigger (fastest disconnect system of all), but this cannot be noticed except by a very skilled rifleman shooting standing at a small mark.

For bolt rifles in general -- Mauser types, M70 -- the Miller single-set trigger is the best I've ever seen. The European double-set and single-sets all allow firing with a trigger unset, but the pull is pretty bad -- which can be changed by making a two-step kickoff lever, one side low to contact the front trigger top with little movement, the other side high for the rear trigger to act against in set functioning. Set triggers can be made

at a reasonable price for most rifles, but special types and high-grade match triggers run high. The average rifleman would faint at the thought of paying $150 or more for a trigger, but it has been done. In a parts drawer I have a custom double-set for a Winchester 52B, made I believe by Robert Milhoan. I was told it cost $140.00 in 1938. I would not *copy* it for that!

Schultz & Larsen, in Denmark, is now making a trigger for Mauser, primarily for target rifle use in England, a direct copy of the Finnish Manttarii which was originally developed for free rifle use but which can be modified easily to single pull, light or heavy pull-off, etc. This might show up in the U.S. eventually. The Manttarii is a double-sear system, with the trigger camming directly on a secondary sear to release the primary sear, which is an override type -- same as the M70 or Remington 700 -- with the cocking-piece face angled and held back by upward pressure. Years ago I used to buy Manttariis for free rifles and make copies myself for rifles the Finnish models didn't fit. It is a good system.

Timney triggers have been made in two types; the first a sliding-sear design in which the sear with angled face moved straight down when released by the trigger, allowing the cocking piece to override. This was a good design but required very close fitting and was undoubtedly expensive to produce. It was superseded for the popular sporters by the more common pivoting-sear design. Probably more of these Timney triggers have been sold than any other make; they have been furnished to European makers, and also copied by them. Timney now makes match-grade triggers for target work, and these should be recommended to sportsmen as well. Doesn't cost much more to go first class.

Canjar's single-set triggers are his standard pivot-sear type with a spring-actuated heavy shoe with a little lever in a notch in the trigger bar which jars off the regular trigger mechanism. Parts are very small, require careful handling, and are not for ham-handed people or those possessing needle-file sets.

The Winchester Model 70 trigger system is, in my opinion, the best which has ever been provided on a factory rifle and is my favorite for all purposes -- once it's adjusted. The trigger leverage is such that ample safe engagement is

present even when reduced to get a cleaner, lighter let-off. In working on these, you never, never, touch the sear nose. Change that 90-degree face (to trigger fulcrum) and you got nothing but trouble. And you can't grind it to recover the angle, for then it has to move farther forward in trigger engagement, the rear of the sear lowers, the cocking-piece moves forward so the safety doesn't work, and probably it will drop back into its notch after firing, locking with the trigger so that when you open the bolt the sear can't depress -- and something breaks. And Winchester will tell you to send the rifle to the factory for new trigger and sear. They won't sell these parts to anyone except their special service stations.

So, work only on the trigger nose. First grind a knife-stone thin enough to work in the saw-cut. Then use the bench grinder, with the trigger on its side on the tool rest or guide, and with the side of the fine-grit wheel reduce the height of the "nose," which reduces the depth of notch and engagement. Keep a uniform depth, of course. Should you inadvertently take off too much, get out the No. 6 cut file with the safe edge and file down the step behind the notch. (You got a hard one that won't file? Put a strip of brass, steel -- any metal that will fit in the notch -- and resign yourself to stoning. The strip of metal protects the face of the notch and its sharp upper edge.)

The Cooey rifle, made by Winchester of Canada, is sort of a cross between the present-day M70 and Remington manufacturing methods, but has the M70 type trigger, complicated somewhat by a haywire safety system. Nothing hard to handle.

The Savage bolt actions have a strange firing-pin and cocking piece design, but the trigger is handled like the 70. Late ones have an adjusting screw through the trigger nose to regulate engagement. Double-set trigger assemblies can be fitted to the Savage without too much work, incidentally.

Remington's trigger mechanism as used on 40X, 700, 721, 722, etc., has had minor changes in shapes of parts, but all can be considered the same. It is an override-sear type, similar in design to most of the patent triggers, but using an alloy trigger simply as a lever to move a hardened steel sear contact, called a trigger connector. These list about a half a buck, so if the

Remington's pull is mushy and requires much engagement because the edges are gone, nobody goes bankrupt replacing the part. Sears don't usually wear much, but they only cost about 60 cents. Adjustment is simple, using the engagement, stop and spring screws in the housing, but remember to use household cement after adjusting so they won't turn in use. Just a fraction of a turn can make a lot of difference. The 40X types with weight adjustment by a screw accessible through the trigger guard loop adjust only by increasing or decreasing spring tension on the trigger itself -- there is no change of engagement.

Sako triggers started out as a M70-type in principle, but now use a Timney-type system. Most foreign arms with patent-type trigger mechanisms use this system. The exception is the English-made BSA. The rifles are superbly accurate, stocks the best modern design, and the trigger is the worst ever put on any rifle. There is no provision whatever for regulation of engagement. There is no place to go -- the trigger must be used to hold the sear down (by pressing forward) to remove the bolt from the receiver. Smooth up anything and you suddenly can't get the bolt out. Two heavy springs, one coil, one helical, work against the trigger at all times (also the sear) so you have three pounds or more of pull without any sear engagement at all. It's a shame. If anybody wants you to fix the trigger on his new BSA Monarch, tell him "No." You can't even be helpful by putting some moly oil or grease in it -- remember, the back of the trigger nose, right below the contact point, has to hold the front of the sear down to get the bolt out, so it can't be very slippery!

So much for the bolt actions. Most autoloaders and pump rifles have similar trigger systems, usually a hammer, connector and trigger, with safety blocking movement of one or two. By the nature of the machine, you just don't have light-pull triggers. However, there is no reason for a really bad pull. Often a spring can be reduced a coil, a notch stoned with a sharp-edged stone (you can grind edges on your slip stones on the bench grinder, in case you didn't know), sides of moving parts polished and wonders will be worked. Quite often much of the trigger pull in such arms is due to just plain friction and light moly grease really helps. Should you grind parts to reduce engagements, be sure you test-fire the rifle, and not with one cartridge at a time -- put three in to find out if the autoloader remains cocked after functioning, and does not Maxim (go full automatic). And be sure the pump doesn't fire by itself when you slam the slide forward on the second shot. If parts change relative positions with the work, the cross-bolt safety may require building up or a new one made to lock properly.

Lever actions are a large family. The old Winchesters, Marlins, Stevens and Savages are no problem, just clean up and judiciously reduce engagement. But the crop of new ones I don't know much about. I have worked on two Winchester 88's. The first one gave a good 3-pound pull in half an hour; after five hours the second one was worse than when I started. Any such system, that is one attached to the lever and moving out of engagement with bolt or firing pin parts, has to vary with fit of lever and all the parts involved. You have a lot of flat parts, friction, push-and-pull fits, accumulated tolerances, etc., that have to be played by ear. Things just aren't uniform enough to say all you have to do is work on one notch or smooth up one part.

As gunsmiths we get somewhat calloused on the matter of triggers. A four-pound pull on a shotgun feels light; we adjust a varmint rifle to two pounds, it feels fine; we get a clean three-pound let-off on a target rifle, it feels perfect. We can snap a rifle twice and are used to the weight range. The customer, handling only his own rifle or rifles with similar triggers, may feel things we do not so it is a good idea to have him on hand to check it whenever possible, while you are working on it -- though you may have to put it together an extra time or two.

Always make the customer put the rifle to his shoulder to try the pull. Anyone can feel movement and added weight if he holds the rifle across his body, like a baby, and squeezes the trigger. In a Model 70 Winchester, holding the rifle this way adds a pound to the pull -- this trigger is supposed to be pulled back, not up. (That's why I put thumbrests on my target stock designs -- I didn't give a damn what the guy did with his thumb, I just wanted to make it uncomfortable for his hand to be anywhere except down, so the trigger was pulled back and the three-pound pull was three pounds.)

Once in awhile the customer goes mental and thinks himself out of phase with the rifle - loses his touch, thinks he's putting pressure on the trigger, but isn't. This really happens. When you think you have a fellow like this, hand him a military rifle -- any military rifle -- and ask him to dry fire ten at a spot on the wall. Should cure him.

Some of these people can get sort of hypersensitive on the trigger finger and feel creep in a set trigger due to concentrating on trying to feel it! You can always tell him to come back tomorrow. Then call your brother-in-law and see if he can get you a job down at the lumberyard. ●

Making a Steel Trigger for the Ruger Number One

Ron Swartley

THE RUGER Number One single-shot has become a classic platform for custom guns the world over. The gun must have a lot of inherent quality, or such well known customizers as Bill Dowtin, Joe Balickie, and Friedrich Wilhelm Heym (of West Germany) wouldn't waste their time on it.

But the gun isn't perfect — nothing ever is. Take as simple a thing as its trigger, for example. It's made of black anodized aluminum. That means that the customizing potential for the trigger is almost nonexistent. There is little you can do to its shape if you want the racy lines of a shotgun-style trigger, a wide target style, or a smooth hunting style. And you can just about forget about gold plating, nickel plating, color case-hardening, nitre bluing, or heat strawing. When the anodizing wears off, about the only thing that you can do is paint it, since most shops refuse to accept such a single part for anodizing. So the Ruger Number One owner is up the proverbial creek as far as trigger customizing is concerned.

Or is he? There is one other option, and that involves the custom building of the trigger assembly itself. Tony Fleming of the JJ Jenkins Enterprises restoration shop in Goleta, California, has come up with a Ruger Number One trigger made from carbon steel. It is attractive and functional, and it allows the customizer to do all those things with it that you can't with the original anodized-aluminum trigger. There is only one minor drawback — you can't make those little postinstallation adjustments on it that you can with the factory trigger. The new trigger has to be adjusted to fit the shooter when it is installed, and then left that way.

For the advanced amateur gunsmith or professional metal worker desiring to make such a custom trigger, the basic steps follow. The Jenkins outfit mentioned above will make and install a bright and shiny one for a hefty 175 dollars, if you think the metal work is beyond yours or your local metalsmith's capability.

First, scribe the outline of the old trigger onto a 1.6-inch-square by 0.300-inch-thick piece of mild carbon steel (1010, 1015, 1018, or 1020 cold or hot-rolled steel will do). Obtain the steel from any fair-sized welding shop.

Machine the top section, using the holes and flats of the upper part as reference points. Leave the bottom area square for easy clamping in a vise.

Shape the lower section (where your trigger finger goes) using a hacksaw and files. Sculpt the metal to the desired shape.

Fit the trigger to the gun, using finish-filing techniques. You'll see from the drawing that the trigger retains the standard Ruger sear-engagement adjustment screw. The weight and overtravel are adjusted in this final fitting.

Finish the trigger according to your particular taste (blued, gold plating, *etc*).

Depending on the quality of his workmanship, the Ruger Number One customizer should end up with an improvement in appearance and a better-fitting trigger.

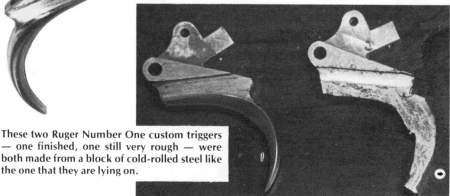

One minor drawback: on a custom trigger made like this one, all adjustments have to be made when it is installed, then left that way. None can be made after assembly of the gun.

These two Ruger Number One custom triggers — one finished, one still very rough — were both made from a block of cold-rolled steel like the one that they are lying on.

Top: issue '03 Springfield firing mechanism.
Below: second prototype of modification made
during late '70s.

SPRINGFIELD
firing mechanism

... a modification to improve reliability, by Ludwig Olson

Taps and Dies

Shortly after this article was written, it was learned that special-order taps and dies, including 9/32-inch size, are offered by B-Square Company, PO Box 11281, Fort Worth TX 76109. This size is approximately .005 inch larger diameter than 7mm, and is the most favorable known for the tap and die to make the Springfield firing mechanism modification. The designation for this tap and die is 9/32x28 (the last figure denoting number of threads per inch).

Roll pins in various sizes, including 1/16 inch diameter for the lock pin, are available from Brownell's, Inc., Route 2, Box 1, Montezuma IA 50171.

THROUGH THE YEARS, the 1903 Springfield .30-06 bolt-action rifle has won the reputation of being basically simple, durable and reliable. There are, however, some high-mortality parts in this venerable rifle, particularly in its firing mechanism. Outstanding among them are the striker and firing pin rod, which were made separately and coupled together. These high-mortality parts are also present in variants of the 1903, such as the 1903A1 and 1903A3.

The idea of making the striker separate from the firing pin rod was a carry-over from the Krag rifle. It was reasoned that the striker could be easily and cheaply replaced in the event its tip would break, but this very seldom happens.

Breakage of the striker and firing pin rod almost always occurs at the weak cutaway areas where these parts are coupled together. It most often happens when the rifle is dry-fired excessively. Such breakage occurred frequently when the 1903 rifle was used in military service and was dry-fired during manual of arms and "snapping-in" marksmanship practice.

Another weak part is the firing pin sleeve, a thin-walled tube covering the area where the striker and firing pin rod are joined. It sometimes splits lengthwise. This breakage is, however, relatively rare.

If the knoblike front end of the firing pin rod breaks off, the rod with attached cocking piece are free to move rearward. Gas from a punctured primer, or ruptured cartridge case, could then drive the firing pin rod and cocking piece assembly rearward out of the bolt.

A means of preventing this unsafe condition was the Sedgley safety firing pin, patented August 10, 1937, by Reginald F. Sedgley (U.S. Patent 2,089,581), and marketed for several years by R.F. Sedgley, Inc., Philadelphia. It was a modification of the issue firing pin rod with a steel collar inserted between the firing pin sleeve and mainspring. The

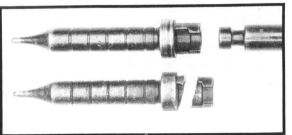

Top: issue striker and firing pin rod. Bottom: a broken striker, the result of dry firing.

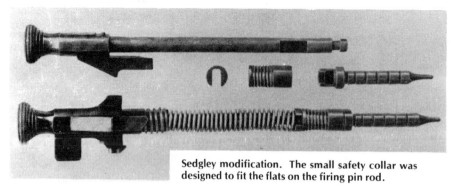

Sedgley modification. The small safety collar was designed to fit the flats on the firing pin rod.

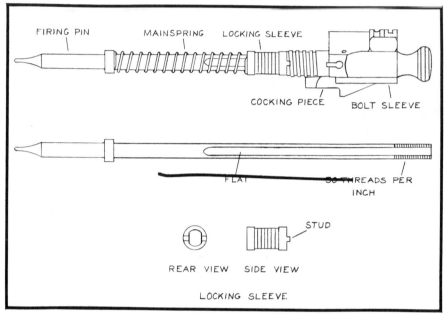

Improved Springfield firing mechanism submitted to the Chief of Ordnance in 1943.

collar engaged diametrically opposed flats on the firing pin rod and prevented the rod from being driven out. There was, however, no change in the firing pin rod and striker where these parts were joined. Also, the issue firing pin sleeve was used. These parts were therefore as subject to breakage as those of the unmodified issue firing mechanism.

Breakage of the firing pin rod or striker where they are joined can also result in the firing pin sleeve and striker being held forward in fire position by the mainspring. With the striker in this position, so that its tip projects from the bolt face, there is danger of a cartridge in the chamber being fired if the bolt is thrust forward smartly. And "slam-firing" with this unsafe condition can occur before the bolt is fully locked. Three accidents as a result of this are recorded in *Hatcher's Notebook,* authored by the late Major General Julian S. Hatcher.

Another fault of the Springfield

firing mechanism is a small amount of end play (about .005 inch) between the striker and firing pin rod. Although such a small amount of play may seem trifling, it cushions the firing pin blow, which is not favorable for best ignition. Some target shooters remove this play by inserting a thin metal shim between the two parts.

These faults have long been recognized by arms designers, gunsmiths, armorers, and well-informed shooters. A few custom gunsmiths and parts suppliers therefore offered a one-piece firing pin threaded to fit the issue cocking piece. In at least one design, the firing pin and cocking piece were joined by a hardened steel cross pin in addition to the threads.

When I was an armorer with U.S. Army Ordnance during the late 1930s, thoughts about correcting faults of the 1903 Springfield often came to mind. This finally resulted in a design for an improved Springfield firing mechanism, which

featured a one-piece firing pin similar in some respects to that of the 1898 Mauser rifle.

A prototype of this firing mechanism, based on my drawings, was made by the late Emil Koshollek, a custom gunsmith in Stevens Point, Wisconsin. This prototype was used extensively for dry-firing, and it worked very well. It was not used for firing with cartridges because the firing pin was made from low-carbon steel and not heat treated.

The one-piece firing pin of the prototype was threaded to fit the issue cocking piece, and the issue mainspring was used. A locking sleeve with internal flats, to fit diametrically-opposite flats on the firing pin, was pushed rearward by the mainspring. Two studs on the rear of the locking sleeve engaged a notch cut across the front face of the issue bolt sleeve. These studs and the mating flats on firing pin and locking sleeve prevented the bolt sleeve and cocking piece from turning on the firing pin.

It was easy to disassemble this firing mechanism without use of tools. The safety was turned to middle position after cocking the rifle, and the bolt was removed from the receiver. After unscrewing the firing mechanism from the bolt, the firing pin tip was rested on a wooden block. The locking sleeve was then pushed toward the front of the firing pin to disengage the studs, and the cocking piece, with bolt sleeve attached, was unscrewed. Finally, the locking sleeve and mainspring were removed from the firing pin.

The prototype was simple, and gave promise of being very durable. However, care was required during assembly to screw the cocking piece on the firing pin so that the rear surfaces of these parts were flush. Failure to do so resulted in improper firing pin protrusion. The prototype was not as foolproof in this respect as the issue Springfield firing mechanism.

Koshollek proposed that a stop be provided inside the rear of the cocking piece to prevent the cocking piece from being screwed too far on the firing pin. A further idea for improvement was to provide only one flat on the firing pin to mate with a single flat inside the locking sleeve. The advantage would be a larger threaded area on the firing pin to engage the cocking piece, and thus help prevent any looseness

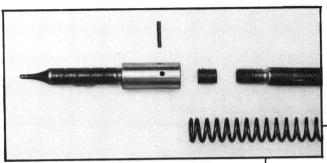

Above: Early version of modified mechanism featured a spacer screw. Right: View of firing pin sleeve, seen from above, shows striker, spacer screw and firing pin rod in end-to-end contact.

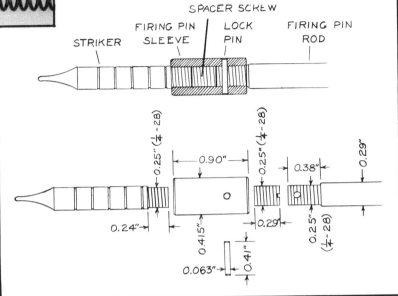

from developing. This feature was used to good advantage in the excellent Mauser B series .22 rimfire rifles introduced about 1935 by the Mauser Works in Germany.

Neither of the above improvements were used in the prototype made by Koshollek. But Koshollek and I planned to include them in a second prototype.

I submitted the prototype firing mechanism to the Office Chief of Ordnance in August 1943. Several weeks later, I received a reply that there was no requirement for an improved Springfield firing mechanism. This reply was not surprising since the M1 Garand rifle had replaced the 1903 Springfield as the standard infantry rifle. Later, when I requested return of the prototype, I was told by a clerk that an ordnance civilian took it when he left Washington on another assignment. His name, appropriately enough, was Fox!

After retiring from the NRA in 1976, I devised a modification of the Springfield firing mechanism which was easier to produce than the one submitted to the Office Chief of Ordnance. The original Springfield striker and firing pin rod are altered for use in this simple modification. These parts can be used even though they are broken where they are coupled together. The issue mainspring, bolt sleeve and safety assembly, and cocking piece are used and require no alteration.

Connecting the striker and firing pin rod is a new firing pin sleeve made from SAE 4140 steel. It is threaded internally full length. Other new parts required are a spacer screw and lock pin.

A lathe is required to make the modification, but the turning and threading operations are simple and straightforward. The rear part

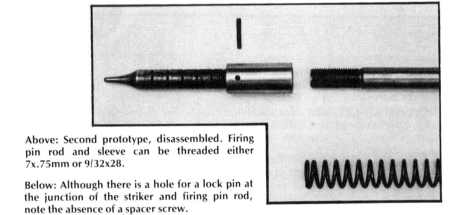

Above: Second prototype, disassembled. Firing pin rod and sleeve can be threaded either 7x.75mm or 9/32x28.

Below: Although there is a hole for a lock pin at the junction of the striker and firing pin rod, note the absence of a spacer screw.

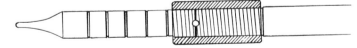

of the striker, recessed to fit the firing pin rod, is cut off flush with the rear end of the striker collar. Turning down the striker collar and threading it to fit the hole in the new firing pin sleeve is next. After cutting off the front of the firing pin rod where its full-diameter portion meets the groove that engages the striker, the front .38 inch of the rod is turned down and threaded to fit the hole in the sleeve.

Of tubular shape, the new firing pin sleeve is .415 inch diameter and .90 inch long. A hole drilled through it lengthwise is threaded to receive

the modified striker and firing pin rod, as well as the spacer screw.

The striker and firing pin sleeve are joined permanently by sweat-soldering the threaded areas where these parts are screwed together. After the threaded areas are tinned, the striker is screwed tightly into the sleeve while applying heat to sweat the parts together. A bottoming tap is then turned into the sleeve from the rear to clean excess solder from the threads. Rosin-core solder is used to prevent rust. Solder is used to prevent the striker from turning in the sleeve, and not to give

311

strength.

Next, the spacer screw is turned into the sleeve to butt solidly against the striker. This is followed by assembling the firing pin rod, bolt sleeve, and mainspring and screwing the rod into the firing pin sleeve. The firing pin sleeve is held in a vise with padded jaws. Turn the rod so that it bears firmly against the spacer screw. The firing mechanism is then assembled to the bolt, and the striker is checked for protrusion from the bolt face. Protrusion should be .050 inch to .070 inch. It can be adjusted to come within these limits by varying the length of the spacer screw.

Final steps in making this modification are to drill the lock pin hole through the sleeve and firing pin rod, and insert the lock pin. I used a 1/16 inch tension pin, commonly called roll pin, for this purpose. It was half an inch long as purchased, and was shortened to .410 inch, or .005 inch less than the diameter of the sleeve.

Tension pins are available from dealers in machine supplies. They are also available from hardware stores, but usually not in 1/16 inch size. It is desirable to use a small-diameter pin to minimize weakening of the sleeve and firing pin rod. The pin is used to prevent the rod from turning in the sleeve and not for strength.

Three prototypes of this firing mechanism were made. Most of the machine work was done by the late William M. Stuart Jr., who was an agricultural scientist, gunsmith and highly-skilled machinist from Beltsville, Maryland. Known for the high quality of his work, he was a shooting companion and close friend of Colonel Townsend Whelen.

The first prototype has 1/4-28 threads for the firing pin sleeve and parts screwed into it. Taps and dies of this size are readily available. It is desirable for strength, however, to use a slightly larger size that comes closer to matching the .290 inch diameter of the firing pin rod. A metric size (7mm) is closest to meeting this requirement. Its .276 inch major diameter is only .014 inch smaller than the firing pin rod. A tap and die of 7x.75mm size were purchased from J&L Industrial Supply, 19339 Glenmore, Detroit MI 48240. They were used in producing the second and third prototypes.

Another feature of the second and third prototypes is a new firing pin rod, made longer than the issue rod so that a spacer screw is not required. The new rod was made from L-size drill rod, which is the same diameter as the issue firing pin rod.

Before unscrewing the cocking piece from the issue rod, it is necessary to grind off the upset portion of the rod at the rear. The cocking piece has thirty threads per inch, not a standard size, and this requires that a lathe be used to cut threads on the new rod. It is necessary, after screwing on the cocking piece, to upset the rear end of the new rod with a ball peen hammer, and then smooth the upset portion with a file and abrasives. Installing a new rod requires considerable effort. It is easier to alter the issue firing pin rod and use a spacer screw, as in the first prototype.

A third feature of the second and third prototypes is that the lock pin extends through a hole at the junction of the firing pin rod and striker. One-half of the hole diameter is at the front end of the firing pin rod, the other half at the rear end of the striker. The hole thus causes virtually no weakening of these parts. It extends crosswise through the firing pin sleeve, as in the first prototype, but the hole is only 1/16 inch diameter and the walls of the sleeve are thick. The hole, therefore, has no practical weakening effect. When using a spacer screw in the sleeve, the hole for the lock screw can be at the junction of the spacer screw and front end of the firing pin rod. This would minimize any weakening effect of the hole.

A drill guide is used when drilling the 1/16 inch hole in the firing pin sleeve. Turned from steel, the guide is cylindrical with the hole for the drill extending lengthwise through its middle. The exterior of the guide is the same diameter as the sleeve.

All three prototypes work very well. They have been used extensively in firing with full-power .30-06 loads, and have been dry-fired approximately five thousand times without breakage of parts. It is expected that those with 7mm threads will prove the most durable. However, the first prototype, which has 1/4-28 threads, shows no problems.

It is intended that this modified firing mechanism not be disassembled unless necessary for cleaning or repair. Disassembly, however, is easy. The chief tool required is a small drift punch to remove the lock pin. In reassembly, the lock pin cannot be fully inserted in the sleeve unless the parts are assembled to give proper firing pin protrusion. This is dependent, of course, on the protrusion being proper when the modification was made.

An important advantage of using the issue striker in this modification is that its tip was specially heat treated to give good durability. *United States Rifles and Machine Guns,* by Colvin and Viall, states: "The point of the striker is hardened and temper drawn in a lead bath to 900 degrees Fahrenheit. This is necessary to make it stand up against the hundreds of blows to which it is subjected during the life of the rifle." Proper heat treatment requires special equipment and knowledge. It is, therefore, beyond the capability of many hobbyists and small shops.

Although this modification does not feature a one-piece firing pin, as in the Model 98 Mauser, the striker, spacer screw, and firing pin rod are assembled tightly to the sleeve so that these parts tend to behave as a single piece. And there is an advantage in having the cocking piece assembled to the firing pin rod with a long threaded connection. Aside from the advantage of tight assembly, there is no breakage of the firing pin rod where it joins the cocking piece. In the Model 98 Mauser, the cocking piece is fastened to the firing pin by means of interrupted lugs. The cocking piece is detachable and is not a perfectly tight fit on the firing pin. There have been instances where the firing pin broke in the lug area, apparently as a result of improper heat treatment. However, such breakage is rare.

Various attempts have been made over the years to reduce the lock time of the 1903 Springfield. Extra strong mainsprings and lightweight firing pin rods and cocking pieces have been used, but with limited success. The cocking cam of the Springfield is steep. Using an extra strong mainspring results in greatly increased cocking effort. There have been no attempts with this modification to reduce lock time, but I plan to work on this in the future.

The firing mechanism in Winchester Model 54 rifles produced up to 1932 is similar to that of the 1903 Springfield. In fact, the striker and firing pin sleeve of these Model 54 rifles are interchangeable with those of the Springfield. So the above-described firing mechanism modification can also be applied to the pre-1932 Model 54.

Firing mechanism modifications described above have proven safe and satisfactory. The publisher and I, however, have no control over work done by others, and are therefore not responsible for any accidents, injury, or damage to rifles which might occur as a result of making modifications covered in this article.

It is recommended that any firing mechanism modification be done by a competent gunsmith equipped to do the job properly. ●

Section 6

PROBLEM SOLVING

BARREL FITTING is generally considered to involve primarily threading, chambering and headspacing, and it does, but quite a few years spent installing new barrels in a custom gunshop have made it apparent that one of the most time-consuming parts of the job is the one that is too-often merely touched upon, or simply ignored — the adjustments and alterations necessary to insure smooth, reliable cartridge feeding.

Immediately after World War II, Springfields, Enfields and Mausers were the most frequent candidates for new barrels, and all would feed .30-06 cartridges — the most popular — without alterations, for they were either originally chambered for this cartridge or the quite-similar 8x57; the almost-as-popular .270, .257 Roberts and 7mm Mauser cartridges could also be chambered in the

FEEDING PROBLEMS...

By PAUL MARQUART

Photos By RICK JAMISON

new barrel without the necessity of any tinkering with the feeding. Perhaps the trouble-free conversions of these cartridges led to a tendency to ignore potential feed problems; but whatever the reason, when an increasing number of customers began asking for various then-popular "Improved" cartridges with body and shoulder configuration greatly changed from the original design, feeding problems became common. How many of those conversions were checked for flawless feeding I cannot say, but many times the customer received the job with feeding considerably less than perfect.

The sharper the shoulder, or the shorter and stubbier the cartridges, the more feeding problems developed. So the gunsmith's problems increased rapidly as the "more compact" factory cartridges began to appear in the Fifties. Though cartridges such as the standard .243 Winchester, .308 and .358 are considerably shorter than older cases such as the .30-06 and 7mm Mauser, they have shoulder diameters larger than the old

ones. In fact, the shoulder diameter of the .243 is, for all practical purposes, the same as the most extremely "Improved" cartridges with absolute minimum body taper.

Obviously, it's a lot easier to push a long, sloping cartridge into a chamber than it is to shove in one that, because of its shortness, enters the chamber at a more-abrupt angle, and has a wide, nearer-square shoulder closer to the tip of the bullet — thanks to a neck that is also shortened. While such cartridges can be made to feed smoothly, they do require special care, and a large measure of patience.

One of the cartridges requiring the most work and time to perfect feeding in bolt actions is the .243 Winchester. A common problem is that the cartridge

Dissimilar cartridges such as the .243 and .378 Weatherby Magnum, above, will function smoothly through the same rifle action, each of which has been properly converted. However, it's obvious that these unlike cartridges cannot be expected to function smoothly without some magazine or action alteration.

A sharp cartridge shoulder coupled with short length increases feeding problems because of the sharp angle at which the cartridge approaches the chamber. Dummy cartridges, such as this .243 which has been continuously used for perfecting feeding, will eventually develop a constriction ring a short distance back from the shoulder. This .243 cartridge has been colored with machinist's layout blue to show the area more plainly. Layout blue is useful to show areas of cartridge stress, which may indicate where a feeding problem lies.

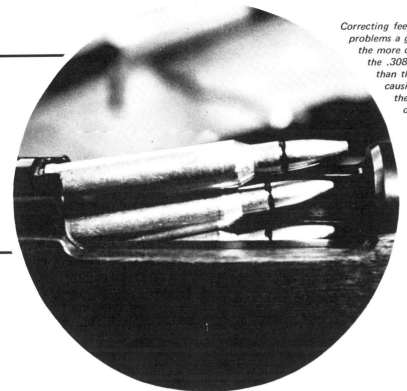

Actions with bolt heads designed like the Mauser and Springfield sometimes will not accept the cartridge head when it feeds up from the magazine and into the bolt face, even though the bolt face diameter is adequate. This problem is caused when the ends of the bolt face lip are not properly relieved, and can easily occur when the bolt face is 'bored out' to accept the magnum head. It is less likely to occur when the alteration is done by grinding, an operation that usually results in a better finish anyway. Sometimes Mauser type extractors are not adequately relieved and the force of an extra strong extractor hook with about 1/32-inch of tension almost prevents the case head from sliding home.

Some years back when Winchester released the .338 Winchester Magnum cartridge it gave the wildcatters a fine short belted case, easily available from the factory, just waiting to be necked up or down. One of the early favorites which resulted was the .30-338 and the conversion of any of the common bolt actions in .30-06 for this "new" wildcat was quite common. I did several hundred of these conversions. The A-3 Springfield

binds at the back end of the chamber as the bolt advances it. Evidence of this problem is the fact that dummy .243 cartridges used in feeding correction quickly develop a distinct constriction ring about 3/8 or 1/2-inch back from the shoulder. This has always been most pronounced with cartridges of about the same minimum body taper and length as the .308 line of cartridges. The .308 seems to feed a bit better than the .243, but not much; perhaps this is due to the larger bullet diameter with resultant lower bullet ogive-to-shoulder angle, and thus a better approach of cartridge to chamber. The prevalence of factory rifles chambered for these cartridges that will induce this constriction, if the same cartridge is fed through the action numerous times without firing (which would erase the constriction), also indicates an inherent feed problem. A small radius, cut at the rear edge of the chamber, then polished, often improves functioning.

The current popularity of short magnum cartridges brings a whole new crop of feeding problems. Not only are there short, minimum-taper cartridges, but increased body diameter as well. This increased body and head diameter necessitates a bolt face conversion so that it will accept the larger cartridge head. After the magnum conversion, the bolt face is sometimes too small to accept the head of a maximum diameter cartridge. This is probably due to the gunsmith altering the bolt face using a cartridge head as a gauge. A headspace gauge, or other plug turned to the maximum head diameter should be used to insure that *any* proper cartridge will be accepted by the bolt face.

was perhaps the most susceptible to the short magnum conversion, with numerous Enfields, Model 70's, custom Mausers, and Model 721 Remingtons also in the running. The bolt face of the Springfield, Model 70, Mauser and Enfield can be easily enlarged for the magnum cartridge head in the following way: A stub arbor is tightly fitted into the rear of the stripped bolt and this arbor is chucked in the lathe. The bolt head is supported in the steady rest. Usually the rear of the bolt needs to be indicated and adjusted to run true as they seldom run true as first chucked. A small high speed hand grinder is held in the milling attachment and aligned with the work. The bolt is rotated at about 75 rpm and the grinder point is fed longitudinally to contact the bolt face, then fed horizontally to enlarge the bolt face recess. This operation often reveals that the bolt face originally was not true and square with the bolt's centerline, sometimes being as much as .003 out-of-square across the extreme width of the bolt face. The bolt face can also be trued at this point, improving the accuracy of headspace measurement and possibly improving accuracy of the rifle. The inside diameter of the bolt face recess should be about .008 to .010-inch larger than the maximum diameter gauge plug or headspace gauge. A cartridge head should not be used for this measurement as many cartridges are considerably under maximum permissible diameter at this point. Obviously, if the recess diameter is inadequate, frequent hangups in feeding can be encountered later on. The lower ends of the bolt face recess lip can also be altered at this time by carefully feeding the mounted grinding point across the stationary bolt face as necessary to provide adequate width and clearance to accept the cartridge. A moment's stoning of the bolt face, followed by a bit of polishing with fine abrasive cloth held on a small screwdriver or wooden paddle, finishes the job. The extractor lip is altered by observing the original contour but shortening as necessary to fit the new cartridge, then polishing.

When converting a rifle action to accept a cartridge with a larger rim diameter; the bolt face must be altered to accept the larger cartridge head. Marquart places a stub arbor in the rear of the bolt so that it may be chucked in the lathe prior to grinding the bolt face. The rear of the bolt is then indicated so that the bolt body will turn true.

The conversion of the Model 721 Remington bolt face from .30-06 to magnum diameter is a bit more involved. Instead of the hand grinder being used, the bolt face is bored out using a lathe bit specially ground to cut the recess required for the Remington extractor. Dimensions of a regular Remington magnum bolt face should be observed and the Remington extractor will then fit. As the ejector normally prevents the extractor from turning within the bolt face and moving out of proper alignment with the receiver ejection port, the larger diameter of the extractor recess in relation to the ejector now eliminates this feature. However, the extractor can still be locked in its proper position by carefully 'staking' the recess lip at two points just beyond the ends of the extractor to effectively prevent the extractor from turning.

Generally, the most common feeding problem stems from improper shape and dimensions of the receiver lips themselves. These lips are intended to restrain the ammo from jumping out of the magazine when the bolt is drawn back briskly. Sometimes there is a fine line between the point that cartridges feed smoothly and the point where they spew out of the action when the bolt is opened, resulting when the gunsmith overdoes the alteration. The latter often happens when an action and magazine with proper width for the original .30-06 cartridge is converted for the nearly cylindrical magnum cartridges such as the full-length .375 H&H necked up to .45 caliber. For such a cartridge the inside width of the magazine box should be increased to permit the loaded rounds in the magazine

Marquart places a small high speed grinder in the milling attachment and feeds the grinder laterally into the bolt face and then horizontally to enlarge the bolt face recess. The bolt itself rotates at about 75 rpm. At this point the bolt face may be checked for squareness; it is not unusual for the bolt to be .003 out of square across the face. Truing the bolt face will result in more precise headspace measurement as well as a possible improvement in accuracy. A bolt face ground in this manner is more likely to feed cartridges properly than one bored out; the ground bolt face usually results in a better finish as well.

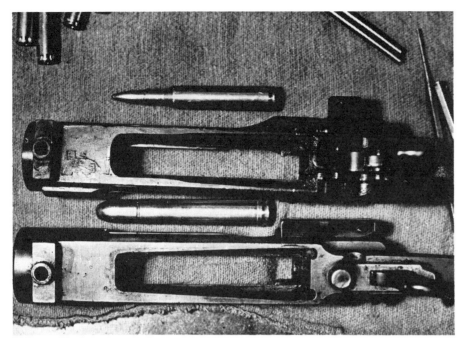

to stagger or be more nearly opposite each other, rather than vertically stacked.

A large portion of time spent perfecting feeding, in most instances, involves the discreet use of the hand grinder. In most conversions, especially when going from a cartridge in the .30-06 category to something like the 7mm Remington Magnum or the .300 Winchester Magnum, the inside width of the receiver opening just below the lips must be increased. The rear surface of the swell on each side of the forward area of the magazine well must also be removed somewhat. These swells were seemingly designed for some sort of feeding help in actions such as the Springfield; but Mauser accomplished smoother feeding without them.

Some of the Mauser receivers appear to have adequate width to accept cartridges in the .460 Weatherby class, yet feed faultlessly with cartridges of much smaller dimensions. Removing metal in the critical areas with a grinder is a cut and try method and one must always be aware that if he grinds out too much, it is impossible to put it back; yet, it is amazing just how wide the inside of the receiver can be and still feed smoothly.

The greatest feeding problem I ever encountered was one connected with the conversion of the Ruger .22 Long Rifle Auto Pistol for the .32 S&W Long cartridge for target use. At one time I did a number of these conversions; and to alter the autoloading action designed for the .22 LR to handle the much larger .32 S&W Long posed considerable problems. The nearly cylindrical .32 with full wadcutter bullet seated entirely within the case had to somehow make an unerring flying leap from magazine to chamber;

target shooters do not appreciate a jam halfway through an important string. One thing those conversions impressed on me was that dimensionally identical conversions simply would not feed identically. One conversion would feed perfectly just as assembled; the next, with apparently the same dimensions, would require many hours to perfect. Obviously, since the differences in these guns were so subtle, often only a minute change is necessary to

correct a feeding problem — so when working on the feed system, don't make chips fly.

It can and does happen that a conversion or re-barrel job comes through the shop that has a real feeding problem. The barrel can be of the finest, headspace and other chamber dimensions near perfect, and yet somewhere someone said that the feeding was "good enough" and delivered it to the customer. He either had been convinced that these usually "don't feed too good anyway" or else was continually dissatisfied with a job which should have performed perfectly from the start. Correcting the feeding is as much a part of the conversion as any other operation, it just takes a lot of patience and a bit of know-how to make all the cartridges feed as they should. ●

Bar stock is used to illustrate how cartridges of different diameter stack in a magazine differently. A magazine designed for .270 cartridges has the cartridges nearly opposing each other while the same magazine loaded with .458 Winchester Magnum cartridges, right, would have the cartridges too nearly on top of each other. If the action and magazine weren't properly converted, the .458 cartridges would not be retained within the magazine by the rails.

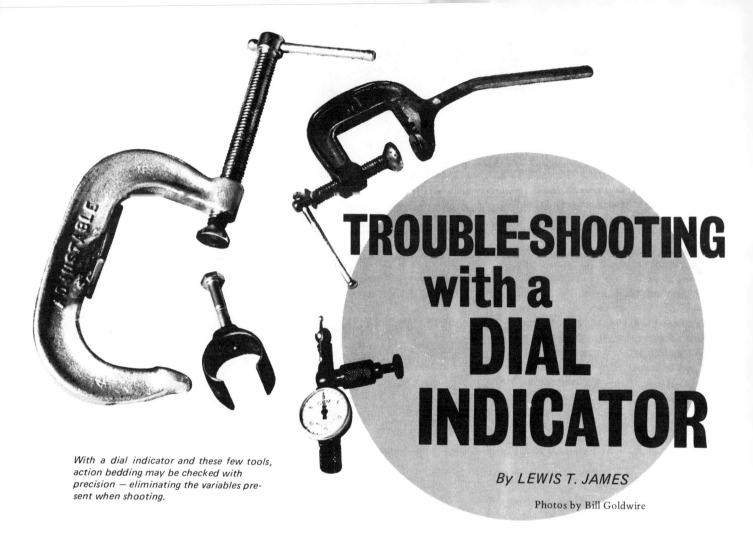

TROUBLE-SHOOTING with a DIAL INDICATOR

With a dial indicator and these few tools, action bedding may be checked with precision — eliminating the variables present when shooting.

By LEWIS T. JAMES

Photos by Bill Goldwire

FOR BEST ACCURACY, a rifle must be bedded properly. That's not exactly earth-shaking news to any student of the rifle; but many are not aware that glass-bedding an action does not automatically insure a perfect action-to-stock fit, or that once bedded properly, it may not stay that way. As a result, there are a lot of epoxy-bedded deer rifles, varmint rifles and even bench rest rifles that don't shoot as well as they could, even if the bedding material has been applied in the right amounts at the right places.

Before accusing me of heresy, consider a couple of often-ignored, and little-known facts: First, *all* epoxy materials, to the best of my knowledge, undergo a slight amount of shrinkage — usually a minimum of one percent — as they "set up." In general, the faster a material hardens, the more it shrinks; and the thicker the layer of epoxy, the greater the measurable effect of shrinkage. In other words, if you have a thick wad of glass or whatever under the tang area "for greater support," and a thin layer under the receiver ring, the percentage of shrinkage will be the same, but the tang will be slightly lower. For this reason, an improved bedding job can be obtained by applying a thin coat of epoxy (even plain epoxy glue) on top of the basic bedding. Shrinkage of the thin layer will be uniform and too slight to affect things.

A second cause of non-perfect epoxy bedding is the wood in the stock. If, after the bedding has hardened, the wood shrinks or warps it will also warp the bedding material. Though different bedding materials vary in their inherent resistance to warpage, virtually all — in the thicknesses used for rifle bedding —

Indication of Bedding Problems

1 2 3 4 5 6

A dial indicator can determine the cause of consistent groups such as these examples — if the problem lies in the bedding, the load is known to be good, the shooting conditions and hold "perfect." (1) Usually caused by the tang area bedding being too low; third or fourth shot will be high; first shot will usually be in the central impact area. (2) Typical of groups when action is bowed by front screw. (3) Tang screw may be slightly loose. (4) Slight looseness of both screws or bedding in extremely bad shape. (5) Front screw slightly loose — tighten a bit after a shot falls near center. (6) "Walking" in one direction can be due to side pressure on barrel, or side pressure on action caused by misaligned or bent action screws.

will bend slightly before breaking. It doesn't take much bending to louse up accuracy, and the pull of a warping piece of wood can be terrific. Bear in mind that the certain way to warp wood is to seal one side absolutely moisture-proof, while leaving the opposite side unfinished, or finished with a substance which can be penetrated by moisture — which is a good description of an epoxy-bedded stock. Even if a bedding job was originally perfect, the effect of wood shifting can be a warped bedding surface — which is one reason why a good rifle may "go sour."

If the rifle is bedded properly, the action should bottom perfectly against the supporting surfaces in the stock, should not bind along the top of the side of the action channel, and should be held firmly in place by the action screws to avoid shifting after each shot. Anything less and it won't shoot right — whether the problem is caused by improper bedding technique, epoxy shrinkage, shifting of the supporting stock wood or compression of the bedding caused by excessive tightening of the screws.

So how do you determine if your bedding is "perfect," other than by shooting — which introduces a host of variables. You can get a pretty good idea simply by standing the rifle on its butt and holding the fore-end tip while lightly touching the barrel, then alternately tightening and loosening each of the stock screws. If you feel more than an almost imperceptible movement something is wrong. Though this test might seem imprecise, most practitioners of this "art" contend that you can feel as little as a thousandth or two of movement.

Although the fingers can detect even slight movement, they aren't precise enough to determine how much, which is why some shooters commonly use a dial indicator to check the action for bedding or flexing. True, the indicator will also show the very slight normal compression of the bedding — which varies with the tightness of the screws and the type of bedding material — but it is probably the best method of making a precision check of the bedding.

If you're going to "trouble-shoot" with a dial indicator, you need to know how to set it up, what the different types of reading indicate, and how giving means of attaching the dial indicator and adjusting it horizontally as

With the dial indicator clamped to the stock, bearing against a clamp attached to the barrel, bedding can be checked by tightening and loosening the action screws.

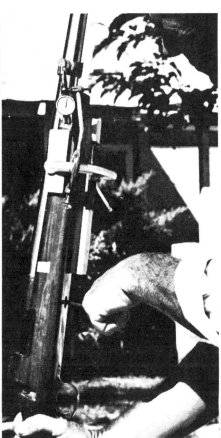

By mounting the dial indicator to read lateral movement of the barrel when the screws are tightened, it will show misalignment of the screws.

This photo shows the detail of comb installation for checking the tang area. Indicator should be pre-loaded and the dial zeroed to show positive or negative.

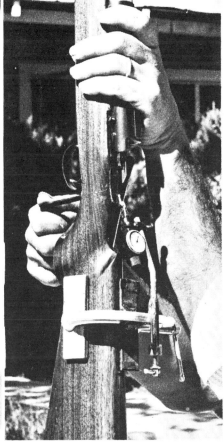

Loosening the tang screw while checking the dial indicator reading will show excessive compression or high points in the bedding.

necessary. Adjusting the indicator to rest on the tang of the action, pre-load the indicator by rotating the indicator slightly on the bar of the "G" clamp. When a reading of about .015 is noted, tighten the set screw and rotate the dial to zero the needle. By pre-loading the indicator, a person will be able to see on the dial any movement of the tang when the screw is loosened or tightened.

Standing the rifle near vertical, and holding it with the fingers around the *receiver ring* and stock, loosen and tighten the tang screw. If the bedding is not quite true, movement will be noted. If the screw is bending the tang, when loosened a positive movement from zero will be noted on the indicator. If .001 or less shows when the screw is loosened, retighten the screw to a zero reading and gradually apply pressure to try to receive a negative reading, and note how much pressure is required.

When more than .0015 positive movement is read, the action is being bent down by the tang screw. This will call for locating and removing the high point in the bedding, or the placing of a shim under the tang of the action. Usually, if I receive a reading of over .002 positive, I will apply a thin coat of bedding compound to the indicated area, brushing the compound with a stiff bristled brush, and let the compound set up before proceeding further.

After loosening the screw and beginning to re-tighten, any negative movement of the indicator will show the compression of the tang into the bedding. A reading of .001 negative has been found to be satisfactory. If great pressure is needed to receive more than this, you are using more pressure than is needed to hold the action in place when the rifle is being fired. If compression of the tang area is noted, depending upon the amount of the reading, either correct with a shim or bedding compound as stated before. When a reading of .0005 positive to about .001 negative is noted, it is time to proceed to the next check point.

A word of caution — be suspicious of an absolute zero reading when the screws are loosened. This reading may be false because the action is being bowed down by the middle screw (if used), by too great a pressure on the front screw, or by the action being wedged in the channel walls. If the

zero reading is noted, loosen the screws slightly and check your readings again. If nothing happens, hurrah, continue on.

At this point, remove the complete rig from the comb of the stock. Placing the barrel band on the barrel roughly an inch from the fore-end tip, tighten the cap screw so it is held in place near the centerline of the fore-end. Now install the "C" clamp and indicator rig on the fore-end of the stock two or three inches from the tip. Adjust the indicator on the bar of the "G" clamp so the lever rests on the cap screw. Pre-load and tighten the indicator as before.

Here is the point where things can be a bit tricky. Much depends on how and where the stock is held to be able to take a true reading. When taking a reading on the tang area, one can grasp the fore-end of the stock or the receiver ring area and not affect the reading of the indicator. For a reading on the barrel, I usually hold the rifle near vertical by grasping the grip of the stock, or placing the butt of the stock in a well-padded bench vise. The reasons for holding by such means are: if held by the receiver ring area and grasping around the stock and receiver, it is possible to have a false reading of the indicator by not allowing the barrelled action to rise from too much pressure on the tang screw, or in the case of an action with a magazine cut, it is possible to bow the action slightly by the hand pressure if the works is not perfectly bedded. When you try to hold by the fore-end, either your hand or arm gets in the way of things, and if you reach around the barrel you will affect the indicator reading. For a piece of steel, a person will be surprised at how little pressure in the wrong places will affect the indicator reading.

Holding the rifle near vertical, "snap" the front action screw loose, and re-tighten slowly. If the action is bedded properly, the screw will "pop" loose when it is untorqued suddenly. If resistance is felt after the first eighth turn, either the screw is binding somewhere, the bedding is being compressed and springing back, or the action is being bowed by one of the screws.

When the screw is first snapped loose, observe carefully the indicator needle. If the action is bedded properly, and the screw tension is near correct, the needle will momentarily show a positive reading of about .002 or slightly less, and return to a zero or near-

zero reading, probably .0005 on either side. This movement of the needle shows the action to be pulled tight in the bedding, but under no bending strain from the screws.

If the indicator needle returns to the negative side after the front screw is loosened, loosen the middle screw slightly, and take a reading. If the action is being flexed by this middle screw the indicator should return to zero. If the middle screw is already loose, the reading on the negative side of zero shows the receiver to be in a downward strain caused by the tang screw. The amount of movement or strain and the location of same will decide the remedy.

A .001 compression of the middle screw area will usually show a .005 to .006 negative reading, too great a movement for top accuracy. We have three choices: scrape the entire bedding area to level it, place a shim in the middle screw area, or lay a thin coat of bedding compound in the needed area.

If the trouble lies in the tang area, the indicator reading is more or less double the actual stress involved. That is, a .002 reading will show a compression of about .001 at the tang. Also, the negative reading can point to a wedging effect of the receiver on the bedding area; proceed carefully so as to make no mistakes as to the location of the trouble.

When the indicator needle jumps to more than .002 on the positive side and stays there when the front screw is loosened, either the front screw has been pulled too tight and the bedding has been compressed between the front screw and the recoil lug (with the most compression near the screw hole in the stock) or the area between the front and middle screws is already low and the action is being bowed down by pressure on the front screw; or there is a high spot somewhere between the front and rear screws.

Compression of the receiver ring area is encountered less frequently than any other problem, due to the size and shape of the receiver ring itself. It usually occurs when one is rebedding an action with "glass" or epoxy material and is "heavy-handed" on the screwdriver or Allen-wrench before the compound is fully hard. The dispersion of the groups caused by flexing at this point seems to be less per .001 than at any other point on an action, but when more than .002 flex is encountered, groups spread in a big hurry.

To check for either of the problems, slowly tighten the front screw to a point where slight resistance is felt, rotate the dial of the indicator to zero with the needle and gradually apply more pressure to the wrench handle. If the bedding between the front screw and the recoil lug is being compressed, the indicator needle will move towards the positive side and continue to move as greater pressure is applied. If the problem is action warpage by the front screw, the needle will start to move toward the positive side but will stop

and return to the zero position and continue to move to the negative side as pressure is applied. Depending upon the amount of movement and the stiffness of the action, either less pressure on the screw or building up the low area will solve these problems. Normally, in a single-shot action you will not run into either of these conditions, but it is quite common to find either on a magazine rifle.

Due to the fore-end reading being magnified by the "leverage" of the barrel, slight variations are more easily detected than when reading "direct"

off the tang. However, reading off the barrel can be confusing because a low spot just behind the front screw will cause the action to bow *downward* when the screw is tightened, but the barrel will move *upward*. Until you're familiar with the basic techniques, it's a good idea to loosen the center screw and leave it loose — this will simplify finding the general problem area. After you've accomplished that much, determining the effect of the middle screw will pin-point the problem. Something else that may help is sketching the action and barrel so you can "see" the effect of high or low points along the bedding surface. ●

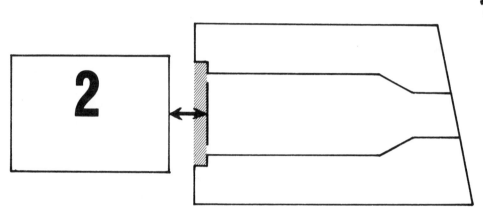

Detecting

Correcting

Effects of

MY RIFLE'S GOT HEADSPACE, reckon I oughtta have it fixed or swap it off. How many times have you heard that? Dozens, I'll wager, and you've probably wanted just as often to do a bit of headspace checking yourself. Many well-used older guns have excessive headspace, and a surprising number of surplus military arms as well. The former from springy actions, and obsolete alloys and heat treatment; the latter from indiscriminate replacement of parts when torn down for cleaning, repair, and preparation for market.

More than a few new-looking rifles built on military actions don't stand up too well in this respect, either. Home fitting of so-called "finish chambered" replacement barrels is often done hurriedly and haphazardly, producing less than perfect results and plenty such with excess headspace are circulating in the used-gun market.

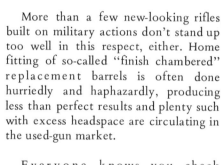

Everyone knows you check headspace with gauges: A "Go" gauge upon which the breech must *close* freely; and a "No-Go" upon which it must *not close*. They are turned from steel, hardened, then ground to final dimensions within very close tolerances. Those for rimless calibers resemble the cartridge case with its neck cut off; those for belted and rimmed calibers are simply "buttons" resembling the head of the case. Unfortunately, few gun buffs buy them, though the cost, from sources like Forster-Appelt, is quite reasonable.

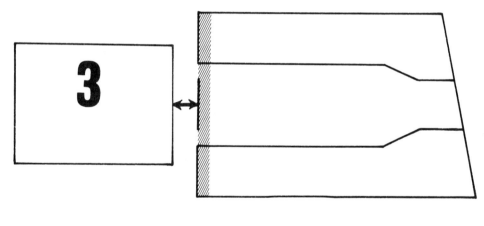

How do they work? As shown in the accompanying drawings, a portion of the chamber supports the cartridge case against the bolt face. The gauge is dropped into the chamber and the breech is closed *gently*. If it closes freely on the "Go" gauge, into its fully-locked position, the distance from bolt face to support surface is over the required minimum and all is well. If it will not close, this distance is too short – not a dangerous condition, but one which will

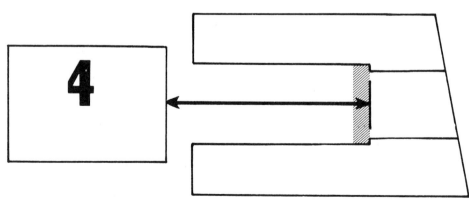

The arrows in the drawings above show the two surfaces between which headspace is measured with different types of cartridges. The shaded area at the right end of each arrow indicates the surface upon which the case is supported. The examples are (1) a rimless case, which headspaces between the bolt and chamber shoulder; (2) belted case, which headspaces on the belt cut; (3) rimless case, which headspaces between the bolt and the face of the barrel; and (4) a straight rimless case chamber, which headspaces between the bolt and end of the chamber. Note that with the exception of the straight rimless case chamber, the forward portion of the case must blow out to fill the chamber area, regardless of the correctness of headspace measurement.

Excess Headspace

By MAJ. GEORGE NONTE

prevent maximum-dimension cartridges from chambering.

If the bolt will not close on the "No-Go" gauge, all is again well -- the distance does not exceed the allowed maximum considered necessary by the factories to insure safety with minimum-dimension cartridges. If it *does* close freely, then a condition of *excess* headspace exists and cartridges will not be properly supported during firing.

I've watched many a man check headspace with good quality gauges, and more than a few got erroneous indications. A "gunsmith" I once knew got an "excess" reading almost every time. He simply opened the breech, dropped the gauge in, and slammed the action shut. Almost any gun will accept a "No-Go" gauge under those conditions. The camming power of the action and the elasticity of steels permit crowding the gauge in, especially in belted chambers where the support area is very narrow.

As any inspector will tell you, gauges must be handled with care if accurate indications are to be obtained. A certain amount of "feel" is necessary and no force may be applied. Accurate gauging for headspace can be accomplished only if these procedures are followed:

Remove extractor.
Remove ejector if of spring-loaded plunger type.
Remove firing mechanism from bolt.
Thoroughly clean chamber, locking lug seats, and bolt face.
Make certain bolt moves freely.
Hold rifle muzzle-down and insert gauge gently into chamber.
Move bolt forward to contact gauge gently, then move toward locked position with as little effort as possible.

Stop as soon as firm resistance is felt. In bolt action rifles, the weight of the bolt handle alone is sufficient for the final movement.

The last two are most important. All locking systems have some camming power during final lock-up, and bolt guns have the most. Because of this, heavy-handed manipulation can easily force the gauge past the proper point, giving an erroneous reading.

Headspace of *rimless* caliber chambers may also be checked from a fired case. Perhaps the simplest method is by dropping the case into a "case gauge" such as those made by Forster-Appelt and L. E. Wilson. The gauge consists of a dummy chamber cut in a steel cylinder, and its head carries two steps. This gauge is intended primarily to determine whether cases or loaded cartridges fall within allowable head-shoulder length tolerances. A case that falls below the bottom step of the gauge *creates* a condition of excess headspace within the gun.

From our viewpoint, the top step is more important. If a freshly fired case protrudes above it, then that case was fired in a gun with excess headspace. L. E. Wilson also makes a micrometer-adjustable variation of this gauge with which the exact amount of excess headspace can be accurately measured, but careful use of a depth micrometer and the standard gauge serves the same purpose.

But, what if you don't have and can't afford that set of gauges, the cheapest of which cost around $5 each? Without them, or without a case gauge you *cannot* check headspace with respect to a known standard.

You can, however, check it with regard to the *particular ammunition* you will be using or the cases you'll be loading in that particular rifle. The procedure is basically quite simple, but requires fair attention to detail and a bit of time. It consists simply of

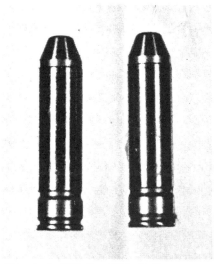

These typical "Go" and "No Go" rimless bottleneck headspace gauges resemble a cartridge with the neck removed. Since each gauge requires careful machining, they are fairly expensive and the average gun buff does not have them.

A second method of gauging headspace is to place a fired cartridge in a case gauge. If the rifle has excessive headspace the case will protrude above the gauge, as shown here.

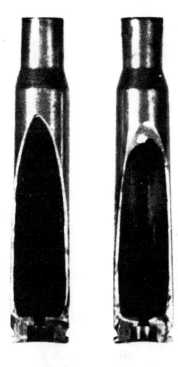

The case at left, above, was fired with .030 excess headspace and shows thinning of the walls ahead of the web. The right case, which shows no such thinning, was fired with normal headspace.

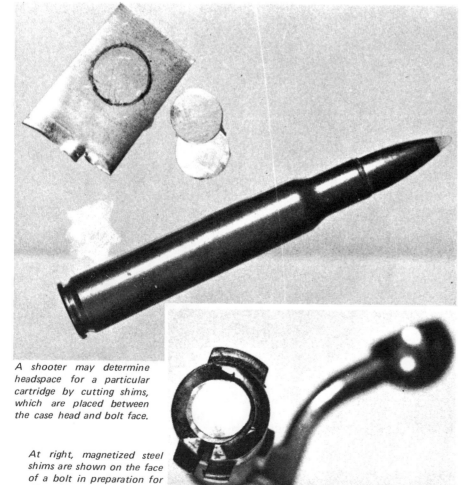

A shooter may determine headspace for a particular cartridge by cutting shims, which are placed between the case head and bolt face.

At right, magnetized steel shims are shown on the face of a bolt in preparation for determining headspace.

determining the amount of clearance between the face of the locked bolt and the head of a chambered cartridge.

Since you can't get into that tiny space and measure it with a yardstick, we use steel shim stock (thin steel sheet made to very close tolerances) between bolt and cartridge head. Steel shim stock in standard thickness of .001 (1/1000-inch), .002, .003, and .005 may normally be obtained from automotive parts supply stores. With it you'll need something to cut it cleanly; if you don't have a small set of tinsnips, tight scissors will do the job, but don't let mama catch you using her best pair. Any thin sheet metal will do if you know or can measure accurately its thickness.

Cut out discs of shim stock that will fit freely into the bolt face recess. Make two each of .001, .002, and .003 thickness. Make certain they are flat, not kinked by the cutting. Sand or file off any burrs resulting from the cutting. The completed discs must stack together smoothly and compactly.

We need some means of holding the discs together and to the bolt or cartridge. Surely you've a magnet of some sort handy, so rub the discs on it to magnetize them. (This won't work with brass shim stock, of course.) They'll adhere to the steel bolt face, but not to the non-ferrous metal case, which won't react to magnetism. Lacking a magnet, a very thin film of grease on the discs will cause them to adhere to the case head when the time comes. The grease will add to the thickness of the disc stack, but not enough to matter.

Select from your stock of ammunition or cases five rounds which are clean, uniform and free from dents or distortion. Make certain rims aren't bent and that primers do not protrude, for either will cause erroneous readings.

Drop one of the selected rounds into the chamber with a .006-inch stack of discs stuck to its head, or the bolt face. Close the bolt gently without force. If it locks completely, excess headspace exists with that particular cartridge. Add discs until the bolt stops just short of full lock-up. Record the shim thickness required. Repeat with the other four rounds to confirm the first reading. If the bolt does not close fully, peel off discs .001-inch at a time until it will. Remember -- *no force.*

If the gun will accept no more than .002 of shim, then headspace is really a bit too tight. You might run into a round or so in that lot of ammunition that will be long enough to chamber with difficulty -- that could be embarrassing if you're facing dangerous game or are in the middle of a rapid-fire string for record. For a permanent fix of this condition, have a *competent* gauge-equipped gunsmith recheck headspace and deepen the chamber if he finds it necessary. You can, though, avoid trouble by simply running all cartridges through the action before going afield and setting aside for casual use any that chamber less than freely.

We've said that .006 clearance is the maximum for industry standards generally allow .006 between minimum and maximum headspace. Actually, if your gun accepts .006 shim over cartridges, the chamber is sure to be more than that much overlong since the odds against you having minimum length cartridges for your test are mighty high.

Much has been said and published about the danger of excess headspace. How dangerous is it? In my personal experience, I've never encountered any gun damage or shooter injury, even when as much as 1/16-inch excess existed -- except when other more dangerous factors existed at the same time. In short, with ammunition of proper pressure level, cases of good quality, and gun in good mechanical condition, a moderate amount of excess headspace presents no hazard.

This is easily explained: The solid head of the case remains confined by the rear of the chamber and bolt face; and the rear portion of the case wall obturates (seals gases) in the usual fashion. Therefore, unless grossly excessive pressures and/or bad brass are involved, gases cannot escape rearward, and no harm will come to the gun or shooter. The most that can happen is that the primer will back slightly out of its pocket upon ignition, after which the case will slide back over it as chamber pressure builds up. This *may* result in a slight primer leak. It will give the *appearance* of excessive pressure -- a badly flattened and distorted primer cup -- even though pressure is normal. Perhaps this has given rise to the reports that excessive headspace increases pressure. 'Tain't so; the effect is actually the opposite.

If excess headspace is merely the result of sloppy chambering any likely amount of it will not affect other mechanical aspects of cartridge case head support. On the other hand, if it has been produced by excessive firing and/or excessive chamber pressures, case head support may have been impaired.

For example, let's say you've a Mauser .30-06 (original caliber) now showing .010-.015 excess headspace. This *could* have been produced by the locking lugs and corresponding abutments in the receiver setting back from excessive pressures and/or less-than-perfect heat treatment. If that's the case, then the bolt face will have moved rearward as much as .020-inch, allowing the case head to protrude that much farther than originally from the barrel breech. This places the forward end of the web perilously close to the chamber mouth, even more so if an excessive radius or bevel exists there. Should you happen to get hold of some cases with webs thinner than usual, a portion of the walls may extend beyond the barrel breech. When that happens, the walls will surely rupture on firing, releasing

gas out into the action to take things apart.

How can you tell if excessive headspace is the result of this sort of set-back? Check first with a bent wire probe to determine if the locking lugs have pounded depressed seats in the receiver abutments. You may not be able to detect such depressions if they are only slight, but if they do exist, they are responsible for at least part of the excess headspace.

A more accurate check on Mauser type actions consists of cutting discs of shim stock that can be layed over the complete bolt face, then closing the bolt on them until you have determined the clearance between the bolt face rim and the barrel breech. This amount, plus the depth of the bolt face recess, is the amount the case head will protrude from the chamber. If this distance amounts to more than 75 percent of the case web thickness, trouble is not very far ahead. This condition can be corrected by building up the bolt face and lugs by the methods to be mentioned later.

Rifles having a coned barrel breech such as the Springfield cannot be

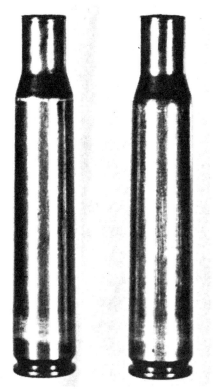

The left case, above, is normal, sized to suit the chamber. The right case has had the shoulder pushed back .030 in a modified sizing die to induce excess headspace for tests.

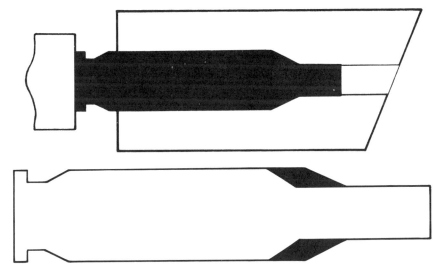

A condition of zero headspace exists when the case is in solid contact with both the bolt face and the support area of the chamber, as shown in the top drawing. In the lower drawing, a rimless case with excess headspace (exaggerated) is illustrated. Upon firing, the shoulder is pushed forward, stretching and weakening the case. A similar condition exists with properly headspaced belted cases which have too much tolerance at the shoulder. An example is shown in the photograph below.

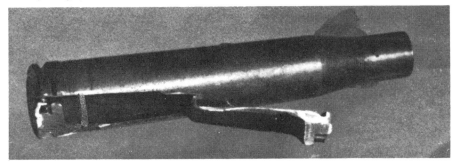

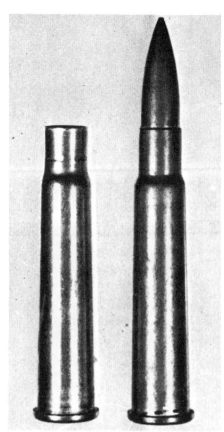

The fired case shows a typical amount of forward shoulder movement in rimmed and belted cases on first firing—about .018-inch.

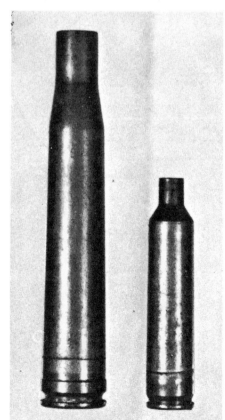

Shown are typical incipient head separations. The left example was caused by excess shoulder clearance with correct headspace on the belt; while the one on the right was caused simply by excess headspace.

checked in this respect except with sophisticated measuring instruments. Altering the barrel breech and screwing it deeper into the receiver is another means of correcting this condition, but it involves first-class lathe and file work.

However, damage to the case will result from excess headspace. Gas pressure forces the head *rearward* against the bolt face, the shoulder *forward* against the chamber shoulder. Generally the front portion, being thinner and lighter, moves first and grips the chamber wall tightest; then the head is forced rearward. This is emphasized by the case first being driven forward by the firing pin blow and primer impulse.

The end result is that the case walls are stretched and thinned, even by initial firing, back just in front of the solid head. The more stretching, the more thinning – and, eventually, at a point depending upon the original wall thickness and ductility of the particular case, the wall will crack or pull apart at roughly a right angle to the case centerline. When this crack extends only part way around the case it is called an *incipient separation*; when the head separates completely from the rest, it is a *separation* or *rupture*. Enough of the case walls remain attached to the head to keep the gases confined.

Generally, separations produce no damage to the gun, though minor erosion or roughening of the chamber wall may occur at the point of separation. The gun will be put out of action, though, for the front portion of the case will remain in the chamber, preventing another cartridge from entering. There are several methods and tools for removing ruptured cases, but we won't go into them here.

This stretching and thinning of the case *always* occurs to some degree in every firing, but does not seriously affect case strength or function except when headspace is grossly excessive, or in rimmed and belted chambers with excess shoulder clearance.

I have produced literally hundreds of incipient and complete separations in Browning machine guns by adjusting headspace to an excess value. In no instance did any damage occur to the gun until the barrel was screwed out sufficiently to leave the case walls unsupported ahead of the web. This, of course, permitted the case to blow out, releasing gas to damage the gun and,

sometimes, the gunner. This condition does not generally occur in sporting rifles, except as already described, even when headspace is greatly excessive.

Probably the only other condition under which it could occur is when a short tenon Mauser barrel is inadvertently screwed into a long-ring action. The 1/8 to 3/16-inch difference in barrel tenon length would leave the case walls unsupported near the head, at the same time creating 1/8-inch excess headspace; a deadly combination guaranteed to wreck both rifle and shooter. Different Mauser models vary this much in tenon length while having compatible threads.

Both belted and rimmed cases are more subject to thinning and stretching than rimless, and this occurs in the same manner when headspace is excessive. However, unlike rimless designs, they are subject to considerable stretching even when headspace is correct. In both cases and chambers, manufacturers generally allow greater shoulder location tolerance in belted and rimmed designs. This is explained simply: in them this location is not critical, while it is in a rimless case. By allowing greater tolerances in non-critical areas, production cost is held down.

Consequently, even when the case is properly supported by the headspacing surfaces, there still exists clearance between case and chamber shoulders. Upon firing, the case walls stretch forward to close this gap, producing the characteristic thinning in front of the solid head. Thus, a separation or badly stretched fired cases do not necessarily indicate excess headspace in rimmed and belted cases.

Okay, suppose you've found that your pet smoke pole does have a few thousandths excess headspace. What to do about it? Send it to a good gunsmith and he'll correct it by setting the barrel back and rechambering. In addition to costing money, that will foul up barrel inletting and change zero. And, all things considered, you might wait as long as six months to get the job done.

If you're a handloader, the solution is relatively simple. First, fire-form cases to fit your chamber. Lightly oil the front half of the cases prior to firing. This will reduce the tendency to separate by allowing the entire case to stretch upon firing. Then adjust the resizing die to suit that particular headspace condition. This consists of using the die so that it does not change the position of the fire-formed shoulder and applies to all bottle-neck cases. In effect, you've lengthened the case body to compensate for the overlong chamber. With rimmed and belted cases, the moved-forward shoulder takes over all or part of the support function. In short, after this treatment the case is supported in the chamber on its shoulder rather than its rim or belt. This cannot be done, of course, with straight cases such as the .458 or .405 Winchester, or the common U.S. .30 M1 Carbine.

Supported in this fashion, the case will undergo no further significant stretching and will not, therefore, progress farther toward separation. Your headspace problem will have been eliminated so long as all cases are properly prepared.

The die adjustment must be made carefully and must be maintained for that particular rifle forever after—or, at least as long as the excess headspace condition exists. If the die should be returned to the standard adjustment, it will push the shoulder back, leaving the case without adequate support. Two or three firings under those conditions will assuredly produce a separation.

Because of the excess shoulder clearance mentioned, the reloadable life of rimmed and belted cases can be greatly extended by using this method of die adjustment. Fireforming the shoulder forward, then keeping it there, prevents recurrent stretching and eventual separation.

In order to demonstrate just what effect excess headspace has on case life, we conducted a few tests. A standard-chamber .30-06 barrel was obtained from McGowen Rifle Barrels and fitted to a M98 action. A single lot of M-2 Ball ammunition was used and firing conducted with headspace increased in .005 increments. This was continued until the limits one might ever expect to encounter were exceeded. Even excessive wear and random re-assembly of military rifles won't produce more than about .030 too much headspace. And, even the most ham-handed amateur rebarreling attempts aren't likely to exceed that.

While it would have been possible to ream the chamber deeper in .005 steps, we chose to create the same condition by setting the case shoulders back the same amount in a shortened resizing die with an oversize neck. In this manner the conditions of neck clearance and bullet jump were kept the same for all firing and chamber pressures were maintained at a more uniform level throughout firing.

Even at the +.030-inch stage, no incipient or complete case separations were produced with the initial firing. The condition of the cases after firing is clearly shown in the section photos. The characteristic thinning and weakening of the case walls is evident however, just ahead of the web, and also can be seen in the photos. In spite of the existence of this internal weakening, the cases *appear* serviceable from a visual external examination. The only sure way to find the damage is with a hook-like wire probe shown in the pix. When this probe is inserted and passed over the damaged area, the depression in the brass can be felt. In short, we concluded that guns with up to .030-inch excess headspace are probably safe for one-time firing of factory loads or handloads in new cases, though we don't recommend.

But, what about reloading those fired cases? 'Tain't generally considered advisable, but we ran some tests anyway. First, we reloaded the cases

One simple method of correcting for excess headspace is to plate or build up the bolt face.

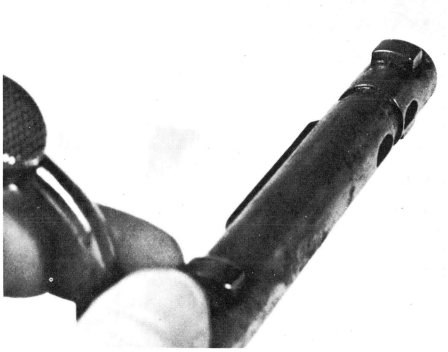

Another method of correcting for excess headspace is to build up or plate the rear of the locking lugs, which then must be carefully honed and fitted to the locking recesses to insure even bearing.

fired with excess headspace, resizing them with the shortened die to return the shoulder to its earlier position, giving the same excess headspace. The result was predictable: incipient or full separation developed in only a few firings. Some cases fired at .030 excess headspace failed after only two or three reloadings, those with less excess lasted a little longer. No damage whatever resulted to the gun or shooter, nor did any gas escape rearward.

Then we worked the other way. The resizing die was adjusted so that it did not shove the shoulder rearward. This resulted in only partial sizing of the case body and was accomplished by smoking the case shoulder. The smoked case was then run into the die only until marks in the soot coating indicated contact with the die shoulder. In this manner it was possible to control shoulder location, not only by not shoving it rearward, but preventing it from migrating forward as the body was resized. Die adjustment was verified by "feeling" the case into the chamber, just as in checking headspace.

In any event, even those cases first fired with .030-inch headspace withstood six "minimum headspace" loadings without measurable further damage or deterioration. They doubtless would have stood more loadings, but we got tired, and called a halt. Probing and sectioning indicated little increase in the weakening process initiated by the first firing.

All of which boils down to this: IF no other mechanical deficiencies exist; IF brass is of good quality and proper hardness; IF chamber pressures do not exceed normal limits; IF the head of the case remains properly supported—you may safely fire new cases in chambers with as much as .030-inch excess headspace. And, IF you fit the case to the chamber by following the die adjustment and resizing procedures we've outlined here, those cases may then be reloaded repeatedly to standard pressures.

This would hold true for an even greater amount of excess headspace so long as the design of the particular gun is such that the extractor will hold the cartridge rearward so the primer can be struck by the firing pin. Spring clip extractors of the Remington type will not do so, nor will several other recent designs. They allow the case to fall too far into the chamber for the firing pin to reach the primer if that much excess headspace exists.

So, we've proved you can do this—but, frankly, any one of the "IF's" we've listed can creep in unknown and cause trouble. You'll be better off to simply correct the excess headspace condition. It isn't all that difficult, depending on the gun involved and the means available to you.

One method that always works is to have the locking surfaces of the bolt or block built up by chrome plating. If your gun swallows .008-inch of shims, adding .004 of chrome to the locking surfaces will move the bolt face forward a like amount, in turn reducing the clearance to a satisfactory .004. Simply strip and clean the bolt, then take it to a reputable plater and ask him for .004 minimum hard chrome on the locking surfaces. Be sure and tell him to mask the rest of the bolt, inside and out. We don't want excess chrome anywhere else. Ask him also if he understands "hydrogen embrittlement." If he doesn't, go to a plater who does. Under certain conditions, the plating process can make the underlying metal brittle. Its effect isn't normally noticeable except on very thin metal, but why take a chance? Make certain you get hard chrome and explain it will be a bearing surface.

Smoke the plated surfaces, then insert the bolt and move it to the locked position while maintaining rearward pressure. Take it out and note from the bright spots whether lugs are making full contact. Stone and polish the plated area until they do, checking frequently to avoid taking off too much. Each time you put the bolt in to check bearing, check the headspace again. This way you'll make certain not to take off too much plate. When headspace checks out okay, you'll surely have adequate lug bearing.

A variation of this method is to have the proper thickness of chrome applied to the bolt face, then polish it down with a hard rubber abrasive rod in a brace or a slow speed power drill. Old time gunsmiths have also been known to silver-solder a disc or two or shim stock to the bolt face and accomplish the same purpose. Contrary to popular belief, the heat required to flow low-temperature silver solder will not damage the bolt head or locking lugs.

If you have tools to remove the barrel, excess headspace can be corrected differently. Obviously, screwing the barrel farther into the receiver will shorten headspace. Modern designs with a separate "barrel bracket"

(as Remington calls it) between barrel and receiver are the easiest to handle. Simply remove the bracket, then reduce its thickness (file or grind) by the amount it is desired to shorten headspace. Screw the barrel back in, checking headspace carefully during the last quarter-turn, and the job is done—if the barrel has no iron sights. If it does, they will have to be shifted.

The M98 Mauser type requires different treatment. In it, the rear face of the barrel seats against a shoulder inside the receiver. Metal must be removed from the barrel breech face to allow it to be screwed in farther. Springfields, M1917 & P14 Enfields, and several older commercial models have Mauser-type extractors seating in a notch in the barrel breech. In addition, a shoulder on the barrel seats on the face of the receiver ring. Metal must be removed from the barrel shoulder to permit screwing it in farther. But, when this is done, the extractor notch will no longer line up with the extractor and the action won't close. Consequently, it is necessary to file the notch wider in a clockwise direction. Not a great deal of metal need be removed since correcting headspace by .007 requires only 1/16-turn of the barrel.

In correcting headspace this way, great care must be exercised. It's very easy to remove too much metal, or to change the angle of the surface from which it is removed. Use clean, fine-cut files and chalk or smoke both them and the work piece frequently; the latter to see where you're cutting, the former to keep the cuts smooth. In filing on a barrel shoulder or extractor notch, grind one edge of the file smooth so it's not cutting into adjoining surfaces.

One other way of correcting excess headspace is sometimes—not often—available. If the gun in question is or was originally military surplus, you might find a nearby dealer with several spare bolts. If so, persuade him to let you try them and determine if one will correct the condition. The odds aren't too much in your favor, but it might work out.

We hope that in this rather lengthy dissertation we've made it clear that mildly excessive headspace isn't necessarily cause for retiring "Old Betsy" or buying an expensive rebarreling job. If your gun shows only .002 or .003, don't get too excited about it. After all, the U.S. Army permits rifles in service until their headspace reaches .004 over the established maximum. ●

Section 7

ODD JOBS

By DON LEWIS

As personal as a toothbrush!

Proper Scope Mounting

MOUNTING SCOPES *properly* is vastly more important than most shooters seem to think. The job takes more than just an old screwdriver or two, even though most modern rifles come already drilled, tapped, and ready for scopes. After fifteen years of specializing in mounting scopes and sighting-in rifles, I know that hundreds of hunters pay dearly for the erroneous belief that mounting a scope is simply a matter of tightening the screws.

The modern rifle scope is superior to any other sight when it is correctly installed *for its user.* Before I closed my gunshop to take up the typewriter, I spent ninety percent of my gunsmithing time in correcting scope problems. I had the opportunity to work on hundreds of rifles, of all calibers, with scope deficiencies ranging from defective mounts to off-center screwholes. But the usual problem had nothing to do with mechanical deficiency; it was simply that the scope hadn't been mounted to fit the person who was going to use it.

This may sound a bit exaggerated. It wouldn't seem that there would be that many ways to mount scopes improperly, causing problems so severe that shooters couldn't use them. Maybe I've worn out the statement that a scope should be as personal as the toothbrush. But the fact remains that the scope mounted properly for its user requires no critical eye-relief adjustment, and the shooter doesn't have to strain or stretch to see through it when the moment of truth arrives. No hunter can shoot better than he can see. If his scope isn't fitted for him, it offers him little more than extra weight.

Back in the early Forties, the switch to the newfangled automatic transmission wasn't easy for drivers; nor will the transition to the scope be easy for the hunter who has had great success with some type of open sight. Getting a scope mounted at least a day or two before the season opens is a step in the right direction — but only a step. The new scope user faces more chances for failure than for success. With all the image sharpness and magnification that the rifle scope offers, it takes time to learn how to see through it. Tossing the scoped rifle to the shoulder a few times isn't enough, although this kind of practice is both helpful and necessary. Actual shooting, from a solid rest, is far more beneficial.

I see no point in going into drilling, tapping, and the simpler mechanics of mounting a scope on a rifle. The average hunter doesn't need to get involved in the technical side of scope mounting, but correct eye relief and focus are extremely important to any scope user. I'm still dismayed to see how matter-of-factly many hunters and even some gunsmiths consider eye relief. They simply center the scope in the rings and force the shooter to adjust to the scope, rather than setting it so the eye relief is right for the shooter as he shoulders the rifle in the usual way.

Sometimes, the scope is shoved as far forward as it will go, so it won't hit the shooter's forehead when the gun recoils, especially when the rifle is a big magnum. In my book, this is ridiculous! No matter how far forward the scope is mounted, the shooter still has to get his eye close enough to see the full field of view. I've seen shooters crane forward to see through scopes mounted far forward — and get whacked just the same.

The scope should be mounted to allow the shooter to place his cheek comfortably on the comb of the stock and see through the scope without any further movement. Even a half inch or less, one way or the other, makes a difference. Since most scopes for hunting big game are mounted long before the season opens, during warm weather, the shooter isn't wearing heavy hunting clothing when he shoulders his rifle. Consequently, the gunsmith who mounts his scope for him can't set the scope to allow him proper eye relief. I've learned to allow for the bulkier hunting clothes the hunter will wear later. This allowance puts the scope a little too close to the shooter's face at the time, but he has comfortable eye relief when he has his hunting gear on.

Focus is as important as one's eyeglasses. If the scope reticle isn't in focus for the shooter, precise aiming is almost impossible. I remember a hunter who stormed into my shop one day. He demanded that I remove his scope, even if I had to burn it off with a torch. When he calmed down, I learned that he had missed two bucks that morning because he couldn't see through his scope. While I adjusted the eye relief for my eye, he went on to say he never had wanted a blasted scope in the first place, since he knew they fogged up at the first sign of rain, but had put one on his rifle against his better judgment only to please his nephew. When I handed him the rifle, he was speechless after one look through the readjusted scope. Several turns of the eyepiece put the reticle into focus for his eye, and he left the shop with a new outlook.

Another time, I had the good fortune of helping an elderly hunter far back in the

> "...correct eye relief and focus are extremely important to any scope user...I've seen scopes shoved forward so they won't hit the shooter's forehead in recoil...the shooter has to get his eye close enough to see the full field of view...and gets whacked just the same."

deer woods. He had slipped away from a deer he thought was legal, but since he couldn't see through the scope, he wasn't sure. When he noticed that I had a scoped rifle, he asked how to hold the rifle to see through the scope. He told me he had borrowed the rifle and had taken for granted that the scope was simply a tube to look through. When I got everything in focus for him, he headed back to find the deer. I'm sure he was carrying more than eighty years on his back, but his departing steps were a full three feet apart.

Squaring the reticle seems insignificant, but it prevents the shooter from canting the rifle. Not every scope user agrees when the reticle is properly squared, so this isn't a job you can do by eye alone. I always considered a squared reticle an integral part of a good mounting job. Since it is a rather complex problem, I used a couple of simple devices to make sure the reticle was square with the action: a crosshair square from the B-Square Company and a simple magnetic protractor level.

The crosshair square, strictly for bolt-action outfits, is nothing more than an L-shaped piece of transparent plastic with a vertical line scribed on the short leg. To use it, remove the bolt from the receiver, press the long leg down firmly on the bolt rails, and align the vertical wire of the reticle with the scribed line on the short leg, which protrudes up past the eyepiece of the scope.

The magnetic level is for lever-action and pump guns; attach it to the flat side of the action and adjust the rifle until the level shows that the flat side is plumb. Then adjust the scope in its rings to make the vertical wire of the reticle also plumb.

(Editor's Note: Don's techniques are much like mine, except that I use a small spirit level for all actions. I first clamp the barreled action in a padded vise, then level it with the small spirit level on the flat bottom of the receiver, the recoil lug, or the flat side of the receiver. A plumb bob hanging from a husky, white nylon line provides the necessary vertical reference line. I look through the scope and align the vertical wire parallel with the nylon line. A house across the street was my first reference — until I learned that its window frames and corners weren't plumb! — K.H.)

Tightening the mount screws properly is not just a five-minute job with a battered, dime-store screwdriver. Base or mount screws that go into the action or barrel should be drawn down evenly and then seated. Many gunsmiths use some form of locking agent or staking compound to keep screws from loosening, but it's not an absolute must. On new actions or first-time mount jobs, metal-to-metal contact holds just as well as a locking agent *if the threads are dry of oil and the screws are*

Getting accustomed to a telescope sight takes more than an occasional peek through the glass. Careful shooting from a rest is practice that will pay off on next season's hunt. And if there is any problem with the scope or the way it is mounted, this is the time and place to find out about it.

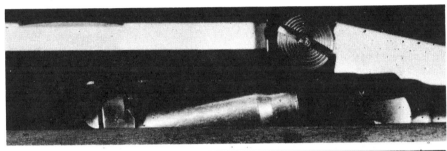

Improper mounting (above) can even cause problems with ejection. This Weaver 53 base is too far to the rear on this Winchester Model 88; the empty case is about to strike the thumbnut on the mount. Below, the mount base is far enough ahead of the receiver port to allow unobstructed ejection of the empty case.

drawn down evenly and seated properly. When the screws or holes are worn, the locking agent (Loc-Tite, shellac, or nail polish) serves as both filler and lock.

Of all the problems I encountered over the years, loose screws ranked toward the top of the list. There seems to be a widespread, built-in fear of overtightening base screws and breaking them off in the action. The truth is that with good screws and a properly fitting screwdriver, there is little danger of this. In tests in my shop, I pushed a torque wrench past sixty inch-pounds without breaking the body of the screw. In every case, when the torque got too high, the head of the screw gave way, usually on one side of the slot.

My tests might have been somewhat crude, but they did prove emphatically that there's a slim danger of overtightening base screws. In time, I

learned to remove problem scopes and tighten the base screws, as a routine. In case after case, that's exactly what it took to solve the problem.

For some strange reason, while base screws are allowed to loosen, screws in the clamp rings are usually far tighter than they need to be to keep the scope from sliding forward when the rifle recoils. Most rings are a half inch wide, or wider, with large clamping surfaces. Consequently, excessive screw pressure is unnecessary and can even damage scopes. I've seen variables clamped so tightly that the power-adjustment rings wouldn't turn.

It's best to pull both clamp rings down evenly. My method was to move from clamp to clamp, tightening the screws a little at a time. Alternating back and forth pulled the clamps down evenly without excessive tension on the tube.

Twisting of the scope tube gets very little attention and seems to be relatively unknown. However, it can play havoc with scopes. A classic case came into my shop 'way back in the late Fifties. I spent several frustrating hours trying to figure out why a new Remington 721 wouldn't zero. When the owner bought the rifle, he had a variable-power scope mounted on it; after going through three boxes of ammo in a futile attempt to zero it, he brought it to my sighting-in range.

Back then, I wasn't all that familiar with some of the more complex scope problems. After splattering half a dozen shots over about eight inches at a hundred yards, I assumed that the problem was either with the rifle or with the scope. Studying the mounting job for a few minutes paid off: I finally saw a small speck of light at the end of the tunnel, and it happened to be a shim under the rear base. I loosened the screws in the rear ring and was amazed to see the scope twist in the ring. It was only a small movement, but enough that I could see the tube turn inside the loosened ring. Curious, I retightened the screws I'd loosened, and without any further remedy, the rifle started shooting the way it should.

After mounting the scope, the gunsmith had needed to level the bases. So he had removed the scope, put a thick shim under one side of the rear base, and forced the scope back on the bases. But the rear ring and base were no longer aligned properly, so tightening the scope on the bases put a severe twist and internal tension into the scope.

Scopes are not just for aging eyes or shooters with vision problems. On the contrary, they are sophisticated optical instruments for aiding both the competition shooter and the hunter. They make the target brighter and sharper, as well as apparently closer to the shooter — which no open-sight arrangement can ever do. But with all the scope offers, much is lost when it is mounted improperly and doesn't fit its user. There is no general way to mount scopes. I still say the scope is as personal as the toothbrush! ●

ultra-light SAKO

Morris Melani

R W Scott

Melani and Scott carried their lightening of this little Sako rifle into the choice of scope and mount: a 6x Burris, Weaver bases, and Tasco rings.

OUR PROJECT to determine just how light a varmint rifle could be — and still be a good varmint rifle — arose from our favorite pastime of hunting jackrabbits, our association in metalsmithing and fiberglass stocks, and increasing curiosity about light rifles and barrel-and-action modifications. What action should we use? How much could we *safely* modify it? Safety would be our foremost consideration as we sought to lighten the barrel and action by removing metal without sacrificing accuracy.

The cartridge would be either a .17 or a .22 centerfire. Caliber .17 possibly

The "butt plate" isn't a plate at all; it's part of the fiberglass shell of the stock, with the glass fibers forming a nonslip surface that suggests checkering.

offered the best choice for coyote; but for shooting other varmints, frequent cleaning of the bore eliminated that caliber. We'd need a .22, and availability of brass favored the .223 Remington — a small cartridge requiring a small action. The Remington action offers several advantages, but the Sako is small and well proportioned to a small cartridge. Its bolt is smaller in diameter; and so is its receiver ring, but why couldn't it be round like the Remington's? Why not make it round? Is there any added strength in the flat bottom or the massive recoil lug? Why not grind all that unnecessary metal off and end-up with a round-bottomed Sako action with a Remington-style recoil lug? We studied the action further to see whether — and where — we might *safely* remove other metal to make it lighter.

Because of the placement of the recoil lug and its possible effect on accuracy, we made this part with its faces parallel within 0.0002 inch. We ground all contact surfaces between centers to ensure precise contact between barrel and recoil lug and between recoil lug and receiver ring.

The most advantageous shape for the action would have the receiver round at the bottom as well as at the top. Thus we not only made the action

lighter but also easier to bed in the stock. We made a mandrel that screwed into the receiver, allowing us to grind it between centers for concentricity. To begin, we took an eighth of an inch off the front of the action to make room for the recoil lug. Then we ground the sides of the receiver up to the scope-mount bases that are integral in this action. In this step, care is essential to avoid obliterating the serial number on the left side and to prevent interfering with any area affecting the attachment of the trigger to the bottom of the receiver.

We carefully milled a slot into the top of the receiver bridge to reduce the weight a bit more.

Because of the new shape of the action, we needed longer screws for the trigger guard and the ejector housing. This gave us an opportunity to replace them with a superior metal with less weight — titanium, which is extremely strong. The original trigger-guard screws weighed two hundred twenty-five grains; the ones that we made out of titanium weigh only a hundred forty grains. The originals — and the sockets threaded to receive them — are metric, so we had to make the new ones on a metric lathe. The weight of the ejector-housing screws was not a major concern; they are quite small. However, because it was necessary to make them longer anyway, we decided to use the lighter titanium because it was stronger. In fact, we remade several small parts out of titanium.

The machining characteristics of titanium required that we use cobalt

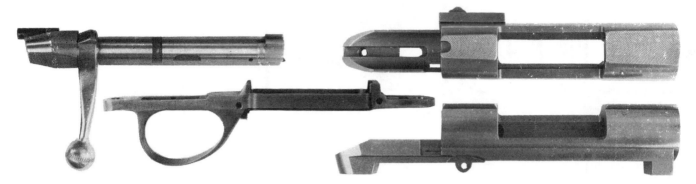

Several details of the ways the action was lightened are clear by comparison of the action parts before (*above*) and after (*below*). Melani and Scott replaced the original trigger guard, remade a number of parts from titanium and aluminum alloy, and added a Remington-style recoil-lug washer after grinding-off the original integral recoil lug to make the receiver lighter.

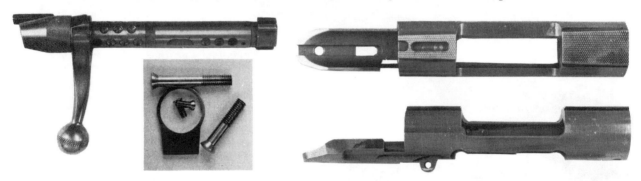

high-speed tool bits with a cutting speed of twenty-five surface feet per minute and a feed of 0.001 inch per revolution.

During the early planning, we determined that we could remove a reasonable amount of weight from the bolt. We decided to lighten it by "Swiss-cheesing" it — milling a series of holes in it. This reduced the weight a pleasing 0.48 ounce. An additional area for weight reduction was in the bolt shroud. Since strength is not its primary concern, we made a new one from lighter aircraft aluminum 7075 T6, which is extremely light and durable with a tensile strength of eighty-three thousand pounds per square inch, a yield strength of seventy-three thousand pounds per square inch, and Brinell hardness of a hundred fifty.

We had to use a little trigonometry to solve the difficulty of machining a blind hole up to an inclined surface. By multiplying the distance from the bottom of the blind hole to the top of the bolt shroud times the cotangent of the angle, which was fourteen degrees, we were able to ascertain the length of 0.775 inch and not mill through the top of the shroud. The machining of this part took considerably less time than we had anticipated — only about an hour — and saved some weight. The weight of the Sako striker assembly with the original shroud was 2.72

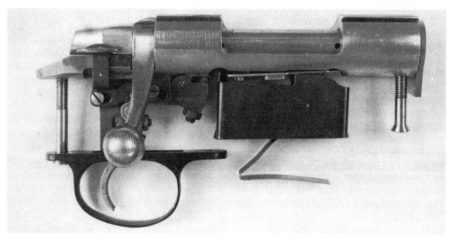

The extensively modified Sako action represents Melani's and Scott's idea of just how light an action of this size can safely be. A good deal of the original steel is gone, but not at the expense of strength in either critical or noncritical areas. The hinged floorplate is gone, in favor of a blind magazine, but the trigger is original and intact.

from light to lighter

component	weight unaltered (*pounds*)	final weight (*pounds*)	reduction (lb	----------- oz)
action	1.965	1.350	0.615	9.84
magazine group	0.430	0.160	0.270	4.32
trigger	0.180	0.150	0.030	0.48
bolt complete	0.490	0.416	0.074	1.18
receiver and bolt stop	0.860	0.612	0.248	3.97
bolt and bolt guide	0.320	0.302	0.018	0.29
striker assembly	0.170	0.108	0.062	0.99
barreled action	4.282 (Sako)	2.625	1.657	26.51
modified Kevlar stock		1.085		
rifle complete	6.320 (Sako)	3.700	2.62	41.92
scope and rings	0.805	0.805		
rifle and scope	7.125	4.505	2.62	41.92

ounces; with our titanium shroud, its weight is 1.73 ounces — a saving of 0.99 ounce.

To save weight in the magazine assembly, we used a Remington Model 700 ADL trigger guard and a blind magazine. We had to shift the magazine up and to the rear to accommodate the new contours of the action and to facilitate feeding. The capacity of the magazine is five rounds — not including a round in the chamber.

From here on, with safety not so deeply involved as it was in our work on the action, we were looking for every way that we could save even a grain of weight. We were also taking a close look at machine time and labor, trying to balance the saving of weight against the time and money that we spent on each part. As it turned out, we gathered a great deal of knowledge about where the maximum weight can be saved at minimum cost to the shooter.

We obtained our Kevlar stock from Al Holland at Brown Precision (Los Molinos, California). A special stock, it had a single layer of Kevlar filled with foam. Holland suggested that we save further weight by eliminating the rubber rifle pad, and he gave us a few tricks in bedding. Kevlar is a DuPont synthetic material made for bullet-proof vests and jackets. It is much stronger than fiberglass but is very difficult to work with. It resists great effort, sharp files, knives, and sand-paper — evidence of its resistance being in the form of frayed fibers that refuse to be cut. In working with Kevlar, the tricks are to apply a light coat of resin over the protruding fibers so that they can be cut off, and to apply a coat of primer over a rough area so that it can be sanded. Fiber-glass stocks are much less difficult.

We used fiberglass flock and resin in the forward recoil area, where strength is necessary. In other areas, we used a product called *micro balloons* with resin, because it is lighter. We formed the shape of a "butt plate" with micro balloons, resin, and two layers of fiber-glass cloth, then applied resin mixed with color to the cloth.

We pillar-bedded the front guard screw to add strength to the stock and support for the action. We free-floated the barrel over a hollow fore-end for better cooling, using a bedding system that Chet Brown has advocated for years — with light but uniform down-ward pressure on the action, without using the guard screws for any pressure.

Our barrel was a Douglas XX blank turned to minimum dimensions on a lathe with a taper attachment, using mist coolant. The tight chamber was reamed with JGS reamers. We crowned the barrel with a small boring tool, from inside the bore to the outside of the muzzle, rather than the old curved hook-style cutter rocked back and forth. This type of crown produces a clean break at the exit of the bullet, with no burr or uneven edge.

Anyone who has mounted scopes on a number of Sako actions soon realizes that the front and rear dovetails don't line up. We were surprised to find that the Weaver drive-on bases lent themselves well to our application. First of all, a person with a little experience can correct the misalignment by flat-filing the tops and sides of both bases at the same time with an eight-inch file. They then provide a parallel V-way like that of a lathe bed for the rings. Granted: other rings and bases may be better, but we chose the Weaver bases along with Tasco rings for their weight advantage. For the same reason, we chose the 6x Burris Mini scope because it was 2.7 inches shorter and 2.1 ounces lighter than the 6x Leupold.

We also made an ultra-light Sako with a *fluted* Douglas XX barrel — it weighs 5.82 pounds! ●

Another approach to a

T HE REALIZATION had been slow in coming, first making itself known a couple of seasons back but becoming more obvious with each passing autumn. It was the knowledge that I was out of shape and would never see that wonderful age of twenty-one again — or thirty-one, either, for that matter. Besides, that was not the whole problem, as one can always walk slower and spend more time glassing an area to make extra sure that he hasn't overlooked a mossy-horned old muley lying in his favorite bed. Of major concern was that my beloved pre-64 Model 70 seemed mysteriously heavier with each passing year.

Whenever the rifle was weighed, it came out at exactly nine pounds, nine ounces. Yet, at the end of a day's hunting, this seemed to increase to at least twenty pounds, with an extra pound added each October. The point was driven home again this past fall while I was trudging up the last hill of the day, the sling cutting into my shoulder to the point that I felt it would have to be surgically removed when I finally got to camp. It was definitely time to look for a lighter rifle.

While there are a great many rifles in the seven-pound class being custom-built today, my main interest is the *way* that the weight reduction is attained. Generally, it consists of shortening the barrel of a standard barreled action to around twenty inches and bedding it in a fiberglass stock, alloy rings and bases being used to mount the scope. I can accept some alloy parts — the trigger guard and floorplate, for example — because on a true hunting rifle, the bluing is soon worn from these parts anyway, and they then do not rust. Alloy rings and bases, in my opinion, are going a bit too far, as I have seen and been told of too many problems traceable to such mounts used on moderately hard-kicking rifles to feel a hundred percent confident in them.

On the subject of stocks, fiberglass is the only way to go, especially on bench guns, varminters, and match rifles, but on hunting rifles? Well, yes, but I just don't like the things on such a rifle. Memory retrieves my first experience of firing a rifle with one of these stocks. The weather was cold and wet, and the stock was also cold and wet, like the inside wall of an old country spring house. They are stable, but I can't help it, I just like wooden gun stocks.

Fortunately for such strange-thinking creatures as myself, there is a way to provide a light, walnut-handled hunting rifle with great resistance to weather-induced bedding changes. This is with the use of an aluminum bedding block — a device used by benchrest shooters before the advent of all-fiberglass stocks — only I have modified it so that a milling machine is not needed in its manufacture. This block can be made by anyone using only a drill press. First however, let's briefly look at the other components of this particular lightweight, since they may be of interest to others who are contemplating a rifle of this type.

This particular arm is quite a bit different than the ordinary light sporting rifle and would be better termed a true hunting rifle. While having classic form and high-quality workmanship, there are none of the niceties of sporting-rifle heritage, such as quick-release floorplates, modified safeties, ultra-light triggers, etc, which always work perfectly until the chips are down, then the impossible seems to happen with frustrating regularity.

If one is really serious about reducing weight and does not have to have a big-cased magnum, the report of which is capable of shaking small pine cones out of their trees at a hundred paces, there is only one action to choose from. This is the Remington 600 as available on a number of different rifles since its introduction in January 1964. It combines a receiver ring of the Remington Model 700 with a bridge area that has been shortened and lightened as much as possible and still keep the bolt from falling out when opened. The only reason I can discover for this action not being more widely used in building light rifles is its bolt handle. Most riflemen get slightly light-headed just looking at the flat, odd-shaped piece of metal.

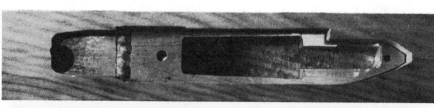

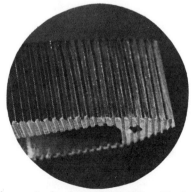

Alignment pins keep the bedding block properly positioned as it is fitted into the stock. A slight gap around the block lets excess glass compound ooze out, allowing the block to be fitted firmly against the bottom of the recess. Evenly spaced saw cuts in sides and bottom of block increase bedding surface and resistance to recoil. Each cut forms a tiny recoil lug.

light rifle
...by Gil Sengel

Some hunting country demands light, flat-shooting rifles — but Sengel wanted a stock of wood, not glass.

Unfortunately, that is usually as far as most shooters have ever gotten — just looking. On an action that has been shortened as much as this one has, there is just no way to have a swept-back handle that does not smash into the trigger hand when the rifle is fired. While some have reported the flat-bottomed knob difficult to grasp, this is more a problem of stock fit than anything else. As bolt rifles get lighter, stocks must fit the individual shooter more closely if quick, accurate follow-up shots are expected. It has been my experience, given a properly fitting rifle, that the Model 600 bolt knob is always there and never seems to slip from the hand when I'm wearing gloves, as some of the round types seem to do.

It is said that with age comes wisdom. Well, I don't admit to being *that* far along yet, but it's been long enough to have acquired a bit of common sense, so I will therefore not even attempt to justify my cartridge choice. Suffice to say that the barrel is chambered for the .284 Winchester, but what it is made of is important. It is a Marquart stainless-steel barrel twenty-two inches long, coming out 0.525 inch at the muzzle. Many may question the use of stainless, but with the advent of shot peening, bead blasting, or whatever you want to call these modern variations of the old sand-blasting technique, there is no

excuse not to have a barrel that is nearly maintenance-free. Many rifles throw the first shot out of the main group if even a speck of oil or grease is in the bore, but if no oil is present, there is a chance of bore or chamber rusting in wet weather. Stainless steel virtually eliminates this worry.

Even though the bead blasting eliminates all glare (much better than a conventionally polished and blued barrel), the white color may still bother some shooters. If this is the case, the problem is very easily solved. While it seems like an unforgivable break with all that is considered holy in gun-building, if one can get to a large specialty paint store, he will discover that there are paints on the market made specially for steel. These can be had in spray cans and require careful degreasing, but when applied properly, I really hate to admit this, but they are nearly as good as a blue job. The trick, if you want to call it that, is to apply a super-thin coat, so thin that the individual dots of paint can almost be seen on the bead-blasted surface if put under a magnifying glass. This finish was also used on the bead-blasted aluminum trigger guard. This paint dries hard as the devil, the only way to get it off being to wear it off — if it is applied properly. It was

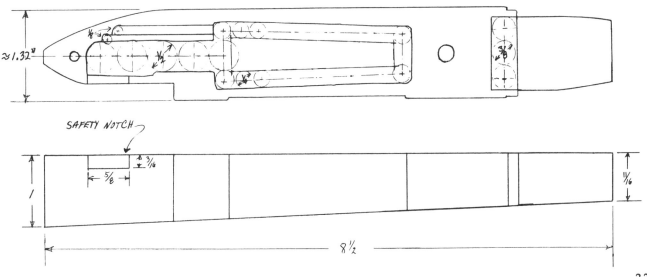

recommended by a local gunsmith who had found that it matches the finish used on many alloy parts. The product I used is made by Zynolyte Products Company in Compton, California, and is of the epoxy type, sold under the name Epoxy Rust-Mate. The color was flat black.

As a point of reference, the above-described barreled action, with trigger guard and all other parts, Conetrol rings and base, and Leupold 4x Compact scope, weighs in at four pounds, twelve ounces. That trigger guard was made in the same way as the bedding block now to be described and is really not necessary, as the aluminum is no lighter than the factory guard. It did, however, allow the bottom of the stock to be rounded up a bit more. To me, this feels better when I'm carrying the rifle in one hand. Now for the stock and that small block of aluminum that will hopefully solve a lot of problems for those of us who still favor those obsolete walnut gunstocks.

When one thinks of bedding blocks, especially for a rifle with a magazine, a lot of time spent setting up and milling away small white chips of metal immediately comes to mind. Perhaps this *is* the proper method from a technician's point of view. However, riflemen are a pretty independent lot, and while the strength of metal sounds good, all that machine work does not. I wondered whether perhaps the bedding-block principle could be modified somewhat to work with a heavy-recoiling rifle, yet be much simpler to make. As it turned out, this is possible and works very well indeed.

My photograph tells pretty much the whole story as to what the bedding block will look like for a Model 600 Remington action. It was made from a piece of scrap aluminum picked up at a salvage yard for one dollar. If starting with scrap, it is absolutely necessary to get a piece of rectangular bar stock with all sides straight and opposite faces parallel to each other. The block in the illustrations measured an inch by an inch and a half and had nearly a dozen holes drilled in it, all of which were cut away except the one in front under the barrel. Of course, new bar stock can easily be found, but it may require purchase of a complete bar (six feet).

The one-inch thickness of the block is just right, but the one-and-a-half-inch width has to be narrowed. My block is a thirty-second of an inch narrower than the diameter of the Remington action. This allows the stock to be inlet to exactly fit the action, yet when this mortise is

deepened for the bedding block, the block drops down without additional fitting. This extra space allows the epoxy to ooze out around the block, ensures no binding, and allows proper alignment during bedding. This is the one time you don't want something to go wrong.

With a little layout blue painted on the top of the aluminum block, the width can now be laid out, followed by the guard-screw holes and the recess for the magazine box and trigger. Actually, all we are doing is copying the inletting of the Remington factory stock but making it a bit lighter. The guard-screw holes are now drilled and the trigger-and-magazine recess drilled completely through the block. When the guard-screw holes are drilled, they should be a close fit to a pair of long, headless guide screws that fit the guard-screw threads. These keep the barreled action in proper alignment with the bedding block and stock when you're glass-bedding, fitting trigger guard, etc. The holes for the guard screws are drilled larger to provide proper clearance only after *all* bedding is complete. If you start the stock from an unshaped blank, the screw holes should be drilled through the aluminum and the blank at the same time. The guide screws are then used to guide the block down into the wood, just as they would be used to guide the barreled action into the wood if there were no bedding block.

Looking at the diagram of the block, the rear hole for the trigger recess is drilled first, then moved forward with the edges of the holes almost touching. The corners of the magazine recess are next, followed by the edges. When the drilling is complete, a bit of work with a triangular file connects the edges of the holes, and the center of the recess drops out. All that remains is to smooth the sides with a large, coarse mill file, out to the edges of the holes. Since the drill press kept the holes straight and at right angles to the top of the block, all is going the way it should.

The recess for the recoil lug and bolt release will *not* be drilled completely through, only deep enough to allow them to clear the action by an eighth of an inch or so. A three-eighths-inch bit was used for the recoil lug, because three holes give the proper width of recess, with plenty of room for glass-bedding compound. Remember, neither the action nor trigger guard will touch this block; its only purpose is to replace unstable wood with metal in a fully glass-bedded stock. How to cut back the edges of those blind holes just drilled? Simply pare them back with light *hand-powered* cuts of your

normal wood chisel to form the rectangular recess for recoil lug and bolt stop. While this may sound somewhat doubtful at first, quality chisels are made from high-speed steel and are much harder than aluminum. I have yet to use aluminum or an aluminum alloy that affected the normally ground wood-cutting edge of my Henckel chisels in any way.

The block can now be narrowed if necessary and the front and rear profiled to match the tang and first inch of the barrel. This is done in the same manner as the inside work, only using a smaller-diameter drill. The use of the proper cutting fluid for aluminum makes all this drilling go much faster. Cutting the clearance notch for the safety arm in the right rear wall of the block now completes the inletting. All that remains is to reduce the thickness of the block at the front to allow the bottom line of the fore-end to taper upward properly toward the fore-end tip. For the Model 600 action, this means a thickness of eleven sixteenths of an inch at the front. This leaves about an eighth of an inch of wood between the bottom of the block and the bottom of the inletting for the trigger guard. With this line scribed on both sides of the block, the greatest part of the excess can be removed with a hacksaw, finishing up with the big mill file and checking frequently with a straightedge.

The aluminum block is then inlet into the stock. After proper depth is reached (one half the barrel diameter), the depth of the recess is increased an eighth of an inch to be sure that there is no contact between the block and the action. Now is the time to slide the block onto the alignment screws of the completely assembled action, to be certain that the trigger assembly and safety do not touch the walls, and that the magazine box does not bind in its recess. With this accomplished, we have one final use for the hacksaw before bedding the block permanently in the stock.

Most rifles using the bedding block, before the switch to fiberglass, were heavy match rifles. Since these were generally in smaller calibers and not subjected to rough use, the blocks stayed in place. Merely degreasing, or roughing the sides a bit with sandpaper, was sufficient. A hunting rifle, on the other hand, especially when it is made as light as possible, creates quite a bit of recoil with heavy-bullet loads at maximum velocities. Also, the weather during hunting seasons is never the best, and the combination of freezing temperatures and sharp recoil are not helpful to the bond between epoxy and nonporous metal. To provide the strongest possible joint between the bedding block and epoxy compound, saw cuts were made all along the sides and bottom of the block. These cuts are of a depth equal to the width of the saw blade and spaced approximately one saw-blade width apart. This effectively triples the bedding surface and provides a mechanical joint with the bedding compound, which should keep the block in place just short of forever.

The block can now be degreased and epoxied into place. An eighth-inch spacer between the action and block ensures that the bedding block goes all the way to the bottom of its recess. Bedding compound will probably have to be added in three or more applications to get everything filled-in properly. A light sanding of all bedding surfaces and a final, very thin application of epoxy should be done last to even up all areas where varying thickness of epoxy caused an uneven surface through shrinkage.

This completes the receiver area, but what about the thin fore-ends generally associated with light rifles? Again, aluminum can be used to great advantage. A piece of half-inch aluminum tubing was inletted the full length of the fore-end so its top surface was an eighth of an inch below the bottom of the barrel channel. Tight-fitting plugs were put in both ends, then it was clamped to the bottom of

its recess, and epoxy bedding compound was poured around it. The barreled action was later assembled to the stock after more epoxy bedding was added to cover the spot left by the clamp, thus completely covering the tube. A hole was then drilled into the tube for the swivel-base nut, and the barrel was free-floated except for the first inch in front of the receiver.

Now it's time to consider finishing-up the stock to its final shape and, most important, its final weight. If the standard European-style lightweight design is used, it is easy to finish-up a rifle under seven pounds total weight. That is if the Remington Model 600 barreled action is used as described. My rifle is just slightly above this, as I like a fuller, more rounded fore-end and wide buttstock for better recoil control. I shoot my rifles quite a bit during warm weather and will gladly trade a couple of ounces for a better-behaving rifle.

Certainly, this seems like a lot of extra fuss just to try to make a basically unstable substance a little more resistant to the whims of the weather. Does it really work? The answer depends upon what the individual shooter is satisfied with. A good case can be made from the fact that properly seasoned and sealed imported walnut is very stable, so long as the completed rifle is not stored in

your bathtub or kept leaning against the outside south wall of the homestead. The only problem is that wood like this is getting *very* hard to come by. Even then, I have noticed one thing about my rifle as opposed to rifles bedded only in wood, or normally glass-bedded. If the guard screws are removed, then replaced and torqued a specific amount, the screw slots always come out in the same place.

How about accuracy? Does this combination of aluminum, paint, and stainless steel give anything away to heavier rifles? All I can say is that this rifle has never yet fired a group over two minutes of angle in which I did not flinch, jerk, or otherwise call the shot out of the group. A recent test session is typical. Several three-shot groups were fired, one shot immediately following the other, then allowing the barrel to cool between groups. Cartridges were loaded with the Sierra 140-grain spitzer and various large quantities of a number of very slow-burning powders. Using proper benchrest techniques for light rifles, the largest group measured one and five eighths inches, the smallest seven eighths of an inch. This is excellent performance, in my opinion, from a seven-pound rifle. Was it worth the work involved? Well, do you know anyone who wants to buy a nine-pound, nine-ounce deer rifle? ●

This is the finished trigger guard-finger lever conversion on de Haas' FBW Model J rifle. This type of trigger guard and finger lever style has been widely used in England and Europe for many years. It has been used on single shot rifles, pistols, shotguns, and break-open guns of all types.

Modifying a Single-Shot Lever

By FRANK de HAAS

A fixed trigger guard and a more comfortable lever are added to a Fix action

THE CLASSIC S-style finger lever as found on a number of both old and new single shot rifle actions is hard to beat. This type finger lever, with the lever doubling as the trigger guard, was the standard style used on the long obsolete Winchester Model 85 and on the Stevens No. 44 and 44½ single shot rifles, and this lever is now also standard on the new Browning M-78, Ruger No. 3 and the Falling Block Works Model Z and J

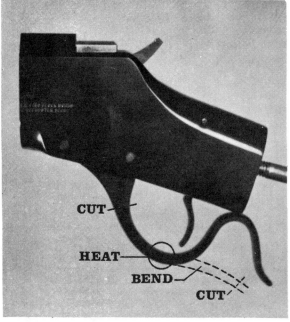

This is the original S-shaped finger lever of the Falling Block Works Model J action. To make the conversion to the separate trigger guard described by de Haas, the lever is removed from the action, heated to red hot at the point indicated, and bent as shown. The end of the S-hook is then cut off and the lever cut in two near the base as indicated. After this, the new trigger guard is shaped and fitted to the receiver, the cut-off piece of the lever shaped to fit around the new guard, and then welded back on the base.

CUT

HEAT

BEND

CUT

actions. On the older rifles which were made with straight gripped stocks, as well as the new No. 3 Ruger, I like the S-shaped finger lever as well as any I have ever used.

This lever is also quite acceptable on rifles having a pistol grip stock, provided the pistol grip is not a full or close-up one. The ideal pistol grip with such a lever is best typified by the rather long "semi" grips as found on the Winchester M-85 and Stevens No. 44 and 44½'s when they were made with a pistol grip stock, and now on the new Browning M-78. I am not at all fond of these long "semi" pistol grips, and on my single shot rifles I like a full pistol grip, one that is well placed in relation to the trigger, one that is useable and "grippable", and one that is no longer or larger in circumference than necessary, and the perfect example of such a grip is on the Ruger No. 1. But with such a grip the S-shaped lever is far from ideal. It just does not fit in.

When I received my FBW Model J action, I was most anxious to get a shooting rifle built on it as quickly as possible and therefore I made no major changes on the action itself. I made the stock for it with a rather full pistol grip and placed it as far forward as its S-shaped finger lever would allow and not cramp my fingers while gripping and triggering the rifle. Despite this, on firing the rifle I found that the S hook on the lever still caused a cramped hold on the grip. In particular, the inverted U loop that formed the S hook was too narrow for my middle finger, even though my fingers are rather slim. At any rate, something about that grip and lever was not to my liking and I proposed to correct this condition by installing a separate trigger guard and altering the finger lever to fit only part way around this guard.

The FBW actions are ideal for making this change. All three models have solid bottoms, with more than ample metal in front of, and behind the trigger opening, to which a separate trigger guard can be attached, and the finger lever is such that it can be altered in just about any way you might want it. In checking my Model J action, I could see that a separate trigger guard of any one of various types and sizes could be fastened to the bottom of the receiver in several ways. It was obvious that perhaps the best procedure was to obtain a trigger guard made for a double barreled shotgun and attach it the same way it is attached to the shotgun. This is usually done by drilling and tapping a hole in the bottom of the receiver about 1/4-inch ahead of the trigger opening to accept the threaded stud on the front of the guard and then inletting the tang of the guard into the bottom curve of the pistol grip and using a wood screw to hold it. I had such a guard on hand but found that the guard bow was too long; in order to get it in the best position in relation to the trigger, I would have to alter it and relocate the threaded stud or use some other method to attach the front of the guard to the receiver. Instead, I decided to use a simple slip-in hook-on method for both the front and rear of the guard.

I altered the double shotgun trigger guard (similar ones made of steel are available from Richland Arms Corporation, Blissfield, Michigan) as needed. I started by cutting off most of the tang and about 1/2-inch from the stud end. Then I heated the front end of the bow to red hot and reshaped it with a brass hammer over a piece of 1-inch diameter iron bar held in a vise. The

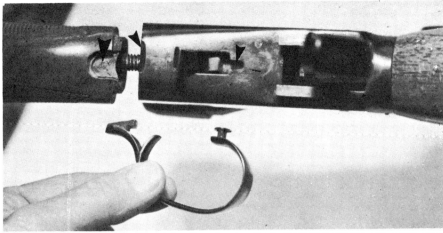

This is a bottom view of the Model J action showing the butt stock loosened and pulled away from the receiver and a side view of the separate trigger guard ready to be attached. The arrows point to the notch made in the front of the trigger opening, the slight bevel on the rear edge of the receiver, and the notch in the stock, to accommodate the new trigger guard.

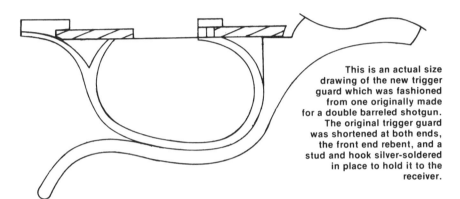

This is an actual size drawing of the new trigger guard which was fashioned from one originally made for a double barreled shotgun. The original trigger guard was shortened at both ends, the front end rebent, and a stud and hook silver-soldered in place to hold it to the receiver.

accompanying drawing shows the final shape. With the internal parts removed from the action, I filed a notch in the bottom of the receiver in front of the trigger hole (see the accompanying photo.) I made this notch just wide enough so that the flat head of an 8-penny nail (yes, a common nail) would slip into it. The stem of the nail under its head was filed smooth and with a No. 27 drill I drilled a hole in the front end of the recurved trigger guard. I cut most of the point end of the nail off, leaving about a 3/4-inch stem on the head and inserted this into the hole. The inside of the bottom of the

receiver was quite rough, and using a 5/8-inch wide flat file through the rear of the receiver, I filed the surface smooth and a little bit thinner. Next I put some silver solder flux on the nail stem, put the nail in place, slipped the guard in place, pulled the nail down snug against the receiver, carefully removed the guard, and then silver soldered the nail in place. The end of the nail protruding in the guard was cut off.

Using a piece of 1/4-inch square cold rolled stock about 1/2-inch long, I filed this to fit the curve on the shortened tang of the guard, and before silver soldering it in place, I notched one corner of it so that it would engage over the receiver edge. I also filed a slight 45° bevel on the bottom rear edge of the receiver the width of the guard at that point. Then I silver soldered this piece in place and filed the notch so that the hook thus formed, plus the nail head stud up front, would draw the guard tightly against the receiver when it was slipped in place. Lastly, I filed away much of the excess metal from the hook, rounded up the end of the tang, filed the nail head thinner to allow the hammer to be fully cocked, and

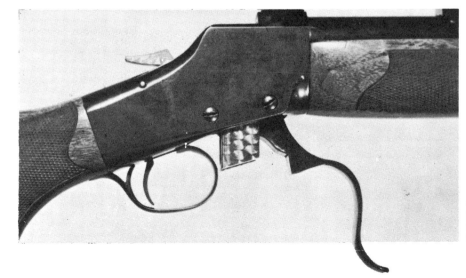

The opened Model J action clearly shows the size, shape and location of the very neat trigger guard and the shape of the altered lever.

343

polished the guard. With the guard in place, I then used small carving chisels to notch the stock, as the stock would actually hold the guard in place.

Now the finger lever had to be altered. Removing everything from the lever, I heated the rear part where it turns down to form the S curve, to red hot and bent it to about the same curve in the opposite direction. The finger levers of the FBW actions are made of a very tough steel, and it cannot be bent cold. It also takes more than a 6-bit hacksaw blade to saw it in two. I then cut the lever off as indicated in the drawing and filed metal from the rear of the finger lever base so it would swing past the front of the new guard. This done, I filed the inside of the cut-off piece of the finger lever flat where it would contact the guard and heated and bent it as necessary to fit the guard.

Welding the finger lever back together was the next step. With the receiver held upside-down in a vise, and with the finger lever base in place on its screw, I put a strip of .03-inch thick metal between the receiver and the rear part of the base to hold the lever base from closing fully.

I then clamped the reshaped lever to the new trigger guard, got everything aligned right, and "tacked" the two pieces of the finger lever together. Then I removed the tacked together finger lever from the receiver and finished welding it. After dressing the welded area down, the lever was put into place, and with the stock also in place, I decided where to cut off the end of the S hook, sawed it off, and rounded up the end with a file. The next step was to grind and/or file the inside of the finger lever to match the curved surface of the new trigger guard. I did this with an elliptical rotary file held in a drill press, with the lever bolted to a piece of two-by-four so I could manage the filing. With the drill press running at low speed and the press adjusted and locked to bring the file even with the lever, the inside of the lever was easily dished out so that the lever would closely fit against the trigger guard. The last step was polishing and blueing the reshaped finger lever and new trigger guard.

Although it involved considerable work, I like this new finger lever and separate trigger guard arrangement on my Model J FBW rifle. The lever is still more than ample in length to easily open and close the action, yet being shorter it does not need so much swinging room below the rifle. When swung open it still has a nice surface for "thumping" with the palm if this is needed to extract a stubborn case, and there is nothing on the pistol grip to cramp the fingers when shooting the rifle.

•

This original Billinghurst picket ball rifle is .40 caliber and weighs 12 pounds; the barrel is 29 inches long with a 1 3/16-inch muzzle.

THOSE OF US who are addicted to the muzzle loading game sometimes make disparaging remarks about the shortcomings of the conventional caplock used to provide ignition on most of the front-loaders in use today. Inefficiency is inherent in the rather complex design of the lock which is, despite a few improvements, little more than an external conversion of the original flintlock that has been in use for more than 200 years.

Most of these cap-snappers consist of eight parts: mainspring, tumbler, bridle, stirrup, sear, sear spring, hammer and plate. Although some of the designers of modern replicas have simplified the lock, it is basically the same as it was in the middle 1800's after the perfection of the percussion cap.

The inefficiency of the traditional caplock is partly due to the long hammer throw, or travel, causing slow lock time. The location of the drum and nipple, or bolster on the side of the barrel is a contributing factor in retarding ignition since the flash from the percussion cap must make a right angle turn before reaching the powder in the bore. Keeping the hole in the drum or bolster clean and dry is a continuing problem, otherwise hang-fires or misfires will be frequent. Sometimes the drum and nipple must be removed for thorough cleaning. Another minus factor for the do-it-yourselfer is the laborious and exacting job of inletting the lock in the stock.

With the numerous shortcomings of the conventional side-lock it may seem surprising that the simpler and more efficient design of the underhammer action hasn't been more widely adopted, especially in the replicas being manufactured today. The answer, perhaps, is that today's muzzle gun buyer wants a rifle of traditional design. And the underhammer is not too well known except to collectors. The Hopkins and Allen, made in several versions by Numrich Arms Corporation, of West Hurley, New York, is the only one using this method of ignition although a majority of the gunsmiths who build slug rifles use the underhammer design.

The originator of the underhammer action is unknown but it seems to have

By HENRY BEVERAGE

making a BILLINGHURST ACTION

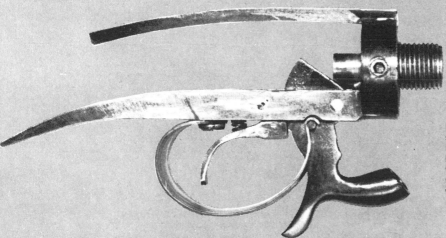

Beverage's completed action is shown with the hammer at full cock. Pulling the trigger disengages the notch in the hammer and the spring/trigger guard throws it forward; the hammer travel to the percussion cap will be 1/2-inch with a 1 1/8-inch barrel.

The shaper eliminated a lot of hand work in making the hammer, mainspring and trigger. Here it is being used to plane down the spring steel to the required thickness for the mainspring.

been developed in New England, particularly in New Hampshire and Vermont. John Brown of Fremont and D.H. Hilliard of Cornish, New Hampshire, Asa Story of West Windsor, Nicantor Kendall and John Pierson of Rutland, Vermont, are a few of the Yankee gunsmiths who used the underhammer form of ignition in making percussion rifles in the middle 1800's. Robbins, Kendall and Lawrence, Windsor, who made muskets for the U.S. Army, also made underhammer pistols.

But is was a New York gunsmith, William Billinghurst of Rochester, who developed this type of action to its highest degree of perfection and earned a reputation for excellence not only in this country but abroad. According to Roberts, in *The Muzzle Loading Caplock Rifle*, Billinghurst made rifles for sportsmen in Brazil, India, Scotland and several European countries. His fame in this country undoubtedly stems from the accuracy of his rifles and the skillful workmanship that characterized his products.

While nearly all of the other makers of underhammer rifles used an internal mainspring, Billinghurst actions were made with an outside spring which also served as a trigger guard. The design is simplicity itself; there are only three major parts, the mainspring, hammer and trigger, all installed on the lower tang.

Billinghurst also made a seven-shot rifle employing the revolving cylinder principle used by Colt in making his famous cap and ball revolvers. He used the underhammer method in making this rifle as he did in producing numerous short barreled "Buggy" rifles. Some of these were of conventional rifle design while others were essentially pistols with detachable shoulder stocks. The man was active in his trade from about 1850 to 1880.

The Billinghurst action has much to recommend it over the traditional caplock. The hammer fall is short, approximately half an inch, and it is fast. Since the nipple is screwed directly into the barrel, ignition is quick and positive: the flash from the exploded cap goes directly to the powder. And if the parts are made from hardened steel there is virtually nothing to wear out.

There is nothing difficult about making a Billinghurst-type action. It can be done with a drill press, hacksaw and an assortment of sharp files. If a shaper, a power grinder and a hand power tool are available the job will be simplified. It does, however, require a lot of careful filing.

I had copied the action from an original Billinghurst slug rifle several years ago in making a pistol; so when it became necessary to make a caplock rifle for a left hand shooter I decided that an underhammer action might be more desirable than a conventional lock designed for the left side. So I borrowed

The mainspring was bent over the form at left, which was held in the bench vise; low heat was applied and the torch was moved back and forth to distribute the flame. The hook in the end of the spring was made by heating that end to a bright red, then laying a piece of No. 36 drill rod over the end and hammering the spring into a groove in the steel block.

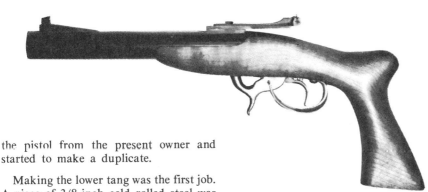

the pistol from the present owner and started to make a duplicate.

Making the lower tang was the first job. A piece of 3/8-inch cold rolled steel was cut to five inches in length and planed to a width of 9/16-inch on the shaper. Half of the length was tapered to 3/16-inch and one side planed in a gradual slope to 1/8-inch at the tapered end to facilitate bending to the shape of the stock. The slot in which the hammer rides was then cut with a 3/16-inch end mill in the lathe by holding the tang in a milling attachment. This slot is 7/8-inch long and 7/32 wide and the forward end is positioned 7/8-inch from the untapered end of the tang. The width was finished to the required 7/32-inch by filing. The sides of the slot must be square with the top and bottom of the tang so that the hammer will ride in perfect alignment with a centerline on the tang.

A slot for the trigger was cut in the rear end of the hammer cut-out. This is 1/16-inch wide and 1/4-inch long and must be centered in the trigger slot. A hacksaw blade with a wide set in the teeth was used to make the cut which was then finished smooth with a point file.

With the tang finished I tackled the hammer. Since this should be made from steel that can be hardened, I got a small piece of die stock from a friendly machinist who makes die casting moulds and planed it to a thickness of 3/8-inch. I then positioned the hammer from the pistol on the block and held it in place with double coated adhesive tape. The two holes in the hammer, one for the pivot pin and one for the mainspring pin, were marked with drills the size of the holes, No. 29 for the pivot and No. 40 for the smaller hole. Holes were drilled through the block after marking with a center punch and removing the adhesive tape. The surface was then sprayed with black lacquer, the shanks of the drills inserted through both pieces and the outline of the hammer to be copied scratched with a stylus.

Rough shaping of the hammer was

This .45 caliber muzzle loading pistol was made by Beverage using a Billinghurst action which he duplicated from an original rifle. The pistol, which weighs 2 1/4 pounds, has a 1x8-inch barrel with an S&W sight. Locating the two holes in the hammer was done by securing the original hammer to the block of steel with a piece of double coated adhesive tape. The hole placements were then marked and drilled with No. 29 and 40 drills.

done with a cutting wheel on the bench grinder. Two square edges were left on the striker end of the block so that it could be held in the shaper vise for planing down the skirt of the hammer to a thickness of 7/32-inch to fit the slot in the tang. Care had to be taken to plane off the same amount on each side so that the hammer would be exactly centered in the slot.

The rest of the cutting was then done with the wheel and a hacksaw and the preliminary shaping done with grinders, files and a belt sander. It was a slow job even with the aid of two hand grinders, abrasive bands, emery points and rotary files. I found that the best procedure was to do a little at a time, checking the shape frequently with the piece being copied.

After the hammer is shaped the hole for the pivot pin can be drilled through the tang. This was done with the No. 29 drill used for the hole in the hammer. The location of the hole through the tang is 3/16-inch from the forward end of the slot and the same distance from the top of the tang. The location must be accurately marked and the tang held squarely in a drill press vise when drilling. Using the shank of the drill for a temporary pivot pin the hammer was inserted in the slot

and found to move freely with no side motion.

The mainspring was made from a piece of 1/8-inch flat spring stock which had been annealed. The finished spring is 3/4-inch wide tapered slightly at both ends. Thickness is .055 in the center; it tapers to .030 on the sides. I secured the piece to a short length of bar stock so it could be held in the shaper vise using Devcon "Two Ton" epoxy for an adhesive. It was then planed down to the required thickness and smoothed by draw filing, then removed from the bar stock by heating.

A pattern the shape of the spring was made by sticking a piece of masking tape to the outside of the pistol spring and cutting to size with a surgical blade and transfering to the spring stock. It was ground to shape with a fine wheel, the hole for the No. 10-32 hold-down screw was drilled and the slot that forms the fingers cut in the opposite end.

To bend the hooks in the ends of the fingers I tapped a No. 10-32 hole in the piece of bar stock and cut a round slot across the bar exactly 3 3/4 inches from the center of the hole. The spring was then secured to the bar with the fingers squarely across the slot, the ends heated red and forced into the slot by holding a broken No. 36 drill squarely across the fingers and striking it with a hammer.

Bending the spring was easy. I had saved the form I'd made years ago when making the Billinghurst type pistol. The spring was attached, heated with a low flame and pulled down over the form by

The trigger was made from one piece of die stock; a hacksaw was used to rough it out; then it was finished with flat files. The lip extends through the tang and pivots on a small pin.

After drilling the holes through the block, the shape of the hammer was outlined with a stylus. Then the hammer was cut to rough shape with a cutting-off wheel on the bench grinder.

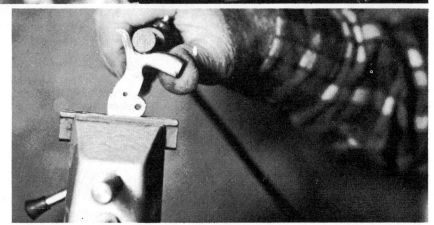

A Dremel hand grinder was helpful in shaping the hammer but filing was necessary in places.

applying pressure to the hooks and tapping lightly with a brass hammer. By moving the torch gradually to distribute the heat an even curve was obtained. The spring was then hardened in oil and tempered deep blue.

The trigger was made from a small piece of the die stock which I planed to 1/4 x 1/2 x 2 inches. Width is 1/4-inch and the trigger proper is approximately 1/8-inch thick but there is a lip on the forward end that fits into the small slot in the tang. A small pin through the lip holds it in place and allows it to pivot. The shaper, a hacksaw and file were used to form the trigger and I did the bending over the end of a round barrel.

The hammer was then placed in the slot, the pivot pin pushed through and the trigger held in place against the edge of the skirt. Holding the trigger in position by hand and with the tang firmly against the drill press table I drilled through the tang and the trigger lip with a No. 52 drill. The trigger would pivot on a pin through the hole. (The tricky part of this operation is doing it without breaking the tiny drill. High rpm and low pressure is the answer.)

With the hammer and trigger held in place with temporary pins I could mark the location of the notch on the hammer skirt which would be engaged by a notch on the trigger. Installing the mainspring and engaging the hooks with the pin through the hammer I pulled the hammer back to full cock position and marked the edge of the skirt where it made contact with the trigger. The hammer and trigger were then removed and a notch filed in the end of the trigger. A similar notch was filed in the hammer after dressing off the skirt above the full cock notch. After re-assembling and checking the position of the two notches the hammer and trigger were again removed, the notches

honed and both pieces hardened and drawn.

In use, the hammer is pulled back against the tension of the mainspring and a coil spring under the trigger lifts the front end so that the notches engage and are held together by the tensions of the mainspring and trigger spring. A slight pull on the trigger disengages the two notches. With a stiff mainspring the hammer fall is very fast.

Billinghurst had a novel method of joining the barrel and action so that they were virtually one piece. The upper and lower tangs and breechblock were a single steel casting which was joined to the barrel by a taper pin driven through the breechblock and the plug extending from the barrel. With the finely fitted stock held to the upper and lower tangs with through screws the lock, stock and barrel had the rigidity of a steel bar.

Since I had no source of a solid casting for the tangs and breechblock I had to improvise with a welded job. I turned a piece of 5/8-inch rod to 9/16 and threaded a half inch on one end with an 18-thread die. A short length back of the thread was turned to 1/2-inch. This was the plug which will be screwed into the barrel.

To make the breechblock I used the end of a 1 1/8-inch barrel blank which had been cut off to get back to the sharp rifling and drilled out the hole to 1/2-inch. The unthreaded end of the plug would go through the hole and be secured by Allen setscrews on opposite sides of the block. The assembly was then fitted to a dummy octagon barrel and the location of an upper and lower flat marked on the round block with masking tape.

Slots were then cut out of the breechblock to accept the two tangs which

348

would be welded in to make a solid frame for inletting into the stock. When completed the job was an acceptable substitute for a Billinghurst.

I made one change in the action. In the original, the trigger spring is concealed in the tang. To simplify, I used a rather stiff coil spring under the hammer, setting it in a 3/16-inch hole in the tang. A threaded 8-32 hole in the underside provided for an adjustment screw if necessary. Final assembly of the action showed that it wasn't needed although it might be at some future time.

It is my intention to rifle the barrel that will be installed on this action, using the old time walking method and a scrape cutter to form one groove at a time. This is a far cry from the present-day method of pulling a carbide button through the barrel and forming all the grooves at one swipe. But there are times when it's satisfying to go back to the beginning. Besides, it has been hinted around here that I need more exercise. This surely will be one way of getting it. ●

building a SCHUETZEN RIFLE

By HENRY BEVERAGE

THIS JOB WAS STARTED as a now-and-then project to utilize some miscellaneous Hi-Wall and Lo-Wall parts that had been collecting over the years. The end result, hopefully, would be a complete action which might be used, sold, or traded — a single-shot action being choice property in these times. But as sometimes happens when I become involved in one of these salvage jobs, the project went far beyond the original target and I ended up with another Schuetzen rifle.

The Old Gun Trader, who knows my weakness for the Winchester single shots, had given me a Lo-Wall frame complete with lower tang and trigger that had originally been on one of the Winder muskets, all of which were the coil spring type. I had a Hi-Wall breech

block from a coil spring action, an extractor, a knock-off and some pins and screws. I needed a coil spring hammer and lever, a coil spring, sear, link, spring and pawl, sear and knock-off springs and a firing pin. Robert Thompson, the Winchester parts man in Clinton, Iowa, supplied the hammer and a flat spring lever, I traded a bullet mould for the sear and the spring-pawl combination and made or converted the other necessary parts.

Making and fitting a coil spring to the hammer and breech block was the most difficult job. The original springs were formed from 1/16-inch piano wire and I believe they were bent cold. Those I've seen were bright, showing no indication of having been annealed and tempered. But since the only spring wire

I could find measured .0725, which was .010 oversize, I annealed the wire before shaping then hardened in oil and tempered blue after fitting.

A jig was made to wind the coils that fit over the hammer pivot studs and to form the loop that goes over the back of the hammer. The coils could be formed easily by winding the wire around the shank of a 19/64-inch drill after bending the loop in the jig. The problem was in fitting the hooks to the tiny holes in the breech block after the coils had been placed around the hammer pivot studs. There is no tolerance here. The arms that extend forward from the coils must be *exactly* the right length and the ears that hook into the breech block must be bent at right angles. The bending had to be done while the wire was red hot or the wire would break. I solved the problem by drilling a hole in a piece of 5/32-inch rod with a number 46 drill, slipping the rod over the end of the wire and heating the wire and the end of the rod when making the bend. It worked, eventually, but I had a small collection

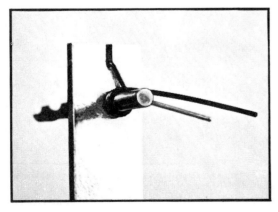

The most difficult part of building this Schuetzen, Beverage says, was making and fitting a coil spring to the hammer and breech block. He used this jig, supported in a vise, with the loop held in place in the slot, two coils are wrapped around a 19/64 drill.

of broken and non-fitting springs before I got two that were acceptable.

That hurdle over, the next job was to convert the flat spring lever to a coil spring type. This was done by fitting a curved ridge over the end of the lever and fastening it with two steel pins and silver solder. The ridge is 1/8-inch thick and 7/32-inch wide. This bears on the spring-loaded pawl in the front end of the frame and provides tension on the lever.

A link from another Lo-Wall was used as a pattern for the one to be made. This was secured to a piece of ¼ by ½-inch tool steel with epoxy cement, the holes drilled and reamed to .195 and the link shaped by grinding and finished with a file. The epoxy bond was loosened by heating and the new link hardened and drawn.

That left only the two flat springs for the sear and knock-off, and the firing pin. I've never made a duplicate of an original Winchester pin. I prefer a straight, spring-loaded pin which is just as functional and much easier to make. An accompanying photo shows the pin and spring.

About the time I had the parts ready to assemble into a complete action Mrs. B decided that since she was no longer shooting it was time to retire her big left-hand Schuetzen before something happened to it. That left me without a .32-40 bench rifle. Obviously, something had to be done about it.

I now had an action, a mongrel perhaps, but tight and in excellent condition, plenty strong for the .32-40 caliber with the loads used in our kind of shooting. I had a partially finished Winchester cheek-piece stock, a casting of a Helm buttplate and some wood to make a fore-arm. So I ordered an 8mm barrel blank in premium grade from Douglas. When it arrived I found the dimensions to be .321 in the grooves and .313 on the lands, very close to the old standard for the .32-40.

These blanks are rough on the outside and must be turned to the diameter wanted for the finished barrel. They are quite hard but will cut to a nice surface. A Carboloy bit set a whisker above center gives me the best results and can be used on several barrels without re-grinding. A follower or steady-rest is essential to avoid chattering and, of course, the turning must be done on centers with the head

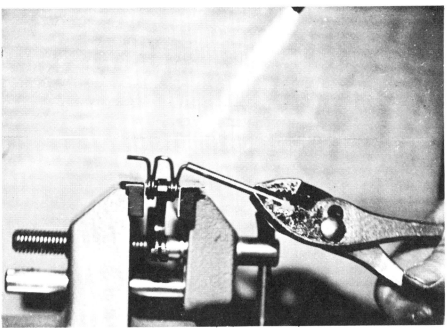

With the coil spring in place on the hammer pivot studs, the hooks that fit the holes in the breech block are bent 90 degrees. A No. 46 hole in the end of the rod is slipped over the end of the wire, heated red and bent. Hooks will be cut to 1/8-inch before assembling the breech block.

and tail stock centers in perfect alignment. In finishing several of these blanks I've found it better to make two or three light cuts the length of the barrel rather than trying to turn to size in one operation. The blanks have been stress-relieved but it is well to avoid unnecessary heating. And they do get warm. Even with a light cut the chips are purple. Cutting oil is helpful but not necessary.

After turning the blank to 1 1/8-inch diameter I smoothed it with a chalked file and gave it a preliminary polishing with fine abrasive cloth. Then I checked for high or low spots by running a dial indicator along the entire length. This showed a straight taper of .003 from breech to muzzle with no high or low spots.

That done, the muzzle end of the barrel was placed in the chuck and the other end on the tail-stock center and the barrel checked for alignment before turning the end to be threaded. The diameter is .935 and the length of the shank .850 but I leave a little extra length for squaring off and fitting after the 16-pitch threads have been cut When a thread gauge shows they have been cut to their full depth, the wire edge, if any, is removed with a fine file held lightly against the shank, and the receiver frame is screwed on as far as it will go by hand. I like to have about two full turns remaining to be taken up

The flat spring lever was converted to the coil spring type by attaching a curved ridge to the forward end. This bears on the spring-loaded pawl in the end of the frame and provides tension on the lever.

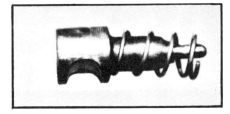

This spring-loaded firing pin is an easily made replacement for an original Hi-Wall or Lo-Wall pin.

351

To eliminate chattering, a steady rest should be used while turning the barrel to size. The rest is moved as the cutting proceeds; care must be used in re-setting the rest to assure the same alignment.

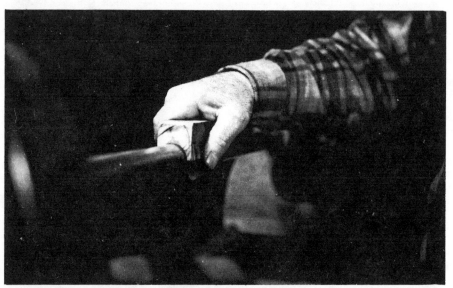

The barrel received a preliminary polish with abrasive cloth under a wood block. Final finishing before bluing was done with 2/0 polishing paper and steel wool.

A dial indicator is used in the lathe tool post to check the barrel for high or low spots.

with a wrench to provide a tight fit against the shoulder of the barrel.

Threading finished, the lathe is returned to normal gear set-up and the length of the shank reduced to .850 with a facing bit. One full thread is now cut from the end of the shank to a depth of .050 to allow for the guide shoulder on the edge of the breech block.

The lever and block are then assembled, inserted in the frame and held in place with the lever pin. The threading and headspace can now be checked by using a wrench for the final turns. A barrel vise is necessary for this job since the barrel is round and must be held firmly against turning under pressure from the wrench.

When the end of the frame, sometimes called the receiver ring, is hard up against the shoulder of the barrel the face of the breech block shouldn't be more than .002 from the end of the barrel. If a .0015 feeler gauge will just slide between the two surfaces it can be considered good. Another method of checking the head-space is to close the action against a strip of paper .003 thick held against the end of the barrel and the block closed against it. If the paper tears when I try to pull it out I call it good enough. On the first trial I had about .004 so I took .002 off the shoulder of the barrel and when I tried it again the paper tore when I pulled it. The barrel was now ready for chambering.

My .32-40 reamer was made for a standard diameter barrel and the integral pilot measured .314. I reduced it to a scant .313 by running it in the lathe on centers and holding a medium cut stone against it. Then the barrel was again aligned with the tail-stock center, supported by the steady-rest and I was ready to start chambering.

There are several methods of cutting the chamber. Some will use drills to start the work. This is an easy way to enlarge the bore before using the reamer. It is also an easy way to spoil a chambering job. Some will use power with the lathe running slowly in the back gears. I prefer to do it the hard way, by hand. I attach two small lathe dogs to the shank of the reamer and feed it slowly into the barrel with the tail-stock screw, making two full turns of the reamer each time it is moved ahead. It's slow work, and hard on the hands, but it gives me full control of the reamer and I can feel the way it is cutting.

I use a mixture of melted lard and turpentine as a cutting oil, applied liberally with a brush. The reamer is removed and cleaned and the chamber cleaned out with a bristle brush after feeding it in a half-turn of the tail-stock screw, approximately 1/16-inch. It sounds like a long job, and it is, but it produces a smooth, clean chamber and doesn't punish the reamer.

The counter-bore for the case rim is cut by the reamer and the cavity checked with an unfired case, or one that has been full-length re-sized. Then the barrel is screwed into the action to check the alignment of the firing pin hole in the breech block with the flash hole in the case. This is done by closing the action, holding the muzzle to a strong light and looking through the firing pin hole. If the flash hole appears perfectly round the alignment is good. If it isn't the block may have to be bushed and a new hole located. I was spared that problem so all I had to do was make the firing pin.

This was made from a piece of 5/16-inch drill rod, which is the diameter of the firing pin hole in all Hi-Wall and Lo-Wall breech blocks. A shank was turned down to 3/16-inch by 9/16-inch, over which the coil spring is fitted. Then a tip 3/16-inch long is turned to the diameter required for the hole in the block. In the block I was using this was .086. The slot for the holding screw was cut with a silicon wheel in the Dremel.

Next and final job to complete the barrel and action assembly was fitting the extractor. There probably is a simple, easy way of doing this. I just haven't discovered it. So I have to use the cut-and-try method. With the barrel screwed tightly into the frame and the breech block removed I place the extractor in position with the lever pin. I then move it against the barrel and scratch the position of the ejecting arm with a stylus. I then remove the barrel from the frame and make the cut-out with a silicon wheel in the Dremel. Repeated cuts and much filing with a square needle file are required before I have a satisfactory fit. The ejector end is then shaped to conform to the chamber and case rim and the fully assembled action and barrel put together. The job was then given a final check-out with a

Cutting the 16-pitch threads after turning the end of the barrel to .935. As always when threading to a shoulder, extreme care must be taken.

Chambering was done by hand. The two half-inch lathe dogs provided a means of turning the reamer as it was fed into the stationary barrel by the tail-stock center.

lightly loaded cartridge while holding the barreled action in the hands. The case ejected easily and the primer indentation was as near center as I had anticipated from my peep-hole check.

I was now ready for the wood-working part of the project. Since I was going to use a pistol-grip stock the lower tang on the action would have to be bent. For this job I used a form made by shaping the end of a piece of 3/8-inch by 2-inch steel bar stock to conform to the curve of the pistol grip. I then tapped two holes in the edge of the bar to accept 10-32 screws. These would go through the holes already in the tang and hold it in alignment with the bending form. The bar was held in a bench vise with the tang secured in place by the screws and the trigger end

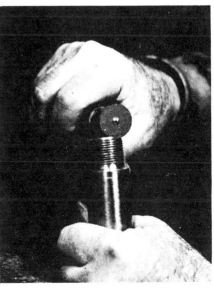

The Dremel was used to cut the slot for the extractor. Finishing was done with a four-sided file.

353

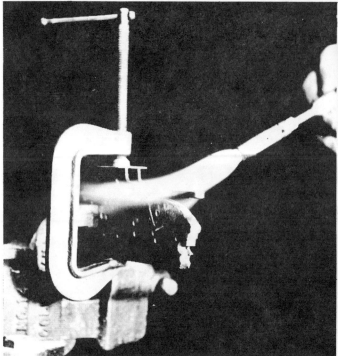

As shown in the left photo, the lower tang was bent over a form shaped like the curved pistol grip of the stock. It was then heated red with an acetylene torch and bent to shape with a brass hammer. In the right photo, a drum sander in a Dremel hand tool provided a good method of fitting the stock to the curved, undercut end of the frame.

held down against the bar with a C-clamp. The end to be shaped was heated cherry red and bent with a brass hammer. I've read somewhere that these tangs can be bent cold. Maybe so. But red heat is pretty good insurance against breakage.

With the tang in place in the frame it could now be fitted to the stock. The most troublesome part of this job is getting a good fit where the wood joins the frame. The curved, undercut ends of the Lo-Wall and Hi-Wall frames require a lot of careful shaping. I've found that a drum sander in a Dremel gives me the best results. Prussian Blue or any of the stock-makers' spotting preparations are

necessary to get a close joint with the frame. The stock had been machine-inletted when I acquired it some years back and I had previously done most of the finishing. But the inletting left a lot to be desired so I decided to bed the action in Devcon plastic aluminum.

The areas around the knock-off and spring and the screw holes were filled with beeswax and the remaining surfaces coated with polishing wax for a release agent. Then the tang channels and other open spaces were thickly coated with the Devcon and the stock and action put together. When the surplus had been removed the job was

laid aside to await hardening.

The stock had been cut for a Helm, or Schuetzen, buttplate which required only slight fitting, most of which was done on a 6-inch sanding drum on a polishing pedestal. Finishing the buttplate, which was a Tenzaloy casting, was done on a belt sander using 200-grit cloth-backed tape and polishing with Dico emery compound on a cloth buffing wheel.

I didn't have a piece of walnut suitable for the fore-arm so I used a piece of maple that showed a little burl in the grain. This was cut 1 3/8-inch square by 11 inches long on the table saw and the barrel channel cut with a one-inch cove cutter. After making several cuts to get the full depth the fence was moved 1/8-inch and another cut made. This gave me a slot the same width as the 1 1/8-inch diameter of the barrel. Moving the fence had left the channel slightly flat in the center but this was shaped out with coarse sandpaper under a one-inch round block.

I roughed the piece to shape with a rasp, smoothed with a rough file and finished by sanding, raising the grain twice with water before applying walnut stain. This gave me a color that closely matched the natural shade of the burl walnut stock. Preliminary applications of Birchwood-Casey Tru-Oil were given

A six-inch sanding wheel provided an easy way of fitting the stock to the buttplate — which can be a mean job.

354

Finishing the Helm buttplate was done on a belt sander using 200-grit abrasive cloth.

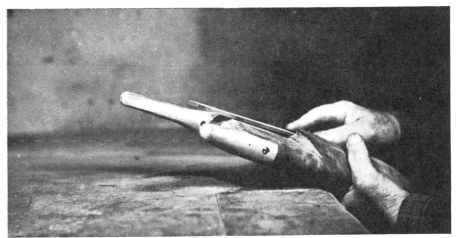

Final fitting of the buttplate to the stock was with a 10-inch flat file.

The channel in the fore-arm was cut on a table saw with a one-inch cove cutter in a molding head.

stock and fore-arm and they were set aside to await final finishing.

Finishing the metal parts of a rifle can be a problem for the amateur or semi-professional gunsmith who lacks the equipment for what is known as hot bluing. He has a choice of taking his work to a shop that does that kind of finishing or doing it himself with one of the cold blue solutions on the market. I decided some years ago that any rifles I restored or built for my own use would be cold blued. Customers' rifles would be finished according to their preferences.

This rifle was blued with Outers' solution, a mixture of selenium dioxide, hydrochloric acid and copper sulphate. It may be no better than some of the other solutions on the market but I've developed a method of using it that gives me excellent results, a deep blue finish that is long-lasting. It costs $1.00 and takes less than an hour to apply.

I start with the metal parts polished with as high a lustre as I can get with 3/0 steel wool. Degreasing is done with alcohol or acetone on a well-saturated cotton swab. When dry the first application of the solution is applied with another swab. I use a liberal amount, going over the parts, especially the barrel, until all streaks have been removed and the solution is standing on the parts. I allow it to dry at least five minutes before washing off with hot water. When it dries I rub it off with 3/0 steel wool and polish it lightly. Another application of the bluing solution is then made, allowed to stand for five minutes and the washing and cleaning operations repeated. I've found that three applications are necessary for a deep blue finish that will stand up under the use I usually give a Schuetzen rifle. This takes the contents of a 2-ounce bottle. After the third application the parts are given a final polish with the steel wool, covered with oil and allowed to stand overnight before assembling.

A few more treatments with Tru-Oil on the stock and fore-arm, hand-rubbed, and the final high gloss deadened with rotten-stone and the job is finished except for attaching scope blocks.

No bullet mould was made for this rifle since I have one which casts a bullet measuring .314 in the body and .322 on the baseband. That should be about right for the .313 by .321 Douglas barrel. Test firing, however, will have to await an improvement in range conditions. As this is being written the snow cover in this neck of the woods is two feet deep. I'll report later if you're interested in the results. ●

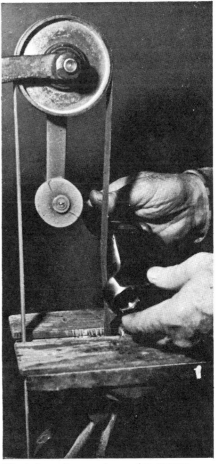

The belt sander was also used to remove the original finish from the frame.

Investment Casting

Resting upon the injection mould are (right to left) trigger-guard pattern, wax pattern, raw casting, and finished casting. Parts shown are brass.

techniques for a small shop

by John Bivins

photographs by H. Armstrong Roberts III

*R*IFLE REPORTED on the complex process of investment-casting firearms parts in an excellent article by Edward Ezell in the November-December 1969 issue. At that time, the recent introduction of Ruger's Model 77 and Number One had focussed new attention upon the trade, although Bill Ruger and his associates had done pioneering firearms casting well back in the Fifties. The general surprise of the consuming public over two major new centerfire rifles with cast receivers, bolts, and breechblocks opened many an eye in the late Sixties.

In fact, the term casting in connection with firearms had less than pleasant connotations to many before that time, and I have little doubt that it has been the obvious and continuing quality of excellent production arms such as the Rugers that have dispelled that onus by now, nearly a decade later. Arms manufacturers are becoming rightfully less reluctant to reveal which parts they cast, since the consuming public has become a bit more enlightened to the fact that investment casting is a valid production process, taking no back seat to more time-honored machining and forging.

Investment casting, in fact, has ensured the longevity of some firearms designs and has enabled others to be created where production costs would otherwise have prevented new arms from ever leaving the model shops. The Ruger sporting rifles are perhaps the best examples. The graceful, sculptured contours of the Number One frame, for instance, could not have been forged and machined at a cost low enough to permit production of the rifle as we know it. The Model 77, with its Mauser-type extractor and corresponding complex receiver cuts, would no doubt have been subjected to design compromises had it not been possible to use a production medium that permits an unusual degree of surface complexity, and even undercuts, without significantly raising cost.

Investment casting has particularly encouraged the development of the blackpowder industry, especially in replication; Val Forgett saw possibilities in the process in the late Fifties, and no doubt the success of Navy Arms since then has been in part due to precision casting. Today, Ruger casts even the cylinders of the excellent Old Army, since casting greatly reduces the cost of producing the convoluted rear face of a percussion cylinder. Casting has even proved an inexpensive source of reliable leaf springs, making the production of all manner of gun locks financially possible. Some still scoff at the notion, but I have been using flintlocks with all major parts cast for some fourteen years, and in that time, I have had but three springs fail, and no other

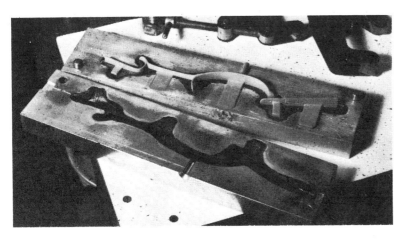

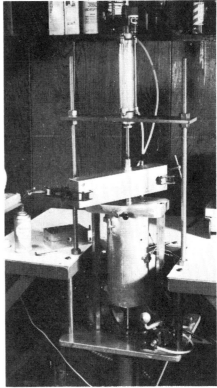

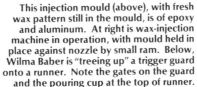

This injection mould (above), with fresh wax pattern still in the mould, is of epoxy and aluminum. At right is wax-injection machine in operation, with mould held in place against nozzle by small ram. Below, Wilma Baber is "treeing up" a trigger guard onto a runner. Note the gates on the guard and the pouring cup at the top of runner.

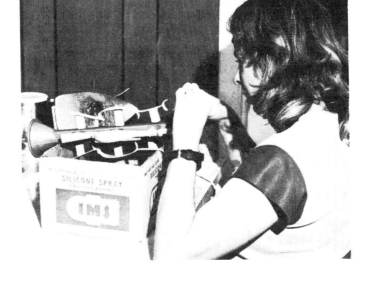

functional parts that I can recall. I don't believe forgings would have had a better record than that.

Of course, investment casting is not a cure for all ills. One thing that I dislike is that it has tended to cause laziness in finishing; manufacturers, and worse, custom gunmakers in some instances, have become satisfied to leave interior and even exterior parts as cast. In locks for muzzleloading arms, such surfaces add nothing to smooth functioning, to say the least, and visually, the result leaves a great deal to be desired. And one sure way to add a really cheesy look to an otherwise good arm is to leave parting lines on the castings.

Investment casting has become financially feasible for the custom gunmaker because of the larger number of foundries operating now and greater competition. One difficulty lies in the need to find foundries small enough to be able to accept the low-volume work of the gunsmith yet advanced enough to be able to produce high-precision castings with good surface integrity. Foundries that have consistently accepted small jobs in the firearms field and can produce good castings include Rimer Enterprises in Waterville, Ohio (the name of this foundry was recently changed to Muzzle Casts, Incorporated, a curious appellation); Oklahoma Investment Casting Corporation, Blackwell, Oklahoma; Tennessee Investment Casting Company, Incorporated, Bristol, Tennessee; and B&H Precision in Blountville, Tennessee. There are many other foundries, of course, and some specialize in firearms work, such as Pinetree Castings, a wholly owned subsidiary of Sturm, Ruger. Generally speaking, larger facilities such as Pinetree are not in a position to accept small jobs.

Custom gunmakers who have made a considerable success of producing investment castings both for their own use and for the trade have been men such as

Lenard Brownell and Al Biesen, and a number of others, particularly shops that do metalwork, are increasingly turning to investment foundries for assistance. I began preparing patterns for casting five years ago, having tired of the time spent in filing and finishing steel forgings for flintlock furniture, and have since expanded my collection of cast parts to nearly thirty-five items, many of which are run in brass as well as steel. Of course, I have considerable financial investment in the patterns and tooling, but the bench time saved has amortized the amount spent many times over. It is difficult now to exist as a custom gunmaker without investment castings, particularly in muzzleloading, unless you can file at the speed of light or can charge a good deal more than most of the market will bear.

Initial problems in having custom investment castings produced lie in pattern and mouldmaking. Some gunmakers have the facilities and skill to produce these items, while others, who lack either equipment or time, must rely on the foundries for tooling-up, which can be considerably more expensive. A certain knowledge of the properties of cast alloys is needed in designing and fabricating patterns. For example, patterns must be oversize enough to compensate for the roughly one percent shrinkage of the injected wax and about two percent shrinkage of the cast part. This three-percent loss in size can be a thorny problem in calculating allowance, and it is compounded by differentials in the mass of various parts of a pattern.

Also, the pattern must be designed so

357

At left, the tree is dipped into the first slurry mix of 325-mesh ceramic particles. It will go through three slurry-dipping stages (center). These have coarser particles, which build up the shell of the mould. The first fine-mesh slurry determines the quality of finish on the final casting. An eighty-mesh sand dip follows, then the trees are allowed to dry on racks (right). These steps are repeated until mould shell is built up to the required thickness.

that an efficient injection mould can be made from it; such moulds must be kept as simple as possible, without an unnecessary number of sections and removable mandrels, or the tooling becomes too expensive and tedious to use. For relatively small production, epoxy-cored aluminum moulds are satisfactory and relatively inexpensive (depending upon the mouldmaker), and they have a life of many thousands of "shots" if they are not abused. "Permanent" moulds of all-aluminum or aluminum and sintered metal are best for large production runs, but their cost is generally well beyond the pocketbooks of custom gunmakers. For longevity of tooling, I prefer to run waxes for casting in my own shop and have a wax injector for the purpose. Using one of my patterns, a ten-inch trigger guard, let's run through the entire process for a bit of a look at what's involved.

The wax injector that I use was designed by Dru Hedgecock of Walkertown, North Carolina, with some input from me, and it's a good size for a custom gunshop in terms of capacity and cost — about fifteen hundred dollars. The purpose of such a machine is to inject wax under pressure into a mould to produce a wax pattern, and this is done by a ram mounted under the unit, actuated by compressed air. The head of the ram pushes up a piston fitted inside a cylinder filled with wax; this cylinder is enclosed within a heavy aluminum jacket, which is fitted with thermostatically controlled cartridge heaters that keep the wax at 140 degrees — about the consistency of mayonnaisse. Hotter wax tends to create "flashing" at mould joints and excess shrinkage, though the relatively cool 140 degrees requires some 150 pounds of head pressure in my three-inch cylinder for clean waxes. The jacket on my machine is hinged to facilitate changing cylinders, which reduces downtime. This could otherwise be a problem, since one of my heavier buttplates, for example, can exhaust a cylinder after no more than twenty-five shots.

At the top of the machine is a small compressed-air ram, which holds the injection mould against the wax nozzle on top of the jacket. Using such moulds requires frequent shots of silicone release spray to prevent the wax pattern from sticking in the mould.

Briefly, the use of an injection machine involves spraying and clamping-up the mould, placing the mould on the nozzle, lowering the top or holding ram, opening the wax valve, closing the valve after a few seconds, raising the ram, and setting the mould aside for cooling. Cooling can require from half a minute to several minutes, depending upon the mass of the part; as the wax cools, it shrinks slightly, facilitating removal from the mould cavities. Various types of waxes are used in the casting industry, each color-coded to indicate different properties. We prefer the pink variety since it has exceptional fidelity of reproduction and readily shows minute flaws when they occur. Waxes are exceedingly fragile and cannot be shipped easily without breakage, which means that if you decide to run your own wax patterns, you'd best be within driving distance of the foundry that is to run your work.

The wax pattern is the heart of the ancient lost-wax casting process known for centuries. Just how it is "lost" in the modern process we'll examine as we go along.

After the desired number of wax patterns are run and packed, I deliver them by car to the foundry. In hot country, that bloody well means you'd best have an air-conditioned car, incidentally, unless you want to arrive with waxes that better resemble Dali sculpture than gun parts. In this case, Bob Roberts, Mark Silver, Paul Forster, and I took a trip to B&H Precision in Tennessee. B&H is a relatively new firm

The autoclave (left) melts wax from shell moulds, then burnout oven (upper right) vaporizes residual wax and improves tensile strength of shell. Finally, the pour (right). Pot is induction furnace, entire liner of crucible being surrounded by a massive induction coil.

run by Jerry Baber and his perky wife Wilma — hard-working types who frequently stay up all night nursing delicate parts through the various stages of the process, with the help of several highly skilled foundry technicians. The Babers, in fact, prefer to work at night, since there is less interference from the telephone.

B&H is a small foundry specializing in firearms parts, and the quality of the steel parts run there has quickly brought in work from a number of armsmakers. Currently run at B&H are various parts for the Shiloh 1874 Sharps, all of the castings for Bud Siler's fine locks, and numerous other parts such as M-14 receivers, parts for .50 machineguns, and massive components that make up the impressive Casull .454 revolver.

Jerry Baber seems a natural for the business, having acquired a certain probing inquisitiveness while working for some years as an electronic engineer in defense systems. He entered investment casting some ten years ago, and the knowledge he has acquired regarding this complex business is impressive.

At B&H, as in any other foundry, the casting process begins with "treeing" the wax patterns. Each pattern is cast with integral tab-like "gates," which permit the pattern to be attached to the tree. The gates perform the dual role of providing an exit for the molten wax and an entry for the molten metal, as we shall see. In any event, the center of a tree is a long square of wax with an integral pouring cup at one end; these runners, like the wax patterns themselves, are made in moulds on a wax injector, of the same wax that the patterns are "shot" from. A metal hook is screwed

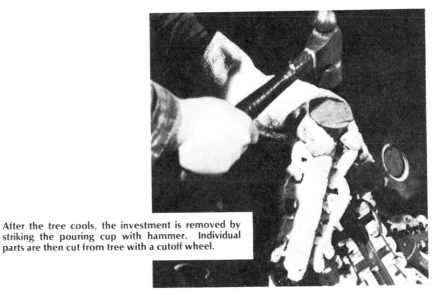

After the tree cools, the investment is removed by striking the pouring cup with hammer. Individual parts are then cut from tree with a cutoff wheel.

into the pouring cup while the runner is soft, enabling the tree to be hung from a rack. Treeing-up the patterns simply involves sticking the gates of the pattern to the runner by melting the ends of the gates slightly with a hot spatula or small soldering iron.

It is of considerable economic advantage to affix as many patterns as possible to one tree. Completed trees are allowed to cool before being sent to the investing or dipping room, and they are also cleaned with methyl ethyl ketone to remove silicone spray from the patterns; the water-based investment material otherwise wouldn't adhere to the pattern later.

The treed patterns are now ready for investment. Two basic methods may be used, either the flask or shell method. The former, more representative of ancient techniques of investment casting, is still used extensively for sculpture, jewelry manufacture, and dental-laboratory work. In the flask method, the wax pattern is surrounded by a relatively large volume of investment material poured around the pattern in the form of a liquid ceramic slurry. When this slurry has dried and hardened, the "green" mould is fired to consolidate it and to melt out the wax pattern. The greatest disadvantage of the flask method is the extensive burn-out time needed, since a fast heat would crack the thick mould before it had cured out.

The greatest percentage of gun parts are produced by the ceramic-shell process. As in the flask method, slurries are used, but only by dipping rather than as deep masses surrounding the patterns. B&H Precision uses three slurries, the first containing ceramic particles of 325 mesh and the next two of a much coarser 120 mesh. The slurries are held in suspension by constant agitation, much like slip used in making cast household ceramics, and they are mixed with a colloidal silica. Number three dipping bath at B&H has an alcohol base to promote rapid drying.

Here's the process of working a tree of patterns through the dipping room. The tree is twice dipped slowly and carefully in number one bath, the 325-mesh slurry that also contains a wetting agent. This first die is the most critical, since it creates the surface that will determine the quality of finish of the casting, hence the finer mesh of the first dip.

While the slurry is still damp, the tree, now covered with white ceramic, is lowered into a vat filled with a special 80-mesh sand, which is aerated from below to loft the sand particles and thereby prevent damage to the delicate waxes. The sand is a silicon carbide that has to be re-fused into silicon oxide and then crushed and reground, making it thermodimensionally stable; its purpose is to add bulk to the

ceramic shell, thus reducing the number of dips required to invest a tree. The sand also provides porosity in the shell, an attribute needed to prevent the entrapment of air in the shell when it is poured full of metal.

After the first dipping and sanding, the tree is allowed to dry for a day. It is then dipped in water briefly, drained, and then dipped again into the number-one slurry and sanded again. After an additional twenty-four hours, the same process is carried out again, but this time the tree goes into number-two, or 120-mesh, slurry and is sanded in a coarser fifty-mesh sand. Four more dippings and sandings follow this for a total of seven dips, the last dip being made in the number-three vat of alcohol-based 120-mesh slurry. Drying between dips is increasingly slower as the mass of the investment builds up; the final shell may be as little as 3/16 to over half an inch thick, depending upon the mass of the part, and when the green shell is dry after the last dipping, it is a self-supporting monolithic coating on the waxes.

In the investment-casting process, when shell moulds are used, the wax is "lost" or melted out in an autoclave, a large and sophisticated steam "pressure cooker" fed by a steam generator that provides a hundred pounds per square inch of pressure at three hundred degrees Fahrenheit. When the trees are inserted into the autoclave, the door is closed and the valves opened, the unit reaching full pressure in eight seconds. The steam pressurizes the shell, penetrating the porous surface; the fast pressure rise is needed so that the wax begins to melt and flow before it has a chance to expand and possibly fracture the shell. After about twenty minutes, virtually all of the wax is melted out, flowing out the bottom of the autoclave into a bucket.

Now the shell is placed in a gas-fired burnout oven at a temperature of 1,400 to 1,600 degrees Fahrenheit for three to five hours, depending upon the nature of the shell. Burning-out vaporizes residual wax on the inside surfaces of the shell, and brings the shell walls up to a tensile strength of four thousand pounds per square inch. The shell may now be cooled and put on the shelf for later pouring, or it may be taken to preheat temperature if it is to be poured right away.

Preheating at 1,800 to 1,900 degrees brings the shell up to the temperature necessary for pouring. The shell is held at this temperature for at least half an hour. When the furnace melt is ready, the shell is simply forked out of the burnout furnace and handed to a foundryman, who places it on the floor for pouring. Though the man handling the shell wears exceedingly heavy asbestos gloves, the white heat of the shell permits no more than ten seconds

of manipulation of the shell before things become uncomfortable. B&H has arranged its burnout ovens close to the furnace to avoid significant drops in shell temperature.

B&H uses an induction furnace, the induction coil housed in the pouring pot itself. The furnace is controlled by a large console, which is actually a solid-state frequency converter, converting sixty cycles per second to three thousand, feeding seven hundred volts direct current to the furnace, switching off and on that heavy "zap" three thousand times a second. This energy creates a powerful 60,000-watt magnetic field in the induction coil and consequently in the bar of alloy placed in the pot. As the alternating flux lines of the magnetic field sweep back and forth, the molecules in the ingot align themselves and follow the sweep, creating friction as the molecules of the alloy are rubbed together. This friction heating, along with resistance in the ingot caused by an eddy current coursing through the bar, melt the ingot down in a matter of minutes.

The melt is checked several times with a handheld pyrometer, and when pour temperature is reached, a quantity of slag fluxing compound (in the case of steel) is dumped on the surface of the melt. The induction coil is actually shut down at a higher temperature than the correct pour level, since the pot loses some heat between shutdown, during fluxing, and just before the pour. In the case of the trigger guard being poured here, the furnace was shut down at 3,020 degrees. Specified pouring temperature for SAE-4140 steel, of which the guards were to be poured, is 2,950 degrees.

When the melt is ready, the shell is quickly forked out of the burnout oven and set on the floor inside a heavy sheet-steel box open at the top. The pour is immediately made, and several other shells are pulled out one after another and poured. A paper cup filled with an organic hydrocarbon compound is then set on the pouring cup of one of the shells, and a lid is quickly fitted to the steel box. The hydrocarbon is converted by the heat to alcohol, which flames off inside the box, driving off oxygen from around the shells. The presence of oxygen around cooling shells can pit steel castings considerably, hence the use of this technique.

This describes a gravity or static-pressure pour, though special applications requiring the flow of alloy into critical shapes may require assistance from either a centrifugal force or vacuum. Dental labs, for instance, commonly use spring-driven centrifuges to insure perfect filling of flasks. Whatever the pour method, correct handling of the procedure is critical if usable parts are desired. For example, many steel alloys expand one percent per hundred degrees of temperature past the melting point; if a melt is allowed to heat too much, the resulting cast parts can shrink unduly or even lose carbon, which causes considerable difficulty in parts that must undergo critical heat-treating.

After cooling, the trees are cleaned of investment by vibration or by simply striking the pouring cup with a hammer. If necessary, a mixture of ninety-percent sodium nitrate and ten-percent sodium hydroxide can be used to dissolve the ceramic binders of the investment; this compound must be heated to nine hundred degrees, and a steel part so cleaned requires a muriatic-acid cleaning afterward. Usually, the tree is simply sandblasted in an enclosed booth after vibrating away the bulk of the investment; the parts are then cut off the tree with cutoff wheels.

Steel castings are then annealed for four to six hours at 1,500 degrees; B&H uses an argon atmosphere to prevent scaling the castings. Annealing leaves SAE-4140 castings at zero on the Rockwell C scale, though they cast at twenty-one. Carbon steel parts generally experience surface decarburization during casting, generally at least 0.007 inch below the surface, and foundries use various recarburization processes for restoring the surfaces when it is needed. Parts that will receive surface machining to any degree often don't need this.

Investment casting is a complex art, requiring considerable knowledge, skill, and financial outlay. We gun nuts should be thankful for the existence of this fine industry. Without it, the future of firearms production at affordable prices would certainly be a dim one. As it is, we still have quality production and custom arms through the assistance provided by precision casting, and these arms need be of no lower quality than guns produced totally from forged and machined alloys. ●

Section 8

CUSTOMIZING

THE CROWNING

DO YOUR OWN CUSTOM

THE APACHE CHIEF'S ancient Henry and the maharajah's Holland & Holland have one thing in common: their owners wanted these rifles to stand out not only from the ordinary but also from other distinctively personalized rifles. One man hammered brass tacks into the stock; the other hired the ablest engravers to cover his rifle with fine scrollwork and inlaid gold wire. One rifle began as a mass-produced arm, "made by the mile and cut off by the yard;" the other was one of a kind from its beginning. Each, in the end, is unique.

Custom gunmakers keep busy making guns for people who want unique firearms. Custom work isn't limited to making rifles in wildcat calibers: custom gunmakers make far more rifles in standard calibers. Nor do they build rifles only from bare actions, from the ground up; much of their work is rebarreling or merely rechambering standard factory-made rifles. Taste is intensely personal, so no single caliber, rifle or finish (or even barrel length!) is ever going to satisfy everybody.

Some special touches are out of the reach of most of us. The Apache Chief couldn't finance the maharajah's double rifle, not even its finishing touches. But he could dress up his own humble rifle, to suit himself. You don't have to be an engraver to give your rifle a distinctive personal touch. You don't have to be a custom riflemaker. You don't even have to have much of a shop. You can make your rifle more interesting and beautiful by any of several treatments of the metal surfaces. You'd like your bolt knob rough, for a good grip, but not abrasive? Checker a band around it, a flat on the underside of it, or a series of circles around it. You want to break up specular reflection on the barrel and on the front-sight ramp? Soft-polish or wirebrush the barrel. Stipple or groove the sight ramp.

You like a dull finish to avoid sending flash signals to game on sunny days? Go easy on the high polish, and have your barreled action glassbeaded.

A tasteful blend of these prefinish treatments will make your rifle stand out from the pack, not only in appearance but in functional practicality as well. Some, you can do yourself; others, you may have to farm out. Either way, the first thing to be done is a good job of polishing.

A well finished rifle is first of all well polished, even on those surfaces that will later be stippled, brushed, or checkered. Good polishing is basic to the final finish of any surface. What you do before you blue determines what kind of finish you wind up with. Your rifle may already be blued, maybe with a factory standard polish and finish, and you want to improve it by repolishing and reblueing. You want all the flat surfaces *flat,* with no ripples or scratches. You want all edges sharp, not rounded over and muted. You don't want any dishing or dimpling around screwholes. You want all lettering sharp-edged and distinct.

You don't have a buffing wheel? Excellent! You're better off, for it's overuse of the buffer that rounds edges, dimples screwholes, makes ripples, and blurs lettering. The buffer is nice for a final touchup, applied ever lightly to brighten the metal, but never to remove pits or scratches.

In polishing, you use finer and finer abrasives to remove irregularities and imperfections from the surface of the metal. On surfaces you intend to leave

unblued ("in the white"), the final grit should be no coarser than No. 500, if you are going to buff for the final gloss. Use finer grit for higher gloss if you have no buffer. On surfaces you intend to give some special texture, you needn't polish with any finer than a No. 320 grit, usually. There is no substitute or shortcut for time and hard work here. You need no magical or mystical ability given only to seventh sons of seventh sons. But you have to want to do the job right, and you have to be willing to take the time required to do it right.

For complete information on proper polishing techniques, study any of the standard gunsmithing books. Basically, you will be using two techniques, each with finer and finer abrasives as you go along. The surface you're polishing determines which technique you use there. Remember, you don't want your abrasives to change any shapes, only to smooth the surface already established. (If the surface is really in bad need of reshaping, you'll do well to reshape it, perhaps with a single-cut file, but never with polishing abrasives. It's one thing to correct mistakes, whoever may have made them; it's another thing altogether to try to cover them up.)

"Hardbacked" polishing requires a hard backing behind the abrasive paper or cloth. A fine file is a good choice for polishing flat surfaces and outside curves. For inside curves, use a dowel, metal rod, or round file. The object is to let the backing determine where the abrasive takes off metal. Soft backing would alter surfaces and edges in all the wrong ways,

One type of "hardbacked" polishing uses a cylindrical piece, such as this dowel, to polish concave surfaces evenly. The serial number on this action is clear and distinct — a result of good polishing technique.

TOUCH
FINISHING OR REFINISHING

By R.L. JAMISON

leaving ripples, dimples, and rounded edges.

After the basic polishing with hardbacked abrasives, you can move on to the "shoeshine" technique for the last stage of fine polishing, but only on outside curves such as the receiver ring and the barrel. Be especially careful not to use the shoeshine technique across sharp edges. The shoeshine polish isn't necessary if you plan to wind up with a soft, dull or matte finish. Bright reflections from rifle steel can ruin your hunt by warning game before you get a chance to shoot.

On hunting rifles, then, the high gloss isn't always what you want. A soft, muted finish can be beautiful, as owners of classic custom arms well appreciate. You can simply leave off the final polishing, if you've gotten rid of all tool and file marks, and have a pretty good soft finish without further work.

For a velvety brushed finish, you may want to wirebrush the barrel and receiver. To do this, move the metal into the bristles of a fine wire brush rotating at a high rpm. The fineness or coarseness of the finish depends on the pressure against the brush and the diameter of the wires in the brush. I use 0.004-inch-diameter wire, in a brush turning at 100 to 1,000 rpm. Be careful to use a wirebrush at the correct rpm rating on the label. Otherwise, the brush can fly apart, throwing wires into you. Also, be careful not to wear loose

clothing that can flap into the wires and get snagged. Wear a face shield or goggles; wires do fly off at times, and they're hard on eyes.

Introduce the metal to the brush in long, horizontal strokes with light pressure. Brush the steel just long enough to get the appearance you want. Overbrushing gives a wavy look, especially on barrels. Be careful to keep the metal below a horizontal line through the center of the brush. This way, you get the right finish without running the risk of having the brush grab the part being brushed. A grabbed part can bounce off the floor before you know it. Or your hand can be slammed into the brush or against the housing or shield of the buffer.

It's difficult to do partial brushing or to mask off areas to be left bright and then brush up to the masking tape. Spot brushing doesn't look as good as some other finishes that lend themselves to spot treatment, so it's best to brush the whole part or none of it.

For a dull finish that comes right up to a sharp border next to a brighter surface, try glassbeading (also called glass peening). This process, which you might have to have done at a local shop specializing in rebuilding auto engines, is a good bit like sandblasting. For our purposes, it's better, because the tiny glass beads don't erode the surface of the steel as sandblasting would. Glass peening is a good term for this process: the beads give the metal a microscopically fine peening. There are several grades or sizes of beads. Fortunately, the sizes I've encountered in most automotive machine shops were right for finishing gun parts the way I wanted them.

These shops usually glassbead parts for a very reasonable price. I've had complete barreled actions beaded for less than five dollars. Be absolutely certain that the man doing the beading knows

"Shoeshine" polishing provides even buffing of surfaces already polished by the "hardbacked" method. Use with the finest abrasive (highest grit number) only.

what you want done, and mask off any areas you don't want beaded before you take the work to him. It doesn't take much blasting to texture gun steel, so masking tape gives enough protection for a good, sharp line of demarcation at the border of the masked-off area (provided the operator is careful near the edges of the tape).

You may want to have the shop blaster glassbead a sample piece of steel for you, to see what kind of finish he will provide, before you commit a valued rifle into his hands. Blued, the glassbeaded surface yields a true "blue," from the irregular reflecting surfaces left by the fine peening. Sights, sight planes, and small parts can be beaded for special effects. I have applied this finish very lightly to nonmating surfaces inside firearms to hold oil better, for better rust prevention and lubrication.

Whereas wirebrushing and glassbeading are great on larger areas, stippling is better suited to smaller areas. For one thing, it's rougher, but can be altogether too rough if you're not careful. For another, it's tedious work if you cover much of an area with it. But it's easy, and you can do it with tools already at hand or with simple punches you can easily make. Center-

The hard backing of the file keeps the emery cloth cutting cleanly and evenly, so the flat surfaces stay flat and the outside curves of this receiver stay curved, with longitudinal lines straight. Hard backing has to be reasonably rigid — not flexible.

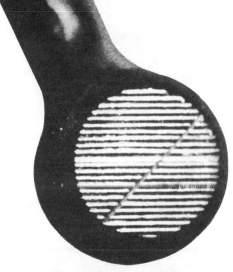

After applying a coat of machinist's layout blue, the author scribed two master lines on the flat underside of this bolt knob. Above, he has cut the first set of grooves with a file. These are not cut to full depth: notice that the ridges between the grooves are not sharp, and the master lines are still visible. In photo at top right, the author cut the second set of grooves with the outside row of teeth of the file set in the second master line. The file has almost reached its full depth. When grooves are cut to final depth, the file will ride the tops of the diamonds without cutting.

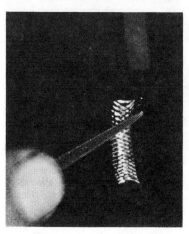

Checkering of curved surfaces requires special care and patience. Surfaces such as triggers are especially difficult. A "tape template," described in the text, has the pattern drawn on it. This tape is stuck on the surface, and the file cuts carefully through the tape, maintaining line spacing. Remains of the tape are then removed, and the cuts finished.

punches and nailsets make pretty good stippling punches, for some applications, just as they are. Old dental picks are excellent for making your own (the punch in the accompanying photograph is an old dental pick). Stippling is a process of roughing the surface with sharp or round-tip punches struck with a light hammer. As the punch indents the metal, displaced metal is raised around the impression, making a rougher surface. Stippling is a more or less random array of closely spaced indentations. Stippling with a round-tip punch is somewhat like a miniaturized version of peening.

You can vary your stippling by the punch you use, the angle at which you hold the punch to the work, and how hard you tap the punch with the hammer. You can vary the effect by spacing the impressions closer together or farther apart. But spacing offers much less variety than the other choices, for stippling quickly becomes crude and awkward in appearance if the impressions are too close together or too far apart.

A sharply pointed punch produces very sharp and rough stippling best suited for breaking up reflections on sighting surfaces or for a fine matte area for decoration. A blunter or more rounded punch held at a more acute angle to the surface produces a broken-up surface that is rough enough to give a good grasping surface without being abrasive. If you do turn up a surface that's too rough for comfort, pass it very lightly across the wirebrush to smooth away just the sharper edges.

Very light hammer taps on a very sharp tool held at a right angle to the work, with the fine indentations spaced close together, produce beautiful shading effects for accenting small areas. In any stippling, uniformity of spacing and evenness of the impressions produce the neatest, classiest finish. Keep the tool poised in position just above the work, holding and guiding it with thumb and forefinger, with your hand resting on the work (or on the vise), and you'll find that very rapid, even stippling is reasonably easy with just a bit of practice. A little care is necessary when you bring your

This is a good medium angle of attack for stippling. Held more nearly vertical, the punch would produce a smoother stippling. Held at a lower angle, it would act more like a plow, producing a rougher surface. Note that the tip is held off the surface, with the fingers acting as a return spring to position the tip again after each blow of the hammer.

stippling up to a border line, but hardly any more than is necessary for smooth, even spacing between impressions.

Don't let the randomness of stippling (as compared with checkering) get away with you; aim for evenness all along, without trying to arrange the impressions in neat little rows, and you'll do well, even around the edges of the stippled area. In stippling the sloping top of a sight ramp, try to avoid making dents that skid down over the sides of the ramp or cause small bulges along the edge of the ramp. You may even want to leave a narrow band of unstippled metal along each edge of the slope, particularly if the ramp is especially wide.

With metal checkering, we come to the roughest finish of all, both in the final surface and the relative difficulty of application. In appearance, metal checkering is sometimes very much like the checkering on stocks. In function, it is even more similar, being useful for improving the graspability of the firearm and quite decorative as well. In

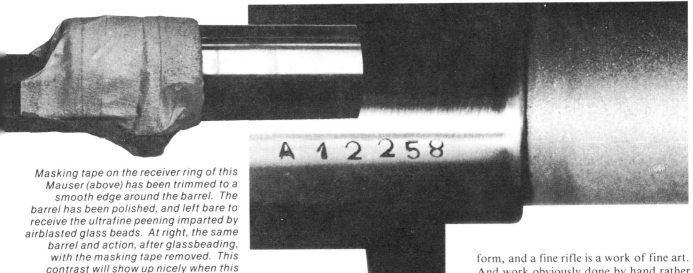

Masking tape on the receiver ring of this Mauser (above) has been trimmed to a smooth edge around the barrel. The barrel has been polished, and left bare to receive the ultrafine peening imparted by airblasted glass beads. At right, the same barrel and action, after glassbeading, with the masking tape removed. This contrast will show up nicely when this barreled action is blued. Careful polishing sometimes sharpens the clarity of the roll marks and stamped numbers on gunmetal.

application, it's somewhat easier than checkering a stock. You'll never want to checker as much area on a metal surface as is common on a stock, and the metal doesn't tend to swerve your cutters away from the desired lines, as the grain in a stock does. As in stock checkering, the pattern is a double array of evenly spaced and evenly cut grooves, with each set of grooves intersecting the other set at a predetermined angle.

Grooving, using a single array of grooves, is a good treatment for some surfaces, often more appropriate for such surfaces than checkering would be. For either grooving or checkering, the best tool is a special checkering file with teeth spaced evenly in whatever number of lines per inch is best for the area you want to checker. On sight ramps, the grooves can be 40, 50 or even 75 lines to the inch. On grip surfaces, where you want more roughness, not merely a reflection breaker, 20 or 30 lines per inch would be preferable. With coarser spacing, grooves will be deeper; with finer spacing, the grooves will be very shallow. Taste and function determine which spacing is best for any application.

An alternative to the checkering file, which you won't be able to use on some gun surfaces, is a homemade template that you make by laying out the checkering lines on a strip of tape. Transfer the tape to the surface you want to checker, and cut the lines one at a time with a knife file, a three-cornered file, or a square needle file.

Carefully lay out both sets of lines on a piece of tape, using the teeth of a hacksaw blade or a thread-pitch gauge, or even a ruler, to space them properly. Peel up the strip of tape and press it into place on the surface you plan to checker. With some

kinds of tape, especially with coarse spacing, the knife file will cut through without a hitch. But some kinds of tape, particularly with closer spacing, tend to pull and snag, peeling away from the steel. If you're using this kind of tape, carefully precut the lines with an X-acto knife guided along a flexible steel straightedge; then file your grooves in the steel. Your first file cuts are simply layout cuts; make them just deep enough at first that you can follow them later. Then, after you've laid out every line, go back over them, filing each line a little deeper and moving on to the next, until the top of each resulting diamond is sharp.

The shape of the diamonds can be varied, in steel, somewhat more than in wood checkering. Square diamonds may be preferable in some small areas, but the most pleasing shape is the 3-to-1 or the 3 1/2-to-1 diamond, with each diamond 3 or 3 1/2 times as long as it is wide. Checkering inside the curve of a trigger, for example, you may have no choice; the tight inside curve may not allow you to make the longer crosscuts required for 3-to-1 diamonds.

None of these surface treatments, alone, will give your rifle a tastefully distinctive finish. Even a good polish looks fairly routine compared to the varied finish treatments on a carefully planned rifle that has a dove-soft luster on the barrel and receiver, a finely stippled rectangle aligned fore-and-aft along the top of the receiver ring, a brightly polished bolt and bolt handle, with fine checkering on the flat underside of the knob, and fine crosswise grooves on the top slope of the front-sight ramp. In the eye of the connoisseur, the rifle is an art

form, and a fine rifle is a work of fine art. And work obviously done by hand rather than by machine signifies an awareness and an appreciation of this art form. The finest displays of such art are those rifles that combine accuracy, fine craftsmanship in the making and fitting of their parts, practicality of function, and tasteful finish.

When you have lifted your rifle out of the ordinary by tastefully personalizing it, the pride of ownership that made you want to dress it up is somehow increased and enriched by the dressing-up you've done. The rifle seems to come to the shoulder more naturally, and it seems to be a bit more cooperative in putting 'em where you aim. This may all be your imagination, but maybe not. Besides, you're probably looking at your rifle for eleven months and hunting with it one month at the most each year. Anything that makes it easier to look at, even a *pleasure* to look at, is well worth the time it took you to add that extra special, final touch that is yours and yours alone. ●

The speed of this wirebrush is 120 rpm. Such a low speed produces a soft luster under the final blueing. Higher speeds produce duller finishes.

METAL FINISHES for the CUSTOM GUNSMITH

By JOHN BIVINS

THE FIREARMS-buying public, so it seems, appears more and more to equate quality in manufactured guns with a mirror-polish blue. No small number of writers have apparently swung to favor this type of finish, all of which seems pretty surprising in view of the fact that less than two decades ago "glitter babies" of the gun world were shied away from due to the fact that they were less than practical for hunting while the sun was shining. Highly polished finishes were also shunned by those who were aware of the fact that bluing wears off such a surface at a greater rate, due to the fact that there is less surface area on a mirror finish to provide the best mechanical and chemical "foot" for bluing oxides. This isn't to say that shiny finishes have no place. . .they certainly do, but not on *all* sporting and target guns, as some manufacturers would seem to believe. Tastes do change, else we would not be saddled with such things as white-line spacers (a modern adjunct which this writer believes is just as useful and decorative as mammary glands on a boar hog), but *use* hasn't changed, and it would be a fine thing if some arms manufacturers would examine their finishing processes they use now. Most of them come up short in comparison with the lustrous blues from the same firms of only a few years ago.

A host of finishing processes are available to the custom gunsmith, of course, many of them far too time-consuming for manufacturers to consider now. . .even though the same processes, such as rust blue, were used by arms companies even as late as the 1950's. Even so, some finishing processes now used by custom smiths to provide the slightly matte finish so desirable on custom work can, in fact, be used in large-production situations with little or no added cost to the product. One such finish should even represent a savings over the mirror polish, as I'll discuss later, and would be a great benefit by providing the shooting public with a more durable and pleasing finish on their guns.

The mainstay of gun finishes today is the so-called "hot" blue or "caustic" blue, consisting of compounds of basic salts such as potassium nitrate, sodium nitrite, and others, sold in prepared form under various trade names and intended to be used at a rolling boil. This type of blue, actually more black than blue, is something of a Johnny-come-lately. Though such blues were known early in this century, they didn't come into the all-encompassing use they enjoy today until after World War II. Even after that date some manufacturers still used earlier finishing processes such as Carbonia, which was a patented system used by Smith & Wesson, Colt, and others to obtain the incredible temper blue once the hallmark of fine handguns in this country. Caustic blue, since it is quite fast, is therefore an inexpensive finishing method, and has virtually supplanted all other methods on the production level, and not always to the good of the consumer.

Virtually all firearms finishes involve oxides in one form or the other, and many of the means of obtaining them, at least for the custom gunsmith, haven't changed for centuries. Basically, the principle oxides desirable are ferrous oxide, or common reddish-brown rust, and ferro-ferric oxide, which has a black appearance on unpolished steel and a blue-black on polished metal. Ferro-ferric oxide, or "blue," is a "magnetic" oxide resulting from a conversion of ferrous oxide by steam or boiling water. The close alliance

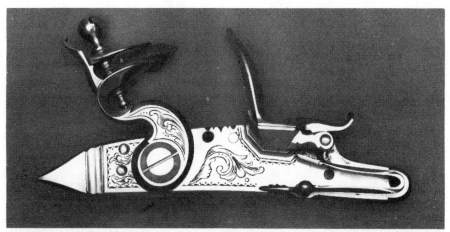

Locks in the 18th Century and before, though casehardened, were often left bright rather than showing colors. This example of casehardening without color is shown on a currently manufactured and customized Siler lock. Photo by Robert Weil.

between the two oxides can easily be seen by the fact that most ancient browning solutions will *also* blue iron and steel, as we shall see.

The exact history of finishing processes is a confusing one, and a subject deserving of considerable thought by arms historians and conservators. The earliest "handegonnes," or shoulder guns, were almost certainly left bright, though some were simply painted with a "japan" varnish, usually a spirit-varnish lightly pigmented with asphaltum. The intent, of course, was to reduce both glare and oxidation. It was not long, however, that gunsmiths discovered that they could make rust work *for* them, by controlling the rust to a fine-grain with chemicals and by using atmospheric controls. The result was an excellent and durable "browne" or "russeting" as it was frequently called by the Seventeenth Century. Formulas for creating browned finishes became part of the "art & mistry" of every working gunsmith. . . hallowed potions to be guarded against the prying eyes of the competition, and woe be unto the lowly apprentice who allowed another trade master to know his own master's browning formula. A vastly imperfect understanding of basic chemistry on the part of gunsmiths much before the 19th Century, however, has left us with a heritage of traditional formulas that seem truly medieval, almost to the extent of having to utter little cries in the dark of the moon while mixing the stuff. Some early browning formulas have as many as five major corrosives and reagents as their working compounds, when often but one or two corrosive agents would have done nicely. No doubt early artificers felt that if *one* corrosive worked, then four together would work four times better, or something like that. Many of the old formulas have been successful to a great degree despite themselves. The earliest formulas were probably simple, often consisting of little more than vinegar or even urine, and today, thanks to the chemists in our midsts, we have returned to simpler. . .and safer. . . formulas than early gunsmiths employed.

Contrary to much current thought, bluing was very much in use early on, probably just as early as brown was. Before the 1830's or so, however, this blue was a *temper* or "fire" blue, brought to the polished metal by holding the part over a low forge or "pit" fire, or submersing it in a heating "agent" such as sand, until a heat of about 600 degrees fahrenheit is reached. Such a heat-source oxide blue was used extensively for the furniture on steel or iron-mounted weapons, and it was a common method of finishing both rifle and fowler barrels. Riflemakers in this country used a fire-blue for barrels much more than is commonly thought, judging from surviving samples I have seen. Gunsmith William Geddy of Williamsburg advertised blued rifle barrels early in the 1750's, and it wouldn't surprise me at all to find that the Brothers Hawken occasionally fire-blued rifle mounts in the 1830's. Make no mistake, however, temper blue, if it is to be even and durable, is a most difficult process. We'll discuss it a bit more later.

As we have noted, the ferrous iron oxide that gives us a good brown on gun steel may be converted to an entirely different black or ferro-ferric oxide by introduction to boiling water. Actually, the water doesn't even have to boil. I have often wondered why rust blue didn't come into use in the 18th Century or before when some idiot like myself tried to brown metal on a hot day when it was raining outside, and discovered that moisture condensation on the metal caused blue spots to appear. No doubt the blue was thought to be the very manifestation of Belial, and the offending barrel promptly taken to the bench and rid of its demons with pumice powder. In any event, that is how rust blue occurs, by simply starting an oxide with what would otherwise serve as a browning formula, and then boiling the part after a period of rusting. The part is also carded with a wire brush or wheel after boiling to remove remnants of the ferrous oxide, and some formulas must be *vigorously* carded unless a mangy blue-brown is desirable. . .as it is in some restoration work, in fact. Though most all browning formulas will also blue, some are more satisfactory than others in respect to fineness of grain and speed. All give the same color.

Rust blue apparently didn't see widespread use anywhere much before the mid 19th Century, even though it must have been known earlier if for no other reason than accident. I'd like to know if any of

The same lock as on the opposing page is shown here rust-blued using the 1841 Ordnance formula noted in the text. Note that though a light source is thrown directly on the lock surface, there is no glare — a distinct advantage on hunting rifles.

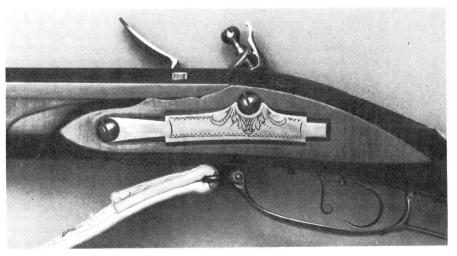

Three different surface finishes are shown on this rifle: rust brown, [the barrel]; fast blue, using Casey's Plum Brown [side plate, trigger guard, triggers]; fire blue [lock screws, sling swivel]. Though bluing was extensively used on early guns, it was generally a fire blue, which usually will not work well on modern steel alloys.

369

The BIVINS DAMP BOX

Mk. II

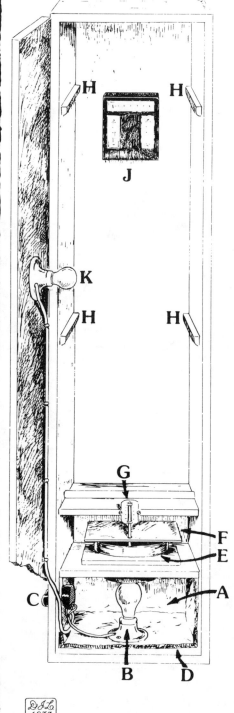

This is Bivins' damp box, which he uses for all rust bluing and browning. The box is constructed of 3/4-inch exterior grade plywood, glued and nailed at the joints. The bottom chamber [A] which is totally enclosed, conceals a single 150-watt bulb in a ceramic socket [B] resting on the floor of the box; the bulb is controlled by a dimmer [C] with a control shaft protruding from the side of the case, and the entire lower heat chamber is lined with asbestos and heavy aluminum foil [D] to prevent heat damage. Placed in a tightly fitting hole in the top of the heat chamber is a medium-sized stainless saucepan [E] filled with water, with two-thirds of the top covered with a piece of sheet brass [F], a meat thermometer [G] reads water temperature, usually set at 140-160 degrees. Barrels and/or barreled actions rest upon the shelf just above the pot, and rests [H] are nailed near mid-point and top of the upper chamber to receive partitioned plywood shelves shown on top of the damp box in the photo for finishing small parts. A dry bulb/wet bulb hygrometer [I] keeps tabs on damp box humidity, and the lightbulb [J] on the door provides both illumination and extra heat; Bivins alternates between 25 and 40-watt bulbs, depending upon the heat needed. Though this box measures 15x15x66 inches, a smaller unit could be used if only breechloaders were to be finished. In use, the water pot should almost touch the light bulb heat source, and the pot should be kept filled. Shelving should be at least four inches shallower than the depth of the box to permit free air circulation. Screen-door hooks keep the door shut tightly.

our erudite readers have insights into such things.

In addition to rust browning and fire-blues, another finish popular from a very early period was case-hardening. Early gunsmiths saved both time and money by fabricating working mechanisms, particularly gunlocks, from soft iron and simply carburizing the surfaces by pack-hardening in charred leather, bone black, and other carbon-bearing substances. This is what old gunsmiths' accounts mean when one finds the entry "steeling a frizzen;" it meant casehardening, or converting the surface iron to steel by the addition of carbon. Such surface-carburized parts were glass-hard on the surface by virtue of having been quenched in cold water, yet .010-.020 below the surface, the part was still soft steel or iron. . .thereby providing a part that was both malleable and hard. This is a very desirable characteristic in my mind, and even with the fine through-hardening tool steels of today, I still much prefer casehardened mild steel for use in fine lock components. All springs, of course, must be through-hardening steel.

Casehardening will, to a good degree, resist atmospheric oxidation, and it was popular among early gunsmiths to leave the locks of fine fowlers and rifles bright. At some point, however, someone discovered that mottled colors could be brought to a casehardened finish by "tampering" with the water which the parts were quenched in when they were dumped from the iron box in which they were pack-hardened in the forge. Someone no doubt noted that as the water in the quenching or "slack" tub became dirty from use, subtle colors began to appear upon the finished gun metal rather than the usual silvery-gray of plain casehardening. Potassium nitrate dissolved in the quench, it was soon discovered, provided brilliant mottling to the surface, especially when the quench tub was aerated by some means. A vigorous stream of bubbles heightened the colors and the patterns they made; what was taking place was simply an instantaneous introduction of oxygen of varying strength to the metal as it was being rapidly cooled, providing the entire spectrum of oxide temper colors, frozen in incredible patterns by cold water. How early color hardening was used, I cannot say, though Lynton McKenzie told me recently that he had seen brilliant color case on the locks of a pair of ca. 1730 French holster pistols. Generally, color case wasn't particularly popular much before 1800, judging from surviving samples of guns in fine condition.

Though casehardening, and even obtaining good colors, isn't really difficult, we won't go into the process here for the reason that it isn't a finish very practical for the custom smith who doesn't have expensive precision heat-treating equipment. Casehardening large parts such as receivers invites warpage unless hardening temperatures are held within a critical range, so this finish, in most shops, is best confined to small parts.

These are the basic working finishes for the gunsmith, all of them with the exception of caustic blue known to one degree or another for centuries, so let's have a look at specifics.

Atmospheric controls are vital to the efficient application of either slow-rust browns or blues. Two years ago, in *Rifle* 36, I discussed the use of the dampbox, in which I used a thermostatic hotplate to heat water to provide a high humidity level inside a sealed chamber, regardless of the ambient humidity of the atmosphere. A damp box is a great necessity in order to provide constant humidity conditions, since you can't do much rusting when the moisture content of the air drops much below 60 percent, and a baroque mess develops if the humidity rises much above 90 percent. Both heat and humidity controls are important; I control the air temperature of the main chamber of my damp box with varying wattages of light bulbs. The more efficient heat source I now use for the water is simply a single 150-watt lightbulb which is controlled by an inexpensive dimmer. See Dave LeGate's sketch and the attendant explanation for details. My box is large to accommodate long muzzle-loading barrels; the gunsmith who only has to deal with breechloaders could well do with a smaller box.

In my rig, I have found that a water temperature range (I measure this with a meat thermometer) of 140-160 degrees and an upper chamber temperature of 90 degrees or so will provide the 80 to 85 percent humidity needed for optimum conditions for most browning and bluing solutions. Each formula, of course, tends to have a humidity level where it works best, hence the need for a dry-bulb wet-bulb hygrometer (cost approximately $20) to keep tabs on the conditions in your box. The wet bulb must be fanned before taking readings for best accuracy, which is why a sling psychrometer is the most accurate. There's no way to use a sling in a damp box, though, unless you have a damnably big box.

Not only do damp box conditions need to be adjusted for different browning formulas; changes in water temperatures and box temperatures need to be made when atmospheric conditions in your shop change radically, as you will find. Such adjustments are usually slight, to either speed or slow rusting. Water must never even approach boiling temperature, or moisture will condense on the metal, with hideous results. Air temperature in the upper compartment must be kept fairly high, also to avoid reaching the dew point inside and causing condensation. In my box I alternate between 25 and 40-watt bulbs in the top for control; the dry-bulb thermometer on your hygrometer will of course give you air temperature readings.

As a matter of safety, bolt your damp box to the wall. You don't want to stumble into it in the dark some night and knock your lovingly hand-polished Hoffman Mauser action off the hooks and into the drink. . .unless you like to stay up until three ayem re-polishing. I prefer thorn branches and snow banks for pleasure.

With atmospheric conditions in hand, let's have a look at six different finishing processes appropriate for fine guns, two of which will be carried out with the aid of the damp box. Regarding surface

Bivins found Rick Schrieber's browning solution to be the best commercially produced for both rust browning and rust bluing. Bivins says it produces a very fast, soft, and fine-grained oxide.

preparation, incidentally, none of these processes except for temper blue require a polishing grit (either hand or wheel) finer than 300. A heavy rust brown or blue or the matte caustic blue, in fact, cover a 280-grit surface just fine. I don't intend to go into polishing techniques here, other than to say that I much prefer hand polishing for *everything*.

Rust Brown

Certainly one of the easiest and most durable finishes available, the old slow-rust brown sees little use today on arms other than muzzleloaders. Before World War I, most fine shotguns with damascus barrels were browned, though some were lightly rust-blued; brown is more attractive on a twist pattern, to my way of thinking.

Here's a formula that I have used for quite a number of years; though it is associated with Harper's Ferry Arsenal

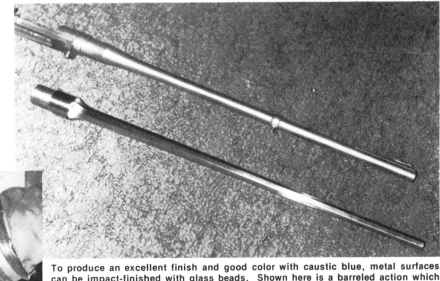

To produce an excellent finish and good color with caustic blue, metal surfaces can be impact-finished with glass beads. Shown here is a barreled action which has been beaded, alongside a new octagon barrel yet to be beaded. The tiny spherical glass beads, which have almost the appearance of flour, are "fired" onto parts surfaces at high speed by compressed air, working in an enclosed cabinet. Some auto shops and almost all aircraft engine shops have bead blasters. Photos by Joe Balickie.

during the mid 19th Century, it no doubt was derived from virtually identical formulas present in the 18th Century:

Browning Solution, US Ordnance Manual 1841

5 oz. ethyl alcohol
5 fl. oz. ferric chloride tincture
1.7 oz. (48.2 grams) mercuric chloride
5 oz. ethyl nitrite, 4 percent alcoholic solution
4 oz. (113.4 grams) copper sulfate
2.5 fl. oz. nitric acid, 70 percent
104 fl. oz. distilled water

This formula makes a gallon, and of course can be cut in proportion if a smaller quantity is desired. One problem ingredient in recent years has been the ethyl nitrite solution, called "sweet spirits of nitre" in the early days, and used as a pharmaceutical up until a decade or so ago. It has gone out of use, and few firms will now synthesize it since it is unstable, so if you are not able to locate it I believe that it can be replaced with an equal volume of ethyl alcohol with no harm to the formula. The 1841 Ordnance solution will give an excellent dark reddish-brown color to just about any alloy of steel, usually requiring six or seven applications spaced four to six hours apart; it's all right to leave parts in the damp box overnight with this brown. Like most browning solutions, it should be kept in a brown glass bottle or an opaque plastic jug. It's poisonous as the very devil, largely thanks to the mercuric chloride.

With the ordnance formula, a medium to heavy oxide suitable for most muzzle-loading work can be obtained by carding between coats with 4/0 steel wool, and you'd best degrease the wool. Much of it seems to be saturated with oil these days, and I for one would like to see someone produce steel wool for gunsmiths that has no oil in it. If anyone knows of any, please write! Parts must of course be degreased before application of the brown. I simply clean parts with toluol (a basic solvent in lacquer thinner) and then go over them again with methanol (wood alcohol) to remove any residue from the thinner. Avoid touching the parts after they're degreased, though the ethyl alcohol in this brown will remove trace amounts of oils. It's also a good idea to run a dry patch down the bore of a barrel that is to be browned, to prevent oil from creeping to the outside; I protect bores from rusting in the damp box by simply swabbing them with a patch soaked in Sherwin-Williams A66 V3 varnish sealer, the stock finish I discussed in *Rifle* 47. This can be removed easily with lacquer thinner after the browning is finished.

If a finer-grain brown is desired, you can card between coats with a wire wheel, using an .004 wire diameter brush, obtainable from Frank Mittermeier in New York. Decreasing the rusting time to three hours per session will also produce a finer grain, and this solution can also be cut as much as 20 percent with distilled water if desirable. For use on damascus

steel, it should be cut considerably. I can't say how much since I haven't tried it on damascus.

To stop the browning salts, either wash the parts in hot soapy water, as I do, or wash with a water and baking-soda mixture. A good final finish results from waxing the parts with Johnson's Paste Floor Wax. For best results, melt a little wax and stir in a little burnt umber universal tinting color first, or you will be left with white spots when the wax hardens. *Do not* be tempted to boil *any* browned parts to stop the rusting action unless you want the parts to turn a matte black. This is at times a good technique for aging when restoring an antique, but it ain't so hot for new work. I wouldn't even soak parts in hot water for more than a very brief period.

The greatest drawback to the Ordnance formula, and to many other old browning solutions, is that it contains mercury salts. Mercury poisoning is one of the most insidious maladies on the books. It's very difficult to diagnose, and, like lead poisoning, it's cumulative. I have become very concerned with this due to the fact that I use large quantities of brown, and I don't fancy becoming senile before I'm forty. For the past couple of years I have been hearing about a solution marketed by Rick Schrieber, whose fine gunsmithing work was featured in *Rifle* 48. Rick is a chemist, well prepared to devise excellent finishes, and some while back he began to market a product he calls "Barrel Brown & Degreaser." The "degreaser" comes from the fact that it apparently contains a detergent, and a strong one at that. I tested this feature, basically being a dubious fellow, and found that it would cut right through a generous smear of oil and immediately begin to brown the metal. . .certainly a boon to the gunsmith, since with this brown there is little need to worry about touching parts during the browning process. Also, this brown is *very* fast indeed; I found that I can finish parts in the damp box in only four applications, spaced three hours apart, and the resulting brown is very fine-grain, with an excellent plum color. Longer rusting periods or less carding will build up the oxide if a heavier coat is needed. Like the Ordnance brown, Schrieber's solution needs 80 percent-plus humidity to work most efficiently, though I found that it would produce a very fine rust at a moisture level not much over 60 percent. Equally as important, this solution contains no mercury, and is not even toxic enough to even warrant a "poison" disclaimer on the label. Rick tells me that the principle corrosive is ferric chloride, and there is a trace of acid present. I've tried a good number of browning solutions over the years, and Schrieber's brown is the very best I have used to date, if my tests with it so far are any indication. I immediately ordered a

gallon, and have no intention of using any other solution in the future unless this brown balks at some particular alloy, which I don't expect it to. I've used it now on 12L14 (low-carbon leaded barrel steel), 4140, and A-2, and it browned all with equal ease.

Rick sells this in 2.5-ounce bottles through various dealers such as Golden Age Arms Co. in Delaware, Ohio; he will not sell these small bottles direct. Due to my prodding, he now has available bulk quantities, quarts retailing at $26.80 and gallons at $87.70, and he will sell these bulk quantities directly to bonafide gunsmiths and dealers *only*, and the discounts are liberal. For the hobby gunsmith, the 2½-ounce bottle retails for $2.75 and will brown four rifles. Schrieber's address is: Laurel Mountain Forge, Box 272, Clawson, Mich. 48017. Use the directions he supplies with each bottle.

Fast Brown

Fast browns, applied by heating the metal until the solution will just barely sizzle when it is swabbed on, are useful for finishing small parts since repeated handling of the parts while slow-browning is avoided. Generally speaking, however, fast browns are less desirable as a finish, since they are less durable and do not always provide as good a color on some alloys as rust brown. I have found that the best color with fast browns is usually obtained when a part is polished; using such a brown on a part with a foundry sandblasted finish can result in a greenish-gray. For best results, parts which have been fast-browned should be left to rust for six or eight hours; this improves surface texture, color, and durability. With a damp box, the parts can be left as little as four hours, but it's best to have the parts directly under the upper-chamber light bulb to prevent any condensation around the powerful browning salts present on the metal.

The standard fast brown of the industry is Birchwood Casey's "Plum Brown," an excellent product which has been around for years. You may rely on their instructions for good results in most cases, with the addition of the extra rusting mentioned above. Avoid excessive heat when using this brown, or you will have a surface buildup of a foamy, yellowish oxide. This, however, is easily removed with a clean swab and more solution, and it must be removed before parts are put into the damp box, if you do decide to "age" the brown.

For those who would like to mix their own, the following formula will give the same results and color as Plum Brown, and it may be used exactly the same way:

Fast Brown

600 gr. Potassium nitrate
400 gr. Bichloride of mercury
500 gr. Potassium chlorate

150 gr. Ferric chloride
150 gr. Sodium nitrate
80 gr. Cupric chloride
900 CC Distilled water

Heat this solution to 140 degrees F., stirring slowly, and let it cool to room temperature. The formula I have calls for the addition of 90 CC of the same ethyl nitrite solution (after cooling) mentioned in the Ordnance formula, but if this isn't easily obtainable, then I believe you can substitute ethyl alcohol in the same quantity with equal results. Also, I don't believe the cupric chloride is particularly needed. This chemical, known as "blue vitriol" in the old days, usually serves as nothing more than a stain. This is needed in a slow-rust solution so that you can see where you've applied solution to bare metal, but I doubt its importance in a fast brown formula. Both this formula and Casey's contain mercury, so avoid both the fumes *and* dust from carding parts. I should mention at this point that making up your own finish solutions is no longer exactly inexpensive, since some of the ingredients have become dear. Check with a drugstore that has been in business for quite some while, and you'll likely find what you need.

Rust Blue

Certainly the finest finish available for fine custom sporting guns, the rust blue, though a little time-consuming, is one of the easiest finishes to use. It is also an appropriate finish on some muzzleloaders of the mid 19th Century and later. I have here in my office a fine little offhand percussion slug rifle by Joseph Tonks of Boston, sporting a beautiful rust-blued barrel.

As I mentioned, virtually every old browning solution will also blue, though some are more efficient than others. I have found that the 1841 Ordnance formula works well, though it should be diluted 15 percent or so with distilled water. An old standby was the simple formula used by A.O. Niedner's shop:

Niedner's Rust Blue
2.5 fl. oz. Nitric acid
2 fl. oz. Hydrochloric acid
1 oz. Nails (clean)
30 fl. oz. Distilled water

To concoct this very strong solution, mix the acids slowly in a stoneware or heavy glass container, preferably outdoors, and add the nails, allowing them to dissolve. The acid solution may then be added *slowly* to the water.

Niedner's formula also works quite well as a rust brown, though for either browning or bluing it seems a little more sensitive to humidity changes than the 1841 Ordnance formula. Proceed with rust bluing just as you do with browning, including degreasing as mentioned before, and be certain that you have a good uniform coat of varnish sealer in bores,

chambers, or other action parts to prevent rusting after boiling. The varnish will hold up nicely in boiling water after it has hardened, but don't expect it to stay on the metal if you dunk the parts in a cleaner such as Brownell's efficient Dicro-Clean! I prefer to use the toluol/methanol method of degreasing, though you must take more care to remove oil from screw holes and "hidden" areas.

When rust bluing, parts are best left in the damp box for no more than three to four hours at a time. . .never overnight. After a rusting session, pop the parts into boiling water for three or four minutes, shake off the excess water, and let them dry. The water must be clear of minerals to avoid a spotted finish, so you must use either distilled water, or, as Jerry Fisher does, rainwater. I have also found that condensate water from an air conditioning system works equally well, but of course it's only available in the summer. If you catch rainwater from your roof, let it rain long enough for dust to be washed away before you put out your barrel.

The boiling apparatus need be nothing more elaborate than a 16-gauge sheet-iron box with the corners welded up, eight inches wide and eight inches high. My box is 45 inches long for muzzleloading use, but a much shorter one can be made for breechloaders. I boil the water on an old range top, with the tank sitting across the two largest burners. A gas burner is much quicker, but not really needed unless you do a volume of rust bluing.

After boiling, parts must be carded, and it's best done with a motor-driven wire brush with .004 wire diameter, as mentioned before. The parts should be carded heavily to remove all traces of ferrous oxide; try to card long parts such as barrelled actions parallel to the part, since cross-carding will show in the blue. Areas inaccessible to the wire brush, such as the inside of a trigger guard, can be carded with 00 steel wool, but you'd best rub *hard*. A good blue can be obtained with no more than five or six applications, boiling, and cardings, but if you like a heavy buildup, as many as eight or ten applications can be used. Preliminary testing with Schrieber's brown mentioned above indicates that it will deposit an excellent fine-grained blue on 4140 steel in four applications, though again further applications are needed for those who like a heavy matte finish. I prefer a fine-grained rust blue since it can be used over engraving without obliterating detail, and it can be used more easily to duplicate old factory finishes, which are usually fine-grained. In any event, use Schrieber's product just as you would Niedner's blue or the 1841 formula.

After the final boiling and carding, rust blue only needs oiling, and it's ready to give you twice the service of a polished caustic blue.

Fast Blue

Fast blue relates to rust blue just as fast brown does to a rust brown, and, as a matter of fact, I suspect that any of the formulas which will brown hot metal will also blue the same metal. I do know that Plum Brown works as an excellent fast blue, using the process described below. Like fast browns, fast blues are not as durable as slow-rust oxides, since the coating is much thinner and the chemical bond with the metal not as strong. However, the appearance is exactly like a fine-grained rust blue. The old standby formula is Clyde Baker's, if you wish to mix your own:

Baker's Express Blue
1/4 oz. Sodium nitrate
1/4 oz. Potassium nitrate
1/2 oz. Bichloride of mercury
1/2 oz. Potassium chlorate
10 fl. oz. Distilled water

This makes a small quantity of blue. Mix the dry ingredients, but do not grind! Potassium chlorate is highly unstable and can detonate under friction. Pour the chemicals into warm water, stir, and let cool. Baker called for the addition of 1/2 oz. of ethyl nitrite, but it's not necessary.

In using the fast blues, parts are simply put into your stove-top tank and boiled vigorously, after of course appropriate degreasing and bore protection. The use of varnish sealer as a bore protecter here is a boon, for if you use plugs in the barrel, trapped air will expand and may cause the plugs to leak.

A small jar of bluing solution is also put into the tank of boiling water (distilled or rainwater), preferably hung on a wire, and allowed to come up to tank temperature. Bluing is carried out by simply pulling out the parts, shaking off the water, swabbing on the blue in fast, long strokes, and returning the parts to the tank for a couple of minutes. They are then removed, shaken off, and carded just as with rust bluing. As with fast browning, the metal must be hot enough for the solution to dry on the metal instantly, or you will get no blue. I find it an advantage to light a propane blowtorch and set it next to the tank of boiling water. I remove a part, give it a couple of slow passes with the torch, then swab on the solution. This is a virtual necessity for small parts, and it helps with larger parts as well.

Four to six applications of Plum Brown or Baker's formula will produce an excellent blue, needing only oiling after the final carding. An entire rifle can be blued in not much more than two hours this way, but I'm not too fond of standing around with my snout in a cloud of steam, so I much prefer rust blue. Harry Pope liked the fast process, though I don't know what formula he used. He did manage to ruin an eye when a tiny bit of

373

solution boiled up and spat out of the jar in the tank, so take care with this stuff.

With both rust blues and fast blues, some alloys and some casehardened surfaces resist taking a good finish easily. When casehardening is present, it's a good idea to put all the parts in boiling water, remove them, and swab them with a 5 percent solution of nitric acid. Boil the parts again briefly, and if they are to be rust blued, let them cool. Proceed with them hot if you are using fast blue. In any event, this very mild etch will lightly frost the surface and give the oxides a "foot."

Temper Blue

As I mentioned before, heat-induced oxides were the primary source of blue for firearms much before the 1800's. A temper blue can be very durable if means can be found to "soak" the part at the temperature at which deep blue occurs. A heating medium is a virtual necessity for this, since heating in an open flame results in a "flash" color that has little surface depth.

Temper blues can be used for large parts such as barrels and actions, if the alloys used have been heat-treated at a temperature *higher* than 600 degrees. Winchester formerly temper-blued the nickle-steel receivers of lever-action rifles, obtaining such a depth of oxide that when it comes off it "flakes" almost like plating, resulting in the familiar appearance of many pre-war Winchester receivers with the finish partially gone. Barrels may also be temper-blued, as I mentioned earlier, but if a heating medium is used a barrel should be heated to 400 degrees or so with a torch before plunging it into the heat bath to avoid possible warpage.

In modern parlance, temper bluing is most convenient for small parts such as screws. "Fire" blued screws showing on a set of silvered, casehardened shotgun sidelocks are the height of London elegance. Needless to say, any part that is to be temper blued should receive a brilliant polish for best effect and color.

Molten lead and other agents can be used to provide a uniform temper blue on parts, but the most convenient agent I have found is common potassium nitrate, which melts at approximately 640 degrees Fahrenheit. Winchester used this chemical for heat bluing in the 19th and early 20th Centuries; a description of its use, written out in a fine Spencerian hand, may be found in Madis' *The Winchester Book*, entitled "Oxidation of Steel and Iron by Nitre." The fellows at Winchester added a bit of peroxide of manganese (a tenth to a twentieth in weight of the amount of nitre used). I don't know what the purpose of the manganese was, and haven't tried it, but I suspect that it may lower the melting point of the potassium nitrate.

When nitre is melted, it's clear as water, and you can simply suspend the polished and degreased part in the stuff on wires, pulling it out when the desired color is reached. Boil the parts afterwards in water to remove the nitre, but take care not to allow even the smallest drop of water to fall into molten nitre, or you will be spattered and burned.

For melting the nitre, I use a smallish 1/8-inch sheet steel box long enough to accept a longrifle guard (about 11 inches) and about four inches wide. Six pounds of nitre is enough to do most work in this box, and I have a lid for the box for use while melting the chemical. It likes to "erupt" through the hard "shell" on top when the bottom has melted, so a lid is advisable.

Different alloys have different temper-color characteristics. Mild steel is the easiest to blue, and can almost be dropped in the tank and left there, while tool and spring steel must be watched closely and pulled out when they near the right color.

Caustic Blue

We come now to the use of that evil stuff which requires all manner of tanks, burners, and alchemic wizardry. . .hot caustic blue. I have no intention of going into this process; it's covered well enough in various books. What I'd like to discuss is the *preparation* of metal that will cause caustic blue to have much the same appearance, if not the durability, of rust blue. Several years ago some custom gunsmiths began experimenting with glass-beading on custom rifles. I don't know who first tried this, but I first saw it on one of Clayton Nelson's fine rifles. Thinking I was looking at a first-class rust-blue, I inquired about the formula, and Clayton just laughed and said that I was looking at a caustic blue over a glass-beaded surface.

Many of the caustic blues that are virtually black to the eye seem to magically become a "true blue" when applied to a beaded finish. I suspect the reason for this is that the minute surface pitting caused by the tiny glass beads shot against the metal at high pressure causes light rays to be reflected off the surface differently, causing the oxide to appear more blue than on a highly polished surface. This may well be the reason also why rust blue is "bluer," since a matte finish is present. In any event, the beaded finish is a timely solution to the gunsmith who wants to reduce finishing work to a minimum, yet produce a finish that has the right color, durability, and luster so desired. . .much in contrast to the space-age glitter of mirror polish, which to some of us is abominable. Beading reduces polishing time to almost zero, and it will remove old finishes and minor scratches.

Joe Balickie has been using this finish exclusively for several years, and I called him a while back for full details. Joe uses equipment at a firm near his shop, Potters Industries, Inc. (Southeast Division, Box 298, Apex, North Carolina 27502). Potters is a large firm specializing in industrial metal finishes, and they apparently were pioneers in the manufacture of glass beads. Joe tells me that Potters is willing to carry out bead blasting for gunsmiths at *very* reasonable rates; contact Frank L. Dray, Potters' regional sales manager, at the address above.

Very briefly, glass-beading provides an excellent surface finish for firearms due to the fact that spherical beads can be regulated through particle size and intensity of application to provide any finish from a bright satin to a deep matte. Other materials used for "blasted" surfaces, such as sand, have angular particles that impart a less-bright surface, even when particle size is small, and angular particles have a tendency to remove pieces of a surface, which beading does not. In other words, areas that have critical tolerances won't be hurt by beading. Further, the beads leave no imbedded particles in metal, and they may be recycled repeatedly. Bead particles range in size from 990,000 to the pound to 864,000,000 to the pound, and are fired on a surface through a compressor-fed "gun" just as sandblasting is done. The operation is carried out in a fully enclosed booth; Joe uses Potters' size AD beads for his work, which I suspect is a medium mesh size. Beads are aimed at the surface at an angle of 45-60 degrees for optimum results.

Since glass beading is fast and inexpensive, and since it makes the use of caustic blue the visual equal of slower, more traditional finishes, it seems to me an ideal production method for manufacturers as well. Certainly, the same effect could be obtained with a 5 percent etch of nitric or muriatic acid, but a great deal more trouble would have to be taken masking areas where this surface finish wouldn't be wanted. Also, acid removes surface, rather than peening it as glass beads do. Beads would be more easily controlled, especially on a critical surface, such as where engraving might be present. In any event, beading, along with the use of caustic blue, seems to be the only really satisfactory firearms finish where speed is a necessity, and it's one of the *few* instances where increased speed and lower cost don't result in a lesser finished product.

There you have it. . .a simplified discussion of six primary finishes useful to the custom gunsmith. With these, I see no real reason to seek other processes. None of these call for strange incantations or medieval witchery to make them work, and they all give a finished surface consistent with what should be considered appropriate on the very finest of guns, custom-made or otherwise. Some of these certainly involve a little more work, but that time spent is more than justified. As for myself, I'd very much like to see more gunsmiths and arms manufacturers making use of these tried finishes. . .and, if they did, perhaps those mirror-finish blues and white-line spacers would sink back into whatever Gehenna they lay in two decades ago, back when guns looked like *guns*. ●

M1 CONVERSIONS

By R. C. SCHUETZ

*B*ACK IN THE EARLY SIXTIES, while sitting at the workbench in my gunshop, I glanced up at the gun rack and sitting alongside my other varmint rifles were two M1 Carbines. The only purpose they had served was to shoot holes in tin cans--but there were several other small caliber rifles that were cheaper to shoot and ventilated tin cans just as well as my carbines. As I took one of them out of the rack, I thought what great sport it would be to hunt fox with such a lightweight rifle, while trudging through three foot deep snow. At that time my gunshop was located in the Midwest and fox were plentiful; our weekends were spent trying to corner the wary little red-haired varmints.

That is when I decided to experiment seriously with the M1 Carbine. In the first conversion I tried, I altered a set of .218 Mashburn Bee chambering reamers so the dimensions would work out with the .30 Carbine case. Then I made up a set of reamers to make a set of dies for the rifle and found that the .30 Carbine case could be necked down in one operation.

The first weekend I used it hunting fox, it was a big success, and everyone that had seen it in action was excited about it. With all that encouragement, it wasn't long before I decided to convert the carbine into a completely sporterized rifle. Since then I have reworked the little rifles in many different ways and converted them to handle several cartridges. There's a lot of interest in doing such conversions, so Editor Neal Knox asked me to explain in detail some of these methods, and the cartridges that we have converted the carbine to.

First of all, if you would like to leave your carbine in its original shape and also use the original barrel, it is possible to rebore the barrel to either .357 Magnum or .41 Magnum. The carbine barrel has enough metal in the outside diameter to be rebored to these calibers successfully for the smallest diameter of the barrel is .600-inch and there is sufficient metal remaining for reboring and re-rifling. We have also found that the .41 Magnum and .357 Magnum operate at the proper pressures so the carbine will operate semiautomatically without problems, though the gas port must be opened up to .085 to bleed the right amount of gas.

In chambering for these two calibers, a ring is added to the chamber, which headspaces the cartridge from the headspace ring to the bolt face. We must also open up the bolt face to the proper diameter to accept .357 Magnum or .41 Magnum cartridges. Half of the outer rim of the bolt face is removed so that it will accept the headspace ring on the barrel. The bottom half of the bolt face is left to strip cartridges from the magazine. This also holds the cartridge forward until it is chambered, so it will not hang up on the spring-loaded ejector.

In most cases, the cartridge feeding

Boring out the carbine barrel to accept a larger rimmed case requires opening the bolt face, leaving the lower edge to strip fresh cartridges from a commercial magazine. Note that the barrel extension lip has been retained to allow the bolt to turn on steel, rather than upon the soft case.

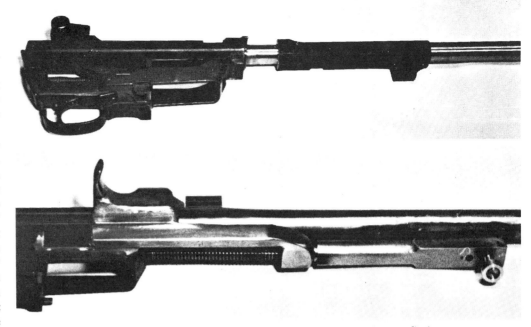

amp has to be rounded off slightly to ensure smooth feeding. When using a rimmed cartridge, the original magazine cannot be used. We use a new 5 shot clip, which can be purchased from one of the companies which manufacture commercial carbines. In the .357 Magnum conversion .38 Special rounds feed well, but pressures are not high enough to operate the rifle as a semiautomatic. We have found that ammunition which is loaded for police departments will work well in the .357 Magnum conversion. One of the largest police departments in the country has been interested in using our .357 Magnum conversion. We worked with them for some time, and they ran approximately 10,000 rounds through it without any problems. However, we have come across a few carbines that have a defect in the receiver threads for the barrel. These will cause some problems when firing, for the bolt will bind due to improper alignment of the bolt and barrel.

When leaving your carbine in its original state and converting it to a smaller caliber than .30, we first cut off the original barrel just in front of the gas piston housing. From there back we bore it out to .610. We then take a new barrel for either .17-30 Carbine or .22-30 Carbine and turn it down to .610 from the thread extension foward. We usually find that customers prefer to have the barrel from 20 to 22 inches in length rather than the original 18-inch barrel. The rifle seems to handle better and balance better with the additional barrel length.

Now that we have turned the new barrel to .610, we can slip the piston

The author's full-scale conversion has the new gas system, allowing no gaps between wood and barrel, tang streamlined and permanently affixed to the receiver, and rear sight dovetail ground off, resulting in a lightweight, streamlined, short-to-medium-range varmint rifle.

When installing a smaller-bore barrel, top, the old gas system sleeve is reamed out to fit the new barrel and sweated into place, but the action and gas system remains essentially unchanged. In an all-out conversion, the author uses his own gas system design, in which the gas works directly upon a piston on a modified operating slide. Size of the bleed-off hole varies according to the cartridge used and the mass of the modified slide.

and operating guide portion of the original barrel on it, and sweat it into place. I have found that it is easier to thread and chamber the new barrel and leave a 1/8-inch thick shoulder to butt up against the front of the receiver before sweating on the old portion of the barrel. If you do it this way, you can install the new barrel in the receiver, and then line up your gas piston and sweat it into place.

Our .22-30 carbine cartridge operates between 40,000 and 45,000 pounds per square inch pressure. We load it with 13 grains of 4227 powder and use a 45-grain .224 bullet. Muzzle velocity is 2,950 feet per second. The weakest portion of the carbine is the bolt. If loaded to over 45,000 psi, you will crack the right locking lug on the bolt. There is always someone that will try to get just a little more velocity out of this little cartridge, and the gun simply will not stand it.

There are a number of things that can be done to the carbine to increase its accuracy. Most of the carbines that I have worked on are very loose fitting in critical areas, such as barrel tension and how securely the action is fastened in the stock. The way the carbine was designed is practical for what it was built for; it can be easily stripped down in the field for cleaning purposes with a limited amount of tools. But we have found that by permanently attaching the rear tang or recoil plate to the back of the action we increase accuracy. The recoil plate normally stays in the stock when the barrel and receiver group are removed. To also help increase the accuracy, you must glassbed the rear tang and the portion of the barrel that is held secure with the barrel band.

Another way to improve the all-around shooting of your carbine when handloading is to make sure of proper headspacing. When using the original .30 carbine cartridges,

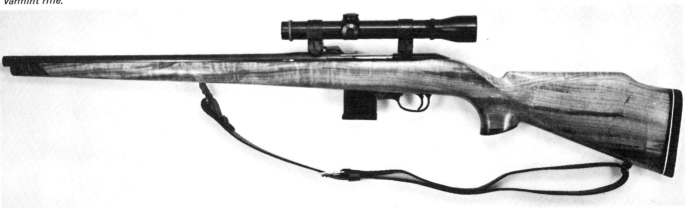

headspacing is from the bolt face to the end of the cartridge case. This is very critical because the locking lugs on the bolt and the locking lug recesses in the action are at a 90 degree angle with the bore. The bolt comes up into line with the lug recesses and locks straight down. There is no camming action when the bolt closes behind the cartridge. Therefore, cases must be full-length resized. But when trimming your cartridge cases during handloading, it is very easy to trim off too much. When we chamber for a shouldered bottleneck cartridge great care must be taken in headspacing.

For the person who wants to completely sporterize his carbine, the following conversion should fit the bill. This conversion eliminates all the military features of the carbine and looks similar to the Model 100 Winchester when it is completed.

The most important part of the completely sporterized carbine is the new gas-operating mechanism, which was designed to operate efficiently with many different cartridges. The original mechanism uses a short gas piston system which starts the operating slide to the rear with a 3/8-inch push—inertia carries it through its bolt-unlocking and extraction operation.

The new operating slide is gas-operated, and the piston seals the gas in the gas piston tube for one inch, and from there back it gradually releases the gas. We experimented with a number of mechanisms for strength and weight, combined with the proper amount of gas bled from the barrel, to operate the rifle efficiently. With this new operating slide and gas mechanism we are able to eliminate most of the military aspects of the carbine.

The main work that has to be done on the action is to remove half of the old operating slide spring housing. By doing this, we make room for the new operating slide, which fits alongside the action and is hidden within the stock. We then remove the lip on the front receiver ring, which is used to hold the upper handguard in place. With the Sporter Carbine the upper handguard is not used. We also attach the rear tang or recoil plate permanently to the rear of the action, as explained earlier, to improve the accuracy of the rifle. We

cut off the long narrow part of the tang, where the tang screw anchors it to the stock, then round off the tang. On the bottom of the tang we drill a new hole for a 10/32 screw. The new screw is put in from the bottom of the stock, just to the rear of the trigger guard. This anchors the action securely and dresses up the appearance of the rifle.

The next step is to thread and chamber a new barrel to be fitted to the action. The new barrel should be turned to .900-inch on the shoulder just ahead of the threads for 1½ inches. The remainder of the barrel is turned to a sporter contour. To get this contour we drop from .900 to .750 over about 2½ inches, then taper out to .600 at the muzzle. These dimensions work out well in either a 20 or a 22-inch barrel.

It is important when threading and fitting the barrel to the action that the half moon barrel extension be put on the new barrel. This extension is a bolt guide, which helps support the bolt when it is being opened under pressure. I have seen some of the original carbines without this barrel extension on them, and without it the bolt must rotate on the cartridge head when operating during firing. This will sometimes disfigure the cartridge case head, or cause the rifle to open hard and not complete its full operation when fired.

We are now ready to install the gas piston housing on the bottom of the barrel. The barrel and receiver group are put into a fixture, and a surface grinder is used to grind a 1½-inch flat on the bottom of the barrel, to which we silver solder the gas piston housing. The gas piston housing is left long enough that the ½-inch forward portion may be drilled and tapped for a 10/32 inch screw, which is used for the front anchor screw to fasten it in the stock. The gas piston is part of the new operating slide and is hollow to accept the operating spring and guide. The operating spring now butts up against the front of the stud on the bottom of the receiver ring, which is used to pin the trigger mechanism to the action. A small hole is drilled in the front of this stud with a number 21 drill to hold the operating spring guide in place.

On our Sporter conversion, we can either install open sights or scope mounts. I prefer the Williams Guide

Sight for the rear sight, or a Williams peep sight made up special to fit in the original carbine dovetail on the receiver. If a scope is preferred, we remove the original sight dovetail on the rear of the receiver and contour it so it will fit a No. 45 Weaver scope mount base. The barrel shoulder just ahead of the receiver ring, which has been turned to .900, works out well for mounting the No. 11 Weaver scope mount base.

When mounting a scope on a carbine, there have been some problems in getting the fired cartridge to clear the scope during ejection. We have found that by altering the nose of the spring-loaded ejector we can effectively change the direction of the cartridge enough to clear the scope. Our sporter stocks also have a high comb, so high scope mount rings can be used, which also gives a little more clearance for the ejected cartridge case.

The sporter stocks that we use are made up for us by Crane Creek Stock Company, Waseca, Minnesota. These particular stocks are stabilized, or special treated in an effort to eliminate warping which will affect the accuracy of the rifle. After we have fitted the barrel and receiver group to the stock there are no holes or gaps between the barrel and the stock, as there is in the original carbine. In order to remove the barrel and action from the stock, the operating rod must be pulled to the rear. By anchoring the barrel and action into the stock at the fore-end with a screw, it is possible to put a nice fore-end tip of contrasting wood, which adds a special touch to the appearance of the rifle.

When these little rifles are completed they usually do not weigh any more than 6½ pounds with scopes on them. Most automatic rifles are in the .243 class and above, and weigh about 8½ pounds, and the next step down in automatics are .22 rimfires. This rifle will fill the gap between the two.

For many years I have worked on all different types and styles of rifles, each having a special purpose in the shooting field—and I have found that the little carbine has its place among sporting guns. A useful conversion of the M1 can provide the hunter with many thrilling moments in the field with an effective, lightweight, low-recoil 100 to 200-yard varmint rifle. ●

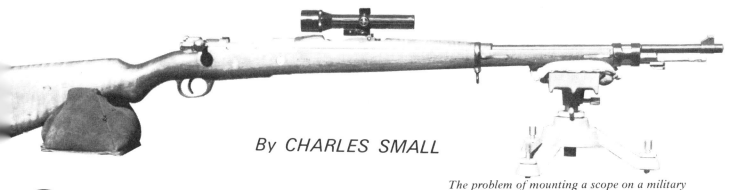

By CHARLES SMALL

The problem of mounting a scope on a military rifle without altering it can be solved by using a long eye-relief scope such as the Bushnell Phantom in a mount which attaches to the rifle's rear sight base. This fine 1909 Argentine Mauser can be tested for accuracy, or even used for hunting, with the aid of the Phantom scope, yet can be quickly restored to its original condition.

Simple Scope Mounts for 'Collector' Military Rifles

Pivot pin milled integral with sight leaf.

Under half of pivot bearing is milled away to provide "under and up" retention of leaf pivot pin.

Sight leaf spring usually inside and part of the base; forward end applies strong upward pressure.

Sight base lug on some Mausers— such as the 1909 Argentine.

DJL 1976

This drawing illustrates the typical Mauser rear sight base. The leaf's pivot pin is milled integral with the leaf — it does not have to be drilled out — the leaf presses down and out from under the lips of the base. Types that have a separate pin which extends through the base bearings may also be encountered. This is easily driven out, followed by the down-and-out removal of the leaf. Some bases also have the rear lug shown — the leaf slider slips under this lug at minimum sight setting.

I HAVE BEEN collecting old bolt action military rifles for quite some time. Not only do they show the development of firearms in various countries, but I also like to shoot them. And keeping within the limits of modern smokeless powder, I always try to duplicate the original loads.

I have been lucky, for only twice did I obtain *unshootable* rifles. I have a beautiful Spanish 1893 Mauser with enough headspace for your whole thumb, and a Siamese Mauser with an oversized chamber near the neck.

The main problem in shooting all of my rifles with any degree of accuracy has been the atrocious military sights. Atrocious because they usually have a tiny V notch in the rear sight and an inverted V for the front. This makes it difficult for me to get a consistent sight picture — and it wouldn't be much better if I had 20-20 vision.

Some idea of what was considered acceptable accuracy for these rifles can be gained by inspecting the Mauser test targets shown in Stoeger's reprint of a between-the-wars Mauser sporting rifle catalog. If you average the spreads for their range of calibers at 100 yards, you find that there is 3 3/4 inches vertical and 2 1/4 inches horizontal dispersion. I think it is significant that the vertical dispersion figure is the largest. Certainly with V notch sights and the inverted V front sight, consistent vertical alignment is difficult.

To really determine what the old soldiers would do, it was necessary to figure a way to mount scopes. I considered unacceptable the conventional solution of bending the bolt handle,

1909 ARGENTINE MAUSER

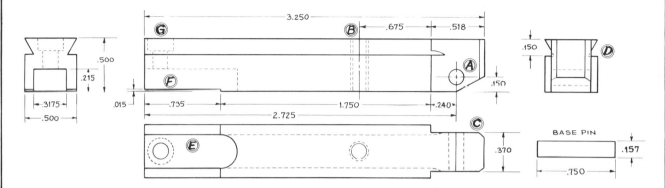

SEQUENCE OF MACHINE OPERATIONS:

A. Drill #22 [.1570] hole; the base pin goes into this hole, retaining scope adaptor to barrel-base through the old sight-leaf pivot bearings. Base pin **is** .157 x .750 steel pin — 5/32" [.1562] can be used.

B. Drill and tap for #8 screw to serve as recoil stop. Use fillister head or socket-head cap screw with head projecting as the "stop." Front transverse screw of Bushnell Universal Mount butts against this. [Stop screw does not project below base.]

C. Mill front tongue of adaptor.
D. Mill 60° grooves for Bushnell Mount.
E. Mill rear slot in adaptor to clear rear lug of the Mauser barrel base.
F. Mill bottom rear clearance [.015] for Mauser barrel base.
G. Mount adaptor to barrel base; locate hole position for #6 screw, drill and countersink adaptor. Drill and tap rear lug of the barrel base to accept the hold-down screw.

At right is the scope base on the 1909 Argentine Mauser. With perhaps a few variations in dimensions, or differences in shape, this type of base will work on other Mauser rifles. Note the forward position of the socket-head cap screw serving as a recoil stop.

installing a new safety and drilling and tapping the receiver. If you go this far, you might as well saw off the long barrel, recrown the muzzle and fit a new stock. You end up spending $150 on a $24.95 rifle, which does not make much sense. The worst part is that the rifle no longer has its original form and shape.

Among the *junk* I have collected are three new rifles — a Chilean 1895 Mauser, an Argentine 1909 Mauser and a 1958 Madsen .30-06. It would be sacrilege to drill holes in these polished receivers and blot out the perfectly formed national crests.

The problem was to mount a scope without permanent alterations and to be able to restore the rifle to its original form with ease.

Solutions often come in a backhanded way. I had acquired four Siamese

Mausers. Two were converted to .45-70's and from this operation, I had two spare barrels. One original rifle had a defective chamber and a chewed-up rear sight; it had the full Siamese markings and I decided to keep it as a decorator. The last one had all of the Siamese markings ground off, but was in perfect mechanical condition.

To put the decorator in good visual condition, I decided to remove the sight leaf from one of the spare barrels and install it on this rifle. The problem was how to remove the leaf. Several gunsmiths told me I'd have to drill out the pin. This I found hard to believe, for most military rifles are easy to disassemble. Then one day I noticed that with considerable force the leaf could be pressed down. While pushing it back toward the receiver at the same time, it

suddenly came loose in my hand. The solution was then obvious — I could simply mount the scope base on the sight leaf.

In my first design, I took a piece of Brownell's aluminum alloy grooved sight base stock and milled the curved underside flat. This was attached to the sight leaf with three 6-48 screws. The leaf turned out to be hardened steel and it took a carbide drill to make the holes. On the Brownell base I mounted a Bushnell Magnum Phantom 1.5X scope.

Sighting-in was by the time honored system of setting the rifle up on sandbags and sighting down the bore and then adjusting the scope for the same picture. When the rifle was fired, the leaf, mount and scope tilted forward from recoil, giving the scope a nasty jar. To fix this was easy. Another 6-48 screw was installed just ahead of the rear of the

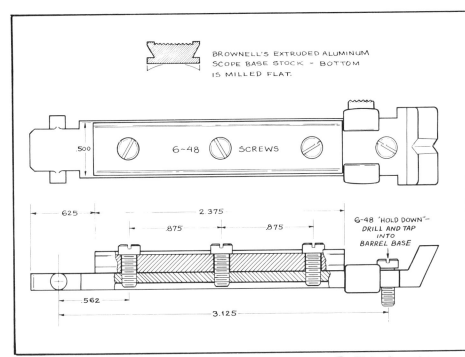

BROWNELL'S EXTRUDED ALUMINUM
SCOPE BASE STOCK – BOTTOM
IS MILLED FLAT.

6-48 SCREWS

.500

.625   2.375

.875   .875

6-48 "HOLD DOWN"–
DRILL AND TAP
INTO
BARREL BASE

.562

3.125

SIAMESE MAUSER

On the Siamese Mauser the sight leaf of the rifle is used for scope mounting, simply attaching the sight base stock to the leaf [which may have to be annealed for drilling and tapping]. This is another typical Mauser sight style. If the original leaf is too nice to treat in this manner, a duplicate may be used in its place. The photo below shows this base fastened on the sight leaf; a 2.5X Bushnell scope is in place.

slider and into the base of the mount. This screw not only served to anchor the leaf, but it also acted as a coarse elevation adjustment.

The next time on the range my 1903 Tokyo Arsenal veteran with the original load equivalent produced 2 3/4-inch groups on the first try, which is not bad considering no attempt was made to check the original bedding, and the bore was far from mint condition. Further, 1.5X is almost no magnification. This test proved that the old rifles were a lot better than their sighting equipment.

If you do not mind putting several holes in military sight leaves, this method is quick and easy. Incidentally, the 6-48 screws were not countersunk. The screw heads above the surface of the Brownell mount contact the lower compression screws of the Bushnell Universal Mount and act as recoil lugs.

With another Siamese Mauser in stock which would serve as the unaltered museum piece, I put a $29.95 Royal Arms semi-finished stock on the scoped Siamese and for good measure bedded the barrel in Devcon. I have not had this rifle on the range as yet, but it should do better than 2 3/4-inch groups.

The Brownell base would not do for my new shiny Chilean and the Argentine rifles because I had only the original sight leaves and did not want to punch holes in them. This would destroy their value on the collectors' market. The solution was easy to devise; simply make a new combined sight leaf and scope base and save the originals.

One evening I milled out of a 1/2 x 5/8-inch aluminum bar the replacement

sight leaf/scope base. This time I mounted the 2.5X version of the Bushnell Magnum Phantom scope. I checked the bedding and adjusted the tension on the guard screws and refitted the front band.

With new cases neck reamed and loaded with the Lee tools and powder charges individually weighed and concentricity checked with a B-Square spinner, I was ready for the range. The average of 10 three-shot groups at 100 yards was 1 1/4 inches with the best group at 7/8-inch.

For good measure, having made an aluminum prototype, I made another from 1/2-inch square tool steel and polished it so that it would be in keeping with the smart appearance of the rifle. Actually I see no reason why aluminum, which is easier to work, is not perfectly satisfactory.

Each of the Mauser variants has a

slightly different rear sight base. The Argentine varies from the Siamese in that there is a post with a lip at the receiver end. This lip fits into a slot on the slider and anchors the leaf in the retracted position. The anchor/elevation 6-48 screw hole is in the center of this post. This does not bother me since the hole is covered when the original sight leaf is in place. Its presence requires two extra milling operations.

Making a new combined sight leaf and scope base will work for most of the military rifles, including the Madsen, except those with aperture sights on the receiver bridge. There is no problem with the GEW 88, the two Kropatschek versions, the Schmidt-Rubin, the Arisaka and the various Mausers.

The mechanical arrangement on the sight of the Schmidt-Rubin Model 1911 7.5mm caliber straight pull is quite different from the Mauser's. The spring

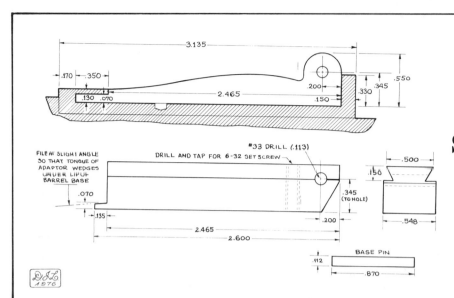

1911
SCHMIDT-RUBIN

The 1911 Schmidt-Rubin requires a base such as the one shown here. Note that this is the 1911 rifle; other Schmidt-Rubin models require different bases.

which presses against the leaf is held in place by a slot in the rear of the mount, plus a dimple in the spring and a corresponding depression in the mount. By using this slot, it is possible to make a replacement sight leaf/scope mount without drilling any holes in the rifle's mount.

This is accomplished by providing a tapered tongue at the rear which is a drive fit in the opening. A 45-degree cut at the front gives the necessary clearance for the tongue to be inserted; then the front of the mount is pushed down for a tight fit against the inside of the front of the rifle's sight base. As a double check, an Allen socket head setscrew was installed near the pin to force the base up tight against the pin.

The coarse elevation adjustment screw on the Mauser units has been eliminated since the mount is held in the vertical plane by the tongue and the pin. It is held in the horizontal plane by being the same width as the inside of the mount.

This Schmidt-Rubin mount was milled from a bar of a hard aluminum alloy whose composition is unknown — it came from my favorite raw material supplier, the local scrap dealer. Either this type of aluminum alloy or steel is required for this type of mount to give adequate strength to the thin tongue.

Using handloads in the 7.5mm, 36 grains of IMR-3031 with a 180-grain Speer round nose bullet in Norma cases, five-inch iron sight groups were reduced to less than half without any alteration to the original bedding.

For the GEW 88, both Kropatscheks and the Arisaka, you do not have to drill into the mount for the anchor/elevation screw. These rifles have a filister head machine screw which holds the leaf spring

in place. If you cannot find a screw to fit, it is easy to retap this hole to fit a standard U.S. screw.

Once the principle is established, it is easy to design the replacement leaf/ mount. One version of the Kropatschek requires the bottom of the unit to be milled at an angle. The Arisaka takes a slot across the unit toward the rear. On the Madsen, it is possible to retain the windage adjustment of the original sight but this requires a slotted hole for the anchor/elevation screw in the replacement leaf/mount.

Machining, using a milling machine or a milling attachment on a 6-inch lathe, is the elegant way of producing these devices. With aluminum bar, a careful workman can produce a satisfactory product with just a few files.

The only rifle in my possession which

defies a solution is the Vetterli-Vitale which has the most awful sight of them all. I once blamed this on Colonel Vitale, but when I saw an original Vetterli with this same abortion, I knew that for once the reliable Swiss had slipped.

I have the original test target for the Argentine Mauser and it's in agreement with the test targets in the old Mauser catalog. If you will attach a Brownell base to the original sight leaf or hack a new one out of aluminum or steel, I am sure you will be pleasantly surprised.

Really, I should not have been too surprised, for the Mauser boys and their successors were not known for shoddy workmanship. They were engineers, not shooters, and evidently did not worry much about the sights as long as they were well made. ●

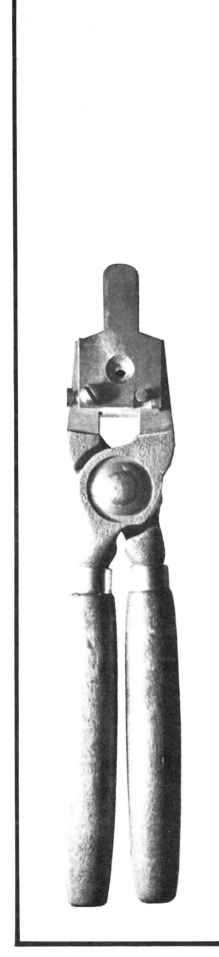

Need bullets for a single-shot;
or want to try a design of your own?
Here's how!

Making a
Bullet Mould

By HENRY BEVERAGE

F I HADN'T BOUGHT the mongrel Pope in the early part of 1964 I probably would never have made a bullet mould. The Pope was a fairly good rifle although not a piece an advanced collector would have cherished. It had a .32-40 Stevens-Pope barrel with an excellent bore, original false muzzle, finely checkered Stevens forearm and a bullet-starter that was too large. The barrel had been fitted to a Winchester Hi-Wall Schuetzen action and buttstock.

There was no bullet mould and none to be had from any of the sources I knew about at that time. So I sought help from my friend, Dewey Bryant. Dewey is one of those old-time, all-around machinists who can make about anything if they have the equipment. A black powder shooter, he had made his own rifles for more than 40 years. And I knew he had made bullet moulds — round ball, slug gun and a few for single shot rifles. So I asked him to make a mould for the Pope. His ans-

was what I should have expected, "Why don't you do it?"

So that's how it all started. Two months and three moulds later, after following Dewey's advice and know-how, I had a 200-grain bullet that would shoot 1-inch groups on the somewhat rare occasions when the Pope and I were fuctioning at top efficiency.

I learned that there is nothing very complicated about the making of a bullet mould. All that's required is a knowledge of what is wanted, some painstaking workmanship, patience and, of course, the equipment to do the essential parts of the operation. Let's see how it's done, or more specifically, how I do it.

The first requirement is a diagram of the bullet to be made. This can be simply a rough sketch showing length and diameters, not necessarily to scale since it is only for reference.

We will make a nose cut-off mould for breech-seating in a .32-40 Winches-

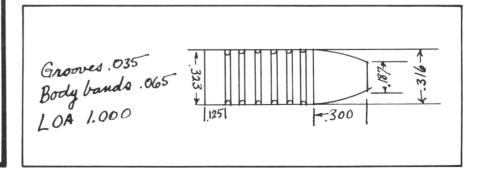

Grooves .035
Body bands .065
LOA 1.000

ter Single Shot rifle. The bore diameter is .315 and the grooves are .322. The twist of the rifling is one turn in 16 inches and experience has shown that the best accuracy can be expected with a bullet one inch long and weighing around 200 grains. We will make the base band .323 to assure a gas seal and the body bands .316 to ride lightly on the lands when seating. The narrow nose band will be .315.

A piece of half-inch drill rod is cut to four and one-half inches, the ends ground smooth and centers marked and drilled with a center drill. This is for the cherry which must be turned on centers.

The rod is turned down to .324, working as close to the dog at the headstock end as possible. The length of the bullet is now marked off. We make a few light cuts about an inch from the tail stock end to serve as a measuring point. This will be the nose of the bullet. We then measure back .875 and scribe a mark, very light, with the point of the cutter. This will allow .575 for the grease grooves and bands and .300 for the nose. The width of the base band will be .125 on a bullet one inch long. The area between the two marks is now turned down to .317. We'll get the final diameters, .323 and .316, by polishing after the grease grooves have been cut and the nose shaped.

To get the radii grooves we want, a cutter bit is ground to a .035 rounded tip. A good substitute is a 1/16-inch cut-off blade with the tip dressed down to .035. This dimension is not of vital importance although the width of the grooves determines the width of the body bands and the suggested dimension has been found to be about right for the bullet we're making.

The first groove is cut at the point where the .323 and .317 diameters coincide and is .012 deep. A good plan is to turn the lathe by hand until the .012 depth is reached then use power for a few revolutions to smooth the cut. These groove cutters are fragile things. The next groove is cut by moving the tool .100 ahead, toward the tailstock, and continuing the procedure until six grooves have been cut, equally spaced. The .012 depth is not a critical dimension, .015 is acceptable but grooves that are too deep cause extraction problems when casting.

We now have six bands and grooves on our cherry. The narrow nose band

Grease grooves are cut in the cherry with a 1/16-inch cut-off blade with the tip thinned to .035 and rounded to give radii grooves.

The photo above shows a profiled cherry in place in the milling attachment ready for cutting the six flutes. A 70-degree beveled cutter is used on the lathe.

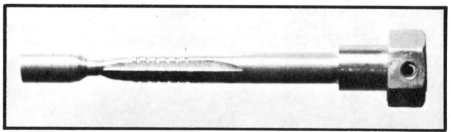

The cherry as it comes from the milling device after the flutes have been cut. The photo above shows the method of attaching the hex nut to the rod to provide six equally spaced cutting flutes.

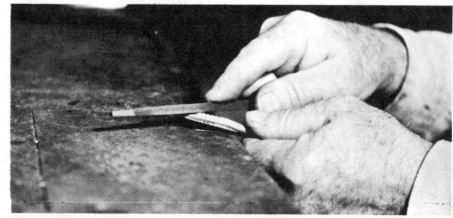

After the flutes have been milled, the cherry must be carefully de-burred and the flutes beveled with a fine-cut file, as shown.

384

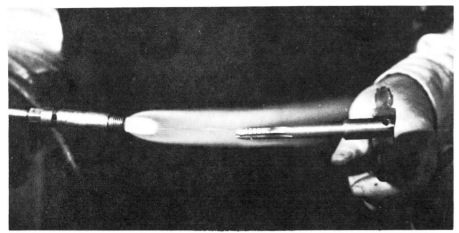

The cherry is heated for hardening using a moderate flame from an acetylene plumber's torch — always from the end. The cherry is held in a long pair of tongs to protect the holder's hand.

Slots for the handles can be cut in a milling attachment on the lathe using a 5/16-inch end mill. A better plan is to have them cut on a milling machine with a circular cutter.

After drilling the alignment pin holes with a No. 14 drill, they should be reamed without removing the blocks from the vise. This can be done with the drill press vise held on the bench or placed in a bench vise.

is provided by turning down the front end of the cherry to leave a band half the width of the body bands. We can now shape the nose.

The method I use is to turn down a short section of the rod to the diameter wanted for the nose end of the bullet. If the finished diameter is to be less than .187 the final reduction is done with the edge of a file. The ogive is roughed to shape with the cutter bit and finished by filing, using an extra-slim-taper fine-cut file and polishing with abrasive cloth. The cherry is now polished to its final size with 240-grit cloth under a flat file. No allowance has been made for shrinkage of the alloy when casting. This is because we are going to cut our mould in brass blocks which will expand slightly when heated, enough to compensate for shrinkage of the alloy. The cherry is now ready for cutting the flutes.

The normal procedure for this part of the operation would be to cut the flutes on a milling machine equipped with a dividing head, using a 60 or 70-degree circular cutter on a horizontal miller or an end mill on a vertical machine. I used this method in the beginning, or rather, I had the job done in a machine shop. But the time involved was too great for one of my impatient nature so I dreamed up a way of doing it on the lathe.

In order to get the milling attachment low enough to permit using a circular cutter I made a tray that fitted snugly over the cross-feed. The shelf to which the milling attachment is bolted sits two and one-half inches below the tool post slot. A tray was then made and bolted to the platform on the milling device after providing holes in the ends to accept a 3/4-inch hex socket and a 3/8x16 screw with one end turned to a 60-degree point. A 5/16 bolt in the center of the base provides an adjustable support for the cherry against the pressure of the cutter.

A hex nut that fits closely into the socket is drilled out to one-half inch, one of the sides tapped for a 3/16-inch Allen set screw and attached to the headstock end of the cherry in which a hole has been drilled for the set screw. The hex nut and socket provide a means of cutting six flutes, equally spaced. An 8-point socket and a square nut allows cutting eight flutes in larger diameter cherries.

The cutter, on a mandrel, is held in

a chuck and the lathe run at slow speed in the back gears. The cutting edge is positioned .005 beyond the center line of the cherry to improve the cutting action and provide a slight hook effect to the flutes. The carriage is then locked in place, the milling attachment adjusted so that a point on the cutter barely touches the cherry and the position marked on the graduated adjusting wheel. This is our starting point. Flutes are cut .050 deep taking out .010 on on each cut. Mark the stopping point. I also mark a stopping point on the cross feed bed so that the flutes will be the same length. A half-inch beyond the base band is ample.

Cutting oil is applied to the tips of the cutter. If a commercial product is not available any good lubricating oil can be substituted. (An excellent cutting oil can be made by melting some lard and diluting it half-and-half with turpentine.) The cross feed is moved slowly to avoid possible chattering and insure a smooth cut.

When the six flutes have been cut the cherry is removed, the end of the rod cut off at the nose and the flutes finished at the ends with a slim-taper file. Roughness left by the milling cutter is smoothed by honing and the flutes relieved (beveled) with a file or a tool-post grinder. I use a fine-cut file.

Relieving the flutes is a painstaking job. The utmost care must be taken not to file or grind into the cutting edges or touch one of the other flutes. A high-intensity light and a bench magnifier are helpful here. The angle of the bevel should be enough to just take out the grease grooves on the side. Burrs in the grooves are removed with a needle file, cutting edges are honed and the cherry is ready for hardening.

Here is where several hours of careful workmanship can be ruined in a few minutes through warpage from heating and quenching. The method that gives me the best results is to use water-hardening drill rod, heated to a dull cherry rod in a moderate flame from an acetylene plumber's torch and quenched *straight down* in a solution of *hot* brine. (A tablespoonful of table salt in a pint of hot tap water is my formula.)

In heating, the flame is applied to the cherry from the end, *never* directly on the sides, and the piece heated as evenly as possible. I sometimes use a furnace but I work more from color than from indicated temperature. Un-

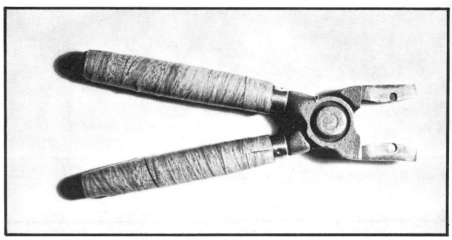

Handles modified for use with the long alignment pins. The ends must be shaped as shown to permit opening the blocks while they are being cut.

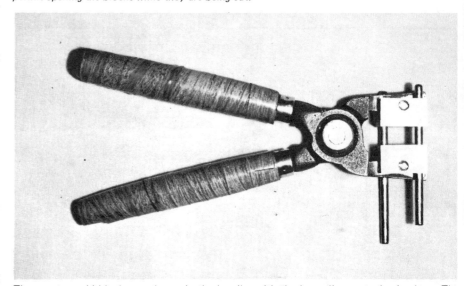

The uncut mould blocks are shown in the handles with the long alignment pins in place. The right-hand half of the blocks slides on the tapered pins assuring positive alignment when cutting the cavity.

The two halves of the blocks after the pilot hole has been drilled.

orthodox, probably, but it works. Slight warpage, if it occurs, can be taken out by honing.

After hardening, the cherry is polished bright with a cloth-backed abrasive disc in a Dremel grinder and drawn to light straw color using a propane torch. Care is necessary here because the color can change quickly to very dark straw or purple which would leave the cherry too soft for our purpose. After drawing, the headstock end, which has been left on for convenience in handling, is removed with a hacksaw. The cherry is then placed in the drill press, checked for warpage, honed if

Cutting the cavity on the drill press with the blocks held firmly on the table. The power is controlled with a foot switch.

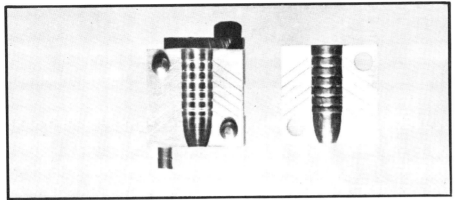

The finished mould blocks, with a bullet in the right half. This shows the fine vent lines running diagonally upward from the grease grooves. The left half shows the base cap in place and the stop pin on the nose end.

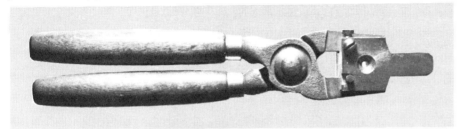

The finished mould. Note the shape of cut-off plate.

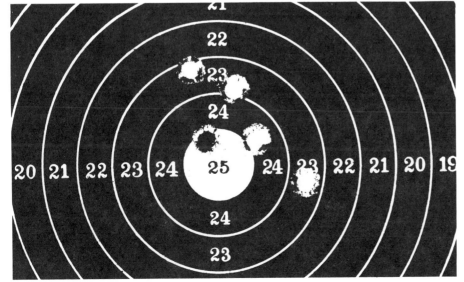

The bullet was test-fired in the Winchester Hi-Wall Schuetzen for which it was made, using original metal sights and an anti-cant device on the barrel. Above is the shooter, Wayne Jordan of New Gloucester, Maine, and below, the test target he fired at 100 yards. Bullet alloy was one part tin and 30 parts lead. Load was 15 grains of 4759 with cork wad over the powder and grease wad in mouth of case; Remington 2 1/2 primers; bullet breech-seated 1/32 inch ahead of case; Pope lubricant.

necessary, and laid aside to await the next step in the operation, cutting the cavity.

The blocks in which the mould is to be cut are made from 5/8x1x1 inch half-hard rolled brass in which a 5/16x 5/16-inch slot has been cut to accept Lyman handles. This should be done on a milling machine using a circular cutter but it can be done on a lathe with a 5/16-inch end mill and the blocks held in a milling attachment.

Holes for the alignment pins are drilled through both blocks with a number 14 drill then reamed with a 3/16-inch straight reamer. This must be done with the blocks tightly held in a drill press vise, being very careful to have the mating surfaces perfectly joined. I check this by holding the vise to a light. If any light shows through the joint the blocks are not square and must be corrected before drilling. Three surfaces of the blocks, top, bottom, and the inside, or mating surfaces, *must* be square with each other before the alignment holes are drilled and reamed.

Hole centers are 5/32-inch from the sides and 3/16 from the top and bottom of the blocks. These are marked with a punch and the holes started with a small drill before using the number 14 for the holes. Light pressure is the rule here to guard against the drill "grabbing" in the relatively soft metal. After drilling through both blocks the holes are *reamed without removing the blocks from the vise.* The alignment pins are then made from 3/16 bronze welding rod and inserted in the block in which the holes were started.

Holes for the screws which will hold the blocks in the handles are now drilled and tapped for 8-32 screws. Hole centers are 5/32-inch from the edges. I drill through with a number 29 drill, go through the top section with a number 18 and countersink for the screw head with a number 1. With the screws fitted we now have a set of blocks in which to cut the mould cavity.

With the two halves of the mould laying face up on the bench I place a piece of thin cardboard on top of the block without the pins and gently tap around the edges with a hammer, also marking the holes. I cut this out on the lines and make cutouts where the holes are marked. The blocks are then put together with the cardboard between the surfaces, placed in the drill press vise and a starting point marked in the center with a punch. The purpose of the cardboard is to guide the pilot drill. The small drill will tend to follow the crack between the blocks.

The nose of our cherry is 3/16-inch in diameter so we'll use a number 15 drill for the first pilot hole. Now, with outside calipers, we measure the diameter of the cherry at one of the grease grooves in the body. We find it is slightly over 1/4-inch so we will use a 15/64 drill for the large pilot. Now drill through the blocks with the number 15 drill, then, using the larger bit, drill down to a point just above where the ogive will start. It is a good idea to start the drilling with a small drill, about 1/16-inch, to be sure the starting hole is exactly centered between the blocks. If the pilot holes are lop-sided, that is, larger on one side of the blocks, our mould cavity will also be 1-sided since the cherry will be guided by the hole. With the holes drilled the blocks are now ready for cutting the cavity.

For this critical job we use a set of Lyman handles that have been specially prepared with the tong ends shaped to permit the use of long alignment pins which go all the way through both blocks. These pins, three inches long, are tapered from .188 to .182 and provide positive alignment when closing the blocks against the cherry. Since the straight reamer with which the holes were finished is slightly smaller on the starting end, the pins will hold firmly in one side of the blocks while allowing the other to slide when the handles are opened and closed. The handles are ground as shown in the accompanying photo and one side of the pivot pin and washer is also ground off flat.

With the driving belts on the drill press arranged for the lowest spindle speed (400 rpm works well for me) the cherry is placed in the chuck and the table moved up until the tip of the cherry barely touches a piece of newspaper on the table. (Remember that this is a nose-cutoff mould.) One of the alignment pins is removed to let the cherry in to cutting position then replaced and both pins are lightly driven into the blocks.

The operation from this point requires the utmost, unhurried care. A foot switch or an extra pair of hands is

necessary for starting and stopping the drill press since both hands are required to hold the blocks in place on the table.

With the blocks held *firmly* on the table, and the pilot hole aligned with the cherry, the power is started and the handles closed very slowly until the cherry begins to cut. A little more pressure on the handles and the cavity begins to take shape. The power is stopped, the alignment pins removed and the chips cleaned from the cavity and the cherry. This procedure is repeated until the cherry no longer cuts. Burrs left by the cherry are removed as necessary using a flat stone or a fine-cut file. We take small cuts at a time rather than trying to do the job all at once. If the cutting is forced the cavity may go off center or cut at an angle. When the cavity is finished the long alignment pins are replaced with the permanent ones, the blocks closed tightly around the cherry and the chuck turned a few revolutions by hand to correct any possible misalignment.

The cut-off plate and the cap over the base are cut from 1/8-inch cold rolled steel plate and are secured to the blocks with 10-32 screws positioned 3/16-inch from the sides on opposite corners from the alignment pins and holes. Locating the sprue hole is done by screwing down the plate tightly, opening the blocks and pin-pointing the center of the nose. After removing the plate and marking the pin-point with a punch, the sprue hole is drilled with a 1/8-inch drill, the plate turned over and the nozzle cavity cut with a 3/8 or 13/32-inch drill. A notch is cut for the stop pin, which can be 1/8-inch rod, and the mould is ready for use.

Testing should be done with the alloy that is to be used for shooting. However, there will be no detectable difference in size between any of the mixes commonly used in single shot rifles. Since brass expands slightly when heated, it usually requires 20 or more castings from a new mould to get a fully filled out bullet which will provide accurate dimensions and weight. The blocks may need venting, which is done by scratching fine lines diagonally upward from the grease grooves in both halves of the blocks.

Now let's see what we have for a

bullet. We were aiming for a base band diameter of .323 and a body measuring .316. After casting 30 bullets from an alloy of one part tin and 30 parts lead we find we have a base band measurement of .323-.3235 and a body diameter of .317-.3175. The weight is 198 grains. The bullet seats easily in the barrel for which it was made although the body is slightly larger than necessary.

The real test of any bullet, of course, is how well it shoots. Maine weather in mid-November is seldom ideal for target shooting and the temperature was only eight degrees above freezing on the day we did our testing. A 5-shot string, after firing two fouling shots, produced a group measuring one and one-half inches between the two widest shots with four staying within an inch. Considering cold hands, cold lubricant and a cold barrel we considered it a good indication of what the bullet would do under normal conditions.

So that's how it's done and what one can hope to get as a result of some careful workmanship. The major pitfalls are warpage in hardening the cherry, drilling the pilot hole off-center and using too much pressure on the handles in cutting the cavity. When a cherry warps badly it is usually smart to throw it away and start over again. They can sometimes be corrected by annealing and re-hardening but as a rule it's better to make a new one.

This method of making a bullet mould is certainly not the ideal procedure. But it is one that works with a minimum of equipment: a very old but still accurate lathe, two milling attachments, a drill press, small shaper and a good assortment of hand tools. Ideally, cherries should be made oversize and ground to the wanted dimensions after hardening, the cavities should be cut in a double-action vise on a vertical milling machine and the blocks should be uniform in size. Uniformity is not possible, however, when making nose cut-off moulds ranging in size from .25-20 to .45-70 so a method that is flexible has seemed to be the most acceptable.

If any of you amateur, or professional, gunsmiths want to try making a bullet mould you can get 5/8x1-inch rectangular brass stock from Metal

Goods, Glen and Ames Sts., Marlborough, Mass. 01752. Specify Free Cutting AL 360. Don't buy scrap brass. You might get a piece of yellow bronze which looks like brass but would be so tough you'd have trouble cutting it. I will be glad to supply blocks such as I use, 1x1x5/8-inch, slotted for the handles and with the alignment pins fitted, for $5.00 a pair (Henry Beverage, New Gloucester, Maine). Blocks shorter or longer than one inch, which require additional machining are $6.50. It is possible to re-cut the old Ideal or Winchester moulds but they require a lot of preparation. I've never seen an Ideal mould that was square on both top and bottom and I've seen some that had the original cavity off-center or cut at an angle. The Winchester moulds are usually square. Uncut Lyman blocks are available, or have been, from Dixie Gun Works, Union City, Tenn., at $4.50 a pair. But these are not adaptable to nose cut-off moulds without plugging the base, which usually results in leakage when casting.

There may be other sources of metal for blocks. Some grades of Meehanite are good, cold-rolled steel can be cut with a very hard, very sharp cherry and some grades of bronze are excellent. But brass, of known hardness and cutting quality, has proved very satisfactory for me. ●

MAKING SPRINGS

By MYRON ROCKETT

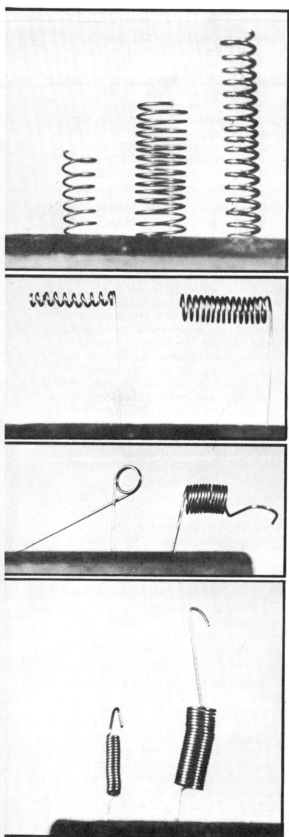

The top photo illustrates three compression coil springs, wound from piano wire. The two compression springs in the photo second from top were also wound from piano wire, but were wound on two different-diameter mandrels — 1/10-inch and 1/8-inch. Two mouse trap springs are shown in the photo second from bottom. The two tension springs, bottom photo, were wound on a 1/16-inch diameter mandrel and a 1/8-inch diameter mandrel.

T ODAY'S SUPER hardware stores usually carry a lot of springs but considering the myriad uses for different types, they can only stock the most common ones. Unfortunately, those who use lots of springs, such as gun tinkerers, soon find that every type of spring needed can't always be bought. You can be sure that in 1700, a Swiss clocksmith or an English gunsmith did not run down to the local hardware store to buy his day's supply of springs. In spite of the inconvenience of not having a local hardware store, those incredible craftsmen managed to build their intricate works with such precision that their clocks and firearms — centuries old — still function flawlessly. Where did those masters get their springs? It should be no surprise that they made them, just as they made everything else they needed — tools included.

It seems reasonable that if a craftsman could make a quality spring two hundred years ago, a modern day craftsman, with much better tools and far superior materials, should be able to do the same. In most cases the only disadvantage the modern craftsman has is lack of know-how. Hopefully, the lack of knowledge will be somewhat alleviated by this article. Don't get me wrong — chances are you won't be able to glance at this account and then roll out a perfect spring on the first try. A perfect spring requires practice, as there are certain skills that must be acquired by doing. Considerable trial and error is usually required to get a spring of the correct dimensions, rate and temper.

The first requirement of spring making is obtaining stock spring metal, which, fortunately, can be purchased specially for this purpose. Either buy your stock from a local gunsmith or at least obtain the name of his supplier. Buying ready-made spring stock is the best bet, but you may want to go one step further and make your springs from scrap metal. I am a bit of a scrounger, so I went out of my way to discover what types of scraps can be made into good springs. Before we talk about scrap metal, let's discuss the production of the spring.

First the coil spring. There are three basic types of coil springs: compression, tension and torsion (or mouse trap). Making all of these springs is exactly the same, the only variable being the spacing of the coils. Find the steel wire of the correct diameter, and wrap it around a mandrel. For a mandrel use a piece of ordinary steel rod, or a bolt; it will take trial and error to find the correct diameter. If you want a spring with an outside diameter of 3/8-inch, a 1/8-inch mandrel might be required — depending on the nature of the spring metal. Secure the mandrel in a vise and fasten one end of the wire to the vise or mandrel with a clamp. Wrap the wire around the mandrel — tightly! I have actually pulled my work bench across the floor while wrapping some coils. If the pressure is released while winding, the coils will not be uniform and the spring will be of second rate quality. Use a pair of vise grips to hold the free end of the wire; regular pliers just are not good enough for this.

Trial and error is the only way to determine the correct spacing of the coils. For some small springs, bolts make excellent mandrels because they allow even spacing of the coils — simply wrap the spring stock into the thread grooves. If the right bolt is not available, make a gauge from a scrap of metal or wood. If the coils must be wrapped with 1/2-inch spacing then cut a 1/4-inch spacer and use it to space the coils while wrapping. With a bit of practice, the spring can be wound evenly — simply by eye. If duplicating an existing spring, the wire must be the same diameter and alloy, and must have the same coil spacing and diameter. When making the spring, make it longer than required to allow for trimming. Wind the wire cold; most springs will work perfectly without heat treating. For heavy coils, the stock metal may have to be heated to allow wrapping on the mandrel. If heating is required, then the spring must be retempered — more on that later.

Generally, leaf springs are a little harder to make than coils. Not because they require greater skill, but because they usually take a bit of elbow grease. The stock steel must be cut into shape with saws and files. The steel sold for this purpose is already soft, but scrap metal will have to be softened by heating to cherry red, then allowed to cool slowly. Cut the metal to the general dimensions, allowing extra length and width for trimming. Leave one end of the spring attached to the stock metal for easier handling. With files, trim and shape the metal to the correct dimensions. File lengthwise on the spring, never across. Filing crosswise will result in uneven taper, as well as scratches that will weaken or result in a broken spring. Generally leaf springs are heavier at their center than at the ends; the taper from the heavy center to the thin ends must be even and smooth, without hollows or humps. After filing, polish the spring. Emery cloth and steel wool should be sufficient. Polishing removes scratches that would prevent even tempering. After polishing, bend the spring, if any bends are required. Use a propane torch to heat while bending. Make the bends gradual, avoiding kinks or twists. Sometimes it is helpful to bend the spring over a piece of metal, such as a screwdriver blade or the corner of a vise. This will allow easier shaping. Allow the spring to cool, then check its shape, making any adjustments that may be necessary.

When the spring is of the correct shape it can be tempered. The best way to heat the spring for tempering is to place the spring on a flat metal plate which in turn is laid on the kitchen stove. Use a thin plate — one that will not warp with heat. A heavy plate will take forever to heat to cherry red. A propane torch can be used for heating, but it is more difficult to

achieve uniform heating. Allow the spring to reach a dull cherry red. If it is over-heated, carbon will burn out of the steel, weakening the spring. A bright red is much too hot! When hot, pick up the spring by an end, with pliers, and quickly dunk and agitate it in a cold solution of brine. The brine is made by super saturating water with table salt. Brine, oil, grease, tallow and various other substances have all been used for quenching springs. Brine will give the hardest temper to the steel, while the thicker solutions will give less temper — in order of their thickness. The spring will now be hard and brittle, and will probably break

The 3/8-inch diameter spring above was wound on the 1/4-inch bolt shown alongside it.

The car antenna wire shown here is being wound cold onto a 1/4-inch concrete drill.

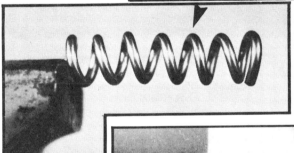

The antenna wire, after being wound as shown above, only needs the ends trimmed before it is used. This spring will compress 1/4-inch under an eighty pound load.

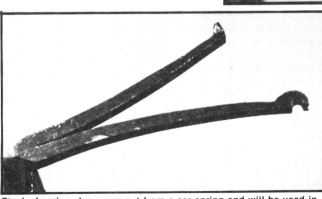

The leaf spring above was cut from a car spring and will be used in a double-barreled shotgun.

This leaf spring was heated to cherry red with a propane torch and then quenched in brine. The brittleness is being drawn here by burning in light oil.

if compressed. The brittleness must be drawn out of the spring. To do this, dunk the spring in oil, then light the oily spring on fire and let all the oil burn off. Once should be sufficient for small springs, but larger springs will require five or six burns. Also, heavy springs can be placed in about 1/8 inch of boiling oil, then the oil is set on fire and allowed to burn completely. After burning off the spring, allow it to cool slowly; it is then ready for service.

I found it harder to find scraps for coils than for leaf springs. However, there are several sources for certain diameters of wire. Piano or music wire is one such source. You can always pluck a few strings out of a piano or a harp; if the owner of the instrument isn't quite that friendly, try a music store. Guitar strings and harp strings come in a fairly wide range of sizes, but do not lend themselves to all types of springs. For heavy duty springs, simply snip the top section from your car antenna. These solid end sections are heavy, but still can be wrapped around the mandrel without heating; all it takes is a bit of muscle, skill and practice. One spring I made from 3/16-inch antenna material is so strong that it takes 80 pounds to compress it 1/4 inch. Try buying one of these super springs in a store!

For leaf springs, all sorts of things can be used. Those blued steel bands used for binding crates and lumber make dandy springs. This material comes in quite a few sizes, and can be used for such things as flat leaf springs in firearms. Saw-blades, whether hacksaw or an old cross cut wood saw, are very good sources for flat leaf springs. For springs that must be cut and filed into shape, leaf springs from wrecked cars are perfect and cost nothing. Cut a slab of leaf spring, soften by heating and slow cooling, then cut the spring and retemper as outlined in previous paragraphs. There are so many sizes of auto and truck leaf springs that it is doubtful that other sources of spring metal would ever have to be explored.

The next time you need a spring, you know what to do. ●

A HANDY CASE-MOUTH GAUGE

by Norman Johnson

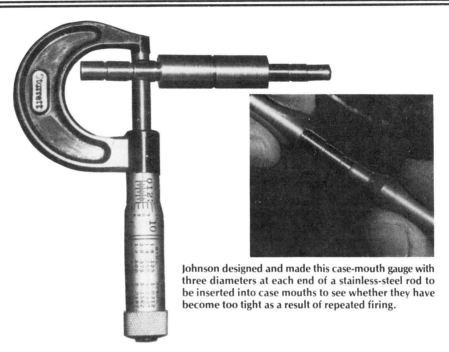

Johnson designed and made this case-mouth gauge with three diameters at each end of a stainless-steel rod to be inserted into case mouths to see whether they have become too tight as a result of repeated firing.

KNOWLEDGEABLE handloaders are aware of the importance of case condition as they carefully prepare their loads. Case inspection, even though overlooked by many, becomes increasingly important in reloading high-intensity cases several times. While some cases tend to flow brass forward, thus causing necks to thicken more quickly than others, all should be checked to avoid possibly dangerous conditions. Excessively thick neck walls can cause the loaded bullet to be compressed or squeezed as it is chambered, sometimes raising chamber pressures to dangerous levels. This condition need not occur if obviated in time — and checking the inside diameter of the case mouth takes but a few seconds.

The best time to check the diameter of the case-mouth opening is after a cartridge has been fired. One can insert a bullet into the mouth of the fired case at this time and reasonably assume, where bullet entry is easy, that a safe reloading condition exists for one or possibly two more firings before further checking is required. The theory here is that when bullet entry into the case mouth is easy, an adequate clearance or tolerance exists between chamber-neck diameter and the bullet. Normally, adequate clearance is provided by manufacturers of

both the firearm and the ammunition, allowing a safe margin for chambering. However, some case-neck walls are near the upper limits of normal, and some chamber necks are near the lower limits in diameter.

Among my rifles, I have two .220 Swifts with such closely fitted chambers, and after two firings with full loads, cases must be neck-turned or reamed to prevent bullet pinching when chambered. At one time, I used the bullet-insertion method to check case mouths for clearance, but now I use a much more convenient method — a gauge especially made for the purpose. It is very easy to use and eliminates holding a smaller bullet in the fingers or a bullet loaded in a case. One can easily make his own gauge in several calibers and sizes to suit his needs, as I did.

A lathe is required to make your gauge, and several calibers can be cut into the same piece of steel if desired. I turned out a case-mouth gauge with six calibers to exact bullet diameter on my first attempt — three calibers on each end. I chose .224, .243, and .257 on one end and .277, .284, and .308 on the other. I left a convenient 1½-inch-long unturned center portion for a handle.

Stainless steel, although not re-

quired, is ideal for making the case-mouth gauge. It resists rust, takes a good finish, and is more wear-resistant, should this be a factor. Turning the steel case-mouth gauge is best performed holding the half-inch steel shaft in a good lathe collet. I used a very sharp carbide cutting tool to turn the shaft down, but a standard tool-steel cutter would suffice. I turned approximately 5/16 inch length to exact bullet diameter for each caliber of the three on each end of the tool. Of course, the smaller caliber must be turned first, preferably remaining held in the lathe collet until all three are completed on each end. I chose to cut a 1/16-inch race at the end of each caliber for better clean-up and measuring. A micrometer or an accurate vernier caliper to measure the turned portion of the shaft to bullet diameter will be a necessary tool in making your gauge.

You may find, as I have, that several of these tools in different calibers — combined or made individually — will be not only handy but a very necessary part of your reloading equipment. You may even elect to make special case-mouth gauges with somewhat greater or lesser diameter than bullet size to fit your specific chamber neck and case dimensions. Either way, it is a tool you will want to have around. ◉

Section 9

MUZZLELOADERS

Precision Assembly of LOCK KITS

By JOHN BIVINS

A LARGE VARIETY of lock kits, both flint and percussion, are available to the muzzleloading gunmaker these days — much in contrast to the relative paucity of such parts even ten years ago. These lock kits vary in quality and ease of assembly, and they also vary considerably in style and grace of design. Some kits will provide a finished lock that is a thing of sculptured beauty, while others have all the grace of a mud fence and will require considerable time cursing over a hot file to make them resemble something that looks like a lock. All kits, however, share a common technology in that they are investment cast in various steels, even the springs. Though some springs are not well designed, and don't always have an ideal flexing geometry, cast springs do give excellent service if properly heat-treated. I have had only two cast springs fill in service over the past ten years; most kit makers provide springs that are already heat-treated to avoid possible problems.

Most, if not all, lock kits on the market can be assembled into a good working unit, but how well the lock functions, and how long its working life will be is determined by the fellow who puts the thing together. Crooked holes, egg-shaped tumbler axles, wobbling frizzen fit, and other such niceties render an otherwise good lock fit only to be used for a shark-fishing sinker — you surely don't want a badly cobbled lock on your gun if you intend to have it go off with any regularity. For both reliability and longevity, a lock needs to be assembled precisely, with a close fit and good polish of its bearing areas. It's not enough for a lock to just function; it should utilize all of the mechanical capability designed into the components. Small assembly flaws have a cumulative effect in reducing ignition time of either a percussion or flint lock, especially in the latter.

Most lock kits assembled today are done so by hobby gunstockers who in general haven't the equipment in their own shops to make lock assembling chores both quick and precise. However, a hobbyist should be able to find access to a good drill press either in a friend's shop or in a high school vocational shop or a local technical school. A 1-inch belt sander speeds work considerably and provides a good surface finish, but such polishing and grinding can be done by

These are the basic hand tools needed for lock work, including small C-clamp; drills: 5/64, 7/64, 5/16; Nos. 29 and 19, 8-32 and 1/4-20 taps; tap wrench; center punch; 5/16 and 11/64 reamers; a special counter-bore with .136 pilot; 1/4x8 pillar files in No. 4 and 0 cut; 8-inch mill file; the special holding jig discussed in the text; and a drill press vise.

The pan screw hole is tap drilled and then counterbored for the screw head. The cut should be shallow to leave excess screw head that may be dressed down later. Note the clamp. The photo at right illustrates tapping the pan screw hole. All screw holes should be tapped by starting the tap in a drill press to insure alignment.

hand. Parts that need precision lathe work, such as tumblers, can be sent to a machine shop with proper instructions; the balance of the tools needed are basically hand tools which will take an investment of some $20-$30 or more, but may be used to assemble quite a number of locks before they wear out.

We'll have a look here at the assembly of a Siler flintlock, done in a manner to get the most out of the lock. The procedure may be used for quite a number of other locks, including percussion locks. Caplocks may vary slightly with the addition of such things as stirrups on the mainsprings and adjustable sears, items which flintlocks seldom have. I illustrate the assembly of a Siler lock here since it is the lock I use for almost 100 percent of my jobs, and it is far and away the best thought-out lock kit on the market — and therefore the easiest to assemble. Bud Siler includes good instructions with his kits, but the instructions are intended largely for those who have no access to machinery other than a hand drill, so with apologies to good friend Bud, let's throw away those instructions and have a look at a slightly different way of doing it. I might add that most of this I learned from Bud back when he was assembling locks, which he no longer does. He only supplies kits.

Monte Mandarino does most all of the lock work in our shop, and the procedure I'll outline here follows his usual efficient method of working, but of course the order of the work can be changed around considerably to suit the individual.

The Siler lock is a lock of Franco-German persuasion, ca. 1760-90 in style, and is made in two sizes, both in flint and percussion mode, and not long after you read this a left-hand version in the large

size, long awaited by gunstockers, will be available. Bud uses 4140 steel for lockplates, both cock and upper jaw, pan, and bridle. The balance of the parts are cast in either spring steel or through-hardening tool steel; screws are turned from low-carbon free-machining screw stock.

Hand tools and bits needed for precision assembly of a large-size Siler lock are a small C clamp; 5/64, 7/64, No. 29, No. 19, and 5/16 drill bits; 8-32 and 1/4-20 taps; (buy 2-flute "gun" taps if you can find them) a tap wrench turned at the top to receive a center (for use in the lathe and drill press); a center punch; 5/16 and 11/64 reamers; a 1/4-inch counterbore with a .1360 pilot (you will probably have to have this ground from a 9/64 pilot; make two while you're about it, since pilots are fragile); 1/4x8-inch pillar files in No. 4 and No. 0 cuts, with safe edges (we use the Grobet files sold by Brownell's), an 8-inch mill file; a holding jig (discussed below), and a drill press vise of good quality. Also needed, though not illustrated here, are 280 grit polishing cloth, 400 grit wet-or-dry paper, a hand vise (optional), a can of anti-scale compound (we use PBC, available from Brownell's; Kasenit Corporation also makes a similar product), a can of Kasenit hardening compound (optional), a small quarter-round needle file for removing parting lines from castings, and access is needed to a 1-inch micrometer, a lathes, a belt sander (optional), and a quality drill press.

Essential to this work is a holding jig for the lock, which is used for drilling, tapping, and reaming holes; this simple jig will insure that all of the holes are straight, to avoid binding moving parts. Our jig is a spartan affair, the base made of a piece of 4x11x3/4 ground aluminum

The small tumbler axle is turned, then the tumbler is faced off.

The sear notches are cleaned up with a No. 4 pillar file. Note that the pillar file has "safe" edges.

When tapping lockplate holes, Bivins uses a drill press center to insure that they are square. Light down-pressure is used on the spindle while starting the tap; after it is started, the drill press is raised, and the tapping is finished by hand.

stock (steel would be fine, if surface ground). On the base are mounted three ground-steel pedestals 3/4-inch high. Two of these are 1 1/8 x 1 3/8, set on the centerline of the base plate, and 3 1/2 inches apart (measuring from the inside edges). The third pedestal is 1 1/8-inch square, and is positioned 1 3/8 inches from the inside edge of the right-hand pedestal; the centerline of this block is set 5/16-inch back from the centerline of the outside pedestals. Behind the outside pedestals are mounted two 40-pound Vlier toggle-clamps (Vlier's part number is 93121); these clamps are also mounted on 3/4-inch pedestals, though the outside pedestals could have been left 2 1/2 inches long to provide extra room for installing the clamps. The pedestals are secured to the aluminum base with 10-32 cap screws. This positioning of the pedestals will allow clamping both a large and small Siler lock, for work on either side of the lockplate. Spacing of the outside pedestals might need to be changed for other makes of lock kits.

We use a 1-inch belt sander for as much lock work as possible; it's particularly useful for leveling and polishing the inside of the lock plate, which must be smooth and free of casting surface characteristics if the mainspring, tumbler, and sear are to have uninterrupted action. An excellent finish may be obtained with the belt sander by using No. 80-grit belts for rough grinding and then finishing with 100-grit belts. For an extra-fine finish on parts that are belt-sanded, however, it's best just to go from the 80-grit belt to hand-polishing, polishing first with cloth-backed 280, backed with a file, finishing with 400 wet-or-dry paper. If you want the lock to have "London" quality inside, 600-grit paper may be used.

Lock assembly begins with belt-sanding the inside of the plate, working around the lug that receives the pan. If the lock is to have the exterior polished, then go ahead and belt sand the exterior longitudinally, since heavy stock removal must be done before fitting the pan to insure a tight fit. The pan is next fitted to the plate by lightly cleaning up the pan casting inside the flange with files. The pan should then slip tightly onto the lock plate, requiring a blow or two from a mallet to drive it home. Pull the pan off and lightly belt sand the bottom of the lug to remove the cast surface. Tap the pan back in place, clamp the lock pan-side-down in the jig, and clamp the pan in position with a small C-clamp. Tap drill the pan screw location with a No. 29 drill, using plenty of cutting oil or tapping fluid — as you should do on *all* drilling and tapping described here. Using the 1/4-inch counterbore, counterbore the hole for the screw head, leaving the cut shallow so that .005-.010 of screw head will be left standing above the surface. Leaving the pan on the lockplate, clearance drill the hole in the lug, setting the drill press stop so that the bit won't pull down into the tap hole in the lockplate. Tap the hole 8-32, using a

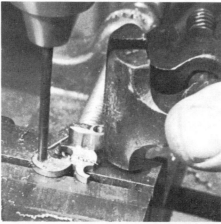

In the photo at left, the plastic indexing plug is shown in place, with the bridle rotated to correct position [bearing against the plug.] In the right photo, the sear screw hole is clearance drilled in the bridle while the bridle is held in a hand vise.

The tumbler hole is reamed, left, then the hole for the small axle of the tumbler. The work must remain clamped so the two holes are in the same axis.

60-degree center in the drill press chuck to center the tap wrench; use a light down-pressure on the spindle while starting the tap; after it is started, raise the drill press and finish tapping by hand. A tap wrench with a center-spot on the top works fine for this, though the B-Square tap wrench works better. A mechanical tapping head is all right with careful use, but they represent an investment of $75-100. In any event, *all* screw holes in the lock should be tapped in this fashion for straightness and evenness of thread unless you have an uncanny eye for starting a tap straight by hand. Some do — I don't.

Install the pan screw, and belt sand it off flush with the pan lug; this will remove the casting gate on the lug at the same time. Go lightly, and remove no more metal than is needed to clean the surface. File the screw off flush with the outside of the lock.

In readying the internal parts for installation, the most important component, which is indeed the "heart" of the lock, is the tumbler. Since investment castings can be out of concentricity as much as .003-.004, the tumbler must be lathe-turned for best results. Hand-filing the axles while the tumbler is spinning in a drill tends to accentuate the "oval" as-cast shape of the axles. Fitting the large axle into the lathe collet, turn the small axle to .1714; this will provide a slip-fit in a reamed 11/64 hole, since the reamer diameter is .1719. After turning the axle, face off the tumbler with the lathe bit just enough to clean it up. Some prefer to turn a bolster ring around the axle at this point, approximately .220 in diameter and .010 high, relieving the rest of the tumbler face. If this is done, a bolster approximately .400-inch in diameter is turned on the opposite side,

around the big axle. This was often done on fine-quality London locks of the late 18th Century, and of course the reason is to reduce bearing area of the tumbler to a very small area to reduce friction. I wouldn't recommend this too highly unless you intend to case-harden the lockplate, since that tiny bolster will tend to wear a ring in an unhardened plate or bridle.

After finishing the small axle and its adjacent tumbler side, turn the tumbler around, and with the small axle held in a collet, turn the large axle to .3120, which will be a slip-fit in the .3125 hole provided by a 5/16 reamer. Face off this side as well, and face off the end of the axle at the square. Center drill the end face of the square, tap drill with a No. 29 drill, and, with an 8-32 tap in the tailstock, start the threads by turning the lathe by hand while advancing the tailstock feed. Finish tapping by hand; this method should insure that the cock screw doesn't pull the cock out of line when it is tightened.

Now you're ready to prepare the other parts. Starting with the cock, hacksaw the casting gate off the back, and belt-sand the inside flat of the cock. Even if you intend to leave the cast finish on the exterior (this works fine for a matte browning job), you should now remove all of the parting lines with needle files. Nothing looks so cheesy to me as lock parts with the parting lines glaring up at you. Now belt-sand the frizzen face, holding the frizzen over the drive wheel of the sander, and remove the parting lines on the front face with files. Lightly belt-sand the bottom of the pan cover, taking care not to remove more stock from one side than the other. Belt-sand the casting gate off the back of the top jaw of the cock, and file off the parting lines.

We usually grind down the screw seat on the sear spring of Siler locks to make the sear spring screw flush with the spring edge, which makes inletting the lock at that point a bit simpler; this is easily done

The front facet of the fly is then dressed down, left, and the side of the fly is filed flush with the side of the tumbler, right.

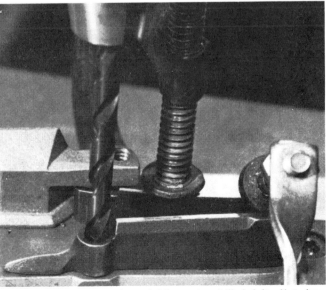

The lockplate, frizzen and pan bridle are tap drilled, left. Note how the frizzen is clamped. At right, the frizzen spring screw hole is spotted with a No. 19 drill [the drill should be running].

on the side of a 1/8-inch cut-off wheel on the bench grinder. For appearance's sake, lightly belt-sand the edges of the frizzen, spring, mainspring, and sear spring. Both the top and bottom of the mainspring should be lightly belt-sanded, and the inside as well. Avoid overheating the spring, since it is already heat-treated. The inside of the mainspring should then be polished out with 280-grit cloth backed on a thin file or sheet-stock scrap to remove the grinding marks, which are at right-angles to the spring — a most definite no-no unless you like to hear the eventual musical tinkle of a breaking spring. The polish marks do not have to be totally parallel with the spring; many old mainsprings, in fact, exhibit diagonal file marks inside, but diagonal cuts don't cause opposing stress points the way right-angle filing or polishing marks do. Should you find a pin-hole near any edge of a mainspring, return it to the maker. That, however, is an exceedingly rare occurrence in a Siler spring.

If you wish, the inside edge of the mainspring may be relieved to the rear of the pivot stud by grinding on the belt-sander; this prevents the entire main beam of the spring from dragging on the lockplate, and many English lockmakers were fond of doing it. However, don't be tempted to take any of the inside edge of the spring off until the spring has been tried in the assembled lock, for reasons we shall see below.

Hand polish the un-machined portions of the tumbler, going over the notches very lightly with a No. 4 cut pillar file to clean up. Infrequently the half-cock notch will need to be cleaned out with a thin escapement file. Don't mess with fullcock notch angles at this point.

Belt-sand both inner and outer faces of the bridle, and file and polish the edges if you desire. The edges don't look bad left as-cast, since foundries commonly sand-blast castings to remove investment.

Using the sander and hand-polishing, finish the sear; a hand-grinder may be used to polish the radius if you have one. Lightly square up the sear nose with the No. 4 pillar file; don't change the angle. The main beam of the sear may be relieved from the rear of the sear screw position back, if desired; grinding away .010 of metal at this point reduces bearing area on the lock plate and tends to give a little better sear action.

Holding the screws between two fingers, polish the lathe marks off all the screw heads, with a strip of 280-grit held flat on a bench-top with the left hand. Finish with 400.

Now, with the lockplate clamped in the holding jig pan-side-up, drill all of the main holes in the lockplate, including the mainspring pivot stud hole, with a No. 29 drill. *Do not*, however, drill the frizzen

spring screw hole at this time. Drill the frizzen spring pivot stud hole with a 7/64 drill. Tap the holes at the rear of the pan 8-32, using the same method outlined above with the pan installation. Drill a screw clearance hole in the front lug of the bridle (No. 19 drill), first drilling a pilot hole with a No. 29 drill. The bridle is best clamped in the drill press vise. Screw the plastic indexing plug supplied with the kit into the sear spring hole, attach the bridle with its front screw, swivel the bridle up until it bears against the bottom of the plastic plug, and tighten the bridle screw. Then, with a new, well-pointed tap, screw the tap into the sear screw hole from the outside of the lock until it lightly marks the inside of the bridle. Remove the bridle, center punch, and holding it in a hand vise over the open jaws of the drill press vise, drill the clearance hole for the sear screw — first with a No. 29, then a No. 19 drill. Re-install the bridle with both screws.

With the pan side of the lock up in the jig, ream the tumbler hole in the lockplate with a 5/16 straight reamer running at slow spindle speed, using plenty of "juice." The center for the small tumbler axle hole in the bridle may now be marked. The best method is to turn a .3120 center punch to shove in from the outside of the tumbler hole. Rest the bridle on something flat and give the punch a little swat with the hammer. If you prefer to save time, you can simply run a 5/16 drill bit into the hole from the outside; the bit will be .0005 smaller than the reamed hole, and shouldn't hurt the good finish of the hole if you're careful. With the drill press running, lightly bear down on the drill, just enough to mark the inside face of the bridle. Without removing the lock from the jig, drill through the bridle with a No. 29 drill, and then follow up with the 11/64 straight reamer. Remove the parts from the lock, and very lightly chamfer the edges of the holes on the inside of the lockplate, using a countersink held in your hand. Now reassemble with the tumbler, and if either tumbler axles bind to a significant degree, put the tumbler back in the lathe and polish lightly until you achieve a firm slip-fit in both lockplate and bridle. You should have to twist the tumbler back and forth to remove it from either hole.

Clamp the sear in your hand vise, the vise holding the perpendicular beam of the sear, and rest the side of the sear flat against the top of the drill press vise, the latter with its jaws slightly open. Drill the sear screw hole first with a No. 29, then a No. 19 drill. For a more efficient operation, you can add a holding clamp to your jig by the means of a toggle clamp and two studs; the screw hole may then be drilled even more precisely.

To fit the cock to the tumbler square, open up the cock tumbler mortise slightly from the rear, giving a slight taper to the

hole. The cock should be a drive fit onto the square, and the end face of the tumbler square should be below the outside face of the cock to prevent the cock screw from bottoming out. Drill and tap (1/4-20) the cock for the top jaw screw, holding the cock in the drill press vise; in fitting the top jaw, file only enough off the back of the jaw for the jaw to be pulled all the way down to its rest by the jaw screw without binding. The top jaw should not be so loose that it can be turned from side to side to any extent.

The Siler cock and top jaw are cast with ridges to provide a firm grip on the flint leather. This works, but isn't exactly traditional. If you prefer the 18th Century usage, file off the ridges and upset a number of rows of teeth using a round-bottom die sinker's chisel or a small cape chisel.

Install the sear and check for good bearing on the tumbler notches. With the sear spring in place, the sear should snap audibly into the notches; if it doesn't, the notches probably need a further bit of cleaning up, though this is rare on a Siler. Don't be concerned with sear angles and bearing at this point.

Dissassemble the lock, and with the small axle of the tumbler held in the "V" of the drill press vise jaws, drill the fly hole with a 5/64 drill, setting the drill press stop to avoid drilling through the tumbler. Install the fly and rotate it all the way to its rearmost position, clamp the tumbler in a bench vise, and file off the front facet of the fly flush with the fullcock "table" — the tumbler flat between the halfcock and fullcock notches. The fly will keep the sear out of halfcock if this isn't done. Then file off the side of the fly flush with the tumbler side. Polish the fly with 280 and 400 — if you can manage to hang onto the blasted thing!

Install the mainspring and check the bearing of the spring hook on the tumbler foot. If the hook isn't bearing on the tumbler evenly, it will either torque the spring against the lockplate or push it away. File the nose of the spring hook until the bearing is even, and polish the nose with 280, 400, and 600. Now the inside edge of the spring may be ground away slightly to reduce the amount of spring bearing against the plate, as I mentioned above.

Strip the lock, and with the lockplate clamped in the jig with the pan down, set the frizzen in place in its closed position and clamp it down hard on the pan with a small C-clamp or parallel machinist's clamp. Tap drill the frizzen with a No. 29 drill, and then run in the 1/4-inch counterbore, leaving the cut a little shallow. After setting the drill press stop, clearance drill the lockplate lug and frizzen with a No. 19 drill, just barely cutting into the pan bridle from the inside. With all the parts still in the jig, tap the pan bridle 8-32. Install the frizzen screw and belt sand off the excess head, holding the frizzen closed so that any excess pan cover is ground off at the same time. After fitting the lock to a stock, you may find that the inside edge of the pan cover may need to be further relieved to avoid scraping the barrel flat; it should clear the barrel by no more than .003-inch.

A close frizzen-to-pan fit is essential. Coat the underside of the pan cover with inletting black or a similar agent and close the frizzen hard. File down the bearing points on the pan until the frizzen has full bearing. No light should show between the pan and frizzen, if the job is done right.

With the lock in the jig, insert the frizzen spring pivot stud in its hole and swivel the frizzen spring up until you have 1/8-inch of spring compression with the frizzen *open*, using the tip of the spring finial as a "pointer." Clamp the spring in this position, run in a No. 19 drill to mark the center, tap drill with a No. 29 drill, and tap the hole. In doing this, you are ignoring the screw index mark cast onto the plate. This should be done since frizzen springs vary, some of them being less "open" than others after heat-treating.

Most of the job is now done. Critical to a long-lasting and good-working lock, however, is heat-treating. Most people who heat-treat lock components do the job with an acetylene torch, or perhaps a Mapp-gas torch (Propane is too cool), but I dislike such a hit-or-miss method. At very least, you should be able to find access to a small electric heat-treating furnace with an accurate pyrometer, perhaps at a dental lab. Or you can send the parts out to be heat-treated in an atmospheric or salt-bath furnace, which is the best method, but heat-treating firms usually have a minimum charge of $15-20, and for that price you could heat-treat 100 tumblers for the same amount you pay to have one done. If you use an electric furnace, you will need to purchase a can of anti-scale compound to prevent scale on critical areas such as tumbler notches. Holding the parts with needle-nose pliers, heat them with a propane torch to about 500 degrees F. (this isn't too great on the pliers!) and scrub them around in the anti-scale powder until the surface is completely covered. Pop the parts in the furnace, take them up to 1,550 F., and using small tongs or an old set of needle-nose pliers, snatch the parts out one at a time and swirl them around in 10W oil. Check each part with a file to make sure that they are hard; a file should not cut them at all. The anti-scale compound, which

has now fused into a ceramic state, can simply be boiled off in water. You will find that you will have a few small spots of scale here and there, with the rest of the surfaces a frosty silver. The anti-scale compound has a tendency to flow a bit under high heat, allowing the oxidizing atmosphere of the furnace to reach bare steel in places. This can be polished off with 280 and 400 paper easily enough.

The frizzen, tumbler, and sear are hardened in this manner. The fly, due to its small size, is best hardened "by the seat of the pants" so that it will not lose heat before reaching the quench. Heat it in the carburizing flame of an acetylene torch, if you have one, holding it by its axle, and keep the part close to the oil while heating.

After hardening the parts, belt-sand off the face of the frizzen a bit, since heat-treating tends to decarburize the surface to a depth of .001 or more, which means that you would get lousy sparking until the soft upper layer is worn away.

Draw (temper) the parts as the lock-kit maker specifies. In the case of a Siler, all parts are heated to 375 F.; the frizzen is removed after one hour and the heat is increased to 425 F.; the tumbler and fly are removed after a half-hour at that temperature and the heat increased to 590; the sear is removed after 1/2 hour at that level. A kitchen oven is all right for this use, but I'd suggest that you verify the calibration of the dial before using the wife's pride and joy, since some ovens can be off 25-50 degrees from the dial setting, which can be disastrous.

Though Bud doesn't suggest it, both his lockplate and bridle, which are 4140 steel, may be hardened; old ones invariably were. The 4140 will harden to approximately RC 58 by heating to 1,550 and quenching in water, though I much prefer casehardening. If you choose the latter, you run a risk of warping the lockplate, though it can be straightened. If you do harden the lock, be certain to drill and tap the lock bolt holes first, and this should be done with the lock in your stock, drilled from both sides between centers, and the lock also tapped while clamped in the lock mortise. Drilling and tapping for lock bolts before inletting a lock is surely inviting a red-eyed monster to sit on the foot of your bed at night while you lie awake wondering how in hell you're going to make screw holes in the stock line up with the lock without boring half-inch caverns through your master-piece.

Frizzens do warp sometimes during heat-treating. Check fit with the pan, and re-fit the frizzen bearing again if necessary; this is usually minor.

I prefer to case-harden both the frizzen

and sear screws. This can be done easily enough by swiping a stainless teaspoon from the kitchen (preferably the one that went down the disposal last New Year's) and clamping the spoon by its handle in a vise. Drop in the screws, fill the spoon bowl with Kasenit, and heat the whole mess up from below until the Kasenit is well melted. Soak it with the torch for a minute or two, and then dump the thing, spoon and all, into cold water.

Assemble the lock, and check for sparking. Silers invariably work best with the bevel of the flint facing up. Stone the full-cock notch with a fine India stone at this point if a lighter pull is needed, though it's best to wait until the lock is mounted in a stock so that you can get the feel on the trigger. If you are using single-lever double-set triggers, leave the pull rather heavy for safety, since you don't need it light anyway. The set triggers will kick it out.

If you find that you have a flint-breaker of a mainspring, now is the time to judiciously grind a bit off the bottom of the spring on the belt sander. Go *slowly* with this, for you want neither to burn the spring nor lighten it too much. The mainspring must be balanced in weight with the frizzen spring. Grind, cock, and snap the lock until everything feels right. I suppose pull weight could be measured for accurate spring regulation, but I don't know what the weight should be. Joe Scorsone, Bud Siler's spring expert and Asheville's resident stockmaker, could probably answer that one.

If you intended to fully polish the lock, exterior and all, now is the time to begin that tedious little chore. Many old locks were left bright by gunstockers originally since they were casehardened, but most have long since acquired a brown patina, of course. Many early locks were also fire-blued, but modern 4140 steel cannot be fire-blued, though a rust blue works very nicely. I have one sitting in the damp box as I type this article.

Most all lock kits, from the lowliest to the grandest, can benefit from customizing and reshaping with the file, if only to give a lock its own personality. Such things as blind-screw frizzen springs, fancy filework on frizzen springs and mainsprings, reshaping of plate, cock, and frizzen, and other goodies can be drawn from fine sources such as Merrill Lindsay's *Master French Gunsmith Designs*, or other such tomes. Customizing, however, is another bedtime tale best reserved for later.

There you have it — a precision-fitted lock certainly equal in quality to most 18th Century originals, and one which will give you long service. If you do as fine a job on the rest of the gun, then you can sit down with a bottle of Jack Daniels Black Label and grin at the wall for an hour. ●

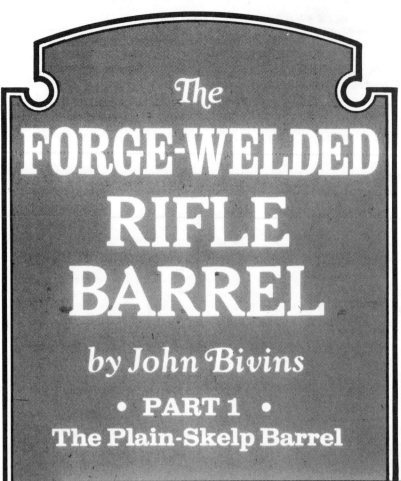

The FORGE-WELDED RIFLE BARREL

by John Bivins

• PART 1 •
The Plain-Skelp Barrel

WE RIFLEMEN are a spoiled bunch in a fair number of ways. Almost anything is available to us at short notice — well, *most* of the time, anyway. We take a heckuva lot for granted. Take barrels, for instance.

Easily one of the least expensive components of a fine custom rifle, a match-grade barrel blank often represents no more than five percent of the total cost of a top-grade sporting rifle stocked and mounted by a competent gunmaker. Consider, however, that it was not until the mid-nineteenth century that barrelmakers had come up with methods that would allow them even to drill a simple hole through a long piece of iron or steel. Before that, tubes had to be made from flat stock wrapped around a mandrel and forge-welded together. A gunshop that had no access to mill-made barrel blanks or powered grinding equipment could easily expend 140 to 180 hours alone in producing a rifle barrel, which meant that a rifle barrel two centuries

Photographs by Armstrong Roberts and Jay Gaynor, courtesy of Colonial Williamsburg. In this extensively restored colonial town, this type of historic riflemaking is but one of the early American trades once again in regular, everyday practice.

Forges like this one at Williamsburg were often built outside the gunshop to avoid both heat and dirt inside the building. This was no doubt warm work at any season of the year.

ago represented just about *half* the total cost of a rifle. In equivalent modern value, that means that the chap who wanted a relatively simple flintlock rifle in 1780 was laying out something like thirty-eight hundred dollars for the completed piece — say fourteen hundred for the barrel, twelve hundred for a fine-quality lock, and twelve hundred for the stockwork.

A good deal has been written about forge-welding barrels over the years; some of the material has been good, some of it balderdash. Of course, writers have been at something of a disadvantage when you consider that they weren't able to talk with anyone who had actually *made* a rifle barrel from scratch — at least in most cases. I've always felt that the person best qualified to write about how something is done is the person who does it. Well, I'm certainly not a barrelmaker, and have no intention of ever becoming one, but I've been fortunate enough to watch several being made by contemporary smiths, so in this, consider me no more than a reporter.

Very few people have the ability and knowledge necessary to forge-weld barrels, for two very basic reasons. First, barrelwork is a trying experience even to a skilled blacksmith who is proficient at most other techniques at the forge. Second, the time consumed in producing welded barrels quite obviously makes them exceedingly expensive, as we've noted, and the completed tube shoots no better than a sixty-five-dollar standard item from a good barrel shop. What then, you say, is the justification for welding a barrel these days? Well, it has no basis in practicality, obviously. What we must consider is that fine handwork and the preservation of "lost" technology is no longer a luxury to us, if we are to maintain perspective in this plastic, disposable society of ours.

The fellow who largely pioneered a new study of forge-welding gun barrels in this country was Wallace Gusler, who for some years was master of the gunshop in Colonial Williamsburg. Wallace began welding barrels about 1963, as I recall; his skill in the art was largely self-taught, which is a monumental tribute to his ingenuity and perception. Wallace left the gunshop five years ago for curatorial pursuits, and barrelmaking along with the other functions of the shop there were left in the capable hands of Gary Brumfield and Jon Laubach.

Rifle barrels in this country, of course, were plain-skelp barrels. That is, formed up and welded from flat stock of plain wrought iron. Nowadays, mild steel such as SAE 1020 is used more often than iron. In Europe, many rifle barrels were made of pattern-welded skelps — "damascus" by any other name — from the end of the seventeenth century to the advent of the breechloader. The making of damascus tubes for shotguns continued to be a large

Barrel skelp is drawn out from rectangular mill stock (top). Flatter is used (above) for truing the skelp, and fuller is used (left) on the swage block, to "fuller" the skelp.

trade until World War One, particularly in the Vesdre Valley of Belgium. There is no evidence that damascus rifle barrels were ever produced in this country, and few if any shot barrels, for that matter. Recently, through the skilled efforts of Daryl Meier and Bob Griffith, the making of damascus rifle barrels in this country has become a reality.

In this issue, we'll look briefly at the production of a plain-skelp barrel, with methods used at Colonial Williamsburg, and next month, we'll study the techniques used in making a damascus barrel by Bob Griffith's methods. I'm indebted to Wallace Gusler, Gary Brumfield, Jon Laubach, and Bob Griffith for their assistance with this, and to Jay Gaynor, Armstrong Roberts, and Bob Griffith for procedural photography.

In the early days, barrelmakers depended heavily on the production of quality wrought iron by blast furnaces and rolling mills. Iron has a structure that's very much like wood: quite fibrous. Some of it is suitable for making barrels, and some isn't, depending upon the amount of slag present, silica content, grain structure, and so forth. Wrought iron was obtained by forging out cast-iron pigs at welding heat under triphammers. Cast iron has a high carbon content, and it is brittle and porous; the heat of forging and drawing out the pigs into long bars drove off much of the carbon, leaving ductile wrought iron. The forged bars were passed through rolling mills at red heat, and then passed again through slitting mills to reduce the long slabs into standard sizes ranging from quarter-inch nail rod up to big squares and various sizes of strap iron, depending upon the need. During the eighteenth century, the greatest quantities of iron came from Pennsylvania furnaces, though other colonies such as Virginia were also producers. Not every furnace was equipped to convert pig iron into wrought iron, though the larger operations generally were. An early blast furnace was a gargantuan operation, involving group work by a considerable number of specialists, and the work was heavy. Large

At left, skelp has been prepared for a butt-weld, is being closed over a mandrel. At right, seam is being welded shut. At far right, welded skelp is being forged into the familiar, traditional octagonal shape.

furnaces were often kept in blast a full nine months at a time, turning night into day with their fiery roar, and they decimated thousands of acres of hardwood in their never-ending hunger for charcoal. Since furnaces used limestone as a flux in smelting iron from the ore, it should be no mystery why the greatest number of furnaces were in the east-coast limestone belt.

Quite a number of techniques were used for making rifle barrels. Some were formed from a single skelp, while others were made up in short pieces, usually three on a rifle barrel, and then lap-welded together, which made it a bit easier to handle the material, since less weight and length were involved. Skelps were both lap-welded and butt-welded at the edges, though the bulk of American barrels I've examined were butt-welded, and most were probably made from a single skelp. The longrifle barrel shown here, being made by Wallace Gusler, started life as a bar of mild steel an inch thick, an inch and a quarter wide, and twenty-two inches long. Early smiths of course would have used wrought iron, which incidentally must be worked at higher heat than mild steel. Obtaining iron sized correctly for preparing skelps must have been a problem in the old days. At least one case is known where a gunmaker actually had skelps prepared at an iron works to his dimensions, tapered out on the triphammer, no doubt. This would have saved considerable work.

Manipulation of the fire is critical in forge work, particularly where welding is involved. Smiths in this country were largely forced to use charcoal for fuel until the nineteenth century. Charcoal is not as good as coal; charcoal isn't "self-containing," burning up quickly and not allowing good control of the heat, and it tends to spark, which makes heat colors difficult to read. Coal was used extensively in Europe and is used almost exclusively today. Good grades of coal suitable for forge work aren't easy to find, however; it needs to be low in sulphur content, free of fines or dust, and easy coking. Coke is made by coal burning in a relatively low-oxygen atmosphere, and the smith produces it by building a tight mound and wetting it, the steam assisting in the coking process. Needed is a dense fire so that oxygen from the bellows will be consumed and converted to other gasses before reaching the workpiece to prevent excessive scaling of the metal. The center of such a fire is somewhat a reducing atmosphere, in other words, and although white flame can be observed in the center, not a great deal of flame can be observed burning in the air. "Green" or uncoked coal is kept on the outside of the fire. Good forgework depends upon constant maintenance of the fire, pulling clinkers, recoking, and keeping the fire a dense mass so that the workpiece can be kept well buried away from oxygen. The metal is protected by the three or four inches of coke surrounding it.

Preparing the skelp is a long and tedious job, since it must be kept uniform and straight to avoid causing additional work during welding the barrel, and to assist in finishing with a truer hole in the welded tube. For a swamped barrel, the skelp had to be tapered in both thickness and width. The barrel in progress in the illustrations was drawn from a twenty-two-inch bar into a forty-inch skelp 3/8-inch thick and 3 5/16-inch wide at the breech, and 5/16-inch thick and 2 5/8-inch wide at the muzzle. Preparing the skelp in the early days was

often the work of three men, the master and two journeymen; the master wielded a small hammer called the mallet, used largely to indicate where he wanted blows landed by the sledges used by his assistants. Naturally, that took considerable coordination in the work. During the drawing process, the skelp must be kept at a bright yellow just under white welding heat to avoid shearing. Drawing distorted the skelp, causing it to skew; it must be worked from both sides of the bar and frequently stood on edge and trued. To finish the skelp, the surface is trued with a flatter, a hammer with a broad, square face that is simply laid on the skelp and driven down with a sledge wielded by a helper. If the barrel is to be lap-welded along the seam, the edges of the skelp must then be beveled, though they are left square for a butt-weld. The face of the anvil is kept clear of scale at all times to keep the skelp as clean as possible.

At dull red heat, the skelp is then "fullered" or bent into an open U, using the swage block, top fuller, and sledge to drive down the top fuller. Like the flatter, the top fuller is a short-handled hammer that has a "passive" role. The skelp is started in the widest grooves of the swage block and taken to successively smaller grooves to proceed with closing the U. A swage block, incidentally, was given the misnomer of "buffalo head" by Ned Roberts in *The Muzzleloading Cap Lock Rifle*. I have never seen that term used in connection with a swage block in early records, and a buffalo head, in fact, was apparently a special stake used in the hardy hole of an anvil for bending curves in strap iron, primarily for gate and railing work.

Fullering is begun on the outside edges of the skelp, working toward the center, to

Journeyman Dave Wagner, left, handles the lengthy chore of rough-reaming on the boring bench. Two weights at wheel end of bench pull carriage and barrel toward turning reamer by chain and pulley. Above, "short bit" roughing reamer is entering bore of the barrel.

Short bit, long bit, and rifling cutter. Leather washers on long bit prevent wooden backer from dropping off when the bit is not traversing the bore.

avoid bending the skelp into a **V** rather than a **U**. Before welding is begun, an approximately eight-inch section in the middle of the skelp is fullered down to the tightest **U** possible, the mandrel is inserted, and the skelp is closed down with the hammer. In the sequence shown here, the mandrel (or "needle" as the English called it) is a half-inch-diameter cold-rolled steel rod drawn three eighths of an inch at one end; the mandrel, of course, is manipulated by the assistant. A smith working by himself can't use a mandrel, and in fact Wallace Gusler made several barrels without using one. The resulting hole left in the barrel blank is then very tiny, requiring considerably more boring to open it up.

The smallest practical mandrel for use in welding a barrel is three eighths of an inch (0.375), according to several sources. If a smaller hole is needed in the welded barrel, then the hole must be closed down from the mandrel size during the process of forging the barrel flats. To obtain a cleaner hole, Gary Brumfield makes initial rough-reaming cuts in a barrel *before* forging the flats and closing the hole; this lessens the possibility of breaking small-diameter rough reamers in a small hole.

The skelp is buried in the fire, and the center section is brought to white welding heat, approximately twenty-three to twenty-six hundred degrees, and the edges of the open seam are fluxed. The flux, when melted, forms a coating on the metal that prevents oxidation, very necessary to avoid closing scale within the weld seam and risking failure thereby. Gusler used a combination of fine sand, borax, and iron filings in making the barrel shown, though plain borax does an adequate job by itself, according to some. At welding heat, the metal makes a faint crackling sound, sparking a bit as carbon is driven off; the skelp is drawn from the fire and carried to the swage block as quickly as possible to

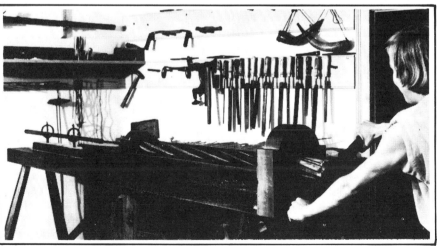

The rifling guide is simply a cylindrical wood form with hardwood strips forming helices, or spiraling splines, to produce the desired rate of twist as the rifling cutter is drawn through the bore.

avoid losing welding heat. The mandrel is quickly inserted, and the weld is started with relatively light but rapid blows of a three-pound hammer; the blows increase in intensity as the skelp begins to cool slightly. The first blows don't need to be heavy, since at welding heat, the metal fuses merely by touching. What is most important is just how the blows are directed on the seam. It's desirable for the seam to close at the bottom first and on the outside last, so that flux, scale, and other impurities are squirted out of the seam as it closes. No more than two inches of tube can be closed at one welding heat, and sometimes less, depending upon the thickness of the skelp. After the seam is completed, the metal has dropped below welding temperature into the yellow range, making a faint frying sound. The smith must know when to stop hammering, or the skelp may split, and not necessarily along the weld. A good eye is also needed, since scale in the joint shows as a darker line on the incandescent metal. As the seam is closed, the skelp lengthens approximately two inches for every ten inches of weld, and the weld seam tends to twist in the process, requiring an occasional straightening. Perhaps the greatest problem in forge-welding is keeping the joint clean and free of scale. So much surface of the metal is continually being lost in the form of ferro-ferric or black iron oxide that the skelp may lose ten pounds or more by the time the barrel is closed the full length — starting from the time when the skelp was a square rod.

Working from the center of the skelp, the skelp is closed and welded into a tube from the middle to the ends. Wallace completed a tube slightly over forty-one inches long in the process shown; an inch and an eighth of the ends was cut off, since the ends of a skelp tend to split as they're closed up. The rough forging then requires straightening, which must be done visually on the outside, since the hole left by the mandrel is too rough to sight through with any accuracy. The barrel exterior is then forged into an octagonal shape at red heat, either on the face of the anvil or in a swage block having octagonal grooves.

Boring was one of the most tedious jobs of the smith who had no power. Nearly thirty hours could easily be expended in rough boring and reaming, and quite a bit of tooling was required. It's not unusual to use a succession of six to eight rough reamers to open the hole in the barrel blank, and during the process, one or two could be expected to break. Rough reamers, or "short bits" as the old-timers called them, took many forms according to the practices of various smiths. The first bits run through the bore are slightly smaller than the mandrel hole, and only skim off high spots; and they are shorter than the larger-diameter rough reamers that follow. The first-cut bits may be no longer than three inches or so, while the final roughers that bring the bore close to final diameter may be as long as seven inches to assist in making a truer hole. The early cuts are problematical

because of scale in the hole, which quickly ruins the bits from the glass-hard surface the bit encounters. To avoid work-hardened spots in the tube, the barrel blank is always annealed to a uniform red heat in the forge and allowed to cool slowly in ashes, else a bit could easily encounter a hard spot and run off unduly.

The rough reamers used by the fellows at Williamsburg are generally formed as tapered squares with file-steel welded to one face to form the cutting edge; the bit blank is then given a hot twist and sharpened up with files, diagonally grooved across the working edges to clear chips, and hardened after it is scarf-welded to a smaller-diameter mild-steel rod. Since the bit has a tapered lead, it follows the hole left by the mandrel, so the barrel must be removed from the boring bench periodically and straightened in places. It isn't possible to straighten a crooked hole with drills or reamers. In the barrelmaking process shown here, Wallace started with a .25 bit three and a quarter inches long, and finished rough reaming with a .56 bit six and a half inches long; he used linseed oil throughout for lubrication, though nondrying oils such as lard oil and the like were probably used more often by early smiths.

All boring or rough reaming, finish reaming, and rifling in a barrel are done from breech to muzzle. This allows for tool wear, since as the tool wears, the hole becomes smaller — or, in the case of rifling, the groovers shallower. The reverse would be very undesirable — a barrel with the bore smaller at the breech than the muzzle. Although a choked bore doesn't necessarily make a rifle shoot better, a funneled bore certainly makes it shoot *worse*. All of the reaming is done on the boring bench, which is fitted with a sliding carriage that can be pulled into the turning bit by weights chained to the breech end of the carriage; Gusler's bench had about sixty pounds pulling the carriage. The barrel is fixed to the carriage in a pair of hoops, wedged tightly at the muzzle end and left a little loose at the breech for a self-centering "floating" effect. At times, the carriage is pulled into the turning bit by hand pressure rather than by weight, especially during finish operations. Oil can be blown into the bore with a blowpipe; dirty oil and chips have to be blown out of the bore after the bit has been pulled back out the breech.

After rough reaming, the barrel is straightened, usually by stretching a taut wire down the bore to locate high spots; the exterior is chalked at the point of bend, and the barrel is hammered or levered as necessary to straighten it. Finish reaming is then done with what the old boys called a "long" or "square" bit, a very precisely filed, hardened square backed on one side with a strip of hickory cut to a semicircular section. The finish reamer, with its backing, is a slip-fit in the hole left by the last roughing reamer. Leather washers are used to keep the hickory on the reamer while it is out of the bore, and as it emerges from the hole, the piece of leather is run onto the reamer to

prevent dropping the backing. The finish reamer makes a fine, scraping cut, and is considerably longer (twelve inches) than the roughing reamers. The amount of cut taken is regulated by strips of notepaper glued to the hickory backing — they are glued on to prevent chips from working their way between the numerous layers, and to keep the paper from working out. Especial care must be taken in using the long scrape reamer to provide enough lubrication to prevent scoring of the barrel wall by a chip, even a small one, caught on the cutting edge. When the reamer reaches the muzzle, it is cleaned and pulled back through the bore with the wheel turning rapidly. The number of paper shims added under the hickory depends of course upon the depth of cut needed to finish up the bore and remove all cuts left by the roughing reamers.

At this point, the bore can be further polished by casting a lead lap and lapping with fine pumice and oil, though this is a practice that seems to have been used more after steel barrels came into use in the nineteenth century, and particularly after forge-welding barrels was given over for deep-hole drilling after the mid-nineteenth century.

The outside of the barrel is usually finished up before rifling, since the removal of metal from the outside of the barrel, even after annealing, could result in stress-relieving that would cause the blank to warp slightly, requiring additional straightening before rifling. Forged barrels are hand-filed at Williamsburg, the flat rough-filed in pairs, checking with calipers, and then the top five flats draw-filed. Many old barrels show no filework at all on the bottom three flats, which is a tribute to the skill of the barrel forger. Large barrelmaking shops with water power finish-ground all flats; this was done with the barrel fixed between centers in a cradle, and likely with an indexing arrangement so that the grinding would be as true as possible and the bore centered in the mass. Despite this, bores on old barrels, even those from barrel mills, are often considerably off-center. Grinding was done with large slow-turning sandstone wheels, and the cuts were made at right angles to the barrel — a fact that can readily be observed on the bottoms of many old barrels. Incidentally, grinding was intended to remove forging marks and true up the flats, not to profile the barrel. Both swamped and straight-tapered barrels were forged to profile, since grinding them that way would have been prohibitive in terms of time and material wasted, and the likelihood of a blank warping would have been greatly enhanced by so much stock removal.

Rifling by hand is a familiar process that remained in use even up to World War Two with such barrelmakers as Harry Pope. Eighteenth-century gunmakers, of course, didn't have sophisticated sine-bar machines and the like for instantly changing the rifling pitch as needed. The wooden guide was generally cut for one twist, and that was used for all the barrels rifled. More than one twist can be cut into a guide, but the index pins would then ride in one or possibly two grooves in the guide, increasing the possibility of slop or torque in the movement of the cutter; this wasn't really practical until after steel guides came into use.

Rifling benches took several forms, ranging from the use of an old barrel as an index in more primitive shops, to the more conventional rigs such as the one shown here that was built by Wallace Gusler. Incidentally, this one is now worn out and has been replaced after fourteen years of service. A somewhat more unusual indexing system was used by Moravian gunmakers in Salem, North Carolina; the eighteenth-century rifling bench used there has a long yellow-pine block as the index head, and the inside of this one-piece block is actually rifled to match the pitch of the guide. This was certainly a difficult way to do it, but it provided a very positive alignment between the head and the guide.

Cutting was done by scrape cutters, or actually "hook" cutters, since they cut on the pull stroke, cutting from breech to muzzle. In the early days, the cutter head frequently had but a single "saw" or cutter. Later, paired and even multiple rifling broaches came into use. The cutters were set on the rifling rod at the same helix as the pitch of the rifling; many old ones were set into hardwood heads. The fellows at Williamsburg prefer to chisel a mortise in a steel head for the cutter, which is better in that there is no tendency for the mortise to enlarge during rifling. Old barrels tend to have seven grooves, although that isn't always the case; the Germans, in fact, were fond of experimenting, and a fair number of *stutzens* were cut with polygroove rifling. Polygonal rifling, in fact, also came into use early.

Rifling cutters in the eighteenth century were more often than not cut with radii to leave round-bottom grooves, though square-bottom cutters were also used. Radiused grooves must be cut slightly deeper than square ones; they are slightly easier to clean, and will take a bit more fouling because of their depth, but they offer no important advantage over square ones.

The cutter head is either made close to bore size, or, as the gunsmiths in Williamsburg do it, the head is shimmed up to bore size with hickory splints wired in place. The first passes of the cutter are exceedingly light, and the cutter is raised on subsequent cycles by slipping bond-paper shims under the cutter. Screw-adjustable "wedge" cutter heads came into use by the mid-nineteenth century and were quicker to use, but the shimmed cutter does just as good work. In either case, rifling is a matter involving good concentration if the grooves are to end up of equal depth. The cutter is pulled through until it is no longer bringing out fine shavings, and the guide is then turned over one groove in the index head, and the next groove started, and so forth. To allow for wear of the rifling cutter, the

order is alternated. If the grooves are cut clockwise one time, they might be cut in the opposite direction or counterclockwise for the next cutting depth, and the starting point might be changed from one groove to another diametrically opposite — all to ensure that the grooves finish up equal in depth and width. The cutter requires constant cleaning and lubrication, and may have to be stoned several times during the rifling of a barrel. Six or seven shims are needed under the cutter by the time the final passes are being made, the number of shims of course determined by the thickness of the stock. Generally, a piece of bond paper is no thicker than about three thousandths; much more than that would cause too heavy a cut on a rifling cutter, and might cause galling or tearing.

Some barrels of the flintlock period that are in fine condition show no finish-reamer marks on the lands, indicating that the barrel was finished off by running a scrape cutter down the lands as well, much in the same fashion that a worn barrel is "freshed" out. Gary Brumfield and Jon Laubach routinely do this on new barrels; the process has the advantage of leaving all machining marks running the length of the bore, and the corners of the lands are left sharp but unburred. Some German rifles were actually finished off with concave lands, or lands with a smaller radius than the radius of the bore; this finishing technique persisted well into the twentieth century, particularly on schuetzen rifles. In any event, lands are cut just as if the barrel were being freshed: a lead slug is either cast or "bumped up" in the bore, a cutter mortised in on the position of one of the lands, and the resulting tool used to make light cuts that remove all reamer marks. The radius of the cutter normally matches that of the bore.

As rifling cutters emerge from the muzzle, they tend to cant slightly, leaving shallower grooves; this may require trimming the muzzle of the barrel back slightly. However, early smiths likely removed most of that when chamfering the muzzle. Modern barrelmakers use a sixty-degree countersink for chamfering, but old barrels were not so treated until well into the nineteenth century. Instead, the lands were simply taken down, probably with files, until no lands were left just at the muzzle, leaving a gradual countersink that ran back into the bore five sixteenths of an inch or more. The grooves were then opened up, usually with round files, just at the muzzle. Opening up the grooves again was done largely for appearance, since the muzzle otherwise would appear to be worn out. The result is a long, sloping countersink that doesn't even look like a countersink in the modern sense, and it allowed a patched ball to be started in the bore with nothing more than the ramrod. Contrary to what you might think, this does not harm the shooting quality of the barrel, but care must be taken to ensure that the "break" point of the counterbore is even. I prefer to finish off all my barrels in this fashion, since it makes the

rifle easier to use, and the muzzle has a traditional appearance. Cutting this "funnel" on the lathe is a better alternative than filing, however.

Breechplugs are forged up, filed, and threaded with a screw plate; the thread shank is left long and given a taper so that it can be started into the screw plate straight. Patent break-off breeches were considerably more work, of course, and they were seldom used in this country on longrifles. In Europe, specialist breech-filers made use of die-forgings for breeches. Probably the most efficient breech was that used by the Mantons; it was recessed on the side, thereby reducing considerably the thickness of barrel wall the ignition flame had to traverse, but it also required a lock with a lug formed in the pan area to fit the breech.

Few breeches on old rifles were threaded much more than three eighths of an inch deep, even on large-bore rifles, though the Germans did often use a long thread shank as much as an inch long, which was counterbored. On large-diameter barrels where a patent breech wasn't to be used, vents were often drilled all the way through the barrel, and then a larger bit was passed back through the barrel from the opposite side, leaving an inside counterbore on the vent, with no more than an eighth of an inch of barrel wall at the vent. The resulting hole in the opposite flat of the barrel was then fitted with a threaded plug that was peened over on the surface to conceal it. This of course couldn't be done on a damascus barrel without spoiling the pattern at that point. Consequently, damascus barrels were usually fitted with a threaded vent liner counterbored from the inside; these were of gold until shortly after 1800, when platinum also came into use. Plain iron barrels, of course, were also fitted with liners, though they are rare on American rifles.

Though it is less convenient to stock up a barrel that has been vented, since lock position becomes more critical, forged barrels must be vented and proved before stocking up, for obvious reasons. In England, rifle barrels were often given a provisional proof — that is, proofed before rifling and even before the exterior was finished. This of course saved labor if the barrel burst or opened a seam. If it did open, it was often possible to insert a mandrel, reweld the barrel, and ream it up to a larger caliber, and this couldn't be done easily if the tube was rifled.

Gusler used to kid blacksmith John Algood at Williamsburg. He'd tell visitors "I proof my barrels with a double charge and two balls. John just pours his full of water to see if they leak." Actually, hydrostatic proofing of barrels is possible, and was practiced by at least one English gunmaker in the nineteenth century.

The making of damascus barrels is considerably more involved in respect to preparing the skelp, and even the manner in which the skelp is welded. We'll have a look at that in the next issue. ●

PART TWO

JOHN BIVINS:

THE FORGE-WELDED

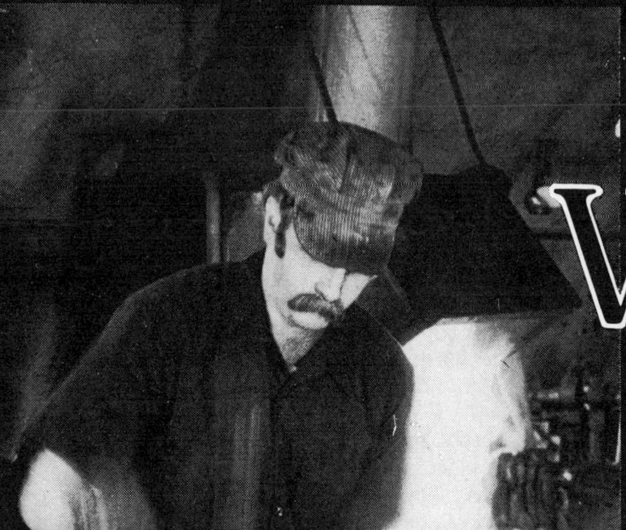

THE DAMASCUS BARREL

IN *RIFLE* 64, WE TOOK a brief look at the production of a plain-skelp rifle barrel, using methods typical of the eighteenth century and before. In this issue, we'll see how one young man working now has managed to successfully forge damascus barrels equal in beauty to fine originals.

Most of us think of shotguns when we think of damascus, but during the muzzleloading period in Europe, particularly during the eighteenth and nineteenth centuries, fine-quality rifles ranging from wheellocks and "jagers" to elegant London-made percussion sporting rifles were fitted with exquisite damascus barrels. A long-standing project of mine has been a late seventeenth-century-style buttstock wheellock, and I was determined to have a damascus barrel for it when I discovered a fellow a few years ago who was experimenting with the process. He'd made a small damascus cannon barrel, a sight that damned near left me speechless. I usually can find many reasons for wending my way to the Fall Nationals at Friendship each year, but meeting artisans following such pursuits are by far the most important reason to me for making that long drive. More on that later.

The term *damascus* when applied to gun barrels is actually a misnomer. True Damascus was actually a high-carbon steel that came into use some time during or before the sixteenth century. It had an international reputation for its use in sword blades, and the best of it was ultimately wrought in Persia. The actual raw material was at first made in India in the form of *wootz,* a primitive form of cementation steel actually made in the forge by using the charcoal fuel of the fire as a source for carbon. The charge comprised both wrought iron and cast iron; this alloy was brought to a heat above welding temperature, the mixture actually melting down. However, the forge fire couldn't be taken to a temperature high enough for a complete melt, and consequently the resulting alloy had areas of differing carbon content. When the steel was refined by forging, wrought into blades, and then etched, the differing amounts of carbon present showed up as "watered" pattern in the steel.

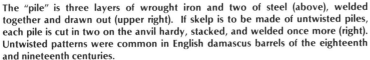

The "pile" is three layers of wrought iron and two of steel (above), welded together and drawn out (upper right). If skelp is to be made of untwisted piles, each pile is cut in two on the anvil hardy, stacked, and welded once more (right). Untwisted patterns were common in English damascus barrels of the eighteenth and nineteenth centuries.

RIFLE BARREL

Damascus was difficult to work, possibly because of its high carbon content; it was prone to shearing under the hammer.

Quite in contrast with true Damascus steel was welded damascus such as that used in gun barrels, and it wasn't a steel at all but a welded material that combined sections of both iron and steel. For gun barrels, sixty percent iron and forty percent steel became a norm by the nineteenth century. The process of making welded damascus (used here with a lowercase *d* to differentiate from true Damascus steel) apparently originated in the Near East by the sixteenth century. Though it was thought to give good texture and strength to gunbarrels, the first motivation for the production of the metal may have been to create a more easily produced version of real Damascus. Of course, welded damascus containing iron wasn't particularly suitable for blades. The metal was sounder than much plain wrought iron, however, because the elements that made it up had been worked to such a great degree by the hammer, thereby driving out impurities.

Little seems to be known about the introduction of damascus into Europe,

though several possibilities exist. Northern attacks by the Ottoman Empire had carried damascus-barreled pieces into Austria in the seventeenth century; the siege of Vienna in 1683 saw some 200,000 Turkish soldiers in arms there, and no doubt after the Ottomans were repulsed, many damascus-barreled pieces remained behind. It seems apparent that many such barrels were used to make up new long guns and pistols after that, particularly in Austria, but it is also evident that European merchants began purchasing and even ordering damascus barrels in Turkey and Persia soon afterward. Damascus rifle barrels were in use in central Europe by the end of the seventeenth century; dated pieces may be found that will pinpoint the use of the metal for rifles, but an exact date can't be assigned here. Whether the first damascus barrels used for rifles were made in the Near East or in Europe is a moot point, but most of those encountered have only European marks on them. It seems probable, then, that damascus rifle barrels were being made in European centers at least by the first quarter of the eighteenth century, and most of them were of twisted skelps. English barrelmakers took up the art by the mid-eighteenth

century, though the English preferred the plainer. barrels resulting from the use of untwisted skelps, and this taste prevailed largely until the end of the percussion era. Also, while Europeans preferred to finish damascus by etching the surface to raise the pattern as the Turks and Persians had done, English gunmakers used a "flush" finish that was more difficult to bring off, especially since their patterns were not so dramatic.

Damascus was brought to its highest development in Liege, Belgium, and the nearby Vesdre Valley by the end of the nineteenth century. Some of the patterns produced were incredibly complex, the result of preparing skelps from as many as a thousand elements welded together, twisted, welded again, and then welded up in a spiral pattern. Damascus persisted on fine sporting guns until after World War Two, but the introduction of fluid-steel barrels on shotguns had sounded the death knell of the art by the 1880s. Incidentally, I'd like to put away one notion that has plagued us for many years, and that is the strength characteristics of damascus. Many writers have solemnly advised us that the metal

Robert Griffith forged this damascus barrel, of both twisted and untwisted piles. Twisted piles show as "watered" patterns on the etched and browned barrel. C.R. and D.E. Getz finish-profiled and bored it to .54 for a wheellock rifle recently stocked by John.

Piles to be twisted are taken to heat and then twisted with a wrench (left). Above are three twisted piles welded together to form a barrel skelp. Note alternating directions of twists.

"eats itself up" from within, finally bursting like a rotten melon. That simply isn't true. Damascus has all of the strength of wrought iron, and perhaps a little more if the welds are perfect, though the spiral welding was no addition to strength in spite of what the old boys believed. Wrought iron has long fibers, and a plain iron barrel opens like a banana peel when it bursts, while damascus lets fly at the edges of the spirally wound skelp when it fails. Both wrought iron and damascus have adequate tensile strength for any conceivable charge of *black powder* if they were well made. The thing that has given damascus such a bad name is that too many idiots have tried to use modern progressively burning powders in damascus tubes. Since smokeless has an entirely different pressure-time curve than black powder, with pressure peaks *farther* up the bore, damascus shotguns occasionally blow just forward of the chambers where the barrels begin to thin. *Good* damascus is safe with black powder.

Bob Griffith, who is a fine blacksmith in Montrose, Pennsylvania, is the smith shown making what is probably the first damascus rifle barrel made in America. Bob became interested in the process while enrolled in the ironworking program at Southern Illinois University in 1974; there he met Daryl Meier, who had been making welded damascus blades before he became involved in the same program. After working with Daryl on various aspects of forging damascus, Bob became interested in the production of gunbarrels, and the result is

shown here in the photographic sequence. The barrel shown was made of untwisted skelps, but during the process, we'll cover the methods used for making twisted-skelp barrels as well.

Preparing the billet or "pile," as the Europeans called it, is the first step in making damascus. The pile was made of alternating layers of iron and steel; for those used to make the barrel in progress here, Griff made up the pile with the outside layers of iron; since iron can take more heat than steel, it serves as an insulating "blanket." The iron he used was old wagon tires. English barrelmakers in the eighteenth century liked to make up iron for the piles from old horseshoe-nail stubs — hence the term *stub twist* — because the nails had been worked down to such an extent at the forge and were freer from impurities. Iron is problematical today, since it is no longer produced in this country, though foreign iron can be purchased in a few places. The steel used here was a low-carbon variety with 0.2 percent carbon and 0.39 percent manganese. This may represent a practical upper limit for carbon content in steel for making damascus barrels, since steels with higher carbon contents can create serious problems of differentials in welding temperatures. The welding temperature of wrought iron is higher than even mild steel, and high-carbon steel is easily burned in the fire when the heat is taken too high.

Griff's five-piece billet, for ease of handling, normally is left with one plate long

to use as a handle. Early barrelmakers simply wired the billet together with iron wire and handled the thing with tongs. The billet is set *on edge* in the fire so that all of the elements come to heat at the same time; when it reaches orange heat, he fluxes the ends of the pile with 20 Mule Team Borax and slowly brings the mass up to welding heat. Griff looks for a milky-white, glossy surface on the metal, and at that point it has reached the same incandescence as the fire. The billet is quickly pulled out and taken to the anvil, where light, rapid blows of the hammer are given to the center of the billet, using heavier blows working toward the ends. The first blows are directed to the center so that flux and scale squirt out the sides and are not trapped inside. No more than ten seconds' working time is available before the pile begins to lose welding heat and must be returned to the fire.

When it is completely welded, the billet is then drawn out from its original six inches to a full foot, with the metal worked at yellow heat. The billet is then cut exactly in half on the hardy of the anvil, and the halves piled one atop the other and welded once again, resulting now in nine laminates. There are actually *ten* layers, but since the outside laminates are of iron, two iron layers are welded together, causing, in effect, the loss of one layer. If a greater number of smaller laminates were required, the billet could then be drawn to twelve inches again, cut, and stacked back on itself once again. For the barrel in progress here, Bob welded another billet to the first one; both had been drawn, cut, restacked, and drawn to eight inches long. The new pile thus yielded seventeen laminates and represented a complete billet ready to be forged to proper skelp size. The skelp pieces are worked down into squares from these completed billets. The length of each section of skelp varies according to the thickness of it, but none used here was much more than twelve to fourteen inches, meaning that a thirty-two-inch barrel can be made up from as many as fifteen pieces of skelp. Of course, skelp pieces can be made longer. The barrel in progress here would have had a skelp sixteen feet long if it had been one piece; it's more convenient to keep the pieces short for ease of handling.

Twisted or untwisted, skelp is wound tightly around mandrel. Welding begins with "jumping up" — driving the white-hot section of barrel straight down on its end, against the face of the anvil.

After the first section of barrel is welded, a new section of skelp is scarf-welded to the end, and another section of wrap is begun.

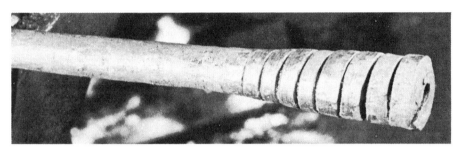

If a barrel is to have a twisted skelp, then a different technique is used after the billet is welded and drawn out to eight to ten inches long. Rather than being halved and restacked, the billet is instead taken to red heat, one end clamped in a vise, and the entire billet twisted with a wrench from one end to the other. The degree of heat used is critical to avoid having iron elements shear. Before twisting, the corners of the billet are lightly flattened with the hammer to avoid causing stress points later. After twisting, a half inch is cut off each end of the billet, since that much of the billet had remained untwisted, being held by the vise and wrench. The amount of twisting varies according to the job, though eight to ten twists per inch produce a pattern consistent with European barrels of the eighteenth century. Actually, the billet must be twisted a bit tighter than needed, since all forging processes after twisting tend to unwind the billet. The number of twists per inch doesn't make the laminates finer in the finished pattern, but it does make the pattern itself finer. Really delicate lines in the pattern are a function of drawing out the billet to greater length, thereby making the laminates thinner before twisting; eighteenth-century patterns, particularly on rifle barrels, were relatively heavy. In fact, only on thin smoothbore tubes is it possible to bring the pattern down to its most delicate appearance.

After twisting and cutting off the ends on the hardy, the billet is then resquared on the anvil to prepare it for welding to other billets; this is done to avoid welding round sections together and possibly leaving voids as the result. The number of twisted billets to be welded together depends upon the nature of the pattern desired. In the photos, Bob is joining three billets to make a fairly coarse pattern. The twisted billets are then welded together; little more than one inch per welding heat can be completely brought together and still ensure a perfect weld with no voids. After welding together, the three-strand billet is then drawn into skelp sizes just as I described the untwisted skelps being prepared above.

Whether untwisted or twisted skelps have been prepared, the next step is to begin the wrap. Though a little unusual, the combination of both twisted and untwisted billets into one skelp was at times used, at least in the eighteenth century; the wheellock

With a bottom fuller in the hardy hole, the weld is consolidated. This barrel is being formed around a mandrel; the finished barrel shown on a preceding page was forged solid, then given a hot twist full-length.

barrel shown was made up this way, showing the candy-stripe pattern of the untwisted elements alternating with the more complex pattern of twisted piles that had been welded to them.

The first piece of skelp is clamped in the vise at one end, with the mandrel clamped next to it, and the skelp is wound around the mandrel at heat and using the hammer, with an assistant holding the mandrel in place. More efficient methods of doing this were used in the old days; the Belgians, for example, did the wrapping in a bottom swage or swage block with a device for holding the skelp to the mandrel. The wrap must be kept as tight on the mandrel as possible, and the coils close to each other,

which is no mean task. The section of wrapped skelp is now fluxed and brought to welding heat for two or three inches of its length and "jumped-up" on the anvil by driving the end of the section of barrel straight down on the anvil face; when the barrel is longer, the skelps are jumped on a steel plate on the floor. Jumping-up welds only the innermost corners of the skelp, since during the wrapping stage, the skelp has become trapezoidal in section, with the narrow face on the outside. One three-inch section of barrel is taken to three separate heats to close the coils as much as possible, fluxing each time, and brushing off scale with a wire brush before returning the piece of barrel to the fire. This jumping-up is

411

done with the mandrel in place, in this case a three-eighths-inch steel rod. Since the length of welded seam in a damascus barrel is so long, extreme care must be taken to ensure that the work is kept clean throughout welding.

Some fifty to sixty percent of the seam between the coils is closed after the third jumping-up; the remainder of the seam is then closed at welding heat with the hammer, with the barrel resting in the swage block. The gap remaining is difficult to close, and three inches of length may take from five to ten heats to close the spiral seam. To avoid sticking, the mandrel is occasionally given a light coat of oil so that it creates its own gaseous envelope, thereby avoiding any possible fusion. After the first section of skelp is completely welded, a second section is started. To accommodate the new wrap, a short piece of the skelp making up the first section of barrel must be left unwelded so that the end of it can be scarfed (chamfered) to receive the similarly scarfed end of the next section of skelp. After the end of the second piece of skelp is welded to the first section of barrel, the skelp is wrapped and jumped-up, and welding proceeds as it is described above. Now, however, there is an additional problem of bringing the unwelded section to proper welding heat without burning, especially when working the welds near the completed section of barrel, since the unwelded coil comes to heat much faster than the welded section. The workpiece must be constantly shifted from side to side in the fire to bring up the consolidated section of barrel without burning the freshly wrapped and unwelded section.

Wrapping and welding continues in this fashion, and when the skelp that will form the muzzle end is attached, the end of it is scarfed so that the muzzle of the blank can be finished-off square and won't have to be cut off. Joints between the skelps are visible as a line to the experienced eye, though most wouldn't see them.

When the barrel has been completely welded, it is forged octagon, annealed, and finished using the same processes used in making a standard U-skelp barrel. If open welds are revealed while boring, more often than not, they can be reconsolidated by forge welding, and in fact Greener mentions that this was a common practice with Birmingham makers.

There are other means of making a damascus barrel, some of which are more practical to use today. One source illustrates what is probably a Turkish or Persian barrel that has a slow spiral to the pattern that actually *reverses* itself — something of a shock to the eye until one understands what was done. In that example, the barrelmaker, rather than spirally wrapping the barrel skelp around a mandrel, had simply forged out the piles, twisting some of them, and then welded the piles together to form a long flat skelp. The barrel was then welded up just in the same manner a plain-skelp barrel would be done. After welding, the smith brought the tube to heat, chucked it in the vise, and gave it a hot twist, alternating the twist direction from one section of barrel to another.

Carrying this idea a bit further, Griff determined that it would be possible to weld a solid damascus bar that could be deep-hole drilled, thereby saving considerable labor and cost. To do this, Griff prepared four long pieces of skelp, each piece composed of one untwisted and two twisted piles to provide an alternating pattern. The four pieces of skelp were bundled and welded together, and the weighty blank was then forged into an octagon full-length. The blank was then taken to heat and given a hot-twist just in the same fashion a pile would be twisted. To ensure solid welds, Griff then worked the twisted blank end-to-end at welding heat, finishing with a heavy round blank. This was the method used for producing the wheellock barrel illustrated here.

Drilling, reaming, rifling, and profiling the blank fell the lot of Dick and Don Getz in Beavertown, Pennsylvania — fine barrelmakers whom we covered in *Rifle* 58. Griff brought the blank down to Beavertown, and I drove up. We spent the next day and a half hovering over that blank like a pair of mother hens, grinning foolishly as lathe or mill cuts revealed each section of figure to the eye, clucking and chortling as the finish reamer left a brilliant, flawless bore finish. The good brothers Getz were more than a little apprehensive that something would go awry, spoiling a piece of work that had an ungodly amount of time in the making, but there was never a bobble. They finally relaxed after we proofed the barrel twice with a hundred and fifty grains of FFg and two patched .535 balls, the mike showing no swelling anywhere.

God only knows what that first successful barrel cost if all the hours of research, trial and error, telephone calls, and the scrabbling about for good coal and iron were all totted up. But it worked, and now if the muzzleloading gunmaker wants something *really* unusual — and has a flush customer — he can contact Bob Griffith at Box 6; Montrose, Pennsylvania 18801, for a true damascus barrel. Griff hasn't set firm prices at this writing, but I feel sure that a finished barrel of a size appropriate for a "jager" or London-style percussion rifle will likely swallow up an honest eight hundred dollars in short order. For less fanciful longrifles, Griff can supply plain-skelp forge-welded barrels for considerably less. He's not likely to be exactly flooded with orders for such special things, nor does he want to be, since there are many other areas of blacksmithing that hold his interest; his ornamental work, in fact, is prize-winning.

Years ago, I asked Wallace Gusler how in the devil he'd perfected so many "lost" techniques working on his own. What he told me was simple enough, but it's carried me a long way. He said, "Well, I figure if they did it then, I can do it now." *Then*, of course, artisans had the benefit of seven years' formal apprenticeship in their trade. Nowadays, most people can't even identify above a half-dozen types of handfiles. Even so, well motivated fellows like Gusler, Brumfield, Laubach, and Griffith have provided us lazier types with the sure knowledge that fine, traditional handwork still represents the innermost core of craftmanship, and will persist. Such things should give us a better perception of the proper uses of modern technology in the trade. ●

Section 10

RESTORATION

New Life for Old Rifles

By HENRY BEVERAGE

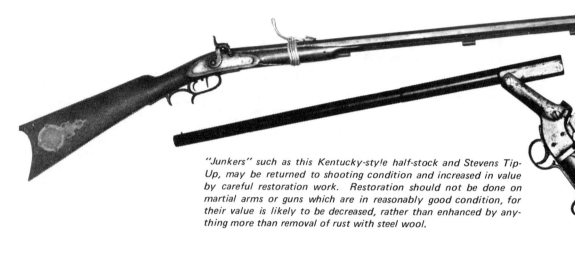

"Junkers" such as this Kentucky-style half-stock and Stevens Tip-Up, may be returned to shooting condition and increased in value by careful restoration work. Restoration should not be done on martial arms or guns which are in reasonably good condition, for their value is likely to be decreased, rather than enhanced by anything more than removal of rust with steel wool.

I KNOW A MAN who gets a lot of enjoyment out of buying old rifles and restoring them to some semblance of their original condition. He frequents the second-hand stores and pawn shops, calls on dealers occasionally and, until a couple of years ago, took in some of the small-town and country auctions. He gave up the latter source because, as he expressed it, "The 'amateurs' are paying such fantastic prices that I couldn't compete."

This man is not a gunsmith. He is just a fellow who needed a hobby and discovered that he enjoyed working with his hands. I wouldn't call him a collector since he seldom keeps any of his restorations more than a few months, selling them at a tidy profit or trading for pieces with greater appeal. He restricts himself to caplocks and flintlocks: rifles, muskets and fowling pieces, but will occasionally pick up an old single shot rifle if the price is attractive.

He first came to me several years ago with an old caplock fowling piece that was in rather rough shape. The wood had been patched at the breech, the fore-stock was split, the barrel was pitted and the hammer was loose on the tumbler. He wanted to know if the gun could be "fixed up." When I told him it could be, he asked if I thought he could do it. I said I was sure he could and, it being one of those afternoons when there were no pressing problems, I showed him what to do.

After separating the lock and barrel from the stock I ran a dowel down the bore and made a pencil mark at the muzzle. I then took the dowel out and held it on the outside of the barrel with the mark at the muzzle. The other end of the rod was opposite the drum thus assuring me that the barrel was not loaded. This test should be a *must* before doing any work on any old frontloader. I've examined several which had powder and ball in the barrel and one old musket was found to be loaded with small rocks and shingle nails. (I've been told that it was common practice years ago for farmers to load these old guns with what was easily available, stand them alongside the shed door against the time when a fox or hawk would appear in the yard. If one never appeared, the piece was never discharged.)

The nipple came out easily and the drum responded after a few drops of Tapfree on the thread, but the breech plug, as usual, required heat before it could be removed. With the breech open we examined the inside of the barrel. A stiff wire cleaning brush dipped in rust solvent loosened the worst of the corrosion, but it required a lot of swabbing with Hoppe's (I now use Hoppe's No. 9-Plus) to find out what the bore looked like. It was rough but shootable if cleaned after each shot.

Because these old fowling piece barrels are so thin, it's a wise idea to polish the inside of the bore with coarse abrasive cloth on a dowel spun by a hand drill, particularly in the lower end of the barrel. Don't expect to polish out all the pits, but this polishing will reveal any really serious pitting that might make the barrel unsafe. If the barrel is too rough, there is not much that can be done with it without relining, which is seldom worth what it costs; usually they are too thin to permit re-boring. If you intend to shoot an old fowler, it's particularly important that the gun first be loaded with a stiff charge and fired while roped to a tire. Most of these barrels weren't overly strong to begin with, and a century of corrosion may have made them potentially lethal.

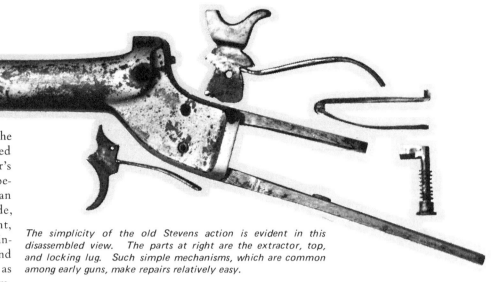

The simplicity of the old Stevens action is evident in this disassembled view. The parts at right are the extractor, top, and locking lug. Such simple mechanisms, which are common among early guns, make repairs relatively easy.

Our next step was to examine the lock. The outside was good, showed some engraving and the lockmaker's name, Jos'h Golcher, was stamped below the drum cut-out. It would clean up nicely with 3-0 steel wool. Inside, the lock was in very good shape, tight, with only some light rust on the mainspring and bridle. A little polishing and some light oil would make it as good as new. I tightened the hammer by shimming two sides of the square hole.

That left only the stock. A new piece would have to be fitted behind the breech on the lock side and I gave the man a piece of scrap walnut that would about match the color and grain of the original and showed him how to chisel out the old patch and fit a better one. The split forestock was just a matter of applying epoxy cement and holding the parts together with tape. The brass fittings, or furniture, as they are called, would have to be removed and the tarnish polished off, the wood sanded and new finish applied.

Not much could be done with the barrel but I suggested that if he wanted to he could take off what remained of the old finish, polish it bright and brown it with Birchwood-Casey Plum Brown, a fast-acting solution that works very well on these old barrels.

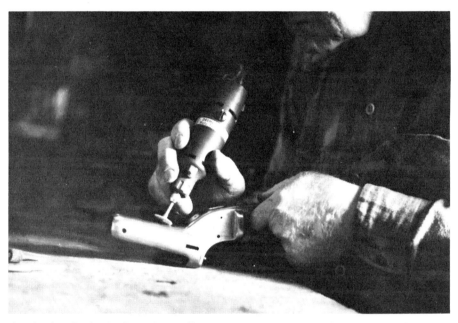

An abrasive disc in the Dremel was effective in removing pitting and the remnants of the original nickel plating on the Stevens. The metal was checked with cold blue to determine that all plating had been removed. Final polishing of the frame was done with a belt sander.

Before the man left with the gun he told me he had bought it on impulse in a second-hand store several years before. While thinking about something for a spare-time project he got the idea of restoring the piece, and a dealer for whom I've done some work sent him to me. I wondered when he left if he would go through with the job and if I'd ever see him again. I did, as often as he picked up an old relic or finished restoring one.

Some of you may like to know what an old-timer in the antique gun game looks for when examining an old firearm with the idea of buying it. We will talk first about muzzle-loading rifles since they are more commonly found and have not yet reached the price levels of the single shots, although original Kentuckies, some of the picket ball rifles, and slug guns by famous makers

Pits in the Stevens barrel were removed with a file and abrasive cloth held under a file, while turning in the lathe. Final polishing was with the belt sander, using crocus cloth. Flats on the breech end of the barrel were draw-filed, as at right, followed by 2-0 abrasive cloth under the file for final finish. Flats on rough octagon barrels can be finished in the same manner.

are now priced beyond the reach of the average old-gun buyer.

The first thing to be considered before purchasing an antique firearm is what it will be used for; whether as a decorator to hang over the fireplace, as a shooting piece, or as a potential source of profit. Many old rifles, muskets or fowling pieces, make good decorators with little or no restoration. A rifle to be used for shooting, or to be re-sold or traded, frequently requires a lot of work to make it safe, dependable and presentable.

And, it must be remembered that a gun which is rare, or in reasonably good condition, or for any other reason commands a high price at the time of purchase, is not a proper subject for restoration. It might look much better, or

be safe to shoot after the restoration, but the value is likely to be sharply decreased, rather than enhanced, as a result of your efforts.

The old admonition, "Let the buyer beware", is a good guideline in the antique gun game. This doesn't mean that anyone having a used gun for sale is a knave. It does mean that the pitfalls are many and varied. They are hidden beneath rust, under old varnish, in the mechanism and in the barrel. But if the potential buyer knows what to look for and keeps his eyes and mind open they can be detected before deciding whether or not to purchase.

Locks should be inspected thoroughly. Check the way the hammer strikes the nipple. It should hit squarely. Does it stay at full cock and half cock? Is it

loose? Have the seller remove the lock so you can get a look at the working parts. Check the tumbler and bridle for looseness and the sear for wear at the tip. Notice whether the parts all look original. If it is a flintlock note the position of the mainspring tip on the tumbler when the cock (hammer) is down and see if the stop on the cock is resting on the top edge of the lock plate. These are little things but they can be troublesome if they have to be repaired or replaced.

Single triggers are usually in good condition. Double-set triggers are often found with broken springs and in some cases the bar may be fractured or the tip badly worn. They are not easy to repair. Parts can be had but they rarely fit. When the adjustment screw is missing there is likely to be a problem

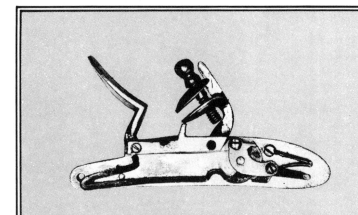

These photos show the basic similarities and differences between typical caplock and flintlock actions. Principal point of wear in the flintlock is the tip of the mainspring, where it bears against the tumbler. The attachment holes in both the hammer and cock are prone to wear, but can be tightened by shimming.

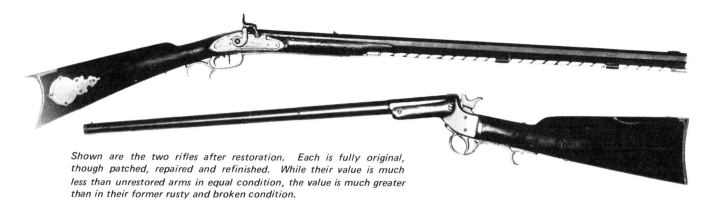

Shown are the two rifles after restoration. Each is fully original, though patched, repaired and refinished. While their value is much less than unrestored arms in equal condition, the value is much greater than in their former rusty and broken condition.

in finding one of the right size and thread.

The *only* way to make a satisfactory inspection of the inside of a muzzle-loading barrel is to remove it from the stock and take out the breech plug. Any of the several kinds of bore lights will provide a rough idea of the condition but they are poor substitutes for the bore-picture you can get by holding a barrel to a strong light and looking through it from both ends. Chances are it won't look very good. Few of them do. After years of black powder shooting and careless cleaning, or none at all, it's a minor miracle when one is found in good shooting condition. Bore condition is not important if the rifle is to be used as a wall decoration, and some collectors don't demand perfection in an otherwise desirable piece.

Imperfections in stocks are usually easy to detect. Scratches are easily removed, dents can sometimes be swelled out with a damp cloth and a hot iron, but when wood is missing it has to be replaced. Clean breaks and splits can be repaired with modern adhesives. Look for tiny checks that can open up when a patchbox or buttplate is removed.

The foregoing applies to all caplock rifles and fowling pieces, to flintlocks of the pre-Civil War era and to caplock muskets. As a general rule all martial arms should be left as is. Their value depends more on the model, the maker and the period than on condition. This is also true of the many breech-loading carbines that made their appearance just before and during the Civil War.

Determining a fair price for an antique firearm depends on many factors; type, age, the maker, condition and the reason for wanting to own it. I have a long-standing idea that a gun is worth somewhere between what the seller wants to get for it and what the buyer is willing to pay. Dickering will often produce a price acceptable to both parties thus establishing, to my mind, the value of the piece at the time of sale. Supply and demand, of course, regulate prices to a great extent, but there are no hard and fast values in the antique gun game.

Now let's look at an old caplock that recently came my way. You've probably heard of things being held together with baling wire. Well, this old rifle was held together with baling twine, the kind that is used for tying

up bales of hay. The gun is a Kentucky-style half-stock and the caliber, .36, would classify it as a squirrel rifle.

The forearm was split from the front end to the lock, a piece was broken off where the lock plate joins the breech, another piece was missing on one side of the forearm and a split in the butt extended to the patch box. The set triggers didn't work and there was considerable rust on the inside of the lock. All of the brass fittings were heavily tarnished and the wood marred in several places. The exterior of the barrel was badly rusted but there were no pits and since it was originally browned, would polish to a good finish. The bore was pretty bad, rusted and pitted.

What can be done with a gun in this condition? Is it worth the time required to restore it plus the cost of having the barrel re-cut? In this case the answer is "yes", which was the reason I bought it. The piece is unquestionably an original Kentucky half stock, made in the 1850's or before, and has a potential value warranting considerable outlay in time.

How did I identify the rifle as a true Kentucky? First: the style, or lines, of

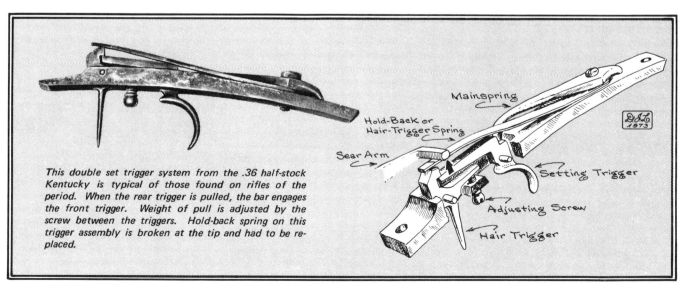

This double set trigger system from the .36 half-stock Kentucky is typical of those found on rifles of the period. When the rear trigger is pulled, the bar engages the front trigger. Weight of pull is adjusted by the screw between the triggers. Hold-back spring on this trigger assembly is broken at the tip and had to be replaced.

the stock are typical early Pennsylvania; second, the seven-groove rifling with wide lands and narrow grooves are average early Kentucky, and third, by the initials and name on the barrel. Some knowledge of types and periods is helpful in evaluating these old smoke poles, but it is not difficult to obtain with a moderate investment in some of the books available.

Restoring the rifle presented no serious problems but considerable time was involved. I first removed all the heavily tarnished brass fittings being careful not to mar the screw slots in the patch box. I've found that a drop of lighter fluid on small screws will loosen the corrosion and make extraction easier. The pins that hold the barrel and some of the fittings to the stock were rusted so I started them with a small punch and pulled them out with pliers.

With everything off the stock I was ready for the repair job. Fortunately, the split in the fore half was a clean break. I coated the barrel liberally with floor polishing wax, placed it in a bench vise then secured the stock in place with the tang screws. The edges to be joined were cleaned with alcohol, coated with clear Devcon epoxy cement and fitted together. When the joint was perfectly aligned I bound the job to the barrel with plastic tape. This is very elastic and held the joined sections firmly together while drying. I gave it 24 hours before removing the tape.

I then removed the old finish with a liquid paint and varnish solvent and a stiff bristle brush. After filing off the ridge left by the squeezed-out cement I was ready for sanding. I like 2-0 grit for the first cleanup, finishing with 3-0, or finer if the wood warrants a really good job. This one didn't. The next operation was to fit a piece into the forearm. After squaring the edge with a file I selected a piece of scrap walnut that seemed to match the color and grain of the stock and made a piece to fill the void left by the missing sliver.

Small chips out of the stock in several places were filled with a wood putty made by mixing sanding dust with a colorless cement and forcing it into the holes with a knife blade. It doesn't make a perfect color match but is preferable to an unfilled hole.

While these patching jobs were hardening I dismantled the lock. It was marked "Henry Parker, Warrented" in

Old English letters and undoubtedly was one of the thousands of caplocks made in England for muzzle-loading gunsmiths in this country. Like most of the English locks of that period, it was nicely made with a long, rather soft-action main spring and long hammer throw. The hammer had a fly to permit the sear to slide by the half-cock notch. Both the hammer and lock plate were lightly engraved. After removing the rust the working parts showed very little wear. Screws were tight in their holes. I smoothed up the face of the plate and browned it with Plum Brown.

The problem with the set triggers was a broken hold-back spring. I made a replacement by heating and hammering flat a piece of spring wire. The heavily corroded brass fittings were first cleaned with the belt sander and finished with an impregnated rubber spindle in the Dremel. Final polishing was done on a buffing wheel. The barrel and tang were so well coated with the original brown finish that all they needed was a brisk rubbing with 3-0 steel wool. I decided that the bore was beyond help. The seven narrow grooves, possibly cut with a hacksaw blade, were badly rusted and the lands were deeply pitted. It would need a reboring job or a new 15/16-inch barrel to make it suitable for any serious shooting, which I don't contemplate at this time. The rifle is a good conversation piece as it is.

There is a mystery about this old gun that intrigues me. On the top flat of the barrel are the initials "A F" in script. According to Kauffman in *The Pennsylvania Kentucky Rifle*, that was the mark of Andrew Figthorn, a Berks County gunsmith who made rifles in the early 1800's and died in 1827.

On the under side of the barrel next to the plug is the name F. Schnader. Frank Schnader is listed in *American Firearms Makers* (Carey) as a Berks County gunsmith, 1839-1852. Also listed by Carey is Henry Parker, a Kentucky Rifle maker at Liverpool, Pa., about 1775. Figthorn and that Henry Parker were too early to have made caplock rifles since that form of ignition didn't come into general use until about 1830. That leaves Schnader as the only one who could have made the rifle. My theory, open to argument of course, is that Schnader used a barrel that Figthorn had previously made and used on a flintlock. That would account for the original Kentucky-type

rifling and the pitting on the outside of the barrel above the drum.

Occasionally an old single shot rifle will be found in a gun store or at an antique auction. I found the Stevens Tip-up in a dealer's cabinet and bought it for a little less than he wanted and a few dollars more than my first offer. The condition was rough but it was tight and everything worked. This is one of the very early Stevens models, patented by Joshua Stevens in 1864, and is an outgrowth of the famous tip-up pistol. This one, however, is not a rifle but a shotgun, chambered for the .44XL Shot cartridge.

The most difficult part of the restoration job on this one was removing what remained of the original nickel plate on the frame, trigger guard and butt plate. I have found that an abrasive disc in the Dremel is effective on the flat surfaces and a small drum with a fine cutting band will get into most of the curved surfaces on any of these old plated rifles or pistols. One problem in removing old nickel plate is knowing when it is all off, the nickel being the same color as the polished steel. When I think I have it all off I give the surface a thin coating of cold blue. The steel takes the blue but any remaining nickel stays bright showing the places I've missed. When all the nickel had been removed I finished with the belt sander and an abrasive rubber polishing point. Final polishing was done on a buffing wheel coated with Dico compound. Old nickel can be removed by a reverse plating process, but that necessitates locating a firm to do the job.

A new barrel hinge screw had to be made, the internal parts cleaned and screw heads polished and blued. The stock was in good condition and required only the removal of the old finish, sanding and three applications of Birchwood-Casey Tru-Oil.

The extractor was unlike those on several Tip-up rifles I had owned in the past, but it looked original, and worked, so I decided not to replace it. Frank deHaas, in *Single Shot Rifles and Actions*, mentions that actions were sometimes fitted with slightly different extractor linkage to facilitate barrel changing when rifles were ordered with extra barrels.

The barrel presented no problem. Although it was heavily coated with rust there were no deep pits and it came out well after the surface was cleaned in the lathe using 240 abrasive cloth under a file. The belt sander was again used for the final finishing with crocus. Three generous applications of Outer's Gun Blue produced a fine finish. A complete restoration job on this gun would require re-plating. As it is, it could be considered a fair sample of what can be done to a century-old relic with a little time.

It would be helpful, of course, if some idea of values and prices could be included in an article of this kind. But any attempt would be meaningless. There are too many factors involved. For one thing, there is the perfectly natural desire of the seller to get what *he* thinks his gun is worth. Ten men with identical guns to sell probably would have ten different asking prices. And the same number of men who wanted the gun would have as many different ideas of what they would pay. This is especially true of the class of guns suitable for restoring, commonly known as "junkers." In my own rather limited dealings in recent years, and in hob-nobbing with traders and collectors, I have concluded that if there is such a thing as a basic buying rule it is: Never pay a seller his first asking price.

I want to add one note of caution. If you take in any of the small-town or country auctions to bid on antique firearms, be sure you know what you are bidding on. If your knowledge is limited, try to take someone with you who does know. The auctioneers are generally honest, but few of them know one gun from another.

Example: In the newspaper ad announcing an auction to be held in a small town not far from my home there was listed a "long barrel Sharps rifle." Such a gun would be a collector's prize. I was unable to attend, but my friend The Old Gun Trader took it in and reported the next day. The rifle was not a Sharps. The name on the lock plate was *Sharpe* and the rifle was just a plain old caplock. Sharpe was a gunsmith and lock-maker in England during the percussion period. The rifle was in fairly good condition and should have been bid in for around $100. It went for $475! The price might have been pushed up by a dummy bidder, but whatever the reason the buyer is in for a rude awakening when he displays his "Sharps rifle" to a discerning collector.

●

Restoring Antique Firearms

ONE SUBJECT that I have avoided writing about, despite a number of inquiries, is the restoration of antique firearms. I have sidled away from the topic for several reasons, the foremost of which is that it is such a damnably complex subject that it takes all of the concentration of a skillful professional to do the work responsibly. In treating a subject that may deal with the care of arms that range from petronels of the sixteenth century to Parkers of the twentieth, one quickly realizes that even a very heavy tome on the subject could not possibly illuminate every aspect of the work.

I don't think that it would be an exaggeration to suggest that a firearms conservator — to be able to treat every material that firearms have been made from, and to understand all of the processes in the technology of the trade over the centuries — would have to develop something like two hundred fifty very specialized skills. Very few people on this earth confidently approach every aspect of firearms restoration, from replacing missing engraved ivory on a baroque wheel-lock to color-hardening the receiver of a Stevens 44. There *are* a few such renaissance men, in fact, but most of us should face the hard facts — and leave to the professionals any critical work that isn't familiar to us.

Fine firearms are not the place to experiment, for quality work is very much a document of its maker and its time, regardless of the century, and therefore deserves all the respect that

To illustrate some of the restoration techniques that he explains in this series of articles, John shows his own work on this much-abused rifle, made in the western Piedmont region of North Carolina by gunmaker John Eagle, who dated it January 14, 1836.

Aside from typical use and abuse, the Eagle rifle had been subjected to both early and recent jackleg work: crude conversion to percussion and a very untidy sheet of brass to cover missing wood, for example.

we can give it. This means that we should learn to understand when it is best to leave something alone rather than to compromise any unique quality that it may have. If we do that, we will have robbed not only ourselves but also students of firearms for many generations to come.

We often use the term *conservation* to mean *restoration*, but the two words are not always interchangeable. In its most current sense, *conservation* often signifies special treatment for stability. Conservation may also include the replacement of missing parts, but usually in a minor sense; the essence of that particular discipline is taken to mean the preservation of a firearm in

the state that it was found in, with an eye to halting or removing harmful factors such as oxidation.

Restoration, however, may take an entirely different approach: it may involve the replacement of missing major parts and even returning every surface of the piece — the *fabric* of the thing, as museum people say — to its original gleaming state. *Responsible* restoration should engender a good deal of earnest soul searching in anyone doing the work. If an arms restorationist doesn't question himself at every turn, worrying about correct procedures and feeling halfway a fool, then sooner or later, he is as like as not to damage irrevocably a priceless

statement of someone else's fine work. As Aesop said, familiarity breeds contempt. A certain humility is part and parcel of the competent restorationist's working manner — to put it just as bluntly.

While conservation is very much a part of restoration, that aspect of the trade is easier to understand — since it embraces, for the most part, a set of tried and proven procedures. So does a great deal of restoration work; but in many instances, even the experts are sharply divided over what might be considered the most responsible way to treat a good piece. Consider, for example, two very different types of antique arms, the British muzzle-loading sporting rifle and the American long rifle. When such rifles were new, there were very basic differences in the way that they were made and finished.

The British piece, whether it was from the hallowed alleys of Fleet Street or from one of the better shops in Birmingham, was a symphony of exquisite inletting, metal fit and finish, fine engraving, and superb finishes — including color case-hardening and fire blue. Most such rifles were returned to their makers periodically for them to refinish those delicate surfaces, and those surfaces were kept crisp.

On the other hand, American rifles were produced for the most part by small shops — often, by one man and his apprentice or journeyman. Both the demand for arms and the lack of specialization here before the nineteenth century prevented most American shops from attaining the level of finish in their work that was common in London. To be brutally frank, American rifles — if we consider

After its barrel had been shortened not once but twice, Eagle's rifle was rebreeched, with a long tang cutting right through the carving (*above*), in stark contrast with its original appearance, which was probably like this other rifle (*right*) from the same gunmaking ''school.'' Similar work helps to provide information on missing elements, but the restorationist usually must depend on the evidence that he finds only on the piece being restored.

This nineteenth-century repair is an iron-wire lacing to reinforce a weak glue joint. The wrap of copper wire and the loss of wood are signs of twentieth-century damage and repair.

them solely as gunmakers' art — were generally indifferently made. Lock mortises were often sloppy, with cavernous sear holes, and barrel inlets in the majority were cut round for most of the length of the stock, having been inletted to fit the octagon only at the breech and the muzzle. As much as I love those long and graceful pieces, I have a good deal more respect for our modern gunmakers who care more about quality work, even where it doesn't show.

To return to my wandering point, however, the antique long rifle as it has survived until today has quite a different appearance from that of its British cousin. It likely never had brilliant temper-blued steel furniture but rather mellow cast brass, and never received tender refurbishing at the hands of its maker. Rather, even though it likely saw a great deal more use than a British piece did, about the only maintenance that it got was the replacement of worn parts and perhaps alteration by conversion to percussion or even having its long barrel cut down to suit shifting styles or uses.

I am continually amazed at the overwhelming evidence of long and hard use on American muzzle-loaders, the wear showing not only just carrying scars and such but evidence of what must have been thousands of shots, in some instances. Some are quite literally worn-out, with locks as loose as a graveyard gate and silver inlays worn quite through. Americans were hard on their arms — and some still are, although the arms aren't getting any less expensive.

Obviously, one must look at the restoration of different types of arms from the viewpoint that best serves the piece at hand. If a fine London flintlock had spent two lifetimes on the American frontier, we would be prepared to accept all of the deep patination and generous surface damage that documented the history of that piece, just as we must with most American rifles. We would work to preserve the

mellowness of age. If the same piece, however, had remained in England since the eighteenth century and had been cared-for in a fastidious manner, we might become concerned with matters of restoring missing areas of original finish or even removing light pitting from and otherwise gleaming case-hardened breech. In the latter instance, we might become more concerned with preserving or even restoring every aspect of its original appearance. With a used-up frontier fowler or even a well worn American long rifle, taking such a tack would be the ruination of the thing.

In this article and in the next two after it, I'd like to examine briefly the variety of techniques that are used in the course of one restoration job on an American rifle. My intent is not to try to make restorationists of any number of readers but to bring up some weighty matters that all of us must consider, whether we are thinking about having an early lock reconverted to flint or dreaming about having the brilliant case colors renewed on a prewar Purdey double. I'll touch on procedure and techniques of repair, replacement, and restoration of finish, on both wood and metal, including techniques for aging where aging is appropriate.

Obviously, if the subject truly demands a huge volume for anything approaching full coverage, I haven't the space here for more than an introduction to the restorationists' art. All the matters of intricate welding techniques, methods of working and decorating the many media encountered on firearms, and the like would fill a very large book — and even then, such a work would best be written by half a dozen experts rather than by one gunstocker who has happened to fix a number of old guns on the side over the years.

The firearm that is the subject of this treatise is a flintlock that happened to have been made about fifty miles from where I live, in Cabarrus County, North Carolina. Though it is loaded with competent — if a little florid — relief carving, good silver inlays, engraved brass furniture, and a long, handsome patch box, this poor rifle had seen about all the ravagement that it could stand and still have merit. And merit it indeed has, even to the extent of being a museum-grade piece, for carved Carolina rifles are quite rare.

None of the major art on the rifle had been damaged, and it is proudly signed on the box lid *made by J Eagle*. John Eagle made that rifle early in his career: a silver comb inlay bears the date of January 14, 1836, and John Eagle — son of gunsmith George Eagle — was born in 1813.

Old John wouldn't have liked to see this specimen of his work. After two major nineteenth-century alterations of something less than gunsmith quality, the thing must have been given to some kiddies to play Daniel Boone with. It had been in the same family since it was made, but it looked so bad that one member of the family came within an ace of giving it to a moving-van man as a tip for his work, since the fellow wanted something to hang over his mantel.

The saving grace of the piece was that it hadn't been "restored" by some well-meaning bloke working with a whizzing Dremel tool and a tube of Plastic Wood or epoxy. What had happened to the rifle was bad enough, but an arms restorationist would prefer to work on an absolute wreck of a gun, rather than on one that had been

Since the barrel of the Eagle rifle had been shortened twice, there is no finish to the forestock molding, which runs abruptly to the cap — always a sign that a rifle has been shortened.

spiffy until it was "improved" along the way by some sport who thought that it would be ever so nice to sand all the dark grime off and draw-file the barrel — or maybe by someone who *wanted* to do the right thing but had read the wrong book.

There is one book on the market — which I shall not name — that makes my teeth grind, for in one chapter, the poor sod who wrote the thing teaches us how to "restore" a pretty decent eighteenth-century French pocket pistol. A sizable piece of wood was missing from one side of the tang, which the fellow replaced — but he was concerned that the other side, which was still intact, was relief-carved. And the solution? Yes: cut the carving off so that the patched side would match. Needless to say, we should consider such things ghastly enough to nauseate a buzzard off a gut wagon.

A project like the Eagle rifle — or any other important conservation or restoration job — starts not with tools but with the eyes and the camera. The work at hand here is *evidence* — evidence of the techniques and skill of the gunmaker, evidence of how the piece appeared originally, and evidence of how it got into the state that we now see it in, which may represent some considerable alteration.

One piece of evidence, in fact, tells us something about the use of antique arms, especially American muzzle-loading rifles, and that evidence is in the fact that many of them are *still loaded*. After all, when a fox was in the hen house, a farmer didn't want to reach for an uncharged piece. And since black powder doesn't materially deteriorate unless it is contaminated by something, it is quite possible to set-off an old charge. I've done so, several times, *after* I'd pulled the load. Check the piece first, and if it is loaded, kill the charge with penetrating oil, with the idea of removing it later (and don't forget).

Responsible work on a historical arm calls for a thorough examination of the piece, inch by inch, and a detailed set of notes about the state of the firearm. After examination should come thorough photographic recording of its details. We must feel the heavy responsibility of documenting everything that we do to a piece — and at the same time showing what we *haven't* done. Aside from full-length shots, shots of both sides of the butt stock and of its top and bottom, also necessary are shots of areas that

obviously need work. Though I can't talk about photographic procedures here (that article should be done by our excellent editor, the Richard Avedon of the gun world), I will mention a couple of things briefly. Record photography should be shot on relatively slow black-and-white film such as Plus-X, with diffused floods or skylight rather than direct specular light, for better control of shadowing to record details. A thirty-five-millimeter camera is all right, but if you have access to a 2¼x2¼ or 2¼x2¾ camera, use that instead.

After the "before" photography, disassemble the piece and photograph its individual parts as needed. I also complete my preliminary notes as I disassemble the arm. During the course of restoration work, I don't necessarily photograph the work unless I'm using some procedure that would be difficult to describe in my final written report.

I also photograph the completed work. I file all of the notes, the final report, the negatives, and the prints in the customer's file, and provide prints if the customer wants to pay the expense. The written report is part of the job, and work for museums is routinely submitted with full photography for the museum's accession files.

If all of this sounds fussy, stop and think of all the implications of doing anything to alter the condition — bad or good — of an expensive arm. If you have your cap set for a Parker A-1 Special, have found both the gun *and* a wheelbarrow full of doubloons, you would want to know just what had been done to that fine thing before you dump your gold at the vendor's feet. Had the elaborate grip checkering been ruined, then later veneered-over and recut? You can bet your last bleeding buck that everything that we do to an old gun alters its value in some way, and not always to its betterment — especially if someone is suspicious about what was done and why. I've seen the reputations of some really fine antique guns destroyed in the market place by scuttlebutt from some individual who mistakenly thought that the piece had been faked in some way.

The cardinal rule of conservation and restoration on all objects of antiquity and art — be they by Rodin or Remington — is *Do no more to the piece than is necessary* to make it stable and presentable, considering the variables that I've already mentioned.

Dismantling an American rifle is the first place where we begin to apply that rule. Absolutely nothing should be removed beyond what is necessary to preserve and repair the piece.

Pins were almost invariably made with a taper, and they are usually rusted fast, often because of the nitric acid used as a base stain. Wood screws were usually hand-cut — in fact, all of them were, before the early nineteenth century — and they may not want to retighten in the wood after being removed, because of rust, deteriorated wood, and a fast helix cut in the threads.

While metal parts do oxidize in places that you can't see, that fact isn't enough reason for me to even think of stripping-off ramrod thimbles, patch boxes, toe plates, and the like *unless* some repair of such elements is warranted. Original pins were often round-headed, the heads protruding slightly above the surface; a hollowed punch should be made for them, and they should be driven out toward their large ends. Screw slots were usually cut with a **V**, and they must be carefully cleaned-out — and screwdriver tips filed to fit them precisely.

Any such fasteners that have to be removed should be numbered and taped to a piece of cardboard, with the correct orientation of each pin duly noted so that they can be returned to their original location and orientation without exchange or damage.

Wood screws that are frozen in place with rust — a particular offender of this sort is the screw that holds the rear of a set-trigger plate — may be loosened by making a "screwdriver" of flat stock that fits the screw slot, perhaps four inches long. Holding the home-made bit with a pair of pliers, heat it above the tip with a torch until you have it just below a very dull red. Allow it to cool slightly and push it firmly into the slot, repeating the procedure several times. Don't ever be tempted to dose the screw with penetrating oil, for that should be used only on fasteners with metal-to-metal fit, and even then very sparingly. More is not better, for you don't want that junk on finishes and in the wood.

When you're working on an antique firearm that doesn't have screws that are either of steel or case-hardened, be aware that you can't cold-work wrought iron; this means that if you use too much persuasion on a rusted screw, you'll wring it off. While a screwdriver bit hand-turned in a drill press is often effective on corroded modern screws, such force would often be too much for early fasteners. Rely on small amounts of penetrating oil. I like Blue Ribbon and buy it when I can find it, for it almost invariably loosens screws if they don't have blind threads that I can't reach — which you might encounter on the lock "side nails" or bolts on a European arm. If one of those is stuck, then you have A Problem. I have my methods, but I hesitate to put them in print lest the faint at heart think that I have all the sensitivity of Attila the Hun.

Guns that are heavily corroded on hidden surfaces are serious problems. Any side lock should be removed very gently by backing the side nails off half a turn at a time, tapping the screw heads very lightly with a small leather mallet. If the edges of the lock plate are badly rusted, though the lock still fits the mortise tightly, you can bet that small pieces of stock around the lock will fracture off as the lock begins to move. Watch the wood closely, and if that happens, remove the broken piece before it falls out, by touching a piece of drafting tape to it. Mark it for later replacement.

That is one situation where you are going to cause damage no matter how hard you may try to avoid it. The same thing is even more likely to happen around a trigger plate, especially a thick set-trigger housing. Trigger plates, incidentally, should be removed in the same manner that a lock is loosened, by tapping lightly on the tang screw. The plate will likely have to be tapped back down flush and restarted several times before the tail begins to lift; don't be tempted to just lever the thing out from the front to the back.

Removing the barrel of a long rifle — even a new one — is a potentially dangerous chore, since the wall of the fore-end of such a rifle is so thin and fragile, especially on an antique rifle stocked in maple. With the tang screws and the pins or wedges pulled, and the lock out, turn the rifle up-side-down with the sights resting on the top of the bench. With a helper steadying the rifle by holding the fore-end, start the stock off the barrel, beginning with the breech, by lightly slapping upward on the top of the wrist.

A really tight or corroded barrel requires some gentle persuasion beyond that. Lifting up on the comb, I tap on the lower forestock with a well padded mallet, and as the barrel begins to move out, I continue tapping all the way down the forestock as necessary to loosen the stock. Lift the comb no more than is necessary to avoid stressing the stock, and proceed slowly with judicious love pats, and the stock usually lifts right off the barrel. Don't even think of standing a full-stock rifle on its butt and yanking away at the nose cap to pull the stock, even on a new rifle, unless you plan to have a two-piece fore-end and don't care where the joint will be.

About the only strength that a long rifle has lies in the support that the barrel gives the stock. Avoid doing any work on the stock with the barrel out, if you can. By no means attempt to remove other parts such as guards or triggers after you have pulled the barrel. After I have removed a barrel and then want it back in the inlet to be able to hold the rifle in the vise, I use two rubber bands cut from inner tube, one at the breech and the other at the muzzle, for temporarily holding the barrel in place. Repeated removals and replacements of pins or wedges lead to trouble — though if you're working with a stock that is fitted with slotted wedges held in place with keeper pins, you'll just have to use the wedges.

Since iron parts such as barrels and trigger plates must be returned to their inlets for work on the stock to be safe, I clean these parts before proceeding with other work; this is especially important if corrosion has built-up on hidden surfaces, for a rough metal surface is hard on brittle inlet edges. Small parts such as locks and the like can be soaked in one of the thin preservatives such as CRC for excellent long-term protection as well as penetrating and loosening rust, though most of the volatile water-displacing oils like CRC are designed to evaporate.

For that reason, I use penetrating oil on barrel surfaces, inside and outside, and apply it several times over three or four days. Use kerosene, if you like, but I like the smell of the stuff about as well as an east wind from a landfill. After such soaking, scrape loose, heavy corrosion off with pieces of heavy sheet brass, say 0.062 inch thick. I cut strips half an inch wide or so and three inches long, and as the edges dull, I toss them in the scrap box and cut more. Sharp-edged brass doesn't hurt patination and finish.

While wrought iron is relatively stable after it has oxidized, unlike carbon steel, leaving heavy patches of corrosion is not good conservation practice — especially if they're under a barrel, where they're not likely to be treated periodically. Where there are such heavy deposits in unseen places, I remove all of the rust. Such cancerous growths often resist scraping with brass, even after repeated scraping and redosing with oil, and — though it's a harsh measure — I take to a phosphoric-acid colloid for removing the junk. Sold in hardware stores as *naval jelly*, such colloids are relatively mild and require repeated application for complete removal of heavy rust. They etch the surface slightly but not to the point of masking original tool cuts and the like.

The side flats of octagonal barrels may also require this treatment because of moisture entrapped in the barrel inlet, but removing corrosion from those places requires refinishing of the side flats. When surface corrosion is heavy, I prefer to do that and be satisfied that the metal is stabilized for many generations to come. Iron or steel treated with phosphoric acid should be neutralized with strong household ammonia, and I'll cover further treatment for long-term preservation later. By all means avoid using this treatment on any visible surface if you can remove heavy encrustations of rust by mechanical means; a very large part of the value of an antique arm lies in the quality of its patination or remaining original finish.

With the Eagle rifle taken down as far as necessary, which included removal of the lock, set triggers, side plate, trigger guard, barrel, and the remains of the shattered fore-end, I catalogued the condition of the rifle. Typically, it showed evidence of four distinct stages in its life.

First, there were good traces of the original finish, including a deep reddish-brown spirit varnish and patches of plum-colored browning on the barrel where wear and corrosion hadn't taken their toll. Second, the rifle showed normal attrition for an American rifle — heavy use. Relief carving at the wrist, tang, and lower ramrod pipe was heavily worn, and the lower part of the forestock was worn to the point of leaving a large coin-silver inlay standing well above the wood and the forward edges of the inlay ground down to a ragged razor edge. That sort of wear *behind* the balance point of the rifle tells us that the rifle was carried for many hundreds of miles across a saddle.

Further, the rifle showed loss of wood forward and behind the lock, brought about by what is often called "dry rot" but is really a destructive fungus that fed hungrily on the animal oils that past owners had slopped liberally down the bore — and allowed to run out the vent and soak into the wood. The fungus broke-down the structure of the wood, and it crumbled away, leaving the usual sickly white, dead look.

The third stage of the rifle's life included normal alteration, clumsy reworking, and careless use that probably occurred after 1850. The rifle was shortened twice, both times at the breech — a usual thing, caused by corrosion. The first time the rifle was shortened, a gunmaker did the job. He carefully remortised barrel-pin lugs in new positions in the stock and carefully centered pin holes. He removed the upper ramrod pipe and set the nose cap back, holding it in place with rivets from the sides rather than from the bottom, as it had originally been held — these bits of evidence telling us that another gunstocker had likely done the job, not Eagle himself. Two upper forestock inlays were lost during the first cutting, which amounted to exactly four and an eighth inches.

For the second shortening, the owner took the rifle to a real backwoods bumbler, perhaps a blacksmith of indifferent skill who fancied himself an armorer. This time, four and five eighths inches was lopped-off, for a grand total of eight and three quarters inches of shortening. The barrel evidently needed a new breech plug then, so this smith beat-out a crude item with the tang an inch and a half longer than the original, meaning that it had to be inlet right through the nice shell carving that Eagle had used in that location. Judging from the quality of the work, the same man "percussed" the rifle at the same time, cutting-off the waterproof pan of the lock to clear a drum.

He did a fairly competent job of beating-out a percussion hammer, but as in the case of the tang, he didn't grace any of its surfaces with file work to finish it. He again moved the nose cap back, and this time, he nailed on through the side rivet holes. He also moved the third ramrod pipe back slightly. Rather than removing the original rear sight and repositioning it

forward to compensate for the shortening, he filed it down and installed a crude new sight on the barrel. The muzzle still remained untouched.

By this time — probably after the Civil War — the rifle likely had wound-up in the hands of family youngsters who wanted to hunt squirrels, and things went from bad to worse. Years of overtightening the lock bolts had compressed stock wood to the point that a leather gasket had to be cut and pinned inside the lock mortise, and a wood screw added under the tail of the lock prevented the plate from wallowing around in the worn mortise. The lock was so worn-out by this time that a blacksmith-made sear was made, the half-cock safety was cut off the tumbler, and a copper shim was placed in the tumbler hole to take-up enormous play in the tumbler.

Inlays were beginning to loosen by this time, so new holes were punched through three of them, and small brass sprigs were cut to hold them down. The upper fore-end split diagonally forward of the ramrod entry pipe, and the joint was *sewn* together by drilling the stock and lacing it up with heavy iron wire. At about the same time or slightly after, the upper fore-end split full-length in the ramrod groove, then the lower forestock cracked for about five inches into the ramrod hole. A generous amount of hide glue was dumped into the joints, and transverse wooden pins were driven through the stock in four places to hold the thing together.

Virtually all of the original varnish finish was worn off the stock by then, except in places where wear normally doesn't occur. Another forestock inlay had fallen off, and a small tear-drop inlay forward of the lock mortise, too. Four silver inlays were now gone, and three others had been defaced with new nails. The two remaining upper thimbles were lost.

By that time, perhaps at the end of the last century, poor Eagle's good work had seen so much use and trauma that it was no longer a working rifle, and no doubt the kids had been given breech-loaders by then, anyway. But grandpa's rifle was put away, not thrown out. Thirty or forty years later, someone found it in the attic, or wherever it lay in exile, and it entered its fourth stage of existence.

Wood under the lock had been broken, probably because the original

mainspring had worn-out and slipped off its stirrup. The broken wood was torn out and a thin brass plate screwed on to cover the hole. More wood had fallen out of the old forestock break, so copper wire was wrapped around the stock to hold the mess in place. Things were pretty crudded-up by now, so someone undertook some light sanding so that "the wood could show." The light sanding was done with hundred-grit paper, right over the metal as well. Fortunately, very little of the butt stock was given such loving treatment. The brass was all shined-up, and the entire rifle was liberally varnished-over with a yellowish synthetic-resin varnish, either an alkyd or a phenolic.

To plug all of the numerous holes in the wood and the gaps in the inletting around the loosened lock and barrel breech, a hard, dark wax was liberally poured on and wiped into the crevices. Then it was ready for hanging over the fireplace, and it probably looked very cozy and Early American unless you got within twenty feet of it. So ended the rifle's fourth phase; in the next two installments, I'll describe a fifth phase — which I hope resembles a second life for this old rifle.

All of this is a very pointed illustration of how any object of material culture provides us with a documentation of how people lived and particularly how they used the objects that surrounded them. In a way, it's this sort of detective work that is the most interesting part of restoring some antiquity. The evidence is all there; we must make ourselves seek it out. I'm sure that I spent a good four hours or so studying this particular rifle before I picked-up anything other than a screwdriver or pin punch.

As a gunmaker, I never tire of studying the evidence of early technology: tool cuts, methods of fabrication, and the like. I particularly like finding mistakes. In the process of determining just how much barrel had been cut from the Eagle rifle, which involved matching-up empty pin-lug dovetails on the barrel with empty pin holes in the stock, I discovered that the old boy had made an error when he pinned the barrel. He had put the top lug too close to the muzzle, not leaving enough room for the long nose cap, so he had to remove the lug, fill the dovetail, and position another farther back. When he installed the cap, he drilled through it with small spade bits for the rivet holes, and the bits left tiny marks on the barrel when they broke through the wood — one of them smack over the blanked-off lug dovetail. That one almost fooled me into believing that the muzzle had been cut back as well, but measurement of the thimble locations showed otherwise.

Such clues are important if we are to do an accurate job, and we must be able to discern just how and when something was done to the piece in its past. Knowing that there was no such thing as pointed wood screws much before 1850, and that wire nails came in after the Civil War, and such academics as the fact that wire nails of that period were slightly oval in section, are the sort of tidbits that we need, to piece a record together. And photography proves that we found such evidence, which some arms student three centuries from now will appreciate.

In the next *Rifle*, I'll move on from matters of philosophy and examination to the repair of wood and metal — and in the final installment, I'll relate some techniques for repairing finishes, artificially aging both wood and metal, as well as taking a look at historical stock finishes and the proper application of long-term preservatives. ●

Restoring Antique Firearms

...continued

IN THE FIRST part of this series (*Rifle* 88), I listed some of the ground rules of arms restoration and gave an account of taking apart a rather bedraggled Carolina rifle, leaving it in pieces at the end of that account. I brought together a history of the rifle's use, based upon the evidence that I found on the rifle alone — a very real demonstration of the fact that all objects of antiquity are documents that can speak to us quite readily if we but listen. This old fellow's vernacular, in fact, must include more than a few groans from its past treatment.

After removing the lock, barrel, guard, and set triggers, I began systematically dismantling all of the secondary elements — parts that had been added to the rifle after it was made. The rifle had suffered through four hard lives, and the evidence of each was intact. The barrel had been shortened — twice — at the breech, and a new tang had been added. After removing the barrel and giving it a light outside cleaning by scraping it with pieces of brass, I removed the drum — taking no special care with it, since it would be replaced.

If a flint rifle is to be left in the percussion ignition that it has been converted to, or if the piece was originally percussion, there should be no attempt to remove its drum until the barrel has been stood on its tang and given a good dose of penetrating oil, down the muzzle and in the nipple if it isn't clogged. If the rifle is loaded, it will need quite a large dose of penetrating oil to soak through the load, to the drum, and I would count on a week of soaking. The drum should always be removed before the breech plug, since plugs were often notched, allowing the threaded shank of the drum to intrude somewhat — rather effectively locking the breech plug in place, though that wasn't the gunmaker's intent.

To remove a drum that is to be saved, I use a small pair of Vise Grips with the teeth blunted and the jaws ground with a bit of a hollow to fit around the drum. I wrap the drum in eighth-inch-thick sheet lead and clamp the Vise Grips on with the tips of the jaws just at the base of the nipple. You don't want to exert any force against the nipple — it would likely shear off — and don't lock the Vise Grips down so tight that they cut the sheet lead and skin the drum. I remove the nipple first, if it isn't frozen — but if any one part of a long rifle is likely to be stuck fast, it's the nipple. Prolonged soaking, with the drum off the rifle, usually loosens it.

If the drum refuses to turn, even after further soaking with penetrating oil, it can almost invariably be loosened with thermal shock — *heat*, that is. Again, *be sure that the piece isn't loaded!* A chap not far from here found-out by the hard way that a Civil War musket barrel that he was welding a tang tip onto had been stuffed with three loads, probably in the heat of battle. All three Minié balls slammed through the cab of his pick-up, since he had the thing lying on the tail gate.

Loosening heavily corroded threaded parts with heat sounds like something brutal, but it need not harm the part if it's done right. To loosen a drum, the breech of the barrel must be heated very rapidly, all around the drum, with a large tip on the oxyacetylene torch. Anything else would heat the mass too slowly, and if the surface temperature rises much above 385 degrees or so, that fine brown patina on the barrel begins to turn a hideous bright red. This isn't heat color but a chemical alteration of the oxides on the surface of the metal — and to remove it later, you'd just about have to go to bare metal.

Since this must be avoided at all costs, move in fast with the torch, play it rapidly around the breech for five to eight seconds, and move it away. The heat expands the mass of the barrel, loosening its grip on the shank of the drum and — at the same time — breaks-down the accumulated "varnish" left in the joint by oils that have deteriorated

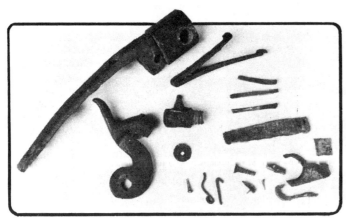

John's investigation into the history of the Eagle rifle required that he systematically remove the materials that had been added by later gunsmiths of the nineteenth (*above*) and repairmen of the twentieth (*right*) centuries.

and oxidized. One such treatment is usually enough; but if it *still* doesn't move, I let the thing cool, dose it again with penetrating oil, and let it sit for another spell before I repeat the process.

Breech plugs that refuse to move can be treated in the same way. Don't be tempted to use much force in trying to loosen them, for it's all too possible to wring a plug off. Use a breech-plug wrench to fully grip the tapering faces of the lug behind the thread shank, with a strip of 0.040-inch-thick brass formed around the lug before you fit the wrench to it. If you have no wrench that fits properly, it's possible to clamp the lug in the jaws of a vise (lined with heavy sheet brass or — better — quarter-inch-thick sheet lead) and then to turn the barrel. Sheet brass 0.060 inch thick should be formed around the flats, with a heavy Crescent wrench used on the side flats from beneath the barrel, and someone must support the muzzle unless you have a telescoping rest to hold it up.

I *always* remove the breech plug and scour the bore out with 00 steel wool and CRC. Many old muzzle-loaders have dirt-dauber nests, scrap paper, and all manner of other things that absorb moisture shoved down their bores — certainly not in the least contributing to the long-term conservation of the bores. For scouring, a bronze brush of an appropriate size, pinned to a hickory rod and then wrapped with steel wool, is quite effective.

On this particular rifle, I elected to simply remove the breech plug with a hacksaw — a rather ghastly method indeed. The breech had been heavily pitted by fulminate

residue from percussion caps and would have required a good deal of surface welding to bring it back to its original dimensions. Since eight and three quarters inches of the breech was *already* missing, I opted to cut just enough away to get back to clean metal, since I planned to return the barrel to its original length.

More on that anon — but I must say here that such a drastic measure quite obviously would *not* be used on a barrel that wasn't to be "stretched" back to length, nor should such a thing be done if the surfaces of the breech are in good condition.

So I plucked-off the offending breech, along with sundry other nineteenth-century impedimenta such as the blacksmith-wrought per-

cussion hammer, the drum, the mainspring from a double-barrel shotgun, pieces of iron wire that had bound an old stock fracture, wooden pins that had helped to hold a longitudinal split together, a woodscrew that had been fitted to the rear of the worn-out lock mortise, a variety of scraps of leather shim, with their tiny wooden pegs, that had been used to reposition the lock in its crushed mortise, and a long strip of leather that had been placed under the barrel to take-up the gap left when the barrel was cut off (the original breech of the tapered barrel was almost three sixteenths of an inch larger).

The real garbage that had to be discarded was part of an early-twentieth-century "face job." The brass plate with its attendant collec-

Since the restored barrel would support the stock while John worked on its restoration, the twice-shortened barrel had to be brought back to its original length — with a section of another barrel carefully welded to the breech end, then dressed-down to final dimensions.

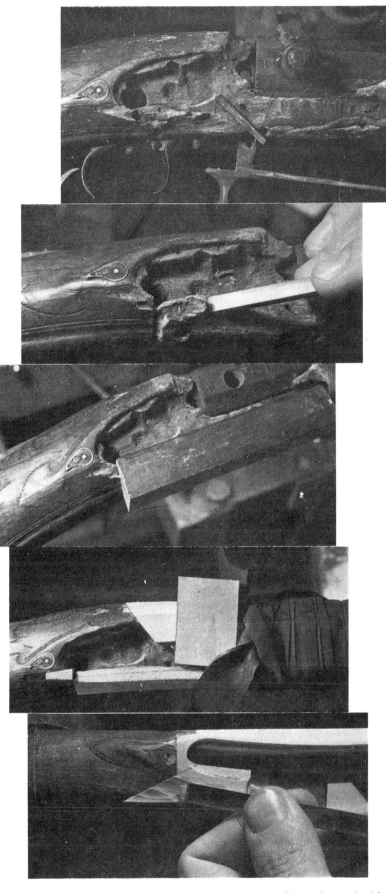

With all of the original parts and later cover-up materials removed from the stock with great care, extensive damage to the stock mortise (*top*) was all too evident. The repair of this damage began (*second*) with the painstaking removal of all unsalvageable wood and the inlaying of new wood (*middle*). A temporary filler block in the lock mortise kept the inlaid pieces of new wood from slipping while all was clamped together with wrappings of inner-tube rubber until the adhesive hardened. Then John trimmed the patches down with a quarter-round gouge (*bottom*).

tion of assorted woodscrews had casually hidden the facsimile of the Carlsbad Caverns that had once been the stock below the lock mortise. The copper wire and small army of wire sprigs had been added to hold the fractured wood together, though the sprigs had caused a number of additional splits. Several fragments of wood simply fell out of the stock when I took the gun down. A pile of dark stuff was part of the hard brown wax that someone had most cunningly applied to every interstice on the rifle.

I photographed all of this junk and then threw it out except for the scraps of wood, the hammer, the drum, the mainspring, and the breech.

I generally elect to undertake the worst part of a job first; if I can get that part past me, the rest seems ever so much easier. On the John Eagle rifle, the worst was the ungodly mess around the lock mortise. As I mentioned in part one, no such work should be done on the stock of a long rifle with the barrel out, since the stock is otherwise exceedingly fragile. To better support and strengthen the stock without straining anything, I felt that it would be better to lengthen the barrel first, so that the barrel inlet would be completely filled, allowing no possibility of twisting the buttstock slightly while I was working on it.

Many long rifles have been cut off, and there is a variety of pros and cons of returning them to their original lengths. It is not a simple or an inexpensive job, and it entails considerable realteration of a rifle — which should be considered very carefully, particularly if the piece is otherwise in fine condition and has been shortened but an inch or two. Radical shortening, as in the case of the Eagle rifle, frequently removed significant elements such as fore-stock inlays, thimbles, and the like, making the rifle ungainly in appearance. Even so, I would rather see a long rifle left as an awkward carbine than see an indifferent job of lengthening both barrel and wood; a poor job of "stretching" is irresponsible and ultimately far more costly in terms of the damage that it does to the rifle.

I determined the original length of the Eagle barrel very readily by matching-up the unused pin lugs and even empty lug dovetails with the original barrel-pin holes in the stock. To prepare a barrel for stretching, I file the breech end off clean and bevel that face about three sixteenths of an inch all around to accept the weld. On the Eagle rifle, I simply cut the corroded breech off. For piecing-in such bobbed-off barrels, I have a closetful of odds and ends of old barrels, and with any luck, I can usually manage to find a piece of the right size to fit a cut-off breech or muzzle.

With the barrel of the Eagle rifle, however, I didn't manage such an easy solution and had to resort to a piece of new barrel. From measuring both the height and the width of the barrel inlet at the breech (with the lock in place), I knew that the original width of the breech was 0.960 inch, so I used a piece of one-inch barrel to replace the missing eight and three quarters inches — actually, after I'd cut a section off, a total of ten and three eighths inches.

While I try to find a bore that is as close as possible to the size of the original, I don't make any great attempt to match the original size exactly. Returning barrels to their original lengths, as far as I'm concerned, is a matter of cosmetics. By using a mandrel for centering, welding clear to the bore with a TIG welder, and then reboring and rerifling, it is entirely possible to have a stretched barrel that is both safe and accurate to shoot, if it's properly straightened and proofed. Many original barrels, in fact, were made in segments and then "jump" welded into a continuous barrel. Such welding methods certainly were no better — and likely not as good — as modern gas-envelope techniques are. However, I am not one who advocates shooting original long rifles. Most of them can not be used without expecting attrition in one form or another, so I do not restore barrels to shooting condition except in very special instances.

The piece of barrel can be welded in place by any of a variety of methods. I've done it with oxyacetylene, arc, and TIG, and I much prefer the TIG because of the quality of the weld and the localization of the heat — especially when some feature such as a signature is near a weld joint. On the Eagle rifle, fellow gunmaker and top metalsmith Mike Ehinger of Stedman, North Carolina, gas-welded the barrel flawlessly.

An easy way to mate-up the two parts is to clamp them in a piece of angle iron, shimming where they

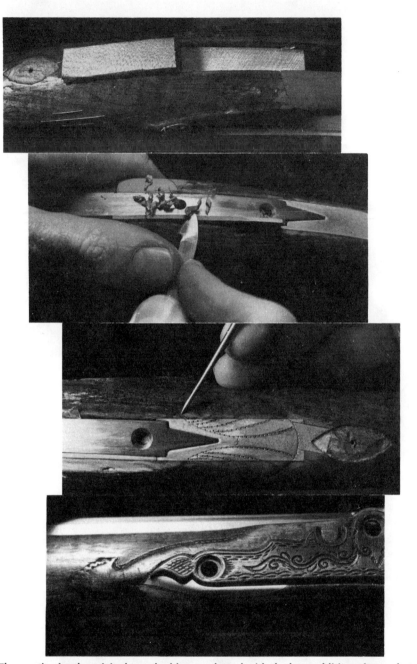

The mortise for the original tang had been enlarged with the later addition of a crude tang; this mortise had to be filled with wood (*top*) before the new tang could be inletted into the stock (*second*), with a shim set in place to fill the extra width of the enlarged mortise. Then John extended the veining pattern from the remaining original carving onto the newly inlaid wood. In a small patch at the front of the side plate (*bottom*), John fitted new wood with a joint line that followed the lines of the carved lock mouldings, to camouflage the line of juncture between new wood and old.

need alignment. The barrel can then be tack-welded in two places, removed from the jig, and welded all the way around. Care is necessary, to keep the heat as even as possible around the mass of the barrel, to avoid warping; and for the same reason, a hot joint should not be laid on a cool surface. If the barrel does warp, however, it's no great shakes to straighten a soft wrought-iron barrel, using a large C-clamp and a pair of steel blocks underneath.

Other things to be aware of: mild

steel rod should be used for the welding, and if an arc is used, the ground should *not* be clamped to the barrel. Further, to save a bit of fuss, breech the new piece of barrel stub before welding it on (for easier manipulation in the lathe).

To provide enough metal to recreate the largest dimension of a tapering barrel, the new piece is usually larger than the original section at the joint. *Filing* a good bit of metal off — over three sixteenths of an inch in the case of the Eagle —

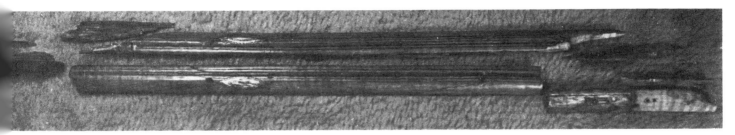

The ravages of time and crude "repairs" had shattered the upper forestock.

With the two halves of the upper forestock rejoined, John strapped it to the lengthened barrel in its correct position.

is about as amusing to me as gobbling cold chitterlings, so I availed myself of friend Dru Hedgecock's three-inch horizontal belt sander — finishing the job with files. With a new breech plug installed (with the correct shorter tang), I was ready to proceed. I placed the barrel in the inlet and wrapped it forward and aft with one-inch strips of inner-tube rubber. The fitting of the missing pin lugs would await restoration of the missing fore-end.

Beginning the woodwork on this rifle involved excising stock wood that couldn't be incorporated into a joint with new material. Joints are a matter all unto themselves. To be effective, and hidden from the eye, the joint between new wood and old must be tight. Butt joints are the easiest to fit, particularly on the compound curves of gunstocks, but they are also the easiest to detect. Rather than to risk an indifferent joint in a tricky place — such as under the lock of the Eagle — I use butt joints. If the figure of the wood or the degree of patination don't allow me to hide a butt joint perfectly, I break up the visible pattern of the joint by veneering over the completed joint with small, irregular — even zig-zag — pieces that fool the eye by robbing the joint of its linear appearance.

This is seldom necessary in an area that is heavily patinated, such as the missing area under the lock of the Eagle rifle. Consequently, I cut-away only enough unsound screw-hole-riddled wood at that point to permit a clean, square juncture for the new wood that is to be added.

Whenever I can, I use old wood for such repairs — not because it has some mystical quality of age or particular coloration but because really old wood tends to be "deader" than new wood and less inclined to move around later. For this patch, I used a piece of straight-grained maple cut from a scrap of mid-nineteenth-century bed post. It is critical that such patches have their grain structure aligned to precisely match that of the stock. To ensure that all of the new additions to this stock —

which eventually amounted to some twenty-four new pieces in a variety of sizes — matched the grain flow of the wood, I spent a bit of time studying just how the blank for this stock had been sawn. The easiest way to determine the exact lay-out of the grain is to remove the butt plate and lightly clean its inlet — this is what I did with the Eagle rifle, making a sketch of the angle of the growth rings before I put the butt plate back on.

With the new piece tightly fitted in place — but not wedged, since brittle stock wood can not stand such stress — I was ready to attach the piece permanently. The adhesives that are to be used in all restoration and conservation deserve a good deal of thought. Because of the nature of handling stress on the stock, and often imperfect joints because of oil-contaminated wood, epoxy unfortunately is the only really effective adhesive for use in restoring firearms. I used the word *unfortunately* because of the fact that it is always considered desirable to make any restoration work *reversible,* for reasons that should be obvious.

Many epoxies are indeed reversible — but only after prolonged soaking in chemicals that would certainly destroy the finish anywhere near a joint. Responsible cabinet makers use reversible adhesives such as hide glue, which is soluble in water, when they refit joints or replace elements on furniture. I haven't found an easily reversible adhesive that has the strength that gunstock joints need, but this doesn't mean that epoxy is a panacea. When we use it, we much be confident that we're

attaching pieces of wood that we can live with later — if we discover that the new patch is incorrectly shaped or finished, it may have to be cut away.

An alternative to removing epoxied joints, however, might be found in a product called *bond-cured epoxy dissolver* (Conservation Materials, Ltd; Box 2884; Sparks, Nevada 89431). This product requires soaking the joint. It might be considered a boon if one encounters a "redo" job that was *first* treated by some idiot whose idea of stock restoration was to fill entire voids with colored epoxy.

Consider, if you will, that a wood-stocked firearm — even one that is in perfect condition — is a very unnatural system. Nature didn't intend for us to attach unyielding metal alloys to organic materials that continually move with atmospheric changes. Stocks therefore split, inlays are rejected like cut-rate liver transplants, and curious gaps develop in embarrassing places. All that we can try to do is to minimize the natural distortion of such a system — not *add to it* with further material differentials that may cause even further damage. In short: keep the use of epoxy to a minimum in restoration work. Never give-in to the temptation to use it to fill large voids or as a bedding compound.

Before I glue such a joint, I often apply a coat of shellac to the original stock wood next to the joint, to prevent epoxy from adhering anywhere *except* the joint. Several coats of liquid floor wax are just as good, providing a better and less messy release agent than most of

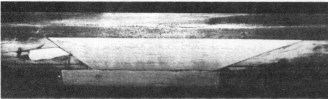

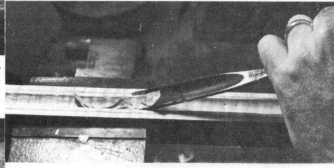

John had to fill a cavernous gap between the upper and the lower forestock (*above*) and replace a missing ten-inch section (*right*) with new wood. Using a ship-lap joint (*below*) avoided cutting more old wood off the stock than was necessary.

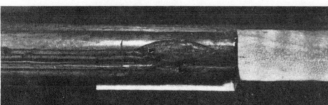

the commercial films. I coat all surfaces of the joint, both new and old, with a thin coat of epoxy spread on with a palette knife. I use gel-type adhesives such as the Acraglas gel sold by Brownell's, since I don't want the stuff running out of the joint.

Don't be tempted to use a five-minute epoxy for anything other than a temporary joint; they haven't the strength of the twenty-four-hour epoxies. The epoxy that I use the most is a twenty-four-hour a-and-b epoxy manufactured by the Smooth-On Corporation of New Jersey; they call it *EA-40* and sell it in convenient tubes. I color it with Brownell's reddish-brown epoxy colorant as needed.

There are few places on a gun stock that allow the use of clamps, and I find that strips of inner-tube rubber hold most repairs in place while the adhesive sets and cures. I first wrap the entire area with waxed paper to prevent leaving great gouts of rubber on the stock when I remove the bands (somehow, "vulcanized curly maple" isn't appealing). Waxed paper is also useful inside inlets. When I add a missing piece of forestock, I simply wrap one thickness of it around the barrel, which is an even more effective means than floor wax for preventing unwanted adhesion.

In shaping-down a new in-fill of wood, one must be exceedingly careful to pick up the contours of the stock correctly. I often do the rough shaping with a pattern maker's rasp, but it doesn't do at all to get near the original stock surfaces in any way. All of the final shaping-down is best done with edged tools. I most frequently use

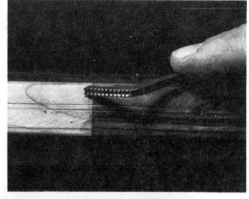

With the mass of the forestock restored, John's next step was to run the moulding on it.

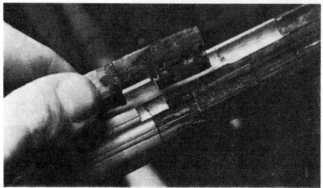

Several small fragments of the original forestock wood could not be reused in their old locations, but some were usable — and useful — as inlaid patches in other locations on the stock.

quarter-round gouges and finish the cuts with a carving knife.

The large patch under the lock of the Eagle rifle actually ran right in to the trigger inlet, which required that the triggers be taken-down and the plate reinlet before I could complete the final shaping. I don't shape new wood down to a metal part with anything other than light paring cuts of the knife, removing the metal for the final leveling of the surface.

No sanding should be done with metal that might be abraded left in place, and grit paper shouldn't be allowed to intrude onto the original surfaces of the stock beyond just what little is required to feather the joint.

Where he had added new wood, John had to recut the lock mouldings. Here, he uses a ninety-degree parting tool to cut Eagle's unusual notched border.

Most long rifles show — to one extent or another — a certain amount of wood damage and loss around the lock mortise. The worst place is just behind the breech, right behind the pan or drum; as I mentioned in the first part of this article, fungus rot caused this damage. In the old days, shooters depended more on oil than on assiduous cleaning with soapy water, as we do now, for preventing corrosion. After shooting, they wiped the rifle out with oil and tow, then often stood the rifle in a corner instead of hanging it up. Oil crept out of the vent or nipple and soaked the end grain of the stock wood next to the lock, encouraging the growth of mold and the eventual destruction of the wood fibers.

We all know the sickly white, crumbling wood that has been damaged in this way. In some cases, this "dry" rot may be trimmed slightly to produce a sound surface that will accept the adherence of a new piece of wood; but some times, the rot is so extensive that the wood must be consolidated before the restorer can add a patch. I have used water-thin marine epoxies that were designed to consolidate insect-infested or rotted wood, but I don't feel any too comfortable about adding such a mass of hard epoxy to a stock.

A better alternative is another product that Conservation Materials, Ltd sells, called *B-72* — an acryloid in pellets, which is dissolved in toluene. It can be reversed by soaking in the same chemical. Since it is more plastic than epoxy, it should not be allowed to build-up on the surface of a joint, where it would create a poor interface with the harder adhesive. Rather, it should be soaked into the wood — not left on it — so that the epoxy bonds well with the wood at the surface.

I didn't have to use a consolidant on the Eagle rifle; instead, I fitted a wedge-shaped piece of wood behind the breech and clamped it in place. I also added new wood above the nose of the lock. To prevent the new pieces from slipping while they were strapped in place, I cut a temporary filler block to fit between the new breech wood and the front pieces.

The lengthening of a tang provides us with one of the most difficult of repairs to hide, particularly since that area of the stock is usually a lighter color than the rest of the stock, because of wear. The tang of the Eagle rifle had been lengthened about an inch and a half, and the new tang was slightly wider than the old one had been. I established the original length from the pattern of the shell carving, the presence of an unused wood-screw hole, and comparison with another rifle that Eagle had made.

I filled the main portion of the secondary or later tang mortise with old wood, matching the grain structure carefully. This, incidentally, took two tries and a good four hours of fussing. I then reinletted the new tang into the stock and with a shim filled the gap left from the wider tang.

Fill-ins of wood can usually fool the eye and hide the joints better if the joint lines curve rather than running straight. I could have made such a joint with the tang mortise by cutting into the shell carving atop the wrist, following the curving veins of the shell. That would have destroyed some original evidence, however. It's preferable to have a new patch visible rather than to obliterate original "fabric," particularly on artistic elements such as carving. However, there are often opportunities to use the outlines of less-important carved features to hide a joint. For example, a patch was necessary at the front of the side plate on this rifle, and I made most of the joint correspond with the line of the lock moulding; the joint is nearly invisible.

I reestablished the punched-in veining of the shell carving on the new wood after the tang patches were shaped-down. Where heavy wear on a stock has obliterated carving, we should not be in the least tempted to recut the missing elements or to "improve" the remaining carving in any way. Some years ago, a customer became more than a little irate over the fact that I had replaced a missing section of stock just behind the lock and then recut the moulding lines just as they had been on the heavily damaged section. Those lines didn't match the opposite side of the stock, but that was the way that the gunmaker had cut them originally. It wasn't for me to correct his mistake, since the very fact that the old-timer had made such a booboo tells us something about how he worked.

The greatest damage to long rifles may often be found on the upper forestock, which is far and away the most fragile portion of the stock. Many stocks were broken in the past by simple removal of the barrel, while others broke or cracked because of poor inletting. If wood isn't supported against the oblique flats of the barrel, it is more than likely to split if the stock is inadvertently hit against a tree — which is bloody easy to do when one is ranging through the woods with a five-foot rifle.

Some stocks came apart because the gunmaker allowed no tolerance for shrinkage or expansion, failing to fit properly slotted lugs for pins or making pin or wedge mortises in the stock long enough to permit movement of the stock. I recently repaired a silver-mounted flintlock rifle that had been broken through the forestock for that very reason, and the fracture likely occurred not many years after the rifle was made. To refit the separated parts of the forestock, I had to remove a full three thirty-seconds of an inch of wood from the forward ends of the lug mortises and a like amount from the slots in the wedge lugs. Now that should teach us a little something about stocking a new rifle.

The upper forestock of the Eagle rifle was an unholy mess — one of those things that you stare at in dismay, wondering whether to throw the whole thing out and add new wood full-length. Original fabric, though, is precious. I could have added a new forestock in probably half the time that it took me to repair what was left, but that would have been irresponsible indeed. Instead, I removed the wire and wooden pins from the stock and separated all of the pieces. I first cleaned them all with toluene to remove wax and other residues and then washed the old hide glue off all of the fracture joints with plain water. I laid the sorry mess out in its proper order and examined all of it to see what could be saved.

At the rear, one section about three inches long could not be used, since its multiple fractures had occurred so long ago that the joints were badly distorted and could not be refitted. Further, the piece looked like Swiss cheese by virtue of the wire that had been used to "sew" the joints together. What I was left with was a sixteen-inch section of forestock in two pieces; this section had four other smaller shattered remains at the muzzle end, one of which could not be replaced. I saved the unusable sections of forestock for a different application later.

After wrapping the barrel with waxed paper, I positioned the remaining forestock section on the barrel in its original position (determined by the pin holes), epoxied the joint, and wrapped the entire thing tightly with inner-tube rubber. After the joint had hardened and the excess epoxy had been removed, I added the three small pieces at the front and at the same time epoxied four longitudinal splits.

Epoxy can be worked into such cracks with 0.001-inch shim stock, or it can be simply blown in under low pressure from an air gun. To pull the joint tight, it's frequently necessary to lay strips of scrap wood along the upper edge of the forestock, at the side flat of the barrel, so that the rubber band pulls down firmly on the side of the stock when it's wrapped. The surface of the stock should be covered with waxed paper first, obviously.

With the remaining section of the forestock made again one piece, a sizable gap remained between that section and the lower fore-end. A good bit more wood was missing from one side of the stock than from the other — and not wanting to replace more than was necessary, I filled the void in three phases: first just below the upper line of the forestock moulding, then on each side of the stock. The lower piece oriented the stock correctly while I made the more difficult side patches, using angular scarf joints.

With the remnants of the original forestock once again pieced back to the lower forestock, over ten inches of upper forestock at the muzzle end remained to be replaced. To match the figure in the original wood, I was forced to spend some time pawing through a large box of remnants of stock blanks, which I save just for such purposes. The figure in this stock wasn't easy to match — it was weak and patchy, and its fiddleback angled slightly forward. I found a piece that matched both the figure and the tangential cut of the stock's grain pattern. After inletting the new piece, I installed it with a sort of a ship-lapped butt joint, both to reduce the cutting of the original wood and to allow a larger and stronger glue joint.

In this particular instance, the fact that the joint would not be contiguous all of the way around the stock would also help to hide the joint. If the joint had been straight across the stock, I would have made it a scarf joint to increase the area of the surface for the adhesive. Although I have used metal pins in such joints in the past, current conservation practice rules against them.

With the ramrod groove run to depth, I shaped the new wood down, then inletted the original nose cap — the nail holes in its sides filled with brass plugs held in place with low-flow silver solder — and riveted it in place with soft copper pins. I then ran the forestock moulding, using a "long jointer" single checkering tool first and then a double-line bordering tool. It's generally my practice to cut such a border as if I'm finishing a brand-new rifle, even though the remaining original mouldings are badly worn and battered. After I achieve the correct form of moulding, I *then* wear and batter the thing down — but that's a matter for the third part of this article.

Butt joints can be hidden readily by veneering over them with small, irregularly shaped pieces of wood. I did some of that on this stock, and that's where the shattered scraps of wood that I'd saved came into useful play. Matching both grains structure and figuration perfectly, they could be sawn into small plugs to cover joints or to add wood where it was missing, obviously matching the stock far better than wood from another source. When small patches must be made, or joints veneered over, and the wood is highly figured, it's often next to impossible to match the figure with a "foreign" piece of wood. I often make no attempt to do so, but instead use a perfectly plain piece as an in-fill, planning to grain it artificially to match later.

Upper fore ends that have been badly shattered and then rebuilt often need more stiffening than the glue joints themselves can provide. To strengthen the stock without causing problems later, a stock liner that is compatible with the natural state of the stock can be added. After cleaning the entire barrel inlet with methanol, I saturate a piece of heavy all-linen drapery material with Franklin's hide glue (available from Woodcraft Supply; Woburn, Massachusetts) and fit it into the forestock full-length. The fabric should be cut to cover the three bottom flats of the barrel only, and it must be pierced ahead of time to clear the barrel lugs. I paint a full-strength coating of glue in the inlet first. The glue to saturate the linen should be thinned a little with water.

I set the fabric in place, wrap the barrel with waxed paper, and push it into the inlet. It's wise, of course, to try that fabric in the inlet *before* dousing the whole business with glue. If the barrel was nicely inletted originally, it may admit no more than the thickness of sheeting linen. In any event, this technique stiffens a pretty wretched forestock considerably yet is easily removable by "painting" the fabric with water. This is most assuredly *not* the place to use epoxy.

In the next installment, I'll treat the finishing and the "distressing" of all this new wood, at the same time taking a hard look at just what the early stock finishes were really like. I'll also go on to matters of metalwork and the curious aging of the metal. ●

Restoring Antique Firearms

CONCLUSION

IN THIS THIRD and final installment, we bring our project to an
end. In terms of firearms restoration, the project was a major one,
with major elements and virtually
all the finish gone, and a good deal
of damage to repair. The entire job,
including the lock reconversion,
used up a bit over 170 hours. For
any antique to warrant that much
time, and therefore the expense, it
must have considerable merit. This
one did, by any standards of American longrifles, and the satisfaction
of saving a piece of high quality is
especially rewarding.

After all repairs are made to the
woodwork, metal surfaces are
treated before proceeding with
stock finishing. Actually, some
metal and wood finishing operations are done concurrently; the
lock and barrel, for example, are
usually being browned and aged
while the stock is receiving its finish.
All metalwork permanently attached to the stock, however, must
be done before the wood is treated,
so we'll outline metal finishing on
the Eagle rifle, and then proceed
with the stock.

Flintlock reconversions are a sore
point with me, due to the fact that
I've seen so many of them done
badly. Buying a handful of investment-cast parts, soldering or screwing a pan to the plate, and hanging
any old cock or frizzen on the plate
just because it happens to be

Compare these views of the restored Eagle rifle to the ones in the first part of this series. In
this and the next four pictures of the restored rifle, it can be seen that John's restoration
was not intended to make the rifle look "new" but to make it appear to have aged with
greater dignity than it had when he received it.

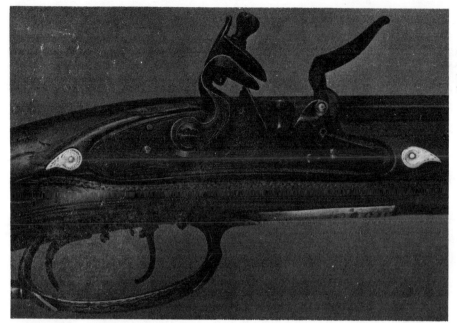

roughly the right size and some-where near the right style just doesn't hack it at all. Unless a lock can be competently rebuilt to flint-lock, it shouldn't be touched, for it's altogether too easy to damage original metalwork irretrievably. And needless to say, a fine 18th century rifle with as-cast 1820-style lock components given a rusty bloom with fast brown is an insult to the rifle itself. Better to leave the piece in its "percussed" state.

There's absolutely nothing wrong with using cast components for reconversion *if* the correct period and style can be matched with castings, or at least modified cast-ings. There are enough cocks and frizzens on the market that very likely a good fifty or sixty per cent of all reconversions can be affected with off-the-shelf parts. There are important points to consider, though. While I have done a number of reconversions that were fully capable of sparking quite well, and some of those are even in use, there's often no need to have a lock fully operable in the sense that it was originally.

A frizzen may be left soft, or old mainsprings that have lost their snap left in that state, especially if the lock is considerably worn and shouldn't be made to bear the strain of being functioned. If a piece is in fine condition, and the lock, though converted to percussion, is still tight and sound, then the lock deserves to be returned to full functioning capability. Even a lock with the tumbler worn out and the screw threads loose, however, should be reconverted in such a way that the parts are geometrically correct. That is to say, the work should be done in such a fashion that *if* the lock were intended for use, it could be made operational by tightening up where needed.

The cock should have the correct throw, with the bottom jaw of an angle that will intersect with the center of the pan with the cock at rest, and the frizzen should be the correct proportional size in relation to the cock. The frizzen should be located so that a flint would strike it normally, even if the lock isn't to be snapped. While there's no space here to explain the niceties of lock design, a close study of original locks will provide an understanding of what should be considered proper geometry and style in a recon-version.

Cast pans often may be used in a reconversion, and at times it's even possible to saw the entire pan section off a new lockplate for use on an old one, particularly in instances where there is a good deal of corrosion on the old plate due to the use of fulminate of mercury caps. Cast pans, however, are generally sold as a separate unit for such purposes. Locks of French and Germanic persuasion usually had separate pans screwed to the plate from inside, which makes for an easier reconversion if the correct size and style of pan can be found. English locks are more of a problem, since British locks after about 1730-40 generally were die-forged one-piece with the lockplate. That means, friend, that a new pan must be *welded* in place inside and out for a correct job. And needless to say, welding on such small parts needs to be done by someone more than a little experienced in delicate work. A good welder with a fine tip on an oxy-acetylene rig, using mild steel rod (coat hanger works fine), can do a perfect job, but I feel that a gas-envelope welding system such as TIG is preferable, particularly since welding heat can be main-tained in a more localized area.

The reconversion on the Eagle rifle was done by Mike Ehinger of Stedman, NC, one of the best in the business, and Mike uses a torch.

Before John started to work on the gun, the fore-end had been broken and shattered. Note that his restoration work here maintains the appearance of "normal aging."

Mike did the metal work on this lock because I *know* his welding ability, and that is the key to the work. The trickiest English lock to do is one with a waterproof pan, such as this lock had. Only the fence remained; both the pan and frizzen bridle had to be cut from solid stock, and it is no mean task to clamp them in place correctly while the part is tacked with the torch.

A one-piece pan is far easier to deal with, but one shouldn't be tempted to use a one-piece pan just because it's easier when there's evidence that something else was there. By the same token, most old locks of any quality tended to have blind screws on the frizzen spring, and inside-mounted frizzen screws. Evidence of such things may always be found, and the reconversion should follow that evidence. Perhaps we can tackle all the considerations of reconversion in a future article.

On the Eagle reconversion, Mike was only able to use one casting: the cock. Pan parts, frizzen and frizzen spring were made from scratch. I have found that there are relatively few frizzen springs on the market that are suitable for reconversions for various reasons, especially on late 18th and early 19th century locks which had roller bearings. Sure, it's a teeth-grinding job to have to make a spring from scratch, but often there's no alternative, and that sort of thing is the very reason why a *good* reconversion is time-consuming and expensive. Damnably few reconversions can be competently done for less than $300 unless the chap doing the work only finds it necessary to eat on Wednesdays and Sundays, and sleeps no more than three hours a night. There are some, of course. They can usually be spotted by their curiously stooped posture and vastly sunken eyes.

There are various techniques for aging and pitting new metal used on restoration jobs, and all of them work to one degree or another. I know one fellow so good with acid that he could probably etch you a relief map of the Sierra Nevada on the breech of a barrel if you wanted. Others like to boil parts in diluted Clorox, which will eat steel like nobody's business. The problem with such corrosives comes when one tries to be selective. A pan or the underside of a frizzen might be well "et," and so might the vent side of a barrel, but not the underside of the pan, front face of a frizzen, or left side of a breech. What to do? Well, the heaviest localized pitting can be done by punching down the surface of the metal with small pointed punches. No doubt a Gravermeister would be dandy for such work, but a hammer is good

While the author believes that tarnished brass mounts should be cleaned, he does not advocate heavy polishing by any means; this patchbox was left with a fair amount of deep patination.

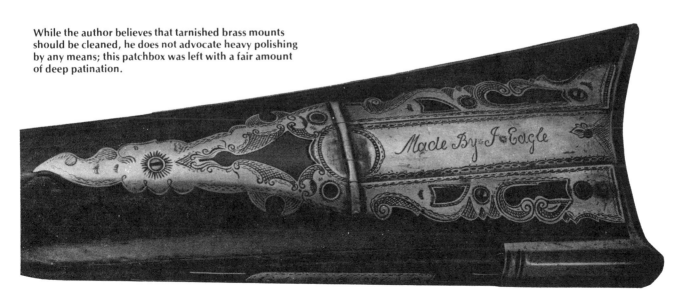

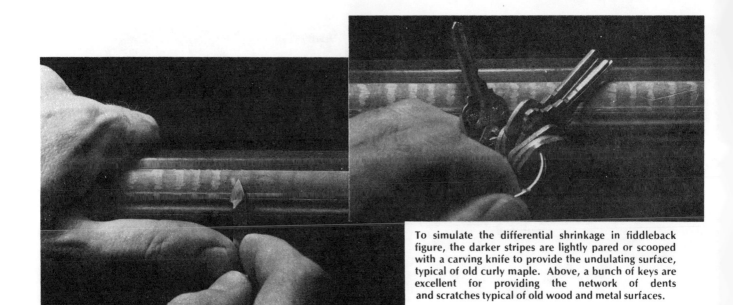

To simulate the differential shrinkage in fiddleback figure, the darker stripes are lightly pared or scooped with a carving knife to provide the undulating surface, typical of old curly maple. Above, a bunch of keys are excellent for providing the network of dents and scratches typical of old wood and metal surfaces.

enough for me. Since such pricks raise up burrs, the area being worked must be polished down, punched again, and so on until the desired effect is evident. For general pitting, I use new 40-grit aluminum oxide one-inch sanding belts. With the grit side against the metal, I beat on the back of the belt with a light hammer, moving the belt to have at new and unshattered pieces of grit. With enough time spent with these two techniques, new metal can be made to look sorry enough to rival Mother Nature's best attempts at oxidation.

Faked pitting isn't enough, however, to provide an aged appearance to a piece which shows heavy use, as the Eagle rifle does. The original barrel surfaces showed numerous dings and scars, which is not so surprising in view of the softness of wrought iron. Accordingly, the new breech section was given a series of similar dents with various objects ranging from a broken hand-vice to the corner of an anvil base. I remember one job where I "stretched" the breech of a barrel, and made the new piece especially convincing by extending a rather embarrassing old surface welding flaw from the original section of barrel onto the new section, using a graver for the job. A vent on a heavily-used rifle should have the appearance of being worn-out and oversize, its outer edges rounded over from corrosion, and the hole well surrounded by good pitting. One of my favorite things to do to the breech of a new barrel which has been stretched is to clamp it in the naked jaws of a machinist's vise and really bear down on the vise

handle. Now, if that gags you out, well it should. But vise jaw marks left on barrels by 19th century bunglers are as common as dirt, and add a certain air of credibility. Make no mistake, though, that sort of aging is really fakery, and must be supported by clear evidence of what was really done. For example, it would *really* be wrong to provide faked cross-grinding marks on the bottom flats of a new barrel breech. Rather, the new barrel section should be left bright underneath and with an obvious indication of where the weld joint is. Perhaps the best way to do that is to run a bit of stainless steel rod into the joint on the bottom flat; the color differential, even on bright metal, will show.

Other things may need judicious buggering as well. Since the Eagle needed a new tang, the new part, to look right, needed the usual damage from improperly-applied wrenches. That is, burred up a little on top just

aft the breech. I did that with a hammer rather than a wrench, and "wore" the burrs down with grit paper. Similarly, screw slots on new screws often must be ruined somewhat, using both a screwdriver and files; this is no fun to someone who likes jewel-like screw heads with perfect hair-thin slots, but if "age" is needed, then one must grimace and do it. For the same reason, the corners of the barrel flats were rounded over as well.

Needless to say, none of these vicious operations would be required for new parts on an arm otherwise crisp and clean, for a newly damaged part would stand out just as badly on such a piece as a perfect part on a well-worn gun. The degree of artificial aging must be determined by the condition of the original surfaces of the piece at hand.

New parts of non-ferrous metals, usually brass or silver, may require

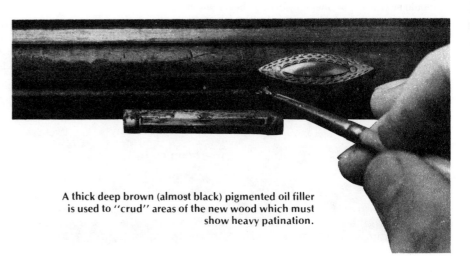

A thick deep brown (almost black) pigmented oil filler is used to "crud" areas of the new wood which must show heavy patination.

a different set of techniques to provide the appearance of age. The three missing upper ramrod thimbles of the Eagle rifle were formed around a mandrel from .045 sheet brass, matching the thickness of the original tailpipe still remaining. I then filed the flats and molded ends to match the original. It's usually my practice to file up such parts as if I were going to finish them as new, then "wear" them with files and abrasives.

The heavy wear on the tailpipe provided a good index to the amount of wear that the new thimbles should show, and I accordingly approached the uppermost thimble with great vigor, since it should show the greatest amount of attrition of all, for that's where the rifle would have been held while loading. The two middle pipes were given a good deal less of the same treatment, but all three new thimbles were scratched up, dented slightly with various objects, and then beat judiciously with a full ring of keys. A close examination of old metal surfaces will invariably show a very complex network of tiny scratches and nicks, and a bunch of keys does that job quite well.

I then blackened the thimbles all over, inside and out, with cold blue swabbed on, and then polished them out with 400 and 600 grit paper. The pipes were then given another shorter session with the jangling keys, then buffed vigorously on a muslin wheel to provide a worn, glazed appearance. That, incidentally, is the *only* job I use a power buffer for in my shop. The pipes were then blackened again, then polished out with Simichrome polish, and they were ready for inletting in the usual manner. A finished pipe is shown here installed below the nosecap on the restored fore-end. As you will recall, the nosecap, though it had survived two barrel shortenings, had been attached at a later time with nails through the sides. The nail holes were plugged with scrap brass tightly fitted and then silver-soldered in place. When such repairs must be made, one must take care not to allow heat to reach the fillet at the muzzle end of the cap, for unless the cap was made one-piece, that fillet was likely soft-soldered in place, and will readily loosen and drop off.

Four silver inlays were missing on the Eagle, three of them forestock inlays. One of the new ones shows in the view with the nosecap. Typically, the original inlays were exceedingly thin, scarcely more than .025, so I had to repeatedly anneal

and hammer a piece of .050 sterling sheet to duplicate the original thickness. Like many Carolina rifles, the Eagle was fitted with forestock inlays embossed with a false wedge head, intended to provide the visual impression of silver wedges fitted through escutcheons of the same metal. After sawing out the inlays with a piercing or "jeweler's" saw, it was a simple matter to make up a wide punch to raise up the false wedge heads; the inlay was placed on a block of lead, and the punch driven into it. The exterior surface was then defined with files, and the inlay drilled for pins.

Making silver nails might seem to be an odious task, but it's rendered quite simple with the use of a torch to form the heads. Holding a piece of .040 round sterling wire in the flame of a torch, the wire will form a ball on the end . . . a small one will do. A head swage is then made by drilling a piece of quarter-inch steel stock with a No. 60 drill, counter-sinking the hole lightly with a 60-degree countersink. The blobby-headed nail is dropped in the swage, and the head forced into the countersink by light blows with a hammer. All that remains is to draw out a point on the other end with a light hammer.

The inlay is countersunk with the same tool used to make the swage, insuring a good fit for the nail. Forestock inlays should be held in place with nails that entirely pierce the side of the forestock; when they strike the oblique flats of the barrel inside the inlet, they are automatically clinched over, insuring that they won't fall out later. This is most assuredly not the sort of place to use an adhesive.

Mother Nature being the easily-displeased sort that she is, wooden stocks are forever trying to shed things made of metal which have forced into it. Unless a piece has been exceedingly well kept, inlays and the like tend to be left standing a bit proud of the surface after a number of years. For that reason, I dubbed over the edges of the new inlays for the Eagle, and when they were inletted I made no attempt to make them perfectly flush. After they were engraved to match the originals, and the engraving worn off where appropriate, I gave them pretty much the same treatment I'd given the thimbles, including dosing with cold blue. If new inlays are being fitted to original mortises, then of course the surrounding stock wood must be masked off before laying on with the keys and other instruments of destruction.

There is really no mystery to providing a good aged appearance to steel and iron parts, if one ponders the problem a bit. Speed is out of the question, though. On the Eagle rifle, the barrel was originally finished with a rich plum-colored brown, most of which had turned quite dark with age, much in the same fashion chemically that we might effect a rust blue today. In other words, some of the reddish-brown ferrous oxide had converted to black ferric oxide. In order to make the long section of new breech match the original part of the barrel, I rusted the new section with several applications of Rick Schreiber's Laurel Mountain brown . . . one of the best on the market, in my estimation, though it's devilishly hard to stop. I then boiled the breech end for about five minutes, turning the thing a nasty matte black. Using 400 grit paper, I scrubbed a good fifty per cent of that off the barrel, especially at the corners of the flats, and then proceeded to brown the barrel normally, carding after each successive coat with a folded-over canvas shot bag. When I saw the color was right, I washed the barrel down thoroughly with ammonia, then hot water and soap, and set the thing aside for a day. Don't be tempted to slosh on oil after browning, for it's better to let the thing sit about for at least a night to see if further oxide will form. If it does, then more ammonia and soapy water is called for, for the last thing we want is for a fine antique to sit quietly rusting away *under* a coat of oil or wax.

The locks on most American rifles were left bright originally, though a few were fire-blued, and by the percussion period not a few were left with case colors. Flint rifles, however, are usually seen with the lock thoroughly brown or even bluish-black with age, and the same techniques described above may be used to age reconversion parts. On a rifle that shows wear, but otherwise has been kept clean, the edges of cocks, frizzen springs, and the like might be polished lightly with 600 grit to show the barest hint of metal below.

It should be perfectly obvious to the reader that the bulk of our discussions here have dealt with finish techniques appropriate to well-patinated arms. Fine antiques with a good deal of finish remaining are far more difficult to deal with, and we'll have to undertake such niceties at a later date. Until then, the reader should be aware that only the most experienced professionals should ever be entrusted with techniques such as re-color-hardening metal, for many reasons . . . some of the most hoary are scale (not nice for engraving), warpage and shrinkage (not nice for inletting fit), and overcarburization or hardening of improper areas such as breech threads (not nice for facial features). The problems, indeed, are manifold when such tricky procedures must be carried out, and one should consider the risk to the arm itself. And I for one do not care in the least, on the other hand, for the "imitation" color hardening done with a torch and a few spoonfuls of interesting pink powder. A clean "coin" finish is far more desirable on aged casehardened surfaces, and certainly far less garish.

Debates will rage forever on whether or not the brass mounts of old arms should be polished or left heavily tarnished. I prefer the former, but with a good deal of reservation. The maker intended them to be bright, or he would have made them of fire-blued or browned iron, but that doesn't mean that old brass surfaces should be made to look mint-new; far from it. If a rifle has tarnished considerably, just as the Eagle had done, I clean the brass with an English product called Dura-Glit, available for $2.70 a can from International Drug Supplies, Inc., 488 Court St., Brooklyn, NY 11231. Dura-Glit is cotton impregnated with mild chemical cleaners and very little abrasive at all, unlike products such as Brasso. Nevertheless, it does contain a certain amount of solvents, including ammonia, that should be kept off stock finishes. I make no attempt to remove all the evidence of surface patination, and I don't try for a hard shine on the parts; I just prefer them clean so that the engraving will show.

For exhibition of brass-mounted arms which will receive little or no handling, museums often lacquer the mounts, but that should be considered impractical for collectors. Instead, coat the brass with a microcrystalline wax such as Renaissance Wax, available from Conservation Materials Ltd., as mentioned before. The same firm also sells a vapor-release substance called Tarn-Guard, which is useful in an enclosed gun cabinet to replace harmful sulphur-bearing air that causes tarnish. The point is that non-ferrous surfaces should be polished as *seldom* as possible, for no matter how mild the cleaning agent, a minute amount of surface is removed at each cleaning. And

since antique arms are precious documents, we'd like their surfaces to be preserved intact for hundreds of years, hopefully.

For silver, an excellent product offered by the 3M Company is Tarnishield, which is very low in abrasive qualities and leaves a chemical coating on the surface which retards tarnish. Pieces entirely mounted in silver, however, are best kept in a sealed cabinet with either Tarn-Guard or camphor blocks (available at the drug store) placed at the top of the cabinet to displace harmful gasses. Initial cleaning of heavily tarnished silver may be carried out with a very light polishing with Simichrome, though that worthy product should never be used in subsequent cleanings, or eventual damage to engraving and crisp edges will result.

Steel and iron parts of antique arms, and that includes the bores of barrels, are best given a thorough soaking with CRC 3-36, available in various quantities from CRC Chemicals, Warminster, PA 18974. A large plumber's supply in my city carries it. After soaking, parts should be drained and dried. I then give all exterior surfaces a light coating of Renaissance Wax before final assembly. Don't allow any sort of oil to pool in locks or other mechanisms, for many oils are deadly to wood. Waxes are far preferable to oils for surface coating, since they attract less dirt, but avoid anything with silicone in it.

With the Eagle's metalwork done, attention was turned to finishing the wood. Some two dozen new pieces of wood had been inletted in the stock or added to it, and the chore at hand with such things is to make them match the original stock wood. Matching isn't merely a matter of coloration and sheen; the new plugs must show the same degree of wear and abrasion that the original stock surface does, or they will stand out like a lighthouse on a clear night. One important item that is often overlooked is that well-worn stocks of curly maple tend to have undulating surfaces virtually the entire length. The folded grain which provides the appearance of fiddleback figure shrinks differentially, the end-grain "curls" which show as the darker stripes often pulling in a bit. This can easily be seen on an old rifle by holding it to the light and squinting down the stock. The ripple can be *felt* even more readily. If large new pieces don't have the same character, then they will appear too level and "dead" next to the undulating old wood.

If a stock has this ripple, I begin my finish operations by lightly staining all the new wood with a yellowish base color. This will provide a mellow under-tone later, but in the beginning the light coloring shows up the dark part of the figure. Using a carving knife, I then very lightly hollow each of those dark curls, even on the forestock molding, and then sand the new wood down with 280-grit paper, allowing the paper to completely round over the edges of all that scooping. Incidentally, this scooping is also used over patches of plain wood, matching the pattern of the figure in the old wood, and will enhance the use of false "graining" later.

While the new woodwork on the Eagle rifle was done with old wood for stability, that did not relieve me from the job of grain raising, for new sections and patches must be quite dead before finishes go on. Even so, additions to an old stock, no matter how old the material used may be, will tend to react considerably more to humidity changes, thereby causing joints to show right through the finish. Ideally, we might like to let a repaired stock sit for six to eight months so that we can cut it down as it rises at the joints, but that's usually impossible to do. In the process of raising the grain, then, we must use enough water on the new pieces to make them move, and hopefully move all they will. Consequently, I really swab the water on heavily, and instead of starting in with a torch right off the bat, I let the stock dry as it will by itself. I then wet it again thoroughly, and when it is almost dry, finish drying with a torch, and then whisker off with 320-grit paper. I then proceed with whiskering as usual, often going through the process five times or so.

Now comes the damage. I study the pattern of dents and scratches on the original wood, and then do my best to duplicate them on the new pieces. If I find a scratch or dent on the original stock next to a new plug, I extend that old damage right over onto the new wood. Splits in the original surfaces which have been stabilized still often show as dark lines, especially if they are old splits; these can be visually extended into the new wood with the point of a knife to provide a substitute "crack." By the same token, the long pores of walnut can be extended right over a new joint with a knife.

As for the dents and dings, one must use one's imagination. As on the new metal surfaces, a ring of keys does yeoman service on wood. Just don't get carried away with your jangling fugue to the point that you distress the new parts more than the amount of surface damage evident on the old parts. After this fervor of banging and clunking, I once again wet the stock, apply the torch lightly, and sand with 400-grit. Some of your minor dings and knife cuts in the new wood may disappear when you do this, and must be redone. The scooping in the figure may also lighten a bit, but that won't hurt.

Matching original stock colors on new wood may be done either with water-based aniline dyes such as those sold by Brownell's, or with toluene / alcohol - based so - called "NGR" (non-grain raising) stains. I prefer the latter, but it seems to be getting difficult to find in all the hues needed. Sherwin-Williams had a system of NGR concentrates they called "Sherwood 500," consisting of basic yellow, brown, red, black and orange. Using the first four of those colors, I've been able to duplicate any original finish color, but I understand that those concentrates have been discontinued. That's the way it goes in this business. . . spend twenty years finding something that works, and they jerk it off the market. Wampler Chemical Company of Harrisonburg, Virginia, has excellent brown and red mahogany NGR stains, and might be convinced to offer other colors if there were enough demand. A mixture of the red and brown will serve to match the color of many stocks; a minimum order is two gallons.

Before we proceed with staining, some things should be cleared up. The whole matter of early finishes is a matter of considerable romantic fiction in many publications, much of it rather akin to that well-known solid matter found about pastures where bulls are known to frequent. We hear all this business about linseed oil used solely as a finish, stains made of soot and oil, and the like. If one takes the opportunity to examine a large sampling of flintlock weapons, both American and European, a different sense of things emerges. What we find is that early gunsmiths preferred varnish finishes, and built-up finishes at that. I have found evidence of such on above ninety-five percent of all American pieces I've examined, if they hadn't been previously stripped. Of course, most old rifles have lost a good deal of their finish due to wear, and close scrutiny may be needed to find traces. As badly done-over as the Eagle rifle was, good samples of a deep reddish-brown varnish was evident under and behind the cheekpiece, and this same finish was found to be perhaps 50 per cent intact on another rifle by the same maker.

What, you may ask, were those varnishes? Well, a lengthy answer to that one would be required if we covered all the finish materials available to early gunstockers and cabinetmakers. Let's try to simplify the thing a bit by saying that early stock finishes were natural resin varnishes, usually made from a hard resin such as copal, which is a product of a certain species of conifer growing in tropic areas. There were many sorts of resins, however, ranging from very brittle to quite soft, each requiring a different formulation of solvents and the like.

Copal varnish was both difficult and dangerous to make. The resin is insoluble in either of the two common solvents of the eighteenth century, turpentine or "spirits" (alcohol), and required heating to some 300 degrees before it could be thinned with turpentine. Since copal is brittle, it required a vehicle which was a drying oil, commonly refined or "boiled" linseed, which would also act as a plasticizer. That is to say, the linseed added elasticity to the finish so that it wouldn't craze so badly with age and dimensional changes in the wood due to humidity shifts. Additional softer resins such as sandarac were often added also; the old boys formulated hundreds of recipes, and many of them were quite good.

Copal varnishes were often rather dark even when newly mixed, and gunstockers more often than not tinted their finishes further by adding such vegetable dyes as Brazil wood, logwood or dragon's blood, all of which provided a deep red cast to a jar of varnish. On a stock, the brownish-amber tint of the copal coupled with the red dye added to the varnish provided a pleasing color indeed. Of course, not all stocks were varnished, and not all that were carried a red tint in the finish film, but that by far was the favored sort of finish everywhere before the mid-19th century. Despite their hardness, the natural-resin varnishes could be rubbed out easily, and the usual application called for numerous thin coats each well-scoured down. The finish was normally used to fill, though old recipes for fillers do survive. One of these was isinglass, which is still used by some violin makers.

In duplicating original colors and finishes, then, we are trying to cope with colors early gunstockers provided by methods often different than what we use today. Stains and dyes were indeed used under finishes, but generally only on light-colored woods such as maple; the favored base stain for that wood, of course, was nitric acid. Vegetable dyes such as the good brown obtainable from boiling walnut hulls were also used. In any event, the reddish varnish applied over such a base stain was the most common finish for maple. As far as I am concerned, nitric acid should not be used on an antique, and due to the amount of neutralization it requires, I don't like it on new stocks either, and haven't used it for fifteen years or more.

Rather than trying to provide a tinted finish film, I mix my base stain to provide all the color needed. After swabbing the color on the new wood repeatedly until the wood either matches or is slightly darker than the old surfaces, I let the stock sit up overnight for the solvents and diluents in the stain to evaporate thoroughly. In the case of the Eagle rifle, the later varnish glopped over the stock and had to be removed with a mild cabinet stripper — I used "Strypeeze" cut a little with mineral spirits — and then the areas which had been scoured down long ago also stained to match the remaining traces of original finish. Of course, areas where colors have been lost by natural wear should be left alone.

Now comes the mud. Some areas of a longrifle stock usually show especially deep patination, such as under the lock. Forestock moldings often are rather plugged with patina, which is really just a combination of ancient filth and degraded finish. Patination is seldom black, but rather an exceedingly deep brown that *approaches* black. Where heavy patination was needed on new wood on the Eagle, such as in the notched lock moldings and next to the trigger plate on the big patch under the lock, and in the forestock moldings, I used a common mahogany - colored pigmented oil filler and dumped enough powdered lampblack into it to turn the muck a *very* dark brown. This goo was then liberally painted into all the appropriate places where sham patina was needed. After letting the stuff sit for a half-hour, I wiped most of it off the surface with a rag. Everything was now nicely clotted up.

For areas of lighter patination, I use common flat black enamel, and dribble just enough bright red enamel into it to achieve the same very dark, almost-black color I wanted in the filler. This enamel is then used for painting the inside of the ramrod groove and for adding a subtle bit of deep toner to areas of the stock which would have had no wear, such as just behind the barrel breech on the lock side, where I'd added a sizeable chunk of new wood to the Eagle. The enamel can be readily feathered out by smearing it around a bit with the fingers, or it can be made rough by dabbing at it as it becomes tacky.

The same paint is used for faked graining. As I mentioned earlier on, it is more often than not impossible to match a curly maple stock with a new plug which also has fiddleback figure. I've found that the best results are obtained by making those plugs of plain wood, though having the *same grain structure*, as we discussed earlier. In the process of distressing the stock, the figure pattern of the old wood is picked out on the new pieces by scooping with the knife blade, as we've just seen. The scoops, which should be of random width to resemble real figuration, are then lightly painted in with our good old enamel patina-in-a-jar. When I say "lightly painted," what I actually mean is that the fake stripes should be virtually dry-brushed on, using a good quality artists' rounded-tip sable. You do not want an appreciable surface build-up of the enamel, for obvious reasons. This technique is also exceedingly useful for hiding butt-jointed repairs, if a fake stripe is allowed to land straight over the joint itself.

With the new wood stained, crudded with mud, and tricked out with artistically shaded patination and cunning phony stripes over the patches, the whole mess is left to harden for a full day. I should mention, if it isn't obvious, that the entirely new upper section of fore-stock on the Eagle was made of fiddleback maple chosen to match the rest of the stock, as discussed earlier. One would hate to tiger-stripe ten inches of stock, and don't you ever believe those old tales about burning tarred string onto plain maple to achieve "curl."

The final finishing of the new wood is as easy as the devil. Since responsible conservation procedures call for reversible materials to be used wherever practicable, finish is one of those areas where that axiom particularly applies. Shellac, actually a "spirit varnish" in 18th century parlance, is the solution. Readily soluble in alcohol, shellac can be removed very easily should the need arise. I use orange shellac, always taking care to buy fresh stuff with a date not more than six months old. Using a 5/8-inch flat sable brush, I coat the new wood, along with sections of the original stock where needed, with a quick application of shellac. After it sits for twenty minutes or so, I very lightly even it out with 0000 steel wool. Another coat, also followed by the light wooling, usually fills maple completely, though walnut may require more shellac unless you smeared your mud around a bit to fill the pores.

For a final finish, I rub on two very light coats of the Express Oil sealer sold by Lowell Manley, allowing a good eight hours between applications. This finish may be lightly dotted about with the fingertips and then rubbed hard with the heel of the hand; keep rubbing until the finish feels almost dry. This hard urethane protects the softer shellac below, along with all of your false ageing, and yet the shellac provides an interface between the wood and the molecule-thick top coating which would allow the easy removal of the whole mess should it be necessary. Hence, our need for reversibility is satisfied. Do *not* be tempted to rub-up an old stock with straight linseed oil, which due to its gumminess and continuing polymerization is no longer considered an acceptable finish material for restoration work. If you like, the newly-finished sections can be compounded just a bit with one of the firm varieties of paste auto wax.

As a final touch, I melt a little beeswax and stir in enough lamp-black to make the mixture pretty dark. While still soft, this wax can be rubbed into thimble pin holes and the like to simulate the ancient crud that usually stops up such orifices. All of these techniques, of course, may be used to thoroughly age a brand-new rifle for those so inclined. I'm not inclined myself, for I've spent the last twenty years trying to duplicate pristine early finishes, but I don't go out of my way to fuss at the fellows who like to have their new flintlock look as if it were run hard and hung up wet.

On a new rifle, I wouldn't fool with the shellac, but would go straight to the varnish sealer, and would do a little judicious wet-sanding on highlight areas, re-staining the wood between coats of finish. Herschel House of Morgantown, Kentucky, is the Past Master of making new rifles that reek of fabulous antiquity. Not a few collectors have been left with red faces over such work, after inquiring just where that "H. House" worked in the pre-Revolutionary period.

With the rifle assembled in all of its new glory, a new ramrod is fitted, whiskered, and then stained with a yellowish-brown NGR stain. After wooling the rod down, give it a thick coat of roofing tar dissolved in mineral spirits, which serves to plug the pores nicely if you let the rod stand for fifteen minutes or so before vigorously rubbing down with a rag. The thing is now done except for completing a detailed restoration report, and making an entire set of "after" photographs to go with the "befores."

As a final consideration, and whether we may be museum curator or collector, we should try to provide proper continuing care for such arms by providing some sort of stable environment. And that doesn't mean, friend, that Betsy should be hung all shiny over the mantel, despite all the romantic depictions of Dan'l Boone's cabin we may have seen. Dan'l, in fact, likely hung his rifle-gun over the *door*, if evidence I've seen in a number of early houses is any indication. By the same token, we don't leave a fine antique gun in the car on a summer's day while we frolic in an air-conditioned gun show. In addition to temperature considerations for anything made of wood, we must also concern ourselves with humidity for the same reasons, and also for the sake of ferrous gun parts. Museums consider an ideal humidity range year-round to fall in the 45 to 55 per cent range, and while it may be difficult for us to maintain such a tight gradient in a household, the attempt should be made.

A gun room should be air-conditioned in the summer, if only with a window unit. It's far better to dehumidify the atmosphere of an entire room than to simply dry the air of a gun cabinet with silica-gel or other such products which must fight the damp each time the cabinet door is opened. Portable dehumidifiers are also useful, and so are dry-bulb wet-bulb hygrometers, which are not expensive. In the winter, humidification of the gun room may be necessary, and open pans of water near heating ducts may be all that's necessary. Humidifiers can be installed in central heating units, but most of them don't seem to last any too long.

Even light is a consideration; strong ultraviolet, such as that radiating from fluorescent lamps or carried in sunlight, can fade stock finishes. The red dyes used in old varnish finishes can be particularly fugitive, or susceptible to fading. If fluorescent is the predominant light in the room, I'd strongly recommend sleeving the lamps with UF-3 tubing, a plexiglas material designed to reduce UV to acceptable levels. Many plastics jobbers can order these tubes in various lengths.

If all these considerations seem fussier than Aunt Matilda ten minutes before her annual DAR meeting, then so be it. If our premise is to respect our antique weapons by finding the correct means of preserving them, then we must perforce think like a professional conservator. That's the name of the game. ●